Enterprise Security Architecture

Enterprise Security Architecture

A Business-Driven Approach

John Sherwood
Andrew Clark
David Lynas

CMP**Books**

San Francisco

Published by CMP Books
an imprint of CMP Media LLC
600 Harrison Street, San Francisco, CA 94107 USA
Tel: 415-947-6615; Fax: 415-947-6015
www.cmpbooks.com, email: books@cmp.com

Designations used by companies to distinguish their products are often claimed as trademarks. In all instances where CMP is aware of a trademark claim, the product name appears in initial capital letters, in all capital letters, or in accordance with the vendor's capitalization preference. Readers should contact the appropriate companies for more complete information on trademarks and trademark registrations. All trademarks and registered trademarks in this book are the property of their respective holders.

The publisher does not offer any warranties and does not guarantee the accuracy, adequacy, or completeness of any information herein and is not responsible for any errors or omissions. The publisher assumes no liability for damages resulting from the use of the information in this book or for any infringement of the intellectual property rights of third parties that would result from the use of this information.

Managing Editor: Gail Saari
Text Design: Gail Saari
Cover Design: David Hamamoto

Distributed to the book trade in the U.S. by:
Publishers Group West
1700 Fourth Street
Berkeley, CA 94710
1-800-788-3123

Distributed in Canada by:
Jaguar Book Group
100 Armstrong Avenue
Georgetown, Ontario M6K 3E7 Canada
905-877-4483

Library of Congress Cataloging-in-Publication Data

Sherwood, John, 1947-
  Enterprise security architecture : a business-driven approach / John Sherwood, Andrew Clark, David Lynas.
    p. cm.
  Includes index.
  ISBN-13: 978-1-57820-318-5 (alk. paper)
  ISBN-10: 1-57820-318-X (alk. paper)
  1. Computer security. 2. Computer architecture. 3. Business--Data processing. I. Clark, Andrew, 1945- II. Lynas, David, 1964- III. Title.

QA76.9.A25S466 2005
005.8--dc22
                                        2005026186

For individual orders and for information on special discounts for quantity orders, please contact:
CMP Books Distribution Center, 6600 Silacci Way, Gilroy, CA 95020
Tel: 1-800-500-6875 or 408-848-3854; fax: 408-848-5784
Email: cmp@rushorder.com; Web: www.cmpbooks.com

Printed in the United States of America
11 12 13 14 15   10 9 8 7
ISBN-13: 978-1-57820-318-5
ISBN: 1-57820-318-X

Dedications

To Amanda, Jason and Mike Sherwood, along with those other close and dear friends who have loved and supported me throughout the length of this project.

To Linda, Catherine and Charlie Clark for your love and encouragement.

To Marie, James, Kathryn and Stephen Lynas for your faith, support and love.

Contents

Foreword

The title of this book brings together three concepts that are overdue for synthesis. The first is the concept of enterprise, meaning the treatment of an organisation, commercial firm or public service as a single entity rather than a set of cooperating departments. It stems from the work of a number of management gurus in the late 1980s and early 1990s, amongst them Porter and Handy. They realised that improvements in competitiveness or services were only going to be achieved by optimising all parts of an organisation in a coherent way and all together, rather than locally optimising at the departmental level. The development of web-based information technologies allowed such optimisation to occur, but usually in an *ad hoc* manner, building on legacy processes and systems. It was not as coherent as it could have been.

At about this time it also was recognised that to improve the alignment of information and communication technologies (ICT) with business processes and to overcome the legacy system issue, an architectural approach to systems design was needed. This, in the hands of Zachman and others, together with a growing appreciation of the value of a systems engineering approach to large-scale ICT infrastructures, generated a structured and coherent approach to the migration of legacy environments to enterprise-wide systems. This approach has been in use for some time, and considerable progress was made at the time of the so-called Millennium Bug in replacing legacy environments with properly designed and engineered systems. However it is a process that continues today, and much improvement remains to be achieved.

The third factor, information and information systems security, has been known about for some time but was not regarded as either a business issue or as a mainstream information systems issue. Frequently, any security that was needed was added after implementation, quite often as a result of a security incident, so the information and information systems security discipline grew up in isolation from business process optimisation and from information systems engineering, except in some special cases such as defence, large-scale finance and banking, and some elements of aerospace. The advent of inter-enterprise working, the pervasiveness of the Internet as the common backbone of a global e-society and the vast increases in computing power, storage and bandwidth brought about by modern silicon and photonic technologies have dramatically exposed the weaknesses resulting from this evolutionary track. Exposure to these weaknesses has the potential to reduce confidence in e-society and e-business to such an extent as to limit the commercial and social benefits that could otherwise be obtained from well-designed, well-engineered and correctly operated secure environments and systems.

I believe society is on the cusp of making a judgement about this issue. This book, with its inbuilt optimism based on a successful set of experiences, will not only help security practitioners provide the benefits expected in their day-to-day work, but it will also help ICT professionals in general to deal with the argument of the gainsayers and doom-mongers.

Hence, the timing of this excellent book could not be better. It provides a well-argued, coherent and complete approach to the issue of how to make an enterprise safe and successful from an information and information systems point of view. The SABSA® framework, the cornerstone of the work, is derived from a mixture of experience and from the synthesis of range of well-proven methodologies and approaches. The use of a 'pervasive use case' will allow the reader to relate the theory to their real-world problems, and also provide them with the basis for the arguments needed to justify investment in their own organisations. Achieving a secure but successful enterprise is a major challenge. The description of the use of maturity models to ensure that an organisation does not undertake more than it is capable of delivering is critical to success. Successful projects, although critical to delivery of benefits, do not by themselves deliver improvements; they do however enable them. The later chapters of the book cover what is needed to run a secure enterprise and to deliver the expected benefits from the security that has been designed into the organisation and its processes. This birth-to-death treatment is unique in my view and it is why this work should be on every CIO, ICT Infrastructure and application development director's desk, as well as that of the newly appointed enterprise security architect.

The built environment which those of us who are fortunate enough to inhabit in the developed world did not happen by accident; it grew from an understanding that co-operative planning, robust, well-designed implementation and safe operation are critical to success. I believe we are approaching that threshold in our virtual environment. What this book gives us is a framework for dealing successfully with all these factors, a framework that is coherently constructed, lucidly described and grounded in real-world experience. Another small step for mankind...?

Professor Brian S Collins

Professor of Information Systems, Cranfield University and Vice President, British Computer Society

Preface

Benefits

As authors we hope that the great benefit of this book to its readers will be the insight that it gives into how to go about the process of developing enterprise-wide security architectures. To most people this is a huge, daunting task. They do not know where to begin, they do not know how to proceed, they do not know how to structure the work, and they do not know how to measure their progress. This book will show them all of these things. They will experience an enlightenment that will open the way for them to begin work on their own enterprise security architecture programme. Reading this book will be an important step on the road to success. It will change their professional lives in a significant way.

We have tried to stay at a relatively high level and have avoided descriptions of technical details that will quickly go out of date. Our intention has been to create a book that will have a long lifetime, and to do this it must be relatively independent of specific technologies and technical solutions. Thus it focuses heavily upon the conceptual and logical aspects of enterprise security architecture. The technical detail on specific solutions has been left to other authors of publications that are very different in their nature. However, we have provided as much help as possible to the reader to facilitate the search for this technical detail. References to other works, to international and Internet standards, to professional journals and to URLs where up-to-date technical detail is likely to be available have been included wherever possible.

The flow of the book follows the structured layers of the enterprise security architecture model that is introduced in the early chapters. There is strong pedagogy, with the layout structured into headings, sub-headings and bullets to make it easy for a reader to scan the pages and pick up the themes quickly. There is also strong emphasis on the use of tables, charts and diagrams wherever possible. This makes for a book that can be read sequentially from start to finish if the reader so desires but which can also be used as a book to be dipped into as a reference text.

The Evolution of Information Security

Information security and its subset, information systems security, are becoming more and more mainstream in their appeal. Information security began life in the military and government arena with very specialised applications in the field of national security. In the 1970s and 80s it became important in the banking industry as electronic banking systems were developed and deployed. During the 1990s we saw the emergence of the Internet, of e-commerce and of many other aspects of electronic business and the use of information systems to manage businesses on an enterprise-wide basis. Thus at the beginning of the 21st century security is a topic that commands wide interest in enterprises wishing to leverage these technological innovations for business benefit.

One thing we wish to make clear at the beginning is that we take a wide view of what is relevant to information security. For those who have an existing view that it covers confidentiality, integrity and availability of information, prepare yourself to be challenged! For example, you will find discussions on topics such as customer service. What possible connection does this have with information security? Well, quite simply, information security has a great impact on the usability of information and communications technology (ICT) systems and upon the experience that users (including customers) have when interacting with these systems. Customer service is closely linked to ease of use, consistency of experience and delivery of expectations. Information security mechanisms for authentication and authorisation can damage these goals beyond repair, and so yes, customer service (and every other business issue) is highly relevant to the development of enterprise information security architecture. In this book information security is approached from a purely business perspective, and so you should expect every business issue to be viewed here as an information security issue.

Information Security Literature

The market for books has responded eagerly to the developing of interest in information security, with a wide range being published about new technologies generally and the security aspects specifically. Most of these books have a very technical focus. At the same time there is growing concern that the technology that attracts so much investment from businesses is not delivering what it promises, and it is clear that the reason is that developments are led from a technical standpoint, not a business one. There are few books that address this issue, either for ICT generally or information systems security specifically.

What is evident in this world of information security is that corporate management teams are becoming impatient with development programmes with ever-escalating budgets and time frames, and ever more disappointing results. We perceive two reasons for this: (1) that there is a lack of understanding of how to link technical development programmes to business needs; and (2) that there is a lack of strategic architectural thinking, which renders the investments in system development incapable of meeting the long-term and wider needs of the business.

There is growing interest in the concept of enterprise architecture as a means to plan, develop, implement and operate business information systems. This interest also extends to the security domain, where enterprise security architecture is becoming more and more attractive to those who are tasked with integrating adequate security into enterprise business systems. Over the next decade we expect this interest to grow substantially, especially if it is fed by the availability of suitable literature on the subject. This book is intended to contribute to that pool of literature. It is written from the perspective of the many years of practical experience that the authors have of working with large organisations in just this field of activity.

How to Use This Book

The book is intended to be the security architects' bible. It will provide a structured approach that can be followed step by step, so as to build an enterprise security architecture that meets the needs of the business. It is intensely practical but at the same time it is a complete theoretical work on how to make information security work. It is our intention that it will become the definitive work on this subject.

The book is organised into four parts:

Part 1: Introduction

Part 2: Strategy and Planning

Part 3: Design

Part 4: Operations

We recommend that the reader treat Part 1 as a text to be read from end to end. In this part of the book we expound our overall philosophy, framework and methodology, and arguably reading only this portion may satisfy a security architect who already possesses a good underlying business and technical knowledge.

In the subsequent three parts we take each layer of the framework described in Part 1 and develop it in detail. These three parts also map onto three phases of the security architecture lifecycle, also described in Part 1. These last three parts are therefore more likely to be used by the reader as reference material, rather than as something to be read from one end to the other.

Part 2 deals with business issues affecting information security and major strategic approaches to solving business problems. It is high-level and truly in the realm of architecture from the point of view of an architect, remaining at a conceptual level of thinking throughout.

Part 3 addresses the more detailed design process at the logical, physical and component architecture levels and will appeal to those readers who have an interest in the more detailed aspects of designing information security solutions.

Part 4 addresses security operations, being the day-to-day operational management of information security within the enterprise security framework. Here we focus on some specific issues but do not attempt to cover every aspect of operational security in fine detail, since after all, there are many good books that already deal with the detail of the operational and administrative aspects of information security management. However, the book would be incomplete without this part being included, since we believe that the power of the book is its unique framework approach to architectural thinking, and some flesh must be put onto the skeleton framework for operational management that was introduced in Part 1.

Since the various parts differ from one another considerably in depth and focus, it is quite likely that many readers will find that some parts of the book appeal to them more than others. This is to be expected, since few people are able to operate successfully at every level of the architectural framework we describe. What we hope is that every reader will find significant value in those parts that address their own sphere of interest, and that the book as a whole will help architecture teams to work more effectively together by understanding the relative roles that different team members play and the value of their individual contributions to the overall integrated architectural process.

It is also important that the reader should appreciate that this book is not a cookbook that provides recipes for all situations. It is much more a book on how to think in architectural terms and how some of the major issues can be approached. You may not find here the solution to your problem, but what you should find is an approach to understanding the real business problem and how that understanding should drive your technical creativity and your process design work.

About the SABSA® Model

The entire book is based upon a six-layer model of security architecture known as SABSA®, an idea first developed by John Sherwood in 1995 and published in 1996 as 'SABSA: A Method for Developing the Enterprise Security Architecture and Strategy[1]'. SABSA® is an acronym for 'Sherwood Applied Business Security Architecture' and was the basis on which the Sherwood team built their world-class consulting skills in this area of security architecture. The starting point for this work was ISO 7498-2 1989[2]: 'Information processing systems – Open Systems Interconnection – Basic Reference Model – Part 2: Security Architecture'. This standard is relatively unsophisticated in terms of business drivers, but it sets out an important framework in terms of security services – the logical architecture, security mechanisms – the physical architecture, and security management – the operational architecture. The Sherwood team added two upper layers to provide a business-driven approach (contextual and conceptual architectures), and a lower layer to map onto real tools and products (component architecture).

Unknown to Sherwood at the time, this work was closely related to work being carried out in the USA on overall enterprise architectures, authored by John Zachman, published by the Zachman Institute for Framework Advancement and known as the Zachman Framework[3]. It is also interesting to note that in 1993 at COMPSEC 93 in London, before the Sherwood team had embarked on its journey into enterprise security architecture, Professor Brian Collins, who has kindly provided a foreword for this book, published a paper[4] with a colleague, Steve Mathews, in which they called for information security to be driven from a business perspective, and many of the factors identified in that paper are to be found in the business-focused SABSA® approach, although we did not at the time make the connection.

John Sherwood presented the SABSA® work at COMPSEC 96 in London and published the follow-up paper on it later that year. At that time he had never heard of Zachman's work. In April 1998 Sherwood was working for an international client as the security architect on a team engaged in developing entirely new global infrastructure architecture. As part of that activity he was fortunate enough to visit a conference entitled 'Enterprise Architecture' in San Francisco, and one of the keynote speakers at that conference was John Zachman. It was in many ways a great experience, because here on the platform was someone else who was doing very similar things but in a much wider context. The similarities between the SABSA® model and the Zachman Framework were amazing, and Sherwood was able to rework SABSA® to incorporate some of the language and ideas that Zachman had talked about in his presentation. However, the original concepts of SABSA® remained pretty much unchanged.

In developing the application of the methods, Sherwood was to be greatly assisted by other members of his consulting team at Sherwood Associates. Both Andy Clark and David Lynas were key players in this respect, and both managed major projects with global clients. David Lynas went on to develop a highly successful training course that is offered on a regular basis by the Computer

---

[1]Reference: 'SABSA: A Method of Developing the Enterprise Security Architecture and Strategy', Computers & Security, Volume 15 No. 6, 1996, Elsevier Science.

[2]Reference: http://www.iso.ch/cate/d14256.html

[3]Reference: http://www.zifa.com

[4]Reference: 'Securing your Business Process', Dr Brian Collins and Steve Mathews of PCSL Consulting, presented at Compsec 93.

Security Institute[5], entitled How to Design a Winning Security Architecture[6]. More recently David Lynas has been presenting a series of training seminars and events in Australia, New Zealand and the Asia Pacific rim under the auspices of ALC Training[7], and his work with clients in that part of the world has led to some of the more recent innovations in the methodology. There were other Sherwood team members who were also important contributors to the work, and in particular we would like to thank Anne Watt, Julie Braun, Krag Brotby and David Watson.

The SABSA® framework is described later in the book and is used as a basis to construct the entire process of security architecture development that the book describes.

Relationship to Other Methods, Models and Standards

We know that some people with a cursory knowledge of the SABSA® approach have wondered to what extent it conflicts or competes with existing methods, models and standards, and the answer to their question is that it does not conflict or compete at all. The reader will find that there are numerous references to these other methods, models and standards and that SABSA® provides an overarching framework that binds them all together into a single holistic view of how to design and manage enterprise security. Nothing in the existing canon of knowledge and wisdom is negated or challenged by the SABSA® approach. Rather, SABSA® provides that final umbrella of unification that enables the security architect to pick and mix from the plethora of available methods, models and standards so as to bring together at the enterprise level a security architecture that is based upon many years of developed ideas from many experts, whilst at the same time providing the means to structure these ideas into a single holistic view.

And Finally...

We hope that you will enjoy reading our book and that it will become one of your primary reference texts as you navigate your way through the process of developing enterprise security architectures. We wish you all success along your interesting journey.

John Sherwood, Andrew Clark and David Lynas

June 2005

---

[5]Reference: http://www.gocsi.com
[6]Reference: http://www.gocsi.com/winning.htm
[7]Reference: http://www.alctraining.com.au

Acknowledgements

This book would not have been possible without the support, encouragement, diligence and constructive feedback provided by many of the practitioners of SABSA® and our clients. We would particularly like to thank those who were there at the beginning when SABSA® and the ideas for this book were formed and those who helped it develop into the mature version that it is today. They include:

Chris Amery	Debi Ashenden	Michael Bacon
Alan Bernstein	Mike Bourne	Tony Bramwell
Julie Braun	Krag Brotby	Brian Collins
Mike Corby	Luc De Clercq	Paul Dorey
Stan Dormer	Marty Edelman	Tim Evans
Hans-Peter Fischer	Jon Fitzgerald	Shaun Fothergill
Ed Fulford	Eric Guldentops	Jacques Hagelstein
Mike Henson	Julien Holstein	Paul Hopkins
Andy Jones	Debbie Joy	Eva Jun
Jenny Kane	Wilhelm Koch	John McGuire
Rob Maines	John Mulholland	Richard Nealon
Dale Newnham	David Nielsen	Kosta Peric
Jane Scarratt	Martin Smith	Peter Stevenson
Paul Stubbs	Angela Taulelei	Steve Thomas
Howard Thompson	Mike Usher	Mark Waghorne
David Watson	Anne Watt	Peter Wenham
Rob Wood		

In addition, we gratefully acknowledge the contribution of others who have helped improve this book by their feedback and guidance. They include:

Niels Bjergstrom	Vince Gallo	Chris Keating
Zika Milenkovic	John O'Leary	Fred Piper
David Roberts	Michael Strang	Steve Temblett
Matt Whelan		

And of course those at CMP Books; Dorothy Cox, Matt Kelsey, Gail Saari, Hastings Hart (for his superb copyediting) and the rest of the team who have done such sterling work to bring this book to publication.

We apologise to those whose names we may have forgotten to include.

We hope you enjoy reading this book on a subject about which we are all passionate. If you spot any errors or omissions we would be grateful to hear from you so that we may make corrections to future editions.

John Sherwood

Andrew Clark

David Lynas

Part 1: Introduction

This book is entitled *Enterprise Security Architecture*. Here we begin by looking at what exactly we might mean by those words. As with all of the parts of the book, we shall start with some dictionary[1] definitions to help us understand the language we are using.

ar·chi+tec+ture n. 1. the art and science of designing and supervising the construction of buildings and similar structures. 2. a style of building or structure: Gothic architecture. 3. buildings or structures collectively. 4. the structure or design of anything: *the architecture of the universe*. – **ar·chi+tec+tur+al** *adj.*

– **ar·chi+tec+tur+al+ly** *adv.*

ar·chi+tect *n.* 1. a person qualified to design and supervise the construction of buildings. 2. a person similarly qualified in another form of construction: a naval architect. 3. any planner or creator: *the architect of the expedition.* [C16: from French *architecte*, from Latin *architectus*, from Greek *arkhitektōn* director of works, from ARCHI- + *tektōn* workman; related to *tekhnê* art, skill.]

se+cure *adj.* 1. free from danger, damage, etc. 2. free from fear, care, etc. 3. in safe custody. 4. not likely to fail, become loose, etc. 5. able to be relied on: certain: a secure investment. 6. *Nautical.* stowed away or made inoperative. 7. *Archaic.* careless or overconfident. ˜*vb.* 8. (*tr.*) to obtain or get possession of: *I will secure some good seats.* 9. (when *intr.*, often foll. by against) to make or become free from danger, fear, etc. 10. (tr.) to make fast or firm; fasten. 11. (when *intr.*, often foll. by against) to make or become certain; guarantee: this plan will secure your happiness. 12. (*tr.*) to assure (a creditor) of payment, as by giving security. 13. (*tr.*) to make (a military position) safe from attack. 14. *Nautical.* to make (a vessel or its contents) safe or ready by battening down hatches, stowing gear, etc. 15. (*tr.*) *Nautical.* to stow or make inoperative: to secure the radio. [C16: from Latin *securus* free from care, from *se-* without + *cura* care] – **sec+cur+a·ble** *adj.* – **sec+cure+ly** *adv.* – **sec+cure+ment** *n.* – **sec+cure+ness** *n.* – **sec+cur+er** *n.*

se+cu+ri·ty *n.* *pl.* ·ties. 1. the state of being secure. 2. assured freedom from poverty or want: *he needs the security of a permanent job.* 3. a person or thing that secures, guarantees, etc. 4. precautions taken to ensure against theft, espionage, etc: *the security in government offices was not very good.* 5. (often *pl.*) a. a certificate of creditorship or property carrying the right to receive interest or dividend, such as shares or bonds. b. the financial asset represented by such a certificate. 6. the specific asset that the creditor can claim title to in the event of default on an obligation. 7. something given or pledged to secure the fulfilment of a promise or obligation. 8. a person who undertakes to fulfil another person's obligation. 9. *Archaic.* carelessness or overconfidence.

---

[1]Collins English Dictionary

Security Architecture

We first look for a definition of 'security architecture' by drawing on the distilled knowledge and wisdom embodied in the dictionary definitions above.

Security architecture is the art and science of designing and supervising the construction of business[2] systems, usually business information systems, which are: free from danger, damage, etc.; free from fear, care, etc.; in safe custody; not likely to fail; able to be relied upon; safe from attack.

A security architect is a person qualified to design and supervise the construction of secure business systems, usually secure business information systems.

This book is about security architecture, in both of the above senses. It has been written for those who are, or who are striving to become, security architects. It has also been written for those who do not themselves aspire to become a security architect but who will commission and accept delivery of security architectural work. They will want to know what to request, what to expect, and how to judge the quality of the deliverables that they receive from their security architects. It is a book for anyone who has any interest at all in security architecture.

---

[2]The use of the term 'business' here has the broadest possible interpretation in this book. It is not confined to systems used by commercial organisations, but is meant to imply that there is some serious intent in having and running the system and that costs, benefits and risks are serious issues that need to be addressed. The word 'business' at least includes any activity of any commercial, industrial, government, educational, or charitable organisation. In some circumstances it could also include private individuals and domestic households, although we do not anticipate that this sector will be a significant consumer of this book.

Chapter 1: The Meaning of Security

If you are to understand 'security architecture' you must first be sure that you understand 'security'. It is a term that is used many times in many contexts and frequently with different meanings. Here the meaning is discussed within the context of this book – that is protection of the business.

In this chapter you will learn about:

- The misunderstanding and conflict that often exists between business users and security advisors and designers;

- The need to ensure that security is in response to perceived business risks and that any other reason for including security is almost certainly invalid;

- The benefit of seeing security not as a cost, but as a business enabler – helping to achieve business objectives.

The Cultural Legacy: Business Prevention

Security has a bad reputation for getting in the way of real business

Security, especially information security, has a bad reputation. Those of us who have worked as information system security professionals in an operational business environment know this only too well. When you walk into the room everyone groans. They say: 'Here come the security guys again! They are going to give us even more passwords to remember, more rules to enforce and they will create even more difficulties in our lives that will prevent us from getting on with real business. Why don't they just leave us alone?'

Some people even call us the 'business prevention' department!

This reputation has developed because of the way security professionals have practised

Is it an unfair reputation? Are we being misjudged and slandered by our colleagues? Well, if we are honest with ourselves, we as a profession probably deserve it all. Not you and me, of course, because we are enlightened. But the profession as a whole has certainly got that reputation because we collectively behaved like that and still behave like that. Now that I think about it, perhaps you and I were also partly responsible, before our enlightenment.

How did it happen? Why did we get this reputation? What did we do wrong?

We need an accurate definition of what we mean by 'security'

Well, in our view, it is because we have not been using a very good definition of the terms 'security' and 'secure'. What do they mean to you? Have you ever had the experience of being asked (as consultants are often asked) by a client or user: 'Have a look at this system; do you consider it to be secure?'

A technical definition of security may not be helpful

Some people, in order to prepare an answer, will start to look at the technical nuts and bolts of the system. They will give opinions on how this and that widget is weak, and how someone could get access to these and those files, and so on and so on. It's a technical analysis of the system, which may or may not be useful. Whether or not it is useful will depend on the answer to an important question. The prudent and experienced security professional will already have asked this question before answering the enquirer. The critical question is: 'What do you mean by "secure"?'

Security can be defined only relative to the value and risk propositions of the business

'Security' is a relative term. There is no absolute scale of security or insecurity. Both terms, 'secure' and 'security', have a meaning only when interpreted as attributes of something that you consider valuable. Something valuable that is in some way at risk needs to be secured. How much security does it need? Well that depends upon the value and upon the operational risk. How do you measure the operational risk? Now you are getting to the real questions that will lead you to an understanding of what you really mean by the term 'secure'.

Measuring and Prioritising Business Risk

Risk is a combination of asset value, business impact, threat and vulnerability

Security is used to protect things of value. In a business environment things that have value are often called assets. If assets are in some way damaged or destroyed, then you will suffer a business impact. The potential event by which you can suffer the damage or destruction is a threat. To prevent threats from crystallising into loss events that have a business impact, you use a layer of protection to keep the threats away from your assets. If the assets are poorly protected (i.e. your security is poor) then you have a vulnerability to the threat. To improve the protection and reduce the vulnerability you introduce security controls, which can be either technical or procedural.

Risk management is a combination of risk assessment and 'risk mitigation'

The process of identifying business assets, recognising the threats, assessing the level of business impact that would be suffered if the threats were to crystallise, and analysing the vulnerabilities, is known as operational risk assessment. Applying suitable controls to gain a balance between security, usability, cost and other business requirements is called operational risk mitigation. Operational risk assessment and operational risk mitigation jointly comprise what is often called operational risk management.

The main objective is to prioritise risks so as to make wise control decisions

Later chapters in this book examine operational risk management in much greater detail (see Chapter 15). The main thing that you need to understand at this stage is that risk management is all about identifying and prioritising the risks through the risk assessment[1] process and applying levels of control in line with those priorities.

Control objectives are the abstract statement of business needs

Not all risks are worthy of implementing additional security and control, either because the potential losses are not significant enough or because the costs of implementing the controls are high compared to the potential losses. What you get from the risk assessment is a set of business requirements for security and control, ranked in some kind of order of priority. These are often expressed as a series of control objectives – abstract descriptions of a business requirement for control. These in turn are used to drive the selection of risk mitigation approaches: broad security and control strategies, logical security services, physical security mechanisms, and eventually the security products, tools and technology components with which you construct your security architecture.

---

[1]Some people make a distinction between 'risk assessment' – by which they mean taking a qualitative view of the risks, and 'risk analysis' – which they mean taking a quantitative view. In this book we shall advocate only qualitative risk assessment. However, we are equally comfortable with the use of 'risk analysis' to describe this qualitative approach, and we do not make a distinction in the definitions of these two terms.

Enablement objectives are another type of abstract statement of business need

Although the term 'control objectives' is well known and widely used, especially within the auditing community, we like to think of a complementary term: 'enablement objectives'. This is to emphasise one of the key messages of the early chapters of this book – that security is primarily all about business enablement and not at all about business prevention. Although 'control' is a valid term, it does lack the imaginative flair that we hope to inspire in those who read this book, and so these phrases are complementary so as to give a more balanced view of what the business objectives really are.

Enablement is often the flip side of control

For example, consider the brakes on a car. The brakes have a clear control function – they are used to prevent the car from going too fast and to reduce the speed if the driver judges that it is too high. However, another way of looking at this function is that having better brakes enables the car to be driven at much higher speeds, because the driver now has the confidence that if the need arises, braking will be fast and efficient. It is a completely different way of viewing the same function – one way is about reducing overall speed, the other about increasing it.

Security should be business risk-driven

By adopting this risk-based approach (in terms of both control objectives and enablement objectives) to developing your security strategy you can more closely align your information systems security with the needs of the business. However, there is much, much more you can do to get value from your efforts. This is only the beginning, and in the following sections we shall look at other ways to build up the business case.

Information Security as the Enabler of Business

Security professionals would like to have a positive reputation with their business colleagues

The reputation that we (information security professionals) would really like to have is very different from the one that we actually have. When we walk into the room we would like to hear: 'Hoorah! Here come the security guys. They're going to help us to meet our business objectives. They're going to help us to realise our wildest dreams by using information and communications technology in new and exciting ways to facilitate business growth, without us losing sleep because of all the risks we would have to take. Our investments in information security are a key success factor for this business. Our information security strategy is critical to the current and future business growth. Invite the guys in, sit them down, give them a drink, and a salary increase.'

We wish!

Not the 'business prevention' department, but the 'business enabling' department.

Your good reputation will depend upon your abilities to serve the business well

But if you do your job properly it could happen. That's what your goal should be. Information security is the enabling technology of electronic business. You have to sell these ideas to your business colleagues and then make them come true. If you don't offer this sort of value to the business then why are you there? What possible benefits does information security have if not these?

New technologies are impacting the way that business is being done

There are several key technologies that are changing the way that business will be done in the future. These include:

- The Internet and the World Wide Web with all its services and protocols, especially the emerging 'web services' protocols;

- Mobile handsets with sophisticated communications and processing capabilities;

- Web-enabled digital television and the prospect of other web-enabled domestic appliances, especially for delivering entertainment and information services;

- Client-server distributed architectures and advanced middleware products;

- High-bandwidth digital communications, including broadband, cable, cellular telephony, satellite and terrestrial broadcast;

- Advanced data networking protocols;

- Wireless communications;

- Public key infrastructure;

- Network computing, thin clients, and mobile code.

The effect is to migrate the point of sale and the point of delivery right into the customer's premises

The major change that we shall see as a result of the deployment of these technologies is the continued migration of both the point of sale and the point of delivery right into the premises of the customer in what is called the B2C (business-to-consumer) model. That is what 'electronic business' or 'digital business' really means. People who want to buy something or transact some business no longer need to make a physical visit to the supplier. They can use some type of information and communications technology system to make contact from their home base. They can browse through virtual shops, looking at virtual products on the virtual shelves. They can click the mouse to examine the product more carefully and click again to select their purchase. The products themselves may be picked automatically in the electronic warehouse and dispatched to the customer with minimal human intervention.

Business-to-business is where most of the initial growth is seen in digital business

More often than not both the supplier and the customer in digital business transactions are business organisations. This is known as the B2B (business-to-business) model. 'Supply chain management' and 'eProcurement' are amongst the most popular phrases used to describe the goals of business organisations in applying this model.

Lack of customer confidence is an obstacle to digital business and eBusiness development

However, the number of possible threats, impacts and vulnerabilities that arise in all of these complex systems is enormous. The major obstacle to the development of electronic business (or digital business) on a huge scale is the low level of confidence that is inspired in the customer community as more and more news items give the grisly details of security breaches.

Think of the major business risks:

- Disclosure of private, personal information, such as details of bank accounts, medical history, personal business interests, etc;

- Fraudulent buyers;

- Fraudulent sellers;

- Theft of payment authorisation details (such as credit card data);

- Errors and mistakes on a large scale (you ordered how many?);

- Disputes that are difficult to resolve because everyone refuses to take responsibility;

- Frustration and loss of confidence in systems that do not work properly.

On-line banking security breaches are very damaging to reputations

Here are a few examples of firms that have experienced some of these risks firsthand. The first one concerns retail on-line banking.

Case Study: The Wrong Accounts

A major retail bank with a global brand name had established an on-line banking service that boasted 1.2 million customers. It had decided to undertake a major overhaul and re-launch of the web site, and as part of this re-launch one of the much-vaunted features was to be improved security. This was at a time when the lack of public confidence in Internet security was suffering heavy battering in the popular press, and the bank had decided to take a pro-active stand on this issue.

The upgrade was implemented over a weekend. On Monday morning customers began to log on to the new service. Several of them (not the majority, just a very few, but plenty to be newsworthy) were presented with the account details of another customer in place of their own!

The technical explanation seems to have been that when two customers logged on at virtually the same time, the second customer was shown the same details as the first. Oh dear!

As soon as the bank became aware of the problem and had verified its existence they shut down the site (at 15:30 on Monday afternoon). The service was closed for several hours and the old version of the system was restored later that evening.

The bank tried to stress that only a very few customers (around 10 in fact) had experienced the problem, but that did not prevent the Tuesday newspapers from carrying the story on the front page with headlines such as 'Security fear shuts on-line bank'.

The embarrassment and the damage to the reputation of the bank were substantial. Perhaps even worse, coming as it did in the midst of a stream of similar incidents and adverse newspaper headlines, the damage to the online banking industry as a whole, and to the growth of eBusiness in general, was also significant.

The second case study relates to a major public utilities company. The story appeared on the front pages of the newspapers in the same month in which the on-line banking incident above was reported.

Public relations management is just as important as technical expertise in the protection of reputation

Case Study: In Denial

A public utilities company selling both gas and electricity had developed a web-based interface for its customers to manage their accounts on-line.

One customer discovered quite by accident that by removing part of the URL on his browser command line, he could display a file that contained the bank account details and credit card details of all of the customers who used this service – approximately 2,500 customers. He had stumbled on this fact by pure chance as he mistyped the URL command.

He immediately telephoned the company, through their customer help line, and informed them of the problem. They did nothing. He telephoned again to find out what was being done, and was informed that 'it could not happen' and that there was no problem. He offered to show them the evidence but they told him to stop annoying them.

In frustration he then copied the file onto his own PC and contacted another web site that specialises in publishing juicy details such as these. They were delighted to help and published the entire file. He then contacted the company again and told them where they could look at their file.

Their first response was to report this gentleman to the police and have him arrested on suspicion of hacking into their system. The newspapers loved this! Eventually they came to their senses, dropped the charges, offered a statement of public thanks to the man for his assistance, and invited him to advise them on security matters in future. (We are not sure that this last point was entirely wise, but then we are seeing here a company that has little idea how to handle Internet security issues. We would hazard a guess that this whole incident was managed from a very technical perspective, with little or no input from people with any real business acumen.)

This incident tells you a lot about business risk and Internet services. It is not just the fact that when these problems occur and they get into the newspapers then the organisation suffers reputation damage. This incident was handled with such crass lack of public relations finesse that you can see immediately that there is more to business risk than technical failure. When the technology fails (as indeed it will from time to time) then there must be an adequate crisis management response that includes the very critical issue of public relations management.

The bank in the earlier case study had some major problems, but at least it knew how to handle them when they occurred.

Here is another banking tale now. This one is of a different nature to the first, and emphasising the broader nature of security as we define it. It actually combines two cases, both very similar in nature.

Scaling and capacity planning are critical issues with respect to service availability

Case Study: Failure to Deliver

(a) A major retail bank had planned and developed a new Internet banking service for its retail customers. The web site was launched amid the usual marketing hype, and people started to use it.

During its first week of operation it was crippled by the surge in demand, and had to be taken out of service several times for several hours at a time to fix the problems. It was hopelessly under-scaled for the level of business that it attracted.

(b) Another retail bank with a very similar market profile to the first one in this example had also planned and developed a similar on-line banking service, but this one was a combination of Internet banking and telephone banking.

Perhaps in response to an analysis of what had happened to the first bank, it delayed the launch of the new service just one day before it was due to go live. Of course by that time it was too late to avoid the humiliation of the newspapers trumpeting this news and the reasons for it.

Both of these incidents underline an important point – that availability of a business service is one of the key goals to be protected and enabled by good security practices, and that security includes anything that has a bearing upon the operational stability and continuity of the business service. Capacity planning and scalability are amongst the issues that must be addressed within the security architecture.

Another case study concerns the movement towards electronic government. In this case the provision of an electronic interface for handling personal tax returns.

Electronic government will only succeed if the citizens can have confidence in the correct operation of the systems

Case Study: A Taxing Problem

A national government personal taxation department launched a new web-based service so that its tax-paying citizens could log on via the Internet and file their personal tax returns on-line.

The service received very large amounts of advance publicity and even more publicity once it was launched. A key goal was to save government money on administration of paper systems, and so financial incentives were offered to users to tempt them to use the service. A modest reduction in the tax bill was to be the reward for filing and paying on-line.

The service was aimed to attract around 300,000 users within its first year of operation. It was therefore very embarrassing for the department concerned to have to admit publicly that the software on the site contained serious bugs that introduced errors into the tax calculations for those using this method.

It seems that errors of several thousands of pounds (in favour of the tax authority, not in favour of the taxpayer) were a regular feature of the calculations, resulting in taxpayers receiving tax demands for far greater amounts of money than they actually owed. If you knew that the service behaved like this, would you use it?

At the same time as this was going on, it was revealed that another computer system that identifies people who may be under-paying their tax and should be investigated, was also malfunctioning. This meant that some people who were quite innocent of any wrongdoing were being identified by the system and subjected to interrogations by investigative tax officers.

If the introduction of electronic government requires the confidence of the citizens in its correct operation, incidents like these are not helping. Electronic government will only succeed if the citizens can see concrete evidence that these issues have been addressed.

Finally, from the same page of the same newspaper where we found the account of the tax problems, here is an insurance group suffering major problems in launching its new service.

Systems integration is a major challenge in the delivery of legacy back-end services through new front-end portals

Case Study: Disintegration

An insurance portal was launched on the web promising consolidated on-line access to a range of household insurance services from several major insurance companies. The marketing budget for this new service has been reported as being 5 million pounds sterling per year.

The launch and the weeks and months following it were dogged by a series of serious technical problems and failures. The site was only partially operational, and the faults and excuses seemed to vary from day to day. An example message was reported as 'Although we can offer a full service for travel insurance, we are currently resolving technical difficulties on home and motor insurance'.

One part of the web site promises: 'Our mission is to make buying insurance quicker and simpler'. So, if that's the key business goal, why isn't the technical department aware of that and performing to a level that supports it?

The public relations speak is well honed: 'It is not that the site isn't working, it's just that some of the insurers have had a problem integrating their systems.'

So here is lesson to be learned – security is not just about confidentiality, integrity and availability. It requires a much wider view to be taken. In this case the overall service was unavailable because of systems integration problems. In our view, control over systems integration is all part of 'security management' and 'security architecture'.

The current environment is a huge opportunity for security professionals to excel

So here is your opportunity to show how good you are. You have the whole world pleading for security of information systems to enable them to do business. You have the technology to provide the solutions. What you must also demonstrate is that you have the associated skills to apply that technology to solving the problems of electronic business.

Technology alone is not enough to produce effective security

You need much more than pure technology. You also need:

- Good understanding of the business needs and risks;

- Strategic architectures;

- Project management;

- Systems integration;

- Security management policies and practices;

- Enterprise-wide security culture and infrastructure.

Adding Value to the Core Product

There are different issues for retail business and corporate business

In the section above we have focused on 'electronic commerce' in a very retail sense of the phrase. Let us now move on to a more corporate view of the electronic business world.

ICT is impacting on traditional bricks-and-mortar companies in several ways

Many companies have been supplying traditional products in traditional ways for many decades. To move very far indeed from the retail end, consider for a moment the civil aerospace industry. The products here are aeroplanes – not something you or I would normally buy for ourselves.

Information and communications technology (ICT) is impacting this industry in two very different ways:

- The products themselves are incorporating more and more embedded ICT systems;

- The support of these products is very information-intensive, and the supply of this support information is becoming more and more automated.

Most traditional industries have similar experiences

We choose civil aerospace as an example because it is easy to see how information and communications technology is critical to this industry. However, almost every industry has a similar story to tell. Electronics are becoming an integral part of many products, and on-line information available to customers is a key aspect of product support.

Customer confidence in safety-critical systems is created and maintained through a comprehensive assurance programme

Case Study: Safety Assurance

First consider the embedded systems in civil aircraft. Not only are aeroplanes very expensive items, but they also carry passengers whose safety is of the utmost importance both to the customers themselves and to those who build and operate the aircraft. The correct functioning of these embedded systems is critical to the success of the business mission.

Assurance of design and implementation, elimination of operational errors and failures and prevention of malicious interference are all absolutely at the heart of providing confidence that the product (and the service that is delivered through it) will function as intended.

The manufacturers and the operators need this confidence – but most of all it is the end-customers (passengers) who need to be confident that they are travelling in a safe aircraft. The way to provide this confidence is through the provision of appropriate quality management and information security practices.

This is a clear example where the key goal is assurance. We shall return to this goal later in our discussions.

The second example looks at the issue of product support during and after delivery.

New ways of working enabled by new technology have a significant impact on customer expectations

Case Study: Raising Expectations

It is said that when you buy an aeroplane you also get a pile of documentation equivalent to the weight of the aircraft. The supply of this information is not only to tell you how to fly and maintain the aircraft. It is to meet the requirements of the industry regulators who enforce strict traceability of all aspects of the design, construction and operation of the plane. The certification of the aircraft as being airworthy depends to a large extent upon this documentation.

The pile of paper equal in size to the plane itself (or however large the pile really is) is very difficult to manage, and so electronic information is replacing it. Electronic solutions require less storage space, are easier to keep up to date, are easier to search for specific items, and are much easier, quicker and less expensive to deliver to the customer (that is, the airline that operates the aircraft).

Not surprisingly the civil aircraft manufacturers are moving as quickly as they can to deliver support documentation to their customers through on-line information systems. When the major manufacturers compete for business, the support of the aircraft during its lifetime is one of the most critical factors to be considered by the airline (customer), since the operational lifetime of good civil aircraft can be anything up to about 30 years. The use of on-line information systems to improve this support is therefore a competitive advantage.

This raises several important information security issues:

– Authenticity of design documents, drawings, service bulletins, etc. Are the electronic documents that were received through the on-line delivery system really from the manufacturer? Customer confidence (and safety) is at stake.

– Information service availability. Once a major airline gets used to a 365 day x 24 hour service[2] and plans its flight operations around a dependence on such a service level, then any failure to meet this service level will result in very unhappy airlines and many potential risks to their own businesses.

Any service that is to be completely successful in this environment in the long term must address these issues. The really challenging aspect is that the potential problems may not emerge at all during the early days of operation. It is downstream, when total dependence has set in, that these problems will become business-critical, and by then it will be too late if the design has not mitigated these risks.

Customer decisions are affected by perceptions of service

These information services that are used to support the core product add real value and become competitive factors for customers making buying decisions. However, customer confidence will be maintained only if these services are secured to an appropriate level, taking into account the business risks.

Empowering the Customers

Customer empowerment means giving the customer choices

We have looked at examples from both the retail world of electronic commerce and the corporate world of electronic business. In all cases we see that electronic information systems are the means to empower the customer to gain greater benefits. These information systems therefore become important competitive factors for the suppliers, because the customers will use their power to select those suppliers who can meet the challenge of providing these benefits.

Understanding the concept of customer service is critical to business success in the new economy

Case Study: Supplying Power to the Customer

The utilities industries have become an interesting example of this phenomenon of empowering the customer through the web.

The product that arrives at your house or your office is essentially a commodity of unvarying quality (provided that service outages have been all but eliminated,

---

[2]In this industry 365 by 24 really does mean every day of the year in a global, multicultural world where religious diversity means that major festivals vary greatly in their timing.

which is the case in most economically developed countries). Electricity sold by one company is indistinguishable from electricity sold by another. The same is true for gas and for water.

Once the industry has been deregulated (as for example in the United Kingdom), there is one company that is responsible for distribution infrastructure and other companies who have relationships with customers and who sell the commodities.

In this environment one of the key things that distinguishes one supplier from another is customer service. The core product remains unaltered. The customer is only ever a couple of mouse clicks away from changing supplier within the comfort of his or her own home, and the only thing that will keep the customer on board (or conversely, that will drive the customer away) is customer service.

At this point you need to look at customer service in its widest possible context. Some points to consider are:

- What do customers see as the intangible aspects of customer service? In other words, how does it feel to do business here? Is it a good or a bad experience?

- How do you manage customer expectations and how high should you build them? (Because if you build them high, you had better be able to deliver to that level of expectation).

- How do you manage customer relationships so as to avoid a confrontational style of relationship (in which customers have complaints) and maintain a long-term service relationship (in which customers remain happy with the service and are content to let it continue indefinitely)?

- What contributes to the 'psychological contract' (as opposed to the legal contract) in a customer service relationship? This is important, because no matter what the strictly legal contractual terms are, there are always customer expectations of service that can never be articulated in a legal document, and meeting these expectations is a matter of trust. The legal document is just a safety net and a definition of the minimum acceptable level of service. In reality people expect much more than this.

- How do you develop consistency in customer service communications across all the people and departments who interact with customers and who therefore have an impact on the customer's perception of service?

- What are the current and projected patterns of communication with the customers and what are the service offers that will be made?

- What are the critical moments of truth in your customer relationships at which the customer relationship is at highest risk because the customer's service expectations are being tested to their limit, and how should you deal with these moments of truth?

So, is the design of a utilities business web site a technical issue? We do not think so. Refer back to the case study in an earlier section that discussed the security breach in a public utilities web site. Had that company understood these concepts of customer service? What do you think?

Once you empower the customers in this way, you have empowered them to leave you on a whim. So the business relationship that you value so much must be protected. Security procedures such as user authentication and login potentially have a major impact on whether or not the user has a good experience using a web site. How personal, private information is protected and safeguarded also affects the customer's perception of the service level being provided, as does the availability of the site and services delivered through it. For these and many other reasons, customer service considerations are a major driver of security strategy and security architecture.

Information security practices can deeply affect perceptions of customer service

Information security is a critical component, without which it will be difficult for suppliers to meet this customer service challenge. Customers will evaluate suppliers not only on the products themselves but also on the means by which those products are marketed, sold and supported. Where on-line information systems are involved, that means that the quality, reliability, integrity and availability of those information services will be key factors in determining which suppliers succeed and which do not.

Service quality and information security are closely linked

To maintain that quality of service, one of the major tools you will need is an effective, risk-based information security programme and a structured information systems security architecture.

Protecting Relationships and Leveraging Trust

Business relationships are based upon trust

There is another security-related dimension to business relationships that we have not yet explored here: the concept of trust. We shall return to this in great detail later on in the book, but for the present time let us take a first glance at the subject.

Trust is a business relationship attribute, not a technical attribute

When you do business with someone, at whatever level (personal or corporate), you establish some level of trust in the other party. You usually evaluate a number of signals that you receive, perhaps over some time, to determine how much you trust this person. How do they present themselves (standard of dress, location and type of premises, eye contact, handshake, etc.)? Have you done business before? How did it go? How long has the firm been established? Can you get a reference from someone else you know and trust (a trusted third party) – someone that already knows this person and can vouch for him or her? And so on.

Technical systems need to protect the trust that exists in a relationship

Trust is an essential pre-requisite to doing business, and trust is entirely a relationship thing. Trust is not created through technical systems but through some mutual knowledge between the parties. However, technical systems are used to protect the trust in the relationship that already exists.

If you trust the source of an information service, you must also be sure that you are talking to the authentic trusted party and not to an impostor

Case Study: Trusted Sources

We return here to our civil aerospace example.

If an airline buying an aeroplane from a major aircraft manufacturer has built up a high level of trust in the product and its supplier, then a drawing or a technical specification supplied by that manufacturer will be trusted to be correct. This trust comes from a relationship that has been built up between the supplier and the customer.

The protection of that trust is through a technical service that verifies the authenticity of such a document when it is delivered electronically through an on-line information system. Thus a digital signature on the received electronic document, supported by a certified public key to verify that signature, is a mechanism that supports an authenticity service, which in turn supports and protects the trust that exists between the parties.

To build an information distribution service for the purpose of distributing aircraft design documents would require this sort of technical approach in order to protect the level of trust that exists at the business level.

Trusted third parties act as intermediaries to introduce business partners to one another

These technical services are no substitute for trust. They do not create trust. They merely protect trust that already exists. However, indirect trust, through a third party (sometimes called transitive trust), is an important part of setting up digital business networks. It is obviously an advantage for both customers and suppliers to be empowered to do business with one another even though they each have no previous direct knowledge of one another. This is where the third-party referee comes into the picture. The third party needs to be trusted by both of the other parties. This trusted third party is then able to play the role of 'introducer' by vouching for each of the two business parties to the other. This is usually achieved by the trusted third party issuing each entity with some certified credentials. This is called a digital certificate and is certified by a digital signature of the trusted third party.

Business relationships are formed in similar ways to social relationships

It's a bit like the situation where you go to a cocktail party at someone's house – someone who is an old friend of yours and with whom you have a long-standing trust relationship, built up through experience and mutual interaction. At the party another guest, someone who you have not met before, nor heard of them, approaches you. It's quite different from meeting this person in a downtown bar or on the street, where you might be very cautious and even suspicious of being approached by a stranger. The first thing you each ask one another is your name and how you know the host of the party. This establishes the credentials – 'Oh, I'm an old friend from college days' or 'I'm his sister-in-law'. It gives the new friendship a kick-start, because you have established that you are both trusted by the host, who in this case acts as a trusted introducer for you both, giving both of you some confidence that it is alright to proceed with a friendship. You can begin to interact with a level of trust that would not be possible in the downtown bar. That's why house parties are such a success!

Business relationships are driven by human factors, not by technology

This trusted third-party mechanism is an important part of human life, both in social interactions and in business relationships. In many cases the two are heavily intertwined. The cynical observer might point out how much business is done on the golf course, but business is primarily about relationships between business people, and it so happens that many relationships are built whilst playing golf.

Mutual trust is essential, and must be protected by technical systems

Many business deals are founded upon a personal introduction by a mutually trusted third party, or upon belonging to some business community that is in some way regulated by a trusted overseer. Thus, when you build information systems, these technical systems can leverage trust that already exists, whether directly or indirectly, and they can protect those trusted business relationships in the course of doing business through this new information system-based medium.

To Summarise: What Does 'Security' Mean?

Security is all about protecting business goals and assets. It means providing a set of business controls that are matched to business needs, which in turn are derived from an assessment and analysis of business risks. The objective in risk assessment is to prioritise risks so as to focus on those that most require mitigation.

Risk is a complex concept, and for any given course of action there is a risk associated doing that thing and a risk associated with not doing it. Thus one must take care not to mitigate a specific risk whilst unintentionally increasing the overall risk to the wider range of business goals and objectives.

In its best possible light, security should be seen as enabling business by reducing risks to acceptable levels and thus allowing business to make use of new technologies for greater commercial advantage.

Security can also be a means to add value to the core product by enabling information services that are essential to the enhancement of the product itself or to the operational support of the product in the field.

Secure information services can empower the customers, enabling them to do business more easily, and providing them with enhanced services that will have competitive value.

Security in business information systems also protects and leverages the trust that exists between business partners, allowing them to establish relationships and to do business in new ways using new technologies.

Chapter 2: The Meaning of Architecture

This chapter explores what 'architecture' might really mean. In particular it examines the essential differences between 'architecture' and 'plumbing'. Both of these disciplines are of great value, but they are the not the same thing. In the world of ICT people sometimes get confused about which is which.

In this chapter you will learn about:

- The concept of architecture as a means to integrate solutions to a diverse range of complex needs, and as a means to manage that complexity;

- Conceptual layered approaches to architecture and the use of architectural reference models;

- The benefits of taking a holistic, strategic architectural approach as opposed to applying point solutions with tactical goals.

The Origins of Architecture

Architecture is best understood in the context of buildings

Architecture has its origins in the building of towns and cities, and everyone understands this sense of the word, so it makes sense to begin by examining the meaning of 'architecture' in this traditional context.

Architecture fulfils the needs of those who experience it

Architecture is a set of rules and conventions by which we create buildings that serve the purposes for which we intend them, both functionally and aesthetically. Our concept of architecture is one that supports our needs to live, to work, to do business, to travel, to socialise and to pursue our leisure. The multiplicity and complex interaction of these various activities must be supported, and this includes the relationship between the activities themselves and their integration into a whole lifestyle. Architecture is founded upon an understanding of the needs that it must fulfil.

The needs that architecture must fulfil are very diverse

These needs are expressed in terms of function, aesthetics, culture, government policies and civil priorities. They take into account how we feel about ourselves and about our neighbours and how they feel about us. In these various ways, architecture must serve all those who will experience it in any way.

Goals, environment, materials and skill are key drivers of architecture

Architecture is also both driven and constrained by a number of specific factors. These include the materials available within the locale that can be used for construction, the terrain, the prevailing climate, the technology and the engineering skills of the people.

This all boils down to three major factors that determine what architecture we will create. These factors are:

- Our goals;
- The environment;
- Our technical capabilities.

The Sydney Opera House could not have been built in piecemeal fashion

Case Study: An Icon of Australian Culture

The Sydney Opera House is perhaps one of the most famous buildings in the world. More than that, it is probably the most well-known example of modern architecture.

How does a building such as this come into existence? Could many small project teams build it, each with its own ideas about how things should be done, each designing its own piece of the building from scratch, and each having a narrow view of the overall business goal as its motivator?

Clearly this would not work. A building of this calibre (whether you are an enthusiast for the design or not) could never be designed and built in piecemeal fashion. The only way that something truly architectural can be created is from a single central vision of its design – an overall concept. Later sections of the book, especially Chapter 10, discuss conceptual architecture at some length.

It is the job of the architect to create the vision and the direction, taking into account the very widest view of all the possible requirements from all possible interested parties. This vision then becomes the road map that guides all others who will work on the project. The architect remains in control throughout, supervising the work and ensuring that the integrity of the architectural design is not compromised at later stages.

Managing Complexity

A major function of architecture as a tool is to manage complexity in large projects

One of the key functions of architecture as a product of the architect is to provide a framework within which complexity can be managed successfully. Small, isolated, individual projects do not need architecture, because their level of complexity is limited and the chief designer can manage the overall design single-handedly. However, as the size and complexity of a project grows, then it is clear that many designers are needed, all working as a team to create something that has the appearance of being designed by a single design authority.

Architecture also acts as a road map for a collection of smaller projects that must be integrated into a single homogenous whole

Also, if an individual project is not isolated, but rather is intended to fit harmoniously within a much wider, highly complex set of other projects, then an architecture is needed to act as a road map within which all of these projects can be brought together into a seamless whole. The result must be as though they were all indeed part of a single, large, complex project. This applies whether the individual projects are designed and implemented simultaneously, or whether they are designed and implemented independently over an extended period of time.

Architecture provides a framework within which many members of a large design team can work harmoniously

As complexity increases, then a framework is needed within which each designer can work, contributing to the overall design. Each design team member must also be confident that his or her work will be in harmony with that of colleagues and that the overall integrity of the design will not be threatened by the work being split across a large design team.

This is achieved through layering techniques and through modularization

The role of architecture is to provide the framework that breaks down complexity into apparent simplicity. This is achieved by layering techniques – focusing attention on specific conceptual levels of thinking, and by modularization – breaking the overall design into manageable pieces that have defined functionality and defined interfaces. This process is also known as systems engineering and is discussed in greater detail in Chapter 5.

Information Systems Architecture

Architecture has been adapted to other spheres of creativity

The concept of architecture in buildings has been adapted to areas of life other than the building of towns and cities. For example one talks about a naval architect being someone that designs and supervises the construction of ships. In more recent times the term has been adopted in the context of designing and building business computer systems, and so the concept of information systems architecture has been born.

Information systems architecture addresses the creation of business computing systems

In the same way that conventional architecture defines the rules and standards for the design and construction of buildings, information systems architecture addresses these same issues for the design and construction of computers, communications networks and the distributed business systems that are implemented using these technologies.

Information systems architecture has influences similar to buildings architecture

As with the conventional architecture of buildings, towns and cities, information systems architecture must therefore take account of:

- The goals that are to be achieved through the systems;

- The environment in which the systems will be built and used;

- The technical capabilities of the people to construct and operate the systems and their component sub-systems.

Architecture addresses a wide range of issues beyond the technical domain

If one accepts this analysis then one is already well on the way to recognising that information systems architecture is concerned with much more than mere technical factors. It is concerned with what the enterprise wants to achieve and with the environmental factors that will influence those achievements.

An inadequate understanding of architecture can lead to failure to deliver business value

In some organisations this broad view of information systems architecture is not well understood. Technical factors are often the main ones that influence the architecture, and under these conditions the architecture can fail to deliver what the business expects and needs.

This book addresses the wider issues, not just the technical dimension

This book is mainly concerned with only one aspect of information systems architecture: that is the security of business information systems. However, in addressing this specialist area the authors have tried to provide as much advice as possible on how to take the broader view. Thus the focus is on an enterprise security architecture, to emphasise that it is the enterprise and its activities that are to be secured and that the security of computers and networks is only a means to this end.

Business systems architecture is the highest-level framework

First, however, here are some general ideas of modern information systems architecture, since a security architecture must fit within this overall framework. Figure 2-1 shows a reference model for the overall business systems architecture[1]. For most people this has several major component sub-architectures, as described in the sections below and as represented in the diagram.

---

[1]This reference model is a creation of the authors of this book. It does not appear in any international standard.

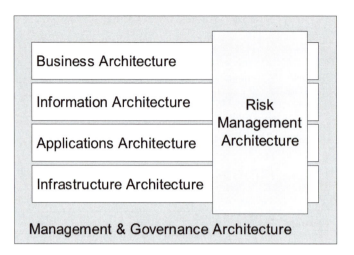

Figure 2-1: A High-Level Reference Model for Business Systems Architecture

Business Architecture

Business architecture is the primary component

The business architecture describes from an enterprise-wide perspective how the business itself is structured into an organisational model, a set of processes, functions and so on. This is the primary architecture of all. The other sub-architectures are all created in support of this single overriding framework of how the business actually works. In other contexts this is often called the 'business model'.

Information Architecture

Information architecture is an abstract representation of the business

The business is represented by information. Every business relationship, every business process, every business transaction, indeed everything about the business, its planning, its control, its management and its success or failure, is represented by information. Information is an abstract representation of something that is real and tangible. This is why information is so important to business, because information is the business, represented in a particular form.

Information architecture is the framework for business information management

The information architecture describes the framework within which business information is created, organised, processed, stored, retrieved and communicated, and in the reference model (see Figure 2-1) it has been represented as the next level of abstraction down from the business itself.

It describes information types and their behaviour

Information architecture describes information types and their overall structured relationships and organisation, information behaviour, information management processes, and physical locations and repositories for information. In particular it identifies and describes the major categories of information that are needed to support the business strategy and goals.

Applications Architecture

The applications architecture supports the information architecture

The applications are the suites of computer programs that carry out actions on business information on behalf of real business users. In the reference model (see Figure 2-1) the applications architecture is shown as the third level, supporting the information architecture, which in turn supports the business architecture.

Applications represent and support real business processes

The applications mirror critical automated parts of the business processes. The applications architecture describes how applications are to be designed, how they inter-operate with one another, and how they are supported within the infrastructure (hardware, software and communications networks). The applications must of course relate to the business processes that they support and the information resources that they create, maintain and process.

Modern applications archi-
tectures are likely to exhibit
certain common properties

Characteristics of modern applications architecture are likely to be:

- Component based – re-usable, generic modules, and hence quickly adaptable to new business needs;
- Service oriented – components offering services to one another;
- Built on a strategic middleware layer – for services integration;
- Offering distributed processing.

Applications architecture
enables business flexibility

The main objective of applications architecture is to enable business processes. It accomplishes that by creating applications that are flexible, economic and responsive to changes in the business.

Infrastructure Architecture

Infrastructure is the logical
and physical medium for
supporting applications

The applications need to be supported on logical and physical infrastructure. The term 'infrastructure' will be discussed in detail later on, but for now it is defined as being inclusive of:

The computer platforms (hardware and operating systems);

The computer networks (cables, lines, switches, routers, etc.);

The layer of software that bridges between infrastructures that have different physical characteristics and presents a consistent virtual interface to the applications. This is commonly known as 'middleware'.

Infrastructure architecture is
highly technical

Infrastructure architecture is at the heart of what most people would recognise as 'technical architecture'.

Risk Management Architecture

Risk management architec-
ture cuts across all others

In the reference model (see Figure 2-1) the four layers already described are represented as lying one on top of another. Cutting right across this layered structure is another front-plane box labelled 'Risk Management Architecture'.

Risk management architec-
ture is pervasive

The reference model represented here is more of a business model and not quite a systems model (although it exhibits some signs of being a framework for information systems design). It is essential to see risk management as a pervasive activity that happens within all of the other four layers. This risk management architecture is close to the notion of security architecture, but it is not quite the same. A more detailed discussion of risk management is provided in Chapter 9 and Chapter 15.

Management and Governance Architecture

Management and governance
architecture is all-pervasive

Finally, surrounding all other components in the reference model (see Figure 2-1) is the all-pervasive piece labelled 'Management and Governance Architecture' and shown in the diagram as a backplane, wrapping around everything else.

It describes how the manage-
ment team controls the
business

The representation of this as an all-encompassing component is critical. It is through this architectural framework that the senior management team controls the business, manages risk, and governs the business use of information, applications, and infrastructure.

Management and governance architecture describes levels of authority and decision making

The management and governance architecture describes the decision-making processes and levels of authority that are assigned to decision-making entities (individuals or committees). It is essentially a model of how power is wielded within the organisation and what span of control is associated with each entity.

Information Systems Architecture Reference Model

Definition of information systems architecture

This reference model for business systems architecture (see Figure 2-1) is a useful conceptual model of the various major components and how they relate to one another. An overarching definition of 'information systems architecture' might be:

> 'A consistent set of principles, policies and standards that sets the direction and vision for the development and operation of the organisation's business information systems so as to ensure alignment with and support for the business needs'

Infrastructure Architecture Reference Model

Infrastructure is a multi-layered technical architecture

However, a more detailed reference model is needed for the infrastructure component, since it is this part in which most of the technology of business systems is focused. Figure 2-2 shows a reference model for this technical infrastructure architecture.

Service integration is middleware plus data management plus common services

The applications sit on top of a layer shown here as 'Services Integration'. This is really traditional middleware plus data management services and a wide range of common services that are made available to applications transparently through the middleware layer. In the detailed discussions about conceptual security architecture later in the book the common services needed within the security architecture are examined more closely.

Data processing means 'platforms'; Information transfer means 'network'

Beneath the services integration layer are two other layers. The 'information transfer' layer is the communications network, and the data-processing layer comprises the platforms, including both

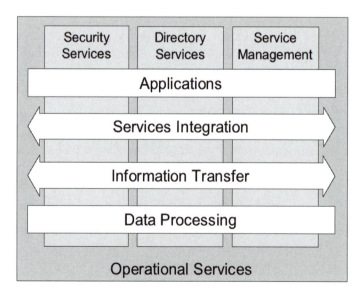

Figure 2-2: Infrastructure Architecture Reference Model

hardware and operating systems, in which the raw manipulation of physical bits and bytes takes place.

There are three pervasive service types

Behind these components the reference model shows three backplanes that cut across all of the other layered components. These service types are pervasive throughout the entire infrastructure:

- Security services (including all services used to control the infrastructure, such as time service);

- Directory services;

- Service management.

'Operational services' means people and the tasks that they perform

Finally, the entire infrastructure model is overlaid on another backplane labelled 'operational services'. The operational services represent the people and the operating processes and procedures that they carry out. Operational services are concerned with people, not technology, but nevertheless are an integral part of the systems infrastructure.

Enterprise Security Architecture

Many organisations have a long history of piecemeal implementations of security

It is the common experience of many corporate organisations that information security solutions are often designed, acquired and installed on a tactical basis. A requirement is identified, a specification is developed and a solution is sought to meet that situation. In this process there is no opportunity to consider the strategic dimension, and the result is that the organisation builds up a mixture of technical solutions on an ad hoc basis, each independently designed and specified and with no guarantee that they will be compatible and inter-operable. There is often no analysis of the long-term costs, especially the operational costs which make up a large proportion of the total cost of ownership, and there is no strategy that can be identifiably said to support the goals of the business.

Case Study: User Authentication

The total cost of ownership of multiple systems is often driven by the complexity of the diverse user authentication methods in use

One of the most commonly occurring examples of how a piecemeal design approach causes business problems is that of authenticating business users to multiple business applications.

Often each application requires a separate user ID, and often enforces different syntax rules so that a user cannot simply replicate an ID across several systems. For each user ID there is a password, again often requiring heterogeneous syntax rules, different change regimes and so on, such that each user ends up with a different user ID and different password for each system.

Setting aside the security implications of this approach (which is a contentious issue often debated by security professionals) the cost of ownership of these applications is adversely affected by the level of user support that needs to be provided simply to ensure that users can login to their authorised systems. The complexity of multiple user IDs and passwords leads to great confusion and many operational problems. The costs include:

- Administering the creation, maintenance and deletion of multiple user IDs and passwords;

- Providing help desk support for a flood of user login problems;

- Lost productivity of the users whilst they are trying to solve their authentication problems.

It is precisely this type of common problem that has led to the adoption of strategic approaches to providing user authentication services across multiple business applications (single sign-on).

True architecture never happens by accident

Those enterprises that suffer these problems are often well aware of the issues, but struggle to find an approach that will make things better. However, the Sydney Opera House could never have been built with this approach. True architecture never happens by accident, and so the enterprise must find skills, methods and tools that help it to succeed with a more strategic architectural approach.

Enterprise security architecture is the solution to the business problems of piecemeal development

An approach that avoids these piecemeal problems is the development of an enterprise security architecture which is business-driven and which describes a structured inter-relationship between the technical and procedural solutions to support the long-term needs of the business. If the architecture is to be successful, then it must provide a rational framework within which decisions can be made upon the selection of security solutions. The decision criteria should be derived from a thorough understanding of the business requirements, including the need for cost reduction, modularity, scalability, ease of component re-use, operability, usability, inter-operability both internally and externally, and integration with the enterprise ICT architecture and its legacy systems.

Business strategy for security is closely linked to operational risk management goals

Furthermore, information system security is only a small part of information security, which in turn is but one part of a wider topic: business assurance. Business assurance embraces three major areas: information security; business continuity; physical and environmental security. Broader still is the view that business assurance is concerned with all aspects of operational risk management. Only through an integrated approach to these broad aspects of business assurance will it be possible for the enterprise to make the most cost-effective and beneficial decisions with regard to the management of operational risk. The enterprise security architecture and the security management process should therefore embrace all of these areas.

The SABSA® model is used in this book as the framework for developing an enterprise security architecture

The authors of this book have been working for some years (since 1995) with a model for enterprise security architecture. This model, known as SABSA®[2] is the basis they have used for major consulting assignments with many clients, and over the years the methodology has been reviewed and refined in the light of experience and in response to new inputs of ideas from various sources. This book is essentially a description of the SABSA® model and its application. The model itself and its derivation are described in greater detail in Chapter 3.

Everything in a security architecture must be a reflection of business requirements

The primary characteristic of this model is that everything must be derived from an analysis of the business requirements for security, especially those in which security has an enabling function through which new business opportunities can be developed and exploited. The model is layered, with the top layer being the business requirements definition stage. At each lower layer a new level of abstraction is developed, going through the definition of the conceptual architecture, logical architecture, physical architecture and finally at the lowest layer, the selection of technologies and products (component architecture) – in other words, the shopping list. In addition the whole area of security management, administration and operations is addressed through the operational architecture.

---

[2] SABSA® is a registered trademark of SABSA Limited. It stands for: Sherwood Applied Business Security Architecture.

The model is generic and defines a process for architecture development – each solution will be unique to the individual business

The model itself is generic and can be the starting point for any organisation, but by going through the process of analysis and decision-making implied by its structure, the output becomes specific to the enterprise and is finally highly customised to a unique business model. The output from applying the model becomes in reality the enterprise security architecture and is central to the success of a strategic programme of information security management within the organisation.

Why Architectures Sometimes Fail to Deliver Benefit – and How to Avoid that Fate

Historical Background

> "Those who cannot remember the past are condemned to repeat it".
> –*George Santayana*

The piecemeal approach to security is commonly found

Many corporate organisations implement technical solutions to business security requirements on a tactical basis. Usually a requirement is identified and a product is sought and acquired to meet that requirement without regard to the broader implications. A point solution is implemented which is often effective in providing some security, but frequently no one is really sure that the security is appropriate to the risk, or that the cost is commensurate with the benefit, or that it meets a wide variety of other business requirements which are not specifically risk-related. Security is often the last thing to be considered in business information system design, and often gets relegated to the status of a few add-on fixes when all other design decisions have been frozen.

Far from rendering business benefits, this leads to business problems

This can lead to many problems. The security solutions are often isolated and incapable of being integrated together or of inter-operating with one another. The variety of security solutions leads to increased complexity and cost of support, and in particular can lead to an exploding workload with regard to administration and management. Worst of all, because there has been inadequate attention paid to the business requirements, the 'solution' can sometimes hinder the business process rather than helping it, and the reputation of security among the business community gets worse and worse.

Good security is business-led and business-serving

Appropriate business security is that which protects the business from undue operational risks in a cost-effective way. If business security is to be effective in enhancing the business process and achieving business goals (and what other possible use could it have?) then the approach described above must be avoided. A much more strategic view should be developed, in which the business requirements are the primary driver for developing effective information security solutions.

The Wider Business Requirements

Information security is only one part of the business assurance picture

For the moment let us return to the issue of information security, using it as an example, whilst remembering that our requirements for business assurance and operational risk management also span the areas of business continuity and physical and environmental security. The same principles developed below can be applied across the entire area of business assurance.

Availability, integrity, authenticity, confidentiality, accountability, auditability

The primary business requirements for information security are business-specific. They will usually be expressed in terms of protecting the availability, integrity, authenticity and confidentiality of business information, and providing accountability and auditability in information systems. To understand these requirements, a detailed analysis of the business processes is required, using as source data information gathered by direct interviews with operational business managers.

Security has to be balanced against other requirements

However, there is much more to the business requirements than pure security and control. Information security provides for the confident use of information for business purposes across the entire organisation. The generic business requirements for an information security solution often include the following:

Usability

The solution must be appropriate to the technical competence of the intended users and ergonomically acceptable to those users.

Inter-Operability

The solution must provide for the long-term requirements for inter-operability between communicating information systems and applications.

Integration

The solution must integrate with the wide range of computer applications and platforms for which it might be required in the long term.

Supportability

The solution must be capable of being supported in the environment[3] within which it has been designed to be used.

Low Cost Development

The solution should be of modular design and hence capable of being integrated into a development programme at minimal cost.

Fast Time to Market

The solution should be capable of being integrated into a development programme with minimal delay.

Scalability of Platforms

The solution should fit with the range of computing platforms[4] with which it might be required to integrate.

Scalability of Cost

The entry-level cost should be appropriate to the range of business applications for which the solution is intended.

Scalability of Security Level

The solution should support the range of cryptographic and other techniques that will be needed to implement the required range of security strengths.

Re-Usability

The solution should be re-usable in a wide variety of similar situations to get the best return on the investment in its acquisition and development.

Operations Costs

The cost impact on systems operations should be minimised.

---

[3]Including number of end users and service delivery points, geographical location and distribution.

[4]Potential platforms range from high-end mainframes, through mid-range servers, down to PCs, workstations, laptops and palmtops. Increasingly, platforms may also include digital TVs, mobile telephones and indeed any consumer electronics goods that provide processing and communications capability.

Administration Costs

The solution should provide an efficient means for security administration to optimise the costs of this activity.

Risk-Based Cost/Benefit Effectiveness

The reduction of risk (the benefit) should be appropriate to the costs of acquisition, development, installation, administration and operation.

Dealing with Conflicting Objectives

Requirements often pull in conflicting directions

One of the most difficult challenges is that these various business requirements are often in conflict with one another. By simplifying the set of wider requirements to a basic set of three – cost control, security and usability – it becomes clear that these three pull against one another in conflicting directions. To obtain higher security or usability will cost more. To increase security often impacts upon usability, and vice versa. Figure 2-3 illustrates this conflict as an eternal triangle in which the three requirements are in constant tension, pulling in opposite directions.

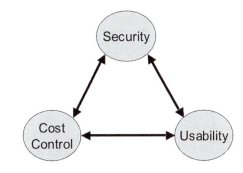

Figure 2-3: The Eternal Triangle of Conflicting Objectives

Enabling Business

Some requirements are specific to the business of the enterprise

Finally there are usually a number of business-specific requirements that influence the security strategy. These include requirements where security has an important role in generating the appropriate level of confidence so as to enable new ways of doing business using the latest advances in information and communications technology, such as:

- Exploiting the global reach of the Internet;

- Using global e-mail and e-messaging;

- Outsourcing the operation of networks and computer systems;

- Providing remote access to third parties;

- Developing on-line business services;

- Delivering digital entertainment products (video, music, etc);

- Improving customer service through integration of information and consistent presentation of a user interface;

- Obtaining software upgrades and system support through remote access by vendors;

- Tele-working, mobile computing, road warriors and the virtual office.

Being a Successful Security Architect

Security architecture must address the wider range of requirements

Unless the security architecture can address this wide range of operational requirements and provide real business support and business enablement, rather than just focusing upon security, then it is likely that it will fail to deliver what the business expects and needs.

Failure to address the wider range of issues is common

This type of failure is a common phenomenon throughout the information systems industry, not just in the realm of information systems security. In this book the whole emphasis is on the need to avoid this mistake by keeping in mind at all times the real needs of the business. It is not sufficient to compile a set of business requirements, document them and put them on the shelf, and then proceed to design a security architecture driven by technical thinking alone.

Successful architecture is business-focused

Being a successful security architect means thinking in business terms at all times, even when you get down to the real detail and the nuts and bolts of the construction. You always need to have in mind the questions: Why are we doing this? What are we trying to achieve in business terms here?

Success as an architect requires strength of character and good communications skills

It will also be difficult to battle against the numerous other people around you who do not understand strategic architecture and who think that it is all to do with technology. These people will constantly challenge you, attack you and ridicule you. You have to be ready to deal with this. You have to realise that being a successful architect is also about being a successful communicator who can sell the ideas and the benefits to others in the enterprise who need to be educated about these issues.

Senior management buy-in and support is a critical success factor

One of the most important factors for success is to have buy-in and sponsorship from senior management levels within the enterprise. Enterprise architecture cannot be achieved unless the most senior decision-makers are on your side. The fruits of the architectural work will be enjoyed throughout the enterprise, but only if the enterprise as a whole can begin to think and act in a strategic way. Creating this environment of acceptance and support is probably one of the most difficult tasks that you will face in the early stages of your work.

Geoff Rob's Ten Rules for the Solution Architect

Finally on the subject of being a successful security architect, here are Ten Rules for the Solutions Architect[5].

Ten Rules for the Solution Architect

Listen and Learn: Clients will appreciate much more your understanding their environment and business requirements fully before you try to sell them your solution. This builds the customer's trust in you.

Lead Diplomatically: In most cases the client is paying not only for a service but also a motivated person to take charge of the situation and provide a clear direction. Always be prepared to give other people time and space to express themselves.

Your Area of Expertise: Understand in depth a specific area of technology and take leadership in it. Collaborate with other leaders who can supplement your knowledge in other areas.

---

[5] Courtesy of its author, Geoff Rob.

Repeatability: Capitalise on work already done for other clients. By using experiences from similar client situations and adapting them to your client's situation, you can deliver a solution faster with a higher success rate.

Market Awareness: Have a global view of alternative solutions available on the market and be able to discuss and compare them with your solution.

Business Sense: Understand the costs and business impacts of the technology and the solutions you are proposing. Keep business benefits and the client's priorities paramount.

Design Acceptance: During the initial part of the design phase, be open and frank with the client and look for acceptance of a solution. This is far better than spending weeks developing something in isolation and then fighting for acceptance later. Discuss design principles and constraining factors and be prepared to defend the design rationale behind your solution.

Don't Go to Extremes: Adopt a common-sense approach to planning and design of a solution and match it to the client's situation. What the marketing hype promotes, or what you think might be interesting to experiment with, may not always be suitable. What is good for one client may not be suitable for others. Keep an open mind.

Best Fit: If a solution is too complex or costly for a client to implement, look at the part that could solve a majority of problems. Suggest an optimal solution that stays within the client's budget and yet brings a maximum of benefits.

Leverage Client's Investment: Wherever possible use the infrastructure already in place to effect transitions. Question the sense of putting in technology for short-term use with doubtful benefits. An example of this is a transitional infrastructure put in place at heavy cost and that becomes obsolete when the project is finished.

Security Architecture Needs a Holistic Approach

Security can be analogous with a chain – one link breaks, the chain is broken

Many people make the mistake of believing that building security into information systems is simply a matter of referring to a checklist of technical and procedural controls and applying the appropriate security measures on the list. However, security has an important property that most people know about but few pay any real heed to: it is like a chain, made up of many links, and the strength and suitability of the chain is only as good as that of its weakest link. At worst, if one link is missing altogether, the rest of chain is valueless.

Complex systems have a holistic design quality and are not described by checklists alone

The checklist approach also fails because many people focus on checking that the links in the chain exist but do not test that the links actually fit together to form a secure chain. The chain is a reasonably good analogy, but the problem is actually much worse than this. Imagine a checklist that has the following items: engine block, pistons, piston rings, piston rods, bearings, valves, cam shaft, wheels, chassis, body, seats, steering wheel, gearbox, etc. Suppose that this list comprehensively itemises every single component that would be needed to build a car. If you go through the checklist and make sure that you have all of these components, does it mean that you have a car? Not exactly!

Complex system example

A car is a good example of a complex system. It has many sub-systems, which in turn have sub-systems, and eventually a very large number of components. Designing and building a car needs a systems engineering approach. (Refer to Chapter 5 for a detailed discussion of systems engineering as a discipline).

Checklists often miss out key questions

Some of the key questions not addressed by the checklist approach to car construction are:

- Can you be sure that all the parts have been designed to work together as one smoothly running system?

- Do you have any assurance that the car has been properly assembled?

- Has the engine been tuned?

- Is the system actually running smoothly at this moment?

- Is there someone at the controls governing the speed, lubricating the moving parts, maintaining its fuel supply and monitoring its performance?

You need a holistic approach

Checklists are not the entire answer. Security architecture, as with all other forms of architecture, needs a holistic approach:

- Do you understand the requirements?

- Do you have a design philosophy?

- Do you have all of the components?

- Do these components work together?

- Do they form an integrated system?

- Are you assured that it is properly assembled?

- Does the system run smoothly?

- Is the system properly tuned?

- Do you operate the system correctly?

- Do you maintain the system?

The analogy of the car as a complex machine that needs a holistic architectural design is much more powerful than the idea of a chain. Security architecture is more like the car, not the chain.

To Summarise: What Does Architecture Mean?

Architecture means taking a holistic, enterprise-wide view, and creating principles, policies and standards by which the system (building, car, ship, business information system) will be designed and built.

The purpose of architecture is to ensure consistency of the design approach across a large complex system or across a complex array of smaller systems. Architectural approaches break up the complexity so as to present greater simplicity and thus make the design activity easier to manage.

One of the ways to simplify complexity is to create architectural reference models that use layering of functionality to break down the complex whole into a series of less-complex conceptual layers.

Enterprise security architecture must be driven from a business perspective and must take account of a wide range of requirements that may often be in conflict with one another. The successful architecture balances the tensions between these conflicting objectives.

Piecemeal approaches used instead of strategic architectural approaches usually fail to satisfy the business needs and to provide true business benefits. Enterprise security architecture needs a holistic systems engineering approach that implies much more than simply satisfying all the points on a checklist.

The successful security architect is an experienced and intelligent person who is a good communicator and can bring together many skills and wide-ranging knowledge from many parts of the team – someone who can grapple with the business requirements and use architectural skill to transform complexity into simplicity.

Chapter 3: Security Architecture Model

The approach to developing an enterprise security architecture that is proposed in this book is based upon a six-layer model. This model is used as the basis of an architecture development process – a methodology. By following the development of the enterprise architecture in line with the layers of the model, the methodology becomes somewhat self-evident. Later chapters provide guidance as to the steps in these various methods.

In this chapter you will learn about:

- The six-layered SABSA® Model of and its relationship to the Zachman Framework;

- The detailed interpretation of each of the six horizontal layers of the SABSA® Model;

- The SABSA® Matrix showing the vertical analysis of each horizontal layer by applying the six critical questions: What? Why? How? Who? Where? When?

The SABSA® Model

Continuing with the analogy of building architecture

To establish a layered model of how a security architecture is created, it is useful to return for a moment to the use of the word in its conventional sense: the construction of buildings.

The architecture model used in this book has six layers

The SABSA® Model comprises six layers, the summary of which is in Table 3-1. It follows closely the work done by John A. Zachman[1] in developing a model for enterprise architecture, although it has been adapted somewhat to a security view of the world. Each layer represents the view of a different player in the process of specifying, designing, constructing and using the building.

Table 3-1: The SABSA® Model Layered Architecture Views

The Business View	Contextual Security Architecture
The Architect's View	Conceptual Security Architecture
The Designer's View	Logical Security Architecture
The Builder's View	Physical Security Architecture
The Tradesman's View	Component Security Architecture
The Facilities Manager's View	Operational Security Architecture

[1]Published through the Zachman Institute for Framework Advancement. Reference: http://www.zifa.com

The layers can also be arranged so that Operational Security Architecture is a vertical bar

There is another configuration of these six layers which is perhaps more helpful, shown in Figure 3-1. In this diagram Operational Security Architecture has been placed vertically across the other five layers. This is because operational security issues arise at each and every one of the other five layers. Operational security has a meaning in the context of each of these other layers.

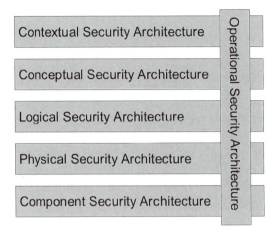

Figure 3-1: The SABSA® Model for Security Architecture Development

Kipling's poem provides six key questions

For detailed analysis of each of the six layers, the SABSA® Model also uses the same six questions that are used in the Zachman Framework and which were so eloquently articulated by Rudyard Kipling in his poem 'I Keep Six Honest Serving-Men'.

I Keep Six Honest Serving-Men

I keep six honest serving-men
(They taught me all I knew);
Their names are What and Why and When
And How and Where and Who.
I send them over land and sea,
I send them east and west;
But after they have worked for me,
I give them all a rest.

I let them rest from nine till five,
For I am busy then,
As well as breakfast, lunch, and tea,
For they are hungry men.
But different folk have different views;
I know a person small-
She keeps ten million serving-men,
Who get no rest at all!

She sends them abroad on her own affairs,
From the second she opens her eyes-
One million Hows, two million Wheres,
And seven million Whys!

The Business View

Before an architect can begin work the business owner has to specify what sort of building is needed

When a new building is commissioned, the owner has a set of business requirements that must be met by the architecture. At the highest level this is expressed by the descriptive name of the building: it is a domestic house, a factory, an office block, a sports centre, a school, a hospital, a warehouse, a theatre, a shopping centre, an airport terminal, a railway station, or whatever. Each one of these business uses immediately implies an architecture that will be different from all the others, an architecture that will fulfil expectations for the function of the building in business terms.

Five more key questions

Having stated *what* sort of building is needed the owner must then decide some more detail about its use:

- *Why* do you want this building? The goals that you want to achieve.

- *How* will it be used? The detailed functional description.

- *Who* will use the building, including the types of people, their physical mobility, the numbers of them expected, and so on?

- *Where* should it be located, and what is its geographical relationship to other buildings and to the infrastructure (such as roads, railways etc)?

- *When* will it be used? The times of day, week, year, and the pattern of usage over time.

Understanding requirements is a prerequisite to effective design

This type of analysis is essential before any type of design work is done. It is through this process that the requirements of the building are established, and understanding the requirements is a prerequisite to designing a building that will meet those requirements.

We take a similar approach in developing an architecture for a secure information system

When designing a secure business information system, the same applies. There are many possible architectural approaches that one could take, but the one that will be the most suitable will be driven from a clear understanding of the business requirements for the system.

- *What* type of information system is it and for *what* will it be used?

- *Why* will it be used?

- *How* will it be used?

- *Who* will use it?

- *Where* will it be used?

- *When* will it be used?

By asking these questions you establish the business requirements

These are the characteristic questions that you must ask. From the analysis of the replies you receive, you should be able to gain an understanding of the business requirements for the secure system. From those you should be able to synthesise a systems architecture and a security architecture that meets those requirements.

The result is the contextual security architecture

In the SABSA® Model this business view is called the *contextual security architecture*. It is a description of the business context in which your secure systems must be designed, built and operated.

Shortcuts that omit this step are likely to result in failure to meet business needs

Any attempt to define an architecture that takes a shortcut and avoids this essential step is unlikely to be successful. Even so, simple observation reveals that many enterprises undertaking architectural work do not take this stage seriously. It is very common for systems architecture work to begin from a technical perspective, looking at technologies and solutions whilst ignoring the requirements.

Technologists are traditionally not good at listening to the business owners and users

It seems to be such obvious common sense that one must first understand the requirements, and yet so few people seem to know how to approach architecture development in the information systems arena. Unfortunately many technologists and technicians believe that they already know the requirements, even though they have a poor relationship with those who might express these requirements.

It is not uncommon for an information systems group to have a poor relationship with business colleagues

The results of taking a shortcut in the requirements-definition stages of an architecture development are abundantly clear. When one looks around at many large corporate enterprises and at their information systems infrastructure managers or applications teams, the relationship with the business community is often strained. For many years the business people have been complaining that the information systems people are unable to deliver what the business needs and that ICT is a serious source of cost with little tangible benefit to show for it. The reason is simple: the business people are right. ICT vendor interests and technical innovations often drive business systems development strategy, rather than it being driven by business needs. Those with responsibility for architecture and technical strategy often fail to understand the business requirements because they do not know how to do otherwise. Ignorance of architectural principles is commonplace.

Following through all the layers in the architectural model is essential to success

This book describes how to take a layered approach to security architecture development. Many of you will be tempted to flip the pages to get to the end sections where some of the solutions can be found. You are in a hurry, and whilst you know that this step-wise approach is correct, you simply do not have the time to linger on the appetisers and starters – you need to get to the meat[2] course. Well, be warned. There simply is no substitute for doing architecture work the proper way. You may try to take shortcuts, but your efforts will most likely result in failure, which costs the business more money, delivers less benefit, and destroys the confidence that business people may have in information and communications technology as the means to enable business development.

Each layer is also analysed vertically using six key questions

In the model presented here, the contextual security architecture is concerned with:

- *What?* The business, its assets to be protected (brand, reputation, etc.) and the business needs for information security (security as a business enabler, secure electronic business, operational continuity and stability, compliance with the law, etc.);

- *Why?* The business risks expressed in terms of assets, goals, success factors and the threats, impacts and vulnerabilities that put these at risk, driving the need for business security (brand protection, fraud prevention, loss prevention, legal obligations, business continuity, etc.);

- *How?* The business processes that require security (business interactions and transactions, business communications, etc.);

- *Who?* The organisational aspects of business security (management structures, supply chain structures, out-sourcing relationships, strategic partnerships);

- *Where?* The business geography and location-related aspects of business security (the global village market place, distributed corporate sites, remote working, etc.);

- *When?* The business time dependencies and time-related aspects of business security in terms of both performance and sequence (business transaction throughput, lifetimes and deadlines, just-in-time operations, time-to-market, etc.).

---

[2]For those who are vegetarian or vegan, please read 'main course'.

The Architect's View

An architect is a creative person with a grand vision. Architects thrive on challenging business requirements. They marshal their skill, experience and expertise to create an inspired picture of what the building will look like. They provide impressionistic drawings and high-level descriptions. The pictures are painted with broad brushes and sweeping strokes. They prepare the way for more detailed work later on, when other people with different types of expertise and skill will fill in the gaps with fine brush strokes.

The architect's view is the overall *concept* by which the business requirements of the enterprise may be met. Thus this layer of the architectural model is also referred to as the *conceptual security architecture*. It defines principles and fundamental concepts that guide the selection and organisation of the logical and physical elements at the lower layers of abstraction.

When describing the enterprise security architecture, this is the place to describe the security concepts and principles that you will use. These include:

- What you want to protect, expressed in the SABSA® Model in terms of a SABSA® Business Attributes Profile?

SABSA® Business Attributes are explained in much greater detail in Chapter 6. They provide the primary tool by which business requirements can be captured in a normalised form.

- *Why* the protection is important, in terms of control objectives?

Control objectives are derived directly from an analysis of business operational risks and are a conceptualisation of business motivation for security.

- *How* you want to achieve the protection, in terms of high-level technical and management *security strategies*?

These strategies set out the conceptual layered framework for integrating individual tactical elements at the lower levels, ensuring that these fit together in a meaningful way to fulfil the overall strategic goals of the business. Such strategies include: the strategy for applications security, the network security strategy, the cryptographic infrastructure strategy, the role-based access control (RBAC) strategy, and so on. For every major area of the business requirements identified in the contextual security architecture, there will be a security strategy (or group of strategies) that supports it.

- *Who* is involved in security management, in terms of entity relationship models, and the trust framework within which entities interact with one another?

The important trust concepts are concerned with the various policy authorities that govern trust within a domain, the policies that they set to govern behaviour of entities in each of those domains, and the inter-domain trust relationships.

- *Where* you want to achieve the protection conceptualised in terms of security domains?

The important concepts here are security domains (both logical and physical), domain boundaries and security associations.

- *When* is the protection relevant, in terms of both points in time and periods of time?

The important concepts are lifetimes and expiration deadlines (of keys, certificates, passwords, sessions, etc.), and the use of trusted time for time-stamping and time-sensitive business transactions. Also important are time-related performance criteria – how quickly things must happen.

The Designer's View

The designer takes over from the architect. The designer has to interpret the architect's conceptual vision and turn it into a logical structure that can be engineered to create a real building. The architect is an artist and visionary, but the designer is an engineer.

In the world of business computing and data communications, this design process is often called 'systems engineering'. It involves the identification and specification of the logical architectural elements of an overall system. This view models the business as a *system*, with *system components* that are themselves *sub-systems*. It shows the major architectural security elements in terms of logical *security services*, and describes the logical flow of control and the relationships between these logical elements. It is therefore also known as the *logical security architecture*.

In terms of architectural decomposition down through the layers, the logical security architecture should reflect and represent all of the major security strategies in the conceptual security architecture. At this logical level, everything from the higher layers is transformed into a series of logical abstractions.

The logical security architecture is concerned with:

- *What?* Business information is a logical representation of the real business. It is this business information that needs to be secured;

- *Why?* Specifying the security policy requirements (high-level security policy, registration authority policy, certification authority policy, physical domain policies, logical domain policies, etc.) for securing business information;

- *How?* Specifying the logical security services (entity authentication, confidentiality protection, integrity protection, non-repudiation, system assurance, etc.) and how they fit together as common re-usable building blocks into a complex security system that meets the overall business requirements;

- *Who?* Specifying the entities (users, security administrators, auditors, etc.) and their inter-relationships, attributes, authorised roles and privilege profiles in the form of a schema;

- *Where?* Specifying the security domains and inter-domain relationships (logical security domains, physical security domains, security associations);

- *When?* Specifying the security processing cycle (registration, certification, login, session management, etc.);

The Builder's View

The designer of the building hands over the work process to the builder. The builder is someone who can take the logical descriptions and drawings and turn these into a technology model that can be used to construct the building. It is the builder's job to choose and assemble the physical elements that will make the logical design come to life as a real construction. This view is therefore also referred to as the 'physical security architecture'.

In the world of business information systems, the designer produces a set of logical abstractions that describe the system to be built. These need to be turned into a physical security architecture model that describes the actual technology model and specifies the functional requirements of the various system components. The logical security services are now expressed in terms of the physical security mechanisms and machines that will be used to deliver these services.

The six key questions again In total, the physical security architecture is concerned with:

- *What?* Specifying the business data model and the security-related data structures (tables, messages, pointers, certificates, signatures, etc.);

- *Why?* Specifying rules that drive logical decision-making within the system (conditions, practices, procedures and actions);

- *How?* Specifying security mechanisms (encryption, access control, digital signatures, virus scanning, etc.) and the physical machines upon which these mechanisms will be hosted;

- *Who?* Specifying the people dependency in the form of the users, the applications that they use and the security user interface (screen formats and user interactions);

- *Where?* Specifying security technology infrastructure (physical layout of the hardware, software and communications lines);

- *When?* Specifying the time dependency in the form of execution control structures (sequences, events, lifetimes and time intervals).

The Tradesman's View

The construction process needs a range of different skills and component parts When the builder plans the construction process, she or he needs to assemble a team of experts in each of the building trades that will be needed: the bricklayer, the plasterer, the electrician, the plumber, the carpenter, and so on. Each one of these brings some very specific production skills and some very specific products to the overall construction process.

Construction requires the integration of many components It is the same in the construction of information systems. The builder needs to assemble a series of products from specialist vendors and a team with the integration skills to join these products together during an implementation of the design.

The component security architecture Each of the integrators is the equivalent of a tradesman, working with specialist products and system components that are the equivalent of building materials and components. Some of these 'trades' are hardware-related, some are software-related, and some are service oriented. The 'tradesmen' work with a series of components that are hardware items, software items, and interface specifications and standards. Hence this layer of the architectural model is also called the 'component security architecture'.

Once again the six key questions The component security architecture is concerned with:

- *What?* Data field specifications, address specifications and other detailed data structure specifications;

- *Why?* Security standards;

- *How?* Products and tools (both hardware and software);

- *Who?* User identities, privileges, functions, actions and access control lists (ACLs);

- *Where?* Computer processes, node addresses, and inter-process protocols;

- *When?* Security step timings and sequencing.

The Facilities Manager's View

The facilities manager runs the building in its operational lifetime

When the building is finished, those who architected, designed and constructed it move out, but someone has to run the building during its lifetime. Such a person is often called the facilities manager. The job of the facilities manager is to deal with the operation of the building and its various services, maintaining it in good working order, and monitoring how well it is performing in meeting the requirements. The framework for doing this is called the 'operational security architecture'.

The operational security architecture

In the realm of business information systems the operational architecture is concerned with classical systems operations work. Here the focus of attention is only on the security-related parts of that work. The operational security architecture is concerned with the following:

- *What*? Ensuring the operational continuity of the business systems and information processing, and maintaining the security of operational business data and information (confidentiality, integrity, availability, auditability and accountability);

- *Why*? To manage operational risks and hence to minimise operational failures and disruptions;

- *How*? Performing specialised security-related operations (user security administration, system security administration, data back-ups, security monitoring, emergency response procedures, etc.);

- *Who*? Providing operational support for the security-related needs of all users and their applications (business users, operators, administrators, etc.);

- *Where*? Maintaining the system integrity and security of all operational platforms and networks (by applying operational security standards and auditing the configuration against these standards);

- *When*? Scheduling and executing a timetable of security-related operations.

Operational security architecture cuts across the other layers

However, referring back to Figure 3-1, there is another dimension to the operational security architecture – its vertical relationship with the other five layers of the model. Thus the operational security architecture needs to be interpreted in detail at each and every one of the other five layers. This is shown in Table 3-2, with some examples of the type of operational activity that is implied with regard to each of the layers.

The Inspector's View

Providing assurance through audit and inspection

There is another view of security in business information systems, the inspector's view, which is concerned with providing assurance that the architecture is complete, consistent, robust and 'fit-for-purpose' in every way. In the realm of information systems security this is the process of security auditing carried out by computer auditors or systems quality assurance personnel.

An integral part of the operational security architecture

However, the SABSA® Model does not recognise this as a separate architectural view. The SABSA® approach to audit and assurance is that the architecture model as a whole supports these needs. The existence of such an architecture is one of the ways in which the auditors will establish that security is being applied in a systematic and appropriate way. The framework itself can provide a means by which to structure the audit process. In addition, security audit and review is addressed as one of the major strategic programmes within the operational security architecture associated with the conceptual layer (see Table 3-1).

Table 3-2: The Operational Security Architecture

At the Contextual Layer	Business policymaking, business risk assessment process, business requirements collection and specification, organisational and cultural development, etc.
At the Conceptual Layer	Major programmes for training and awareness, business continuity management, audit and review, process development for registration, authorisation, administration and incident handling, development of standards and procedures, etc.
At the Logical Layer	Security policymaking, information classification, system classification, management of security services, security of service management, negotiation of inter-operable standards for security services, audit trail monitoring and invocation of actions, etc.
At the Physical Layer	Development and execution of security rules, practices and procedures, including: cryptographic key management, communication of security parameters between parties, synchronisation between parties; ACL1 maintenance and distribution of ACEs2, backup management (storing, labelling, indexing, etc.), virus pattern search maintenance, event log file management and archiving, etc.
At the Component Layer	Products, technology, evaluation and selection of standards and tools, project management, implementation management, operation and administration of individual components, etc.

[1]ACL: Access control list
[2]ACE: Access control entry (in an access control list)

The SABSA® Matrix

The six key questions that have been asked at every layer to provide a vertical analysis

In the above sections, each of the six horizontal layers of abstraction of the architecture model (contextual, conceptual, logical, physical, component and operational) has been examined. Each of the sections has also introduced a series of vertical cuts through each of these horizontal layers, answering the questions:

- *What* are you trying to do at this layer? – The assets to be protected by your security architecture;

- *Why* are you doing it? – The motivation for wanting to apply security, expressed in the terms of this layer;

- *How* are you trying to do it? – The functions needed to achieve security at this layer;

- *Who* is involved? – The people and organisational aspects of security at this layer;

- *Where* are you doing it? – The locations where you apply your security, relevant to this layer;

- *When* are you doing it? – The time-related aspects of security relevant to this layer.

These six vertical architectural elements are now summarised for all six horizontal layers. This gives a 6x6 matrix of cells, which represents the whole model for the enterprise security architecture. It is called the SABSA® Matrix (see Table 3-3). If you can address the issues raised by each and every one of these cells, then you will have covered the entire range of questions to be answered, and you can have a high level of confidence that your security architecture is complete[3]. The process of developing an enterprise security architecture is a process of populating all of these 36 cells.

Table 3-3: The 36-Cell SABSA® Matrix

	Assets (What)	Motivation (Why)	Process (How)	People (Who)	Location (Where)	Time (When)
Contextual	The Business	Business Risk Model	Business Process Model	Business Organisation and Relationships	Business Geography	Business Time Dependencies
Conceptual	Business Attributes Profile	Control Objectives	Security Strategies and Architectural Layering	Security Entity Model and Trust Framework	Security Domain Model	Security-Related Lifetimes and Deadlines
Logical	Business Information Model	Security Policies	Security Services	Entity Schema and Privilege Profiles	Security Domain Definitions and Associations	Security Processing Cycle
Physical	Business Data Model	Security Rules, Practices and Procedures	Security Mechanisms	Users, Applications and the User Interface	Platform and Network Infrastructure	Control Structure Execution
Component	Detailed Data Structures	Security Standards	Security Products and Tools	Identities, Functions, Actions and ACLs	Processes, Modes, Addresses and Protocols	Security Step Timing and Sequencing
Operational	Assurance of Operational Continuity	Operational Risk Management	Security Service Management and Support	Application and User Management Support	Security of Sites, networks and Platforms	Security Operations Schedule

Detailed SABSA® Matrix for the Operational Layer

When one examines the lowest layer (operational security architecture) of Table 3-3, and refers back to Table 3-2, it becomes clear that this operational layer can be further broken out into a SABSA® Matrix mapping to each of the five layers above. In other words, there are operational aspects associated with each of the contextual, conceptual, logical, physical and component layers. This more detailed insight into the operation security architecture is provided in Table 3-4.

---

[3]Although there may remain a potential issue regarding consistency and lack of conflict between all the various cells.

Table 3-4: The Operational Security Architecture Matrix

	Assets (What)	Motivation (Why)	Process (How)	People (Who)	Location (Where)	Time (When)
Contextual	Business Requirements Collection; Information Classification	Business Risk Assessment; Corporate Policy Making	Business-Driven Information Security Management Programme	Business Security Organisation Management	Business Field Operations Management	Business Calendar and Timetable Management
Conceptual	Business Continuity Management	Security Audit & Assurance Levels; Measurement, Metrics & Benchmarking	Incident Response; Disaster Recovery; Change Control Programme	Security Training, Awareness and Culture Development	Security Domain Management	Security Operation Schedule Management
Logical	Information Security; System Integrity	Detailed Security Policy Making; Policy Compliance; Monitoring; Intelligence Gathering	Intrusion Detection; Event Monitoring; Process Development; Security Service Management; System Development Controls; Configuration Management	Access Control & Privilege Profile Administration	Application Security Administration & Management	Managing Application Deadlines & Cut-off
Physical	Database Security Software Integrity	Vulnerability Assessment; Penetration Testing; Threat Assessment	Rule Definition; Key Management; ACL Maintenance; Back-Up Admin; Computer Forensics; Event Log Admin; Anti-Virus Admin	User Support and Help Desk	Network Security Management; Site Security Management	User Account Aging; Password Aging; Crypto Key Aging; Administering Time Windows for Access Control
Component	Product & Tool Security & Integrity	CERT Notifications; Research on Threats & Vulnerabilities	Product Procurement; Project Management; Operations Management	Personnel Vetting; User Administration	Platform, Workstation and Equipment Security Management	Time-out configuration; Detailed operation sequence

To Summarise: The Security Architecture Model

The SABSA® Model for Security Architecture Development used in this book has six layers:

- Contextual security architecture – the business view;

- Conceptual security architecture – the architect's view;

- Logical security architecture – the designer's view;

- Physical security architecture – the builder's view;

- Component security architecture – the tradesman's view;

- Operational security architecture –the facilities manager's view.

The operational layer can be visualised as cutting across the other five layers, since there are operational aspects to each of these layers. Each of these six layers is further analysed by asking six basic questions:

- What?

- Why?

- How?

- Who?

- Where?

- When?

Combining the horizontal layered analysis with the vertical analysis of the six key questions produces a 36-cell table called the SABSA® Matrix.

There is another architectural view – the inspector's view. For an enterprise security architecture this is the view taken by the security auditor. In the SABSA® Model this is treated this as an integral part of the operational security architecture and so it does not have a separate layer in the model.

The SABSA® Matrix provides a framework for developing and documenting your enterprise security architecture. Each cell must be addressed in turn (although not necessarily in strict sequential order). Thus a security architecture document might well be structured with a chapter for each row of the matrix and a section within the chapter for each cell in that row. By taking this approach you can have a high level of assurance that your security architecture is comprehensive.

Chapter 4: Case Study

The intention of this book is to provide a highly practical guide, relating the work as much as possible to the real-life environment and experiences of the readers. It therefore draws on as many case studies as possible. Some case studies are small one-off affairs, usually drawn from real examples that the authors have encountered across many different industry sectors. However much of the case study material has been consolidated into a single fictional case study: Intergalactic Banking and Financial Services Inc (IBFS).

In this chapter you will learn about the IBFS case study that is used to provide examples in many other chapters.

Intergalactic Banking and Financial Services Inc

Here the initial outline of IBFS is described. As the book unfolds, new information about IBFS is presented in those chapters where it is relevant, building up throughout the book into a cohesive, detailed picture of a global financial services institution.

Through the examples of IBFS the intention is to develop a pragmatic description of how to go about developing an enterprise security architecture. It will provide the reader with a clear general framework that can be applied specifically and uniquely in any business environment, whether or not that business is in the same industry as IBFS.

Intergalactic Banking and Financial Services Inc and its employees are all entirely fictitious. Any resemblance to any real organisation or people is purely coincidental. On the other hand, the fiction has been constructed based on a wide variety of experience in this industry, and so hopefully everyone in the industry will recognise it as being realistic.

Overview of Intergalactic Banking and Financial Services Inc

Intergalactic Banking and Financial Services Inc (IBFS) is a global group of companies. As its name suggests, its business interests cover the entire range of banking and finance products and services throughout the business world.

IBFS business sectors include:

- Retail banking (current accounts, direct debits, standing orders, debit cards, credit cards, cheque payments, Internet payments);

- Corporate banking (current accounts, foreign exchange, treasury, payments);

- General insurance (household, motor, travel, healthcare, etc.);

- Life assurance;

- Pensions;

- Personal investment products (unit trusts, annuities, special investment products in each country or region);

- Savings, loans and mortgages;

- Asset management (managing a portfolio of investments on behalf of clients);

- Custody and other agency services;

- Securities trading (buying and selling stocks, shares and bonds);

- Corporate finance (advising on mergers, acquisitions, divestments and stock market flotations);

- Invoice financing (factoring – providing finance against the collateral of a sales ledger for a percentage of the ledger value).

IBFS is global, with many different companies established in 84 countries. It therefore has to deal with a wide variety of multi-cultural, multi-lingual and multi-time-zone issues.

IBFS markets and sells its products and services through a variety of channels, including branch offices, independent agents, newspaper and television advertising combined with a call centre, and increasingly, the Internet (World Wide Web and e-mail). It is this latter development of the business that is driving a project to define an enterprise-wide security architecture.

Early Internet offerings from IBFS included some web-based systems that were very tactical, with small market penetration, designed and operated by small project teams inside some of the business units. Now IBFS needs to take a much more strategic approach by developing infrastructure (both technology and process) that will enable a wide range of new business applications. This enterprise security architecture initiative is part of that strategic development.

Interviews at IBFS

The enterprise security architecture project at IBFS is under way. To get a good insight into the business issues that face IBFS, the business analysts in the architecture team have conducted several interviews with senior managers with a view to understanding the business requirements for the enterprise-wide security architecture for IBFS businesses.

The following interview notes summarise the main messages that were picked up by the team during the interview process.

Interview with David Smith, Group Chief Executive Officer

David Smith is based in New York. At the age of 52 he has been in the banking industry since he graduated from Harvard. A 'New Yorker', he has had career postings in London, Frankfurt and

Hong Kong. He has been at IBFS for 10 years, the last four in his present position. He has overseen the recent growth of the organisation through a series of major acquisitions.

David Smith: Interview Notes

'IBFS is a global company with many important brands and a reputation that has been developed over more than a century. We are owned by our shareholders, and we have a commitment to them to maximise their financial returns over the time of their investment. We achieve this by investing for the long term in people and technology and in developing, marketing and selling superior products and services. We aim to maintain lasting relationships with our customers by providing value for money and excellent service.

'The banking industry more than almost any other is based on trust. Customers give us all their money and ask us to look after it for them – how much more can you trust an organisation? If we were ever seen to breach that fundamental trust, then our relationships with customers and our reputation in the marketplace would suffer enormously. You can withstand a few isolated incidents, but if there is a constant tide of events where trust has been breached, then you're finished. In all our information systems the protection of that trust must be a primary business requirement.

'Our business strategy is based upon maintaining our leadership position in the marketplace. To achieve this we continue to restructure our organisation and re-engineer our business processes to keep abreast of a rapidly changing and developing financial services market. At the present time we are focused on harnessing new technologies, both to improve our efficiency in existing business sectors and to enable new lines of business and new methods of marketing and distribution. In particular the Internet is enormously important, and we will continue to invest heavily in these technologies so as to stay ahead of the curve. This will enable us to leverage a competitive advantage of being first into the marketplace with new products and services.

'We are also well aware of the reputation damage that can occur in this industry sector when customers suffer losses at the hands of their bankers and insurers. We continue to maintain a strong policy of legal and regulatory compliance and to exhibit due diligence at all times in handling the affairs of our customers.'

Interview with Juan Carlos, Chief Operating Officer

Juan Carlos, age 45, is currently based in the London office of IBFS. He finds that this location provides him with the best access to colleagues around the world who are in different time zones, straddling as it does the time gap between the Far East and the Americas. Although he has been at IBFS now for seven years, previously he had senior management experience in a global retailing chain.

Juan Carlos: Interview Notes

'As Chief Operating Officer one of my main concerns is the need to operate our business on a truly global scale. That means that we have to be both multicultural and multi-lingual. We also have to operate in all time zones and in accordance with all religious calendars, which really does mean 365 days by 24-hour operations. Someone, somewhere is always at work.

'The geographical spread also means that we have to organise ourselves in virtual teams, in which team members rarely meet face to face and often have their working hours overlapping only briefly because of the different time zones. To achieve success in this environment we must leverage information and communications technology to its fullest extent.

'I try to encourage my team of managers to invest their time spent on overseas trips in building strong relationships with their people, rather than frittering such valuable face-to-face time on today's operational issues (unless of course there is a specific crisis that has prompted the trip). Operational management has to happen every day, whether you are there or not, and so we have to create the best environment for communicating well at a distance. Technology, however good it is, always interferes with that special communication that you get face to face, and that means that we need to develop good relationships that can support us during those times when our only means of communication is by using technical systems.

'Having said all that, new technologies come along all the time and some of these offer significant improvements in the quality of personal communications, so I am always keen to have our technical folks evaluate new technologies and recommend those that we should be adopting to bring us closer together in spirit whilst remaining geographically separated.'

Interview with Rosemary Brown, Senior Vice President, eBusiness

Rosemary Brown joined IBFS when the insurance group where she was employed was acquired three years ago by the IBFS group. She is age 48 and has been in insurance since leaving school at age 16. She worked for a London-based firm that over the years became global. Rosemary still has a keen interest in the insurance side of the IBFS business but now also has responsibility for developing digital business channels right across the group's business activities.

Rosemary Brown: Interview Notes

'In the good old days we used to control this business. We used to tell our customers what products and services they could have, where and when they could obtain them, and how these would be delivered. That is all changing. This business is being turned on its head. In the future it is the customers who will be in control. They will lead this business sector and they will determine its characteristics. We must listen to them and follow.

'That means that we must be acutely sensitive to the needs and expectations of our customers and potential customers. The Internet has empowered people and extended their choice. They will use that power to choose the providers with whom they feel most comfortable. We must never forget that on the web a customer is only a few mouse clicks away from transferring their business to another provider.

'"Customer relationship management" and "customer service" have become buzzwords, and with good reason. The experience of a customer in interacting with us to do business, whether it be person to person, over the telephone or via the Internet, will determine whether or not that customer will continue to do business with our company. Not only that, but they will expect smoothness and consistency in all these different interfaces, and they will expect us to know the things about them that they have already told us. Once we know their name and address, we should never, ever ask for it again unless it is to change these details. Similarly, we should always be aware of all of our previous dealings with this customer, especially all the accounts, insurance policies and investments that he or she holds with us.

'My greatest challenge is gaining control of those aspects of customer relationship management in a business environment as diverse as this one, where there are many different application development projects being spawned by many different business units. If any one of those projects goes off doing its own thing regarding customer information management, then the enterprise-wide customer relationship management initiative that I own will be badly damaged.'

Interview with Helmut Meyer, Group Chief Financial Officer

Helmut Meyer is age 54 and is based in the Frankfurt office of IBFS. He has been a finance man all his working life and is steeped in experience. He started out at the age of 18 in a sales invoice finance company as a credit controller, during which time he saw most of the tricks that customers try to pull and learned how to deal with difficult people. From there he moved in financial operations management in a couple of hi-tech companies before joining the Bank Treasury Department at the age of 35. He has risen through the ranks of IBFS to his present position as Chief Financial Officer, where he rules with an iron hand.

Interview Notes: Helmut Meyer

'The competitive pressures in this industry squeeze our margins all the time, and so profitability and cash flow are always under close scrutiny. For example, we have a substantial investment in office property to support our global business operations and we are keen to realise some of those assets and make better use of our office space worldwide.

'The financial services business is very fluid these days, with new partnerships and joint ventures being spawned all the time. These arrangements sometimes have a short lifetime, depending on market conditions, and so we are in a constant state of change with regard to mergers, acquisitions, divestments and joint ventures. If one part of the business is no longer profitable or if it is no longer part of our core business strategy, then I might want to recommend to the board that we sell it off. Alternatively we sometimes may wish to grow a business simply to sell it off later at a profit. In all these cases we have to be careful to ensure that we can integrate and disintegrate the ICT systems and network infrastructure that the businesses use, depending upon current business strategy. In my view flexibility for an ever-changing business strategy is one of the most important drivers for our information systems decision-making.

'I'm afraid that I'm rather sceptical about security. It has cost us a lot in the past without any demonstrable benefits. Any plans that we develop under this architecture initiative must be subject to a clear analysis of costs and benefits. I want to see a clear demonstration of a return on our investment. I'm not convinced that much of what we call "security" has any real business benefit, and in some cases it seems to me that it actually hinders the business.'

Interview with Brian Jones, Senior Vice President, Marketing and Distribution

Brian Jones came to his present position via the investment banking arm of the group activities. He is based in New York but he has marketing people in every major financial district around the world and so finds himself travelling frequently. He started out as a bond trader and made a name for himself as a star trader with a keen eye for good business opportunities. He quickly became the leader of a new group specialising in certain types of derivatives on the futures market. Now, at the relatively young age of 43, he leads Marketing and Distribution for the entire IBFS Group, despite his obvious lack of formal training or experience in marketing. What he brings to the position is a highly intuitive and intelligent understanding of the financial services marketplace. He is a powerful strategic thinker who has created a team that has the broader set of marketing skills that are needed.

Brian Jones: Interview Notes

'An important part of the IBFS business strategy in recent years has been to develop joint venture partnerships, especially with companies in similar business sectors but in different regions of the world where we had not previously had a strong presence. The benefits for IBFS are mainly concerned with ready access to new large markets. Our partners benefit from the external investment and the capability to grow the infrastructure to leverage their market position even more effectively than before, especially in the cross-selling of a wide range of financial products to existing customers. The joint venture concept requires a special approach to security. Both IBFS and the partner concerned need to give the other access into business information systems, but at the same time they need to maintain their independence and their own control. We share some things, but not everything. Our security architecture must address this issue.

'I am also very concerned about the usability of business systems, and in particular about the difficulty that security often imposes on legitimate business users. We have to get this right in future. There is nothing that discourages a user more than the endless layers of user IDs and passwords that many of our systems require. We have had lots of complaints from our network of agents and independent financial advisors (IFAs) about these difficulties, and it really is turning into a competitive issue. If our systems are difficult to use and those of another provider are much easier, then we should not be surprised if the agents and IFAs prefer to use those other providers. Using our systems has to be a pleasant, interesting and productive experience for the users; otherwise they will look elsewhere for service.

'We often use a special product line to attract new customers, usually by luring them away from other providers. Favourites are low-interest credit cards, high-interest savings accounts or low-cost motor insurance. The intention is that once we hook them in we can cross-sell a wide range of other products and services. If when they interact with our systems it turns them off again, then it has all been wasted effort.

'As an example of the types of problem I am talking about, we have had a history of complaints that when we have special regional or conditional offers such as 0% interest on credit card balance transfers from other banks, we do not follow through, the systems are not changed properly or on time to match these needs and we do not deliver on promises to customers.'

Interview with Ranjit Patel, Chief Information Officer

Ranjit Patel started his professional career in the US in the telecommunications sector, working first for US-based telcos and later, as the market developed during the 1990s, for a large networking company providing both voice and data services to global customers. One of those customers was IBFS, and after taking some 'gardening leave' to satisfy various contractual arrangements he moved from the network service provider to IBFS. He is now still only age 39 but has risen meteorically to become Chief Information Officer for the group.

Ranjit Patel: Interview Notes

'The IBFS information systems applications architecture is in the process of being revised. Like many organisations in this industry sector we suffer from the problems of legacy applications that have a stovepipe architecture. That is to say that they each have their own interfaces and their own data repository, and it is very difficult to integrate them together or to share data between them. The business imperative towards customer relationship management (CRM) means that we must be able to provide a single central data repository for customer data, and that this repository must be shared across all applications. Our new applications architecture is based upon the provision of a data warehouse to fulfil this central repository function. All new applications will be architected around this concept, but of course we have some major technical challenges ahead of us to integrate some of the legacy applications into this new architecture.

'We have many legacy systems in which we have made major investment over decades. Continually changing those systems in a rapidly changing business environment is a major challenge. For example, many of our major global and Fortune 100 clients are in the habit of requiring that we transfer huge sums of money instantly in order for them to take advantage of better interest rates in a particular country on any given day – they may even transfer the funds to another institution. Unfortunately, these clients can have many different accounts of many different types in many different subsidiaries, and most of the systems that contain the information are long-established legacy systems. Worse still, many are batch-processing systems, which are not engineered to give a real-time, fully integrated picture of the total available funds for the client. That exposes us to a double risk: We can transfer the funds without sure knowledge that they are available, or we can upset the major clients on whom we rely. However, throwing away our legacy systems would be unacceptable and the cost of re-engineering every system is prohibitive. This is the most major and pervasive issue that our architecture team faces.

'When you start to think deeply about what the business wants – in particular the desire for a consistent, easy-to-use interface for customers, agents and employees alike, and that this consistency must span different applications and different access channels – then you soon realise that "single sign-on" is a mandatory strategy, not something that would be nice to have. We may not move to single sign-on in one simple step, but we do have to have an architecture that allows us to move more and more towards this goal in the future. If not, then our ideas about CRM and about a pleasant experience for our users when they interact with our systems will all come to nothing. My colleague Brian Jones (SVP, Marketing and Distribution) often raises this issue at the Architecture Board meetings.

'Business strategy often moves quickly, sometimes presenting us with major changes of scale, both upwards and downwards. Mergers and acquisitions often increase the scale of the business operations, although they also bring about rationalisation of ICT services and facilities. There are also occasions when the market conditions change and a business unit needs to be downsized. This means selling off a business activity and having to remove the applications in that area from our infrastructure and onto someone else's infrastructure, so we need flexibility in the way the infrastructure architecture works.

'Another major driver or constraint on security architecture is the business strategy of outsourcing all operational services that are not regarded as core businesses. This especially applies to ICT services. We shall of course always own our business applications and their data, but increasingly we shall not be responsible for operating the platforms and networks on which these applications are hosted. Some of our mainframe-based applications are already outsourced, and we shall be putting out an invitation to tender later this year to outsource our wide-area network. We even have a feasibility study in progress right now to look at outsourcing the desktop PCs to a third-party service provider. When we develop new applications, especially web-based applications, then right from the beginning these will probably be hosted by third-party service providers.

'The guiding principle for our security architecture must be that any platform and any network can potentially be outsourced. The architecture must enable this to happen with minimum disruption and minimum impact on the ownership, policy-making and policy enforcement for each of these physical domains. It must also allow us to manage some of the interesting issues that arise with regard to liability and service level management.'

Interview with Ho Siew Luan (Sarah), Director of Compliance

Ho Siew Luan is age 35 and works for IBFS in her native Singapore. She has extensive international experience, having attended university in the UK where she obtained a first class law degree (and also adopted the name Sarah Ho for convenience), and later in the US where she acquired an MBA. Subsequently career appointments have taken her to locations including Washington D.C., Hong Kong and Sydney. As Director of Compliance for IBFS she has to oversee compliance in all 84 countries where the group operates, working closely to co-ordinate the individual activities of the local compliance officers in those territories so as to deal with the different, sometimes conflicting, requirements of the legislation and the regulators in those various countries.

Ho Siew Luan: Interview Notes

'Compliance is a major business driver these days. There have been too many spectacular failures by major financial institutions to take care of clients' monies properly. At IBFS we are involved in a broad span of lines of business that fall under the auspices of a number of different regulators, even within one country. Added to that we are a global company with business operations in more than 80 countries, and each one has a different legal and regulatory regime. There are also major international regulations aimed at preventing and detecting money laundering, and in the European Union we have a very comprehensive set of legislation covering data protection (the privacy of personal data that we collect in the course of our business). At this time we are also evaluating the effect of the New Basel Capital Accord (Basel II) and the response that we shall have to make to that new regulatory regime in the area of operational risk management.

'Insider dealing is another area where the industry is very sensitive. In IBFS we have both a corporate finance business, advising clients on mergers, acquisitions, takeovers and market flotations, and a securities trading business where money is made by buying and selling stocks and shares. It is imperative to separate the information in corporate finance from the people in securities who could use that inside information to make illegal deals.

'All of this is very challenging, but our board of directors is very committed to strong governance and executing these responsibilities with due diligence. That means that we must build a strong culture of compliance with the laws and industry regulations in each of our operating countries. We must also build into our systems and processes a series of technical and procedural control mechanisms that provide us with assurance that we are indeed compliant. To be able to prove our compliance beyond reasonable doubt we must also be able to bring reliable documentary evidence before a regulator or a court of law.'

To Summarise: IBFS Inc

The description of IBFS in this chapter is the basis for an ongoing case study that runs throughout the book. The interviewees were:

David Smith	Group Chief Executive Officer
Juan Carlos	Chief Operating Officer
Rosemary Brown	Senior Vice President, eBusiness
Helmut Meyer	Group Chief Financial Officer
Brian Jones	Senior Vice President, Marketing and Distribution
Ranjit Patel	Chief Information Officer
Ho Siew Luan (Sarah)	Director of Compliance

Chapter 5: A Systems Approach

The proper and rational design of security architecture is achieved by taking a systems approach. This will ensure that the end result is consistent with the business needs and that the design process is properly executed. The systems approach advocated in this book is based upon well-established systems engineering principles.

In this chapter you will learn about:

- The meaning of the term 'systems engineering';

- The basic techniques used in a systems approach to simplify complexity, including: sub-systems; top-down decomposition, black-box modelling and logical flow analysis;

- The kinds of behaviour a systems approach implies: good documentation, peer review and good communication;

- The basic concepts of a systems approach: objectives, environment, resources, the parts of the system, their activities, goals and measures of performance, and systems management;

- The control system concept of a feedback control loop, used in many security sub-systems;

- Advanced system modelling techniques: business process engineering, dependency tree modelling and finite state machine modelling.

The Role of Systems Engineering

Systems engineering is 'A rational approach to decision making related to the solution of complex problems in engineering planning, design and operation"

Earlier chapters have discussed the need for the structured design of information systems within an enterprise and the subsequent realisation of an enterprise security architecture. Such architectures should

- Meet the goals (requirements) that you define;

- Operate successfully within the systems environment;

- Be manageable, with system performance being measurable.

Developing such an architecture demands that you should:

- Understand clearly the boundary of the system that you are securing;

- Make rational and traceable decisions as to how the architecture should be realised;

- Consider all aspects of the system at all times in the development process so that deficiencies can be identified and remedied with minimal impact.

Systems engineering is the most relevant approach to designing digital business systems

Since the very survival of an enterprise in the world of digital business may depend on your ability to design and implement systems securely, you need to adopt an approach that will support you in this exercise. The most relevant approach is that of systems engineering. Boardman defines systems engineering as '*a rational approach to decision making related to the solution of complex problems in engineering planning, design and operation*'.[1]

The aim here is to apply systems engineering thinking, not to reinvent systems engineering

Defining and expanding the practice of systems engineering and its associated techniques is well beyond the scope of this book. Indeed Checkland states in his 30-year retrospective of Soft Systems Methodology: '*SSM has been ill served by its commentators, many of whom (sic) demonstrably write on the basis of only a cursory knowledge of the primary literature*'.[2]

The description here is a high-level summary of the systems approach

The authors certainly do not wish to fall into that trap! In this chapter they simply seek to promote the practice of systems thinking that leads security architects into adopting a systems approach to the way that they consider the analysis and design of security architecture.

Systems engineering practices are useful tools for the security architect

The chapter draws on several systems engineering practices and expands on those that serve the security architect well in the pursuit of a satisfactory design and implementation.

Why a Systems Approach?

Managing Complexity

Complexity is a primary issue

Almost invariably business information systems are highly complex. One area of complexity is the frequent need for a new system to be integrated with a legacy system, which itself has often grown organically since its initial design and implementation. On top of this, the new system itself is often highly complex, especially as expectations of what can be achieved with technology are advancing all the time. You must have techniques that make this level of complexity manageable.

Top-Down Decomposition

Top-down decomposition of the system into sub-systems enables complexity to be transformed into simplicity

The systems approach fundamentally views the entire system as comprising a number of smaller sub-systems. Each of these (being a system in its own right) can be further broken down into sub-sub-systems, and so on. This is known as top-down decomposition of the system. This provides a way of masking the complexity and presenting the architect or designer with a relatively simplified view at each level of decomposition. The architect or designer can focus on a narrow, simplified field of vision without falling into the trap of neglecting the wider issues of the overall complexity. Each level of decomposition presents a manageable piece of work. If you want to eat an elephant, then the only way is by taking it in small pieces, one at a time.

Black Box Modelling

The 'black box' concept is another aspect of systems decomposition and analysis

Another implicit result of the top-down decomposition process is that each system component (each sub-system) is seen as a black box. This means that you do not see what is inside the box. Its inner workings are hidden. You simply see that the box has inputs and outputs, and that the box performs some defined function on the inputs that transforms them into outputs (see Figure 5-1).

---

[1]Boardman J. 1990, *Systems Engineering*, Prentice Hall, p 2. (ISBN 0-13-504416-2)
[2]Checkland P, 1999, *Systems Thinking Systems Practice*, p 42. (ISBN 0-471-98606-2)

Figure 5-1: The Black Box Concept

Black boxes take an input and transform it into an output

This black box concept also helps you to see complexity with greater simplicity. You can accept the black box as a component of the system, exhibiting a defined function with a defined interface to other similar components (other black boxes at the same level of decomposition). At another time you can look inside the box to examine the next level of detail down, where you may well find smaller black boxes with finer granularity of function, and so on.

Black boxes assist in creating simplicity from complexity

Thus, through top-down decomposition into black-box sub-systems, the system can be analysed into multiple layers, each with a different granularity of detail, each providing the architect or designer with a simplified, focused area of work.

Logical Flow Analysis

Systems can be analysed into a logical flow through a series of black boxes

The next thing to recognise is that systems have a logical flow. Analysis of this logical flow is closely related to the decomposition process already described. What you get at each level of decomposition is a series of black-box components, each with functions and interfaces, linked together in a logical flow pattern, such that the output from one box becomes the input to next and so on. Figure 5-2 provides a graphical example.

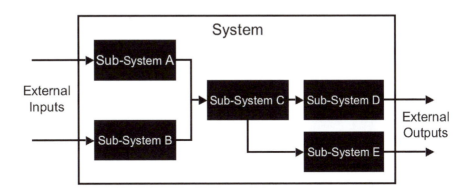

Figure 5-2: An Example of System Analysed Into Sub-Systems

A systems approach provides a structured framework in which to work

These are some of the basic ways in which a systems approach helps to simplify complexity and provide a structured framework within which to think about the system and design system solutions.

What Does the Systems Approach Make You Do?

Documenting the Ideas

Write down what you really need

Following a systems approach makes you do several things – one is probably the simplest task to describe, and the most challenging to execute – *to write down what you really need.*

If you can't write it down, you haven't thought it through

It is a truism that *if you can't write it down, you haven't thought it through*. So often one experiences presentations where new projects are being described in the early stages of planning where the presenter has not really understood the scope and interdependencies of the system they are proposing. The simple act of writing these early ideas down forces you into identifying the whole context of the system and identifying problem areas.

'Writing down' includes both diagrams and text

'Writing down' means a mixture of descriptive text, bulleted lists and diagrammatic representations of the system using the basic modelling techniques described above. Sometimes more advanced modelling techniques are needed, and some of these are explored in a little more detail later in this chapter.

Peer Review

Structured review and feedback is a peer-review process

Once the models and descriptions have been developed to a first draft, problem areas are identified. The systems approach also provides mechanisms to address these and to manage their resolution. Structured review and feedback is a process that allows identification of problems, possible solution approaches and the refinement of system goals. It is a peer-review process that scrutinises all the synthesis of one person or team, subjecting it to analysis and constructive criticism by another person or team of similar professional standing. This approach sharpens the thinking of the entire team and actively promotes collaborative teamwork.

Communicating Ideas

Communication and preservation of ideas

With the system properly defined and documented, the systems approach allows you to communicate your ideas and approaches to others who need to consider them in the planning and execution of projects. The modelling techniques are a key part of this communication process. The critical descriptive information is preserved not just for the immediate short term but also in a form that will be beneficial to follow both on future projects and on the review of existing projects.

Later chapters in this book show you how to follow a systems approach step by step in the development of a security architecture.

The Need for Systems Engineering in Security Architectures

Systems engineering addresses complex problems

Systems engineering, as Boardman shows[3], provides for the balanced investigation and resolution of complex problems arising out of large-scale systems.

Modern business systems are becoming more and more complex

As businesses grow in the early part of the 21st century, the dominant technical influence behind business change is the increased level of globalisation brought about by major improvements in telecommunications. Businesses can now undertake commercial transactions, on a global scale, in real-time, with parties that they have never met, through the Internet. This explosive growth in telecommunications has brought with it an ever-increasing complexity in the mechanisms used.

Complexity is destabilising unless you have tools to manage it

This complexity can prove destabilising for a business if the interdependencies of the processes and mechanisms are not clearly understood. This applies to the systems as a whole and to the security architecture in particular. Without doubt these new business systems are both large-scale and produce complex problems in their design, implementation and operation.

Systems engineering techniques provide the tools for managing complexity

Systems engineering can provide a rigorous and coherent approach to understanding these complex problems and their proper resolution.

---

[3]Boardman J. 1990, *Systems Engineering*, Prentice Hall (ISBN 0-13-504416-2)

Some Basic Concepts

The system seen as a collection of component parts and actions

The concept of a system implies a collection of component parts that act together in such a way as to accomplish a set of (declared) objectives. Boardman[4] gives a set of five basic considerations to apply when thinking about the meaning of a system:

- Total system objectives;
- The system's environment;
- The system's resources;
- The parts of the system, their activities, goals and measures of performance;
- The management of the system.

Objectives

System objectives should be mapped to business requirements

You express system objectives as the business requirements that the system should satisfy. In formulating these requirements it is of prime importance that proper consideration is given to how the performance of the system will be measured so as to demonstrate the extent to which it is satisfying those requirements. If you cannot measure whether or not you are hitting the objectives, you are not managing the solution adequately – more of this in later sections.

Starting with only technical objectives is a common fault

In the experience of the authors, systems designers frequently start from a set of technical requirements that do not reflect accurately the needs of the business and do not lend themselves to easy compliance measurement.

Incorrect objectives lead to poor solutions

If the task of stating the system objectives is not properly undertaken, then the resulting design and implementation may be at best adequate and at worst completely useless.

Environment

The system environment is outside of your control, but you must consider its influences

If you consider that the system you are designing is bounded and that you can control those elements within the boundary, the environment represents the area outside the system boundary but within which the system must operate and which has an *influence* over its operation. Figure 5-3 shows this diagrammatically. The system designer, whilst not in control of the environment, must recognise its influences and design the system to respond appropriately to them.

Resources

System resources are within the system boundary

System resources lie within the system boundary and are the means by which the system operates and achieves its objectives. In simple information system terms they are represented, for example, by the machines that process information, their operators and users, the power that drives them and the consumables that they use.

Parts of the System – Sub-Systems

Top-down decomposition into nested sub-systems reduces overall complexity

The concept of sub-systems as components of a super-system

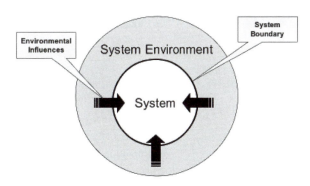

Figure 5-3: The System and Its Environment

---

[4] See Footnote 3 in this chapter.

has already been introduced in an earlier section of this chapter. A major activity in systems engineering is to decompose large-scale systems into their smaller component parts (sub-systems) whose behaviour can be modelled and measured in line with the objectives of the system as a whole. By undertaking this task, the systems architect is able to reduce the complexity of the modelling of the system as a whole, thus making it easier to understand system behaviour.

Sub-system design must take account of overall system goals

In the experience of the authors, the maintenance of the overall system objectives when delegating the design and implementation of a sub-system is frequently overlooked. This can result in the development of a sub-system that, while meeting its entire design brief, fails to fulfil business expectations. It is precisely this sort of error that can be avoided through diligent use of systems engineering.

Management

Management implies the ability to measure

In order to manage a system you must first be able to measure its performance against the system objectives. This implies both a set of measurable system parameters and a method of measuring and reporting them. Measurement and metrics are discussed in greater detail in the next section.

System management includes a wide range of activities:

- Setting system objectives;

- Collecting metrics on system performance against those objectives;

- Analysing and evaluating the metrics;

- Making and implementing decisions (both design decisions and operational decisions) based upon the analyses and evaluations;

- If necessary, reviewing and resetting the objectives.

Management is concerned with ensuring that the objectives are met

Thus the operating and performance plans for the system should ensure that it fulfils its objectives and that proper reviews are undertaken to ensure that the system maintains optimal performance.

'Performance' here has a wide meaning

'Performance' in this context has a very widest interpretation, meaning 'fulfilling all of the system objectives'. There are obvious measurable performance attributes such as throughput, latency, response time, percentage up-time and so on, but in this wider interpretation many other attributes are also included that would not normally be associated with the concept of performance. For example, maintaining the confidentiality of business information, protecting its integrity and holding users accountable for their actions are all system objectives that you might expect to be specified as part of a security architecture. Hence, system management also implies being interested in how the system performs in fulfilling these and other similar objectives.

Business Attributes provide a technique for normalising objectives and measuring performance

The concept of abstract system attributes is used extensively in the SABSA® methodology described in this book. In Chapter 6 you will encounter a full definition of a large collection of Business Attributes of this type. Not only does this technique allow you to normalise any real business model into a conceptual model based on standard abstract business attributes, but it also provides the mechanism by which you can measure performance against the objectives. For each business attribute there are suggested suitable metrics and ways that these might be measured (see Chapter 6). From this you can evaluate whether or not the security architecture is indeed meeting the stated objectives, and whether or not it needs to be changed in some way to perform better.

The Control System Concept

Control loops are used in control systems

Within any properly managed system there is some type of control loop. The study of control systems is in itself a complex subject, embracing feedback control loops, feed-forward control loops and many other more advanced control system concepts.

Feedback control is the most common

In this chapter only the simplest of these is presented – the feedback control loop – since it is by far the most common control concept that you will encounter. Figure 5-4 shows an example of a very simple feedback control loop.

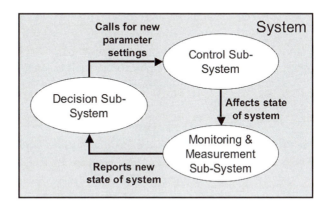

Figure 5-4: A Feedback Control Loop in a System

A feedback loop is constructed from three basic sub-systems

In this example the system includes three sub-systems (there may be other sub-systems, but this discussion focuses only on the feedback control loop). These are:

- The control sub-system – exerts control (e.g. in a heating system the component that controls how much heat is to be generated, by turning the heating on or off, or by increasing or decreasing the rate of heat output)

- The monitoring and measurement sub-system – measures the state of the system, which in turn is affected by the actions of the control sub-system (e.g. in a heating system the component that measures the temperature);

- The decision sub-system – makes decisions based upon the measurements provided by the measurement sub-system (e.g. in a heating system, the component that decides whether the temperature is above or below a set point);

Measurement information is fed back through a decision module to a control module

There is a continuous feedback of information. The control system changes certain system parameters and sets them to certain levels. As a result of this action, the state of the system changes. The monitoring and measurement sub-system measures and reports the new state. This information is fed to the decision sub-system, which decides whether or not the new state is the required one (the set point). If it is, then it will call on the control sub-system to do nothing. If the reported state is unsatisfactory then it will call on the control sub-system to bring about more change in the state, until the set point is reached. The measurements are fed back to the decision module which feeds back instructions to the control module – hence the term 'feedback loop'.

Control loops are used to manage security in business systems

This control loop concept is of critical importance in managing the security of a business system. In later chapters you will see many examples of the application of this fundamental systems concept.

Using the Systems Approach in Security Architecture

A systems approach helps in the design of secure systems

By focusing on the critical concepts that help you to understand a system you are guided into considering the areas that are relevant when designing, for example, a new secure business application.

Broad Strategic Objectives

Use broad business-based definitions of objectives

The objectives (business requirements) of the application should be aligned with the overall strategic business requirements of the sponsoring organisation. Too often the brief for the application is narrow-minded and forces the design into a rigid, tactical implementation that cannot be changed subsequently to deliver the real benefits that were originally expected. As an example, inter-operability with other systems and consistency of the user interface are the type of wider strategic requirement that often get overlooked if the project specification has a very tactical focus. It is through a series of 'tactical projects' with too narrow a scope in the objectives that enterprises often find themselves with a diverse technical environment and a high total cost of ownership.

Environmental Influences

Always include the environmental elements

There are elements in the environment surrounding the system that may be beyond the control of the system architect but which have a major impact on the ability of the system to meet its objectives. For an architect to ignore these elements simply because they are beyond his or her span of control is a serious shortcoming. The existence of these elements must be recognised and they must be included in the system modelling, because the system must respond to them and operate within the constraints that they impose.

Threats are environmental; vulnerabilities are within the system

For example, the threats that might put the security of the system at risk are properties of the system environment – they come from the outside[5]. However, the vulnerabilities that might be exploited by the threats are properties of the system itself – weaknesses in the way that it is built or operated. The system designer must recognise the threats that exist and in response must design a system in which the vulnerabilities to those threats are minimised within certain cost constraints. If you ignore the threats, it is impossible to understand what might be the vulnerabilities.

Simplifying Complexity

Use decomposition into sub-systems to reduce complexity

It is generally the case that various components of the system can be decomposed into smaller self-contained sub-systems. Through this process the systems architect can ensure that logically related functions are implemented together, thus allowing the sub-system to be tested separately to confirm compliance with its objectives. Through this type of action the complexity of testing of the system as a whole can be simplified.

---

[5]There is a potential semantic contradiction here, inasmuch as people who interact with the system are defined as being part of the system, not part of the environment, and people can pose a threat. However, people who do not interact with the system are part of the environment. There needs to be a distinction drawn between people who are authorised to interact with the system and can be regarded in that interaction as being part of the system, and people who are not authorised (who pose the threat). In this context 'unauthorised' includes people who are authorised for certain interactions but are interacting in unauthorised ways, or authorised people making human errors in the way they interact. Thus authorised interactions and the people who make them are part of the system, but unauthorised interactions and the people who make them are part of the environment and are also threats to the system.

Measuring Performance Against Objectives

The management of the system lies at the heart of its operational success. One critical aspect of this function is the collection of performance data to ensure that the system is operating in line with the objectives. It is important to include sufficient *meaningful* monitoring and measurement in the management process to allow this reconciliation to be undertaken.

Case Study

Presented here is a description of a client application where the lack of a systems approach led to the designers pursuing an erroneous course of action that failed to deliver benefits in line with the business requirements.

Overview

The Securities Trading Division of IBFS (see Chapter 4) ran a financial trading application that market analysts used to gather and consolidate information on the securities markets. A recent routine internal audit revealed that the system administration, which had originally been undertaken at the main system processor on a locally connected terminal, had been upgraded to allow the administrators to log on remotely from any user terminal.

Since the system had now changed to operate internationally (the previous design had been limited to a single office) the remote administrators' logon credentials (user IDs and passwords) were being sent in the clear across untrusted networks. Indeed *all* the other user's logon credentials were also being transmitted in the clear on the same network.

The application data being transmitted on the network was not considered sensitive since it was believed to be public-domain material that the company was post-processing and consolidating for internal use.

The audit observation highlighted that company security policy required all user passwords to be suitably encrypted when sent across untrusted communications links. Thus the remedial action planned by the client was to install hardware encryption devices at all entry points into the network so that all the paths through which these credentials could travel would be encrypted thus preventing their compromise in transit.

This case study is examined here from the perspective of a consulting team that has been asked to provide support to help plan the design and implementation of this global encryption scheme, as recommended by the audit report.

Initial Observations

At first it was noted that the scope of the data paths to be protected extended worldwide. To protect this network by encrypting the entire data transmission bandwidth would be prohibitively expensive and operationally impractical. The dynamic nature of the network meant that network routing changed over time and thus encryption devices would need virtually constant maintenance. Considering the problem in a systems way revealed some interesting information:

Scope of the System

An interesting question - how should one 'bound' this system? It turned out that the initial application designers' brief had been to produce an application that:

– Provided the market analyst, on the desktop, with consolidated financial information from three sources;

– Allowed market analyst access into the company's research database of previous historical financial information;

– Operated within the UK, using the existing communications infrastructure, but capable of expansion internationally;

– Was developed in accordance with the company's standard security operating practices.

The consultants' first try to assess what has gone wrong. What has led to the adverse audit report?

Analysis of Shortcomings

1. There was no structured or formal specification for the system. It had been built using a Rapid Application Development (RAD) approach in a correspondingly short development time. The system documentation was limited to administration and user manuals.

2. It was clear that the original designers had considered the original scope of the system as the financial trading application alone. They had delivered a system that, according to their limited remit, had been successful. However, by considering only this limited set of functionality they had delivered a point solution that, while working for this application alone, did not deliver the maximum benefit to the organisation as a whole. It certainly did not provide any flexibility for supporting extended business needs in the future.

3. The original conception of the system boundary had been short-sighted. Expanding the system boundary to be the entire company and considering the real *business requirements* pertinent to the financial trading application provided a very different view.

The consulting team now reworks the definition of the business requirements, taking a more strategic view and looking for the broader set of business requirements beyond the immediate tactical needs.

Business Requirements

The real business benefit delivered by this application was through the consolidation of a substantial amount of real-time financial data together with historical trend information stored on the company's own database and other research data sources. Providing the traders with such a well-rounded picture enhanced their ability to make sound trading judgements based on the most complete and timely data available. The principal business requirements were straightforward:

- The company made money through timely trading of various securities on their associated markets and thus wanted to *maximise its chances of success*. It had been limited in its trading scope and wanted to *expand to trade in global markets* rather than the limited markets open to it at the time.

- Its current main trading area office space was costly and it wanted to *make better use of facilities* that it already owned in other parts of the country.

- It wanted to make sure that it was using *the most up to date and correct information* as the basis for its trading to maximise returns.

- It wanted to *reduce the overhead cost* of running its computer networks as this was starting to dominate its operating expenses.

- It wanted to increase the number of transactions it made through the use of additional trained staff as soon as possible.

Next, by interviewing the management team, the consultants derive from these broad strategic business requirements some new specific system objectives.

Total System Objectives

The system should:

- Provide real-time financial information to the market analysts with the minimum of delay. In no event should this delay be more than five seconds from its provision by the information provider.

- Ensure that the information received by the market analysts should be correct and complete.

- Make trades based on user requests within five seconds of the analyst committing to the trade on their screen.

- Support 100 simultaneous users without performance degradation, and up to 150 users with no more than a 30% reduction in response times.

- Be capable of enhancement and upgrade to support additional users without a need to change the basic system architecture.

- Be available 99.99% of the time during the normal working week (defined as opening of business in Asia on Monday and close of business in the USA on Friday).

- Be fully accessible to any authorised user in any of the company's offices worldwide during the normal working week.

- Operate consistent with the needs of company compliance monitoring, including the provision of full accountability for all trades through the provision of a tamper-protected audit trail of all trader actions.

— Use the most cost-effective computing and communications infrastructure available without compromise of security as defined in the company's security policy.

The last two requirements are the only ones that the business managers who were interviewed considered relevant to security – in reality *all* are relevant to security, but only the last one reflects why the team had originally been asked to review the project (the password problem). It turns out that this problem is easy to solve as part of a proper overall system design.

Review of the Design: Functional Problems Identified

1. In the light of the review of the requirements it becomes clear that the original design had no insight into the need for timeliness of delivery of information. In fact a review of the operational system showed that the financial information was being delivered to the desktop up to two minutes after it was required.

2. There had been no planned expansion of the system outside the geography of the UK. It appeared that the original application had been funded through one business manager's departmental research fund and that there was a disincentive for her to spend any more than she absolutely needed to serve the needs of her department.

3. The system had a hard-coded maximum of 64 users.

4. Although the correctness and completeness of the information being processed was used to drive the trading process, there were no checks within the system to ensure the integrity of the business critical information being delivered.

Referring back to the discussion earlier in this chapter about the need to consider the system environment as well as the system itself, and the resources available to the system, the consulting team find that these are major issues with respect to the original thinking behind the design of this system.

Review of the Design: The System's Environment

The system used a communications infrastructure provided by a third-party supplier. There appeared to be no Service Level Agreement between the company and the supplier. Response time of the network to support the required transaction turnaround had never been discussed.

Review of the Design: The System's Resources

The hardware on which the trading application was hosted was shared by many applications. There was a simple round-robin form of task scheduling that ensured that all the tasks were run in sequential order and that they all received some share of the processing and I/O available.

The main processor was fitted with an uninterruptible power supply (UPS) and fault-tolerant hard disks.

The traders' desktop machines were not fitted with UPSs or any form of fault-tolerant storage. However, the application used local storage on the traders' machines to cache information being sent to and received from the main processor.

The consulting team now looks at how the complexity of the design has been managed and how it was intended that the achievement of the objectives would be measured.

Review of the Design: The Sub-Systems, Their Activities, Goals and Measures of Performance

The system documentation gave no insight into how the design had been decomposed into anything other than the most high level sub-systems – principally the main processor and the traders' processors.

There had been substantial work done on streamlining the user interface to ensure that the information presented to the analysts was clear and unambiguous.

There had been no attempts to produce any form of performance model or availability model for either the main processor component or the traders' component.

Review of the Design: The Management of the System

A systems administrator undertook the management of the system. The primary management task defined in the documentation was to administer user accounts (add, modify, delete) and take regular backups of the system data to tape.

There were no performance-measuring tools available that would show how well the system was behaving, and there were no simple auditing tools available to show how users had acted in processing trades on the system.

The consulting team now has all the information that it needs to analyse and report on what was wrong with the original system design.

Critical Shortcomings of the Design

What is most apparent when reviewing the business requirements is the overwhelming need for high performance, high reliability and high integrity in this system. At no previous stage had the company seen the need to produce any form of performance or availability model of the system to review how well it met both specifications and the business requirements.

Of particular interest is the arrangement for outsourcing the (external) communications infrastructure. The decision to use this third-party service had been taken by the Information Systems Department with a view to reducing costs and allowing the business to concentrate on core business. This was in line with the overall business strategy of the company, but the lack of a formal service level agreement with the supplier meant that the performance of this component of the system was completely outside the control of the company. Additionally there had been no review of how this decision may introduce business risks to the applications using the infrastructure.

The recommendations of the consulting team are that a complete redesign exercise should be undertaken, based upon a proper systems approach, taking into account the wider requirements of the organisation.

Using a Systems Approach to Redesign the System

IBFS was not fully committed to following a systems approach to re-engineering the whole business (this is frequently the case), but was prepared to sponsor the re-engineering of the trading system using a systems approach that reflected the high-level needs of the business as a whole.

It is left to the reader to compare and contrast how different the real business requirements were compared to those considered in the initial implementation and how different things might have been with a little more structured work earlier.

Conclusions

It was clear that the original application had been designed and implemented with a very limited set of boundaries. In particular the role of the system in the context of the business as a whole had not been properly considered. As a result the completed application fulfilled the spirit of its original specification (as a business sub-system), but its overall performance and contribution to the business would have been much improved if it had been the subject of systems thinking and the business had employed a systems approach. However, it is only fair to point out that this additional rigour would probably have had an impact on the overall project budget, but you usually get no more than that for which you are prepared to pay.

Advanced Modelling Techniques

Advanced techniques for those with a deeper technical interest

For those who have a deep technical background or interest there is included here a section on some of the more advanced system modelling techniques. If you are not especially technical in your outlook then you may choose to skip over some of this material. The three sections are arranged in order of increasing difficulty: business process engineering, dependency tree modelling and finite state machines. In each case the section provides only a brief overview. If you want to take the study of these techniques further then you will need to seek out specialist texts on each subject.

Business Process Engineering

Business process engineering applies system concepts to business

Business process engineering or business process re-engineering is the application of a systems approach to the architecture of the business itself. A business process is a system (or sub-system) that takes inputs and transforms them into outputs that have value to the business.

Examples of business processes are:

- Manufacturing a food product from raw materials;

- Assembling a motor car from components and sub-assemblies;

• Processing transaction data against a master database of customer bank accounts.

Certain processes are common to many enterprises

In any typical enterprise involved in a business process engineering exercise there are certain common processes that you might expect them to define. These might include:

• Acquire customer order;

• Fulfil customer order;

• Collect revenue from customers;

• Manufacture products;

• Acquire and store raw materials;

• Pay suppliers.

A meta-process is used to manage processes

There will also be at least one special process that is itself used for managing the business processes. Such a process management process is called a meta-process. Sometimes the highest-level processes are expressed simply as: the sales process or the manufacturing process, and in some texts these too are referred to as meta-processes.

Business process engineering uses top-down decomposition

Using the top-down decomposition methods already discussed, each of these high-level processes can be analysed into sub-processes, and at each level of decomposition there is the potential to take the decomposition down to yet another level of detail. The exact number of levels of decomposition will depend upon what the enterprise needs in practical terms to be able to engineer the processes successfully.

Business process engineering leverages new technology

Why is this so important? The current fashion for business process engineering has been driven by the obvious failure of a functional model of the business and by the fact that in introducing new technologies, it simply doesn't work to replicate a manual process with a technical solution. The introduction of new technology provides the opportunity and the impetus to re-engineer completely the business process around the technology, and hence leverage its real power.

Business processes are built up from individual functions

First consider the functional model versus process model of business. The functional model organises the enterprise according to what people do. There is a sales department, production department, finance department, and so on, each fulfilling a different function. The problem with this model is that no one department has oversight of the real way in which the business operates. The real business is a series of processes, and each process calls upon different functions along the way. Thus a process called Fulfil Customer Order might involve several departmental functions:

• The sales department has the information on what the customer ordered;

• The production department must produce it;

• The quality assurance department must check it;

• The warehouse department must store it;

• The logistics department must arrange the shipping.

Which department has overall control? None of them! And there lies the problem.

Business processes need to be managed at a process level, not just a functional level

If on the other hand, the business is organised on a business process basis, then there is a process owner who oversees the successful operation of each process, ensuring that each function is co-ordinated so as to deliver the process on an end-to-end basis.

This has a significant effect on business continuity management, which is the subject of a more detailed treatment in Chapter 17.

Case Study on Business Process Failure

The Case of the Missing Taxis

A television-broadcasting organisation had its studios located in a capital city, some number of kilometres from the central government offices and parliament building. The current affairs programming required that politicians regularly visited the studios to give interviews, often at short notice in response to breaking news items. The way most of these politicians travelled to and from the studios was by means of a taxi.

The overall business process of running current affairs programmes involved many functional departments, but it had not been recognised as a business process, and its criticality to the overall success of the organisation had not been assessed. More specifically the significance of the individual functions within the process was not understood and no one person had overall process ownership.

A woman secretary who was located in the basement of the studio building carried out one specific function. She used to arrange the taxis that brought the politicians to and from the building. She worked for the facilities manager, a functional department that looked after the building in general and took care of most of the ancillary services – such as ordering taxis.

In a cost-conscious world every job is up for review – is it really needed? The facilities manager looked at his staff head count. There was a woman whose only job was to order taxis! Surely this was excessive luxury if ever there was one – people can order their own taxis – and so she was 'let go'.

What happened? The entire process of getting politicians to the studio on time for interviews fell apart. The core business purpose of the current affairs section was destroyed overnight.

And the lesson is … make sure that every single function in an end-to-end critical business process is afforded the same level of criticality as the overall process that it supports. You only need one function in the middle of process to fail, and the entire process is broken. Moreover, any attempt to manage business continuity in an environment where business process engineering is not part of the culture has a questionable chance of success.

Some of the major benefits[6] of a business process engineering approach are:

- The ability to provide cost accounting for each stage of the process:

    - To calculate the total cost of the process;

    - To identify the high-cost sub-processes;

---

[6]Summarised from a paper entitled 'Process Based Auditing' by Stan Dormer. See www.ink-e-media.com

- To look for alternative, lower-cost implementations of sub-processes through automation, integration, re-sequencing or outsourcing.

- The ability to make a value-chain analysis on each process:

  - To understand where the enterprise adds real value (i.e. core business);

  - To understand what activities or sub-processes could be outsourced because they are not adding real value (i.e. not core business).

- The ability to carry out process analysis:

  - To test if re-sequencing the sub-processes can economise on execution time or operational costs;

  - To assess the risk of failure at each level of sub-process and thus look for more robust implementations of vulnerable sub-processes;

  - To identify significant control points in the process;

  - To eliminate hidden unnecessary complexities;

  - To ensure all decision points are clear, that the decision parameters are known at the time of the decision and that the decision criteria are well-defined.

Dependency Tree Modelling

Higher-level systems depend on their constituent lower-level components

This technique provides a means to examine the way in which system behaviour is affected by a series of interdependencies. Higher-level systems (or super-systems) are dependent upon the functioning of lower-level sub-systems. However, the way these dependencies work depends upon how they are combined – in series or in parallel.

The AND relationship

Consider the simple system in Figure 5-5. It comprises two sub-systems that operate in series. Both sub-system A and sub-system B must be operational for the overall system to work. The system depends on BOTH A AND B being functional.

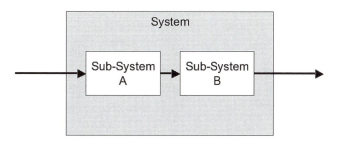

Figure 5-5: Sub-Systems in Series – the AND Relationship

The OR relationship

Now look at Figure 5-6. This time the sub-systems are connected in parallel. If either one of these sub-systems is functioning, then the overall system is working. The system depends on EITHER A OR B.

AND increases risk; OR decreases risk

This has huge implications for resilience and failure in systems. The AND relationship between sub-systems increases risk of system failure, because if one component fails, the entire system fails, whatever the status of the second component. However, the OR relationship decreases risk of

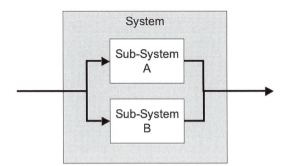

Figure 5-6: Sub-Systems in Parallel – the OR Relationship

system failure, because if one component fails, the other will carry on servicing the system and keeping it going.

Can be applied to sophisticated risk modelling

These basic ideas have been developed into a sophisticated dependency modelling toolset by Professor John Gordon of Concept Laboratories Limited. One of its main applications is the computation of risk in complex systems.[7]

Finite State Machine Models

Traffic light systems have finite states

Consider a set of traffic lights. The system can be in one of three states: red, amber or green[8.] You have only one state at a time, they are mutually exclusive and there are a finite number of possible states, all of which can be described. To change from one state to another is called a state transition. The transition from one state to another is caused by an event. In the case of the traffic lights there is an internal timer that is set when a new state is entered. When the timer runs out, the light changes to the next colour. In each stable state the system waits for an event. In a more sophisticated traffic light system a vehicle approaching may also generate an event. A state transition diagram can be used to represent the sequence of states and state transitions. See Figure 5-7.

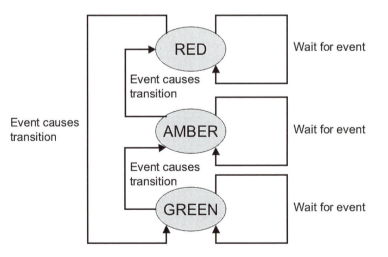

Figure 5-7: The State Transition Diagram for Traffic Lights

---

[7] See www.dependency.com for more information.

[8] In some countries (especially the UK) this is not quite true – some poetic licence is used here for simplicity.

Finite state machine is another system modelling tool

The state transition diagram is similar in appearance to the logical system flow diagrams discussed earlier in the chapter, but the meaning of the diagram is entirely different in this case. The following sections explain the terminology and meaning.

The model comprises states, state variables, state transitions and events

When a system is modelled as a finite state machine, it is conceptualised as a series of stable states in which the system can be found to exist from time to time. At any given time the system is in only one of these possible states. Each state is described by the values of a number of state variables. (In the case of the traffic lights, there would be a state variable called lightColour which has three possible values: red, amber or green). The system changes state from one to another, triggered by an event, such as an external interrupt or an internal timer expiring. The change of state is known as a state transition. In changing state, some or all of the state variables will change in value.

All of the finite number of states must be identified

The term 'finite state machine' is used because, for a given system, there are only a finite number of states in which it can find itself. In developing a finite state machine model it is therefore essential that the designer should first identify *all* of the possible states.

Predicates govern the selection of the appropriate outgoing event

Some incoming events may lead to a number of possible outgoing events. The selection of the appropriate outgoing event is governed by the value of one or more predicates. These are Boolean variables holding the values true or false. Logical expressions that combine these predicates through AND, OR, NOT, NOR and XOR operations are evaluated to determine which outgoing event is to be selected.

Specific actions are local responses to incoming events

Some of the actions needed in response to an incoming event are local rather than being outgoing events. These are referred to as 'specific actions'. They could include such actions as 'start timer' or 'increment counter'.

FSMs behave atomically

Finite state machines operate in an 'atomic' mode. This means that states are indivisible. The system is in one state or another but cannot be somewhere between the states. This also means that when an event occurs that will cause a state transition, all functions associated with that event must be processed in full before another event can be accepted for processing. Any further events must be queued up until this processing is complete.

FSM modelling is applied to interactive protocols in systems

What types of system should be modelled as finite state machines? The most common type of candidate for this type of modelling is an interactive communications protocol between two or more sub-systems. Indeed, if such a system is designed without producing a finite state machine model, it is likely that at some stage the system will fail because it enters a state that the designer has not foreseen and for which there are no planned actions!

Security architectures embody many interactive protocols

Examples of interactive communications protocols that you find in security architecture include:

- Cryptographic protocols;

- Authentication protocols (such as password protocols);

- Handshaking protocols;

- Two-phase commit protocols in distributed databases;

- Any protocols for the distribution, replication or duplication of some security-related data (perhaps for backup purposes);

- Any synchronisation protocols between two application sub-systems.

Finite State Machine Case Study

A Password Authentication Protocol

Consider a simple password authentication protocol by which a user logs in to a computer application. For absolute simplicity this arrangement is conceptualised as a system with two sub-systems: the Prover (that must prove its identity) and the Verifier that must verify the identity of the Prover.

There is an initial registration protocol by which a new Prover is introduced to the Verifier and registered on the Verifier's database of known Provers. This protocol itself needs to be modelled as a finite state machine to ensure that it is complete and robust. However, here it is assumed that this has been achieved and that the Verifier already has a database of known Provers. Figure 5-8 shows the system as described.

Consider now the Prover. How many possible states are there for this sub-system? The following states must be included:

- IDLE state – doing nothing;

- WFLP state – waiting for an incoming 'login prompt' event after an outgoing 'wake-up' event;

- WFID state – waiting for an incoming 'user enters ID' event after a 'login prompt' event;

- WFPP state – waiting for an incoming 'password prompt' event after a 'user enters ID' event;

- WFPW state – waiting for a 'user enters password' event after a 'password prompt' event;

- WFLC state – waiting for a 'login completed' event after a 'user enters password' event;

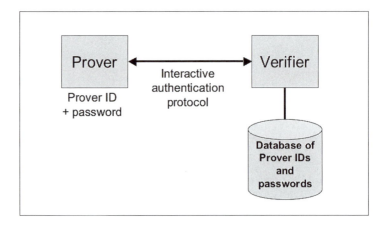

Figure 5-8: The System for Password Authentication

- WFLO state – logged in and working after a 'login completed' event, thus waiting for a 'logout' event or 'activity timeout' event or a 'session timeout' event.

This rather basic state model is a good example of the types of states that you might encounter. There will be others that you would want to include, because here no analysis has been included of error conditions (such as incorrect ID or password) or individual timeouts on any of the intermediate states. To build a truly robust system, every possible state and every possible event must be identified and included in the model. This example is being kept simple so as to demonstrate certain aspects of the technique, and it is not intended to be a comprehensive tutorial on finite state machine modelling.

The state transition diagram is shown in Figure 5-9. This allows you to appreciate visually the relationships between events, states and the transitions from one state to another.

As well as the state transition diagram, other aspects of the model are documented through a series of tables. These tables include:

- The incoming events table – describing the event name, the interface through which it is received and its meaning;

- The outgoing events table – describing the event name, the interface through which it is sent and its meaning;

- The states table – describing the states and their meaning;

- The predicates table – describing the predicate names and their meanings and values;

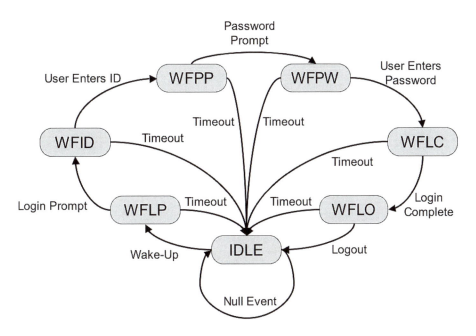

Figure 5-9: The State Transition Diagram

- The specific actions table – describing the local specific actions;

- The state variables table – defining the state variables, their data types and their ranges of values;

- The event/state table, mapping all the possible events to all the possible states and showing the results of each event on each state.

Consider now the Verifier sub-system. This is not analysed in detail here, but you can quickly see that the Verifier has a more complicated set of states and state variables to maintain. The Verifier must handle the expiry of passwords, which then need to be changed, which involves yet another protocol to be modelled. The Verifier must also handle the expiry of accounts, the blocking of accounts because more than three attempts have been made to get the password right, and must handle all the possible error conditions that can arise, and so on.

The finite state machine modelling technique provides the tools by which this can be done, systematically, methodically and completely.

FSM modelling is a tool for guaranteeing high levels of assurance in systems

Finite state machine modelling is a very powerful and advanced tool. It provides the means for systems engineers and architects to analyse precisely the very complex interactions in an interactive system. Without such a technique it is doubtful that one would be able to build robust interactive systems of this type. The use of this approach allows the designer to establish a detailed model of an interactive system in which a high level of assurance is required regarding its functionality.

Types of high-assurance system

High levels of assurance are needed in several types of system:

- Safety-critical systems, where malfunction can cost lives or injuries;

- High-security systems, where malfunction can have a massive business impact;

- Basic infrastructure systems (such as data communications networks) which support a wide range of business applications and which are fundamental to the continuity of business operations.

Exhaustive Model Checking

High levels of assurance require comprehensive model checking and possibly formal specification languages

In order to gain the very highest level of assurance, the system should be first modelled as a finite state machine[9]. Then the model should be processed through an automated model checker that will exercise every possible state and every possible event to ensure that the model is truly robust. However, if the model is incorrect (e.g. a particular state or event is missing) then the model checker will not normally be able to detect that. Additional techniques such as formal specification languages may be needed to prove the correctness of the model itself, but these are way beyond the scope of this book.

---

[9]It is important to recognise a practical problem that can arise in large complex systems – the state explosion problem, in which the number of possible states increases exponentially as the size and complexity of the system rises. One way to manage this problem is to create a tiered sub-system model and to be careful in specifying the scope of each sub-system so as to limit the number of states in each. The difficulties then arise when events from one sub-system trigger state-changes in another sub-system. By using tiered black box sub-systems it may be possible to contain the explosive complexity of the FSM model. However, this is well beyond the scope of the overview in this chapter.

This section offers a brief introduction to FSMs, not a comprehensive treatment of the subject

This chapter has introduced the subject of finite state machine modelling and explained its main concepts, but this is not meant to be a comprehensive tutorial on how to use finite state machine models. Those who wish to take this further are recommended to refer to the literature on the subject. Most serious texts on data communications protocols contain a section dealing with this approach.

Other Advanced Modelling Techniques

New security-specific techniques such as trust modelling and domain modelling will be introduced later in the book

Throughout this book many of the system modelling techniques described in this chapter are applied in various contexts. Some new advanced techniques that are very specific to the modelling of security architectures are introduced in later chapters. These include trust modelling and security domain modelling. When you encounter these approaches you will see similarities with the material already discussed. Much of the advancement of security architecture as a discipline depends upon the development of new and innovative modelling techniques and tools that allow you to solve new types of complex problems.

To Summarise: A Systems Approach

A systems approach means taking a comprehensively structured approach to your thinking, ensuring that all aspects of system behaviour and its influences are considered, and thus ensuring maximum delivery of business benefit.

To achieve this you must:

- Understand the system boundary;
- Make rational, traceable decisions;
- Consider all aspects of the system.

The systems approach is characterised by addressing complexity and simplifying complexity through:

- Top-down decomposition;
- The black box concept;
- Logical flow analysis.

A systems approach implies certain behaviours by the architect or designer:

- Writing it down;
- Structured peer review;
- Communicating and preserving ideas.

The basic concepts of systems engineering are:

- System objectives;
- System environment;
- System resources;
- Sub-systems;
- System management.

Security systems and sub-systems often employ the control system concept using a feedback control loop with three sub-systems:

- Control sub-system;

- Measurement sub-system;

- Decision sub-system.

Using a systems approach in developing security architectures requires the designer to consider:

- Broad-based business objectives;

- Environmental considerations;

- Reducing complexity;

- Meaningful monitoring and measuring.

There are also a number of advanced modelling techniques that can be applied in developing security architectures. These include:

- Business process engineering;

- Dependency tree modelling;

- Finite state machine models;

- Other advanced modelling techniques such as trust modelling and security domain modelling that are introduced in later chapters of this book.

Chapter 6: Measuring Return on Investment in Security Architecture

The previous chapter emphasised the need to be able to measure and monitor performance. This next chapter builds upon that idea by looking at the measures of business performance that can be associated with security architecture. Increasingly, senior management teams are looking for business cases in advance of making a major investment in new developments. A key performance indicator that they are looking for is some measure of return on investment, or at least return of value. This chapter examines several approaches that can be adopted for evaluating the return on an investment in an enterprise security architecture.

In this chapter you will learn about:

- Interpreting the notions of return on investment and return of value in the context of a security architecture programme;

- The concepts of measurement, metrics and monitoring and the use of a dashboard to display key performance indicators;

- The Balanced Scorecard approach to measuring enterprise performance;

- The SABSA® Business Attributes approach to measuring enterprise performance;

- The use of Capability Maturity Models for measuring enterprise performance;

- Benchmarking enterprise security architecture and security management practice against external measures.

What Is Meant by 'Return on Investment'?

Return on investment is concerned with evaluating the payback

'Investment' means spending some resources now (money, time, effort) so as to gain a payback at a later time. The length of time before the payback occurs can vary from a few days to a few years. 'Return' means the payback itself. So here is one of your key difficulties: You invest in security, the security is good, the payback is – nothing happens! Yes, that's right – there are no security incidents, because the security is working well.

Insurance is not a good analogy for security

Some security professionals attempt to sell security to senior management on the basis that security is like insurance. This approach fails to recognise the true nature of both security and insurance. Insurance is not a preventative measure. You take out life insurance policies precisely because you know death to be a risk that ultimately cannot be avoided. But the policies contribute nothing to the quality of your life, nor do they extend life. Those who use this insurance analogy to justify security usually set an expectation that nothing of value will happen and thus they contribute significantly to the perception of security as a business inhibitor.

If security is good, there are no incidents – nothing happens – which makes it hard to demonstrate benefit

This somewhat contradictory proposition can be very damaging to your business case for security, since 'return on investment' means that something happens. More than that it means that you can measure the something to get an evaluation of how much return on investment you are getting. Whether you like it or not, if you are to convince senior managers that security adds value to the organisation, you must be able to demonstrate the added value and to measure the added value.

'Return of value' is perhaps a more useful phrase

You may be better off using the term 'return of value' rather than 'return on investment', since this already gives a clue that things are not so simple. However, having decided that you will demonstrate and measure a return of value, you now have to find a way to achieve that measurement. This chapter focuses on this issue.

Why Do You Need Metrics?

Some famous quotations about measurement

Consider what some others have said about metrics and measurement:

'If you can measure what you speak of and can express it by a number, you know something about your subject; but if you cannot measure it, your knowledge is meagre and unsatisfactory.'
> Lord Kelvin

'The ability to measure is one of man's great capabilities.'
> F. D. Rossini

'Measure what is measurable and render measurable that which is not yet measurable.'
> Galileo Galilei

'If you can't measure it, you can't manage it.'
> Peter F. Drucker

The 'can't measure, can't manage' maxim from Drucker is especially useful

These all shed some light on the subject of this chapter, but Peter Drucker's message, being the more contemporary of the set, is perhaps the most germane. It is clearly such common sense and is absolutely at the heart of modern management theory. Applying it to security architecture, if you want to manage security, then you need to measure the effects of your actions – meaning you need to measure security in some way.

Many people need measurements

Now consider this in more detail from the perspective of several key groups of people in an organisation:

The information security manager needs measurements

The information security group manager needs to know how the security management programme is going:

- What has the team achieved?
- Does the team add value to the organisation?
- How can I demonstrate how valuable we are?
- How can I justify the department's budget?

- How can I motivate the team to achieve more?

The team members need measurements

The individual team members also need to know how things are going:

- Are we getting anywhere?

- Can I feel a sense of achievement to boost my morale?

- Can I see my career developing?

- Can I measure my achievements at my next staff appraisal?

Senior managers need measurements

Senior managers need to measure success:

- What sort of assurance can be demonstrated that the security of our systems is adequate?

- Can I show that due diligence has been exerted?

- Are we ahead of the others, or behind the others, or are we comfortably in the middle of the pack?

- Are we fulfilling the corporate governance responsibilities?

- What sort of return am I getting from my security investment?

Measuring security performance can be challenging. The SABSA® Business Attributes Profile provides a useful approach

The need for measurement and metrics is clear, but information security managers often struggle to provide useful metrics. Here the SABSA® Business Attributes Profile is introduced as a solution. It uses a series of business attributes that have been developed by the authors entirely based on practical experience in consulting to major organisations on enterprise security architecture – but first a look at some other theoretical concepts.

The Security Management Dashboard

The concept of an instrument panel or dashboard is useful

Complex engineering systems such as motor vehicles and aeroplanes provide a means to feed back a wide range of information to the people who are in control of the systems. In an aircraft this is called the 'instrument panel'; in a car it is called the 'dashboard'. These panels have many dials and gauges, each of which provides a measure of some critical parameter of the system – speed, altitude, fuel level, engine temperature, air pressure, etc.

The measurements and the reporting of them is an important element in feedback control loops

It is time to recall the feedback control loop model that was discussed in Chapter 5, shown in Figure 5-4. The instrument panel in an aircraft reports the measurements that inform the pilot of the status of the aircraft. The pilot makes the decisions and implements them through the controls (rudder, flaps, etc.). These alterations to the controls affect the parameters measured, and the pilot continuously monitors the panel and makes changes to the controls in order to fly the aircraft. This is a classic example of a feedback control loop.

The dashboard provides the means to assess the status of the security management process

Just like the aircraft pilot, you need a kind of instrument panel or dashboard for security management, measuring and reporting back the level of effectiveness of your previous decisions and helping you to make new decisions that will maintain and possibly improve that effectiveness. The measurements that you choose become the displays on your conceptual dashboard. Figure 6-1 shows this diagrammatically.

The domains of activity follow accepted wisdom

The choice of strategic, tactical and operational objectives in this diagram is based upon the Harvard Business School philosophy that in order to be successful in business you need to be successful in all these three domains:

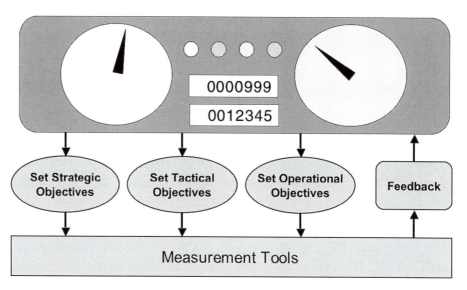

Figure 6-1: The Security Management Dashboard

- **Strategic planning and management** – setting out long-term goals and plans for reaching those goals. Strategic goals tend to take a year or even several years to reach. However, a strategic programme is something that might have a beginning but never ends. Strategy-focused organisations tend to be in a state of constant change, and their success depends upon their ability to manage that change programme.

- **Tactical planning and management** – setting medium-term goals and plans to achieve those goals. Tactical goals usually take several months to reach, and tactical programmes have both a beginning and an end. You know when a tactical programme has been completed. Projects are typically tactical initiatives that take you further towards the strategic goals. Alternatively, sometimes you need to do things on a purely tactical basis, without a specific strategy in mind, because there is an immediate problem that current strategy does not address and you need to do something now. Later this gap can be addressed by new strategies.

- **Operational planning and management** – deals with the day-to-day job of keeping the business running. Operational work is based upon repetitive procedures that make up business processes. These processes and procedures were more than likely developed through tactical projects, which in turn were driven by strategies.

Success depends upon diligence in all three domains

The Harvard Business School philosophy is simple –you cannot afford to neglect any one of these streams of activity, and a successful business operates simultaneously on all three levels.

There are a number of ways to provide the measurements

Returning to the dashboard concept, to make this work in practice you need the appropriate tools and metrics to provide the information displayed on the panel – and for all three domains of planning and management. Before introducing the SABSA® Business Attributes Profile methodology as a means to provide these measurements, other potential approaches that you might want to consider are introduced. In particular, the Balanced Scorecard approach has merits.

The Balanced Scorecard Approach

Balanced Scorecard is a general business performance measurement methodology

The concept of the Balanced Scorecard (BSC) was developed and published in 1993 by Robert Kaplan of Harvard Business School and consultant David Norton. Balanced Scorecard is a strategic tool for senior executives to measure and improve organisational performance. The thrust of Kaplan and Norton's thesis is that traditional financial measures such as return on investment or earnings per share are good only for reporting results and that these metrics are not very useful in helping to make the effective strategic decisions that lead to the results.

BSC combines financial measurements with other more qualitative methods

The Balanced Scorecard approach has become very popular and a central theme of mainstream management science. It now has a similar standing to business process re-engineering. The advantage that it offers is to combine both financial and operational measures of performance into a single framework that 'translates a company's strategic objectives into a coherent set of performance measures'[1]. It has been specifically applied to ICT management[2] and to ICT security management[3].

BSC translates strategy into performance measures

'Balanced scorecard is a tool that translates an organisation's mission and strategy into a comprehensive set of performance measures that provides the framework for a strategic measurement and management system.'[4]

There are four perspectives for the measurements

Kaplan and Norton's BSC offers four perspectives on the measurement of performance:

- **The Financial Perspective** – covering the traditional measurements of cost per unit, revenue growth, profitability, gearing, etc.

- **The Customer Perspective** – covering both subjective measurements (such as customer satisfaction surveys) and objective measurements (such as customer acquisition rates, customer retention rates, etc.).

- **The Internal Process Perspective** – focusing on efficiency measures such as how long it takes to answer a customer query, fulfil a customer order; open a new customer account, etc.

- **The Innovation and Learning Perspective** – addressing the need to change and adapt constantly through measurements of investment in training, innovation processes, etc.

The four perspectives form a layered architecture model

These four perspectives are in fact a kind of architecture model, as shown in Figure 6-2. The scorecard is simply a series of statements of goals (intentions) and matching measurements (outcomes) in each of the four perspective domains, providing a balanced view of what the organisation needs to achieve.

Quoting again from the Balanced Scorecard Collaborative web site (see Footnote 4 previously):

Here are some of the benefits of using BSC

'Organisations benefit from the use of Balanced Scorecard in the following ways:

- Clarify the vision throughout the organisation;

- Gain consensus and ownership by the executive team;

- Provide a framework to align the organisation;

---

[1]Robert Kaplan and David Norton, 'Putting the Balanced Scorecard to Work', Harvard Business Review, January-February 1996.

[2]Robert Gold, 'The Balanced Scorecard and IT Management', Compass America White Paper 1999.

[3]Stan Dormer, 'IT Security Management: A New Look at the Deliverables', Information Security Bulletin June 1999.

[4] Quoted from the web site of the Balanced Scorecard Collaborative at www.bscol.com

- Provide structure for multiple initiatives;

- Drive the capital and resource allocation process;

- Integrate the strategic management process across the organisation;

- Focus teams and individuals on strategic priorities.

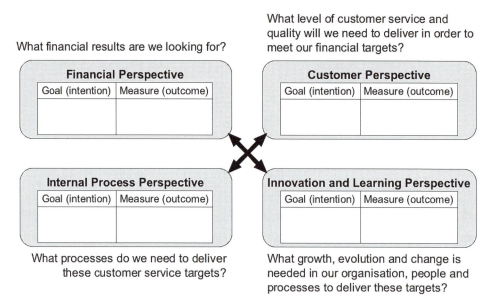

Figure 6-2: The Architecture of Balanced Scorecard

BSC is the first step towards becoming a Strategy-Focused Organisation

'The Balanced Scorecard is a powerful framework to help organisations rapidly implement strategy by translating the vision and strategy into a set of operational objectives that can drive behaviour, and therefore, performance. Strategy-driven performance measures provide the essential feedback mechanism required to dynamically adjust and refine the organisation's strategy over time. The Balanced Scorecard concept is built upon the premise that what is measured is what motivates organisational stakeholders to act. Ultimately all of the organisation's activities, resources, and initiatives should be aligned to the strategy. The Balanced Scorecard achieves this goal by explicitly defining the cause and effect relationships between objectives, measures, and initiatives across each perspective and down through all levels of the organisation. Developing a Balanced Scorecard is the first step in creating a Strategy-Focused Organisation5. Creating a Strategy-Focused Organisation is based on five principles:

- Translate strategy into operational terms and performance objectives;

- Align the organisation to the strategy;

- Motivate the people by making strategy everyone's job;

---

[5]Strategy-Focused Organisation is a concept owned by the Balanced Scorecard Collaborative.

- Adapt to make strategy a continual process of change;

- Mobilise the resources for ongoing change through executive leadership.

Strategy-Focused Organisations operate on five principles

'The five principles of the Strategy-Focused Organisation illustrate how Balanced Scorecard adopters have taken their groundbreaking tool to the next level. These organisations have used the Scorecard to create an entirely new performance management framework that puts strategy at the centre of key management processes and systems.

Table 6.1: Business Drivers for IBFS RTSS

Driver No	Business Drivers
BD1	Protecting the reputation of IBFS, ensuring that it is perceived as competent in its sector
BD2	Providing support to the claims made by IBFS about its competence to carry out its intended functions
BD3	Protecting the trust that exists in business relationships and propagating that trust across remote electronic business communications links and distributed information systems
BD4	Maintaining the confidence of other key parties in their relationships with IBFS
BD5	Maintaining the operational capability of IBFS's systems
BD6	Maintaining the continuity of service delivery, including the ability to meet the requirements of service level agreements where these exist
BD7	Maintaining the accuracy of information
BD8	Maintaining the ability to govern
BD9	Preventing losses through financial fraud
BD10	Detecting attempted financial fraud
BD11	Providing the ability to prosecute those who attempt to defraud IBFS
BD12	Ensuring that the solutions provided for securing electronic business services include a clear and unambiguous definition of responsibilities and liabilities for all parties at every stage of the transaction.
BD13	Providing and maintaining the ability to resolve disputes between IBFS and any other parties, quickly, efficiently and with minimum cost
BD14	Ensuring that information processed in IBFS's systems can be brought to a court of law as evidence in support of both criminal and civil proceedings and that the court will admit the evidence, and that the evidence will withstand hostile criticism by the other side's expert witnesses
BD15	Ensuring that the information security approaches used in the systems directly support compliance by IBFS with commercial contracts to which IBFS is a party
BD16	Ensuring that IBFS is at all times compliant with the laws and industry sector regulations, and that the information security approach in the systems directly and indirectly supports legal compliance
BD17	Maintaining the privacy of personal and business information that is stored, processed and communicated by IBFS's systems
BD18	Protecting against the deliberate, accidental or negligent corruption of personal and business information that is stored, processed and communicated by the systems
BD19	Ensuring that an entity that makes a business transaction cannot later deny having made the transaction, and that the entity will be bound by the contractual obligations associated with making the transaction
BD20	Ensuring that all users can be held accountable for the actions that they take in making use of their access privileges

Driver No	Business Drivers
BD20	Ensuring that all users can be held accountable for the actions that they take in making use of their access privileges
BD21	Ensuring that access privileges are designed and implemented in such a way as to minimise the risk of a single individual having excessive power that could be abused without easily being detected
BD22	Providing a means by which IBFS can monitor compliance with its various information security policies and can detect, investigate and remedy any attempted or actual violations of those policies
BD23	Providing assurance of the correct functioning of IBFS's systems and sub-systems
BD24	Providing for the setting of policy and the control and monitoring of compliance with policy by the authorities vested with responsibility for corporate governance in the system environment
BD25	Protecting other parties with whom IBFS has business dealings from abuse, loss of business or personal information
BD26	Ensuring that employees using the system are only granted authorised access within need-to-know and need-to-use privileges
BD27	Ensuring the system security solution is cost-effective and provides good value for money
BD28	Ensuring that the security of IBFS's information is dependent only upon its system security measures and not on the security competence of any other organisation
BD29	Ensuring that the granularity of system security services is appropriate to business need
BD30	Preserving the ability of authorised business users to maintain a high level of productivity
BD31	Ensuring that information security interfaces are easy and simple to use
BD32	Utilising, where possible, commercial off-the-shelf products to build information security solutions
BD33	Ensuring that security services can be extended to all user locations, to all interface types and across all network types that will be used to support delivery
BD34	Maximising the economic advantage of the enterprise security architecture
BD35	Supporting security services through electronic communications, without the need for physical transfer of documents or storage media
BD36	Ensuring that system security solutions comply as far as possible with internal and external standards and best practices
BD37	Ensuring that the security architecture is independent of any specific vendor or product and is capable of supporting multiple products from multiple vendors
BD38	Ensuring that the security architecture remains compatible with new technical solutions as these evolve and become available, and with new business requirements as these emerge, with a minimum of redesign
BD39	Adapting the security architecture to counter new threats and vulnerabilities as they are discovered
BD40	Ensuring that the required internal and external cultural shift is achieved to support the security architecture
BD41	Ensuring accurate information is available when needed
BD42	Minimising the risk of loss of key customer relationships
BD43	Minimising the risk of excessive loading on insurance premiums due to negligence on IBFS's behalf or lack of due diligence

BSC is highly suited to new strategies and organisational alignment

There is considerable harmony between BSC and the aims of a security architecture programme

'In general, situations where there is a lack of focus or direction, a new strategy, or a need to achieve organisational alignment to a common vision, are conducive to the Balanced Scorecard approach."

All this is very harmonious with what has been said in this book so far about the need for and benefits of enterprise security architecture. The Balanced Scorecard is discussed here because it is worthy of your consideration as an approach. Should you want to pursue this, you are recommended to the Kaplan and Norton reference and to the BSCOL web site for further information.

Business Drivers and Traceability

Which of the many possible metrics that could be displayed on the dashboard should you choose?

If security is difficult to measure, risk may be easier

Each and every business is a unique complex system. Like the aircraft with its instrument panel there are many different parameters that you can measure and report to the pilots. So, which parameters should you choose, and what metrics should you use for each of these?

In the many years of experience of the authors of working with large corporate clients they have always approached the drivers for security from a business risk perspective. If security is difficult to measure, then risk, being a kind of opposite of security, provides a measurement method that is less difficult. Risk assessment has been a central theme of management science for several decades, and there are many methods and approaches around from which to choose.

Risks tend to be the negative side of Business Attributes

In carrying out many risk assessments the authors have discovered that each business risk may be expressed as the opposite of a business virtue – something to be protected and upheld. In the SABSA® methodology these virtues are called Business Attributes, and at the time of writing there are 85 of these attributes that have been identified and defined. Each Business Attribute is a distillation of practical experience in assessing business risk and classifying those risks under useful headings.

Business drivers for security are closely related to these Business Attributes

From this the authors learned that the best way to assess business risk is to first define the business drivers – things that the business needs in terms of security. The best way to help you to understand these concepts is through example. The following case study will illustrate the approach.

Case Study: IBFS Real-Time Settlement System (RTSS)

IBFS are introducing a new back-office computer system to carry out real-time settlement of front-office transactions. Several brainstorming workshops have been carried out to collect all of the business drivers for security in this system. The results of these workshops have been collated and tabulated in Table 6-1.

Business drivers are part of the contextual security architecture

A layered architecture approach gives bi-directional traceability

These business drivers are in fact the opening statement of the contextual security architecture – more of which is discussed in Chapter 9.

One of the major benefits of the multi-layered architecture model introduced in Chapter 3 is that it provides bi-directional traceability. You begin with the contextual security architecture (business drivers), and you work through a series of abstractions to develop the component security architecture and the operational security architecture. *This layered framework ensures that every component and every operational procedure is there because at the top of the model there is a business driver that eventually is satisfied by these elements.*

Every solution is traceable back to and justified by some business requirements

If you need to answer the question 'Why are we doing it this way?' then the answer will always be found by tracing back to the business requirements and the rationale at every level that links that traceable development path through the layers. Thus the method provides traceability to provide full justification for each and every part of the security architecture – it is always based on business need.

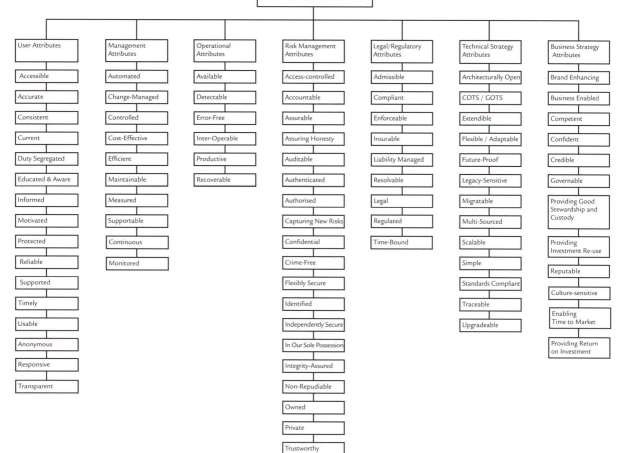

Figure 6-4: Taxonomy of Business Attributes

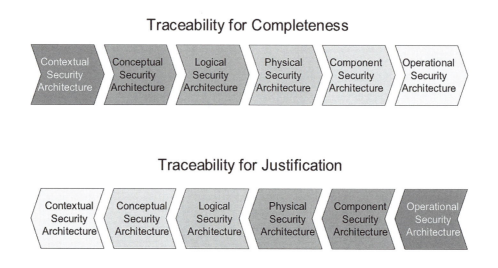

Figure 6-3: Two-Way Traceability

Business Attributes and Metrics

The taxonomy of Business Attributes is based entirely on practical experience

Although every business organisation is unique, the same types of business drivers are seen again and again in different organisations, even in different industry sectors. This led the authors to compile the Taxonomy of Business Attributes based entirely on an analysis of the practical experience with clients. Figure 6-4 shows a summary of this taxonomy as a diagram, and Table 6-2 provides detailed definitions for each Business Attribute.

New Business Attributes are added as experience grows

One thing you should recognise straightaway is that whilst this taxonomy is extensive, it is almost certainly not complete. It is not unusual for one or two more Business Attributes to be added as a result of completing another client assignment. At the time of writing the total number of attributes is 85. Be prepared to add and define your own Business Attributes if it seems that there is a gap when you look at your business requirements[1].

The taxonomy is classified under seven headings

The Business Attributes have been arranged in seven major classes, again derived entirely from practical experience:

- User Attributes – relating to the users' experience of security in the system;

- Management Attributes – the security requirements for managing the system;

- Operational Attributes – concerned with security that protects day-to-day operations;

- Risk Management Attributes – comprising the usual extended set of security requirements to identify and manage business risks;

- Legal and Regulatory Attributes – covering compliance issues;

- Technical Strategy Attributes – addressing the strategic aspects of technical architecture;

- Business Strategy Attributes – what the senior managers and the board want to see.

Business Attributes can be used in one of two ways

The Business Attributes can be used in one of two ways:

- As a pick-list to prompt your thinking on business drivers – i.e. start with the Business Attributes list and use it to create your list of business drivers;

- As a crosscheck for completeness of your business drivers – i.e. start with a list of business drivers (created in some other way) and cross-check against the Business Attributes list.

A one-to-one mapping between Business Attributes and business drivers is not a necessity

However, there is not necessarily a one-to-one mapping between business drivers and Business Attributes, depending upon how your business drivers are expressed. It is quite possible for one business driver to map to several Business Attributes and for one Business Attribute to be associated with several business drivers[7].

Traceability is derived from the cross-mapping of Business Attributes and business drivers

Whether the relationships between Business Attributes and business drivers are one-to-one or many-to-many, the ability to demonstrate the relationship is fundamental to the bi-directional traceability discussed in the previous section and represented in Figure 6-3. The cross-mapping is necessary to demonstrate:

- Justification – every business driver (requirement for security) listed in the contextual security architecture is valid because it is shown to support or increase a business asset or value (the Business Attribute);

- Completeness – the list of Business Attributes is shown to be complete because each is the conceptualised desired return from at least one active business driver.

---

[6]The authors would also like to hear from anyone who has extensions to propose: http://www.sabsa.org.uk/

Table 6-2: Business Attributes Definitions and Metrics

Business Attribute	Attribute Explanation	Metric Type	Suggested Measurement Approach
User Attributes	**This group of attributes are related to the user's experience of interacting with the business system.**		
Accessible	Information to which the user is entitled to gain access should be easily found and accessed by that user.	Soft	Search tree depth necessary to find the info
Accurate	The information provided to users should be accurate within a range that has been pre-agreed as being applicable to the service being delivered.	Hard	Acceptance testing on key data to demonstrate compliance with design rules
Anonymous	For certain specialised types of service the anonymity of the user should be protected.	Hard	Rigorous proof of system functionality
		Soft	Red team review[1]
Consistent	The way in which login, navigation and target services are presented to the user should be consistent across different times, locations and channels of access.	Hard	Conformance with design style guides
		Soft	Red team review
Current	Information provided to users should be current and kept up to date, within a range that has been pre-agreed as being applicable for the service being delivered.	Hard	Refresh rates at the data source and replication of refreshed data to the destination
Duty-segregated	For certain sensitive tasks the duties should be segregated so that no user has access to both aspects of the task.	Hard	Functional testing
Educated and aware	Users should be educated and trained so that they can embrace the security culture and have sufficient awareness of security issues that their behaviour is compliant with security policies.	Soft	Competence surveys
Informed	The user should be kept fully informed about services, operating procedures, operational schedules, planned outages, and so on.	Soft	Focus groups or satisfaction surveys
Motivated	The interaction with the system should add positive motivation to the user to complete the business tasks in hand.	Soft	Focus groups or satisfaction surveys
Protected	The user's information and access privileges should be protected against abuse by other users or by intruders.	Soft	Penetration test (Could be regarded as hard, but only if a penetration is achieved. Failure to penetrate does not mean that penetration is impossible)
Reliable	The services provided to the user should be delivered at a reliable level of quality.	Soft	A definition of 'quality' is needed against which to compare
Responsive	The users obtain a response within a satisfactory period of time that meets their expectations.	Hard	Response time
Supported	When a user has problems or difficulties in using the system or its services there should be a means by which the user can receive advice and support so that the problems can be resolved to the satisfaction of the user.	Soft	Focus groups or satisfaction surveys

Independent audit and review against Security Architecture Capability Maturity Model[2] |
| Timely | Information is delivered or made accessible to the user at the appropriate time or within the appropriate time period. | Hard | Refresh rates at the data source and replication of refreshed data to the destination |
| Transparent | Providing full visibility to the user of the logical process but hiding the physical structure of the system (as a URL hides the actual physical locations of web servers) | Soft | Focus groups or satisfaction surveys

Independent audit and review against Security Architecture Capability Maturity Model (see Footnote 9) |
| Usable | The system should provide easy-to-use interfaces that can be navigated intuitively by a user of average intelligence and training level (for the given system). The user's experience of these interactions should be at best interesting and at worst neutral. | Soft | Numbers of clicks or keystrokes required.

Conformance with industry standards – e.g. colour palettes

Feedback from focus groups |

Business Attributes	Attribute Explanation	Metric Type	Suggested Measurement Approach
Management Attributes	**This group of attributes are related to the ease and effectiveness with which the business system and its services can be managed.**		
Automated	Wherever possible (and depending upon cost/benefit factors) the management and operation of the system should be automated.	Soft	Independent design review
Change-managed	Changes to the system should be properly managed so that the impact of every change is evaluated and the changes are approved in advance of being implemented.	Soft	Documented change management system, with change management history, evaluated by independent audit
Controlled	The system should at all times remain in the control of its managers. This means that the management will observe the operation and behaviour of the system, will make decisions about how to control it based on these observations, and will implement actions to exert that control.	Soft	Independent audit and review against Security Architecture Capability Maturity Model (see Footnote 9)
Cost-effective	The design, acquisition, implementation and operation of the system should be achieved at a cost that the business finds acceptable when judged against the benefits derived.	Hard	Individual budgets for the phases of development and for ongoing operation, maintenance and support
Efficient	The system should deliver the target services with optimum efficiency, avoiding wastage of resources.	Hard	A target efficiency ratio based on: (INPUT VALUE) / (OUTPUT VALUE)
Maintainable	The system should capable of being maintained in a state of good repair and effective, efficient operation. The actions required to achieve this should feasible within the normal operational conditions of the system.	Soft	Documented execution of a preventive maintenance schedule for both hardware and software, correlated against targets for continuity of service (such as MTBF[3])
Measured	The performance of the system against a variety of desirable performance targets should be measured so as to provide feedback information to support the management and control process.	Hard	Documented tracking and reporting of a portfolio of conventional system performance parameters, together with other Business Attributes from this list
Supportable	The system should be capable of being supported in terms of both the users and the operations staff, so that all types of problems and operational difficulties can be resolved.	Hard	Fault-tracking system providing measurements of MTBF, MTTR[4] and maximum time to repair, with targets for each parameter

Business Attributes	Attribute Explanation	Metric Type	Suggested Measurement Approach
Operational Attributes	**This group of attributes describe the ease and effectiveness with which the business system and its services can be operated.**		
Available	The information and services provided by the system should be available according to the requirements specified in the SLA.	Hard	As specified in the SLA
Continuous	The system should offer 'continuous service'. The exact definition of this phrase will always be subject to a service level agreement (SLA).	Hard	Percentage up-time correlated versus scheduled and/or unscheduled downtime; or MTBF, or MTTR
Detectable	Important events must be detected and reported.	Hard	Functional testing
Error-free	The system should operate without producing errors.	Hard	Percentage or absolute error rates (per transaction, per batch, per time period, etc.)
Inter-operable	The system should inter-operate with other similar systems, both immediately and in the future, as inter-system communication becomes increasingly a requirement.	Hard	Specific inter-operability requirements
Monitored	The operational performance of the system should be continuously monitored to ensure that other attribute specifications are being met. Any deviations from acceptable limits should be notified to the systems management function.	Soft	Independent audit and review against Security Architecture Capability Maturity Model (see Footnote 9)
Productive	The system and its services should operate so as to sustain and enhance productivity of the users, with regard to the business processes in which they are engaged.	Hard	User output targets related to specific business activities
Recoverable	The system should be able to be recovered to full operational status after a breakdown or disaster in accordance with the SLA.	Hard	As specified in the SLA

Business Attribute	Attribute Explanation	Metric Type	Suggested Measurement Approach
Risk Management Attributes	**This group of attributes describes the business requirements for mitigating operational risk. This group most closely relates to the security requirements for protecting the business.**		
Access-controlled	Access to information and functions within the system should be controlled in accordance with the authorised privileges of the party requesting the access. Unauthorised access should be prevented.	Hard	Reporting of all unauthorised access attempts, including number of incidents per period, severity and result (did the access attempt succeed?)
Accountable	All parties having authorised access to the system should be held accountable for their actions.	Soft	Independent audit and review against Security Architecture Capability Maturity Model (see Footnote 9) with respect to the ability to hold accountable all authorised parties
Assurable	There should be a means to provide assurance that the system is operating as expected and that all of the various controls are correctly implemented and operated.	Hard	Documented standards exist against which to audit
		Soft	Independent audit and review against Security Architecture Capability Maturity Model (see Footnote 9)
Assuring honesty	Employees should be protected against false accusations of dishonesty or malpractice.	Soft	Independent audit and review against Security Architecture Capability Maturity Model (see Footnote 9) with respect to the ability to prevent false accusations that are difficult to repudiate
Auditable	The actions of all parties having authorised access to the system, and the complete chain of events and outcomes resulting from these actions, should be recorded so that this history can be reviewed. The audit records should provide an appropriate level of detail, in accordance with business needs.	Soft	Independent audit and review against Security Architecture Capability Maturity Model (see Footnote 9)
	The actual configuration of the system should also be capable of being audited so as to compare it with a target configuration that represents the implementation of the security policy that governs the system.	Hard	Documented target configuration exists under change control with a capability to check current configuration against this target
		Soft	Independent audit and review against Security Architecture Capability Maturity Model (see Footnote 9)
Authenticated	Every party claiming a unique identity (i.e. a claimant) should be subject to a procedure that verifies that the party is indeed the authentic owner of the claimed identity.	Soft	Independent audit and review against Security Architecture Capability Maturity Model (see Footnote 9) with respect to the ability to authenticate successfully every claim of identity.
Authorised	The system should allow only those actions that have been explicitly authorised.	Hard	Reporting of all unauthorised actions, including number of incidents per period, severity and result (did the action succeed?)
		Soft	Independent audit and review against Security Architecture Capability Maturity Model (see Footnote 9) with respect to the ability to detect unauthorised actions
Capturing new risks	New risks emerge over time. The system management and operational environment should provide a means to identify and assess new risks (new threats, new impacts or new vulnerabilities).	Hard	Percentage of vendor-published patches and upgrades actually installed
		Soft	Independent audit and review against Security Architecture Capability Maturity Model (see Footnote 9) of a documented risk assessment process and a risk assessment history

Business Attribute	Attribute Explanation	Metric Type	Suggested Measurement Approach
Confidential	The confidentiality of (corporate) information should be protected in accordance with security policy. Unauthorised disclosure should be prevented.	Hard	Reporting of all disclosure incidents, including number of incidents per period, severity and type of disclosure
Crime-free	Cyber-crime of all types should be prevented.	Hard	Reporting of all incidents of crime, including number of incidents per period, severity, and type of crime
Flexibly secure	Security can be provided at various levels, according to business need. The system should provide the means to secure information according to these needs, and may need to offer different levels of security for different types of information (according to security classification).	Soft	Independent audit and review against Security Architecture Capability Maturity Model (see Footnote 9)
Identified	Each entity that will be granted access to system resources and each object that is itself a system resource should be uniquely identified (named) such that there can never be confusion as to which entity or object is being referenced.	Hard	Proof of uniqueness of naming schemes
Independently secure	The security of the system should not rely upon the security on any other system that is not within the direct span of control of this system.	Soft	Independent audit and review against Security Architecture Capability Maturity Model (see Footnote 9) of technical security architecture at conceptual, logical and physical layers
In our sole possession	Information that has value to the business should be in the possession of the business, stored and protected by the system against loss (as in no longer being available) or theft (as in being disclosed to an unauthorised party). This will include information that is regarded as intellectual property.	Soft	Independent audit and review against Security Architecture Capability Maturity Model (see Footnote 9)
Integrity-assured	The integrity of information should be protected to provide assurance that it has not suffered unauthorised modification, duplication or deletion.	Hard	Reporting of all incidents of compromise, including number of incidents per period, severity and type of compromise
		Soft	Independent audit and review against Security Architecture Capability Maturity Model (see Footnote 9) with respect to the ability to detect integrity compromise incidents
Non-repudiable	When one party uses the system to send a message to another party, it should NOT be possible for the first party to falsely deny having sent the message, or to falsely deny its contents.	Hard	Reporting of all incidents of unresolved repudiations, including number of incidents per period, severity and type of repudiation
		Soft	Independent audit and review against Security Architecture Capability Maturity Model (see Footnote 9) with respect to the ability to prevent repudiations that cannot be easily resolved
Owned	There should be an entity designated as owner of every system. This owner is the policymaker for all aspects of risk management with respect to the system and exerts the ultimate authority for controlling the system.	Soft	Independent audit and review against Security Architecture Capability Maturity Model (see Footnote 9) of the ownership arrangements and of the management processes by which owners should fulfil their responsibilities, and of their diligence in so doing
Private	The privacy of (personal) information should be protected in accordance with relevant privacy or data protection legislation, and so as to meet the reasonable expectation of citizens for privacy. Unauthorised disclosure should be prevented.	Hard	Reporting of all disclosure incidents, including number of incidents per period, severity and type of disclosure
Trustworthy	The system should be able to be trusted to behave in the ways specified in its functional specification and should protect against a wide range of potential abuses.	Soft	Focus groups or satisfaction surveys researching around the question 'Do you trust the service?'

Business Attribute	Attribute Explanation	Metric Type	Suggested Measurement Approach
Legal & Regulatory Attributes	**This group of attributes describes the business requirements for mitigating operational risks that have a specific legal or regulatory connection.**		
Admissible	The system should provide forensic records (audit trails and so on) that will be deemed to be admissible in a court of law, should that evidence ever need to be presented in support of a criminal prosecution or a civil litigation.	Soft	Independent audit and review against Security Architecture Capability Maturity Model (see Footnote 9) by computer forensics expert
Compliant	The system should comply with all applicable regulations, laws, contracts, policies and mandatory standards, both internal and external.	Soft	Independent compliance audit with respect to the inventories of regulations, laws, policies, etc.
Enforceable	The system should be designed, implemented and operated such that all applicable contracts, policies, regulations and laws can be enforced by the system.	Soft	Independent review of: (1) Inventory of contracts, policies, regulations and laws for completeness (2) Enforceability of contracts, policies, laws, regulations on the inventory
Insurable	The system should be risk-managed to enable an insurer to offer reasonable commercial terms for insurance against a standard range of insurable risks.	Hard	Verify against insurance quotations
Legal	The system should be designed, implemented and operated in accordance with the requirements of any applicable legislation. Examples include data protection laws, laws controlling the use of cryptographic technology, laws controlling insider dealing on the stock market, and laws governing information that is considered racist, seditious or pornographic.	Soft	Independent audit and review against Security Architecture Capability Maturity Model (see Footnote 9) Verification of the inventory of applicable laws to check for completeness and suitability
Liability-managed	The system services should be designed, implemented and operated so as to manage the liability of the organisation with regard to errors, fraud, malfunction and so on. In particular the responsibilities and liabilities of each party should be clearly defined.	Soft	Independent legal expert review of all applicable contracts, SLAs, etc.
Regulated	The system should be designed, implemented and operated in accordance with the requirements of any applicable regulations. These may be general (such as safety regulations) or industry-specific (such as banking regulations).	Soft	Independent audit and review against Security Architecture Capability Maturity Model (see Footnote 9) Verification of the inventory of applicable regulations to check for completeness and suitability
Resolvable	The system should be designed, implemented and operated in such a way that disputes can be resolved with reasonable ease and without undue impact on time, cost or other valuable resources.	Soft	Independent audit and review against Security Architecture Capability Maturity Model (see Footnote 9) by legal expert
Time-bound	Meeting requirements for maximum or minimum periods of time: e.g. a minimum period for records retention or a maximum period within which something must be completed.	Hard	Independent functional design review against specified functional requirements

Business Attribute	Attribute Explanation	Metric Type	Suggested Measurement Approach
Technical Strategy Attributes	**This group of attributes describes the needs for fitting into an overall technology strategy.**		
Architecturally open	The system architecture should, wherever possible, not be locked into specific vendor interface standards and should allow flexibility in the choice of vendors and products, both initially and in the future.	Soft	Independent audit and review against Security Architecture Capability Maturity Model (see Footnote 9) of technical architecture (conceptual, logical and physical)
COTS and GOTS compliant	Wherever possible the system should utilise commercial off-the-shelf or government off-the-shelf components, as appropriate.	Soft	Independent audit and review against Security Architecture Capability Maturity Model (see Footnote 9) of technical architecture (conceptual, logical and physical)

Business Attribute	Attribute Explanation	Metric Type	Suggested Measurement Approach
Extendable	The system should be capable of being extended to incorporate new functional modules as required by the business.	Soft	Independent audit and review against Security Architecture Capability Maturity Model (see Footnote 9) of technical architecture (conceptual, logical and physical)
Flexible and Adaptable	The system should be flexible and adaptable to meet new business requirements as they emerge.	Soft	Independent audit and review against Security Architecture Capability Maturity Model (see Footnote 9) of technical architecture (conceptual, logical and physical)
Future-proof	The system architecture should be designed as much as possible to accommodate future changes in both business requirements and technical solutions.	Soft	Independent audit and review against Security Architecture Capability Maturity Model (see Footnote 9) of technical architecture (conceptual, logical and physical)
Legacy-sensitive	A new system should be able to work with any legacy systems or databases with which it needs to inter-operate or integrate.	Soft	Independent audit and review against Security Architecture Capability Maturity Model (see Footnote 9) of technical architecture (conceptual, logical and physical)
Migrateable	There should be a feasible, manageable migration path, acceptable to the business users, that moves from an old system to a new one, or from one released version to the next.	Soft	Independent audit and review against Security Architecture Capability Maturity Model (see Footnote 9) of technical architecture (conceptual, logical and physical)
Multi-sourced	Critical system components should be obtainable from more than one source, to protect against the risk of the single source of supply and support being withdrawn.	Soft	Independent audit and review against Security Architecture Capability Maturity Model (see Footnote 9) of technical architecture at the component level
Scaleable	The system should be scaleable to the size of user community, data storage requirements, processing throughput and so on, that might emerge over the lifetime of the system.	Soft	Independent audit and review against Security Architecture Capability Maturity Model (see Footnote 9) of technical architecture (conceptual, logical and physical)
Simple	The system should be as simple as possible, since complexity only adds further risk.	Soft	Independent audit and review against Security Architecture Capability Maturity Model (see Footnote 9) of technical architecture (conceptual, logical and physical)
Standards-compliant	The system should be designed, implemented and operated to comply with appropriate technical and operational standards.	Soft	Independent audit and review of: (1) The inventory of standards to check for completeness and appropriateness (2) Compliance with standards on the inventory
Traceable	The development and implementation of system components should be documented so as to provide complete two-way traceability. That is, every implemented component should be justifiable by tracing back to the business requirements that led to its inclusion in the system, and it should be possible to review every business requirement and demonstrate which of the implemented system components are there to meet this requirement.	Soft	Independent expert review of documented traceability matrices and trees
Upgradeable	The system should be capable of being upgraded with ease to incorporate new releases of hardware and software.	Soft	Independent audit and review against Security Architecture Capability Maturity Model (see Footnote 9) of technical architecture (conceptual, logical and physical)

Business Attribute	Attribute Explanation	Metric Type	Suggested Measurement Approach
Business Strategy Attributes	**This group of attributes describes the needs for fitting into an overall business strategy.**		
Brand-enhancing	The system should help to establish, build and support the brand of the products or services based upon this system.	Soft	Market surveys
Business-enabled	Enabling the business and fulfilling business objectives should be the primary driver for the system design.	Soft	Business management focus group
Competent	The system should protect the reputation of the organisation as being competent in its industry sector.	Soft	Independent audit, or focus groups, or satisfaction surveys
Confident	The system should behave in such a way as to safeguard confidence placed in the organisation by customers, suppliers, shareholders, regulators, financiers, the marketplace and the general public.	Soft	Independent audit, or focus groups, or satisfaction surveys
Credible	The system should behave in such a way as to safeguard the credibility of the organisation.	Soft	Independent audit, or focus groups, or satisfaction surveys
Culture-sensitive	The system should be designed, built and operated with due care and attention to cultural issues relating to those who will experience the system in any way. These issues include such matters as religion, gender, race, nationality, language, dress code, social customs, ethics, politics and the environment. The objective should be to avoid or minimise offence or distress caused to others.	Soft	Independent audit and review of: (1) The inventory of requirements in this area to check for completeness and appropriateness (2) Compliance of system functionality with this set of requirements
Enabling time-to-market	The system architecture and design should allow new business initiatives to be delivered to the market with minimum delay.	Soft	Business management focus group
Governable	The system should enable the owners and executive managers of the organisation to control the business and to discharge their responsibilities for governance.	Soft	Senior management focus group Independent audit and review against Security Architecture Capability Maturity Model (see Footnote 9) for governance
Providing good stewardship and custody	Protecting other parties with whom we do business from abuse or loss of business or personal information of value to those parties through inadequate stewardship on our part.	Soft	Independent audit, or focus groups, or satisfaction surveys
Providing investment re-use	As much as possible the system should be designed to re-use previous investments and to ensure that new investments are re-usable in the future.	Soft	Independent audit and review against Security Architecture Capability Maturity Model (see Footnote 9) of technical architecture (conceptual, logical, physical and component)
Providing return on investment	The system should provide a return of value to the business to justify the investment made in creating and operating the system.	Hard	Financial returns and ROI indices selected in consultation with the Chief Financial Officer
		Soft	Qualitative value propositions tested by opinion surveys at senior management and boardroom level
Reputable	The system should behave in such a way as to safeguard the business reputation of the organisation.	Soft	Independent audit, or focus groups, or satisfaction surveys
		Hard	Correlation of the stock value of the organisation versus publicity of system event history

Notes for Table 6.2

[1] A 'red team review' is an objective appraisal by an independent team of experts who have been briefed to think either like the user or like an opponent or attacker, whichever is appropriate to the objectives of the review.

[2] The type Architectural Capability Maturity Model referred to is based upon the ideas of Capability Maturity Models described in the later parts of this chapter.

[3] MTBF: mean time between failures

[4] MTTR: mean time to repair

[5] The terminology used in this SSE-CMM model for 'risk' and 'exposure' is, in the view of the authors, very confusing and shows poor clarity of thinking. Readers are warned to take care in attempting to reconcile these uses of the terms here with those used elsewhere in this book.

The actual metrics you use must fit into your specific business model

You will need to define your own measurement approach and the associated metrics that fit your specific business. To help you, in Table 6-2 there are some suggested ways that metrics might be constructed and measurements taken. This will be needed when you get to the Manage and Measure phase of the feedback control loop in the security architecture lifecycle that you will encounter in Chapter 7.

There are hard, quantitative metrics and soft, qualitative metrics

There is a distinction between hard metrics, where the measurements are good solid numbers and the measurements are objective, and soft metrics where the measurements are of a qualitative, subjective nature. Not all Business Attributes lend themselves to hard quantitative measurement.

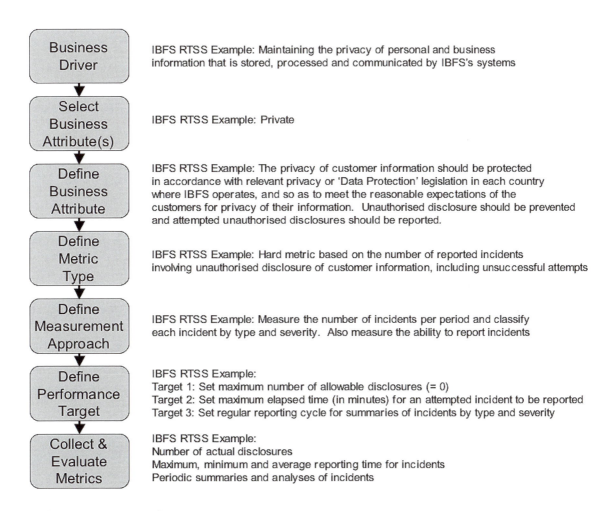

Figure 6-5: Defining a Metrics Framework

Table 6-3: Examples of IBFS RTSS Business Drivers Mapped to Business Attributes

Business Driver (From Table 6-1 above)	Supporting Business Attributes (From Figure 6-4 and Table 6-2 above)
BD1	Credible, Reputable
BD8	Controlled, Governable
BD17	Access Controlled, Authenticated, Confidential, Identified, Private

Table 6-4: Examples of Business Attributes Mapped to IBFS RTSS Business Drivers

Business Attribute (From Figure 6-4 and Table 6-2 above)	Associated Business Drivers (From Table 6-1 above)
Private	BD17
Informed	BD5, BD30, BD31
Non-repudiable	BD3, BD4, BD13, BD14, BD19

Setting Up a Metrics Framework

Having selected the Business Attributes, you need to select your measurement approach

Once you have defined your business drivers and selected the Business Attributes that are associated with them, the next step is to define the measurement approach and the performance targets to be used for each Business Attribute so as to collect and evaluate your own metrics. The suggestions in Table 6-2 will help you with this, but you will need to be creative in applying the technique to your own business. The performance targets that you choose must be specific to your organisation and your business. The interpretation and evaluation of the metrics that you collect will then tell you how your enterprise is performing against those performance targets.

Further examples

In Table 6-5 there are some more examples to help you along. These examples also refer back to the business drivers for the IBFS RTSS case study in Table 6-1. Additionally, one of the case study examples (Business Attribute 'Private') has been set out in a detailed flowchart in Figure 6-5 to help you understand the process by which you should set up the metrics framework, including the measurement approach and the performance targets.

The metrics provide the means to monitor ongoing performance of the security management programme

The metrics that you collect are used on an ongoing basis to measure conformance of the security management programme with the performance standards that have been set at this stage. They become an important tool used in the Manage and Measure phase of the security architecture lifecycle that you will meet in Chapter 7.

Independence of the reporting should be preserved

There is potentially an issue to be considered here regarding the consumption of the reported metrics – to whom should they be delivered? If, for example, the metrics show up failings on the part of a specific manager, then it is probably not a good idea for those metrics to be delivered to that manager, who may then have the opportunity to cover up the failings. You need to give some careful thought to the independence of the reporting line, similar to that afforded to internal audit reports.

Table 6-5: Example Metrics Framework for IBFS RTSS

Business Attribute	Business Driver	Metric Type	Measurement Approach	Performance Target
Private	BD17	Hard	Reporting of all unauthorised disclosure incidents, including number of incidents per period, severity and type of disclosure	Zero successful attempts at unauthorised disclosure. Alerts of unauthorised access attempts, produced and delivered to <systems manager name> and <business owner name> within <X> minutes. Summary reports of number, severity and type of unauthorised access attempts to private data produced and delivered to <systems manager name> and <business owner name> monthly
		Soft	Independent audit and review with respect to the prevention of unauthorised disclosure of private information	System passes review by <independent legal and forensic authority> to a degree deemed acceptable by <Group Legal> to prevent prosecution under EU Data Protection legislation
Non-repudiable	BD5, BD30, BD31	Hard	Reporting of all incidents of unresolved repudiations including the number of incidents per period, severity and type of repudiation	Exception report detailing all incidents of repudiation produced and delivered to <business owner name> for validation Audit trails recording the detail of all transaction-based information required to provide non-repudiable proof and accountability, available to <business owner name> on demand
		Soft	Independent audit and review with respect to the ability to prevent repudiations that cannot be easily resolved	Independent audit and review by <Group Internal Audit/Group Legal> with respect to the ability to provide proof of the transaction flow and individual accountability on all transactions
Informed	BD3, BD4, BD13, BD14, BD19	Hard	Awareness programme	Adherence to quarterly awareness program plan produced by <business operations manager name> and agreed with <business owner name>
		Soft	Focus groups or satisfaction surveys	Monthly report on all customer feedback relating to level of awareness produced and delivered to <business owner name> and <business operations manager name> Report from quarterly customer and non-customer focus groups delivered to <business owner name>

Maturity Models Applied to Security Architecture

Capability maturity models have been developed at Carnegie Mellon University

The concept of a Capability Maturity Model[6] (CMM®) was developed at the Carnegie Mellon Software Engineering Institute[7]. The idea is that the development of an organisation in any specific domain of expertise and knowledge begins in an immature state and passes through several levels of maturity as the organisation gains experience. The generic maturity levels of the model are described in Table 6-6.

Table 6-6: The Carnegie Mellon Capability Maturity Model

Maturity Stage	Description of Maturity Stage
Initial	The process is characterized as ad hoc, and occasionally even chaotic. Few processes are defined, and success depends on individual effort and heroics.
Repeatable	Basic project management processes are established to track cost, schedule, and functionality. The necessary process discipline is in place to repeat earlier successes on projects with similar applications.
Defined	The process for both management and engineering activities is documented, standardized, and integrated into a standard process for the organization. All projects use an approved, tailored version of the organization's standard process for development and maintenance.
Managed	Detailed measures of the process and product quality are collected. Both the process and products are quantitatively understood and controlled.
Optimising	Continuous process improvement is enabled by quantitative feedback from the process and from piloting innovative ideas and technologies.

CMM uses a domain structure called Process Areas

In applying the model to a specific domain of activity, each of the levels or stages of maturity is usually decomposed into several key process areas (PAs). Thus in the Software CMM (SW-CMM®) there are the following Process Areas at the second level:

- Requirements Management;

- Software Project Planning;

- Software Project Tracking and Oversight;

- Software Subcontract Management;

- Software Quality Assurance;

- Software Configuration Management.

At other levels of the SW-CMM the process areas are different, becoming more sophisticated as you increase in maturity.

CMMs have been developed in several application areas

There are several applications of the CMM model to specific areas of measurement. Versions of the CMM currently supported (in various stages of development) by the Carnegie Mellon SEI include:

- SW-CMM: Capability Maturity Model for Software;

- P-CMM: People Capability Maturity Model;

- SA-CMM: Software Acquisition Capability Maturity Model;

[6]Capability Maturity Model is a registered trademark of Carnegie Mellon University. See www.sei.cmu.edu/cmm/

[7]Carnegie Mellon Software Engineering Institute: www.sei.cmu.edu

- SE-CMM: Systems Engineering Capability Maturity Model;
- IPD-CMM: Integrated Product Development Capability Maturity Model.

System Security Engineering Capability Maturity Model

The CMM concept has also been developed for system security engineering

These ideas obviously have an application to security management and security architecture. There has been work done on a system security engineering capability maturity model (SSE-CMM) by the International Systems Security Engineering Association (ISSEA)[8]. This work is now an ISO/IEC standard (ISO/IEC 21827).

The SSE-CMM uses both Capability Levels and Process Areas

The SSE-CMM Model Description Document describes a total of 22 Process Areas, divided into two groups – Security Engineering PAs and Project and Organisational PAs, shown in Table 6-7. The treatment here is slightly different from the approach in the SW-CMM. In the SSE-CMM the Process Areas are subdivided into groups of Base Practices, a small example of which is shown in Table 6-8. The Process Areas apply at all Capability (maturity) Levels, but each Capability Level is subdivided into Common Features that span the entire range of Process Area domains, and each Common Feature is further subdivided into Generic Practices (see Table 6-9), again spanning the entire domain space.

Table 6-7: SSE-CMM Process Areas

		Process Area
SECURITY ENGINEERING	PA01	Administer Security Controls
	PA02	Assess Impact
	PA03	Assess Security Risk (see Table 6-9 for Base Practices example)
	PA04	Assess Threat
	PA05	Assess Vulnerability
	PA06	Build Assurance Argument
	PA07	Coordinate Security
	PA08	Monitor Security Posture
	PA09	Provide Security Input
	PA10	Specify Security Needs
	PA11	Verify and Validate Security
PROJECT AND ORGANISATIONAL	PA12	Ensure Quality
	PA13	Manage Configuration
	PA14	Manage Project Risk
	PA15	Monitor and Control Technical Effort
	PA16	Plan Technical Effort
	PA17	Define Organization's Systems Engineering Process
	PA18	Improve Organization's Systems Engineering Process
	PA19	Manage Product Line Evolution
	PA20	Manage Systems Engineering Support Environment
	PA21	Provide Ongoing Skills and Knowledge
	PA22	Coordinate with Suppliers

---

[8]www.issea.org

Table 6-8: Example of SSE-CMM Process Area/Base Practices

PA03	Assess Security Risk
Goals	1. An understanding of the security risk associated with operating the system within a defined environment is achieved
	2. Risks are prioritized according to a defined methodology
BP.03.01	Select the methods, techniques, and criteria by which security risks, for the system in a defined environment, are analysed, assessed and compared
BP.03.02	Identify threat/vulnerability/impact triples (exposures)
BP.03.03	Assess the risk associated with the occurrence of an exposure5
BP.03.04	Assess the total uncertainty associated with the risk for the exposure
BP.03.05	Order risks by priority
BP.03.06	Monitor ongoing changes in the risk spectrum and changes to their characteristics

This provides a fine-grained two-dimensional matrix of cells in which the organisation can be assessed for compliance with each Process Area/Base Practice (the domain dimension of the matrix) at each Capability Level/Common Feature/Generic Practice (the capability dimension of the matrix). This matrix can be used to visually track progress toward maturity (see Table 6-10).

Table 6-9: The SSE-CMM Generic Practices

Capability Level	SSE-CMM Maturity Description	Common Features/Generic Practices
Level 1	Performed Informally	1.1 Base Practices are Performed GP 1.1.1 – Perform the Process
Level 2	Planned and Tracked	2.1 Planning Performance GP 2.1.1 – Allocate Resources GP 2.1.2 – Assign Responsibilities GP 2.1.3 – Document the Process GP 2.1.4 – Provide Tools GP 2.1.5 – Ensure Training GP 2.1.6 – Plan the Process 2.2 Disciplined Performance GP 2.2.1 – Use Plans, Standards, and Procedures GP 2.2.2 – Do Configuration Management 2.3 Verifying Performance GP 2.3.1 – Verify Process Compliance GP 2.3.2 – Audit Work Products 2.4 Tracking Performance GP 2.4.1 – Track with Measurement GP 2.4.2 – Take Corrective Action

Capability Level	SSE-CMM Maturity Description	Common Features/Generic Practices

Level 3	Well-Defined	3.1 Defining a Standard Process
		
		    GP 3.1.1 – Standardize the Process
		
		    GP 3.1.2 – Tailor the Standard Process

		3.2 Perform the Defined Process
		
		    GP 3.2.1 – Use a Well-Defined Process
		
		    GP 3.2.2 – Perform Defect Reviews
		
		    GP 3.2.3 – Use Well-Defined Data

		3.3 Coordinate the Process
		
		    GP 3.3.1 – Perform Intra-Group Coordination
		
		    GP 3.3.2 – Perform Inter-Group Coordination
		
		    GP 3.3.3 – Perform External Coordination

Level 4	Quantitatively Controlled	4.1 Establishing Measurable Quality Goals GP 4.1.1 – Establish Quality Goals

		4.2 Objectively Managing Performance
		
		    GP 4.2.1 – Determine Process Capability
		
		    GP 4.2.2 – Use Process Capability

Level 5	Continuously Improving	5.1 Improving Organizational Capability
		
		    GP 5.1.1 – Establish Process Effectiveness Goals
		
		    GP 5.1.2 – Continuously Improve the Standard Process

		5.2 Improving Organisational Effectiveness GP 5.2.1 – Perform Causal Analysis

Table 6-10: SSE-CMM Matrix

This chart is used to track progress on developing the organisation's security capabilities

Definition of a Process Area	A Process Area:

- Assembles related activities in one area for ease of use;
- Relates to valuable security engineering services;
- Applies across the life cycle of the enterprise;
- Can be implemented in multiple organization and product contexts;
- Can be improved as a distinct process;
- Can be improved by a group with similar interests in the process;
- Includes all base practices that are required to meet the goals of the process area.

Definition of a Base Practice

A Base Practice has the following properties:

- Applies across the life cycle of the enterprise;
- Does not overlap with other Base Practices;
- Represents a best practice of the security community;
- Does not simply reflect a state-of-the-art technique;
- Is applicable using multiple methods in multiple business contexts;
- Does not specify a particular method or tool.

Tables show examples of the practices used in SSE-CMM

Table 6-9 shows the Generic Practices. Table 6-7 provides the detailed list of Process Areas. The full breakdown of Process Areas into Base Practices is very detailed and has been omitted here, but can found at the SSE-CMM web site16. A small example is given in Table 6-8. Table 6-10 shows the matrix mapping between Generic Practices and Process Areas.

The CMM concept is very good, whether or not you use this specific version of it

For more information on the SSE-CMM you are recommended to the materials available on the SSE-CMM web site[9]. You may find the methodology a little on the heavy side. The downloadable PDF document entitled SSE-CMM Model Description has 336 pages, which gives you a clue as to level of detail! However, the concept of the CMM is a good one, and you could easily create your own simplified version for internal use – something that the authors have helped client organisations to do from time to time.

CobiT™ Capability Maturity Model

CobiT is an open standard for the IT Governance Institute

The CobiT[10] framework is an open standard for control over information technology, developed and promoted by the IT Governance Institute, under the auspices of ISACA[11]. This framework identifies 34 information and communications technology (ICT) processes, a high-level approach to control over these processes, as well as 318 detailed control objectives and audit guidelines to assess the 34 ICT processes.

---

[9] www.sse-cmm.org

[10]CobiT: Control Objectives for Information and related Technology

[13]ISACA: International Security Audit and Control Association. See www.isaca.org and www.ITgovernance.org

Table 6-11: The Maturity Levels in the CobiT CMM

Level	Title	Description
0	**Non-Existent**	Complete lack of any recognisable processes. The organisation has not even recognised that there is an issue to be addressed.
1	Initial	There is evidence that the organisation has recognised that the issues exist and need to be addressed. There are, however, no standardised processes but instead there are *ad hoc* approaches that tend to be applied on an individual or case-by-case basis. The overall approach to management is disorganised.
2	**Repeatable**	Processes have developed to the stage where different people undertaking the same task follow similar procedures. There is no normal training or communication of standard procedures, and responsibility is left to the individual. There is a high degree of reliance on the knowledge of individuals, and therefore errors are likely.
3	**Defined**	Procedures have been standardised and documented and communicated through training. It is however left to the individual to follow these processes, and it is unlikely that deviations will be detected. The procedures themselves are not sophisticated but are the formalisation of existing practices.
4	**Managed**	It is possible to monitor and measure compliance with procedures and to take action where processes appear not to be working effectively. Processes are under constant improvement and provide good practice. Automation and tools are used in a limited or fragmented way.
5	**Optimised**	Processes have been refined to a level of best practice, based on the results of continuous improvement and maturity modelling with other organisations. ICT is used in an integrated way to automate the workflow, providing tools to improve quality and effectiveness, making the enterprise quick to adapt.

The CobiT Management Guidelines

The IT Governance Institute has also built on this framework to produce Management Guidelines for CobiT[12], comprising:

- Maturity Model;
- Critical Success Factors (CSFs);
- Key Goal Indicators (KGIs);
- Key Performance Indicators (KPIs).

CobiT Key Indicators

Key Goal Indicators and the Key Performance Indicators have been defined using the Balanced Scorecard approach (described above, earlier in this chapter).

The CobiT CMM

The CobiT Maturity Model is based upon the Carnegie Mellon Software Engineering Institute model and defines six levels of capability maturity, as shown in Table 6-11.

The CMM is used to benchmark the enterprise

The application of the CobiT CMM is geared towards benchmarking the ICT management performance of the organisation – something discussed in more detail in the next section below. To achieve this the CobiT Framework proposes four measurements against the CMM levels:

- The current status of the organisation — where the organisation is today;
- The current status of (best-in-class in) the industry — the comparison benchmark;

---

[12]Downloadable from www.isaca.org

- The current status of international standard guidelines — additional comparison benchmark;

- The organisation's strategy for improvement — where the organisation wants to be.

Visual presentation of the benchmarking results

These are assessed under each of the 34 Process Areas defined in the CobiT Framework, and the results can be either tabulated or presented in visual representations, as shown in Figure 6-6. The 34 Process Areas of CobiT are classified under four Domain headings:

- Planning and Organisation;

- Acquisition and Implementation;

- Delivery and Support;

- Monitoring.

For more detailed information on the CobiT Framework you are recommended to the ISACA or IT Governance Institute web sites[13].

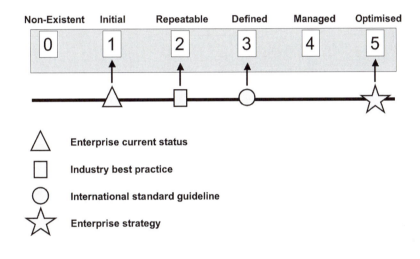

Figure 6-6: The CobiT Benchmarking Scale

Applying CMMs to Measure Return on Investment

A CMM can be used directly to report progress to senior managers

Capability maturity models of the type described above can be another valid way to address the issue of measuring the return on investment in security architecture. Whilst this approach is normally applied only to management processes, the authors have personal experience of also applying it to measure the level of strength (in place of maturity) of technical security mechanisms (in place of process areas) included in the architecture.

Using a CMM requires some sophistication on the part of the management team

However, using capability maturity models does imply a level of sophistication and education in the senior management team, who must first buy into the idea of the maturity model as a valid measurement tool, and must understand what the various capability levels mean, so as to be able to interpret reports about how much the capabilities of the organisation have been improved. It also requires the senior management team to accept and to recognise that reaching a given level of

---

[13]See www.isaca.org and www.itgovernance.org

maturity in a given domain or process area represents a valid business goal and is therefore a useful measure of return on the investment. This might not suit all organisations.

It is not always appropriate to aim for the top of the scale

It is also important to recognise that reaching the highest level of maturity might not be the right goal for your enterprise. The key to applying these techniques successfully is to use the maturity levels as a means to determine where on the scale you want to aim and why. This theme is explored in the next section on benchmarking, in which an objective measurement scale is used to determine where you are now and where you want to reach, which will not always be the top of the scale.

Benchmarking Security Architecture

Benchmarking measures performance against an external standard

The concept of benchmarking was introduced in the previous section. Benchmarking is the practice of measuring the performance of the organisation against some external standard. The question being addressed is 'How are we doing compared to everyone else?' A follow-up question is often 'Now we know where are on the scale, where is it that we want to get to? So, the enterprise measures the external benchmark and its current position and sets a target of where it wants to be. Figure 6-7 shows this diagrammatically.

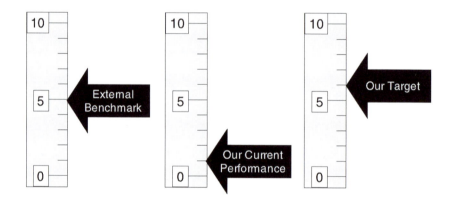

Figure 6-7: Benchmarking the Enterprise

What should you use as the external benchmark? There are several possibilities:

- An external best practice or good practice baseline standard such as:

    - ISO/IEC 17799: A Code of Practice for Information Security Management14;

    - ISO/IEC 21827: Systems Security Engineering Capability Maturity Model (discussed in detail in the previous section);

    - CobiTTM: Control Objectives for Information and related Technology15.

- Compliance with a legislative or regulatory requirement such as:

    - Government Information Security Reform Act (US);

---

[14]See www.iso.org

[15]See www.isaca.org

- Directive on Data Protection and aligned national legislation (EU);

- Directive on Privacy and Electronic Communications and aligned national legislation (EU);

- Health Insurance Portability and Accountability Act, 1996 (US);

- Gramm Leach Bliley Act[16] (US);

- Sarbanes-Oxley Act17 (US);

- Basel II: New Basel Capital Accord18 (Banking sector).

- Recent surveys and other publications such as those provided for members of specialist organisations:

  - ISF (Information Security Forum) Survey19;

  - I-4 (International Information Integrity Institute) publications and reports20;

  - CSI (Computer Security Institute21) annual survey and also the IPAK Self-Assessment Kit.

You need self-assessment for benchmarking

Whichever one you choose, the benchmarking method depends upon your carrying out a self-assessment of your organisation against the standard of your choice.

The benefits of benchmarking play to your need for measuring return on investment

The benefits of measuring and benchmarking security architecture and the security management process are closely linked to your aims in providing a way of evaluating return on investment:

- Demonstrates added value;

- Builds the business case;

- Justifies expenditure;

- Sets objectives to motivate the team;

- Helps you to understand what you are achieving.

To Summarise: Measuring Return on Investment in Security Architecture?

Return on investment or return of value are the measures commonly used by senior management to evaluate the business case for a particular investment proposal. For security architecture investments to be subjected to this evaluation, some objective measurement techniques are required.

The Balanced Scorecard method is one possible approach. It provides a balanced view between four perspectives of the enterprise:

- Financial perspective;

---

[16]See www.ftc.gov/privacy/glbact/. The Gramm Leach Bliley Act addresses the privacy of customer information.

[17]The Public Company Accounting Reform and Investor Protection Act of 2002. See www.sec.gov.

[18]See the Bank for International Settlements at www.bis.org. Basel II addresses the management of operational risk in financial institutions.

[19]For members only – see www.securityforum.org

[20]For members only – see https://i4online.com

[21]See www.gocsi.com

- Customer perspective;

- Internal process perspective;

- Innovation and learning perspective.

For each of these perspectives a scorecard is constructed, setting out the goals (intentions) of the enterprise and the objective measurements of how those goals were met (outcomes).

Another approach is based upon SABSA® Business Attributes, which are classified under seven headings in the taxonomy of attributes. There are currently 85 attributes defined in the taxonomy, each with suggestions for measurement approaches and metrics that can be defined. Some of the suggested metrics are hard and quantitative, whilst others are soft and qualitative. In the SABSA® approach, the use of Business Attributes enables two-way traceability between the business drivers for security and the way that the enterprise security architecture is constructed at the component and operational levels.

Yet another approach is to apply a Capability Maturity Model, similar to those devised by Carnegie-Mellon University for measuring software engineering practices. These provide a two-dimensional analysis of capability versus domain. Both the System Security Engineering Capability Maturity Model and the CobiT Capability Maturity Model are potential candidates for use.

Finally, the enterprise may choose to adopt one or more of these techniques to benchmark itself against a series of external standards, using an assessment of the external benchmark, an assessment of the current position of the enterprise, and a target for the desired position of the enterprise, all measured on a notional benchmarking scale.

All or any of these techniques can be used to measure the benefits to the enterprise of investments in security architecture and can therefore be used as measures of return on investment or return of value.

Chapter 7: Using This Book as a Practical Guide

The primary purpose of this book is to provide the reader with a practical guide to developing an enterprise-wide security architecture within an organisation. This chapter focuses on this practical aspect, pointing out some of the key steps and deliverables and describing how to plan and execute the process itself.

In this chapter you will learn about:

- The SABSA® Development Process and how it is derived directly from the SABSA® Model;

- The SABSA® Lifecycle for security architecture development and how that maps onto the SABSA® Model;

- The detailed processes and sub-processes that comprise the top-down decomposition of the four individual phases of the SABSA® Lifecycle;

- The detailed process flows that you should follow in applying the SABSA® methodology;

- The way in which the various layers of the SABSA® Model are integrated into the final enterprise security architecture.

The authors have given considerable thought to how they should best present the material in this chapter, since it is after all, the detailed description of the SABSA® Development Process itself, and therefore very much at the heart of the whole book. The SABSA® Model was introduced in Chapter 3, and already at that stage terminology and concepts embedded in the SABSA® Matrix were introduced but not fully explained. The concept of the Business Attributes Profile has been fully explained in Chapter 6, but other major concepts such as the trust model, the domain model and many others still remain without detailed explanation. Now, in this chapter, many of those terms and ideas appear again, and still there is no opportunity to explain them in detail, because each one deserves a large section of a chapter – chapters that come later in the book. This may cause some frustration to some readers, although the authors hope that this will be minimal.

The only alternatives would have been either to explain all the individual pieces first and then present the process framework afterwards (a bottom-up approach) or to distribute the process descriptions throughout the book so as to position them alongside the detailed descriptions. After due consideration and weighing the advantages and disadvantages of each way of structuring the book, the authors have chosen to focus the entire process description in this one chapter and trust that the reader will benefit from finding all this material grouped together and having the entire framework described before the details of the framework are populated. It will certainly benefit those readers who want to use the book as a reference work, rather than as a text to read from start to finish.

Using the SABSA® Model to Define a Development Process

The SABSA® Model previously introduced is the basis of the development process

The SABSA® Model described in Chapter 3 and shown in diagrammatic form in Figure 3-1 implies by its layered structure that there is a layer-by-layer development process. At its simplest, this process flow is shown in Figure 7-1.

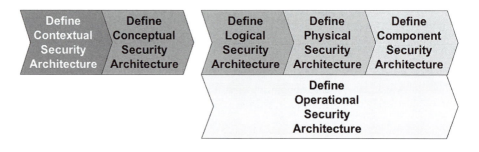

Figure 7-1: The SABSA® Development Process

Development is sequential, except for the operational layer

The implied process flow is that successive layers are developed in sequence, except for the operational security architecture layer. This operational security architecture is developed in parallel rather than sequentially, although this activity cannot really begin until the conceptual security architecture has been defined. Thus you will see the combination of sequential and parallel flow as shown in Figure 7-1.

There is a natural sign-off and buy-in milestone after the conceptual layer

To take the implied process a stage further, there is a natural break in the continuity of flow between the conceptual and logical layers. The conceptual security architecture (the architect's vision) is the conclusion of what is called the Strategy and Concept phase, within which high-level strategy is developed and agreed on. It is essential to gain buy-in and sign-off to these strategic visions before heavily committing resources to what follows. The end of the conceptual security architecture activity is therefore a milestone at which to stop, draw breath and reach consensus. The break in the diagram shows this milestone.

The design phase follows the sign-off and buy-in milestone

Once the contextual security architecture (business model) and the conceptual security architecture (architect's vision) have been agreed on and there is clearly broad buy-in from all interested parties, then these concepts can be realised through a more detailed Design phase of work. This encompasses the definition of the logical, physical, component and operational layers of the SABSA® Model.

Completion of the design phase is another major milestone

The completion of the design constitutes another major milestone, with sign-off and agreement being needed before you move on to the Implement phase in which you actually construct the systems and processes that have been designed.

After implementation comes the manage and measure phase

Finally, after implementation the Manage and Measure stage will handle the operational management of your implemented systems and processes and tell you whether or not they are really meeting the original business requirements. This is the governed by the operational security architecture that has already been designed, by which management and measurement are achieved.

The four phases form a cycle – an architecture lifecycle

These four phases of activity form the SABSA® Lifecycle, in which the operational Manage and Measure phase leads back to a potentially new Strategy and Concept phase, where new business requirements are formulated, based upon the operational experience.

Thus the diagram shown in Figure 7-2 represents the SABSA® Lifecycle for security architecture.

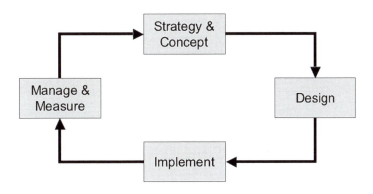

Figure 7-2: The SABSA® Lifecycle

Each phase is described in detail below

The following sections examine each one of these four SABSA® Lifecycle phases in greater detail, looking at the process steps in each one.

Strategy and Concept Phase

The diagrams show the detailed processes

This section focuses on the Strategy and Concept phase of the SABSA® Lifecycle. Figure 7-3 explains the symbols used in the subsequent process flow diagrams, and Figure 7-4 and Figure 7-5 show the detailed process flows of the sub-processes within the Strategy and Concept phase, and the deliverables that are generated.

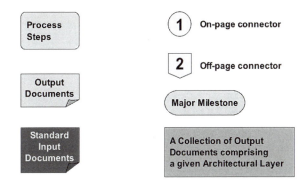

Figure 7-3: Key to Symbols Used in Process Diagrams

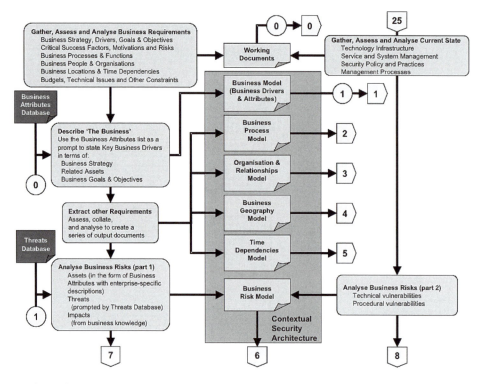

Figure 7-4: Developing the Contextual Security Architecture

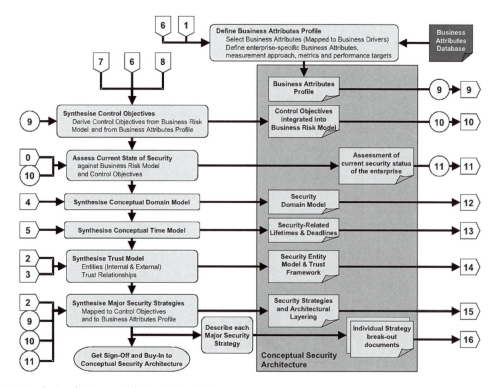

Figure 7-5: Developing the Conceptual Security Architecture

You begin by collecting business requirements

The Strategy and Concept phase begins with you collecting comprehensive business requirements and understanding your existing technology infrastructure. Chapter 8 examines the detailed techniques for gathering this information, but for the present time assume that it can be collected and collated satisfactorily.

The information gathered is based upon the answers to the six questions that were identified in Chapter 3 in the context of the business and its current infrastructure:

- What?
- Why?
- How?
- Who?
- Where?
- When?

The business requirements populate the first row of your architecture matrix

The results of this investigation provide the data that populates the first (contextual) row of the SABSA® Matrix shown in Table 3-3 in Chapter 3. This row is reproduced here in Figure 7-6, along with the second (conceptual) row, to remind you of their structure.

	Assets (What)	Motivation (Why)	Process (How)	People (Who)	Location (Where)	Time (When)
Contextual	The Business	Business Risk Management	Business Process Model	Business Organisation & Relationships	Business Geography	Business Time Dependencies
Conceptual	Business Attributes Profile	Control Objectives	Security Strategies & Architectural Layering	Security Equity Model & Trust Framework	Security Domain Model	Security-Related Lifetimes & Deadlines

Figure 7-6: The Contextual and Conceptual Rows of the SABSA® Matrix

The format as a row in the matrix is for presentation only – the information is physically held in a series of working documents

There is no need for you actually to format the information like this. The SABSA® Matrix serves the purpose of ensuring that your thinking is both structured and complete. The quantity and structure of the actual data that you gather at this stage may be different from that which is required for formally documenting your contextual security architecture, and so it is the substance of a series of working documents. These are your field notes that provide the raw source data from which your subsequent analysis and synthesis takes place. The working documents are not considered to be formal deliverables and are therefore not listed in the schedule of deliverables below. Some working documents will be pre-existing enterprise documents, some will be interview notes, whilst others will be notes that summarise information from a variety of sources. There are no specific recommendations made for how these working documents should be formatted, structured or organised, since they are of an *ad hoc* nature.

By analysing and synthesising you create the deliverables

The results of the various analyses and syntheses developed from your working documents become the contents of your Contextual Security Architecture and your Conceptual Security Architecture, as can be seen in Figures 7-4 and 7-5 and are the deliverables. These deliverables are summarised below.

Contextual Security Architecture Deliverables

- The business model – business drivers, including business assets, goals and objectives, mapped to SABSA® Business Attributes;

- The SABSA® Business Risk Model in the form of a risk assessment matrix, driven from the SABSA® Business Attributes;

- The business process model;

- The business organisation and relationships model;

- The business geography model;

- The business time-dependency model.

Conceptual Security Architecture Deliverables

- The SABSA® Business Attributes Profile, including the selected Business Attributes, their detailed definitions within the context of this enterprise and its business, the metric types and measurement approaches to be used and the performance targets for each metric, as described in Chapter 6;

- The SABSA® Business Risk Model, extended to include a statement of the control objectives;

- Assessment of the current status of security against the SABSA® Business Attributes Profile and associated control objectives;

- A description of the architectural layering to be employed, and the major security strategies and concepts mapped to the control objectives;

- A series of break-out documents, each describing a major security strategy;

- The security entity model and trust framework;

- The security domain model;

- A list of security-related lifetimes and deadlines to be addressed at lower layers.

Detailed flow charts of activity are shown in the diagrams

The step-by-step process by which you work through the development of the Contextual Security Architecture and the Conceptual Security Architecture is shown in Figures 7-4 and 7-5 respectively. Each diagram maps the flow of activity, the sources of information and the production of the deliverables listed above. Figure 7-3 shows the key to the symbols used in these diagrams.

The process diagrams are arranged in columns

These process flow diagrams are arranged so that all the input sources are on the left-hand side and all the outputs on the right-hand side. The sub-process activities are in a column just to the right of the inputs. The deliverables are all shown as documents and grouped in a column to the right of the sub-processes, surrounded by a box that is labelled according to the appropriate layer of the SABSA® Model.

Off-page connectors indicate the linkage to other flowcharts

You will notice that there are off-page connectors on the process flow diagrams that lead to subsequent flowcharts for the later stages of the SABSA® Development Process. There is also one off-page connector that is numbered '25' that comes all the way back from the final flowchart of the manage and measure phase – feeding back operational information into the gathering of the information on the current status. This is not relevant in a first green field development but is very important when an architectural development is building upon previous foundations, as implied by the loop structure of the SABSA® Lifecycle shown in Figure 7-2. Under these circumstances understanding the current status is important.

The flowcharts show key input sources

In Figure 7-4 you will see two input sources: the Business Attributes Database and the Threats Database. You have already encountered the Business Attributes in Chapter 6. This input in Figure 7-4 refers to an up-to-date list of Business Attributes, their generic descriptions and their possible metrics, as discussed in the earlier chapter.

The Business Attributes Database is applied twice

At this point in the SABSA® Development Process the Business Attributes are used only to prompt your thinking on business drivers and related assets, not to develop the full Business Attributes Profile. That comes later, when they are used again at the conceptual layer (see Figure 7-5) to develop the Business Attributes Profile, which includes all the chosen Business Attributes along with their enterprise-specific definitions, the metric types, the measurement approach and the performance targets. The Business Attributes Profile is the conceptualisation of the real business strategy, drivers, assets, goals and objectives.

The Threats Database prompts your thinking on risk assessment

The Threats Database is an up-to-date list of threat types and threat agents to prompt your thinking in carrying out the risk assessment. This database is described more fully in Chapter 9, where there is a detailed discussion on operational risk assessment. See also Chapter 15 for a more detailed view of operational risk management.

How Does the Strategy and Concept Phase Fit Together?

Fitting together the two layers of this phase

It is absolutely critical that you should understand what is going on at this level of the architecture model, since so much of what you are trying to achieve in developing your enterprise security architecture depends upon the foundations that you build at this stage. Figure 7-7 is included in order to help you with further insight into how it fits together.

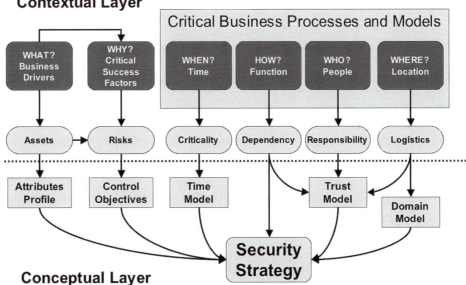

Figure 7-7: How the Strategy and Concept Phase Fits Together

The assets of the business are conceptualised in the Business Attributes Profile

The description of what you are trying to protect at the business level is embodied in the business drivers. These include business strategy, business goals and business objectives. These drivers are seen as the business assets when conducting a business risk assessment. At the conceptual layer they are represented in the form of the Business Attributes Profile.

The success factors and mitigation of risks are conceptualised as control objectives

The risk assessment itself examines what puts the assets at risk. This is also closely linked to the critical success factors for the enterprise – those factors that influence its success as opposed to the risks that might bring about its failure. These are all concerned with why you want security – your motivation behind the security architecture. At the conceptual layer success factors and risk mitigation are combined into a representation in the form of the control objectives.

The entire business model drives the security strategy at the conceptual layer

The when, how, who and where questions are concerned with a series of critical business processes and business models. These bring out aspects of the business model that are concerned with issues such as criticality, dependency, responsibility and logistics. All these feed into the various conceptual models at the conceptual layer, including the time model, the trust model and the domain model. Everything from the contextual layer feeds into the conceptualisation of the security strategy – or rather a series of linked security strategies.

Design Phase

Design only begins when you have sign-off to the Strategy and Concept phase

Now it is time to look in detail at the Design phase of the SABSA® Development Process. You should enter this phase with an agreed, signed off, conceptual security architecture, based upon an agreed, signed off contextual security architecture. This is critically important, since you must not start on detailed design work without knowing that you really do have the support of the business in defining their requirements and the wide support of the technology leadership team in agreeing on the strategic, conceptual approaches to the security architecture. These matters are discussed again in more detail in Chapter 8.

Sometimes your work must begin somewhere in the middle of the process, utilising earlier work that precedes it

In some programmes, you do not have the luxury of starting at the beginning and ending at the end – you have to start at some point in the middle of the process, building on work that others have done before you. This work may or may not fit easily into the process model that is described here for the development of an enterprise security architecture. Thus, in these circumstances you would need to introduce a couple of extra process steps called:

- Review and validate business requirements/contextual security architecture;
- Review and validate conceptual security architecture.

If you have to start in the middle, you should validate previous work

If you find yourself in the situation where you must begin in the middle, wherever that may be, then you will need to be creative in introducing an appropriate set of validation steps to ensure that you are building on sound foundations already built by someone else. If the review and validation shows inadequacies in these foundations, then you should propose some re-work steps, basing your business case upon the results of your review and validation activity.

The design authority takes responsibility for the integrity of the design

Be careful! If you, as the architect, build your house on sand instead of rock, then it will probably fall over later on, and you will take the blame! If you are ordered to proceed against your own better judgement, make sure that you carefully document your advice and lodge it where it can be retrieved and authenticated if (when?) the building starts to subside. Issues such as design authority are discussed in Chapter 8.

Once again it is time to be reminded of the elements of the SABSA® Matrix that must be addressed in the design phase. These are reproduced in Figure 7-8.

	Assets (What)	Motivation (Why)	Process (How)	People (Who)	Location (Where)	Time (When)
Logical	Business IInformation Model	Security Policies	Security Services	Entity Schema & Privilege Profiles	Security Domain Definitions & Associations	Security Processing Cycle
Physical	Business Data Model	Security Rules, Practices & Procedures	Security Mechanisms	Users, Applications, & the User Interface	Platform & Network Infrastructure	Control Structure Execution
Component	Detailed Data Structures	Security Standards	Security Products & Tools	Identities, Functions, Actions & ACLs	Peocesses, Codes, Addresses & Protocols	Security Step Timing & Sequencing
Operational	Assurance of Operational Continuity	Operational Risk Management	Security Serv ice Management & Support	Application & User Management & Support	Security of Sites, Networks & Platforms	Security Operations Schedule

Figure 7-8: The Logical, Physical, Component and Operational Layers of SABSA® Matrix

Logical Security Architecture Development Process

The detailed development process is shown in the flowchart

Referring back to the conceptual security architecture development flowchart in Figure 7-5, there are a number of off-page connectors that provide the links into the next layer – the logical security architecture layer. These reappear in Figure 7-9, where the process steps for developing the logical security architecture are mapped.

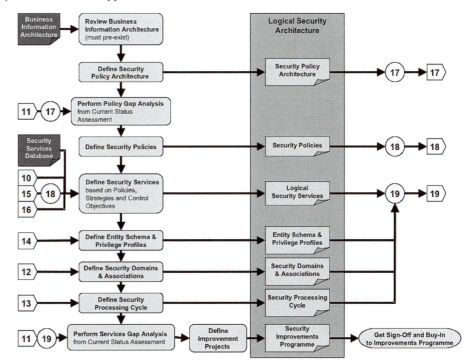

Figure 7-9: Developing the Logical Security Architecture

Again those with a keen eye will have spotted that there is a potential mismatch between the 'what' cell of the logical layer as shown in the SABSA® Matrix (see Figure 7-8) and the output from the process shown in Figure 7-9. Where does the business information model come from and what is it?

The business information model is a prerequisite

The business information model, or information architecture (refer back to Chapter 2 for a description of this, and to Figure 2-1 for its position in the reference model), is not within the scope of a security architecture programme to create. You need it, and without it you will find it hard to proceed, but for the purposes of this book it is assumed that this is pre-existing and has been developed as part of a wider enterprise architecture programme.

The business process model is a prerequisite

There are parallels here with the business process model in the contextual security architecture – which is also well beyond the scope of a security architecture programme to create but which is equally important to its success. Once again you have to assume that a business process model pre-exists. If the organisation has no process model and indeed has no real concept of business processes in its culture, then some of the risk assessment work done at the contextual layer may be faulty. This is because it will not have been possible to identify critical functions that interrupt critical processes. You may wish to refer back to the case study on the Missing Taxis in Chapter 5 to remind yourself of how this happens.

Logical Architecture Deliverables

- Security policy architecture – a hierarchical model of policy documentation and how it fits together;

- The individual security policies, or at least templates and guidelines for their production;

- A list and description of the logical security services to be provided within the security architecture, with a mapping to the control objectives and major security strategies that they are intended to satisfy;

- The entity schema to be applied in the enterprise-wide (logical) directory, with associated models for privilege profiles, authorisations, authentication attributes, etc.;

- The specific security domains with a description of their logical make-up, their individual security policies and the security associations that exist both intra-domain and inter-domain;

- A description of the logical security processing cycle;

- An improvements programme to gain short-term advantages and to deliver early wins from the security architecture programme.

Functional Specification

A functional specification is part of the logical architecture

Functional specifications are usually associated with specific projects

Those readers with an experienced eye will be asking – 'what about the functional requirements specification? Surely that is part of the logical architecture.' And indeed you are correct, it is.

However, at this stage you are designing the architecture from an enterprise-wide perspective, by creating a blueprint or road map that will guide individual development projects and ensure that they all follow the same architectural guidelines. You are not at this stage attempting to define

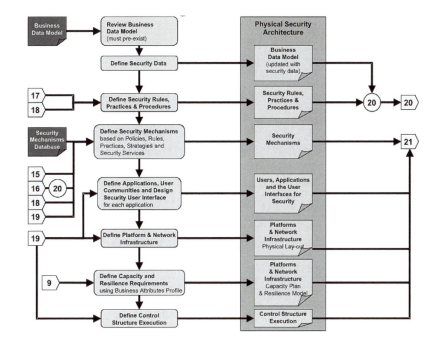

Figure 7-10: Developing the Physical Security Architecture

every possible business project in detail, and hence you are holding back on defining functional requirements. The intention is to provide an architectural framework within which every business project will be designed, and at that detailed design stage you will require a definition of the functional requirements of the project.

Where future projects conflict with the architecture, a resolution process is needed

Should it transpire that the functional requirements of a project are actually in conflict with your overarching architecture then you will have misjudged the architectural requirements. It happens. Not everything you do is perfect. So you will need an architecture maintenance process, which is discussed in more detail in Chapter 8. This maintenance process will, amongst other things, resolve any conflicts between the architecture and a new project.

Physical Security Architecture Development Process

The detailed flowchart shows the development process

The sub-process steps for developing the physical security architecture are shown in Figure 7-10. Once again there are inputs in the form of off-page connectors from Figure 7-9. There are also two other inputs: the business data model, assumed to be pre-existing, and the security mechanisms database, which is described in detail in Chapter 12.

Physical Security Architecture Deliverables

- An updated business data model, describing any new data types required by the security architecture (such as passwords, usernames, certificates, etc.).

- A statement of the security rules, practices and procedures that will be required. At this stage the details of the procedures and practices will not be written. The statement will describe only certain procedures and practices that will be needed to implement the policies defined at the logical layer. Templates for creating these procedures and practices may also be defined here.

- A list of the security mechanisms that will be needed to implement the logical security services from the layer above. Different mechanisms will be used in different contexts for the same service, and an indication of where each selected mechanism should be used can be defined at this stage. However, the number of security mechanism types should be minimised to avoid complexity and to provide generic, re-usable, modular approaches to the construction of new infrastructure and applications.

- A list of applications and user communities, with a security user interface design for each type. In the future, as more applications are added, this may need to be updated. As with the security mechanisms, the number of user interface types should be minimised to avoid complexity and to provide generic, re-usable, modular approaches to the construction of new applications. A user interface module with a defined API would be a good architectural approach.

- The physical layout of the platforms and networks, probably in diagrammatic form. This is a physical representation, defining the number of physical computer boxes, physical communications lines and physical networking equipment items – how many, what type and where.

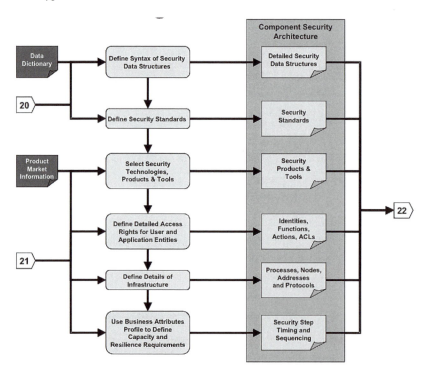

Figure 7-11: Developing the Component Security Architecture

- A statement of capacity planning. Given the throughput of the devices, the processing power of computers and the bandwidth of communications lines, how many of each will be required to handle the expected load?

- A description of the resilience model provided by redundancy of boxes and connections. The resilience model is integral to the physical layout model, providing redundant capacity in resilient configurations.

- The control structure execution model needed to execute the logical security processing cycle from the layer above.

Component Security Architecture Development Process

The detailed flow-chart shows the development process

The sub-process steps for developing the component security architecture are shown in Figure 7-11. The off-page connectors on the input side are from Figure 7-10. There are also two other inputs: the data dictionary, assumed to be pre-existing, and the security products market information, assumed to be available externally from product vendors and market analysts.

Component Security Architecture Deliverables

- An updated data dictionary, defining the syntax rules of all the data structures required by the security architecture;

- A framework for security standards and a list for all the security standards that are required – although the detailed content of the individual standards will probably not be developed at this time;

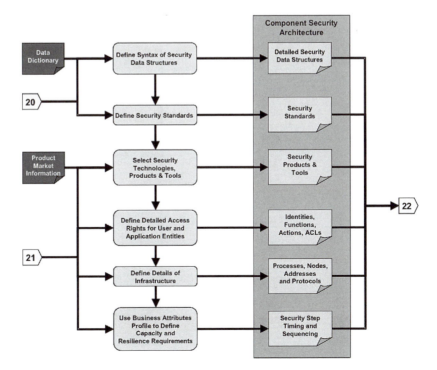

Figure 7-11: Developing the Component Security Architecture

- A list with descriptions and specifications of all strategic technologies, products and tools that have been selected, with guidance for project teams as to how, why, where and when they should be used;

- A naming scheme and a framework for defining roles, identities, access privilege profiles (also known as permissions or authorisations), authorised functions and actions and guidance on building access control lists that represent these parameters;

- Detailed design of the security infrastructure, including the application processes to be run, the platform nodes on which these are to be hosted, the handling of both logical and physical addressing schemes, and the protocols to be used in inter-process and inter-node communications;

- Detailed specification of procedural step timings and sequences needed to implement the control structure execution model from the layer above.

Operational Security Architecture Development Process

Operational people must be involved in designing the operational security architecture

Whereas the development of the first five layers described above is very much an architecture design team activity, the design of the operational layer needs major participation and input from the teams that will have operational responsibility during the lifetime of systems built to this architecture.

At this stage you develop only the framework for the operational processes

The security architects therefore need to involve their operations colleagues in the work, so that what is designed will be workable. It will be up to those operational teams to define the detailed procedures and so on, but at this stage you need to lay out a framework of what processes,

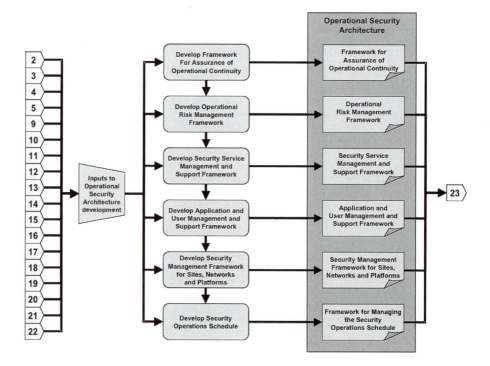

Figure 7-12: Developing the Operational Security Architecture

procedures and activities are needed and how they relate to one another. These are based on the framework seen in Chapter 3, Table 3-4. Figure 7-12 shows the process steps for the development of the operational security architecture.

Operational Security Architecture Deliverables

- Framework for assurance of operational continuity:
    - Business requirements collection process;
    - Information classification scheme;
    - Business continuity management process or programme;
    - Information security management process;
    - Systems integrity management process;
    - Database security management process;
    - Software integrity management process;
    - Product and tool security and integrity management process.
- Operational risk management framework:
    - Business risk assessment process;
    - Corporate policymaking process;
    - Measurement, metrics and benchmarking process;
    - Security assurance framework;
    - Security audit process;
    - Detailed policymaking process;
    - Policy compliance monitoring;
    - Intelligence gathering;
    - Vulnerability assessment;
    - Threat assessment;
    - Penetration testing;
    - Ongoing research into threats and vulnerabilities;
    - CERT notification management process.
- Security service management and support framework:
    - Business-driven information security management programme;
    - Incident response process;
    - Disaster recovery process;
    - Change control process;

- Intrusion detection service;

- Event monitoring service;

- Security process development programme;

- Security service management process;

- Development controls programme;

- Configuration management process;

- Operational procedures, including:

  - Rule definition;

  - Key management;

  - ACL maintenance;

  - Backup administration;

  - Information forensics;

  - Event log administration;

  - Anti-virus administration.

- Product procurement process;

- Operational management process;

- Project management process.

- Application and user management and support framework:

  - Business security management organisation structure:

    - Roles;

    - Reporting structure;

    - Responsibilities.

  - Security training, awareness and culture development programme;

  - Access privileges (permissions) management framework:

    - Role-based profile definitions;

    - User identity management and registration;

    - User account and privilege administration;

    - Personnel vetting.

  - User support and help desk framework.

- Security management framework sites, networks and platforms:

  - Business field operations management;

  - Security domain management;

- Application security administration and management;

- Network security management;

- Site security management;

- Platform, workstation and equipment security management.

• Framework for managing the security operations schedule:

- Business calendar and timetable management;

- Security operations schedule management;

- Management of application deadlines and cut-offs;

- Time-dependency management:

  − Password lifecycle;

  − Account lifecycle;

  − Cryptographic key lifecycle;

  − Defining the time-dependent context for access control.

- Operations sequencing.

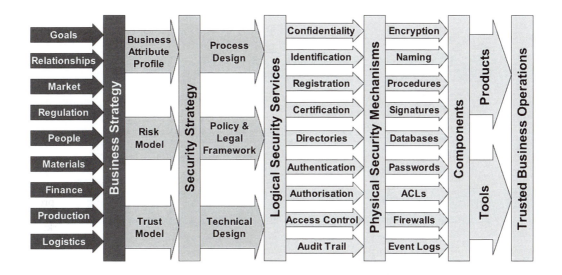

Figure 7-13: How the Strategy and Concept/Design Process Fits Together

How Does the Strategy and Concept/Design Process Fit Together?

Further insight into how it all fits together

It is time to take stock again. Figure 7-13 provides another graphical model to give further insight into how all the architecture model and the derived processes fit together.

Case study example on directory architecture

Here is some insight of each stage of the strategy and concept and the design phases through a case study at Intergalactic Banking and Financial Services Inc.

Case Study – Directory Infrastructure Project at IBFS

The CIO, Ranjit Patel, has decided to embark on a directory infrastructure project to put in place a global directory service to support all IBFS applications.

He has first commissioned a study to identify all types of business entity. These include:

- People;
- Corporate legal entities;
- Organisational units;
- Sites;
- Equipment items;
- Computer systems and applications.

The analysis of these business entities forms the contextual architecture of the directory infrastructure.

The concept is simple – that the entire set of business entities and their relationships will be logically represented through a directory infrastructure and that this infrastructure will be built in the form of a relational database compliant with an internationally recognised standard such as X.500. Access to the directory services is to be gained through the enterprise-wide middleware – which is being developed as another company-wide infrastructure project, shown in Figure 7-14.

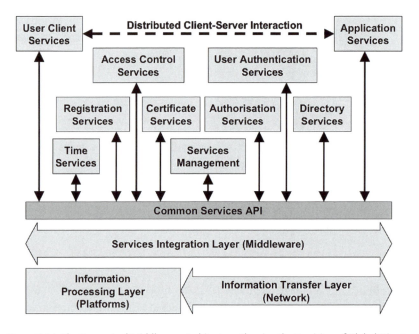

Figure 7-14: The Conceptual Middleware Architecture Showing the Provision of Global Directory Services

The directory service itself is to be built in the conceptual form of a meta-directory – a directory of directories, as shown in Figure 7-15. This is because IBFS already has a number of legacy directories that pre-exist this project, all of which must be integrated into the global service but which are still needed in their present form to support legacy applications. In addition, it is too difficult and expensive to re-engineer these directories, and so the meta-directory approach provides a means to integrate them as they are, supporting legacy applications whilst still providing a completely new directory interface to new applications.

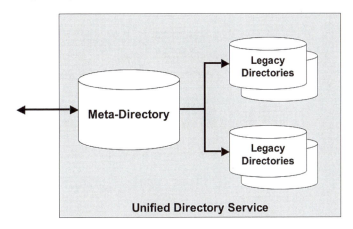

Figure 7-15: Conceptual Meta-Directory Architecture

At the logical layer the business entities are modelled as a directory schema. This logical model represents each entity as a unique entity name and a set of attributes[1] that describe the entity. The entities are related in a branching tree structure in which the naming convention describes a path from the root of the tree through a series of nodes to the entity being identified. Entities can be at intermediate nodes or at the leaves of the tree branch. The full path name is called the distinguished name of the entity and is a unique name. Some of the attributes can be alias names, often used in a local context without ambiguity. Other attributes might include access rights, digital certificates, cryptographic keys (stored encrypted), passwords (stored encrypted), and so on. Figure 7-16 shows a simplified version of how the schema is organised.

Another issue to be addressed in defining the schema is the possible inheritance of properties by entities. This happens in two ways:

- By attributes being defined as entities in other sub-trees, and thus the entity having the attribute inherits the properties of that attribute;

- Entities at a lower level in a sub-tree inherit properties from an entity at a higher level.

Transitivity of trust between entities must also be addressed. Together with inheritance, these can have a huge impact on the effectiveness of the trust models, because some entities can become endowed with trust that is not supposed to be there.

---

[1]Do not confuse the word 'attribute' used here, meaning a descriptor of a directory entity, with the use of the word elsewhere in this book in the context of the Business Attributes Profile – which is an entirely different usage.

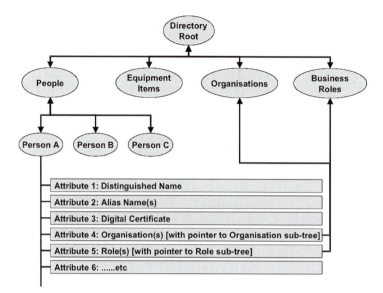

Figure 7-16: Directory Schema Logical Structure

The physical architecture of the directory is concerned with the following aspects of design:

- The detailed naming standard to be applied;

- Physical storage of the directory database;

- Resilience of the database by mirroring;

- Replication of the directory data from masters to slaves to make it locally available without creating bottlenecks and bandwidth problems, to provide the required performance, availability and response time;

- Access protocols (such as LDAP);

- Physical layout and location of equipment.

Figure 7-17 shows many aspects of the physical architecture.

The component architecture comprises whatever directory products have been selected.

The operational architecture of the directory includes the following:

- Backup and recovery of directory data;

- Directory security management (privacy, authentication, access control and auditing);

- Synchronisation and replication strategy;

- Directory administration, maintenance and support;

- Monitoring and directory management.

Figure 7-18 shows a summary of the six-layer architecture model focused on the directory architecture. Each layer in the diagram shows what is addressed

at that layer. The operational layer is divided into five sub-layers, one for each of
the other layers to which it relates.

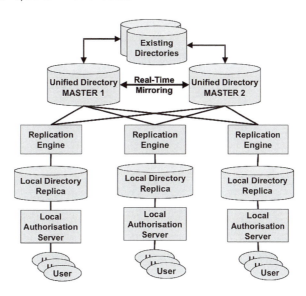

Figure 7-17: Directory Physical Architecture

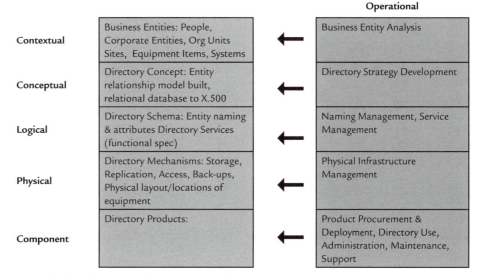

Figure 7-18: The Overall Layering of the Directory Architecture

Implementation Phase

*Infrastructure projects rarely
get business support*

Anyone who has experience of trying to implement infrastructure projects will know already that it
is notoriously difficult to gain business support for these. Who is going to pay? Where are the
business benefits? What is the return on investment? And so on. Business units are prepared to pay
for projects that are directly related to a business initiative that they have conceived in response to a

perceived business opportunity. These projects get budget, whereas pure infrastructure projects rarely do.

Thus, it is unlikely that a major strategic enterprise-wide security infrastructure will ever be implemented as a single project. You would be wise not even to try to take this route. What is more likely (and more sensible) is that the architecture provides a blueprint and a road map that guides a whole series of separate implementation projects, each of which is driven by a specific business initiative and funded by a budget associated with that initiative. Some of these projects may themselves be infrastructure projects, such as building an integrated, enterprise-wide, unified directory service, provided that someone can get the wider buy-in for such a project (which does sometimes happen).

Implementation of architecture is fragmented – one project at a time

The reality is that implementation will usually be fragmented in this way. Thus the main purpose of the security architecture is to ensure that this fragmentation does not lead to a piecemeal approach to design. Despite the fragmented projects, the overall systems environment should maintain its architectural integrity – provided that the architecture has been created and documented, and provided that project teams refer to it and are guided by it.

Architecture governance is needed to ensure that projects comply

This last point raises the issue of architecture governance – ensuring compliance with the architecture by individual projects, through a mechanism called the Architecture Board. This is discussed again in more detail in Chapter 8.

The detailed flowchart shows the implementation process

Accepting that implementation will be fragmented, you still need to address how the Implement phase of the SABSA® Lifecycle will be managed. Figure 7-19 shows a detailed flowchart showing some of the most important sub-processes and their key deliverables.

The key deliverables[2] include:

- The implementation plans:
- Specifications for build;
- Procurement plans;
- Change management plans;
- Project plans;
- Quality plans;
- Test plans.

The deliverables from the implementation itself:

- Operating guides;
- Support documentation;
- Training materials;
- Traceable change history;
- The test reports.

---

[2]The scope of this book is architecture rather than implementation, and whilst it is important to discuss implementation issues as part of the overall SABSA® Lifecycle, it is beyond the scope of the book to describe these implementation deliverables in any detail.

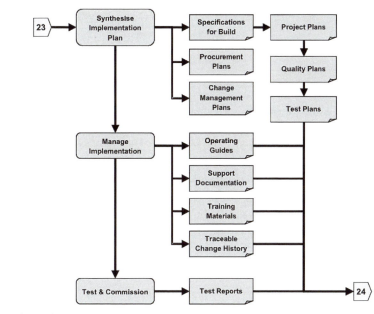

Figure 7-19: The Implementation Process

Manage and Measure Phase

Manage and Measure is concerned with operational aspects

The final phase of the SABSA® Lifecycle is Manage and Measure. This is where you see the architecture in operation. Aspects of the operational security architecture have already been discussed in this chapter and in earlier chapters, and Part 4 of this book is entirely devoted to this area. There is therefore little to say here on the subject, other than to entreat you, the security architect, to take this aspect very seriously.

Operational costs are usually the greatest contributor to total cost of ownership

When you look at the total cost of ownership of security architecture, this is where the bulk of the cost is to be found. In large organisations, with user communities running into many tens (even hundreds) of thousands of people, the cost of managing and administering user access privileges is huge. The complexity of organising a user help desk function for that size of community is enormous. When you, the architect, design something, perhaps the single most important question you should address is: 'How much will it cost to operate this?' It will usually be far more than it ever cost to design and to build it. When you look at the SABSA® Business Attributes Profile, you should check that you have addressed those Business Attributes such as scaleable, cost-effective and supportable.

Measurement is required to feed back to senior management the success story

The 'measure' part of this phase is also critically important. There has been a detailed discussion on measuring return on investment or at least return of value in Chapter 6. Part of your operational security architecture should be a process by which you can measure performance against the design goals embodied in the Business Attributes Profile. The purpose of these measurements is to provide feedback to the senior management team – 'Look boss, it's working!'

The detailed flowchart shows the management and measurement process

Some of the most important sub-processes in the Manage and Measure phase are shown in Figure 7-20. The key deliverables are:

- Operational reports;

- Event reports;

- Incident reports;

- Penetration test reports;

- Gap analysis reports;

- Improvements programme plan.

Security architecture must live and breathe – it changes over time

Finally, the security architecture must live and breathe. It is not a document written once and then carved in tablets of stone so as not to be changed. As time progresses there will be new business requirements, unforeseen by even the most forward-looking architect. There will also be new technical solutions, and at some point you may decide to make a step change and migrate from an old solution to a new one. There will also be lessons learned from experience that show you with hindsight that you could have done things differently to better advantage, and in some cases this will drive changes in your thinking and in your chosen solutions. To accommodate all of this you will also need an architecture maintenance process – something that is discussed in more detail in Chapter 8.

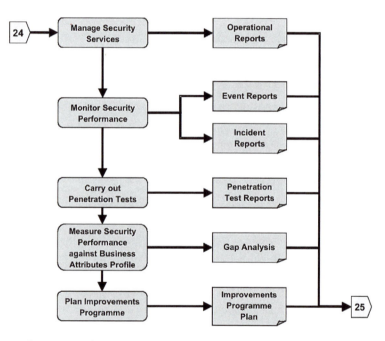

Figure 7-20: The Manage and Measure Process

To Summarise: How to Use This Book as a Practical Guide

The SABSA® Development Process is derived directly from the SABSA® Model.

The first two layers of a security architecture based on the SABSA® Model are developed first, after which there is a major milestone at which senior management sign-off should obtained to gain approval of and buy-in to the contextual and conceptual security architectures.

The development of these first two layers forms the Strategy and Concept phase of the four-step SABSA® Lifecycle.

After this milestone comes the development of the logical, physical, component and operational architectures. These development activities are grouped together under the Design phase of the SABSA® Lifecycle. At that point the SABSA® Development Process is complete.

The next step in the SABSA® Lifecycle is the Implement phase, followed by the final phase, Manage and Measure.

Each of the four phases of the SABSA® Lifecycle is broken down into detailed process flowcharts showing the input sources, the process steps, the deliverables at each step and the outputs to other subsequent process steps.

The SABSA® Model and the way that it is used to drive the SABSA® Development Process ensures that the individual layers of the security architecture closely integrate with one another.

Apart from the development work itself, there are significant political, organisational and cultural issues that the security architect must face, especially during the execution of the Implement and Manage and Measure phases of the work.

Chapter 8: Managing the Security Architecture Programme

Following directly from the discussion in Chapter 7 on the practical process of developing your security architecture, this chapter looks at another equally practical aspect – how to manage the architecture programme itself. This focuses largely on the political and cultural issues that need to be addressed if you are to succeed. It picks up and expands upon a number of points already introduced in the previous chapter.

In this chapter you will learn about:

- How to go about influencing the opinion, behaviour and attitudes of a specific group of people;

- Selling the true business benefits of a security programme;

- How to approach senior management to gain their buy-in, support, sponsorship and budget approval;

- Building and managing an effective security architecture team;

- Using the Fast Track™ approach[1] to get started on a security architecture programme quickly;

- Planning and managing the security architecture development programme;

- Collecting the information that you require to develop an enterprise security architecture;

- Reaching a consensus view on the conceptual security architecture so as to get sign-off and buy-in before moving forward with the Design phase of the SABSA® Lifecycle;

- Exerting architectural governance and ensuring compliance with architectural standards through an Architecture Board and through the formal delegation of design authority;

- Maintaining the security architecture over its extended lifetime;

- How to maintain the long-term confidence of senior management during the elapsed time of a long development project.

---

[1]Fast Track™ as applied to a Security Architecture Development Workshop is a trademark of SABSA Limited.

- Security awareness-raising activities – focus on the key messages for the specific group that you want to target.

Now that you know how to say it, what do you want to say?

So now that you know how to approach your audience, what is it that you want to say? Assuming that you are speaking to a senior leadership team, here are some topics that might interest them. However, you must decide what fits your situation. Rarely can this sort of thing be lifted directly from a textbook.

Ensuring That You Solve Business Problems

Identify specific business problems in your organisation and explain how you can help to solve these problems

The SABSA® methodology presented in this book is business-driven. It identifies business requirements and business problems, and from this you develop solutions to those business problems. When you present your business case, make sure that you identify the specific business problems in your organisation that will be addressed through your security architecture, and explain in business language how the solutions will bring specific business benefits.

Maximum Return on Investment

Build a return on Investment model specific to your organisation

Your organisation already invests to some extent in security for business information systems, and senior management knows this. You can tell them what it already costs. A major benefit of the architectural approach is to maximise the return on investment and optimise the cost/benefit ratio. In Chapter 6 you have seen some specific ways to present this approach. Make sure you develop these ideas in the context of your organisation and its specific business.

Economies of Scale and Standardisation

Leverage the fact that senior management already understands economies of scale

Economy of scale is well understood by senior management, so leverage this understanding. Some of the key points to make are:

- Lower cost of acquisition because you can minimise the number of different components and leverage the bulk purchasing capabilities of your procurement team;

- Lower cost of support because you minimise the number of different product types to be supported by setting corporate standards;

- Lower cost of training because you minimise the number of different tools and products on which your people need to be trained.

Improved Corporate Governance

Remind the directors that you are protecting their personal liabilities under the law

Corporate governance means control over the enterprise by the board of directors and other senior executives, fulfilling their legal responsibilities to safeguard the shareholders' funds that have been entrusted to them for investment and growth. At the most extreme end of the scale, corporate governance is about keeping the directors out of jail! You need to remind them of their personal legal responsibilities and show them how your work is contributing to their personal safety under the law.

Selling the Benefits of Security Architecture

You need to sell your programme to the senior management team

Generally speaking it is the senior management team to whom you must sell the benefits of the work that you are proposing in a security architecture programme. So you need to think about how you should go about getting their attention.

How sell an idea and influence opinion

When you want to sell an idea to anyone so as to influence their opinion or their behaviour, there are certain ground rules that should be followed so as to increase your chances of success.

Rules for Influencing Opinion or Behaviour

– Address your remarks, your document or your presentation only to the group of people whose opinion or behaviour you seek to influence. Do not attempt to make your communication a catch-all for everyone.

– Speak only in the language, concepts and terminology used by the group whose opinion or behaviour you wish to influence. Avoid the use of language, concepts and terminology with which they are unfamiliar.

– Address only those issues that are of interest to the group whose opinion or behaviour you wish to influence. Avoid issues that are not of interest to them.

– Focus on presenting a set of key messages that you want them to assimilate. Craft the communication around these key messages.

– Prioritise your material, presenting the most important messages first. If their attention span is short, or if they are distracted by something else during the communication, then at least they will have received your most important message before you lost their attention.

These rules for communicating are unfamiliar to those with a traditional scientific education

To someone with a background in communications, these rules will seem trivial, but to someone with a scientific or technological education they may well be completely new and somewhat counterintuitive. This is because scientists and technologists are traditionally taught to develop a logical argument, to present the steps in order, and to deliver the conclusion at the end. However, senior business people are much more likely to want the bottom line first, because this allows them to make a rapid judgement on whether to invest further time on this topic or move on to something more important. You need to grab their attention first with the meat of the communication. Remember that you may only ever get one chance to get your message across to a senior audience, so take it before it runs out of time.

A successful security architect applies these rules in many different ways

The application of these rules is very wide, and they are relevant to many aspects of being a successful security architect. Some examples:

• Writing security policies (of which there is more discussion later in the book) where you want to influence a specific group of users – speak only to that specific group in their language and prioritise your material according to their interest.

• Writing the executive summary of a proposal, where you want to sell the benefits – begin your summary with the most important benefit that you want the reader to understand.

• Writing the executive summary of a consulting report, where you want to make recommendations – start with the most important recommendation.

Better Risk Management

One of the demands of corporate governance is that the directors properly manage risk – financial risk of all types, strategic risk and operational risk. In this last category, operational risk, information systems related risks contribute a significant proportion of the risks to be addressed.

Quite apart from any legal pressures to do so, a diligent management team will want to manage business risks appropriately. You could even argue that the job of a senior manager is mostly about managing business risk. It also plays strongly to the need for good corporate governance mentioned in the previous section.

Good security architecture helps in these endeavours by:

- Providing consistent risk assessment across all parts of the organisation;
- Providing consistent risk mitigation across all parts of the organisation;
- Providing levels of mitigation and control that are commensurate with the level of risk, as determined by those with responsibility for managing the business.

Operational risk management is discussed again in greater detail in Chapter 9 and Chapter 15.

Improved Preparedness for Formal Audit

It depends on the culture of the organisation as to how the internal auditors are perceived. In some places people shake in their shoes as the auditors arrive, fearful of the effects of a bad audit report. In other places it is not so. In some cultures the auditor is the policeman, in others she or he is the helpful internal consultant working with the business to improve control.

Whatever the culture in your organisation, it is universally the case that people do not like to receive negative audit comments. Thus you can leverage this desire for a clean audit. Having a well-founded security architecture is a sure way to get the auditors on your side. Indeed the internal audit team can be strong allies when you are building your business case, so do not be afraid to get them involved in the entire programme.

Then there is the external audit. This has a different function – to safeguard the shareholders and make sure that the management team is investing and managing their funds wisely – but it can also be used as a lever to sell the benefits of security architecture. Here again, nobody likes a bad audit report, and careers have been known to falter and even terminate for this reason alone.

Influencing the Financial and Business Analyst Community

The power exerted by business analysts has grown extensively over the last decade. This community works either for a division of one of the large investment banks or for one of the specialist business analyst companies such as The Meta Group, Gartner Group or Forrester Research. These companies specialise in identifying and analysing emerging trends in technology and their impact on business.

Senior leadership teams are usually very aware of what the analysts are saying because the share-buying community read their reports and are heavily influenced as to which stocks and shares they purchase. Thus, in order to keep the listed share price buoyant or to promote a forthcoming market flotation, senior managers must ensure that the company receives the public approval of the analysts.

Quote the analyst reports to support your case

To maximise the effect of this powerful lever, read the analyst reports on corporate security and ICT security and quote from them in presentations and reports that you make to the senior leadership team. Also be aware of what the analysts are saying about your own organisation, and pick up on any specific levers that you can identify here.

More Flexible Response to New Business Opportunities

Fast time to market is often an important business driver

Increasingly there is pressure of time on the developers of a new business system to meet a deadline and to get the new system operational quickly so as to grasp a market opportunity. The ability to do so often brings competitive advantage. This 'fast-time-to-market' driver needs to be addressed in your security architecture.

Security architecture helps to promote a fast turnaround on projects

By creating a security architecture in the form of a road map, you prepare the way for meeting these aggressive time targets. This is because a well-conceived security architecture provides modular solutions for new business initiatives, enabling them to be created quickly and reliably, because most of the problem solving has been done up front, even if the construction has not been finished.

Common security services and mechanisms are the key success factors

In a security architecture it is the provision of common security services implemented through common security mechanisms that helps to deliver this quick turnaround. This approach can be sold as a worthwhile investment that will support the business needs for speed.

Development speed must also be traded against assurance – security architecture helps here too

Another point to make is the need to balance speed of development with assurance. The risk of missing the business deadline trades off against the risk of putting into production a poor-quality system that will fail under load and cause embarrassment and interruption to the business. Risk management is never simple, since mitigating one risk almost always increases at least one other risk. This is just another example of this effect. However, the provision of a security architecture allows you to swing the balance further towards the speed end of the scale whilst still maintaining a reasonable level of assurance – thus improving the overall risk management stance.

More Flexible Response to Business Reorganisation

Frequent business reorganisation is commonplace

Most businesses today are likely to experience major organisational changes, brought about by mergers, acquisitions, divestments, joint ventures, outsourcing arrangements or other partnerships of various types.

Monolithic security architecture presents an obstacle, but domain-based security architecture makes reorganisation easy to manage

If the corporate information system security management has been organised on a monolithic basis, then these changes are very difficult to accommodate. If, on the other hand, there is a security architecture in place that is based upon a series of business domains interacting with one another but capable of being managed independently, then there is little difficulty in accommodating these changes. New domains can be added. Existing domains can be removed. Domains can be changed in their scale and scope.

Security domains are a key concept of the methodology

This whole topic of security domains is discussed in detail in Chapters 10 and 11. The application of these concepts in the security architecture delivers huge business benefit in terms of the flexibility to reorganise the enterprise on short notice.

Reduced Operating Costs

Operating costs usually dominate the overall cost model

The operating costs of any business system are likely to be where most of the total cost of ownership is to be found. It is often possible to collect data on the operational costs of legacy systems and to demonstrate how greedy they are in consuming the revenue budget. If you can then make reasonable predictions about the cost savings to be gained by implementing an enterprise-wide security architecture, you have a strong business case to present.

Look out for places where there are high operating costs and where the security architecture can provide large cost savings

Places to look for the high costs are:

- Running the help desk function to support users and solve their operational problems. The more diverse the technology environment becomes, the exponentially greater is this cost, to the extent that with no architectural control, user support becomes impossible at some level of diversity and complexity. Remember the principle described in several earlier chapters – that a major function of architecture is to bring simplicity in place of complexity.

- User administration (adding, deleting, amending user details). In a systems environment in which users are registered on multiple different and distinct systems or applications, the total workload is equal to the work of administering each user registration, multiplied by the number of registrations. An enterprise security architecture that provides a single database of user registrations can therefore deliver huge operational cost savings, as well as improving the overall level of control by reducing the risk of forgotten dormant user accounts.

- System administration – another potentially manually intensive activity, unless the system management architecture has been designed for high levels of automation and centralisation of those functions that need human attention.

Improved Productivity Through Better User Support

Statistics on how long it takes to resolve user problems are often available

Another aspect of running a help desk function is the time it takes to fix a user problem. This is often measured as a mean time to repair (MTTR). The statistics are usually easily available because there is a trouble ticket management system in use that records all incidents, their reporting time and their resolution time.

Use the available statistics to assess how much productive time is lost through user problems

Have a look at how many hours or days are required to resolve the average user problem. Then have a look at the average number of problems per week or month. Then, assuming that the user is unable to carry out certain types of work until the problem is resolved, you can calculate the loss of productive time. You might need to introduce a weighting factor for users who can do some of their work without system access and are therefore not completely unproductive during the downtime.

Make sure the security architecture specifically addresses these productivity losses

Now you should design an architecture that targets this problem, aiming to reduce the complexity and difficulty of resolving user problems. If you can make a convincing argument that the new architecture will bring about such reductions, you have a powerful business case in terms of cost savings, productivity increase and thus return on investment.

The concept of a standardised desktop configuration is often used to optimise the help desk efficiency

To address this specific problem many organisations have moved towards a common operating environment (COE), sometimes also called the standardised desktop. This strategy restricts the hardware and software configuration of user desktop systems to a limited number of instances that are all supported by the help desk. Each specific user system is also registered and the configuration known by the help desk. When a support call comes in, the help desk already knows precisely what the user has configured and can get to the root of the problem much more quickly. The savings on help desk resources and lost user productivity can be enormous.

Case Study: The Operational Cost of User Login

(This refers back to the IBFS case study material in Chapter 4.)

In interview, Brian Jones, Senior Vice President, Marketing and Distribution at IBFS said, 'There is nothing that discourages a user more than the endless layers of user IDs and passwords that many of our systems require. We have had lots of complaints.'

IBFS had not yet established formal measurements and metrics to demonstrate the extent of this problem, and a short consulting exercise discovered a number of valuable measurements that could be analysed effectively to produce a proposal for important 'quick wins'. The primary sources of information were IBFS's system inventory, a range of logs from a variety of platforms and applications, and historical help desk call statistics.

IBFS had a clear business requirement to authenticate users of its systems and services. However, like most large organisations, authentication was achieved through the deployment over a long period of time of a large number of tactical point solutions. Each system and application had its own user naming standards, password rules and authentication protocols, and a specially trained support group with skills in the appropriate technology administered each system independently.

The consultants examined the costs of three different elements of the authentication service:

- – User set-up;

- – Day-to-day login activity;

- – Problem management and support for the authentication service.

Base Information

Total number of IBFS system users = 120,000

Annual staff turnover = 15%

Average number of different user IDs and passwords per user = 5

Number of working hours in business day = 8

Number of working days for each employee or contractor in a business year = 220

User Set-Up

Each year the number of new users (employees, contractors, etc.) at IBFS is 18,000 (15% of 120,000).

These users average five different accounts, therefore the support teams have to create 90,000 new accounts each year.

Administration at IBFS is relatively efficient, so the actual resource effort to set up each account (view request, check authorisation, create the account record, allocate group memberships, and advise the new user of their identity and initial password) takes on average just 120 seconds.

90,000 setups at 120 seconds require an annual resource cost of 3,000 hours.

Login Activity

Taking into account the use of five different identities or passwords on average, inactivity timeouts, and the need in daily working to switch from one application or system to another, the average total number of logins per user on a daily basis was found to be 20.

The average time taken for each login (time to remember the correct identity, the correct password, enter both to the system, and get an acceptance response from it) was calculated at 15 seconds. Again, this is a relatively short time for a large complex environment.

Each day the user community at IBFS spends a total of 10,000 resource-hours just logging in (120,000 users * 20 logins each at 15 seconds per time). That equates to 2,200,000 resource hours per year.

Problem Management

It came as no surprise to find that not every login at IBFS was successful. On average it was found that just 1% of logins failed for some reason. Each of these had to be repeated in order for the user to gain access, and the average time taken for a repeated login (including puzzling over the reason for the failure) was found to be 60 seconds.

This adds another 88,000 resource hours per year spent just logging in.

Total Resource Effort

Excluding the capital expenditure of procuring authentication systems, the time spent in initial deployment of new systems, and the staff costs needed to support existing systems, the cost of using the authentication systems at IBFS was:

User Setup	3,000 resource hours per year
Login Activity	2,200,000 resource hours per year
Repeat Logins	88,000 resource hours per year

TOTAL = 2,291,000 resource hours per year

Based on an average eight-hour day and 220 working days per year, this figure represents more than 1% of the total resource available to the company – just spent logging in!

However, this is not by any means the whole story. Continuity of operations at IBFS is fundamentally important, particularly for the staff in the trading and dealing rooms. Effective productivity was found to an important requirement for all the senior managers interviewed throughout the organisation.

Lost Productivity

Since three failed login attempts in a row will lock the user account, after two failures users are advised to contact the help desk. 10% of those who fail to login at the first attempt also fail on the second attempt, meaning a total of 2,400 failed login reports to the help desk every day.

Due to the importance of continuity of operations at IBFS, the Security Administration team and the help desk team have to comply strictly with the terms of a four-hour service level agreement (SLA) with the business.

Even though some organisations may find four hours to be a very rapid turnaround, it has a potentially devastating effect on the total cost of ownership of the authentication service. This is because of lost productivity: for an employee, access to the system is a prerequisite to performing their job. If they are unable to login for any reason, they can only be doing one of three things – using someone else's ID and password (which renders security totally ineffective), nothing at all (which causes the employee to be totally ineffective), or perhaps even worse, while they are doing nothing productive they are actively and openly complaining about security being a business constraint!

The relevant metrics are:

SETUP: 18,000 user support requests per year, each with a four-hour service time. This means that there is a maximum of 72,000 resource hours of lost productivity.

PROBLEM MANAGEMENT: Each of the 2,400 failed second attempt logins per day is reported to the help desk for resolution. That means a maximum service time of 9,600 hours per day equating to a potential loss in productivity of 2,112,000 resource hours per year.

The total potential impact on productivity (even if help desk meets its performance targets) is 2,184,000 resource hours per year – again more than 1% of the total available resource.

Thus a total of more than 2% of the available human resource was being used (wasted?) on logins and associated support and problem resolution.

The Quick Win

Centralised, single-identity authentication understandably became a major strategy for IBFS. However, a short-term tactical project was initiated within the framework of the strategic solution defined by the conceptual security architecture. Its purpose was to identify those existing elements of the legacy authentication systems that could be quickly integrated and rationalised, if only partially so.

The result was not full-scale secure single sign-on but a reduction in the average number of identities per user from five to just four. At first glance this is not a fantastic result, but the impact was a 20% reduction in the total cost of ownership – more than enough to create an almost instant return on investment for the project and gain visible credibility and support for the security architecture project.

Support for Outsourcing Strategy

Outsourcing ICT operations, including certain security management operations, is popular

Outsourcing of non-core business activities is a popular strategy in many organisations, and ICT operational services are high on the list of potential candidates. The operational management of certain security management activities is one example of the type of service that can be outsourced.

Outsource the operational implementation of security policy – not the setting of security policy

However, outsourcing security management needs care. One has to distinguish between the outsourcing of policymaking and control (which is not recommended) and the outsourcing of purely operational services that are the implementation of policy already made. It is perfectly feasible to outsource such operational services. Managed intrusion detection and reporting is an example of such an outsourced service that enjoys a certain amount of market popularity.

Design the security architecture keeping in mind an outsourcing strategy for security operations

To gain the best business advantage from outsourcing these types of service, it is essential to ensure that the security architecture is suited to these arrangements. The need for business-driven security architecture therefore follows from this primary business driver – to outsource operational service wherever possible. Chapter 10 returns to the subject of security in relation to outsourcing strategy.

Reduced Total Cost of Ownership

Cost saving has already been identified in earlier discussions

Several areas where good security architecture can help to control costs have already been discussed. These include:

- Cost of user administration;

- Cost of system administration;

- Cost of user support and the help desk function;

- Cost of lost productivity through unresolved user security problems;

- Cost of lost productivity through time lost in complex security user interfaces with multiple logins and authentication.

Make sure you identify the potential cost savings specific to your organisation

There are potentially many more areas where you can identify costs associated with security management that is inappropriately designed and operated. Try to build as complete a picture as you can of what types of cost exist and how large they are. Being able to demonstrate in hard figures how the total cost of ownership can be reduced is a powerful argument in support of a security architecture programme.

Leveraging Trusted Business Relationships

Trust is an attribute of relationships. Technical systems are used to protect that trust

Trust (as you will see later in Chapter 10) is an attribute of relationships. It is not something that is created through a technical system (unless the system supports the building of a relationship).

However, technical systems are frequently used to communicate between parties who have already established a level of trust in their relationship, and so the technology must support and protect that trust.

Business is based on trust. Electronic and digital business also need to support and protect that trust

Business is based on trust. To do business with someone else you have to have some level of trust in the other party, otherwise you would not feel comfortable about the business transaction and its possible outcomes. Electronic business or digital business also requires that trust. Applying ICT to the provision of these types of service leverages the trust that you have established by other means – but only if you can guarantee that the trust will be properly supported and guarded through the intervening ICT system.

Key security services are used to provide this protection of trust

This is where the security architecture becomes critical. To protect the trust in a relationship that underpins business that will now be transacted across an electronic network, you need certain security services (such as data confidentiality, data integrity protection, authentication, non-repudiation, etc.). The provision of these services, so as to leverage trust in digital and electronic environments, is what the security architecture sets out to achieve. This is yet another major business driver for the security architecture and therefore also a means to sell its benefits.

Consistent User Experience

The login process is often a source of major frustration through inconsistencies in the user experience

One of the great criticisms of security services in existing business ICT systems is the complexity and variety of the login process. Users of all types, including internal business users, external users in customer or supplier organisations, and even technical support users, all find this to be a problem. It causes great frustration. It also tempts people to subvert or circumvent the security mechanisms because they feel that they obstruct their legitimate business activities. Finally it wastes huge amounts of productive time, both directly through time taken to login, and indirectly through the help desk support that is needed to resolve the plethora of problems that this complexity brings.

Standardising the login user interface is one of the major benefits of a security architecture

One of the key benefits of an enterprise security architecture is the provision of a standardised, consistent user interface for handling security functions (such as login), thus reducing frustration and cost, and making it so much simpler to do business.

Single sign-on offers the most efficient login interface but is controversial with regard to its vulnerability of a single password

At best this single user interface will also offer single sign-on, so as to tackle the problems of multiple passwords to be remembered, the difference in syntax rules for passwords and user identifiers between systems, and the different lifetimes that different systems enforce for password change. There is an argument that suggests that single sign-on is a weakness because a single password gives access to all the user's authorised systems and applications. It is a debate that cannot be objectively resolved – people simply feel differently about these risk issues. However, in the opinion of the authors, the benefits of single sign-on from both a cost perspective and from the perspective of helping a user to look after his or her password properly are easily demonstrated. Your decision on this issue will depend upon whether you consider these benefits are outweighed by the risk of a single password being compromised.

Although multi-factor authentication can solve the technical vulnerability of a single password, it still raises many other significant issues

There is another approach to solving the single password vulnerability – by providing two-factor or even three-factor authentication. This requires the authorised user to be issued with some kind of token device, or to use some biometric technique for proving authenticity, or both. Whilst these approaches solve the technical vulnerability issue regarding passwords, they are even more controversial than the single password. Firstly there is the added cost – of acquiring and deploying additional equipment at the user terminals, and of the tokens to be used. There is also the operational cost of distributing the tokens, reissuing them after their lifecycle expires, and providing help desk support to deal with all the additional user problems created by these added complexities. On top of that, there is the issue of user acceptance – because people do not want extra stuff to carry around in their pockets, and they are also liable to leave the token at home ('Sorry, it's in the pocket of my other suit'). They are also often resistant to new gadgets that increase the complexity of their login procedure.

Getting Sponsorship and Budget

Getting sponsorship depends upon being able to sell the benefits to budget holders

Of course, the key to getting sponsorship and budget is to be able to sell the benefits of the security architecture programme, and hence much of what has been said in the previous section is applicable here. The people to whom you must do this selling are the major budget holders – getting them on side, getting them to sponsor the work.

Key influencers of budget holders are also a good target for you

There is another important type of target to aim at – those who themselves may not own the budget, but who are able to influence the budget holders. Such senior people in the organisation can become the champions of the cause, raising the issues with individual decision makers and at key meetings, perhaps by ensuring that the agenda includes the appropriate items.

Here are some points that might help to persuade those whose support you seek

Bearing in mind what has already been discussed in the previous section, here is a list of some of the most important points that you might consider raising, either with decision makers or with potential key influencers.

- Point out the increasing tendency in the regulatory and legal regime for directors (including non-executive directors) to be held personally liable and accountable for corporate losses where risk management practices are called into question;

- Relate the security and risk control requirements to the overall investment in business ICT systems and associate the security budget with protecting the investment;

- Use the materials discussed in Chapter 6 to create return on investment or return of value models that support your budget requests by showing the payback;

- Draw parallels with other ongoing, non-revenue-producing business functions such as marketing and accounting to ensure that they understand that this is not a one-off project but a lifetime commitment;

- Link the security architecture budget to achieving the business mission and realising the vision and to supporting the organisation's critical success factors;

- Point out any history of positive contributions that demonstrate the value of the security programme;

- Point out any marketing edge or competitive advantage to be gained from the security architecture programme;

- Prepare a business impact analysis to point out the potential damage that can be expected if inappropriate and insufficient information security is applied (see Chapter 9 and Chapter 15 where risk assessment is discussed in detail);

- Prepare an analysis of previous losses;

- Draw attention to best practice statements in external standards and analyst reports and link these to due diligence and corporate governance;

- Leverage the points made in the previous section:

  - Improved productivity;

  - Reduced operating costs;

  - Reduced total cost of ownership;

  - Economies of scale and standardisation;

  - Better, consistent risk management;

  - Improved preparedness for formal audit;

  - Improved corporate governance;

  - Influencing the analyst community;

  - Greater flexibility for reorganisation;

  - More flexibility to meet business opportunities in a timely manner.

- Identify any other specific business benefits that are unique to your organisation (and therefore not covered here) that you can present in support of your budget requests;

- Remember also the rules for influencing opinion or behaviour (earlier in this chapter) and apply them to your communications with those you wish to influence.

Building the Team

The security architecture programme is a team game

A security architecture programme is a team sport, as are most business endeavours! That means you need to give some thought to the right configuration for your team, since different people with different skills play in different positions on the playing field. First of all, it is important to define what is meant by a team.

Definition of a team

A team is two or more employees who are organisationally empowered to:

- Establish objectives;

- Make decisions about how to achieve those objectives;

- Undertake tasks to meet the objectives;

- Be accountable (individually and collectively) for the results.

Team Roles

Belbin's research into team roles provides a very useful model

R Meridith Belbin developed the theory of team roles in management teams more than two decades ago[2] and it has since been adopted and quoted by many others who have followed[3]. In this theory, based upon experimental observations, there are eight different roles defined. Belbin observed that successful teams contain all eight of these roles, and some of the roles can be filled only once. The essentials of Belbin's theory are summarised below, but for more detail you should go to the reference sources[4].

---

[2]R Meredith Belbin, 1981 *Management Teams*, Butterworth Heinemann.
[3]Gordon and Rosemary Jones, 1995, *Teamwork*, Appendix 9.
[4] www.belbin.com

Belbin's Team Roles

- **Plant** – creative, innovative thinker, producing ingenious new ideas and novel strategies. Bright, radical and provocative, but not all their ideas are very practical. They are usually introverted and work alone, thinking intensively. The plant is the ideas engine of the team, although not really team-oriented themselves. Only one plant is needed in the team – having two is counterproductive. A plant will often need a good *co-ordinator* to draw out the best ideas, a good *monitor evaluator* to reject the infeasible ideas and a good *resource investigator* to find ways of making the good ideas work in practice.

- **Co-ordinator** – not necessarily intellectually outstanding but carries the respect of others. Is a broker of harmony and consensus amongst the team members. Draws the team together again and refocuses it on the job in hand if a conflict has divided it. Can be the overall team leader and leads in a quiet, understated way. Dominant without being over-assertive. Goal-oriented and has personal energy and enthusiasm that motivates the team as a whole.

- **Resource Investigator** – not an original ideas person, but very good at picking up other peoples' ideas and making them work in practice. As the name suggests, she or he is good at looking for resources beyond the immediate team, probing for information wherever it can be found. A resource investigator has strong interpersonal skills – sociable, friendly and fairly extroverted. Thinks on his or her feet and is adaptable, finding ways to make things work when failure looms. Also an explorer, an improviser and a negotiator.

- **Monitor Evaluator** – intelligent, discerning and objective. Capable of resolving debates and conflicts between the innovative members by showing a dispassionate attitude and the ability to weigh the facts objectively and decide upon which is the best of competing ideas. Not themselves an achiever but an excellent judge. Intellectually stronger than the *co-ordinator* and therefore able to evaluate the ideas of others.

- **Shaper** – highly motivated, a high achiever with a lot of nervous energy. May be the team leader but in a very different leadership style to a *co-ordinator*. The *co-ordinator* is highly moral, whereas the shaper is so strongly goal-oriented that he or she will reach these by whatever means it takes, legitimate or not. Aggressively extroverted, single-minded, impatient and often critical of others if they appear to be obstructive. Personifying the 'JDI'[5] culture. Having more than one shaper in a team is usually counterproductive, because they are likely to experience interpersonal relationship problems between them.

- **Team Worker** – hard-working, conscientious, good communicator, trusting, sensitive, caring, putting group objectives and success above personal ambition. Perceptive and diplomatic, and interested in

---

[5] JDI – 'just do it'

maintaining a smooth-running harmonious team – hence playing an important role to help smooth over conflicts between other team members of different personality types. Can be the team leader and often makes a good senior manager, especially if more junior line managers are *shapers*.

- **Completer-Finisher** – pays attention to detail, tying up loose ends. Hard-working and conscientious. Consistent and self-disciplined. Needed in the final stages of a project when the bright-ideas people have gotten bored and want to move on to the next bright idea. Tenacious, even to a fault when they refuse to give up when a project should be abandoned.

- **Implementer** – similar to a *completer-finisher* in personality. Attentive to detail and well-organised, preferring order and routine. Capable of directing other team workers, implementing the work others have devised and designed. Tending to be emotionally well-controlled. Less anxious about detail than the *completer-finisher* and more focused on strategic success, with a high capacity for hard work that often means they are left to carry the load that others find too heavy.

Research shows that teams based objectively on these roles are more successful than those selected by subjective intuition

Perhaps one of the most startling outcomes of Belbin's research was that during the later experiments, when the role types had already been identified, the researchers would gather a group of people together, and once the group had got to know one another, they would ask them to self-select their best team – the strongest team to perform a competitive team task in the experiment. Once the group had selected its own A-team, the researchers would select the B-team from those who remained, using their analysis of role types to configure this second team. In the team competition that followed, the so-called B-team always won!

Subjective selection of team members does not usually produce the right mix of skills

The problem with picking teams is that people tend to pick people who are like them and to whom they are socially (or even sexually) attracted. Unfortunately, this does not result in a balanced team according to Belbin's theory. You need to bear these things in mind when configuring a team for any type of project, including your security architecture programme. The benefits of getting this right can be enormous, as can the costs of getting it wrong!

Examples of poor team configuration are common

A quick run through your own past experiences and a look around you at your place of work will probably reveal that these theories are much neglected in practice. If you want to make a difference, this is one way you can almost certainly succeed.

Teambuilding

In knowledge-based working, team members must be empowered and must buy in to the team objectives

In the traditional industrial economy the model for leading and supervising teams tends to have been one of giving instructions and having those instructions carried out. In the knowledge-based economy, and in particular amongst those who work in a knowledge-creating environment, this approach is unlikely to work. Key words that differentiate the new style of teamwork are 'buy-in' and 'empowerment'. The team members must understand the objectives of the team and must become stakeholders in the results (hence the term 'buy-in').

Empowerment must include some risk-taking and incorporate a tolerance of mistakes

Empowerment is the delegation of authority to input new ideas, make decisions and execute them. It involves trust and encouragement from the team leader and a tolerance of mistakes. Mistakes should be owned by the team as a whole and used as a joint learning experience – the characteristic of a 'no blame' culture, where individuals feel safe enough to take some well-judged risks without fear of retribution.

Team development has four identifiable phases

Team formation is not an instantaneous thing, because teams grow into cohesive units through organic processes. BW Tuckman[6] identified the four phases of team development as 'forming, storming, norming, performing'.

- Forming – getting acquainted, understanding the objectives, establishing ground rules for operating, each seeing his or her place in the group;

- Storming – having interpersonal conflicts, competing for attention and influence, reconciling divergent interests;

- Norming – becoming cohesive, developing a team identity and team spirit, sharing, cooperating and collaborating, where team goals override individual considerations;

- Performing – experiencing strong team loyalties and working with a high degree of creativity and productivity on the tasks in hand.

Effective teams have certain characteristics

An effective team is most often characterised by:

- Joint accountability and tolerance of individual mistakes – a 'no blame' culture;

- Deep sense of involvement in and loyalty to the team effort – team members feed off each other's enthusiasm;

- Consensus about key decisions and a joint commitment to those decisions;

- Clear group consensus about the goals and objectives;

- Conflicts being brought into the open and dealt with;

- Alternative ways of thinking and new ideas being welcomed and evaluated with an open mind;

- Leadership associated with respect and confidence from the rest of the team.

Team dynamics are nothing new, but they will impact the success of the security architecture programme

The discussion here has summarised much of the well-known conventional wisdom on team behaviour. Of course there is nothing specific here to a security architecture programme, but if you fail to address these team issues, then your security architecture programme will suffer because of it.

Getting Started: Fast Track™ Workshops

Getting everyone started and ensuring their buy-in can be challenging

One of the challenges that you face in the early days of an enterprise security architecture programme is that it is quite difficult to explain to people what you are planning to do. Such a programme is a big thing and is hard to explain in a three-minute elevator pitch[7]. Yet, to launch the programme you need to gain buy-in from a number of key players.

You could use this book – get everyone to read it!

One way to help them to understand what you are planning is to give them this book to read (not your copy, don't be a cheapskate; get them their own copies!) However, reading this book may not appeal to all the people you need to get on your side. One thing that the authors have done successfully in a number of organisations is to run Fast Track™ workshops.

---

[6] BW Tuckman, 1965, *Psychological Bulletin*, 63, 384-399.

[7] The theory goes that if you have a pet project or idea, you must always have ready the three minute explanation and pitch for support, so that if you meet the CEO in the elevator and he or she says 'How are things going', you have roughly three minutes before the elevator opens and the CEO gets out, in which time you try to explain your idea and win their support.

The authors have successfully used Fast Track™ workshops to overcome this challenge

The workshops themselves are usually scheduled over a contiguous five-day period – a single week, starting Monday morning and finishing Friday afternoon. During the workshops a certain amount of training material is presented – explaining much of what is written in this book. However, the most important part of the activity is that after each presentation of a section of the material, the Fast Track™ participants carry out a workshop exercise to apply the material in the context of their own organisation.

Fast Track™ gets the key players to experience every aspect of the programme in a short time

They are beginning to work on the actual security architecture programme, but only a little work is done in each area. Over the entire week they get exposed to every aspect but only to get a taste of what is involved. Usually this work also reveals that much more research is needed to collect the definitive information about the organisation and its business requirements or to bring the design process to useful conclusions.

The workshops are based on small syndicate groups

Typically there will be a group of between 10 and 16 people. Often the workshop sessions are organised around small syndicate groups (say three groups of four) that each tackle a different but related aspect of the work. After (say) an hour of brainstorming in the syndicate groups, each group then reports back to the assembled full group. The work is done using flipcharts, and these are used for the presentations. The presentations often promote useful debate amongst the others who were not in that specific syndicate group, and so everyone gets some exposure to all of the work done.

Each topic is treated in turn

Then the group moves on to another presentation from the facilitator (consultant) followed by another syndicate workshop and so on through the week.

Some types of people such as senior managers attend only a restricted subset of the workshops

Because the areas of work are of interest to different groups around the organisation, the overall workshop is structured so that different groups attend different sessions. For example, there are some of the sessions in which the facilitators want to involve some senior managers. These sessions address the strategic business vision and how this drives the business requirements for security. This is usually done on Day 1, and may be a couple of hours, or half a day or perhaps a whole day, depending upon how much time you can get the senior leadership people to commit to it.

Every Fast Track™ is tailored to the specific needs of the client organisation

Each Fast Track™ seminar is usually tailored to the specific needs of the organisation, and this varies because each will be at a different stage of development when the seminar begins and will have different ideas about scope. It is also essential not to start cold on the first day of the workshops, so the overall package that Fast Track™ delivers begins with five days of consulting up front so that the facilitators can understand the specific requirements. This includes tailoring the workshop programme and making sure that it addresses the issues that most interest the client organisation.

There is a post-workshop report that summarises the output from the workshops

There is then a follow-up of five more consulting days after the workshops during which the facilitators take all the output from the intensive week's activities and write it up in an organised tidy format to present back to the client organisation. This post-workshop report includes a draft project plan that was developed during the final session on the Friday afternoon, which sets out the future programme of work, with resources allocated and some estimates of durations and target dates.

The objective of Fast Track™ is to create a realistic programme plan

The objective of the whole package is to introduce the organisation to the SABSA® approach and methodology, to help the key players to appreciate the scope of the work to be done and to help them make realistic plans for taking the programme forward.

The outline description of a Fast Track™ package is as follows:

Prior to the On-Site Programme

Your business is unique in its objectives, functions and processes, infrastructure and culture, customer and user expectations, and the way that it handles information and information systems. It therefore has unique requirements for security that must be met by the security architecture in a dynamic, flexible, scaleable and usable manner.

To maximise the benefit of the on-site **Fast Track**™ program, the consultants must:

- Gain an initial understanding of the organisation, its goals and objectives, through research and an analysis of documents supplied in advance by the **Fast Track**™ host;

- Gain an initial understanding, through an analysis of documents supplied in advance, of the current security and technology environment or the position of any architecture program that has already commenced;

- Gain an initial understanding of the roles of all of the proposed **Fast Track**™ participants and their objectives;

- Draft, prioritise and agree on the specific **Fast Track**™ objectives and deliverables;

- Draft, structure and agree on the five-day program and its detailed contents;

- Compile and customise all presentations for delivery during the five-day on-site program;

- Design and produce appropriate detailed workshops for delivery during the five-day on-site program.

During the On-Site Program

As development of the outline architecture progresses, each **Fast Track**™ workshop reveals important new issues, tasks and priorities. Just like the security architecture itself, **Fast Track**™ must be sufficiently flexible and dynamic to deliver to the specific needs of its participants. This requirement introduces a real-time consulting element to the program. To meet it the facilitating consultants must be prepared to invest resource long after the participants' working day has ended in addition to delivering the agreed five-day program during working hours. Tasks may include:

- Customisation of planned presentations to meet new objectives;

- Development of new or replacement presentations to be introduced into the program;

- Customisation of participant workshops to meet new or refined objectives;

- Development of new or replacement participant workshops to be introduced into the program;

- End-of-day status meetings to review progress against objectives and to plan mechanisms that must be introduced to meet altered priorities or objectives;

- Review workshop output and document key architecture components.

After the On-Site Program

On completion of the on-site program, work must begin on a **Fast Track**™ report that summarises the output from the program and provides sound independent consulting advice on appropriate next steps. The post-program deliverables will vary according to the focus and structure of the on-site program, but they may include items such as:

- Documented summary of the business case for security architecture development activities;

- Documented summary of a plan to collect and verify the full set of security business requirements;

- Documented summary of the outline presentations and draft reports developed during the on-site program, and advice on progressing these to definitive and detailed architecture plans;

- Summary of existing physical, component, and operational architecture and a high-level gap analysis against stated strategic architectural requirements;

- Advice on a means to integrate the security architecture with any existing or in-progress developments of business or technology architecture;

- High-level implementation and migration strategy;

- Summary of key performance indicators (KPI) for security;

- Documented draft project plan to communicate key tasks, milestones, and future deliverables, together with any key dependencies revealed from an analysis of the on-site program;

- Documented draft project plan summary illustrating what is needed to complete the security architecture, when it is needed and what resources are required.

If you want to explore this approach, please make contact

If you are planning to go ahead with a security architecture programme and you think that the Fast Track™ approach would be useful way to start, then please get in touch with the authors[8]. They will be pleased to advise you.

---

[8] http://www.sabsa.org/

Programme Planning and Management

Professional programme and project management is an essential ingredient for success

There is no intention to reproduce here a tutorial on project and programme management. However, it is worth saying that this activity is something to be taken seriously and something that needs a professional approach. Professional project management requires attention to detail, a very logical mind and the assertiveness to say 'No, these estimates are unrealistic' when required. One thing is certain – without a proper project plan the estimates for both time and budget will be way off the actuals. You are recommended not to attempt to cut corners on this aspect of programme management.

Being a good team leader does not necessarily imply good project management skills

Not all team leaders are good at formal project management, even though they are excellent team leaders. Consider what has already been said about team roles and Belbin's theory (earlier in this chapter). A Shaper may well be the energetic, charismatic leader who drives this security architecture programme along. Spending hours of detailed work on a project plan and maintaining that plan in up-to-date condition is not generally what one expects a Shaper to do – so, if you are the leader and you fit the Shaper profile most closely, make sure you delegate the task of formal project planning and resource management to someone whose skills profile is appropriate.

Collecting the Information You Need

You will need to collect certain information about the organisation

There are two major sets of information that you will need to collect:

- Information about the business;

- Information about technical infrastructure, systems and applications.

Information about the Business

Collecting information on the business is critical to the SABSA® process

Collecting information about the business is critical to the success of the entire SABSA® process. In the experience of the authors there are two main approaches that can be used:

- Structured interviews with business managers;

- Reference to existing materials.

Of these, the first is by far the most useful and the most productive.

Structured Interviews with Business Managers

You need to get access to the most senior managers that you can reach

The interviews should be with the most senior business managers to whom you can get access. To achieve this some pre-selling will be needed. Their first response when asked for a meeting will be along the lines of 'Why can't you see my technical manager?' You first have to convince them that it really is them with whom you need to have a discussion and that you need to explore what they perceive to be the most significant business risks and the most pressing needs to protect corporate information. You must make it plain that you do not want to ask technical questions (and having made such a promise – do not ask any!).

Use a senior champion to help secure the interviews with the right people

By far the easiest way to get these interviews arranged is to use the influence of a champion who is a peer or even a more senior person than the target interviewee. This is where the role of the influencer that was discussed in an earlier section of this chapter really comes into its own.

A senior management interview is a great opportunity

An interview with a very senior manager is a superb opportunity, but it carries some risks too. The main opportunities are:

- To build a relationship with a senior executive who will, through this relationship, become a friend and an ally;

- To sell the benefits of the security architecture programme at a senior level, developing buy-in, support and endorsement, and perhaps recruiting another champion to carry your flag and defend your position;

- To gain real insight into the strategic direction of the organisation and how that will drive business requirements for information security;

- To ensure that you are hearing business requirements from key decision makers, and thus getting a true picture, especially when it comes to looking to the future of the organisation and its upcoming business opportunities and strategies;

- To understand the risk issues that really concern the senior management and to get some perspective on the relative ranking of risks;

- To validate the input gathered at less senior levels to ensure that what you are being told at those levels really is true, and not just wishful thinking;

- To communicate to senior management that you are approaching this programme from a business perspective, that you understand business issues, and that the value proposition is based upon providing business benefit. Once they understand that this is your philosophy they should be much more supportive and much more willing to discuss these matters with you.

It also carries some risks

Some of the main risks are:

- Time will be restricted – you may only get half an hour, so you will need to be focused on presenting your case succinctly and getting the information you need, all in a short time.

- If you stray outside the domain of interest of the interviewee you will damage your reputation and you will find it difficult to get another meeting.

- Such meetings tend to be a one-shot opportunity – if you blow it, there are rarely second chances.

- You may raise expectations that you cannot later deliver. Be careful not to do this. Make sure that you underline the benefits to be gained from using a high-quality process without promising specific outcomes that you cannot possibly predict.

- Involving senior management brings with it visibility and exposure to their scrutiny. This is good when things go well but can be irritating when they go badly.

- You may speak in terms and concepts that are not understood. You need to prepare carefully to ensure that this does not happen. Speak in the language and concepts that are familiar to the interviewee. (Refer back to the earlier discussion on how to succeed in influencing people).

Here are some ideas on the types of questions to use in a senior management interview

So, what questions should you ask of a senior manager? Once again it is difficult to be prescriptive. You will need to tailor your interview plan according to the specific needs of your own organisation. However, here are some ideas that might help you:

- I want to understand your role as fully as I can. What are the four or five bullet points that describe your management responsibilities in the organisation?

- Who are your key advisors, whose opinion you are most likely to seek when considering a decision?

- What are the mission and the vision for your particular part of the organisation?

- What are the main risks facing this organisation as a whole and your part of it in particular, and how do think those risks can best be mitigated and managed?

- Is there anything that keeps you awake at night – any inhibitors or constraints to achieving your mission or things that you are really anxious about that should be addressed – perhaps through this security development programme?

- What do you expect to be the development of the organisation and its business over the next one to five years, and how far ahead does your strategic planning window stretch?

- What will be the main factors influencing this industry and this organisation over the period of the strategic planning window?

- To what extent do you think that reorganisations, mergers, acquisitions and joint ventures will characterise the future landscape of this business?

- What new technologies do you see coming over the horizon that will have major impacts on this business?

- In particular the Internet and its associated technologies continue to evolve and develop – how do you see this affecting this business?

- How do you think technology will change the way that we work and the way that we do business?

- It is often said that information is power. Do you think this is true and if so, how powerful is information in this business?

- If a hostile investigative journalist were digging around for dirt on this organisation, how would you feel? Is there anything that would worry you? Anything that you need to be especially careful about?

Some questions can be very sensitive	This last question may draw a blank response, because you may not be sufficiently trusted to know the true answer!
The questions here will provide you with a general idea of the type of approach to take	These questions should give you some idea of the general tenor of the questions to ask, even if they are not exactly the right questions for you. The key to a successful senior management interview is to ask only about the areas that will be of direct interest to this person in doing their job – so keep things at a high level and leave the interviewee scope to reply at whatever level of detail they choose. Use the replies to frame the next question, picking up on areas of interest and backing off areas of disinterest.
Encourage an open response	Remember that the primary purpose of the interview is to hear the views and concerns of the interviewee. It can be difficult to gain access to such senior people, and the time frame of the interview is likely to be short. Maximise the time available for the interviewee to talk by minimising the length of your own questions and comments. Questions should be open in order to encourage valuable detail rather than simple yes or no responses.

Validate your understanding of the information provided

The information you receive is of primary importance to the development of the contextual business requirements for the architecture. Any misunderstanding that is not corrected but allowed to filter downwards through the architecture model will result in components and operational processes that do not meet the real needs of the business. The information received (and your interpretation of what that means for security) must be properly validated. There are two ways in which this can be achieved. The first is to provide the interviewee with a copy of the interview notes or the initial draft of the business requirements that result from the full set of interviews, or both, and ask them to verify the contents.

Executives and managers can have conflicting requirements

The second approach is to hold a brief consensus-building workshop based on the initial draft of the requirements document. This approach is particularly useful if the senior managers have differing requirements and priorities – as they often do. In the experience of the authors it is not unusual for a team of executives to have almost unanimous views that turn out to be incorrect.

Case Study: A US-based eLearning Provider

During a consulting assignment to develop the contextual security architecture for this client, the consultants interviewed all eight members of the executive board.

In asking a question about the potential impact of a specific risk scenario, seven of these executives believed it to be a negligible risk that required no action. To the eighth, however, it was a catastrophic scenario, but there had never been any apparent reason for him to discuss his specialist knowledge of this scenario with his colleagues because he assumed they understood the risk as he did.

A brief, facilitated consensus workshop allowed the consultants to give this executive a platform to discuss the issue, and it resulted in enterprise-wide consensus of high-priority actions to be taken within the security architecture program.

Understand the best way to record interview results

Another important challenge is that of interview logistics. Particularly in situations where there are a potentially large number of stakeholder interviews, the formatting and recording of the interview results is critical. Information must be recorded quickly so that interpretation and meaning is not lost over time while additional interviews take place. It must also be recorded and stored in a consistent format so that comparisons can be made and patterns determined.

The skill of the interviewer is critical – make sure you use on-the-job training to develop these skills

In the end it will be the skill of the interviewer that makes or breaks the success of the interview. In this respect there is no substitute for practical experience. Here then is an opportunity to develop the skills of more junior members of the team by conducting the interviews two-handed. One, more-experienced interviewer, to ask the questions, parry the challenges, keep the momentum going and be quick on the feet as the direction twists and turns, and a second, less-experienced interviewer to act as scribe, take detailed notes and say very little, but to watch, listen and learn.

Some senior interviewees can be quite hostile

You must also be ready for the fairly hostile interviewee. The authors have had personal experience of this, and this next case study is a recounting of one such personal experience:

Case Study: An Experience of Interviewing the Chief Financial Officer of a Global Materials Manufacturer

We got stuck in traffic and were several minutes late for the 10:00 am interview. He made it quite clear that we had a drop-dead limit of 11:00 am because he had a teleconference arranged for that time. His office was large, nicely furnished and very tidy. His desk was enormous, highly polished and completely clear. A personal assistant scurried in and out, radiating efficiency. This was a man so clearly 'in charge' that it was quite intimidating in itself.

We apologised for being late, accepted a coffee from the PA and introduced ourselves. Another manager in the company had arranged the interview (we were there as consultants) and some excellent pre-selling had informed the CFO why we were there and what we wanted to discuss. He was very pleasant but blunt. He sat back in his chair and said:

'I can't see any need for information security in this firm. There is nothing secret about our business. The most competitive thing is the price list, and we all find out each other's prices as soon as they come out anyway. I don't know why we just don't all fax each other a price list and save ourselves a lot of trouble.'

Hmmm. This was going to be tough. We hesitated just a little, and then we took up the challenge. It's a long time ago now and the exact details are blurred, but somehow we turned it around. Maybe we asked the question about the hostile investigative journalist and 'How do you feel about him or her being able to get to anything he or she likes?' We certainly talked about publishing stock-market-sensitive information on company performance and the demands of the financial regulators. However, the trigger that really caught his imagination was when we discussed integrity and reliability of financial records and how systems downtime can increase 'debtor days'.

It was perhaps one of our finest moments, because when his watch alarm went off at 10:55, he didn't make us go till dead on 11:00. By that time he had agreed that information security was really important for the firm. He had also given us a considerable amount of useful information about the real business requirements, and he had become a strong supporter of the cause.

It just shows the huge benefits that can result from an interview with the most senior executives. Opportunities like this are absolute gold dust.

Reference to Existing Materials

Existing documents and reports can be a good source of material, especially the annual report and accounts

There are many documents that a company produces that contain much of what you want to know. If you cannot get access to senior managers directly, then try to get access to what they have written. One good place to look is the annual report and accounts of the company, where you will find out what the senior management team has written for the benefit of the shareholders, much of which is very useful in the context of your work.

Other existing documents are also potentially very useful

Apart from the Annual Report and Accounts, other possible sources include:

- Audit reports, both internal and external;

- Press interviews and reports;

- Analyst reports;

- Consultant reports;

- Mission statements, vision statements and associated support documentation;

- Strategic vision documents;

- Previous risk assessments;

- Industry reports on legal and regulatory drivers.

In your organisation there will be other specific sources that you can identify

These are just some of the sources you might consult. In your own organisation and in your specific industry you will have a much more precise idea as to where to look for this information.

Collecting Technical Information

Technical information is relatively easy to collect

The collection of technical information is relatively straightforward, provided that you ensure that you refer to authoritative sources. This means:

- Interviews and brainstorming workshops with technical managers;

- Reference to current technical documentation.

The relationship with technical managers is also significant in getting agreement about solutions

There is little more to say on collection techniques since the discussion has covered the basics of interviewing in the section above with regard to collecting business information. However, your relationship with the technical managers has much more significance in terms of obtaining their buy-in and consensus agreement about the technical solutions that you will synthesise later in the security architecture programme. The next section addresses the approach that you might take to this community of technical managers.

Getting Consensus on the Conceptual Architecture

You will need to gain consensus on the conceptual security architecture

Getting consensus agreement to the conceptual security architecture is a major milestone in the programme. You will have collected all your information on the business requirements, analysed it and presented it in the form of the contextual security architecture. Now you synthesise a conceptual view of what the solutions will look like – the conceptual security architecture.

The clear division of lifecycle phases is to emphasise this point

One of the reasons for a clear phase definition between the Strategy and Concept and Design phases of the SABSA® Lifecycle (see Chapter 7, Figure 7-2) is that this is a point at which you must obtain sign-off from the technical management community before you proceed to more detailed design work. You cannot proceed beyond this point without the support and buy-in of this group.

You must build and maintain strong relationships with the key players

The way to tackle this is to build strong relationships with these people as early as possible. You may already have such relationships in place, but even if you do, you need to prepare the ground for this sign-off phase. A series of meetings with the key players will enable you to collect technical information or at least find out where the detailed authoritative sources are to be found.

Find out what makes them tick

Far more important, these meetings will allow you to engage these individuals as early as possible on the subject of security architecture. You can find out their general approach and opinions:

- Do they have any concerns?

- Are they pre-disposed for or against any particular approaches?

- What will you need to do to get their agreement to the conceptual security architecture?

- What level of influence do they expect to have?

- What type of involvement in the process do they expect?

- Who are their key allies and opponents?

- What specific 'buttons' do they have that you will need to 'push'?

Foresee difficulties and manage expectations

This type of intelligence information will help you to foresee any conflicts and difficulties before they arise. It also provides you with the opportunity to manage the expectations of the technical managers, without whose support your security architecture programme will falter.

Gain consensus through open forum workshops

When you get to the point of synthesising the conceptual architecture, you will need to involve this group actively. The best way is to arrange workshop sessions where you can present the ideas that you have, expose them to open debate, get all the inputs from all perspectives – systems development, procurement, operations management, etc. – and then hopefully through those discussions reach a consensus. Without such consensus the security architecture is likely to remain a paper exercise.

Pre-selling the ideas ensures success at the workshops

Pre-workshop preparation is also critical. It is dangerous to go to any open forum of the type just described without a clear idea of what all the players in the room think beforehand. So, you need to pre-sell your ideas. Make sure that you continue to leverage strong relationships with each person individually. Have one-to-one meetings to expose your ideas and get input. Work offline to overcome objections and difficulties and present new versions, until you are fairly confident that when you get them all in the same room for the workshop, the discussion is a mere formality.

Politics and diplomacy are necessary to your success

You may not like it, but politics and diplomacy are essential to your success in a complex programme of this type.

Architecture Governance and Compliance

Security architecture is a strategic road map that should be followed by all projects

The purpose of a security architecture is to provide a road map to be followed by individual projects serving individual business initiatives. The architecture provides the overall strategic direction across the enterprise, and the projects follow that direction. They are also the vehicles by which certain pieces of strategic infrastructure get constructed.

To be successful, there must be a way of ensuring that all projects comply with the architecture

It is all very well having a strategic enterprise security architecture, but if nobody ever takes any notice of it, then it is all wasted time and effort. This leads to the subject of governance, compliance and enforcement. How do you make the projects comply with the architecture?

Controlling budget sign-off is a good tool to ensure compliance

One of the key levers that can be pulled here is budget approval. If you don't comply, you don't get budget approval! That still needs a mechanism to approve both the architectural standards and the compliance of individual projects with those standards. Such a mechanism can be created through an Architecture Board.

The Architecture Board

The Architecture Board is the mechanism by which compliance is governed

The Architecture Board is a kind of steering committee, ensuring that the overall direction for architecture in the organisation is set and that individual parts of the organisation follow the strategic direction. It is more likely to be a success if the remit of the board is all of ICT architecture rather than just security architecture, since it is difficult to see how the board may gain sufficient power and teeth otherwise.

The Architecture Board approves the architecture and approves projects as being compliant

The Architecture Board has two main functions:

- To approve architectural standards, road maps and guidelines and to ensure that these have been developed with the strategic interests of the business uppermost in priority;

- To review individual project proposals and designs to ensure that they are compliant with the architectural standards set by the board, and to approve budget for those projects only if the compliance criteria set by the board are met.

Here are some ideas on membership of the Architecture Board

The potential members of the Architecture Board include (but are not restricted to):

- At least one senior business manager;

- The head of ICT services;

- The head of ICT operations;

- The head of ICT systems development;

- The chief ICT architect (if such a position exists);

- The most senior member of the information security expert team;

- The head of internal audit;

- A senior representative of the finance team who has authority to control budget sign-off.

A possible substitute for the Architecture Board is an ISO17799-style steering committee

If there is no possibility of an overarching Architecture Board for all of ICT, then it may be possible to have some regulation through an Information Security Management Steering Committee of the type suggested in ISO17799.

Design Authority

The Design Authority is a single person accountable to the Architecture Board for compliance of a given project

The Design Authority role is usually vested in a single person, such as the chief ICT architect or the project director. This person takes ultimate responsibility for ensuring the integrity of the overall design and of the design process through which it has been produced. Since, for any given project, the design must be compliant with the architectural standards, it is the Design Authority who is accountable directly to the Architecture Board for compliance. Thus the Design Authority is an important player in the overall architecture governance process. This person will attend Architecture Board meetings to present items relevant to the project, but otherwise may or may not be a permanent member of the board.

Architecture Maintenance

Despite the durability of an architecture, changes will be needed

Although architecture is a relatively static thing, being a standard that is durable and pervasive across many projects, inevitably it must also live and breathe in the real world, and in the real world things are constantly changing.

Business requirements change over time

Your security architecture is driven by business needs, and these change over time. One of the aims of your architecture is to build in sufficient flexibility to handle unforeseen business requirements, but after some time it will become necessary to rework certain aspects of the architecture based upon new and emerging business drivers.

New technologies emerge and need to be integrated because of new benefits they bring

New technologies emerge too, some of them being more successful than others. In some cases the emergence of technology itself changes the direction of business, the Internet being a prime example. So, from time to time there will have been sufficient technological change to force you to rethink your architectural decisions. This is especially true at the component layer where new products and tools come onto the market offering new solutions. In some cases the changes are so major that they may well affect your conceptual architecture, by providing the means to realise concepts that were previously infeasible with the technology available at that time[9].

Practical operating experience also exposes flaws and suggests new approaches

Practical operating experience is also a major driver of change. Architectural and design decisions that were taken on a theoretical basis are then tested in real-life operations, and sometimes they turn out to be flawed. When this happens, you need to revisit the issue and maybe change the overall guiding architecture to correct the problem.

Architecture maintenance should be under the governance of the Architecture Board

So, you need a process and a mechanism by which the architecture can be reviewed and maintained. The Architecture Board has a major role to play here, since it is this body that has responsibility for approving the architectural standards. This includes approving changes to those standards. Thus, when a change is proposed, it should be documented, with the business case, and brought to the Architecture Board for approval. If the changes involve significant budget expenditure, this too falls within the remit of the board.

Long-Term Confidence of Senior Management

In Chapter 7 under the section on Logical Security Architecture development there was a brief mention in a single bullet point of delivering 'quick wins' to demonstrate continuous value. This is actually a major issue in managing the expectations of senior managers and maintaining their confidence over a prolonged period of time.

The authors of this book have had much experience of working with clients on enterprise security architecture development. Not all experiences are good in the sense that a bad experience is unpleasant. However, all experiences, both good and bad are good for you since they teach you valuable lessons. Here is one lesson that the authors learned some time ago through a bad experience.

Case Study: Senior Management Losing Its Religion

The client was a large corporate organisation. The information security manager had heard our description of our methods and was converted to our Religion. He became a Believer and we were very pleased. He engaged us to do some preparatory work on consulting with 'The Business' and the results were encouraging. This exercise enabled us to assemble an initial report that described a lot of things from a contextual security architecture – reasons why this organisation needed security from a truly business perspective.

The knowledge gained from this exercise was then used to put together a presentation to the senior executive team – the CEO and his immediate reports. Our sponsor meanwhile had been doing a lot of internal selling, preparing the ground, winning support and ensuring that when we made the presentation to the CEO and his executive team, they would be ready for it. The whole plan thus far worked well and was well-executed. We gave the presentation and they were impressed. In fact they bought the concept and gave it their support. The

---

[9]The recently announced developments in hardware processor architecture from Intel may well be in this category – discussed in more detail in Chapter 13.

budget was created and programme was planned. We had converted them to our Religion and now they too were Believers.

And so off we went to get on with The Work. It took a long time and we were making steady progress, but the costs were racking up as time went by. We made a fatal mistake. We did not go back and preach our Religion. We did not tell of the Miracles that we had performed. We did not carry the Good News back to the CEO and executives. They could see the costs in the management accounts, but they could not see any benefit. They lost their Religion, they stopped being Believers and they pulled the plug on The Work.

Quick Wins

You must maintain the momentum of senior management support

The moral of this sorry tale is simple: you must build into your programme a series of deliverables that deliver visible, tangible benefit to the business. Some people call these quick wins or early victories. They must come on a regular basis at intervals of no more than two months, preferably less. When they come you must organise an internal public relations programme to ensure that all of the senior management sponsors, supporters and critics alike receive the good news. By doing this you maintain the momentum that you built up at the beginning, and you maintain the confidence of the senior management team that they made the correct decision in approving this programme of work.

No flow of deliverables will lead to loss of confidence

If you fail to deliver a series of identifiable benefits at regular intervals, as in the case study, then as far as the senior management team is concerned you are spending money and nothing is happening. No business benefits are being delivered. Their confidence wanes and eventually, as the authors found to their cost, they lose all confidence and stop the work.

Manage expectations

Managing senior managers' expectations and keeping their confidence buoyant are key tasks that you must not neglect if you want to succeed.

To Summarise: Managing the Security Architecture Programme

There are many political and cultural issues that need to be addressed if your security architecture programme is to succeed.

You must sell the benefits of your security architecture programme at all levels of the enterprise but especially at the senior management levels. To do this effectively you need to understand the fundamentals of how best to influence people and change their attitudes, opinions and behaviour. You also need to point out the specific benefits that will appeal to the senior management team whose support you need.

The reasons for selling the ideas to senior management are to gain their support and to get their sponsorship and budget approval. You can do this directly, by addressing the budget holders, or you can do it by winning the support and championship of key influencers, who will then influence budget holders on your behalf.

The security architecture programme is a team event, and you should give due consideration to the configuration of your team, the skills profiles of the individual team members and the team dynamics. There are many research studies and team models that can help you with this, including Belbin's Theory of team roles.

Sometimes it can be difficult to get started on a major security architecture programme because it is difficult to tell others what it will involve. One approach successfully used by the authors is to run Fast Track™ workshops to kick start the process.

Programme planning and management is something described in detail in many other texts and hence is beyond the scope of this book. However, getting this part right is an important success factor for the security architecture programme.

To collect the business-related information that you will need there are two main alternatives: interviewing key business managers face to face (which is the best approach) or referring to existing materials, especially those written by the key business managers and executives.

It will always be important to gain consensus on the conceptual security architecture before any detailed design activities begin. To achieve this you need to address the issues of politics and diplomacy amongst the technical management team, through building relationships with them as individuals and through design workshops in which the key players participate.

The security architecture will have little value unless individual projects adhere to the architectural standards. This can be achieved through a suitable architecture governance process, using the mechanism of an Architecture Board that approves projects and enforces compliance through control of project budgets.

Another function of the Architecture Board is to oversee the architecture maintenance process, and to approve changes to the architecture as and when these become necessary through significant changes in either the business need or the technical solutions available.

Finally, a critical success factor for a security architecture programme is maintaining the long-term confidence of the senior management who have sponsored the work. They need to see frequent benefits being delivered in the form of quick wins and it is essential to organise the flow of deliverables on this basis.

Part 2: Strategy and Planning

This part of the book is entitled *Strategy and Planning*. It is about how you develop the contextual security architecture and the conceptual security architecture. First take a look at what exactly is meant by these words, starting with some dictionary definitions to help you understand the language being used.

strat+e·gy *n. pl.* ·gies 1. the art or science of the planning and conduct of a war. 2. the practice or art of using stratagems, as in politics, business, etc. 3. a plan or stratagem. [C17: from French *stratégie*, from Greek stratēgia function of a general: see **STRATAGEM**]

strat·a+gem *n.* a plan or trick, esp. one to deceive an enemy. [C15: ultimately from Greek strat‾egos a general, from stratos an army + *agein* to lead]

plan *n.* 1. a detailed scheme, method etc. for attaining an objective. 2. (sometimes pl.) a proposed, usually tentative idea for doing something. 3. a drawing to scale of a horizontal section through a building taken at a given level. 4. an outline, sketch, etc. 5. (in perspective drawing) any of several imaginary planes perpendicular to the line of vision and between the eye and the object depicted. ~ vb. plans, plan+ning, planned 6. to form a plan (for) or make plans (for). 7. (tr.) to make a plan of (a building). 8. (tr.; takes a clause as object or an infinitive) to have in mind as a purpose; intend. [C18: via French from Latin planus flat; compare PLANE, PLAIN].

con+text *n.* 1. the parts of a piece of writing, speech etc., that precede and follow a word or passage and contribute to its full meaning: it is unfair to quote out of context. 2. the conditions and circumstances that are relevant to an event, fact, etc. [C.15: from Latin contextus a putting together, from *contexere* to interweave, from com- together + *texere* to weave, braid]

con+text+tu·al adj. relating to, dependent on, or using context: contextual criticism of a book. –con+tex+tu+al+ly adv.

con+cept *n.* 1. something formed in the mind; abstract idea; thought. 2. Philosophy. a. a general idea of something formed by mentally combining all specific parts and characteristic features. b. an abstract notion, theoretical construct, or directly intuited object of thought. [C16: from Latin conceptum something received or conceived, from concipere to take in, CONCEIVE]

con+cep+tu·al *adj.* of or characterised by concepts or the forming of concepts. –con+cep+tu+al+ly adv.

Strategy and Planning

Now applying the dictionary definitions: Strategy in a business context is 'the practice of the art or science of using plans or stratagems to conduct a war' against business problems. Planning is the development of a 'detailed scheme, method etc. for attaining objectives'.

Thus, in developing the first two layers of a security architecture based on the SABSA® Model, Strategy and Planning means understanding business problems, and creating a strategic vision and a set of schemes, methods and ideas for solving those problems.

Contextual Security Architecture

The dictionary tells us that 'contextual' means 'relating to, dependent on, or using context'. Specifically, the contextual security architecture relates to and is dependent on the context in which the security architecture will be created and used – the conditions and circumstances in which you need security – in your business context.

This means that you must investigate, examine and analyse all the aspects of the business context of your organisation that create a need for security, and use this context to drive your thinking at subsequent layers.

Conceptual Security Architecture

Again from the dictionary, the conceptual security architecture is 'of or characterised by concepts or the forming of concepts'. These concepts are 'abstract ideas and thoughts formed in the mind' of the security architect.

Following the collection of information and the analysis of that information that characterise the contextual layer, at this conceptual layer the security architect synthesises new ideas. The architect develops abstractions of the material facts to create a vision of how the solutions to business problems will be planned, designed and implemented.

The conceptual security architecture is one of the most creative phases of the security architecture development process, since it is at this stage that the strategies and plans are decided for the entire programme.

Chapter 9: Contextual Security Architecture

The key to success in the SABSA® methodology is to be business-driven and business-focused. The business strategy, objectives, relationships, risks, constraints and enablers all tell you much about what sort of security architecture the organisation needs. This analysis and description of the business itself is called the contextual security architecture. This chapter will help you to focus on what it is you need to find out in order to construct your own contextual security architecture for your organisation.

In this chapter you will learn about:

- How information security can enable business activities that would otherwise be too risky;

- How digital business has developed and where it is going, and how good information security is needed to protect business activity in the digital environment;

- How all modern business activities, being so pervasively dependent upon information and communications technology, require adequate information security to guarantee their operational continuity and stability;

- How safety-critical systems which use computers or electronics as part of their control logic need to be secured so as to ensure the safety of those who might be put in danger by a system malfunction or by a deliberate compromise of the system functionality;

- The business goals, success factors and operational risks that drive the requirements for information security;

- Operational risk assessment achieved through a process of risk modelling, threat assessment, business impact assessment and vulnerability assessment, followed by risk prioritisation and providing the information required to support risk mitigation decisions;

- The types of information security services that need to be integrated into business processes;

- How organisational structures and business relationships of all kinds affect the needs for information security;

- The location-dependence and time-dependence of business security requirements.

Business Needs for Information Security

SABSA® Matrix cross-reference

This section is relevant to the cell of the SABSA® Matrix entitled The Business on the Contextual row and in the Assets column (see Chapter 3, Table 3-3 and Chapter 7, Figure 7-6). It also provides background for developing the deliverable entitled Business Model (see Chapter 7, Figure 7-4).

ICT has become pervasive in modern businesses

In modern business, information and communications technology has become pervasive. It would be difficult to find an office-based job today that did not involve the employee using a computer system at some stage. Even in factories, workshops and construction sites, information and communications technology can be found in abundance. This tells you that:

- Modern enterprises are totally dependent upon information and communications technology (ICT).

- Which must mean that:

- Modern enterprises are totally dependent upon information.

To protect its information and its information processing capabilities, the enterprise needs to provide information security.

The value of information security is related to the business value protected

Information security has no intrinsic value of its own. Its only possible value is that it protects something that has explicit value to the business. Therefore you must begin the process of defining your enterprise-wide information security architecture by first identifying the things that you consider to be valuable that are affected by information security. These are the business assets that need to be protected by providing suitable security for business information and for business information systems.

This chapter provides a list of important things to investigate

This chapter provides a checklist of things that you will probably want to investigate in your enterprise. It is not for this book to tell you how important these might be, and you will need to investigate and prioritise them through meetings, interviews and document reviews, as has been discussed in earlier parts of the book.

Business drivers identified in this chapter are the primary inputs of the SABSA® Methodology

Each of the issues raised in this chapter is a potential business driver for information security, as referred to in the SABSA® process description in Chapter 7 and shown in Figure 7-4. From these initial business drivers you then derive your Business Attributes, which in turn drive the Business Risk Model, the Business Attributes Profile and the Control Objectives. The business drivers are the primary input to the process.

Security As a Business Enabler

SABSA® Matrix cross-reference

This section is relevant to the cell of the SABSA® Matrix entitled The Business on the Contextual row and in the Assets column (see Chapter 3, Table 3-3 and Chapter 7, Figure 7-6). It also provides background for developing the deliverable entitled Business Model (see Chapter 7, Figure 7-4).

Information security can enable business that would otherwise be too risky

One of the key areas of business need for information security is where there are new business activities enabled by information and communications technology or perhaps new ways of executing old business activities, again enabled by ICT.

Electronic Publishing

Electronic publishing needs security to protect against unauthorised copying

Electronic publishing is a new concept born of the Internet age. The digital delivery of the written word or the pictorial image replaces traditional publishing on paper. One of the business issues that must be addressed is the protection of copyright and the prevention of unauthorised mass copying and redistribution of the materials. An electronic publishing business needs security mechanisms to control copying and redistribution to ensure that only those who have paid for the material are authorised to access it.

On-Demand Entertainment

On-line music and movies also need protection against theft of the material

Moving on a stage further from electronic publishing, the whole sphere of multi-media technology now offers a number of ways in which sounds (mostly music) and movies can be delivered in digital format, directly on-line to a personal computer or digital TV. Once again the issue facing such businesses is how to take advantage of this new business opportunity without losing control over the copying and redistribution of the materials.

All digital entertainment media have this requirement

The music industry has faced something of a crisis over the electronic distribution of pirated digital copies made from CDs. The movie industry and the computer games industry both have similar issues.

Value-Added Information Services

Restricting access to a value added service makes it a commercial proposition

People need information for all sorts of reasons to support their lifestyles. They need general news information, weather information, travel information, financial information, business information, sports news information, entertainment information and much more. Collecting, collating and presenting this information creates a business opportunity in its own right – being an information provider. By adding value through personalised profiles, customised searches and the like, information providers can develop a competitive edge in the market for these services. However, for the business to be viable they need to sell their services, and so they need to restrict access to these services to authorised subscribers.

Remote Process Control

Electronics is widely used in process control

Electronics has been used in factories and manufacturing plants for some time. From a simple electronic control valve in a chemical plant to a fully automated robotic assembly line in a car manufacturing plant, there are countless applications of all shapes and sizes.

Once the control is removed to a remote location, security becomes an important issue

Security is not really an issue so long as the electronic control mechanisms are all contained locally within the physically secure enclosed plant. However, increasingly these control elements are being connected to networks so that they can be managed from remote locations, and then a problem arises. Potentially dangerous manufacturing processes can be controlled using standard technologies and protocols. A hacker can potentially intercept and hijack these remote communications and take over the plant. Now security becomes a major issue. What is worrying is that new adopters of these technologies are often blissfully unaware of the security issues and serious risks.

Case Study: Remote Control of an Electrical Power Plant

We had cause to visit an electrical power plant in a small island economy where there is only one, small electricity company that owns only one generating plant. The company is a friendly, family sort of place and everyone gets on well together in a professional, efficient way. However, they are not really exposed to some of the dirtier aspects of life in the bigger world. During the conversations they proudly explained to us how they now had complete control of the entire plant from a computerised control room. More than that, Harry, the deputy power plant manager, who is a bit of a whiz with ICT, could now control the plant from his laptop computer in his living room at home, dialling up to the control room. So we asked the question, 'What sort of security do you have to protect that?' They had never considered the question before. The benefits were clear, but the risks were not.

It is a bit unfair to single out this small company for naivety – it just happens that this was whom we met. However, if we went to a similar company of a large size serving half of the USA, would we get a different answer?

You do not have to run a factory to have remote process cortrol issues

Some of you will be reading and thinking, 'This does not apply to us, because we do not have manaufacturing processes.' Well, extend the thinking just a little bit:

- Do you run a data communications network?

- Do you run remote computer systems?

- Do you have a network management centre and perhaps a systems management centre?

- Do you use standard network management protocols (such as SNMP[1] version 1) for managing your network?

Network management is a case of remote process control

If you have answered 'yes' to any of these questions then you have a remote process control problem. Network management using SNMP is a classic case. The managed elements are spread throughout the network – in a global organisation those physical objects are spread across the world. They are managed from the control centre by using a protocol, usually SNMP. There are three basic elements to SNMP, or any remote management protocol:

- GET messages, to enquire about the current status of a managed device;

- SET messages, to set up and configure the parameters of the managed device, on-line;

- TRAP[2] messages, for a managed device to let the control centre know of an unexpected event (or at least an asynchronous event).

Many network management systems have a very poor level of security

The only mechanism in SNMPv1 to authenticate these messages is a fixed password called the community name, which is sent in cleartext (no encryption) and which is common to a group of devices. So, if someone wants to take over your network and, for example, close it down (or close down parts of it), all they have to do is to intercept the message path and either change existing SNMP messages or insert their own SNMP messages, and they can take over the control of your network. This is a major vulnerability of which many organisations seem to be unaware.

Supply Chain Management

Large businesses are often dependent upon successful management of the supply chain

Some businesses have complex supply chains, and these need careful proactive management. Take for example a large retail superstore that sells thousands of different lines. These various lines come from a wide range of suppliers. To protect against not being able to obtain an item because of a problem at the supplier, there will probably be multiple suppliers of many of the lines. These

---

[1]SNMP: Simple network management protocol – one of the suite of Internet protocols
[2]A TRAP message is similar to an interrupt in a computer system.

suppliers in turn have their own suppliers, who have theirs, and so on. There is an entire chain of suppliers upon which the superstore depends for supplies.

ICT is frequently used to improve supply chain management

Information and communications technology has impacted on these types of complex businesses in two major ways. First, there are specialised computer applications for managing this complex database of information. The application shows current orders, past history, seasonal patterns, etc., and in the more sophisticated versions there is a facility for supply chain event management – providing visibility of the supply chain both upstream and downstream and reporting problems. Second, the communication of commercial information between suppliers and customers, such as orders, acknowledgements, invoices, remittance notices, etc., is often completely automated in electronic format, with the traditional paper documents having been dematerialised some time ago.

Where It is applied, there are many security issues to address

The range of security issues here is wide. Availability, integrity and confidentiality are all important. If you consider this type of supply chain management application and run down the list of Business Attributes (see Chapter 6) you will find a high number of them that apply here.

Research and Information Gathering

The Internet and the web are frequently used for research purposes

The Internet has transformed research activities. Where libraries full of books, journals and documents were once the only way of searching for information, on-line web sites and sophisticated databases have replaced a great proportion of the services that the traditional library used to provide. Scientific research, other intellectual areas of research and business intelligence gathering all now rely heavily upon electronic sources of information, often made available through the Internet.

Trust in the sources of information is an issue

These new ways of gathering information and searching for specific items are much faster than the old ways and provide a much wider scope for the searches. There are some issues about authenticity, since anyone can publish anything on the Internet, and there is no certainty that it is either true or accurate. This implies care about what sources are to be trusted and perhaps some method of authenticating those sources.

Authentic service providers who charge for services need to protect their revenue

There is also an issue for the providers of authentic, specialised information about how to sell this service and charge subscription fees, so access control and authentication of authorised users is an issue for them.

Digital Business

SABSA® Matrix cross-reference

This section is relevant to the cell of the SABSA® Matrix entitled The Business, on the Contextual row and in the Assets column (see Chapter 3, Table 3-3 and Chapter 7, Figure 7-6). It also provides background for developing the deliverable entitled Business Model (see Chapter 7, Figure 7-4).

'Digital business' is post dot-com terminology

'Digital business' is the term that has emerged, largely promoted by The Gartner Group, as the respectable descriptor to replace what was previously known first as 'e-commerce' and later as 'e-business'. These terms have fallen into disrepute because they are associated with the boom and bust phenomenon of the dot-com era – mostly with the bust. However, 'digital business' is slightly different in that it takes a more realistic view that electronic business rarely exists in isolation and is in fact just another dimension of business, alongside traditional bricks-and-mortar-based business.

'Digital business' can be defined[3] as:

'Digital business' defined

'Leveraging the value of information in its digital form. Digital business is an approach to maximising information leverage on two levels:

- A strategic, business level – "How can we use information to do business in new ways that create value for our customers, our shareholders and our employees?"

- A technology level – "How can we build a single platform for capturing, managing, analysing, using, and sharing our information?"

The lifecycle of the dot-com rise and fall

It is worth taking a few moments to consider why the dot-com disaster happened at all, because it has some bearing on what you are trying to do in building an enterprise security architecture. The history of the events is insightfully portrayed in Figure 9-1, which comes from Gartner[4]. It shows a path of market enthusiasm (more like hype) from the original technology trigger of the Internet and the WWW, followed by a huge Peak of Inflated Expectations, down to the Trough of Disillusionment. What is expected after that is a gradual recovery of confidence based on realistic expectations (the Slope of Enlightenment) to a stable state in the Plateau of Profitability.

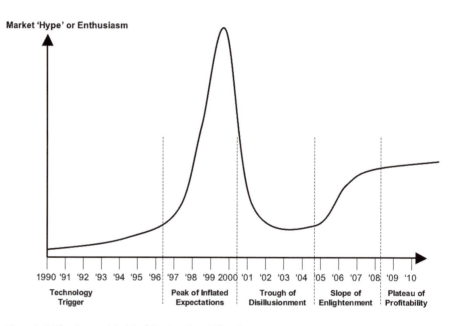

Figure 9-1: The Gartner Model of the Dot-Com Lifecycle

Reasons for the dot-com phenomenon

Some of the reasons for the huge hype and subsequent crash were:

- The rapid proliferation of the Internet and web technologies tempted enterprises and their investors to focus on the technical medium rather than on the business drivers. The goal for many was (and is) to build a great web site and encourage lots of traffic. The problem is that there is little cause-and-effect connection between web traffic volumes and revenue growth or profitability.

3This definition is quoted from the web site of Ceritas Digital. See www.ceritasdigital.co.nz

4Gartner Strategic Research Note: 'Fear and Loathing: The E-Biz Trough of Disillusionment', C. Rozwell, April 2001.

- The focus has been on integrating external partners such as customers and suppliers, giving them access to internal systems. There has been almost no attention paid to re-engineering the internal processes or dealing with the needs of the employees who operate them. The result is that the apparent hi-tech automation is actually window dressing and that behind the external window called the web site, there is no real integration and processes are often manual and antiquated. Thus transaction costs have not been driven down, and efficiency has not been driven up.

- The desire to jump on the dot-com bandwagon led to lots of quick-to-market tactical projects with no attention paid to architecture. The era spawned many people with business cards that carried the title eBusiness Architect, when in reality these folks were little more than ICT system plumbers, who had no concept of architecture or why you might need it. Hence in most cases there is no integration of eBusiness with the CRM or data warehouse initiatives, and there is no common infrastructure, which means that technology investments made are rarely capable of being leveraged for further investment and development.

- The overall result of all these effects is that the total cost of ownership is very high and the return on investment is very low – even negative.

What you need to do next to recover after the dot-com crash

For organisations that now want to climb the Slope of Enlightenment so as to reach the Plateau of Profitability the way forward is clear:

- The integration of business processes must be engineered right through the internal workings of the enterprise providing end-to-end efficiency and transaction cost management;

- All business information must be integrated and shared across all functional departments and applications, moving towards a truly knowledge-driven business;

- The integration of technology projects must be driven to the maximum through an enterprise architecture providing common services, common interfaces and common delivery channels to all business applications.

Enterprise security architecture is part of the recovery process

Your efforts to build an enterprise security architecture are entirely in harmony with this approach.

Some of the specific areas where eBusiness has been relatively successful are discussed in the following sub-sections, together with some of the main security issues for each.

eBanking

Banking has been an early adopter of information and communications technology for many years

Electronic banking is perhaps one of the most successful forms of electronic business. This success is probably due largely to the fact that the banking industry has always been amongst the earliest adopters of information and communications technology, and as an industry is therefore probably the most experienced in its application to business development. This experience seems to have paid off.

Banks are also very experienced in the deployment of information security

Banks have also had the longest commercial experience of applying information security. They deal almost exclusively in financial information, for which the security requirements are very clear – fraud prevention, client confidentiality and service availability. However, the detailed requirements for securing eBanking systems go much deeper than these three. Refer back to the business drivers for the IBFS RTSS case study in Table 6-1, Chapter 6. What you see there is a comprehensive and typical set of business drivers that any bank might come up with in connection with any new business information system, especially one for eBanking.

There are always new exploits emerging

Despite the level of experience that the banks have in offering secure on-line services, their opponents are always coming up with new modes of attack, and the security architecture is sometimes inadequate to face up to the challenge. Consider the following case study:

Case Study: IBFS Internet Bank – Gone Phishing

Like many of its competitors IBFS has a successful Internet bank (IBFS iBank) and has registered several millions of customers for the service. The bank uses several standard URLs to provide access to various components of this service, and these are well published so that customers and prospective customers can contact the iBank web site. The web site is carefully designed using the bank logos and corporate colours for marketing purposes, and customers easily recognise the site when they log in.

Recently the bank discovered that someone had set up a web site with a URL that was quite similar to its own, and then launched a fake web site that was an accurate copy of its own authentic site. This was not sufficient in itself to catch the bank's customers, so to lure the customers toward the hook (as in various fishing techniques) the fraudsters sent out mass spam e-mails to millions of e-mail addresses. The message appeared to come from the IBFS iBank and read[5]:

Important message to all customers

Please read this important message about security. We are working very hard to protect our customers against fraud. Your account has been randomly chosen for verification. This is requested to us to verify that you are the real owner of this account. All you need to do is to click on the link below. You will see a verification page. Please complete all fields that you will see and submit the form. You will be redirected to the IBFS iBank home page after verification. Please note that if you don't verify your ownership of account in 24 hours we will block it to protect your money. Thank you.

The attack was simple: Many people who received the e-mail were indeed customers of this bank (the others probably just felt confused and deleted the message) and many were fooled by the apparent diligence of the bank to protect them against fraud (nice double bluff, eh!). The rather barbed threat to block their account also ensured that they acted promptly. They clicked the link to the fake site and amongst the fields to be filled in the submitted form were the user name and password. These were captured at the fake site, and the fraudsters simply logged into the real customer accounts and emptied them of all funds.

The implications of this masquerade are enormous. A customer receives the mailing, goes to the 'new' site, enters his or her login ID, password and any other

---

[5]If the grammar and style of this message seem a little bit dodgy, that is because (apart from the name of the bank) it is an exact copy of a spam that was sent out on 5 February 2004 purporting to come from one of the large UK retail banks.

authentication information (mother's maiden name etc.), and the fraudsters have now stolen the access credentials for the real account. It is a classical example of the decoy attack. The fraudsters can change the password and lock out the real customer, and of course they can steal the money from the account. The potential business impact is not restricted to the loss of the money. The credibility of the IBFS iBank and of Internet banks in general is put in jeopardy.

This type of attack has come to be known as the phishing fraud and at the time of writing in early 2005 it remains a major problem for all Internet banks.

Scary or what? The underlying problem is not that Internet banking is inherently unsafe, but that the security architecture of Internet banks in often unsuitable for the range of threats that they actually face.

If you are thinking 'Ah, but the bank would be using SSL' then think again. Think very carefully. SSL provides a secure tunnel between the client web browser and the web server. It provides server-side authentication – if you care to check the certificate in detail, but anyone can buy a valid certificate, so what does that prove? The fake phishing sites all run SSL and have a valid certificate issued by one of the regular certificate authorities. The user credentials are fully protected by the SSL tunnel all the way to the rogue server, making sure that they arrive safely at the fraudulent site ready for the theft. Standard SSL as it is usually implemented offers no protection at all against this attack.

To counter this threat a different architecture is needed – ideally one that provides an authentication hand-shaking protocol between the client PC and the web server without revealing the client-side secret(s) to the server. The big mistake in most implementations is the basic assumption that you can trust the server provided it has a valid certificate, and that if you can see a little padlock on your browser screen everything is OK, neither of which assumptions is valid.

eProcurement

Electronic purchasing is a popular application with many benefits

Supply chain management has been discussed in an earlier section. eProcurement is a sub-set of that discipline. eProcurement involves automated purchasing systems using software applications that are web- or Internet-based. A business user with a common web browser can log into an eProcurement system to view vendor offerings and catalogues, and place orders.

- The process benefits can be:

- Faster transmission of orders;

- Accurate order tracking;

- Efficient processing of orders;

- Faster reconciliation of deliveries and payment of invoices;

- Lower transaction costs;

- Comprehensive purchasing reports.

The main benefit is bringing rogue buying under control

However, in companies that have implemented eProcurement, the major business benefit that they all report is quite different – that moving to eProcurement brings rogue buying under control overnight, forcing employees to stick to centrally negotiated procurement deals and preventing them from buying from unauthorised sources. They frequently report huge cost savings (in the order of 20-40%) from this effect alone[6], which is quite interesting, because it means that the technology can be used to exert additional security and control over simple business processes where control has been traditionally difficult.

Fraud prevention is the main security focus

As with any financial system the major business requirements for security focus around fraud prevention, integrity, accountability, secure audit trails and service availability.

eGovernment

eGovernment should provide better service to the citizens

Most governments in the developed world are moving towards providing on-line services for citizens to interact with the many government departments and agencies that are part of modern living. Typically an individual has to interact with 30 or 40 of such agencies over a lifetime, and in most cases he or she has to re-submit all their personal information to each one. eGovernment is therefore seen as a tool for providing 'joined up government', where once the government knows about you in one department, all other government departments also know the same information. That should lead to greater efficiency in the government departments, and less irritation for the citizen (unless he or she is into benefit fraud and tax evasion).

There are also concerns about government exerting too much control over citizens

This integration of information across all departments is controversial. Some quite rightly see the dangers of moving towards a Big Brother state where the government can monitor your every move. Others point out the cost savings and the benefits to citizens in being able to get sensible replies and consistency in their interaction with the government.

There are many security requirements for successful eGovernment

The security requirements for these eGovernment services are demanding. Authentication of the citizen is critical, especially as so many of them have the same names. The rise in identity theft in particular raises some interesting issues here, for once a fully computerised identity is stolen, it may be difficult to correct the problem. Protection of privacy of personal information is also critical, and in the EU carries the weight of the data protection laws behind it. Integrity and accuracy are also very important, as is service availability.

Operational Continuity and Stability

SABSA® Matrix cross-reference

This section is relevant to the cell of the SABSA® Matrix entitled The Business, on the Contextual row and in the Assets column (see Chapter 3, Table 3-3 and Chapter 7, Figure 7-6). It also provides background for developing the deliverable entitled Business Model (see Chapter 7, Figure 7-4).

Revenue Generation

Revenue generation depends upon operational continuity

Business that is dependent on computer systems to run its core business processes is dependent upon these systems to support its revenue stream. If the systems stop, then so does the revenue. The continuity of service of such business systems is therefore totally critical to the survival of the business. Questions that you should ask include:

- How much revenue is lost if this system is unavailable?

- How long will it take to recover the service?

- What is the total revenue loss that would be sustained at that level of recovery?

---

[6]Several presenters at the conference 'Oil & Gas eProcurement Strategies and Solutions' in Aberdeen, June 2000 discussed these levels of saving.

- How long would it take before the business was in trouble with both cash flow and recognisable revenue?

Then look at all the threats that could bring down the service and consider what sort of architecture you need to protect the business from this risk.

Customer Service

ICT has been applied to improve customer service levels and to make customer service into a competitive issue

A frequently made point in support of using corporate web sites and other on-line information systems for customer interaction is that you can differentiate your business not on the core product, but on the levels of customer service that you wrap around it. It is this effect that has allowed the deregulation of the utility companies in some countries. After all, electricity and gas are homogenous products – whoever you buy them from they all look the same. It is the pricing tariffs, the methods of payment, the analytics on your account, the ease of interacting with the supplier for problem resolution, advice on energy usage and so forth that make one supplier different from another.

If you raise expectations of customers, you must deliver to those expectations

So, many enterprises have adopted technology as a way to improve customer service. In doing so they have raised the expectations of their customers, and once raised they are difficult to lower again. If you lead the customer to believe that you can offer a certain service level and then you fail to deliver it, then the customer loyalty fades quickly. Remember, this is the Internet and every customer is only a few mouse clicks away from changing their supplier.

If customer service is a key differentiator, it is worth protecting

If customer service is a key differentiator in your business, you will want to make sure that the security architecture supports the continuity and quality of service that you have led your customers to expect.

Market Reputation

Reputation is difficult to measure

Reputation is a difficult thing to quantify. To some people, for a commercial enterprise, it is reflected by the stock price, but this is probably too simplistic. So how can you measure reputation? You probably cannot find a hard numeric metric, so you must be satisfied with a qualitative approach.

Operational incidents do impact on reputation, but how much?

It is certain that operational incidents do have an affect on the reputation, but the question is, how much? A single incident or even a series of incidents of limited scope do not generally destroy the reputation of an organisation. Reputation is a long-term thing. It takes years to build. Apart from certain catastrophic types of incidents (such as a financial institution defaulting on the investments made by its customers) the reputation will survive a short-term battering. However, at some point in time short term begins to look like long term. The transition point is hard to predict, but once you get there, the reputation tends to flip very quickly from good to bad, a catastrophic failure where the collapse happens quickly and without warning.

Reputation failure is unpredictable – so you must limit the risks that you take with it

Given that reputation failure exhibits this unpredictability, you have to be a brave person to take risks with it. Most organisations that have a good solid reputation recognise that this is probably their single most important and most valuable asset, even though it does not appear on the asset register and its value cannot be seen on the balance sheet. So protecting that reputation becomes one of the most critical of the business drivers. (See Chapter 6, Table 6-1 where reputation appears as the first business driver in the list for the IBFS case study).

Protecting reputation is an individual thing

In your organisation you need to ask around in the senior management circles to get a feel for how reputation is viewed, how it is valued, and how resistant it is thought to be in the face of damaging incidents. What do people think could cause material damage to the reputation of the organisation? Then you will know how to treat it in prioritising your business drivers.

Management Control

Management information helps you to keep control of your business

Keeping control of your business is the main job of management at all levels. In order to achieve that, the management must have information – 'management information'. This is usually in the form of reports and analyses of how the business is performing. This information is usually generated by business information systems.

Management information needs to be accurate and timely

The key security requirements for management information are integrity (is it correct?) and timeliness (do you receive critical information in time to make business decisions that can keep you in control of what is going on?) Confidentiality is also an issue to the extent that you probably do not want to share this type of information with outsiders. If yours is a company whose shares are quoted on the stock market then there are probably regulatory reasons to keep this management information confidential since it can lead to insider trading of your shares, which is illegal.

Operating Licences

Some regulated industries require an operating licence

In some industries you need some kind of licence to operate in business at all. These industries are mostly those where the health and safety of the public is an issue (such as civil aviation, pharmaceuticals, and health care) or where the security of the public's money is an issue (such as banking, insurance and investments). If you are in a regulated industry then you will know about it. You will also know what the regulatory and licensing conditions are that apply to your enterprise.

Regulation is a strong business driver for information security

You need to analyse these business drivers very carefully to assess the extent to which they affect your information security requirements. Noncompliance can lead to censure, to fines and in the end to withdrawal of your operating licence. You must decide how this will drive your enterprise security architecture.

A few industries are mentioned above as being sensitive to licensing and regulation. As a specific detailed example the following case study describes one of the issues in the global pharmaceuticals industry.

Case Study: Pharmaceutical Industry – 21 CFR Part 11

Title 21 of the Code of Federal Regulations Part 11 (21 CFR Part 11) is the section of the United States government rules and regulations document that applies to all the Food and Drug Administration (FDA) program areas and applies to the security and use of electronic records and electronic signatures.

All organisations and persons within the United States who market, or intend to market, pharmaceutical products, pharmaceutical systems, or participate in pharmaceutical research, must comply with the controls, procedures and requirements for using computer applications, systems and devices detailed in 21 CFR Part 11.

The goal of the regulation is to ensure the trustworthiness, privacy and reliability of electronic data, documents and signatures transmitted to the FDA. These transmissions occur when:

- The FDA requires a timely review and approval of safe and effective new medical products so as to protect and promote public health;

- The FDA needs to conduct efficient audits of required records;

- The FDA needs to pursue regulatory actions.

The regulation requires the applicable organisations and persons to demonstrate their ability to develop and maintain reliable and secure computer systems, in addition to having sound business practices and processes around these systems.

The regulations set forth in 21 CFR Part 11 became effective on August 20, 1997. 21 CFR Part 11 applies to all FDA program areas but does not mandate electronic record keeping. 21 CFR Part 11 describes the technical and procedural requirements that must be met if a person or company chooses to maintain records electronically and use electronic signatures. 21 CFR Part 11 applies to those records required by the FDA predicate rule and to signatures required by the FDA predicate rule, as well as signatures that are not required but that appear in required records.

Employee Confidence

In organisations where the employees are key to success, you need to maintain their confidence

There are many stakeholders in a modern enterprise, and amongst the most important of these are the employees. This is especially true for companies in the knowledge economy, where the main company assets really are in the talents of the employee community. So, in order to protect the strategic future of the enterprise, you have to ensure that the employees have confidence in the organisation, and that they will remain committed, loyal and happy to stay in your employment. A key question that they all ask is, 'Are our jobs safe?'

Professional employees are tuned into management performance, including security management

Professional employees tend to be watchful and critical of the competence of the senior management. They look at the policies that are made, the personal examples that are set and most of all, they look to see whether or not the senior management seems to know what it is doing and whether it is really in control of the business. Overall lack of control, poor policymaking and inability to implement sensible policies eat away at employee confidence. Security management is a part of this picture, and to maintain the confidence of the employees you need to make sure that you perform well in this area.

Employees need to feel trusted and empowered to do their work

Set against that, the employees also want to feel that they are trusted and that their requirements for ease of working have been considered. Thus a security culture that treats employees as potential criminals and which makes their work difficult to execute will work against you. There is a need for sensitivity and balance by ensuring that whilst free access to everything is not granted, employees find it easy to use the systems and they are empowered to do their work. You should focus on the User and Management Business Attributes list in Chapter 6, as these will help you to build a Business Attributes Profile that meets the needs of your user community.

Employees must be protected against personal abuse and false accusations

There is another aspect to employee confidence – that the employees feel protected against personal abuse. There are a number of themes in information system security that affect this:

- Sexual harassment, which can happen through the e-mail system with suggestive remarks or pornographic images. The company needs to address this in the security policy and to enforce a culture of acceptable use of inter-employee messages.

- False accusations of computer misuse – the company needs to ensure that employees are accountable for their actions but cannot be falsely accused. This means building in strong authentication and providing audit trails that ensure an innocent employee cannot be reasonably suspected of someone else's misdeeds or even 'fitted up' by someone else.

- Private personal information stored on corporate information systems must not be disclosed to unauthorised persons, either inside or outside the organisation. Apart for being a legal issue in many countries, this is something that will undermine employee confidence quickly.

Personal privacy in the use of corporate systems is a sensitive issue

Reasonable personal use of corporate information systems and personal privacy are contentious issues, especially with respect to e-mail. Is the employee entitled to send private e-mails through the company system and if he or she does, is the company allowed to spy on these activities? The legal position differs from country to country, and the moral position is also variable between cultures. For companies operating on a multi-national basis these legal and moral variations create problems with regard to setting a company-wide policy.

Case Study: Republic of Ireland

Not only do laws and regulations sometimes conflict between countries, but occasionally they conflict within countries. In the Republic of Ireland, corporate governance guidelines require executive managers to monitor what is going on throughout the business, but the regulations on personal privacy forbid them from monitoring employee e-mails.

Reasonable personal use of corporate systems is probably a wise middle ground to seek out

Long ago, before the absolute pervasiveness of the telephone and before the age of the mobile telephone, the same issue surrounded the use of company telephones. Sensible companies allowed employees to make reasonable low-cost, short calls to arrange their personal life, because the alternative was to have employees leaving the office to go to a call-box to make these calls, which makes a huge hit on both productivity and morale. Now there is the same debate about e-mail. It is clearly a reasonable thing for employees to communicate during the working day with family, friends and outside agencies to make arrangements about their lives. The problem is where to draw the line, since it is clearly unreasonable for an employee to spend a lot of time on this. It is also clearly unreasonable for an employee to spend a lot of time surfing the web for personal reasons, or for an employee to use the company computers to run the accounting system for his or her private business. You have to address these issues, decide what position you will take, set a policy, publish clear guidelines so that people know exactly where they stand, and implement the policy with fairness across the employee community.

Shareholder Confidence

Shareholders have several windows through which they see the workings of the organisation

Those who invest in your business need to be kept happy. Their happiness is associated with how well their investments are being managed, which means how well the company is being managed. Shareholders tend to be at arm's length with little direct visibility of company management. There are, however, several windows through which they look to see how things are going:

- The annual report and accounts from the board of directors;

- The external auditor's annual report, made especially to inform the shareholders and to protect their interests;

- The reports of the business and financial analysts who make recommendations on buying and selling shares.

Corporate governance is an issue for shareholders

Shareholders are not concerned with detail, but they are concerned with the general ability of the company management to manage the business, to deliver profits and to grow the assets. Corporate governance – the ability of the senior management to control the business – is what gives shareholders confidence.

Satisfying the auditors and analysts is the key to maintaining shareholder confidence

To maintain the confidence of shareholders your main aim must be to satisfy the external auditors and the analyst community, and you can do this by making sure that your security management programme complies with the views of these groups. You must pay attention to audit points and take decisive action to satisfy the auditors, and you must listen to what the analysts say and act accordingly.

Other Stakeholders

Some organisations do not have shareholders

Not every organisation is owned by shareholders. The most obvious exceptions are government organisations, owned by the government, and charitable organisations run by a board of trustees. Each model of ownership has its own specific set of stakeholders, and you must decide what the ownership framework looks like in your organisation. Whatever it is, it will have an impact on the needs of your enterprise security architecture.

Government organisations are susceptible to sweeping changes reflecting political policy changes

For example, in government, a change of leadership or even more likely a change of party following an election, will quickly lead to a change of policy and a major reorganisation, with some departments being amalgamated, others being split, new departments being created, and so on. The business driver for these events is purely one of political presentation to the electorate, yet those responsible for organising and managing information security must be able to respond flexibly and swiftly to the whims of their political masters. If the security architecture is monolithic, then this could be difficult indeed, and so a finely granular domain structure suggests itself at the conceptual security architecture level. These business drivers must be understood.

Safety-Critical Dependencies

SABSA® Matrix reference

This section is relevant to the cell of the SABSA® Matrix entitled The Business, on the Contextual row and the Assets column (see Chapter 3, Figure 3-3 and Chapter 7, Figure 7-6). It also provides background for developing the deliverable entitled Business Model (see Chapter 7, Figure 7-4).

Safety-critical systems defined

Safety-critical systems are those whose failure may cause injury or death to human beings. Many such systems involve computer-controlled or electronic-controlled electromechanical sub-systems, and it is these that are of interest in this section.

Remote Communications to Safety-Critical Systems

Hacking into remote communications to safety-critical systems is a major security issue

One very important aspect of safety-critical systems has already been addressed in the earlier discussion in this chapter about the need for securing remote control systems for factories, plant, robotic machinery and so on. Any application of process control that involves the use of remote data communications is at risk from an opponent intercepting the communications and hijacking the control. This also applies to the remote management of computer systems and network devices, and hence any business application supported on a remotely managed computer or data communications network is vulnerable to attack.

Applied cryptographic techniques provide a large part of the solution

The means of securing remote communications to prevent these types of attack lies in the use of cryptographic techniques to ensure complete authenticity of the instructions issued to the control target. Some protocols have standard optional features to implement these security mechanisms, but the ability to do so then depends upon vendor support for those mechanisms having been built into the managed devices. Not all vendors feel able to justify the extra cost of such support, and in a competitive market place where price is an issue such extras are often not regarded as economic. Only where there is an explicit safety-critical need (or some other explicit business driver) will the expenditure be justified for many organisations.

Authentication of communications to a remote safety-critical system is a particular requirement

There is an increasing tendency to introduce information and communications technology into complex engineering systems – especially into the design of both civil and military aircraft. Here safety-critical issues are paramount. Aircraft sub-systems are often engineered with triple redundancy to reduce to a negligible amount the risk of failure. However, if remote digital data communications between ground stations and airborne flight vehicles are to be used, then security issues raise their heads again. The designers of such systems need to consider the authentication of any communications to ensure that an opponent cannot hijack the aircraft by remotely hijacking the data communications.

Authentication of support documents in the civil aviation industry is also important to prevent all methods of logical attack

There is another aspect to safety-criticality in this business domain. Civil aircraft are operated by a large number of airlines around the world – probably a hundred or so separate organisations. They maintain their aircraft according to the service bulletins and other technical support documents issued by the aircraft manufacturers. The major manufacturers have adopted information and communications technology as a tool to distribute the large volumes of documentation that they publish to support their products, with many clear business benefits being experienced by both the manufacturers and the airlines. However, here is another method by which an opponent may try to attack the industry – by substitution of authentic documents with false ones. Strong authentication of the electronic documents is needed to prevent this style of attack, which could threaten the safety of commercial flights.

Systems Assurance

Assurance of correct working is a key requirement for safety-critical systems

Another important aspect of security with regard to safety-critical systems is that of systems assurance. This is concerned with reaching high levels of assurance that the system has been implemented correctly and will function as expected and as laid down in the functional specification. The areas of application include:

- Nuclear power stations and other nuclear installations;
- Dangerous chemical plants, oil refineries and other manufacturing plants;
- Aircraft systems and air traffic control systems;
- Weapons and defence systems.

The main issue is assurance of no unwanted functionality

In most (ordinary) systems it is sufficient to be sure that the system will perform all the functions laid down in the functional specification and that it is easy to test that it does. You simply write out a test specification that covers all the functions, all the expected inputs and all the expected outputs and run through the tests to demonstrate the correctness of the system. In safety-critical systems this is not sufficient, because the potential problems are not with expected inputs and outputs but with unexpected situations. It is much more difficult to establish that the system does not have any unwanted functionality in response to certain input scenarios, of which there are potentially an infinite number.

*Security of safety-critical
systems has demanding
requirements*

Safety-critical security requirements are demanding, and it remains an area in which there is much active research. Information and communications technology will be used more and more for these types of application, and there is a need to understand how to ensure that the systems do not endanger human life.

Business Goals, Success Factors and Operational Risks

*SABSA® Matrix cross-
reference*

This section is relevant to the cell of the SABSA® Matrix entitled Business Risk Model on the Contextual row and in the Motivation column (see Chapter 3, Table 3-3 and Chapter 7, Figure 7-6). It also provides background for developing the deliverable entitled Business Risk Model (see Chapter 7, Figure 7-4). The section looks at some of the key areas where the enterprise faces risk and is motivated to develop an information security response.

Brand Protection

*Brand is one of the most
valuable assets of any
organisation*

A brand is something that takes a huge investment of time and money to develop. The concept is one of a business name or product name, perhaps accompanied by a pictorial image, which carries a message of reliability, quality and trustworthiness. It is closely related to reputation. The brand is a major investment and therefore must be considered as major asset, to be protected and further developed. Information security management plays an important part in this by supporting the overall strategic, tactical and operational development of the enterprise. Information security failures can lead to brand damage.

Fraud Prevention

*Fraud is nothing new
– but there are new ways to
commit fraud*

Fraud is ubiquitous. It happens in every industry, in every size of organisation, at every level of the management hierarchy, and it has existed for as long as there has been business. So, a fraud carried out using a business information system is just another manifestation of an age-old problem – manipulating business information to hide dishonesty and theft.

*Computer systems can be a
means to commit fraud*

Computer-related fraud is perpetrated by abusing business computer systems that support business transactions (banking, electronic commerce, ordering, etc.) or those that represent business positions (stock control, inventory, asset portfolios, financial accounting, etc.). The effects of these frauds can be large or small, from large-scale bank funds transfer frauds, down to fiddling a travel expenses claim. They also vary from the single fraud to the systematic fraudulent collection of small, unnoticed amounts (sometimes called a 'salami fraud' because it takes a thin slice at a time).

*'Computer fraud' is
committed by people, not
computers*

Computers do not commit fraud. They are merely one of the many tools that can be used by humans to commit fraud, and in that respect, computer-related fraud is just the same as any other type of fraud. Fraud usually happens in situations where there is an opportunity (access, skill and time) combined with motivation (need, justification and possibly the challenge).

Fraud prevention is relevant to every single business in the world, and information security is needed to prevent the abuse of business information systems to commit fraud.

Loss Prevention

*There are many operational
risks that can lead to
business losses*

Potential business losses arise from many different operational risk areas. Information security management is one of the key competence areas in any organisation that will help to manage and mitigate a wide range of these risks. There is a fairly comprehensive taxonomy of operational risks in Table 9-2 in a subsequent section of this chapter, together with their mapping to the information security domain.

Business Continuity

Business continuity management requires security management of systems to ensure continuous service

Perhaps the most commonly experienced and most feared risk with regard to using computers in business is the system failure that leads to interruption of business operations. It can lead to delays or in some cases complete failure to meet the service level expectations of customers, suppliers, employees, shareholders, regulators, etc. If key business information services are disrupted, then so are the business processes that depend upon them.

Business continuity is a key business driver for the information security architecture

Service interruptions can be caused by accidental system failures, by wilful neglect and poor operating practices, or by malicious interference and sabotage. The entire security architecture is focused on upholding the set of business requirements that can be collectively classified under 'business continuity'. These requirements are common to every business at some level of criticality.

Strategic Business Development

Security architecture supports strategy

The best way to illustrate the link between strategic business development and the information security programme is to look at a specific case study example.

Case Study: A Major Healthcare Administration Agency

This is an administration agency within a national government department. Its strategic goals are:

- Protect and improve citizen health and satisfaction;

- Purchase the best value health care for citizens;

- Promote the fiscal integrity of the agency programmes;

- Provide leadership in the broader public interest to improve health;

- Promote citizen understanding of the agency and its programmes;

- Foster excellence in the design and administration of the agency's programmes.

These six strategic goals are to be accomplished by meeting more specific strategic objectives:

Customer Services

- Improve citizen satisfaction with programmes, services and care;

- Enhance citizen programme protection;

- Increase the usefulness of communications with citizens;

- Increase the usefulness of communications with business partners, service providers and other agencies;

- Ensure that programmes and services respond to the health care needs of citizens.

Quality of Care

- Improve health outcomes;

- Improve access to services for under-served and vulnerable citizen populations;

- Protect citizens from substandard care.

Programme Administration

- Build a high-quality, customer-focused team;

- Enhance programme safeguards;

- Maintain and improve the agency's position as a prudent programme administrator and an accountable steward of public funds;

- Increase public knowledge of the financing and delivery of health care;

- Improve the agency's management of information systems and technology.

Business strategy calls for good governance and accountability

If you examine these strategic goals and objectives they paint a picture of good governance, sound management and clear public accountability. The infrastructure that supports these goals and objectives must include:

- Good operational risk management practices;

- Protection of the trust relationships that exist between the agency, beneficiaries, health care providers and many other parties;

- Protection of the confidentiality, integrity and authenticity of electronic communications and information transfers that are involved in the automation of the health care business processes;

- Protection of the privacy of individual beneficiaries with regard to their health records;

- Maintaining continuous service availability;

- Authenticating all parties in eHealthcare communications and holding all parties accountable for the electronic transactions made in their name.

Thus the information security programme is a major contributor to success in meeting these objectives and reaching these goals.

Legal Obligations

Legal factors are another major business driver for information security architecture

Organisations have many legal obligations, and failure to meet these obligations represents a major area of operational risk. The situation is much more complex for companies who are multi-national and international in their business operations, since each operating country has different laws, some of which are in conflict across national borders. Many of the laws and regulations have a direct or indirect linkage with management of information security. It is not possible to list all the relevant laws and regulations for all the countries and all the industries, but here is a list of the important areas that you need to examine in your domains of operation:

- Compliance with criminal law;

- Compliance with civil law;

- Regulatory compliance relevant to the industry;

- Compliance with contractual obligations;

- Management and mitigation of legal liabilities;

- Civil liability[7] caused by failure to maintain a reasonable level of security[8].

The Business Attribute Profile will help you to identify the relevant legal drivers

In order to make sure that your enterprise security architecture takes into account all the legal and regulatory drivers, you will need to build a Business Attribute Profile (see Chapter 6) that specifies the attributes and relevant metrics to describe your business needs. In doing this you will need to confer not only with business managers but also with your legal representatives who can give detailed advice. In certain regulated industries (such as banking) there may also be a compliance officer or a compliance department that can give detailed advice on regulatory matters.

Confidence of Key Stakeholders

Every business has many key stakeholders

An earlier section of this chapter has already discussed the need to maintain the confidence of both employees and shareholders in order to maintain the operational continuity and stability of the organisation. However, there are other key stakeholders whose confidence you must protect. These include:

- Customers;

- Suppliers;

- Employees;

- Investors;

- Regulators;

- Bankers;

- Government agencies.

Maintaining stakeholder confidence is a key driver for your security architecture

You need to examine each of these in turn in some detail to tease out the many information security drivers that are associated with each one.

Operational Risk Assessment

SABSA® Matrix cross-reference

This section is relevant to the cell of the SABSA® Matrix entitled Business Risk Model on the Contextual row and in the Motivation column (see Chapter 3, Table 3-3 and Chapter 7, Figure 7-6). It also provides background for developing the deliverable entitled Business Risk Model (see Chapter 7, Figure 7-4). The section looks at the basic modelling of risk and how such models can be used to carry out a risk assessment. This will help you to develop your Business Risk Model.

Operational risk defined

The exact definition of operational risk is often debated and not entirely standardised, but an emerging standard definition is one developed by the Basel Committee on Banking Supervision[9] as follows:

---

[7] See 'Downstream Liability: The Next Frontier', Mark Rasch, COSAC 2003. www.cosac.net

[8] Including the failure to prevent certain events, failure to warn about the iminence of certain events, failure to notify after certain events have occurred and failure to monitor certain events.

[9] See 'Working Paper on the Regulatory Treatment of Operational Risk', Basel Committee on Banking Supervision, September 2001 – part of the developments of the New Basel Capital Accord, sometimes known as 'Basel II'. See www.bis.org

Basel II Definition of Operational Risk

'The risk of loss resulting from inadequate or failed internal processes, people and systems or from external events'

Risk assessment is needed for the contextual security architecture

There is a full discussion of operational risk management in Chapter 15. However, you need to be introduced to the techniques for assessing operational risk at this stage so as to be able to develop the SABSA® Business Risk Model. This model is an important deliverable of the contextual security architecture development process (see Figure 7-4 in Chapter 7).

Risk Modelling

To assess risk you need a suitable model

Risk is a complex concept, familiar to everyone in every aspect of daily life, yet surprisingly difficult to describe without a theoretical analysis. The most commonly accepted model for risk involves some basic concepts:

- Assets – things that are of value to your business that you want to protect;

- Threats – potential damaging events that put your assets in danger;

- Impacts – the potential outcome of a threat materialising and causing damage to your assets;

- Vulnerabilities – weaknesses in your operational business procedures or systems that will allow a threat to materialise and exploit an asset, causing an impact.

Estimating the likelihood of an event is complex

The likelihood of a risk event occurring is some complex combination of:

- Level of threat (the likelihood of the threat event materializing in a given period of time);

- Level of vulnerability or weakness (the likelihood that a threat event will succeed in exploiting your business assets thus causing an impact).

Risk Assessment

Risk assessment is an important part of the methodology in this book

In order to manage risk you first need to identify the sources of risk (threats) and assess their significance (the likelihood of the risk event and the impact on your business assets should it materialize). Risk assessment is an important part of the SABSA® process as described in Chapter 7 (see Figure 7-4) in which the Business Risk Model is one of the key deliverables (see also Chapter 3, Table 3-3). You will therefore need to adopt a risk assessment methodology to develop this business risk model. A simple-to-use method that the authors have used when carrying out risk assessments is presented here. You could use any other method that is already adopted by your organisation.

Quantitative threat assessment is unrealistic for most organisations

Assessing the level of threat is notoriously difficult. Threats exist outside your span of control – the world is simply a dangerous place, and all that you can do is to recognise the threats and identify them and their sources (threat agents). Without access to reliable, consistent, complete data on previous loss events, statistical analysis provides little useful guidance on the probability of a threat materialising. Additionally, as has been already mentioned, observation of past events is not necessarily a good guide to how the future will be.

Intelligence gathering is also unrealistic for most organisations

Another way to assess threats is to gather intelligence information from a network of intelligence agents and to process that information, as is done in law-enforcement and national security agencies. However, commercial organisations do not have access to this type of intelligence and in any case, it only applies to certain types of threat posed by criminals, terrorists and the like. It does not help with the wide range of operational risks that are not based on malicious intent.

Vulnerability assessment is much more realistic

Assessing the vulnerabilities (weaknesses in how your business is operated) and the associated impact (the level of damage you would sustain if a threat event successfully exploited your vulnerabilities or weaknesses) is much easier, since both these things are within your span of control. Thus risk assessment methodologies in commercial organisations tend to focus on assessing these aspects, usually qualitatively (low, medium, high). Analysing threats in commercial organisations is limited simply to identifying the threats without quantification.

A typical risk assessment method

The steps in a commercial risk assessment methodology are usually:

Step 1:   What are your business assets?
  • Identify and value these assets.

Step 2:   What possible threats put your business assets at risk?
  • Identify the possible threats.

Step 3:   For each threat, if it materialised, what would be the business impact on your assets?
  • Identify and quantify these impacts by relating back to your asset list.

Step 4:   If the impact is significant enough to trouble you, what vulnerabilities or weaknesses might there be that could allow this threat to exploit your assets causing an impact?
  • Identify and quantify these vulnerabilities or weaknesses.

Step 5:   Can you reduce these vulnerabilities or weaknesses by introducing additional controls?
  • Identify the possible control strategies and quantify the cost (total cost of ownership) for these controls.

Step 6:   What is the cost/benefit analysis derived from the level of reduction of potential business impact (benefit) weighed against the cost of additional control?
  • Quantify the benefits and costs.

The purpose of this type of risk assessment is to:

  • Understand the risk profile in detail;

  • Make well-informed risk management decisions.

Threat Modelling Framework

To understand threats you need a modelling framework

In order to make your understanding of threats as informative as possible when trying to foresee all possible threats that face you (and understand their respective impacts) some kind of threat modelling technique is needed to help structure your thinking.

A taxonomy of threats is included to help you

To achieve this you need a taxonomy framework for classifying threats so that you can reasonably expect to address a checklist of all possible areas of threat whilst attempting to synthesise a comprehensive list of the actual threats that face you. The classification scheme allows you to build up a database of known threats and to use this as a means to prompt your synthesis in specific risk assessment exercises. It can be extended over time as operational experience teaches you more about the threat environment. You will see the part played by the Threats Database in the SABSA® process in Chapter 7, Figure 7-4.

The threat classification scheme that is presented in this chapter is two-dimensional, comprising threat domains and threat categories.

Threat Domains

The definition of operational risk (see earlier definition from Basel II) implicitly suggests that there are four principal domains of risk to be considered:

People;

Processes;

Systems;

External events.

The SABSA® approach to risk assessment uses these domains as an initial classification for threats and threat agents that are relevant to operational risk assessment. Table 9-1 provides more detail.

Table 9-1: Threat Domains and Threat Agents

Threat Domain	Description of Domain	Threat Agents
People	Losses caused by: Malicious violation of internal policies Negligent violation of internal policies Human errors	Current employees Past employees People under consideration for employment
Processes	Unintentional losses caused by: Deficiency in an existing procedure Absence of a suitable procedure Failure to follow a defined procedure	Employees Customers Suppliers Service providers Agents Partners Members of the public
Systems	Unintentional losses caused by: Unforeseen breakdown of technical systems Insufficient resilience in technical systems	Technical failure through 'fair wear-and-tear' Technical failure through inadequate design or poor implementation
External	Losses caused by: Natural disasters Man-made disasters (unintentional) Malicious actions of third parties Negligent actions of third parties Legitimate actions of third parties	Natural events Accidents Malicious third parties Negligent third parties Legitimate third parties whose business interests conflict with ours

Threat Categories

The second dimension is the threat category, based on experience and observation

As a secondary classification of threats the SABSA® approach uses a series of threat categories. The selection of these categories is entirely arbitrary and is based upon practical experience only. The categories chosen could be changed without violating any theoretical principles. Table 9-2 shows the taxonomy of threats classified by domains and categories. This is the Threats Database referred to in Chapter 7, Figure 7-4. Each category maps to one or more of the threat domains. There is no specific logical mapping of a category to the domains. The category and domain mappings are indicated in columns 2 – 5 in Table 9-2 by the smiley face ☺ symbol. The list is not necessarily comprehensive, and new categories could be added if that becomes necessary or desirable.

Table 9-2: Taxonomy of Threats – the Threats Database

Threat Category	Domain Mapping				Description	Examples	Information Security Mapping
	People	Processes	Systems	External			
Facilities and Operating Environment	∗		∗	∗	Loss or damage to operational capabilities caused by problems with premises, facilities, services or equipment.	Business interruption from one of many possible threat scenarios and threat agents	Inadequate business continuity management and ICT disaster recovery
						Data processing service interruption	ICT systems outages through inadequate disaster recovery
						Communications interruption	ICT systems outages through inadequate disaster recovery
Health & Safety	∗	∗	∗	∗	Threats to the personal health and safety of staff, contractors, suppliers, agents, customers and members of the public	Unsafe operating environments with safety hazards unmanaged	Poor installations and operational management in ICT operations rooms
						Criminal or terrorist attacks on individuals	Weak logical and physical security leading to unauthorised disclosure of private address details, travel itineraries, etc.
						Safety-critical systems failure	Inadequate protection for process control systems for automated factory processes, machine tools, power generation, etc., including automated secure vaults and other specialised machinery
						Infectious diseases spread in the workplace	Non-availability of key staff due to local epidemic

Threat Category	Domain Mapping				Description	Examples	Information Security Mapping
	People	Processes	Systems	External			
Information Security	*	*	*	*	Unauthorised disclosure or modification to information, or loss of availability of information, or inappropriate use of information	Unauthorised disclosure of corporate-confidential or customer-private information	Weak logical security, weak physical security and weak operating procedures
						Unauthorised modification, deletion, duplication or replay of corporate or customer information	Weak logical security, weak physical security and weak operating procedures
						Unauthorised or inappropriate use of corporate or customer information	Weak logical security, weak physical security and weak operating procedures
						Unauthorised or inappropriate use of personal employee information	Weak logical security, weak physical security and weak operating procedures
						Loss of availability of internal corporate or customer information	Inadequate resilience, backup and recovery in ICT systems
						Malicious denial of service attacks causing loss of services	Inadequate physical and logical security
						Inability to hold people accountable for their actions	Inadequate policies and guidelines and inadequate audit trails in ICT systems
						False repudiation of completed transactions	Lack of non-repudiation services and mechanisms in ICT systems
Control Frameworks		*	*		Inadequate design or performance of the existing risk management infrastructure	Lack of adequate cost accounting	Inadequate cost accounting in ICT projects
						Lack of measurement of efficiency	Inadequate measurement and reporting efficiency of systems and processes
						Theft and fraud	Inadequate control of unauthorised activity on ICT systems

Threat Category	Domain Mapping				Description	Examples	Information Security Mapping
	People	Processes	Systems	External			
Legal & Regulatory Compliance	∗	∗	∗		Failure to comply with the laws of the countries in which business operations are carried out, or failure to comply with any regulatory, reporting and taxation standards, or failure to comply with contracts, or failure of contracts to protect business interests	Failure to comply with EU data protection legislation or similar legislation in other countries	Inadequate attention to privacy laws affecting personal information
						A change in the law or industry regulations in one or more countries leads to a breach of the law or industry regulations in all or part of the world	Inadequate architecture to enable upgrade, extension, change, enhancement of ICT systems to deal with changes in regulations, and inadequate early warning research
						Inconsistencies in the legal and regulatory framework lead to being in breach of the law or of industry regulations in all or part of the world	Inadequate research into the legal environment for this business initiative
						Operating rules for a service are found to be in breach of the law or industry regulations in all or part of the world	Inadequate research and drafting of operating rules for the service
						Contractual disputes	Weak or inadequate contracts
						Deliberate, wilful or grossly negligent breach of regulations or of the law of the operating country	Weaknesses in operating procedures and an inability to control the behaviour of staff
						Failure to comply with the taxation regime in one or more countries	Inadequate reporting of tax details

Threat Category	Domain Mapping				Description	Examples	Information Security Mapping
	People	Processes	Systems	External			
Business Strategy		*		*	A strategic business plan fails to meet its expected targets	Expected market fails to emerge as forecast	Poor market research for ICT services and weak forecasting techniques
						Competitors are more successful	Poor marketing of ICT services
						Inadequate marketing for the business mission	Poor marketing of ICT services
						Technology is in breach of patents	Poor research into patent position and inadequate contracts on liability, responsibility, etc.
						Key technology suppliers suffer business collapse	Dependence on single source suppliers and lack of multi-sourcing
						Future technologies fail to emerge as expected	Poor information research and forecasting
						Inter-operability failures with regard to other key players in a developing market	Misjudgement of standards selection
						Long-term operational service failure destroys market confidence and the opportunity is lost forever	Inability to manage and solve operational problems with poor leadership
						A merger of two businesses fails because integration proves to be too difficult and expensive	Failure of the due diligence process to assess the costs and difficulties of integration
						Consortia or joint ventures fail because of disagreements between members or because members withdraw to pursue other strategies	Weak buy-in from participants and inadequate contracts to tie up liabilities and responsibilities

Threat Category	Domain Mapping				Description	Examples	Information Security Mapping
	People	Processes	Systems	External			
Corporate Governance	∗	∗	∗		Failure of directors to fulfil their personal statutory obligations in managing the company and protecting the interests of shareholders	Lack of internal policy	Inadequate leadership and policy setting from senior levels
						Failure to take timely action when a major strategic project gets into difficulties	Lack of due and timely diligence, inadequate reporting to senior management and lack of leadership in solving operational problems
						Failure to comply with internal policies	Poor implementation of systems and processes and inadequate internal audit
Public Relations	∗	∗			The negative effects of public opinion, customer opinion, market reputation and the damage caused to the brand by failure to manage public relations	Loss or interruption of services to customers	Inadequate resilience, disaster recovery, continuity and crisis management
						Failure to meet customers' expectation for service delivery	Inability to manage and solve operational problems
						Failure to meet the market's expectations for rate of roll-out following launch	Inadequate project management and strategic planning
						Failure to meet the market's expectations of what a warranty means in practice	Inadequate marketing of ICT services, raising false expectations
						Loss of market and customer confidence caused by media reports of operational failures in service delivery	Inadequate crisis management, including public relations management
						Loss of market and customer confidence caused by media reports of serious security breaches	Inadequate crisis management, including public relations management
						Hostile reporting by investigative journalists	Inadequate protection of internal confidential information from access by hostile external parties

Threat Category	Domain Mapping				Description	Examples	Information Security Mapping
	People	Processes	Systems	External			
Processing and Transactions	*	*	*		Problems with service or product delivery caused by failure of internal controls, information systems or through weaknesses in operating procedures	Poor integration of processes	Need to maximise integration of software applications and eliminate 'islands' of functionality
						Lack of conceptual thinking in systems planning	Inadequate ICT systems architecture
						Transaction failure	Inadequate exception reporting and transaction recovery in ICT systems
						Reconciliation failure	Inadequate exception reporting in ICT systems
						Unauthorised trading	Inadequate authorisation, identification, authentication and access control in ICT systems
Product Liability	*	*			A product or service sold and delivered fails to meet the required standards for suitability for the client needs	Poor advice given to clients	Inadequate information content management
						Mis-selling of financial products	Inadequate information content management
						Failure to meet contractual service levels	Inadequate attention to fulfilling the SLA for ICT services
Behavioural	*				Problems with service or product delivery caused by lack of employee integrity, or by errors and mistakes	Data input errors	Inadequate data input validation
						Business operations mistakes	Inadequate ICT operations procedures and operations management

Threat Category	Domain Mapping				Description	Examples	Information Security Mapping
	People	Processes	Systems	External			
Technology		*	*		Failure to plan, manage and monitor the performance of technology-related projects, products, services, processes, staff and delivery channels	Failure to meet business requirements	Inadequate business requirements specification on ICT development projects
						Failure to integrate with business processes	Need for ICT projects to support and integrate with business processes
						Technical integration failure	Must successfully integrate chosen ICT product components
						Inadequate technical architecture	Inadequate ICT systems architecture to ensure flexibility in response to changing business requirements
						Lack of technical standards for construction	Badly designed and constructed ICT systems
Project Management	*	*	*		Failure to plan and manage the resources required for achieving tactical project goals, or leading to failure to complete the project	Cost overrun on projects – missing business budget targets	Inadequate cost management on ICT development projects
						Time overruns on projects – missing business targets for time-to-market	Inadequate time management on ICT development projects
						Project failure – project stopped or withdrawn	Need to ensure technical feasibility of ICT projects
						Post-delivery project failure	Need to ensure that ICT projects can be successfully be integrated with the business operations

Threat Category	Domain Mapping				Description	Examples	Information Security Mapping
	People	Processes	Systems	External			
Criminal and Illicit Acts	*			*	Loss or damage caused by fraud, theft, wilful neglect, gross negligence, vandalism, sabotage, extortion, etc.	Fraud by internal staff	Inadequate prevention of Trojans, back-doors, etc., introduced by ICT developers
						Fraud by external parties	Weakness in logical security, physical security and operational procedures
						Theft of equipment	Weakness in physical security and operational procedures
						Destruction of corporate assets	Weakness in logical security, physical security and operational procedures
						Extortion	Inadequate protection of private and confidential information gained from unauthorised access to ICT systems
Terrorism, War and Similar Events				*	Loss or damage caused by malicious physical attack by hostile forces	Loss of business operations centres and the operational capability	Inadequate redundancy and resilience in the design and implementation of ICT systems and data centres
Human Resources	*	*			Failure to recruit, develop or retain employees with the appropriate skills and knowledge, or to manage employee relations	Key person dependency	Poor transparency of processes and lack of cross-training for people to deputise and step in for other key workers

Threat Category	Domain Mapping				Description	Examples	Information Security Mapping
	People	Processes	Systems	External			
Supply Chain	∗	∗	∗		Failure to evaluate adequately the capabilities of suppliers leading to breakdowns in the supply process or sub-standard delivery of supplied goods and services; also failure to understand and manage the supply-chain issues	Loss of key services supplied by third parties	Inadequate resilience of third-party service provider relationships, including outsourcing of ICT and communications services
						Disputes with third-party suppliers	Inadequate provision of strong contracts for ICT service suppliers addressing all aspects of security management and operations management, escalation, problem resolution, liability, responsibility, etc.
Management Information	∗	∗	∗		Inadequate, inaccurate, incomplete or untimely provision of information to support the management decision-making process	Poor management information systems	Inadequate reporting from all ICT systems
Ethics	∗	∗		∗	Damage caused by unethical business practices, including those of associated business partners; issues include racial and religious discrimination, exploitation of child labour, pollution, environmental and so-called green issues, behaviour to disadvantaged groups, sexual harassment, etc.	Uncontrolled publishing under the name of the organisation	Inadequate content management to avoid offensive materials in e-mails, on web sites, etc.

Threat Category	Domain Mapping				Description	Examples	Information Security Mapping
	People	Processes	Systems	External			
Geo-Political	*			*	Loss or damage in some countries, caused by political instability, by poor quality of infrastructure in developing regions or by cultural differences and misunderstandings	Breakdown of normal working life	Inadequate resilience and disaster recovery to prevent ICT operations being interrupted
						Breakdown of national or local infrastructure	Inadequate plan for dealing with power outages and telecommunications outages
Cultural	*	*	*		Failure to deal with cultural issues affecting employees, customers or other stakeholders; including language, religion, morality, dress codes and other community customs and practices	Sexual harassment	Inadequate polices and procedures to discourage and if possible prevent inappropriate or pornographic content in e-mails
						Language problems	Lack of flexible language modules for all ICT applications
Climate, Weather, Environment and Geology				*	Loss or damage caused by unusual climate conditions, including drought, heat, flood, cold, ice, storm, winds or by geological instability such as earthquakes and subsidence	Loss or damage to operational facilities	Inadequate site selection for data centres

Threat Scenarios[10]

To gain greater insight into threats you can construct threat scenarios

In order to gain a more detailed insight into the specific threats that you wish to consider, the taxonomy of threats classification framework can be used to prompt ideas about threat scenarios. These scenarios provide a much richer set of information against which to make risk management decisions than you would get with a simple list of threats. Each scenario is described by a number of qualitative parameters. Table 9-3 and Figure 9-2 show the framework for describing a threat scenario. Tables 9-4 to 9-7 contain supplementary information for this framework. All of these tables are based on pragmatic principles rather than any theoretical framework and can be amended or extended as a result of further operational experience.

---

[10]Many of the concepts and ideas used in this section are drawn for the work of Andy Jones of the University of Glamorgan, UK, as published in his presentation at Compsec2002 in London and expanded in a paper in Information Security Bulletin, Vol 8, Issue 4 (May 2003). However, the authors have restructured some of Andy's ideas and used them in a somewhat different way.

Table 9-3: Framework for Describing a Threat Scenario

Parameter	Description	Example
Specific threat	A threat selected from Table 9-2	Unauthorised code inserted into an application to either: Defraud the Organisation Sabotage the Organisation
Threat agent	A threat agent suggested by Table 9-1 but defined in more detail as in Table 9-4	Disaffected employee working in the systems development team
Capability	Level of resources expected to be under the control of the threat agent, as suggested by Table 9-5	Full skill set and tool set required for the task
Motivation	What motivates the threat agent, as suggested by Table 9-6	(1) Personal gain (2) Revenge
Opportunity	Description of the opportunity or level of access available to the threat agent	Full access to development code and development environment
Catalysts	Events or changes in circumstances that make the threat agent decide to act, as suggested by Table 9-7	Redundancy of employee Redundancy of a friend of the employee Employee runs up debts
Inhibitors	Factors that may deter the threat agent from executing the threat, as suggested by Table 9-7	Fear of being detected, losing job and gaining a criminal record
Amplifiers	Factors that may encourage the threat agent to execute the threat, as suggested by Table 9-7	Belief that the rogue code can be hidden and covered and not attributed to an individual

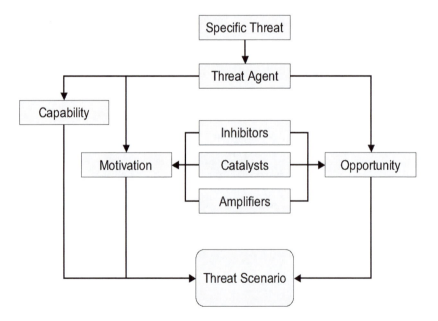

Figure 9-2: Framework for a Threat Scenario

Table 9-4: Threat Agents	
Threat Agent Groups	**Specific Threat Agents**
Natural Events	Wind
	Electrical storm
	Earthquake
	Flooding from rainwater, rivers, tidal surges, storms
	Volcanic eruptions
Accidental Events	Fire
	Flooding from burst water pipes or tanks
	Explosions caused by malfunction of processes or services
	Structural collapse or damage from external impact by aircraft or heavy vehicles
	Structural collapse or damage from other assorted causes
Technical Failures	Equipment failure from fair wear and tear
	Equipment failure from poor design or implementation
Individuals	Human errors made by our employees
	Human errors made by employees of other organisations (customers, suppliers, partners, agents)
	Human errors made by members of the public
	Gross negligence by our employees, past, present and future
	Malicious actions by disaffected employees, past, present and future
	Malicious actions by individuals belonging to external third-party organisations
	Malicious actions by external individuals, including:
	Criminals
	Hackers
	Terrorists
External Organisations	Malicious actions by third-party organisations including
	Organised crime syndicates
	Terrorist groups
	State-sponsored action groups
	Competitive commercial organisations
	Political pressure groups

Table 9-5: Threat Agent Capabilities

Capability	Explanation
Finance	Money to finance the threat activities
Technical equipment	Computers, specialised networking equipment, etc.
Software	Software tools to perform detailed analysis, probing and penetration of systems
Facilities	Buildings, services and general support
Expertise	People who are educated and trained in the techniques to be applied in mounting the threat activities
Literature	Books, manuals and other documentation containing details of how to mount the threat activities
Experience	People with previous experience of mounting the threat activities

Table 9-6: Threat Agent Motivations

Class	Motivation
Personal Gain	Financial gain
	Revenge
	Gaining knowledge or information
	Exerting power
	Gaining peer recognition and respect
	Satisfying curiosity
	Satisfying antisocial personality traits
	Terrorising certain target groups or individuals
	Enhancing personal status within one of the groups list below
Group Gain	Furthering the aims of political groups
	Furthering the aims of criminal organisations
	Furthering the aims of religious organisations
	Terrorising certain target groups
	Gaining competitive advantage

Table 9-7: Catalysts, Inhibitors and Amplifiers

Inhibitors	Catalysts	Amplifiers
Fear of capture	External events that trigger a response	Peer pressure
Fear of failure	Changes in personal circumstances creating a 'need'	Fame
Insufficient access limiting the opportunity	Step changes in level of access increasing the opportunity	Easy access providing high level of opportunity
High level of technical difficulty	Step changes in level of difficulty through new technologies and tools	Ease of execution because of low level of technical difficulty
High cost of participation	Step changes in level of cost	Low cost of participation
Sensitivity to adverse public opinion	Dramatic changes in public opinion and cultural values	Belief in sympathetic public opinion

Risk Prioritisation

The main reason to do risk assessment is to identify the most important risks in order of priority

It is not possible to mitigate all of the risks all of the time, because you have limited resources with which to do so. What you need to know is which risks are the most dangerous and hence on which ones you should focus your scarce resources for mitigation and management. The main reason for carrying out a risk assessment is establish this ranking of importance. The objective is to come up with a ranked list of risks showing the order of priority.

SABSA® Risk Assessment Method

A qualitative method of risk assessment is described here

The SABSA® approach to risk assessment is to adopt a qualitative measurement method that classifies risks into a series of bands. The following steps describe the method. Table 9-8 provides an example of how these steps are applied and is an example of what is called the Business Risk Model in Chapter 7 (see Figures 7-4 and 7-5). It is based upon the ongoing IBFS case study (see Chapter 4).

SABSA® Risk Assessment Method: Step 1
Business Drivers and Business Attributes (Assets)

The assets are those things of value to your business that you wish to protect and uphold. The SABSA® approach uses the business drivers and Business Attributes concepts to capture the notion of assets. These are then turned into a statement of business requirements for security. See the first four columns in Table 9-8 for the example.

The business drivers used here are samples drawn from the IBFS case study in Chapter 4. Specifically, the business driver 'The customer is king' is drawn from the interview with Rosemary Brown, Senior Vice President, eBusiness and 'We must comply with the law' comes for the interview with Ho Siew Luan, Director of Compliance.

SABSA® Risk Assessment Method: Step 2
Threat Assessment

The SABSA® approach takes the view that since detailed threat assessment is too difficult for a commercial organisation to achieve, the approach should be binary – does this threat affect you or not? Thus you make a list of threats or threat scenarios that you consider to be the relevant threat model for your business. The Business Requirements derived in Step 1 are used to help frame the statement of a threat that will prevent that requirement from being met. (See column 5 of Table 9-8).

NB: The sample table is short and simple, but you should remember that for a given business requirement there may be several threats that put it at risk, and each should be reported in the table by simply splitting the row at that point.

SABSA® Risk Assessment Method: Step 3

Impact Assessment

Once the business requirements and the threats are stated, the next step is to assess what would be the business impact that would result from each threat materialising. This is first stated descriptively (see column 6 of Table 9-8) and then rated on a simple qualitative scale (see column 7):

Table 9-8: An Example Business Risk Model – from the IBFS Case Study

1	2	3	4	5	6	7
ID	Business Driver	Business Attributes	Business Requirement	High-Level Threat	Business Impact	Impact Value
BD001	**'The customer is king'**					
BD001-1	Customer experience impacts competitive advantage or disadvantage	Usability	Security features of any customer-facing business system must not create difficulties in use	Customer becomes frustrated by difficult login processes and other security features	Many customers go somewhere else where the experience is easier	H
BD001-2	Business in the future will be customer-driven	Trustworthy Private Confidential	Customers who provide private information must be confident that it will be protected from disclosure	Customer details disclosed to unauthorised parties, and this becomes generally known	Wide loss of customer confidence Censure or prosecution by the regulators Eventual loss of operating licence	H
BD002	**'We must comply with the law'**					
BD002-1	Data protection legislation	Compliant Private Confidential	Must comply with data protection legislation	Customer details disclosed to unauthorised parties, and this becomes generally known	Wide loss of customer confidence Prosecution by the regulators	H

H – High impact: could potentially do great damage to the business

M – Medium impact: could do significant damage to the business

L – Low impact: could do only minimal damage to the business

SABSA® Risk Assessment Method: Step 4

Vulnerability Assessment

Now comes the assessment of the strengths and weaknesses of your systems, processes and culture. (See columns 8 and 9 of Table 9-8)

The trick here is to try to ignore any additional controls that you have already put in place but to assess the vulnerability as if nothing special had been done. This is called the green field vulnerability assessment. This is often difficult because people always want to explain how they have already done enough to prevent the threat from materialising, but it does help in the development of the security architecture to assess the contribution of all the planned controls over an above the green field situation before any security is built.

8	9	10	11	12	13
Potential High-Level Vulnerability	Green Field Vuln Value	Green Field Risk Cat	High-Level Control Objectives	Target Vuln Value	Mitigated Risk Cat
Multiple logins and authentications, each requiring a new password	H	A (Red)	Establish consistent, easy-to-use authentication and login procedures	L	C (Green)
Inadequate control over privacy of information	H	A (Red)	Establish strong physical security surrounding all customer data, in transit, during processing and in storage Establish strong logical security surrounding all customer data, in transit, during processing and in storage	L	C (Green)
Inadequate control over privacy of information	H	A (Red)	Establish strong physical security surrounding all customer data, in transit, during processing and in storage Establish strong logical security surrounding all customer data, in transit, during processing and in storage	L	C (Green)

The aim of this exercise here is to state some control objectives at the conceptual security architecture level and to use these to drive through the detailed design of controls at the logical, physical, component and operational security architecture levels. This architectural development has different objectives from a security review of an existing system. This same risk assessment method can be applied to conducting such a security review, but there are differences in how you do it. These are described in Part 4 of the book under the operational security architecture (see Chapter 15), since conducting a security review is an operational activity, not an architectural development activity. Hence the subtly different approach.

Once again a simple qualitative scale of measurement is used:

H – High vulnerability: easily exploited by the threat

M – Medium vulnerability: possible for the threat to exploit

L – Low vulnerability: very difficult to exploit by the threat

NB: Under Step 2: Threat Assessment, it was pointed out that there may be more than one threat against a given business requirement, meaning you will need to split the table. Similarly there may be several vulnerabilities mapped to each threat, and once again you will need to split the table at this point to address each vulnerability individually.

SABSA® Risk Assessment Method: Step 5
Risk Category

In the SABSA® approach the prioritisation of risk is based on four risk categories. These categories are calculated directly from the impact rating and vulnerability rating, using the chart in Figure 9-3. Table 9-9 provides more detail as to the meaning of each category. The green field risk category rating is entered into column 10 of the Business Risk Model (see Table 9-8).

It is also very helpful to colour-code the background of the table cell according to the severity of the risk, producing a traffic light system of risk reporting that is easily understood. The colour codes are shown in Figure 9-3 and Table 9-9.

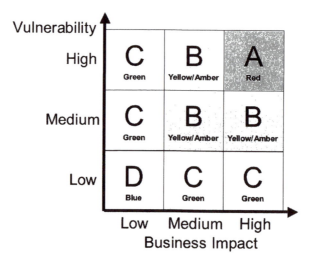

Figure 9-3: Mapping Risk Category to Impact and Vulnerability

Table 9-9: Risk Categories

Category	Colour Code	Description	Required Actions
A	Red	Severe risk	Immediate corrective actions are required either to reduce the vulnerability or to reduce the impact level, or both. These risks are of the highest priority.
B	Yellow or Amber	Significant risk	Appropriate corrective actions should be planned and executed so as to reduce the vulnerability or the impact level.
C	Green	Acceptable risk	These risks are acceptable, because either the vulnerability is at its lowest possible, or the impact is minor, but they should be monitored to ensure that they do not creep into the B category.
D	Blue	Negligible risk	No action needed.

Risk Mitigation

Risk mitigation is the process of setting control objectives and implementing controls through the security architecture

The five steps of the SABSA® risk assessment and prioritisation method cover only the first 10 columns of the Business Risk Model (Table 9-8). Column 11 refers to control objectives, which are part of the conceptual security architecture (see Chapter 7, Figure 7-6). Column 12 gives the target vulnerability after the mitigating controls are applied, and Column 13 shows the mitigated risk category calculated from the target vulnerability. In Chapter 10 the Business Risk Model is discussed again so as to populate these last three columns. This is where you will begin to construct your response to the risks that you have assessed, by designing strategies for risk mitigation and control.

This is a key contextual/ conceptual interface

Columns 10, 11, 12 and 13 of the Business Risk Model represent one of the key interfaces between the contextual security architecture and the conceptual security architecture.

Business Processes and Their Need for Security

SABSA® Matrix reference

This section is relevant to the cell of the SABSA® Matrix entitled Business Process Model on the Contextual row and in the Process column (see Chapter 3, Figure 3-3 and Chapter 7, Figure 7-6). It also provides background for developing the deliverable entitled Business Process Model (see Chapter 7, Figure 7-4). The section looks at some of the sub-process elements that have generic security requirements. This will help you to identify the security requirements that are driven by your business processes.

Business Interactions

Interactions require identification, authentication and authorisation

Interactions between business entities have the following specific security requirements:

- Entity identification: ensuring that each entity is uniquely identified and that there can be no confusion as to which entity is interacting. This requirement is usually met through a naming scheme that ensures uniqueness.

- Entity authentication: proving that an entity claiming to be of a certain identity (the claimant) is actually that entity. The standard of proof required is according to the satisfaction of the other entity in the interaction (the verifier).

- Entity authorisation: once an entity has been uniquely identified and authenticated, the requirement is to restrict the actions to those that have been authorised.

The entities involved in the interactions may be:

- Individual human entities (users);
- Corporate entities (entire businesses or business divisions or departments);
- Logical entities (such as applications, acting on behalf of individuals or corporates).

Business Communications

Methods of communication have an important effect on your security architecture

Communication is an important part of many business processes. The following checklist reminds you of many of the methods used.

- Point-to-point telephone calls;
- Telephone conference calls;
- Mobile telephones;
- Video conferencing;
- Fax communications;
- Dial-up data communications;
- Leased line data communications;
- Broadband data communications using ADSL;
- Cable television;
- Satellite television;
- Local area networks;
- Wide area networks.

The applications also drive the security architecture

The applications of these communications methods include:

- Home banking;
- Corporate office banking;
- Home shopping;
- Internet and web access;
- E-mail;
- On-line chat;
- Corporate networking and distributed applications;
- File transfer;
- On-line transaction processing;
- Remote database access;
- On-demand entertainment.

You need to look at threats, impacts and vulnerabilities for each form of communication

Each method of communicating has its own particular threats and vulnerabilities, and each application has its own business impacts. In developing the Business Risk Model it is essential to consider the ways in which business processes are implemented and the types of technology that they employ to create systems.

Business Transactions

There are many forms of electronic business transactions

Use of electronic on-line communications to transact business may include the following types of electronic transactions:

- Contracts negotiation and agreement;
- Distribution of catalogues of goods and services;
- Specifications;
- Orders;
- Invoices;
- Payments;
- Transfers of ownership;
- Information delivery;
- Electronic publishing for product support.

You need to examine your transactions to define your security reuqirements

Your own list will contain many more transaction types, often specific to your own business. In developing your Business Risk Model you will need to examine each transaction type in context – what are the assets at risk, from what threats, what business impacts could result and what are the potential vulnerabilities?

Organisation and Relationships Affecting Business Security Needs

SABSA® Matrix cross-reference

This section is relevant to the cell of the SABSA® Matrix entitled Business Organisation and Relationships on the Contextual row and in the People column (see Chapter 3, Figure 3-3 and Chapter 7, Figure 7-6). It also provides background for developing the deliverable entitled Organisation and Relationships Model (see Chapter 7, Figure 7-4).

Organisational drivers for information security

Some of the aspects of Business Organisation and Relationships that you will need to examine in order to derive your business drivers and business requirements for security include:

- Management hierarchies and their effect on authorisation, governance and control;
- Integrating the supply chain – trusted interactions between suppliers and customers, the trust model that represents them and the risk model associated with these relationships;
- Outsourcing ICT operations to a third-party service provider – managing security policy making and its implementation, and the risk model that accompanies an outsourcing strategy;

- Strategic partnerships – how close you get, how much information you share, the liabilities implied by such a partnership and other aspects of the Business Risk Model;

- Joint ventures – how much information is shared and how much is segregated (JVs pose difficult problems where you collaborate on some fronts but compete on others. The development of a security domain model is essential to address these issues.);

- Mergers, acquisitions and divestments – whether the security architecture easily support changes in the overall structure of the enterprise (Once again the use of a security domain model makes these requirements much easier to address than if the security architecture is monolithic.).

Location Dependence of Business Security Needs

SABSA® Matrix cross-reference

This section is relevant to the cell of the SABSA® Matrix entitled Business Geography on the Contextual row and in the Location column (see Chapter 3, Figure 3-3 and Chapter 7, Figure 7-6). It also provides background for developing the deliverable entitled Business Geography Model (see Chapter 7, Figure 7-4).

The Global Village Marketplace

The Internet has made business much less dependent upon relative location of the players

The Internet has created the so-called global village in which everyone from an individual, through small businesses, medium-sized businesses, right up to the largest businesses has access to the same marketplace, either as a customer or as a supplier. This has effectively removed many of the traditional barriers associated with location. However, it has introduced some interesting challenges for securing the business, since you can no longer see, feel and touch the other parties to your business transactions. This distance and remoteness has a huge impact on the management of trust relationships, and will provide a key business driver for your Business Risk Model.

Remote Working

Many people now work from remote locations

Another modern development fuelled by Internet technology is the trend towards workers no longer being located in corporate offices. People can often work from home (teleworkers or telecommuters). Those who travel on business (the road warriors) can keep in touch using telephones and e-mail and have a virtual office that moves around with them, based on a laptop computer and a mobile telephone. This introduces a broad set of requirements to secure remote business information processing and communications in hostile environments connected over long-distance third-party networks.

Virtual teams are spread across the world using ICT to communicate

Even those who do work in corporate offices may find themselves working in virtual teams, where the group consists of people in different countries and different time zones working as a team using information and communications technology as the means to communicate and to hold together the team and its activities. Some of the team may be inside a corporate office somewhere in the world, and others may be working from home, from a hotel room, from an airport lounge or from their car.

Data networks connect distant physical offices into a single logical office

It is certainly common for large organisations to have multi-site offices, often in different countries, and for these offices to be linked by corporate data networks supporting on-line communications between various parts of the business.

Some virtual companies have no office at all

In some cases you will even find virtual companies who have no corporate offices at all where everyone is a home worker or road warrior, but these tend to be small hi-tech companies in the knowledge economy.

More business drivers

All of these potential modes of remote working are key business drivers for the Business Risk Model.

Time Dependency of Business Security Needs

SABSA® Matrix cross-reference

This section is relevant to the cell of the SABSA® Matrix entitled Business Time Dependencies on the Contextual row and in the Time column (see Chapter 3, Figure 3-3 and Chapter 7, Figure 7-6). It also provides background for developing the deliverable entitled Time Dependencies Model (see Chapter 7, Figure 7-4).

Time-Related Business Drivers

- Business transaction turnaround times. The security architecture must support these. In particular security mechanisms must not slow down response times beyond business tolerances.

- Business transaction lifetime. These affect the mechanisms that you apply to secure business transactions. The security mechanisms must have llifetimes exceeding those of the transactions that they secure with a tolerable margin of safety.

- Business deadlines. For example, banking cut-offs and stock-market closing times may have an impact on how the security architecture is to be implemented. In particular the provision of secure time-stamps on certain types of business transactions may be a fraud-prevention mechanism to detect attempts to manipulate business cut-offs. Perhaps the most extreme type of example would be placing a bet on a horse race after the race has finished and the result is known – there may be parallels in your business.

- Record retention times. The security architecture needs to ensure that data can be retrieved and read and used right up to the end of the period, which is often a regulatory requirement. One of the main threats here is the withdrawal of support for old storage media technologies. You may have archived copies of electronic documents on old tapes or disks stored in a vault somwhere, but do you have the sub-systems to read these items? Consider the disappearance of 8-inch and 5-inch floppy diskette drives.

- Response to customers. It must be within a time that they expect. This is another example of the need to ensure that security mechanisms and procedures do not delay the business responses beyond an allowable tolerance threshold.

- Just-in-time operations. These are needed for manufacturing operations where stock levels are kept to an absolute minimum to maximise cash flow in the business. If the security mechanisms were to cause delays that meant JIT deadlines were missed, this would have a damaging effect on business continuity.

- Time to market. This means balancing the risk of going to market with a product or service that may not be perfect in terms of its security against investing more time to get the security to an acceptable level whilst missing a business opportunity. Risk management is never easy, and mitigating one risk will always increase at least one other risk. Always be aware of the risk of doing something versus the risk of not doing it.

Time-Based Security[11]

Consider an attack on a secure system. The time taken to break into the system depends upon how much security there is. No security, zero time. Some security takes a short time. High security takes a long time. It is an easy concept to understand.

Now as soon as the attack begins there is some kind of detection sub-system that starts to work. It takes a finite time for that sub-system to detect and notify management that an attack is happening (to raise the alarm). Once notified, it then takes management a further finite time to react to the alarm and to repel the attack. The effectiveness of the security, or the exposure, can be calculated in terms of time, being a mathematical relationship between these parameters. The outline of the mathematics is shown below:

Time-Based Security

P is the Protection Value measured in time (= the time that the system will resist attack – the time it takes to break into it)

D is the Detection Value measured in time (= the time it takes for the system to raise the alarm)

R is the Reaction Value measured in time (= the time it takes for the system management to react to an alarm)

IF P > D + R THEN the system is secure and the attack will fail

IF P < D + R THEN the system is exposed and the attack will succeed

E is the Exposure Value measured in time (= the time during which the system is exposed and the attack can cause damage)

E = D + R - P

The point of all this is that by measuring these time-based parameters you can begin to design systems that are more secure and less exposed. In particular the aim is to reduce both D and R as close to zero as possible and to use this as a means to select components in the component security architecture.

To Summarise: Contextual Security Architecture

Information security is a great enabler of business activities. It allows you to create solutions to business problems and to mitigate business risks down to a level of acceptability, such that these otherwise risky business activities can be carried out safely. The description of your business needs for information security is called the contextual security architecture.

Information security is especially applicable in all types of digital business where the application of information and communications technology is used to create new ways of doing business. Specific applications include electronic publishing, on-demand entertainment, value-added information services, remote process control, supply chain management, research and information gathering, eBanking, eProcurement and eGovernment.

---

[11]As exemplified in the book: *Time Based Security* by Winn Schwartau, published by Interpact Press 1999, ISBN 0962870048, but these ideas have been around for a long time before Mr Schwartau's book.

Information security is also essential to maintaining operational continuity and stability in the business. The key dependencies include revenue generation, customer service, market reputation, management control, qualifying for operating licences in regulated industries and maintaining employee confidence and shareholder confidence.

In safety-critical business systems, information security contributes to their safe operation by protecting remote communications against accidental corruption or malicious attack. It also contributes to providing assurance of the correct operation of such systems.

There are many business goals and success factors that are protected by information security architecture and many operational risks that are mitigated. The most important of these goals include brand protection, fraud prevention, loss prevention, business continuity management, strategic business development, fulfilling legal obligations and maintaining the confidence of key stakeholders.

In order to assess and manage operational risks you need suitable methods and processes. You need a suitable model of risk in terms of assets, threats, impacts and vulnerabilities, from which you derive a method of assessing and analysing risks. The objective is to prioritise your risks and manage them by mitigating the most important ones.

The SABSA® Business Risk Model is business-driven, with each business driver being derived from a detailed examination of your business activities. The SABSA® Business Attributes Profile helps to begin this process. As well as the core business activities you must also examine your business processes, your organisational structure and relationships with other organisations, the location dependence of your business, and its time dependency.

Chapter 10: Conceptual Security Architecture

The conceptual security architecture is where the security architect really starts to add value. At this stage you have gathered and analysed all the necessary information about the business of the organisation. What is needed now is a vision of the future – a conceptualisation of the types of solution that will satisfy the business needs. If you get this part right, then everything else should flow with ease. If you get this part wrong, nothing at the lower layers of the architecture will ever fix it. This chapter describes some of the key areas where you will need to apply your conceptual creativity.

In this chapter you will learn about:

- The importance of conceptual thinking;

- How to develop the SABSA® Business Attributes Profile as a means to conceptualise the real business and its requirements for security;

- How to extend the SABSA® Business Risk Model so as to integrate a set of control objectives that are a conceptualisation of the business needs for risk mitigation;

- How to use architectural layering techniques and how to apply these to a variety of situations;

- A layered architectural model of security infrastructure and how to determine which services are best placed at which layers of this layered infrastructure model;

- Some of the major security strategies that you will need to include in your conceptual security architecture;

- The concept of a security entity and how entity relationships are characterised by the amount of trust between the parties;

- A method of analysing complex trust relationships into simple components;

- The concept of a security domain and how this concept can be used as a powerful modelling tool to represent a real business;

- Some important lifetimes and deadlines that affect security;

- How to assess the current state of your enterprise security architecture as a basis for planning a programme of quick wins.

Conceptual Thinking

Conceptual architecture is about being able to design the forest rather than the trees

There is a skill called conceptual thinking that is essential to being a successful architect. The key to mastering this skill is learning to stand back from the trees and being able to see the forest. Conceptual architecture is very much at the level of the forest. Individual trees, or even small groups of trees should not distract you. You are however concerned with the overall shape and size of the forest, the overall mix of tree species and the way they are to be grouped to create habitats for humans and wildlife alike. You are also concerned with the overall texture of the forest – the balance between wooded areas and clearings, the structure of the firebreaks and pathways and the density of planting in certain areas – and so on.

Conceptual architecture is about the big picture

You are concerned here with the big picture, the helicopter view and the strategic plan for your security architecture. You must not be concerned with the details – they will come later. The conceptual architect is a visionary and a missionary – someone who can create a new vision of the future and sell that vision to others, leading the intellectual thinking of the architecture team and its clients.

This book is designed to help you be a successful security architect

If this seems challenging – it is! However, in writing this book the authors are attempting to help you to address this challenge. Their intention is that by sharing their experience with you, you will be able to grow into this role. Good luck!

Business Attributes Profile

SABSA® Matrix cross-reference

Please refer to Chapter 3, Figure 3-3 and Chapter 7, Figure 7-6, the SABSA® Matrix – Conceptual Layer, Assets column, where you will see a cell entitled Business Attributes Profile. In Chapter 7, Figure 7-5 this also appears as key deliverable of the conceptual security architecture. This section explains in detail how this Business Attributes Profile is used as the key tool for conceptualising the business assets that need protection in an information security architecture.

The taxonomy of Business Attributes captures many years of practical experience

The concept of Business Attributes and metrics was introduced in Chapter 6. These Business Attributes have been compiled from the extensive experience of the authors of working with clients. The experience reflects work done with numerous clients in many countries and different industry segments. Over the course of that work it has become clear that although every business is unique, there are many commonly recurring themes. This experience has been used to create a taxonomy of Business Attributes, shown in Figure 6-3 and defined in more detail in Table 6-2 – see Chapter 6.

Business Attributes are used in two different ways

During the contextual and conceptual security architecture phases, as mapped out in the flow charts in Chapter 7, Figure 7-4 and Figure 7-5, the Business Attributes Database (represented by Table 6-3) is used in two different ways:

- To prompt your thinking on business strategies, business drivers, business assets, goals and objectives (contextual phase – Figure 7-4);

- To map Business Attributes to business drivers in the Business Risk Model (conceptual phase – Figure 7-5) using the risk assessment methodology defined in detail in Chapter 9 – see also Table 9-8.

Your Business Attributes Profile is a conceptual representation of your business

The Business Attribute Profile is the complete set of Business Attributes that you believe represents your business, mapped to business drivers and business risks, and with a measurement approach for producing metrics and specific performance targets defined for each one. An example of this is shown in Chapter 6, Table 6-5.

The Business Attributes Profile is a powerful tool

This profile is a powerful tool that allows any unique business to be translated into common terminology and normalised. The profile selects only those Business Attributes that apply to this specific business (creating new attributes if there are found to be gaps). The taxonomy provides a checklist of possible attributes. The Business Analysts can decide whether or not a given attribute should be included in this specific profile. The senior executives will usually need to sign off on the overall Business Attributes Profile.

The Business Attributes Profile is an important part of your conceptual security architecture

The Business Attributes Profile is an important conceptualisation of the real business and forms a core part of the conceptual security architecture. It appears in the first cell of the second row of the SABSA® Matrix shown in Table 3- 3 in Chapter 3 and Figure 7-4 in Chapter 7.

The Business Attributes Profile provides the target for the measurement phase

It also allows the selection of metrics that are used to set performance targets as an integral part of the Business Attributes Profile that can later be measured to answer the question: 'Did we hit the target?' This too is at the choice of the business analysts, using either the suggested measurement approaches in the detailed definitions of the attributes in Chapter 6 (see Table 6-2), or creating new measurement approaches if this seems more appropriate. Once again, the performance targets usually need to be signed off at senior executive level.

This integrates the Manage and Measure phase with the Strategy and Concepts phase

Thus the Manage and Measure activity in the SABSA® Lifecycle is based upon the Business Attributes Profile that was set out during the Strategy and Concept phase of activity and which has been customised specifically to conceptualise this unique business.

Control Objectives

SABSA® Matrix cross-reference

Please refer to Chapter 3, Figure 3-3 and Chapter 7, Figure 7-6, the SABSA® Matrix – Conceptual Layer, Motivation column, where you will see a cell entitled Control Objectives. In Chapter 7, Figure 7-5 this also appears as key deliverable of the conceptual security architecture – the control objectives integrated into the Business Risk Model. This section explains in detail how the control objectives are used as the key tool for conceptualising the mitigation strategy to address the identified business risks.

Control objectives state the desired result of implementing controls

A control objective is a statement of a desired result or purpose to be achieved by implementing controls within a particular business activity. Controls are implemented through policies, organisational structures, processes, practices and procedures, and through technical systems.

Control objectives can be generic good practice or specific to a business need

A control objective can be stated in response to specific business requirements for control, or it can be a generic 'good practice' statement that should be applied to all businesses. This latter use of control objectives is at the heart of the CobiT[TM1] Framework, which focuses on generic ICT control objectives.

Control objectives conceptualise the Business Risk Model

The SABSA® Methodology uses control objectives as a means to conceptualise the mitigation strategy developed through the Business Risk Model. During the contextual security architecture phase you build a Business Risk Model as exemplified in Chapter 9, Table 9-8. Like the Business Attributes, the control objectives are a means to take a unique real business and normalise it into common terminology and abstract concepts that can be used to drive more detailed design work, free from the confusion that unique real business detail can create.

The control objectives form an interface between the contextual and conceptual layers

In Table 9-8 there were three columns to be filled in at this later stage. You now decide upon the control objectives that best express your needs for security and control and insert them into column 11 of the Business Risk Model. This is an important interface between the description of the real

[1]CobiT: Control Objectives for Information and related Technology. See www.isaca.org

business (the contextual security architecture) and the description of a conceptual model of the business (the conceptual security architecture). Columns 12 and 13 of the Business Risk Model (Figure 9-8) are used to record the target vulnerability after the planned risk mitigation has been applied and the new overall risk category that results from that new reduced vulnerability level.

There are several sources of generic 'good practice' control objectives

In selecting your control objectives you can either create your own (and you will probably need to do this at least some of the time) or you can draw upon other sources of standard control objectives such as:

- ISO/IEC 17799: 'A Code of Practice for Information Security Management'[2];

- ISO/IEC 21827: 'Systems Security Engineering Capability Maturity Model'[3];

- CobiT™: 'Control Objectives for Information and related Technology'[4];

- ISF's[5] 'Standard for Good Practice'[6];

- 'IT Baselines Protection Manual' published by Bundesamt für Sicherheit in der Informationstechnik (BSI)[7].

The control objectives form a core part of the conceptual security architecture

Like the Business Attributes Profile, the control objectives form an important conceptualisation of the real business, and are also a core part of the conceptual security architecture.

Security Strategies and Architectural Layering

SABSA® Matrix cross-reference

Please refer to Chapter 3, Figure 3-3 and Chapter 7, Figure 7-6, the SABSA® Matrix – Conceptual Layer, Process column, where you will see a cell entitled Security Strategies and Architectural Layering. In Chapter 7, Figure 7-5 this also appears as key deliverable of the conceptual security architecture.

There are many approaches to layering and security strategy

There are many security strategies that you can adopt and many ways in which you can layer your security architecture. This section examines some of these possibilities in some detail, at a conceptual level. Figure 7-5 also refers to a number of individual strategy breakout documents. These are individual descriptions of each of the major strategies that you decide should be included in your conceptual security architecture.

Security architecture is not the same as software architecture

There is one word of caution needed for those readers who regard themselves as software architects. This section has very little to do with software architecture. Where it does address that concept, it is made explicitly clear. Thus when you examine the various layered models of security architecture, you must resist the temptation to translate them into software designs – they are not software designs. This chapter is about conceptual security architecture, not software architecture, and these layered models are conceptual models, not detailed logical designs.

---

[2]See www.iso.org

[3]See www.sse-cmm.org

[4]See www.isaca.org

[5]ISF: Information Security Forum

[6]See www.isfsecuritystandard.com

[7]See www.bsi.de

Multi-Layered Security

Increased effectiveness is achieved by multiple layers of security of different types

People often refer to the onion-skin model of security, where layer upon layer of defence is built up one on top of another. That analogy has been transformed here to simplify the diagram. Consider an electrical cable with the conductor in the centre, and layer upon layer of insulation built up around the conductor. The concept is shown in Figure 10-1. The conductor represents the information assets (which are themselves a conceptualisation of the real business) that you wish to protect. Around that are multiple layers of security, each at a different level of detail. Closest to the assets are security controls that act directly on the information assets – cryptographic controls. As you move outwards the controls become more and more generic, until at the outer layer you have responsibilities, organisation and policy.

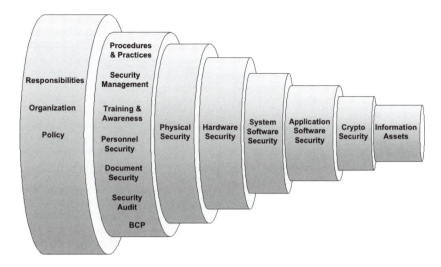

Figure 10-1: Multi-Layering of Security

Multi-layering of security avoids any single point of failure – if one control fails, another will be effective

The primary reason for this multi-layered approach is to ensure that there is no single point of failure in the security measures. If one measure fails to stop a security incident, then there are others that do the job in a different way. The multiple layers provide a reasonable level of assurance that there are multiple ways of preventing security breaches. This is a fundamental principle that is strongly recommended that you adopt in your security architecture.

Multi-Tiered Incident Handling

Improved effectiveness is also achieved through multi-tiered security services

Another way to improve the effectiveness of your security is the provision of multi-tiered security services for dealing with potential security incidents. First you try to prevent them. If that fails, you need to contain the effects. You also need to detect an incident and raise the alarm, then react to the incident to recover from its effects and restore the status of business as usual. You also need to collect evidence to track events, assist with restoration and use for forensic purposes. In addition, the entire process needs a level of assurance that it all works correctly. Figure 10-2 shows this multi-tiered approach in diagrammatic format.

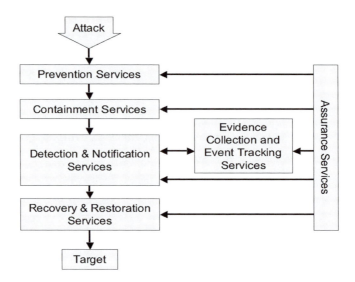

Figure 10-2: Multi-Tiered Security Services

A comprehensive list of security service is in Chapter 11

A full list of security services classified under these broad tier-headings is contained in the description of the logical security architecture in Chapter 11. In creating your security architecture you should aim to have a mix of security services that provides adequate coverage in each of these tiers of this conceptual model.

Security Infrastructure Layered Architecture

You need some security infrastructure to support security services

The provision of security services requires some security infrastructure. This should comprise:

- Common security services delivered to applications through a common applications security services API;

- Security middleware to integrate and deliver the common security services across distributed applications;

- Security services on platforms (systems);

- Security services embedded in the network.

The infrastructure architecture should be layered

Figure 10-3 shows the layered architecture of the infrastructure and the security services at each layer.

Network and platform security is distinct from application security

An important feature of this diagram (apart from showing the common services and their integration) is the recognition that platforms and networks are separate elements and quite distinct from applications. They form the foundation upon which the middleware and applications are built.

The distinction of security domains for networks and platforms supports an outsourcing strategy

It is quite possible that in many organisations both the platforms (meaning hardware boxes and their operating systems) and the networks may be outsourced for operations by a third-party service provider, if not immediately then at some future date. Thus they must be treated as separate security domains[8] under the control of separate security policy authorities with separate security policies, so that no disruption or major operational difficulty is encountered at the time of outsourcing.

---

[8]See the section in this chapter on Security Domains.

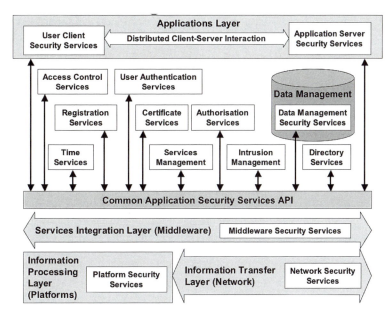

Figure 10-3: Layered Security Infrastructure Architecture

The Common Security Services API[9] Architecture

To facilitate integration of real-world components you need a common security services API architecture

Figure 10-3 shows a common application security services API. In the real world, hardware and software are often provided as off-the-shelf components by vendors. The actual interfaces to these devices are usually vendor-specific. To integrate these various products into your architecture you need to construct the enterprise common security services API as a series of layered APIs, as shown in Figure 10-4.

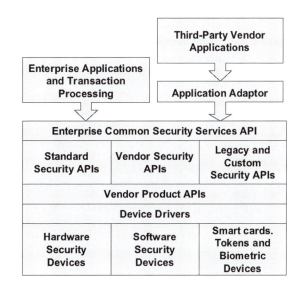

Figure 10-4: Multi-Layered Common Security Services API Architecture

---

[9]API: application program interface

The API model is purely conceptual

This layered API framework is a conceptual model only. It is not meant to imply any specific software development method and should be equally applicable in object-oriented software environments as it is in more traditional software development. The developers can use this conceptual approach to drive their actual software design.

To make this API model work, the software architecture itself has to be properly designed

It is essential to realise that this model implies a sound overall software architecture, too. The upper software layers of the model have to be designed from the beginning to be able to support the extensibility and functional substitution at the lower levels. This is simply good software architecture, but there are unfortunately many software developers who do not seem to understand layered architectures. Instead they build monolithic application software in which low-level mechanisms (such as a smart card data set) are hard-coded into the business logic of the application. The implementation of a common application security services API as described here should have the beneficial effect of preventing that sort of sloppy software design and introducing instead proper architectural principles governing the development of software.

This requires some in-house development

The layer labelled Enterprise Common Security Services API is maintained in-house by your systems development team, or, if you do not have an in-house systems development capability, by a contracted systems house. Having that standard interface allows all your in-house-developed or custom-developed applications to see exactly the same API, whatever underlying products are chosen.

This approach allows the integration of components from many different vendors

The underlying products can be drawn together from a number of different vendors, each with its own proprietary interfaces. The products can also be changed and replaced without the applications needing to be changed, since all the integration is done within the API architecture. This architectural approach effectively decouples the applications from the underlying product APIs, preserves flexibility and limits development costs.

Third-party applications are integrated using an application adaptor

There still remains the issue of third-party applications, which like the lower-level products have their own vendor-specific API. These can be integrated into the entire API architecture by constructing application adaptors for each one.

Application adaptors are software modules that provide a conversion interface

Application adaptors are software modules that convert the calls from the third-party application APIs into the standard calls of the enterprise-common security services API. With this additional sub-layer the entire range of applications (in-house and third-party) can be integrated with the entire range of common security services.

Common security services are integrated as if they were applications

The common security services are also likely to be supported by vendor products (such as PKI products, directory products, etc.), and these can be integrated in exactly the same way as the applications. The best way to look at these common security services is to view them as pseudo-applications with their own APIs.

Application Security Services Architecture

Applications security architecture is a specialist area

The previous section discussed the delivery of common security services to applications through layered infrastructure architecture. The applications part of this deserves a more detailed discussion.

Legacy applications are often constructed on a stovepipe architecture

If you examine the range of legacy applications in most organisations you will find that each one has been independently designed, developed and implemented. Each is unique, and this uniqueness shows up especially well in respect of the way these applications are secured. However, the problem goes much deeper than just security. What you find is that each application has its own database and its own registry of users, and that these are very difficult to share with other applications. This situation is often described as a stovepipe model, in which each application is contained in a vertical stovepipe, allowing information to flow into and out of the application at the end of the pipe but preventing any cross-flow between the applications. Figure 10-5 provides an illustration of this concept.

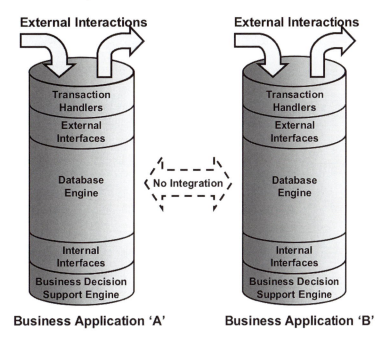

Figure 10-5: The Stovepipe Model of Legacy Applications

The 'stove-pipe' architecture arises through lack of planning and coordination

This model was not planned – it just happened this way as a result of independent, uncoordinated developments. It is this limiting situation that has driven many organisations to take on the concept of strategic architecture to ensure that there is an overall vision of how applications are built, and more particularly, how they can be integrated with one another when the business needs such integration.

This stovepipe approach makes integration difficult

The digital business revolution has also drawn particular attention to these legacy problems, because the building of digital business systems usually means integrating a web-based front end with several legacy back-end systems. In the stovepipe model this can be very difficult indeed.

Modern architectural thinking leads to the daisy model of application architecture

To address the problems posed by the poor integration characteristics of the stovepipe applications, ICT architects are taking a much more strategic view. In this view, there is a common infrastructure that is shared by all applications. The most important part of this infrastructure is the provision of a central data repository, shared between the applications, and often referred to as a data warehouse. Around this central data repository are a number of common services, again shared by applications because they are common – needed by all applications. A good example of a common service is printing. The central repository is also surrounded by the individual applications, each of which makes use of the central data repository and the common services. There are also common external interfaces, such as the web interface. This model has been represented as a daisy, as shown in Figure 10-6. Both the common services and the applications are integrated through a series of common interfaces (APIs), as shown earlier in Figure 10-3.

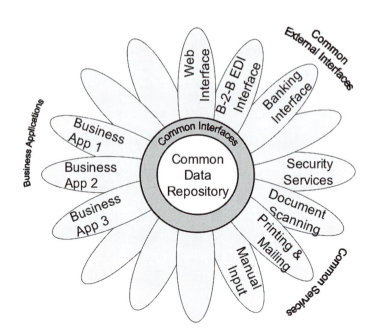

Figure 10-6: The Daisy Model of an Integrated Applications Architecture

The 'daisy' architecture concept is well-aligned with providing common security services

This model harmonises perfectly with the desire to identify and centralise a series of common application security services as shown above in Figure 10-3. They simply take their place alongside other common services that applications need.

Placing of Security Services in the Architecture Layers

Which security services are appropriate at which layer?

In the infrastructure architecture model presented in Figure 10-3 the discussions have focused so far on the common security services provided to applications. However, there are other layers in this model where security service can and should be provided. These include:

- Middleware security services – within the middleware layer itself;

- Data management security services – provided within the databases and possibly considered as part of the middleware security services;

- Network security services – within the network;

- Platform security services – within the individual platforms.

The question now arises – which security services are appropriate at each of these layers, including the application layer? The next five sections address this question.

Security Services in the Applications Layer

Application security is about authorisation

The main focus of application security is to address the question of who is allowed to do what within the application, and how much. That is authorisation.

You need an authorisation process

Authorisations are created through some suitable management process where business users are granted privileges. These privileges include things like:

- Application functions they are allowed to use;

- Application data they are allowed to read, update and create;

- Limits on application transactions they are allowed to make (especially financial transactions);

- Dual control on some sensitive transactions where a second person is also needed to authorise the transaction;

- Sometimes there is a context-based set of rules governing the location of the user for certain activities (e.g. head office desk versus hotel dial-up) or the time of day or day of week when the activity is carried out.

Logical access control enforces authorisations   Authorisations are then enforced by the system through a logical access control service.

Front-end authentication   As a front end to access control, you also need authentication to prove that the claimant really is the authorised party.

Back-end audit trails   As a back-end to access control you also need audit trails to tell you historically who did what and when.

Security administration for creating and editing   You also need tools for creating and editing the authorisations and reviewing the audit trail. This activity is often called security administration.

The Six As of application security   Application security services can be summarised under the Six As:

- Authorisation (the process of granting a privilege);

- Authentication (the process of verifying identity);

- Access control (the process of making access decisions based on checking authorisations and authenticating identity);

- Audit (the process of writing, storing and reviewing records of all access attempts, decisions and outcomes);

- Administration (administering privileges and all associated activities);

- Application-to-application communications security.

Legacy systems are often self-contained and difficult to integrate   Legacy applications and third-party vendor applications are often characterised by having their own unique, in-built access control sub-system. Integration of these sub-systems between applications is usually a nightmare. The holy grail of application security architecture is therefore the ability to integrate all applications under a single sub-system for the Six As, using the integrated API approach described above.

An integrated application security architecture has major benefits   Some major benefits of a wholly integrated architecture are:

- Single window for user administration – leading to a reduced training need, reduced support, higher productivity and lower costs of administration.

- Single authorisation database – leading to a single registration for each user instead of multiple registrations, lower administration overheads, better control over total user privilege, less risk of dormant accounts, and the ability to block or delete a user's access to all applications from a single action (for leavers).

- Single sign-on for the users – providing better password control (this problem is well known and much debated, so no detailed discussion is presented here).

Role-based access control is a conceptual approach needed to deliver these benefits

The major architectural approach for providing this integrated, single administration window, single authorisation database, single sign-on model is through role-based access control (RBAC). This is discussed in more detail below in the section entitled Authentication, Authorisation and Audit Strategy.

Application level communications

Application-to-application communications needs some further explanation. In Figure 10-3 this is shown as distributed client-server interactions but it could be any type of application-level end-to-end communications. Whatever the precise mechanisms used, many applications send files, messages or transactions to other applications, and these need to be protected during transmission. The security services needed are:

- Confidentiality;
- Integrity;
- Authenticity;
- Non-repudiation.

Network security and applications communications security are not the same thing at all

There are those who would argue that this type of security falls into the domain of network security – which is discussed a little later on. The authors disagree with that proposition because:

- The network does not understand application data structures (it sees only a payload of unknown structure) and therefore cannot apply structure-dependent security mechanisms (which are needed for three out of the four security services listed above).

- The network is frequently owned and operated by a third party, providing commercial network transport services to the organisation that owns the applications and their information. You cannot outsource the protection of applications data to someone who knows nothing about the applications and who has no way of controlling them.

Network security protects network resources; application security protects application resources

The rule is very simple. Network security is needed to protect the network. Application security is needed to protect the applications. These four application communications security services are all provided on an end-to-end basis through the use of cryptographic techniques. The integration of the cryptographic sub-systems (usually vendor products) needed to deliver these security services is achieved through the enterprise common application security services API in the normal way, as described earlier in this chapter.

There is widespread use of data encryption in network layers

Nevertheless there is a widespread school of thought and practice that says you should put data encryption into the network layers, not the application layer. The whole concept of a VPN is built on this principle. The section headed Security Services in the Information Transfer (Network) Layer later in this chapter provides a more detailed analysis of the issues.

Security Services in the Middleware Layer

Middleware organises the logical service view of a distributed system

The function of middleware is to provide transparency of certain common services for distributed applications. Specifically, client and server applications do not need to know the details of each other's locations (the physical, server view of life) because the middleware handles all that stuff transparently, and provides the application with a logical, service view of life. The location and distribution of the servers does not matter to the application and is hidden within the middleware.

The objectives for middleware are to enable:

- Seamless interactions between application components via a set of common, consistent APIs;

- Node, service and data location transparency;

- Scalability and extensibility;

- Reliability and availability;

- Vendor, platform, operating system and networking protocol independence.

Middleware commonly deals with the following types of basic services:

- Remote procedure calls (RPCs) from client to server;

- Inter-process messaging management (message queuing and message passing);

- Object request broker (ORB) management;

- Data management;

- Load balancing between physical servers for logical services;

- Inter-process resource sharing;

- Prioritisation of application services;

- Security services management.

There are two approaches to providing security services within the middleware layer:

Explicit Security Services:

Explicit security services – called explicitly by the application through an API

Explicitly requested by applications through explicit security API calls. In this case the application is aware of the security service and of the results of any security events (such as the success or failure of a verification of a digital signature).

The application may need to receive a result for its own use

The application makes requests and gets reports back again. This is necessary to meet certain types of business requirements (for example, where an application needs to store its own audit trail of digitally signed transactions for evidence purposes, and where the signature keys used belong to and are in the explicit control of the application users.

Implicit Security Services:

Implicit security services – provided by the middleware transparently to the application

Provided from within the middleware transparently without the explicit knowledge of the application. These are provided using resources (such as encryption and authentication keys) that belong to the middleware itself rather to the application and its users. These services are needed to provide adequate security within the middleware infrastructure, over and above anything that might be requested by an application, and the decisions about applying security are made by the middleware.

The middleware has physical location knowledge and can apply location-dependent context rules

For example, when the middleware finds a server on the same physical platform, it will not be necessary to encrypt the inter-process communications. However, when a remote procedure call is to be made to another physical server, the request and response may need to be protected from eavesdroppers in their journey over the network.

The objectives of providing security within the middleware are to:

- Provide a secure infrastructure upon which applications can run;

- Offer explicit security API calls to applications;

- Enforce logical and physical security domains and domain policies (see the section later in this chapter on the Security Domain Model;

- Protect itself from logical attack;

- Be capable of creating a trusted operating environment for entities that have established trust relationships.

Middleware security services are provided independently of any other layer

Middleware security services, both explicit and implicit must be provided completely independently of any security services provided in lower layers, such as in the information transfer (network) layer. This is because it is dangerous to rely upon the existence of security services in another layer which is completely beyond the control of this layer, and which cannot even be monitored by this layer to ensure that the security services are available and switched on. This view also harmonises with the principles explained for providing security in the information transfer layer (the network) – see later in this chapter.

Explicit security services are called through the common security services API

Explicit security services in the middleware layer include all those listed as security services for the applications layer (see above) and are called through the enterprise common application security services API. These services are discussed in greater detail in Chapter 11, Logical Security Architecture.

Implicit middleware security services include the following:

- Entity authentication for entities making use of the middleware infrastructure;

- Entity authorisation and role management;

- Logical domain access control based upon entity roles;

- Physical middleware node-to-node mutual authentication;

- Physical middleware node-to-node confidentiality of transmitted data;

- Physical middleware node-to-node protection of message and object integrity;

- Traffic flow confidentiality, preventing the application traffic flows from being analysed for source, destination, volumes and timing;

- Real-time security monitoring, intrusion detection and reporting.

There may be constraints on implementing the middleware security architecture due to lack of functionality in vendor products

At the time of writing there are some limitations on the ability to implement this range of implicit security services due to the lack of functionality in vendor middleware products. There are also limitations that arise through performance constraints and the need to support legacy applications. However, it is the intention here to help you to specify a target security architecture, which will not necessarily be capable of full implementation on Day 1.

Middleware security requires cross-platform inter-operability

One of the important prerequisites for middleware security services is inter-operability across multiple platforms, which requires either middleware security service standards to be defined and adopted, and where there are multiple standards supported, the provision of suitable translation services from one standardised environment to another. This translation service is the role fulfilled by the Application Adaptor shown in Figure 10-4.

Data Management Security Services

Data management has its own special security requirements

Among the basic service types that are listed above in describing the function of middleware is data management. This has special requirements for security.

Data management must implement authorised (controlled) access to data

Data management has a dual role: It provides both access to the application information resources and protection of these information resources. The key to achieving these apparently contradictory goals is authorisation, and the provision of appropriate security services within this layer is critical to the success of the overall applications architecture.

The data management function embraces the following components:

- Metadata management;
- Relational database management;
- Object-oriented database;
- Management systems;
- Database access;
- Data warehousing;
- Data mining;
- Transaction processing monitoring.

Data management sub-system security services

Thus the important security services required in the data management sub-systems are:

- Access control to data at the object level, using labelling mechanisms within the metadata as a means to match data object classification to subject access privileges, based upon subject roles (see a later section for a discussion on role-based access control). In conventional databases this can include access control at the level of databases, tables, views, records, fields and stored procedures, with privileges granted according to database function (select, insert, update, delete, execute).

- Authorisations based upon business need and the segregation of write access (for making transactions and other updates) as against read-only access for information retrieval, analytics, etc.

- Data availability protection, using a variety of backup and restoration techniques.

- Data integrity protection within databases, to maintain a high level of confidence in the quality, accuracy and cleanliness of stored data. There are various security mechanisms that can be applied, including:

  - Atomic transactions, commitment, recoverability and serialisability;

- 'Before image' and 'after image' journals with checkpoints, rollback and roll-forward to restore a database to a specific business position for business continuity purposes;

- Field contents validation;

- Field limits validation;

- Two-phase commitment of distributed database transactions;

- Using database views[10] as an access control mechanism;

- Using stored procedures[11] and triggers[12] to provide secure encapsulation of sensitive functions and prevent access to powerful functions in native form;

- Using triggers to enforce special access rules at the specific object or subject level (such as time-context-based access control for time of day, day of week, or preventing subjects who are both employees and customers from updating their personal records for fraudulent purposes – for example, as in the case of an electricity supply company, where an employee might potentially alter the record of the amount of electricity consumed in his own household).

- Data confidentiality protection, ensuring that stored data is only revealed to authorised subjects.

- Authentication of SQL requests and responses (and other database access mechanisms: OQL, Java, Smalltalk, C++, etc.), especially for remote database access (RDA).

Data management sub-system security management services

The important security management services required in the data management sub-system include:

- The process for designating the sensitivity and criticality of data (data classification);

- The designation of stewardship roles and the execution of these roles;

- The use of standard naming conventions for data objects as a part of an integrated data architecture;

- The support for standard data formats to provide inter-operability with other organisations (such as support for XML[13] formats).

Security Services in the Information Transfer (Network) Layer

Information transfer (network) sub-layering

The information transfer layer is often referred to as the network. It comprises several sub-layers: a sub-net (OSI layers 1 and 2), a network layer (OSI layer 3) and a transport layer (OSI layer 4).

---

[10]A database view is a restricted sub-set of a table.

[11]A stored procedure is a series of database commands bound together as a procedure, given a name and executed as if it were a single atomic transaction – the entire procedure has to be completed.

[12]A trigger is a stored procedure that is automatically executed whenever a predetermined logical condition is met – such as: IF 09:00 < time < 18:00 THEN trigger = daytime ELSE null.

[13]XML: extensible mark-up language

- **The Sub-net:** provides physical transmission, transmission media access control, link level protocols (framing protocols such as HDLC, Token Ring or Ethernet) for error detection and correction, flow control, etc., and bridges and switches for network segmentation and traffic control.

- **The Network Layer:** provides network naming, addressing, directory and routing control, and network protocols (packet protocols such as IP) for transfer of data units between physical platforms. The network layer also provides remote access services using dial-up sub-net connections and protocols such as PPP or SLIP.

- **The Transport Layer:** provides end-to-end flow control, error control and session management for transfer of data units between applications (such as is provided by TCP).

Network management embraces the managing of security services in the network

There is also a need to provide network management, which is addressed from a security perspective collectively with systems management (see the later section entitled Security Service Management Strategy).

Network topologies include:

- Local area networks;

- Campus area networks;

- Metropolitan area networks;

- Wide area networks;

- The Internet;

- Intranets;

- Extranets.

The goals for security in the information transfer layer are:

- To provide high-quality, highly reliable and highly available connectivity to its users;

- To protect these reliability, quality and availability attributes;

- This includes the protection of the network management flows (DNS, ICMP, SNMP, etc.);

- To prevent theft of bandwidth by unauthorised users and to enforce payment for services by authorised users.

Network security is not there to protect applications or their data

The information transfer layer security does not exist to protect the confidentiality, integrity, authenticity or non-repudiability of higher layer protocol data units, including middleware objects and messages and application layer messages. In the view of the authors it should be a fundamental principle of your enterprise security architecture that these higher layers will provide their own protection for confidentiality, integrity, authenticity or non-repudiation.

Separation and independence of application security and network security is the best architectural approach

The provision of application security within the network layer would be architecturally unsound, because it locks application security into network technology dependence, and it can never be truly end-to-end. When network technologies change, the application security is put at risk. Also, there is absolutely no control over application security in the application layer if it relies upon security in the network layer.

These segregation concepts are controversial

This is a controversial area in which there is widespread misunderstanding of how network and application security works, especially amongst the vendor community. Many vendors of network security products try to sell these products on the basis that they will protect application data (as an example, you are invited to examine any commercial brochure for an IPSec networking device or a firewall device).

The VPN concept provides limited protection of confidentiality of data being transported

There is some limited merit in providing a transparent confidentiality service in the network (in the form of a virtual private network – VPN), but this only affords protection against the real outsiders in the external domain. It does little to protect the confidentiality of information inside the enterprise domain. When one examines the range of security incident surveys that are published, from all sources, from all countries, on every occasion, these surveys agree that a significant proportion of security incidents arise from inside the enterprise. Thus focusing protection only against the external opponent is wholly misguided.

Other types of protection beyond confidentiality of data are not possible in the network layer

When you move from a pure confidentiality service on to integrity, authenticity and non-repudiation services it is actually impossible to provide these services to applications by embedding the services in the network. Few people understand this, but consider for a moment the authentication of transactions between applications. If this were to be attempted in the network layers the following problems will result:

- If there is an authentication failure, there is no mechanism available to report this to the application, yet it is the application that needs to know that this event has happened, and it is a decision to be taken by the application as to how to handle the event.

- Applications need to authenticate specific application data structures such as whole transactions. If authentication is carried out down in the network layer there is no guarantee of a one-to-one mapping between an application protocol data unit and a network protocol data unit. Depending on various factors such as the size of application data unit, buffering, line speeds, traffic density, multiplexing, and so on, an application protocol data unit may be fragmented over several network packets, or several application data units may be aggregated as a batch in a single network packet. Thus there is no one-to-one association between a single transaction and a single authenticator. If there is an authentication failure, what is it that has failed? Which transaction is rejected? There is no easy way to resolve this.

- Applications usually store audit trails as evidence of business transactions successfully completed. If digital signatures are applied, and if there is a contractual liability associated with the use of this signature, then it is essential to store not only the message, but also the signature that is associated with it. In this way, if a dispute arises after the event, the message and the signature can be re-verified by a trusted arbitrator and used as evidence to resolve the dispute. If the signature has been created and verified in the network layer, then it is not stored (how could it be, networks do not store information, they just deliver it), and there is no evidence of what happened. Network security is a real-time thing. It works on data in transit at the time and then it is gone. This does not meet the business requirements for providing security to applications.

Network layer security mechanisms have limited value

What this tells you is that technologies such as SSL, TLS and IPSec have limited uses. They do have uses, but they are not the panacea for solving security requirements that the vendors would have you believe. When you use these technologies you must be clear that they are appropriate to the requirements that you are hoping to fulfil.

Even when you apply encryption mechanisms in the network layers to provide confidentiality of application-level data, there is still the problem that the application has no visibility of whether or not the encryption is turned on. It is a leap of faith that the transmitted data is actually being protected by encryption. There have been many instances where network encryption gets turned off and application data continues to be transmitted in clear. Sometimes it is a network technician naively trying to improve network performance, other times it is a failure of an equipment item or failure of a procedure. The following case study is an interesting example of this type of problem.

Quoted from 'The Guardian' (a UK national newspaper) Friday 7 November, 2003, by Chris McGreal in Jerusalem.

Dr. Strangelove goes live as secret Israeli missile test is mistakenly shown on TV.

Reality television has finally caught up with the Israeli military. But the country's generals had no idea that their every move was being watched, their secret missile codes broadcast to their enemies or their conversations potentially overheard from Libya to Iran.

For two days this week, Israel's communications satellite accidentally beamed a live feed from the control room of a highly classified test missile firing, meaning that they could be viewed by anyone in the Middle East with the simplest satellite dish.

Four of Israel's most senior generals and their foreign guests were shown in the control room discussing the relative merits of weapons systems and whom they might be used against. Officials were seen punching in launch codes, and the latest missile control equipment and maps were on full display to anyone viewing.

At one point, believing they were in a secure area, Israeli officials were heard discussing access codes to defence industry computers.

The broadcast went out when someone – as yet none of the various agencies involved wants to accept responsibility – failed to encrypt the live feed that is sent from one weapons-testing control room to another via the satellite.

The mistake became known to the broader public after an Israeli television station taped the preparations and the missile launch over 48 hours, and then broadcast segments to the nation.

The Israeli newspaper Yedioth Ahronoth called it 'one of the most embarrassing fiascos ever to happen to the security establishment'.

However, returning to the valid deployment of network security services, the strategic principles for providing security within the information transfer layer are:

- Network security policy:

  - Defining network domains;

  - Assigning domain ownership;

- Setting domain security policy;
  - Training and awareness on security policy and its implementation.
- Network domain segregation:
  - Security gateways (firewalls) at domain boundaries;
  - Security rules for firewalls to reflect domain policy.
- Network component redundancy and resilience:
  - Diverse routing;
  - Redundant equipment items;
  - Multiple access points;
  - Bandwidth on demand.
- Network entity authentication:
  - Mutual node-to-node authentication within the network (router to router);
  - External entity authentication at the network boundary;
  - Operator authentication for network service management.
- Network entity authorisation:
  - Roles associated with external network entities;
  - Service profiles for roles.
- Network boundary access control:
  - Security gateways (firewalls) to control traffic flows into and out of network domains;
  - Service restriction rules.
- Connectivity control:
  - Authorisation for connections;
  - Change control;
  - Physical and logical security standards for all network nodes.
- Network management security:
  - Authorised operator entities;
  - Access control;
  - Secure 'get' and 'set' protocols;
  - Remote authentication of operator entities;
  - Integration with the system management architecture;
  - Integration with existing management infrastructure and organisation.
- Network resource integrity protection:

- Software development lifecycle controls;

- Production controls;

- Delivery and installation controls;

- Configuration control;

- Operational lifecycle;

- Configuration data integrity;

- Routing table integrity;

- Change management.

- Network security monitoring and intrusion detection:

  - Signature-based intrusion detection;

  - Event logging and analysis at routers, firewalls, gateways, servers and other network devices.

- Network security incident handling:

  - Reporting;

  - Confirmation;

  - Escalation;

  - Response;

  - Recovery;

  - Analysis and lessons learned.

- Network vulnerability research:

  - Collecting, collating and analysing CERT advisory notices;

  - Intrusion testing (penetration testing);

  - Internet intelligence gathering (who is talking about us on the net and what are they planning?).

Security Services for the Information Processing Layer

Processing layer refers to platforms

This layer is concerned with the architecture and standards of the processing platforms, operating system services and peripherals.

- Platform and peripheral types include:

- Personal computers;

- Terminals and VDUs of all types;

- Printers and plotters;

- Various I/O devices – document scanners, digital cameras (still and video), digital audio recorders, transponders, barcode readers, smart cards and biometric devices;

- Network interface devices;

- Network computers;

- Data network devices – switches, hubs, routers;

- Voice network terminals and other devices – telephones, fax machines, PBXs (and PABXs), cell phones;

- Specialist security devices – HSMs, PIN pads;

- Process control devices – plant controllers, control room consoles;

- Mobile workstations (notebook or laptop PCs);

- PDAs (personal digital assistants or palm-top computers, sometimes with integrated mobile telephony capability);

- Mid-range servers – file servers, database servers, multimedia servers, data push servers, applications servers, optical disk servers, mail servers;

- Storage devices – magnetic disks, RAID arrays, optical disks;

- Mainframe hosts and servers.

Platforms also have operating systems

There is also a wide range of possible operating systems in use on these various hardware platforms.

Principles of platform security

The strategic principles for providing security services in the information-processing layer are:

- To reduce vulnerabilities in the information processing platforms and infrastructure;

- To segregate and isolate production platforms and environments from those used for development and testing;

- To provide and maintain highly trusted execution environments for highly sensitive data processing;

- To provide secure storage environments for highly sensitive non-volatile stored data.

Platform security services

The major security services to be provided at the information-processing layer are:

- Physical security of the installation site to prevent theft, unauthorised physical access to the platform or malicious destruction;

- Environmental protection of the installation: electrical power protection, fire prevention, detection and quenching, flood prevention, structural stability, humidity and temperature control;

- Local user authentication with passwords and possibly smart cards or other tokens, and possibly biometric devices;

- Local user access control, based on local authorisations, provided by the operating system;

- Local audit trails;

- Cryptographic services provided by local cryptographic sub-systems (hardware and software);

- Remote interaction with central security services such as cryptographic key management, digital certificates, role-based access control;

- Anti-virus services for prevention, containment, detection, reporting, restoration and recovery of virus and other malicious software attacks;

- Content filtering services to support the implementation of acceptable use policies with regard to pornography, racially abusive messages and other socially unacceptable materials;

- Change control;

- Configuration control;

- Regular scanning to detect unauthorised changes to the configuration;

- Backup and recovery planning;

- Systems management (including operations management, security administration and many other services).

Authentication, Authorisation and Audit Strategy

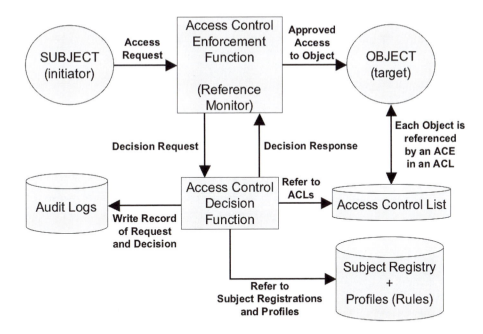

Figure 10-7: A Conceptual Model of an Access Control Sub-System

Generic access control sub-system architecture

The main components of an access control sub-system are shown in the form of a conceptual model in Figure 10-7.

These components are:

- The subject – a party requesting access, which can be a human user or an external system acting on behalf of a user;

- The object – the resource to which the subject is requesting access. The object can be a data structure (such as a file or a database record), an application function, a computer system, a peripheral;

- The access control enforcement function – which intercepts all subject requests to access objects and implements the decisions as to whether these requests will be granted or denied;

- The access control decision function, which makes the decision as to whether the access request will be granted or denied;

- The subject registry containing all the information on registered subjects including their names, their authentication data and their access privileges;

- An access control list (ACL) associated with each object listing the subjects or groups of subjects that are allowed to make access to that object;

- The audit logging sub-system, which stores comprehensive data on all requests for access, whether or not they are successful in being granted.

Access control decision making process

The decision is based upon a series of sequential questions:

- Is the subject registered?

- Has the registered subject been successfully authenticated?

- Does the subject's privilege profile contain an authorisation to access this object?

- Does the access control list attached to the object authorise this subject to be granted access?

Integrated access control in many legacy systems creates architectural problems

The traditional model of a legacy business computer system is one in which each system or application has its own built-in logical access control sub-system. Thus all the functions in the conceptual model above are implemented in each target system. There are many problems with this approach:

- Subjects that need access to many target systems need to be registered separately on each one, multiplying the amount of administration work needed to handle registrations and thus increasing the cost of security administration;

- Subjects with multiple registrations may be given inconsistent access privileges on different systems, and there is no way to cross-check for consistency;

- Subjects whose privileges need maintenance, as in the case of a change of job, need to have each and every registration updated, further exacerbating the administration overload and increases the risk of introducing inconsistencies in privileges;

- Subjects who leave the organisation need to be deleted from every registry on every system, creating a risk that at least one registration will be missed, leaving a dormant account that can be abused by hackers.

A strategic role-based access control architecture can alleviate these problems

To avoid these problems a strategic architectural approach is needed. This involves a centralised authentication service and the implementation of role-based access control (RBAC). The main features and principles of this strategic approach are:

- A single central authentication service is set up that authenticates all subject requests on behalf of all target systems.

- Subject registrations are thus decoupled from target system registries and each subject is registered only once on the centralised authentication service registry.

- This removes the problems of increased workload to handle multiple registrations and also the risk of losing consistency and the risk of leaving dormant accounts;

- A business analysis of all subject activity is carried out to define a number of subject roles. These might easily be mapped onto job functions and job descriptions. Roles are essentially business-based. This provides a highly practical way of ensuring that users are granted (and restricted to) the access privileges needed to fulfil their jobs.

- Each subject is allocated one or more roles and these are stored in the centralised subject registry. Also in the subject registry are stored the target systems to which each user has been authorised for access.

- Each target system is now set up to register roles rather than individual subject names in the access control lists (ACLs) associated with the objects in the system. These roles rarely change and are mapped inside the target access control sub-system onto local objects. More importantly, each target system now has only a handful of role registrations rather than many thousands of individual subject registrations. The administration of these target system profiles is now a rare and lightweight task.

- The precise mapping of a role onto a set of system objects depends upon the outcome of the analysis of business activities to determine what functions and data are needed to fulfil the business duties associated with a specific role.

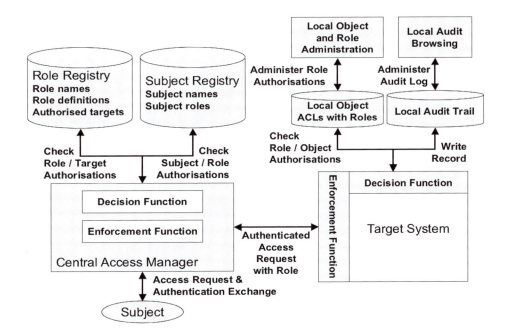

Figure 10-8: Role-Based Access Control

- In order to be able to hold every subject accountable for his or her actions, subject specific information is passed across to the target server along with the access request, and this is stored with the event history on the local audit trail at the target system. Browsing tools are also provided to interpret this information so that a subject name can be associated with the events in the log, even though there is no local registration of the subject name.

The use of roles decouples users from target applications for the purposes of administration

Figure 10-8 shows the decoupling of the access control sub-system using the RBAC approach. The role is the key mechanism that enables this decoupling. Compare this diagram with the closely coupled approach in the previous figure (Figure 10-7).

CAM decisions

In Figure 10-8 both the central access manager and the target system have both a decision function and an enforcement function. At the central access manager the decisions to be taken include:

- Is the subject registered?

- Can the subject be authenticated?

- Has the role requested by the subject been authorised for that subject?

- Has the target system requested by the subject been authorised for that role?

CAM enforcement

The central access manager enforces the subject to be confined within those decisions – meaning that unregistered, unauthenticated subjects are turned away, as are subjects who requested role is not authorised or for which the requested target system is not authorised for the role.

Target system decisions

The target system also makes decisions:

- Has the role been authorised to use the requested functions?

- Has the role been authorised to make the requested type of access to the requested objects?

Target system enforcement

Based on these decisions, the target system also enforces the rules, disallowing any unauthorised requests

RBAC brings many benefits

The major business benefits of role-based access control are:

- Static roles definitions, which require little maintenance. Individual subject privileges are liable to change frequently as business duties change, people join, people leave, whereas role definitions are much more stable. This means that security administration of access privileges at a target application server is reduced to a low level.

- Ease of administration of users and their privileges, since these are concentrated into a single central registry and privileges database, stored and published within the directory service (see below under the Directory Services Strategy). There is only one repository of subject attributes to be administered rather than one at every target system.

- Low administration overhead, because multiple user registrations at multiple target servers are eliminated.

- Single sign-on for users, because they interact with a central authentication service, are authenticated and are then issued with session or transaction credentials to be processed by the target application server. No matter which service they request, they are always authenticated through the central authentication, authorization and access control service, called here the central access manager (CAM).

- Stable security policy because a role effectively defines a logical security domain to which all users mapped to that role belong.

- Stable, auditable configurations at target application servers, which require almost no access control maintenance.

- Flexibility in interpretation in different sub-domains according to the policy of the local domain authority, because each target server has its own local policy that applies to a given role.

- Improved control over the joining, moving and leaving of subjects (users) and the administration of their access privileges under these conditions of change, since there is a single repository of subject names and associated privileges which can be edited through a centralised security administration service. This prevents the accidental failure to remove user privileges that are no longer required.

Remote communications between the distributed parts of the RBAC sub-system is protected by cryptography

Using the RBAC approach, the entire access control system is now highly distributed across many platforms and so some security mechanisms are required to protect the interactions between these physically separated parts of the overall system. This protection is achieved by applying suitable cryptographic protocols. These can be based upon the facilities of a PKI, or they can be entirely based on symmetric cryptography (as in the case of Kerberos, which is just such a protocol). These protection mechanisms are described more fully in Chapter 12 (Physical Security Architecture) and Chapter 13 (Component Security Architecture).

User-to-machine interaction is also decoupled from the network communications to the authentication server

A further aspect of the RBAC approach is the decoupling of the user-to-machine interface and the machine-to-machine interfaces (see Figure 10-9). Many of the traditional authentication and access control systems have been built such that the user enters a secret password at the terminal or client workstation and this is then transmitted in clear over the network to the target server where it is checked. The obvious vulnerability in this approach is that the passwords can be intercepted and stolen as they travel through the network (such as by using a sniffer tool).

Network transmission of passwords is replaced by cryptographic authentication exchange protocols

To avoid this vulnerability, the transmission of the password is replaced by a cryptographic authentication exchange protocol between the client workstation and the central access manager (CAM). A similar protocol is used between the CAM and the target system. Provided that the

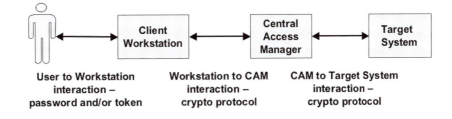

Figure 10-9: Decoupling the User from the Remote Authentication Server

cryptographic protocol is robust, interception is no longer any help to an opponent. The password is only used in the immediate human-to-machine interface at the physical workstation. Once entered into the workstation, client agent software (that forms part of a client-server authentication application) processes the password to initialise the authentication exchange protocol. The exact mechanism depends upon the protocol used.

Decoupling has the added advantage of architectural flexibility for future upgrades

Any single one of the mechanisms (user-to-client, client-to-CAM, CAM-to-server) can be replaced with another mechanism without interfering with the working of the others. This allows great architectural flexibility to embrace future technologies, especially in the areas of user tokens, biometrics and cryptography.

Two-factor authentication with token devices can be used to strengthen the user-to-machine interaction

Further strengthening of the user-to-machine authentication process can be achieved by using token devices of various types, although at some stage there is usually an entry of a password or PIN by the user, so these additional tokens make little difference to the conceptual model already described. The key common strength of all these methods lies in the cryptographic protocol replacing the cleartext password transmission. The use of tokens together with a password or PIN is often known as two-factor authentication, because you need to have both to succeed.

Biometrics offers some interesting possibilities but is immature and controversial

Another possible approach to improving the user-to-machine authentication is to use biometrics, although this approach is good deal more controversial than you may think. A more detailed discussion of these various mechanisms is in Chapters 12 and 13 where the physical and component security architectures are described.

Security Service Management Strategy

There are two issues to be addressed here:

- The management of security services;
- The security of service management.

Managing security services

The management of security services includes:

- Provisioning of security parameters and privileges for users;
- Provisioning of security parameters for application systems;
- Provisioning of security parameters for embedded systems in equipment such as routers;
- Routine security operations to maintain the corporate systems in a state of compliance with security policy and standards;
- Security monitoring and intrusion detection to detect security incidents and collect information relevant to the problem management process;
- Security incident and problem management to recover and restore secure operations following a security incident. Stages include:
  - Reporting;
  - Confirmation;
  - Escalation;
  - Response;

- Recovery;

- Analysis and lessons learned.

- Some help desk functions to support users with respect to their interaction with the security of corporate systems, especially to resolve security-related operational user problems;

- Managing the accounting for security-related services, such as registration and certification services;

- Security vulnerability research:

  - Collecting, collating and analysing CERT advisory notices;

  - Intrusion testing (penetration testing);

  - Internet intelligence gathering (who is talking about us on the net and what are they planning?)

Securing management services

The security of service management includes:

- Authorisation of operator entities that will perform service management functions. Special service management roles should be created, and the role-based access control service should be used to enforce a separate logical security domain for service management, with sub-domains enforced by each individual role.

- Segregation of critical duties to protect the corporate information systems environment against the malicious actions of any single individual working alone. This should be achieved through the definition of service management roles so as to segregate duties between mutually exclusive roles.

- Local and remote authentication of operator entities;

- Access control to service management applications for the management of:

  - The information transfer layer;

  - The information processing layer;

  - The middleware layer;

  - The applications layer.

- Secure service management protocols, protecting both:

  - The authenticity of a service management message source;

  - The authenticity of service management message contents;

  - The confidentiality of service management message contents.

- Independent monitoring and audit of security operations management;

- Integration with the overall systems management architecture;

- Integration with existing service management infrastructure and organisation.

The TMN model for service management architecture

There is a commonly used multi-layered service management model known as the

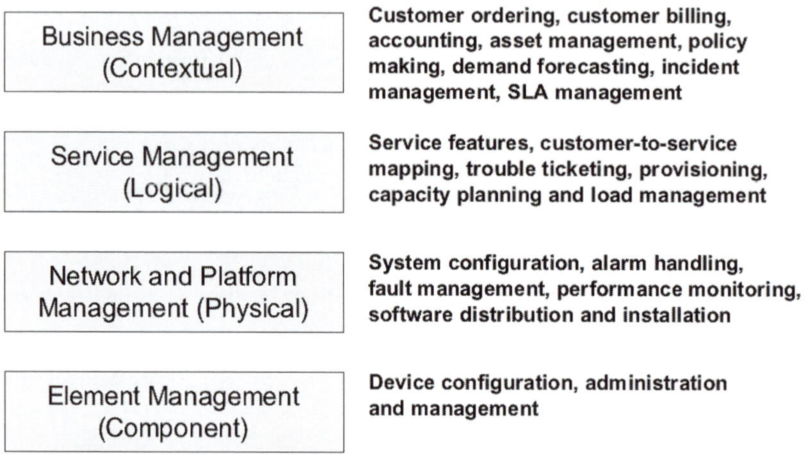

Business Management (Contextual)	**Customer ordering, customer billing, accounting, asset management, policy making, demand forecasting, incident management, SLA management**
Service Management (Logical)	**Service features, customer-to-service mapping, trouble ticketing, provisioning, capacity planning and load management**
Network and Platform Management (Physical)	**System configuration, alarm handling, fault management, performance monitoring, software distribution and installation**
Element Management (Component)	**Device configuration, administration and management**

Figure 10-10: The TMN Model for Service Management

Telecommunications Management Network (TMN) Model. Figure 10-10 shows this four-layered model in outline, with an indication of how its layers map to the layers of the SABSA® Model.

TMN is in harmony with the SABSA® approach

It is interesting to see how closely the TMN Model maps to the SABSA® model. Because of this it is a useful guide to developing a security services management architecture. However, the development of this model into a full-scale service management architecture would provide sufficient material for another book of similar size to this one, so only a passing reference to the TMN Model is made here.

Other standards for service management architecture

Other useful references on this subject are BS15000[14] (also being considered for international standardisation as ISO 15000) entitled IT Service Management. The IT Infrastructure Library (ITIL)[15] was created by the UK Government and forms the basis for implementing BS15000. It is a definitive reference source on ICT service management that has been widely adopted across Europe, Asia and Australasia. One of the ITIL publications is specifically dedicated to security management[16].

System Assurance Strategy

Systems assurance defined

System assurance is concerned with the correctness, reliability and proper operation of the system. There are a number of strategic areas of control that help you to provide the required level of assurance:

- Control over systems development;

---

[14]See www.bs15000.org.uk

[15]See www.itil.co.uk

[16]*ITIL Security Management*, published by The Stationery Office, 1999, ISBN 011330014X

- Control over production systems operations;

- Software integrity protection and anti-virus controls;

- Content filtering to keep out unauthorised and illegal data (such as pornography, for which the enterprise may incur legal liability);

- Protecting the integrity of mobile code (such as Java applets, ActiveX, scripts);

- Functional testing;

- Penetration testing;

- Security auditing.

Cross-reference to Chapter 17

Each of these is discussed in detail in Chapter 17, since they are part of the ongoing operational security architecture.

Tools used to develop high assurance

For constructing systems with high levels of assurance, such as in the case of safety-critical systems, there are a number of additional tools and approaches needed. These include:

- Redundancy of components;

- Fault-tolerant architectures;

- Formal methods of specification and proof;

- Probabilistic risk assessment and fault-tree analysis;

- System modelling using finite state machine models (see Chapter 5) and exhaustive model checking;

- Tamper-resistance to defend against malicious attack;

- Human factors analysis, looking at the user interface.

Cross reference to Chapter 9

You should also refer back to Chapter 9 for the section on Safety Critical Systems and within that to the sub-section on Systems Assurance, where some of the key requirements are discussed.

Directory Services Strategy

Directory service is one of the common security services in the example of security infrastructure architecture

In Figure 10-3 earlier in this chapter 'Directory Service' is shown as one of a number of common security services needed within the layered security infrastructure architecture. This is because the directory service is a critical piece of infrastructure without which it is difficult to deliver many other security services. It is the centralised repository of much security-related information about system objects.

Directory objects

In the context of describing directory services the word 'object' has a very broad meaning. It includes all classes of object, including user-class objects, which are called subjects in other parts of this chapter. Where the term 'subject' is used in other parts of the chapter, in this section it is referred to as a user-class object.

Directory functions

The main functions of the directory service in supporting other security services are:

- Holding registered details of all objects of all object classes in the form of a distinguished name plus a variety of attributes. This constitutes a directory entry.

- The directory attributes of objects include all location and contact details, credentials, roles, privileges, certificates, authentication values, status information, state variables, cryptographic keys and so on. Any secret values (such as keys and authentication values) may be stored in encrypted form. They may also be stored in physically secure repositories away from the other attributes, since the logical structure of the directory says nothing about its physical structure. The logical and physical architectures of the directory service are quite distinct.

Directory Services Strategy: Management

Directory access control

The directory service needs to be subject to sophisticated access control, so that directory users gain access only to subsets of entity credentials for which they are authorised. Secure directory access methods require user authentication and cryptographic protection of the data exchanges.

Directory integrity and availability

The integrity and availability of the directory service must also be protected, almost at all costs, since without the directory service almost no other service can remain operable.

Directory security management strategy

Thus the directory service integrity and availability are of the utmost criticality. Suitable directory security management must be applied. This may include:

- Physical access control to the directory servers and their location;

- Environmental protection to prevent fire, flood, structural instability and other environmental problems from interfering with directory service availability;

- Sophisticated service management and monitoring of the directory and its service availability;

- Logical access control with a severely limited set of privileged users;

- Strong user authentication for privileged directory administrators and operators;

- A highly resilient directory service physical infrastructure:

  - No single points of failure;

  - Replication of records from the master directory server to a series of slave directory servers, providing both resilience in case of a single component failure, and performance handling through load sharing and local request handling.

Important management issues for directory architectures

There are several important management issues that must be addressed in directory architectures:

- The directory service must be inter-operable with other directory infrastructures, which implies conformance to industry standards such as LDAP or X.500.

- The overall directory service may need to integrate many existing legacy directories implemented to a variety of standards. This can best be achieved by use of a meta-directory – a directory of directories.

- The directory must be able to limit transitivity of trust and inheritance of privileges to avoid the problem of uncontrolled inheritance, in which everything gains access to everything else.

- The directory service architecture must support specific performance characteristics such a high read-to-write ratio in the directory enquiries.

- The directory service architecture must be capable of running the service in a highly (usually globally) distributed environment.

- The directory service must be almost infinitely extensible and scaleable to accommodate future growth.

- The directory service architecture must support regular extensive replication of updates.

Directory Services Strategy: Objects

Directory object types   The directory service must support both entity objects and file system objects. These two primary types of objects will be subject to separate but inter-related security policies.

- Entity objects represent abstractions of such entities as users, roles, groups and hardware. For example, a user is represented by a user-class object.

- File system objects present the standard hierarchical file system and are called container and leaf objects (see below).

- Access to both types of objects must be controllable by a variety of attributes and provide support for controlled inheritance.

Entity classes   Entity classes might include:

- Business organisational entities;

- User entities;

- Application entities;

- System entities;

- Hardware equipment or platform entities;

- Site and building entities;

- Logical service entities.

Directory schema   All object relationships in the directory must be controllable by a hierarchical directory schema. All object classes must support multiple properties (or attributes). The attributes store and provide information about objects.

User-class attributes   For example: in the case of a user-class, this includes information such as:

- Distinguished name;

- Home directory;

- Telephone numbers;

- E-mail address;

- Login scripts;

- Public key certificates;

- Roles.

Using security equivalence for ease of administration

All rights granted under the directory should be created by security equivalence to a standard template for that type of object – usually a sub-class. That means that when you assign a security equivalence to a directory object, that object acquires the same rights as another object or group (in this case a template). If the rights assignment changes for one object (in this case the template) it also changes for all the security-equivalent objects. This greatly simplifies objects rights management and avoids the creation of inconsistencies. By editing the template you automatically edit all those objects created as equivalent to it.

Users with multiple contexts require multiple user-class objects

You should not try to create objects with partial equivalence or subsets of equivalence to represent partial overlaps in privileges. Users with requirements for different authorisations in different contexts will require multiple user-class objects to be created to represent them. For example, a user who is both a customer and an employee of the enterprise should be registered twice, once under each context. However, these objects must cross-reference one another to ensure that mutually exclusive authorisations are not allowed (such as a finance clerk operating his or her own customer account).

Directory structure and objects

Objects in both X.500 and LDAP directories are defined as either container objects or leaf objects, depending upon their position in the hierarchical directory information tree (DIT).

- Containers correspond to directories in a hierarchical file structure;

- Leaf objects correspond to files in the hierarchical directory;

- An object belongs to either a container or a leaf object, depending on the class to which it belongs, as defined by the directory schema;

- Names of objects are created from the complete path to the root starting at the leaf;

- Object relationships and access rights are based on a security equivalence list;

- The algorithm is based on the follow sequence of steps:

  - All users are security-equivalent to the pseudo-object named (Public);

  - Users are security-equivalent to all container objects in the path of their user object to root including themselves and root;

  - Users are also security-equivalent to objects explicitly set equivalent by the administrator (such as the template described above).

- To meet both security policy and architectural requirements, only security administrators should be allowed to create and delete directory objects in containers;

- System administrators can modify non-security-related object attributes in the systems under their purview;

- Users can modify only non-security-related personal information in their user objects such as telephone numbers and address.

PKI Strategy

PKI will have its day again

At the time of writing PKI is languishing in the Trough of Disillusionment – see Chapter 9, Figure 9-1. However, it is reasonable to assume optimistically that in the lifetime of this book it will climb the Slope of Enlightenment and reach the Plateau of Profitability, in which case you need to consider your PKI strategy.

PKI Strategy: What Is Public Key Cryptography?

We shall describe only the basic principles

It is not an intention here to provide a detailed description of how public key cryptography works, since there are many books on the market where such a description can be found. However, it is essential to ensure that all readers understand some basic principles to inform their understanding of PKI strategy.

What public key cryptography provides

Public key cryptography utilises complex mathematics to create an asymmetrical cryptographic relationship between two parties. These techniques have great benefits in providing the following security services:

- Authentication;

- Integrity protection;

- Encryption key management;

- Non-repudiation.

Digital signatures

For authentication and integrity protection purposes, each party generates a public-private key pair using software (or hardware) provided for the purpose. The private key is used for calculating digital signatures on messages to be sent to other parties. The public key is given to the other parties so that they can verify these digital signatures.

Public key encryption

For the management of encryption keys, a different public and private key pair is usually used. The keys used for authentication are not used for encryption, and the keys used for encryption are not used for authentication. However, the precise rules on these issues are set in the certification authority (CA) certificate policy (CP) and certificate practices statement (CPS).

Non-repudiation requires a trusted third-party arbiter

Non-repudiation is possible because each party has a unique signature key. Hence digital signatures (which can also be verified by the trusted independent certification authority) can be uniquely linked to the party that created them, which removes the opportunity for that party to later claim that the signature was made by someone else and is a forgery.

Conditions for the scheme to work

To make this scheme work securely, the following conditions must be met:

- The private signature key must not be disclosed to any other party, including trusted third parties, since if there is any chance that this may have happened, the owner of the signature key can accuse others of forging his or her signature, and non-repudiation cannot be achieved.

- Thus the signature key must be generated inside a computing device in the possession of the owner of the key, and it must never be exported from this device.

- Every participant in the scheme must have their own unique, private signature key.

- The public keys of all participants must be certified by a trusted certification authority to ensure that fake keys cannot be introduced into the system through man-in-the-middle attacks.

- The certified public keys of all participants in the scheme must be published or distributed so that they can be used to verify signatures.

- Every participant must have a cryptographic sub-system with which to generate keys, verify digital certificates, sign messages and verify signatures on messages.

- There must be local authentication of users and local access control at the client subsystem to ensure that an unauthorised party cannot abuse a user's private signature key to forge the user's digital signature.

- There must be a means to revoke certificates that have been issued and which now need to be withdrawn.

- There must be an audit trail of received messages with their matching digital signatures so that any disputes can be resolved.

- The trusted certification authority acts as a trusted party in resolving repudiation disputes and sets up a process to support this requirement.

- To preserve the digital signature audit trail, digital signatures must be applied before encryption of the message, so that the encryption can be stripped off leaving the signed message.

PKI Strategy: What Is Public Key Infrastructure?

PKI defined   To support the use of public key cryptography it is essential that all participants in the business community have access to some public key infrastructure (PKI) as follows:

- A universally unique naming standard through which every entity can be uniquely identified;

- A registration authority (RA) that registers all *bona fide* members of the business community;

- Key generation software or hardware for every participant;

- A certification authority (CA) that certifies all public keys of members of the community in the form of digital certificates;

- A certification procedure that prevents the introduction of false keys for certification;

- A directory service through which to publish the certified public keys (digital certificates) of all participants;

- Provision by the CA of a service to inform relying parties (those who verify a digital signature and rely upon its veracity to accept a business transaction) when a digital certificate has been revoked, which can be achieved by publishing certificate revocation lists (CRLs) which are batches of revocations updated periodically, or by providing an on-line inquiry service in real time;

- Expiry dates on all certificates;

- A trusted time service for generating time and date stamps for certificates and other cryptographic protocol units;

- Cryptographic software or hardware for every participant so that they can verify certificates, sign messages, encrypt messages, exchange symmetric keys, decrypt messages and verify signatures;

- Interoperable standards[17] for cryptographic algorithms, digital certificate syntax, key block syntax, digital signature syntax and encrypted message syntax;

- Hierarchical certification and cross-certification of CAs to extend the chain of trust across the business community;

- A trusted time service to ensure that all parties can verify times and dates accurately, and can rely upon time as a security parameter – often used as a 'nonce value' to prevent undetected replays of previous messages and transactions;

- Management procedures, policies and practices for registration and certification.

PKI Strategy: The Way Forward

PKI strategy for the future

In formulating your PKI strategy, the following points require your consideration:

- PKI is really a business issue, not a technical one. The problems that have beset many of those who attempted to implement a PKI during the Peak of Inflated Expectations (see Chapter 9, Figure 9-1) arose because they implemented a solution looking for a problem. They had no idea how to use the technology to gain business benefit, so they had large costs and no return on that investment.

- The first thing you must do is to build conceptual trust models of how your business works or how you want it to work when you move into the digital business space. The next section of this chapter gives you guidance on how to do this.

- You also need to have clear process models of how your digital business will work, so you can see where technology can add value and where there is a need for technology integration.

- Having built these models, you then need to look at how to map them onto the elements of a PKI:

  - How many types of digital certificate will be needed?

  - What will be the certificate policies and practices associated with each type?

  - What are the risks associated with the use of each certificate type (a full risk assessment is required)?

  - How will each of these risks be controlled and mitigated?

  - How will private keys be generated and owned?

  - What sort of directory infrastructure will be needed for certificate distribution and management?

---

[17]Even with agreed technical standards in place, there is still an issue of true inter-operability between products from different vendors. The EU-funded EEMA PKI-Challenge Project has attempted to address this issue. See www.eema.org

- What degree of inter-operability and integration across organisational units will be expected?

- Do you really need a centralised PKI, or would it be better to develop separate islands of PKI, each with a specific purpose?

- What type of trust brokerage is required from the CA and RA and what is the value proposition for each party to the relationships? (In the next section of this chapter these issues are explored in detail.)

- Do you want to run a CA in house or would it be better to look for a managed service from a specialist supplier (in effect a supplier of trust)?

- How will the PKI elements be integrated into real business applications? (This is an area where many early adopters of PKI failed completely.)

- Having sorted out the overall technical approach, you should then build a cost model, including not just the acquisition costs but also the operational costs. Try to evaluate the total cost of ownership.

- Build your business case by identifying the business benefits. This inevitably means that you will not build a global PKI that will satisfy every possible need. You will build a PKI that has a specific purpose within a specific business initiative.

- Given the constraints of the previous point, to make all your future PKI projects compatible with one another you should develop an overall theoretical PKI architecture and use this as a guiding framework for implementing each individual PKI project as it comes along. In other words you tackle the problem of eating the elephant by taking just one bite at a time.

Security Entity Model and Trust Framework

SABSA® Matrix cross-reference

Please refer to Chapter 3, Figure 3-3 and Chapter 7, Figure 7-6, the SABSA® Matrix, Conceptual Layer, People column, where you will see a cell entitled Security Entity Model and Trust Framework. In Chapter 7, Figure 7-5 this also appears as key deliverable of the conceptual security architecture. This section discusses in detail some important conceptual models of entities and their trust relationships.

Security Entities

Security entities defined

A security entity is something or someone that can take actions in a business environment. These actions need to be controlled through authorisation processes and through technical and procedural controls that enforce the authorisations. Security entities are of several types:

- Individual personal entities (people);

- Corporate entities (organisations or organisational units, whether legally recognised as entities or not);

- Application or system entities – automated processes that act on behalf of personal or corporate entities.

Security entities as subjects

'Security entities' are equivalent to 'subjects' – as the term is used in discussing access control models – see the earlier section of this chapter on Authorisation, Authentication and Audit.

Security Entity Naming

Global unique naming of entities

Each security entity must be identified with a globally unique name to ensure that there will never be confusion about which entity is being referenced. However, local alias names are also permitted for use in the local domain where the alias is unique within the local domain but not necessarily unique within the global domain.

The directory as repository for entity information

The directory is the repository for holding information on all security entities, including their globally unique (distinguished) name, any alias names, and all other attributes including security attributes. This is discussed earlier in this chapter under the heading of Directory Services Strategy.

Security Entity Relationships

Entity relationships

Security entity relationships are characterised by the information flows that represent the relationship. There are three major types of entity relationship that you must consider:

- Unilateral relationships – in which one entity broadcasts or publishes information and other entities may receive it at their choice;

- Bilateral relationships – in which two entities make a specific contract (either formal or informal) to transact business and exchange information;

- Multilateral relationships – in which a number of entities participate in a group relationship under an agreed set of rules.

Trust in entity relationships

Each of these security entity relationships implies a certain degree of trust (which is discussed in detail below).

Understanding and Modelling Trust

Trust in the merchant-customer relationship

Consider a simple business model. A merchant has goods to sell and advertises them on the web. A

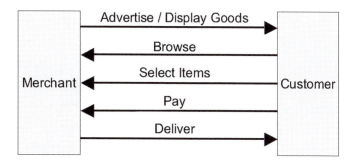

Figure 10-11: A Simple Merchant-Customer Relationship

web interface allows customers to browse the site, look at the goods, select what they want, place an order, and (in the future perhaps[18]) make an electronic payment by sending a digitally signed

[18]The model proposed here is at least a generation beyond the current model of using traditional plastic credit cards in a 'cardholder not present' mode. It would perhaps be implemented by means of smart cards on which user private keys were stored and which were capable of making digital signatures on business transactions.

authorisation message to take money out of their bank account. Figure 10-11 illustrates the model.

What needs to be protected here? What is the security that you require and what function does it serve? The answer can be summed up in a single word – **TRUST**.

Two-way trust

The key security-related issue with all relationships between business entities is trust. In the simple merchant-customer business model the trust is implicit in the relationship between the seller and the buyer. It is also two-way trust, where both must trust each other. Now examine some of the ways that trust characterises this relationship:

Buyer trusts merchant

The buyer must trust the merchant to:

- Offer goods that are of reasonable quality for the given price;

- Actually dispatch the ordered goods, once the payment has been made;

- Not repudiate the receipt of a payment that has been received;

- Dispatch the correct number of units ordered for the agreed price;

- Dispatch the same quality goods that were described on the web site;

- Accept the return of the goods and refund the money if the goods fail to meet expectation once they are seen and handled;

- Handle after-sales complaints about failure of the goods to live up to pre-sales claims made about durability, fitness for purpose, and so on.

Merchant trusts buyer

The merchant must trust the buyer to:

- Pay for the goods and have enough money in his bank account to cover the price;

- Not make vexatious or false claims about the quality of the goods;

- Not repudiate receipt of the goods that have been delivered;

- Not repudiate the order that was placed by the customer;

- Not repudiate the payment authorization.

Trust is a relationship attribute, not a technical attribute

This list is not meant to be exhaustive, but it serves to show you that trust is a multi-faceted thing and that trust flows in both directions in many business relationships. It is essential to understand that trust is an attribute of relationships between business entities (people or corporate bodies[19]) and that trust is not a technical attribute[20].

Levels of trust are variable

It is also quite clear that the types of trust and the levels of trust (and levels of assurance of trust) vary enormously from one business transaction to another. Each and every business relationship is unique in this respect. For example, if you buy a hot dog from a stall at a street market, you might wonder if it is fit to eat. However, you will not worry about whether the stallholder really

---

[19] Inter-corporate trust is also heavily linked to the trust that exists between the individual people that represent those corporate bodies and who transact business on behalf of those corporate entities.

[20] However, you might talk about a trusted system as being one which has been designed and tested to certain criteria that allowed you to trust its operation, and in this sense only you might consider trust to be a technical attribute.

owns the hot dog and has the right to sell it, nor will you question whether he will be there tomorrow in case you have a complaint to make. At the other extreme, if you are buying a house then you will employ a lawyer at significant cost to investigate every last detail of the ownership, the local planning regulations and the prospects for future peaceful undisturbed residence in the house once you have purchased it. Only when you have developed a high level of trust in the vendor and the claims made will you even sign the contract, and that will be filled to its brim with conditions and get-out clauses in case the information turns out to be false. Trust is not homogenous across all business relationships.

If trust can be sold as a service, who is the customer?

So, consider, in a business transaction, who is the customer for trust? The answer to this question will give you an insight into how a trusted third party might sell trust services as a business opportunity in its own right. That is, you will understand the value proposition and business opportunity for a *trust broker*.

Specific examples show the way

The answer to this question will be unique to the specific trust relationship, so consider again the simple earlier example, with a merchant selling goods over the web. Some very specific aspects of the trust model are used here so as to illustrate the point.

Buyer trusts claims of quality

Take for example the issue of quality of goods. Who is the customer for trust in this respect? Clearly it is the buyer of the goods. He is the one who must rely on the claims made by the merchant regarding quality.

Seller trusts good faith on payment method

As another example, who is the customer for trust with respect to payment for the goods? Here it is the merchant who must trust that the payment will be honoured and will not be repudiated by the buyer. The merchant must rely on the electronic payment turning into real cash.

Trust implies a claim by one party that is relied upon by the other party

A pattern is emerging here – there are parties who make claims and other parties who have to rely on those claims. This can be conceptualised this into a simple model of a claimant and a relying

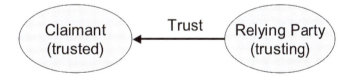

Figure 10-12: Simple One-Way Trust Relationship Model

party. The relying party is the trusting party who trusts the claimant. The claimant is the trusted party, who is trusted by the relying party.

One-way trust is the lowest common denominator of all trust relationships

After analysis, most[21] trust relationships will boil down to this simple one-way trust model. Figure 10-12 shows the model visually.

Real business relationships imply complex two-way trust – which can be analysed into simple components

Of course, a business relationship between two entities will usually be characterised by complex two-way trust, which comprises several individual types of trust, each possibly at a different level of

[21]The authors were tempted to say 'all trust relationships' but thought better of it because there may be some that do not submit to this analysis, although they cannot think of any at present.

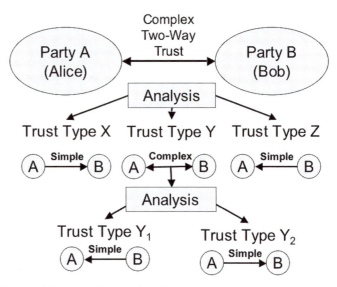

Figure 10-13: Hierarchical Decomposition of a Trust Model

assurance. Each of these types can be identified and possibly further analysed until there is only an array of simple one-way trust models aggregated together. Figure 10-13 shows how this top-down decomposition of trust might be made. At the bottom of the analysis tree can be found only examples of simple one-way trust relationship models, as shown in detail in Figure 10-12.

Protecting Trust Relationships – Trust Brokers and PKI

Looking for solutions for protecting trust

Using this analysis technique you can reduce everything to a series of simple one-way trust relationships, which makes life a lot easier. You will want to protect these trust relationships with technical and procedural solutions, and some of these will include PKI-based solutions. However, PKI is not the answer to every problem, and there are many other ways to protect trust that in some circumstances will be more appropriate to the business need.

PKI plays a part

Part of the process of architecting the digital business infrastructure is to understand where PKI is the right solution and where it is not. However, for the moment the focus remains on PKI to carry through the ideas from the previous section of this chapter and to see how it can be used to protect this simple trust model to which all other complex trust models[22] can be reduced. It is then possible to analyse the previously posed question, 'Who is the customer for trust?' against this single simple model shown in Figure 10-12.

The relying party is the customer for trust broker services

Clearly it is the relying party that needs to purchase trust services. The claimant has only a passing interest in these services in that he wants to be trusted, but it is without doubt the relying party who must be convinced that the trust is real. This means that the relying party must have a business relationship with the trust broker and must enter into a contract with the trust broker by which the trust broker agrees to provide certain trust brokering services and the relying party agrees to pay for them[23].

---

[22] It has not yet been shown that transitive trust can be similarly reduced in this way, but the discussion will deal with this later.

[23] As a useful analogy, consider escrow arrangements. The escrow agent is the trust broker and the buyer (relying party) is the one who might need to call on the escrowed items if the supplier (claimant) defaults on

Trust brokers must offer liability cover to add value

To provide a high level of assurance regarding the trust service being offered, the trust broker must also offer a remedy if the business transaction goes wrong. The trust broker must guarantee that he will take responsibility for the trust and more importantly, will take *liability* for it. So trust broker services provide the wheels for digital business transactions, but when the wheels start coming off, the trust broker has to be responsible and liable, otherwise what was the value of the trust service?

Original academic models of trust services were flawed

In the late 1970s and early 1980s, when the concept of public key cryptography was being discussed in technical textbooks on cryptography, it was assumed that the business opportunity for running a certification service would be in selling digital certificates. However, when you perform this rigorous analysis of how trust relationships really work, it becomes clear that this original assumption (that has contaminated thinking ever since) was deeply flawed. Selling certificates is not where the business opportunity lies.

Trust services have to be based on a true business model

A trust broker provides the certificate to the claimant, but the customer for his trust services is the relying party. If he makes a contract with the claimant and sells him a service, it has minimal value,

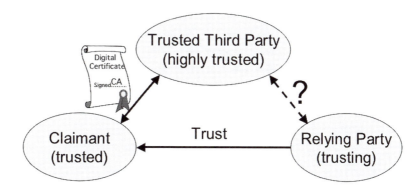

Figure 10-14: No Value for the Relying Party

and the real need for a trust service remains unsatisfied, because the relying party got nothing at all (see Figure 10-14). And that is why the original technical publications had it all wrong.

Trust broker services must meet the needs of the relying parties

We have already said that real business transactions are complex and involve two-way trust, such that both parties are simultaneously both claimant and relying party. But when you analyse this complexity into its constituent elements, there is only one element to be found – the simple reduction previously discussed. So, whatever the business application, you must create trust broker services that meet the needs of the relying parties, recognising that this will include all parties to a multi-party transaction. How can this be done?

Trust Broker Models that Work

The trusted transaction as the unit of 'product'

The key to understanding the true business model is recognising that what a trust broker can sell is a *trusted transaction*. The business model is like that already used for conventional credit card transactions (no, this does not mean using credit cards over the web – it means the way that credit cards work in general). Consider a credit card issuer that decides it will make money by selling credit cards to its customers. This is the equivalent of selling certificates. How sustainable would such a

---

the contract.

business be? Exactly! Which is why banks *give*[24] you a credit card (provided that you meet the registration criteria).

The credit card analogy shows how it should work

How do they make money then? Well, every time you use your credit card to buy something, they take a percentage of the transaction value from the merchant. Why would the merchant pay this percentage? Because the credit card company offers in return a guarantee (subject to the merchant having followed proper procedures) that the merchant will get his money, whatever the status of the card, the cardholder or the account. If it is a stolen card, and the merchant takes all reasonable steps to check for authenticity of the cardholder, then the credit-card company takes the hit. The merchant is protected, and so is the authorised cardholder.

The services on sale are trust and liability management

What is on sale here is *trust* and *liability management* – which is exactly what you are looking for in digital business. Translate this plastic model into a digital model. The digital certificate is the equivalent of the plastic card. You can apply for one, and you must be registered and pass certain verification tests about your true identity, your credit worthiness, and so on. If the registration authority is satisfied that it *trusts* you, you will be issued with a digital certificate by the certification authority. This combination of RA and CA is the equivalent of the credit card issuer.

There may be a registration fee

In practice there are many possibilities for the RA and CA to be the same organisation or different organisations working together under an agreement, but that sort of detail is beyond the scope of this discussion. There may be a registration fee to cover administration costs and to deter vexatious applications, but essentially the RA and CA make little money from issuing digital certificates.

The relying party wants assurance from the trust broker of trust in a given claim by a claimant

It is when you use the certificate to do digital business that they will get their revenue, just like with the cards. The relying party wants to know, 'Can I trust the claim being made by the claimant?' (Whatever the nature of that claim might be). In some cases it is simply a claim of a given identity. In other cases the claim will be that the claimant will behave under certain agreed rules and conditions, that he will pay his debts and that he will in general not cheat the relying party.

Transitive trust

The trust model here is what is known as *transitive trust*. It works like this:

- The trust broker trusts the claimant. This trust is established through the registration process.

- The relying party trusts the trust broker. (Here is the core of what it takes to be a successful trust broker. Relying parties have to trust you enough to pay you for the trust services that you offer. You live and die by your reputation.)

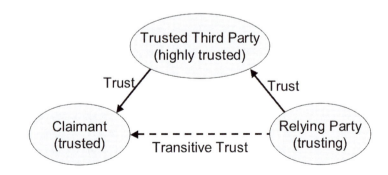

Figure 10-15: Transitive Trust Model

---

[24] There may be an annual subscription fee of a few dollars, but this is not industry-standard and where it is applied is controversial. It is also not how credit card companies make serious money.

- Hence, by transitivity, the relying party trusts the claimant and also trusts the claims that he makes.

Transitive trust can be reduced to a series of simple one-way trust relationships

Figure 10-15 shows this transitive trust model at its simplest. We maintain that this model also submits to the hierarchical analysis used earlier and that it can be treated as a triangular combination of three complex two-way trust relationships, each of which can be reduced to a series of simple one-way trust relationship models, as before.

Pricing and service packaging are commercial issues

Depending upon the business service, there will be different pricing and payment models for these trust services. For payment transactions in digital business the price will probably be based upon a percentage of the transaction value (as with credit cards). However, digital certificates and trust-broker services will cover a much wider range of services than just payments.

E-mail trust services are more likely to be subscription services

For example, using PKI to secure an e-mail service, proving authenticity to the recipients (who for this part of the relationship are relying parties) and privacy to the senders (who are also relying parties in this other respect) requires a different approach to pricing the service. Both senders and receivers are more likely to be charged an annual subscription for the trust services, although some sort of usage metering is also possible.

Analysing a business application to determine the trust services

Whatever the business application, it will need to be analysed on the following criteria:

- Who are the relying parties? (Remember that all parties are probably relying parties in some respect and that the relationship must be analysed to reduce it into a series of simple one-way trust relationships where reliance is clearly identified).

- How much do the relying parties need to trust? And hence how much value will they associate with the trust broker service? And hence how much will they pay for it? And how can 'gold service' trust be differentiated from mere silver or bronze?

- How can you unit-price and bill for the service in a way that reflects the value and is also easy to deliver and administer?

Trust service providers need to understand their market

The answers will be variable, according to the business model being supported. However, those who want to be trust brokers had better have a clear and accurate set of answers. And for those who want to purchase these services, they had better influence their trust brokers to produce the right services for their needs. In most business areas, there is long way to go yet on both these fronts.

Authorisation certificates provide a mechanism for trust brokers to communicate their trust

From a technical perspective the relying party will go on-line to the trust broker and ask if the claim being made by the claimant can be trusted. The trust broker will verify the claim by appropriate investigation and will respond with a trusted message, giving authorisation to accept the claim (or not). This trusted message is often referred to as an authorisation certificate or a privilege attribute certificate. The technical standard most likely to be used to implement this is the X.509 Attribute Certificate.

Managing the lifetime of authorisation certificates is a business risk-driven issue

The authorisation certificate must have a limited lifetime, controlled by a trusted time stamp embedded in its own data structure, and after that lifetime expires the authorisation that it carries is automatically revoked. There is then a business decision to be made as to how long (or short) that lifetime should be, and of course there is a risk assessment involved in making that decision. By extending the lifetime you potentially increase flexibility, but at the same time you increase the risk that the user authorisations that underpin this authorisation certificate will have been revoked since it was issued.

Total real-time risk exposure can be monitored

A further development of this authorisation certificate lifetime risk management approach is for the trust broker to monitor the total real-time risk exposure due to current 'in-flight', unexpired authorisation certificates.

Real-time authorisation addresses several architectural issues

This real-time authorisation of business transactions by the trust broker also provides solutions to several other major problems that are posed by the conventional textbook model:

- Certificate revocation lists (CRLs) are almost certainly unscaleable in large business communities. This on-line authorisation model does not require CRLs because the transaction will always be authorised in real time by the certificate issuing authority. Hence this scalability issue disappears[25].

- The CRL also raises questions about how current it is and about the relationship between currency and liability. If you check a certificate against a CRL that has aged a little, and the certificate has actually been revoked since the CRL was issued, who will be liable for the transaction that was trusted on the basis of a revoked certificate? There is no easy answer to this, but with on-line authorisation, there is no CRL, and hence no problem. You go right back to the issuing authority to get a specific authorisation that includes verifying that the certificate has not been revoked.

- If liability management is associated with issuing certificates, it is impossible to track what the instantaneous risk exposure is at any one time. If people can use certificates to claim value, how many times can they use them and up to what total value? However, in the on-line authorisation model you can track the in-flight transactions that are at risk and you can monitor and manage the overall instantaneous risk exposure. Much better!

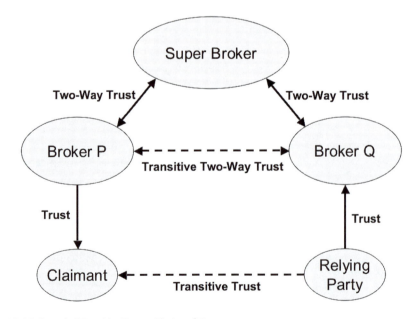

Figure 10-16: Extended Transitive Trust – Chains of Trust

---

[25] However, it is replaced by another scaling challenge. The bandwidth and processing to handle this on-line model is very significant, especially as you imagine very large business communities.

Extended Trust Broker Models for PKI

Multiple trust brokers

The model shown in Figure 10-15 assumes that there is a single trust broker that has both registered the claimant and is known to and is highly trusted by the relying party. There are many cases where this will not happen. The claimant has registered with one trust broker that is unknown to or not well trusted by the relying party, and the relying party trusts a broker that has not been adopted by the claimant. After all, we all live and work in a free market where there will be many trust brokers with many differentiated offerings.

Chains of trust

One solution would be that every claimant has to obtain certificates from every trust broker that could be used by a relying party with which he wants to do business. This is impractical. What is much more likely is that trust brokers will develop levels of trust in each other and that through these higher level trust relationships, the concept of transitivity can be used to create an extended transitive trust relationship, sometimes known as a *chain of trust*. Figure 10-16 shows an example.

Identrus – the solution adopted in the banking industry

One industry that has developed a good understanding of trust and trust brokerage is the banking industry. This is because banking is based entirely on trust between bank and customer. Who else do you trust enough to look after all your money and to give it back again when you ask? So are these concepts being rolled out in banking? Yes indeed they are. The organisation most obviously responsible is a consortium of very large banks called Identrus[26].

Levels of Trust

Variable levels of trust

There is one more thing that needs to be discussed on the concept of trust – and that is the potential need for different levels of trust for different business situations.

Strength of registration process is the key to trust

The level of trust that can be associated with a business transaction is directly related to the level of trust that the parties can have in the digital certificate that has been used to broker the transaction. This in turn is directly related to the strength of the registration process by which that certificate was granted and issued. How much validation was done regarding the identity of the claimant? How much verification of trustworthiness was carried out?

Low assurance registration

On the one hand there might be situations where self-registration is the appropriate way for a given business application. You go to a public web site, you fill in a form with your name and other details (Micky Mouse, George Washington... whatever), you 'click and go' and you automatically get a certificate sent to your e-mail address. A slight improvement on this click-and-go process might be to check that the name and the e-mail address are related, but this may not work in all cases.

High-assurance registration

At the other end of the trust scale you apply for a certificate in writing and you experience something like the process for getting your first passport. You need a birth certificate, probably a social security number and written references independently procured from citizens of upstanding positions in society who will testify that they have known you for at least 10 years. For certain applications you will also need a banker's reference to testify to your credit-worthiness and your credit history over an extended period. Just to make certain, independent checks will also be made for a criminal record. Now that's serious registration!

Verifying credentials often involves transitive trust

As an aside, the use of birth certificates, passports, driver's licences, banker's references, personal referees and the like are all examples of transitive trust, where an independent trusted third party (or a document issued by such a trusted third party) is being used to verify some aspect of your claimed identity or trustworthiness.

---

[26]See www.identrus.com, where you will find full details of both the business models and the technical models used.

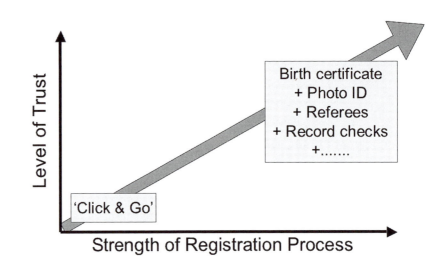

Figure 10-17: Level of Trust versus Strength of Registration

The relationship between level of trust and registration strength

Figure 10-17 shows the relationship between the level of trust and the strength of the registration process. Table 10-1 provides a more detailed view of the possible strengths of registration available to you.

Table 10-1: Assurance Levels for Registration Processes

Registration Assurance Level	Implications for Level of Trust
Self-registration	This allows very quick sign-up for customers on a click-and-go basis. It is suitable only for services publicly available within the user's environment (possibly a closed business environment) where the only service provider interest is in collecting general information on how many and which users are registering for the service. There can be no attempt made here to ensure that the registered user is the authentic owner of the name claimed. However, this approach may be suitable for certain web-based services.
E-mail registration	This again allows quick sign-up by allowing the user to be authenticated based upon the possession of an e-mail address with a given domain name embedded in it, indicating that the user belongs to an organisation with that domain name. The level of authentication is weak, and the use of the domain name credentials will not cover all situations, especially for staff with other e-mail addresses. However for certain low-assurance applications this may be suitable.
Web-based credit card registration	In this case the user self-registers but proves more about his identity by supplying a valid credit card number. This is still a relatively weak registration process in which it is easy to supply a fraudulent card number (which may or may not exist), but for low-assurance applications where small payments are involved and a level of fraud can be tolerated, this may be a suitable method. Suitable applications will include low-value information services.

Registration Assurance Level	Implications for Level of Trust
Telephone confirmation	Adding a telephone confirmation process can augment each of the previous three methods of registration (self-registration, e-mail registration and web-based credit card registration). The user is telephoned at a number obtained independently of the initial registration ('out of band'), and certain details are verified in the conversation. This eliminates certain types of impersonation.
Postal registration	In this case the entity sends an application for registration through the post, enclosing documentary evidence of identity and membership of the given business community. The policy of the registration authority determines the strength of this process, specifying whether copies or original documents are required and how many documents of what type must be presented. In the USA, there is an additional strength and implication to using postal registration. Use of the postal service as a means to defraud constitutes mail fraud, which is a federal offence, therefore adding additional risk mitigation potential.
Personal registration	This is where an individual must attend in person to a registration office and present credentials for verification (birth certificate, passport, membership certificate, driving license, proof of address). The registration process can be made as rigorous as is required for the business environment and is entirely up to the registration authority in determining the registration policy. High-value transaction or order-execution systems will require strong registration processes. They will also require strong user authentication mechanisms, such as smart cards or biometrics.
Transferred registrations	Existing client databases can be used as sources of registration data. In this case previous registration details obtained for another purpose are accepted as suitable and are transferred to this application. The strength of the registration is entirely dependent upon the strength of the original registration and upon the level of maintenance to the database to keep its details up to date.
Delegated or multi-tiered registration	In this case a registration authority registers a sub-registration authority that is delegated with the responsibility for registering users within its own domain. These delegated registration authorities are often known as local registration authorities (LRAs). There could potentially be several levels or tiers of delegation. The overall strength of the registration depends upon each and every one of the processes at each level in the hierarchy.

Different levels of trust leads to different classes of digital certificates

These very different needs for levels of trust and for appropriate registration processes to accompany them will lead to the provision of different classes of digital certificate designed for different purposes. The purpose for which the digital certificates are intended, and the trust and liability management that can be associated with them are described in documents called the Certificate Policy (CP) and the Certificate Practices Statement (CPS).

The market for trust levels is still emerging

We may see the emergence of a gold/silver/bronze type of hierarchy. We may also see the emergence of certificates that are restricted to certain groups of activities within a given vertical sector of the market. We can be sure that there will be differentiation of trust level, but exactly how the market will respond with service offerings is hard to predict at present. It is an issue that any potential service provider should actively consider.

Security Domain Model

SABSA® Matrix cross-reference Please refer to Chapter 3, Figure 3-3 and Chapter 7, Figure 7-6, the SABSA® Matrix, Conceptual Layer, Location column, where you will see a cell entitled Security Domain Model. In Chapter 7, Figure 7-5 this also appears as key deliverable of the conceptual security architecture. This section explains in detail the concept of security domains.

Security Domains

The security domain concept is very powerful The security domain concept is a very powerful modelling tool. Here is presented a definition what it means and an explanation of the terminology and concepts used in that definition.

Security domains defined A security domain is a set of security elements subject to a common security policy defined and enforced by a single security policy authority[27]. The activities of a security domain involve one or more elements from that security domain, and possibly elements of other security domains.

Security element A security element may be a security entity (as defined in a previous section of this chapter – i.e. a subject) or a security object (such as a data structure – field, record, file, database – or a physical system or sub-system – computer, disk drive, printer)[28].

Security policy and security policy rules A security policy expresses security requirements for a security domain in general terms. Security policy rules are derived from the security policy during security engineering activities. The security policy rules interpret the security policy in definite terms that can be incorporated into security mechanisms, which in turn deliver security services that are used to implement the security policy.

Security policy authority A security policy authority is responsible for setting and implementing the security policy within the domain. For example, in a domain of registered users, the registration authority is the domain security policy authority.

Inter-Domain Relationships

Isolated security domains Two security domains are said to be *isolated* from each other if they have no data objects in common and no activities in common and therefore cannot interact.

Independent security domains Two security domains are said to *independent* of each other if they have no data objects in common and the activities within each security domain are constrained only by their own security policies and the security policy authorities of each are not constrained to coordinate or harmonise their security policies.

Agreements between independent domains Two or more independent domains may enter into agreements to coordinate sharing of information among them.

Sub-domains and super-domains Security domain A is a *sub-domain* of another security domain B (and hence B is a *super-domain* of A) if and only if:

* The set of elements of A is a sub-set of or is the same as the set of elements of B;
* The set of activities in A is a sub-set of or is the same as the set of activities in B;

---

[27]This formal definition and its expansion over the following sections are taken from ISO/IEC 10181 – Security Frameworks for Open Systems, 1996.

[28]Logical systems or sub-systems such as applications may be regarded either as subjects or objects depending upon the context.

- Jurisdiction for A is delegated from the security authority of B to the security authority of A;

- The security policy of A does not conflict with the security policy of B. A may introduce additional security policy if required, but only if permitted under the security policy of B.

Trust in Domains

Trusted entities in a domain

An entity is said to be trusted for some classes of activity in the domain, in the context of a security policy, if the means of enforcing the policy depend upon the entity behaving in a particular way. The security policy defines which entities are trusted, and for each trusted entity the policy defines the set of activities for which the entity is trusted. An entity trusted for one set of activities is not necessarily trusted for all activities in the domain.

Conditional and unconditional trust

The security policy may require a mechanism to detect misbehaviour by a trusted entity. A trusted entity that can misbehave without the violation of policy being detected is said to be *unconditionally trusted*. A trusted entity that can violate the policy but not without the misbehaviour being detected is said to be *conditionally trusted*.

Trust is not necessarily two-way or transitive

Trust within the domain is not necessarily mutual (two-way) and not necessarily transitive. Transitivity of trust is usually defined technically by the security policy but is also heavily dependent upon the relationship.

Secure Interaction Between Domains

Secure interaction rules

To be able to exchange information between domains the domain policy authorities must agree a set of security policy rules governing this interaction – known as secure interaction rules. These jointly agreed rules form part of the policy rules of each individual domain.

Agreed security services, security mechanisms and security information

To implement the secure interaction rules the policy authorities also need to negotiate an agreement on a set of common security services and common security mechanisms as well as on the security information items to be exchanged (for example as part of a mutual authentication exchange protocol).

Policy relationships in sub-domains

If the interacting domains are both sub-domains of the same super-domain, then the super-domain policy authority may impose the secure interaction rules or it may allow the sub-domains to negotiate their own set of secure interaction rules, depending upon the terms of the super-domain's own security policy.

Security Associations

Security association defined

A security association[29] is a set of shared security information items and attributes (such as state information and rules) that describe a relationship between two or more entities. The security association governs the provision of security services involving interaction between the two entities. A security association implies the existence of secure interaction rules and the maintenance of consistent security-related state variables for both entities. State variables can be passwords, sequence numbers, cryptographic keys and so on[30].

---

[29]The formal definition here is taken from ISO/IEC 10745: Upper Layers Security Model, 1993.
[30]For a full discussion of finite state concepts, refer to Chapter 5.

Logical Domains

A logical domain maps onto groupings of logical entities, such as entities sharing an application, a business community or a privileged group of entities.

Logical domain boundaries are usually protected by logical access control – role-based or otherwise.

Physical Domains

A physical security domain maps onto groupings of physical entities. It is usually a site, a platform or a network.

Physical network domain boundaries are usually protected by firewalls. Doors, locks, gates, guards and so on are usually used to protect physical site domain boundaries. Tamper-resistant computing devices are used where a physically trusted and secure domain is required to protect sensitive code execution, such as handling cryptographic keys.

Multi-Domain Environments

A given environment can support multiple overlaid domains of different types.

Example 1: A distributed application is a single logical domain, but because of is physical distribution, it may span several physical network domains, including the Internet and several private networks.

Example 2: A single host computer is a single physical domain, but it may simultaneously host several different applications, each of which is a separate logical domain.

Applying the Security Domain Concept

The application of these concepts to real-world business situations requires some discipline but provides a powerful modelling tool. The following guidelines will help you to make the best use of this tool:

- Make sure that your specification for a given domain is clear and explicit;

- In particular make sure the definition of the domain boundary and the domain interfaces are clear so that there is no confusion as which elements and activities are included and which are excluded;

- Make sure you identify the domain security authority for each domain and that this authority really does set and implement security policy governing the domain;

- Be prepared to consider sub-domains and super-domains, since real-world situations are often found to reflect these structures;

- Many real business environments involve multiple domains, often overlaid and overlapping. Although this complexity may seem daunting, the domain modelling approach gives you a method by which you can unravel the complexity and reduce it to a set of simple domains, each of which is well defined. It suggests a top-down analysis similar to that which was applied in analysing trust relationships earlier in this chapter. Once completed, the domain model provides a clear conceptual model of the real business that you can work with easily for design purposes;

- When designing control points such as firewalls and logical access control systems, make sure you cover all the domain boundaries and all the domain interaction points;

- Do not forget that there is always a surrounding domain called 'the universe' that is a super-domain of all domains that you will define and which should be regarded as completely hostile, with no security policy, no domain authority and containing untrusted security elements.

New Security Paradigm for Digital Business

Digital business means opening up the enterprise

Here the security domain concepts are applied to help you see how you can open up your enterprise to support the new business requirements that digital business is thrusting upon you.

The fortress mentality is an age-old security model

Security models date back to the days of fortified castles and cities. This traditional model is based upon the concept of a strong perimeter wall that entirely surrounds and encloses the area to be protected. The walls are high, there are battlements on top from which soldiers can fire missiles at potential attackers and there are strong gates that remain closed against enemies but which can be opened to allow access to authorised people and traffic. It is a model that has worked well and is well understood, and there are many implementations of this conceptual model in the familiar real world. In particular business computer systems have been built and secured along these lines for several decades.

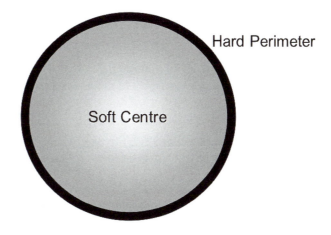

Figure 10-18: The Eggshell Model of Security

Many legacy business systems have an eggshell model of security

We might describe this conventional approach as the eggshell model of security. The perimeter of the enclosure is a hard shell, but the inside is soft. Once you break through the hard perimeter, everything is easily consumed. Figure 10-18 shows this basic conceptual model. Most existing business computing systems have been constructed like this, on the basis that the aim is to allow access to resources only to those who are already inside the perimeter, and to prevent any type of access to those resources from outside the perimeter.

For digital business you need something different from the eggshell approach

When you consider doing digital business, you find that the traditional eggshell security model does not work well at all. You have to do something different because for digital business you must allow outsiders to gain access to your business computing systems. How can this be done without undue risk?

Often one tries to modify an existing model by making some adaptations. For example, the eggshell model has a continuous perimeter, but you can go back to the idea of the fortified city with its strong gate. The gate can be opened for an authenticated, authorised friend but can be closed against all foes. In computer system terms this is the concept of a security gateway. See Figure 10-19 for a conceptual representation.

Figure 10-19: The Eggshell Perimeter with a Gateway

However, this classification into two categories of friend (a trusted party) or foe (an untrusted party) is too crude. In real business life trust is not a binary quantity. Trust is measured on a continuum and you can trust your business associates and partners to varying degrees (as has been discussed in some detail in an earlier section of this chapter). If you trust another party, there is a qualifying statement that tells you how much you trust them. And based upon this level of trust, you will want to grant them greater or lesser access to your systems and resources for the purposes of doing digital business. This already tells you that a security gateway (a firewall) alone is probably not enough.

There is a tendency with the firewall mechanism to make a binary decision: trusted or untrusted? That means that once through the gate of the strong perimeter, the outsider can do pretty much anything that an insider can do. Even if the decision-making process at the gate is sound, the binary approach to classifying trust does not map onto the real business model of trust.

The new security model that you must build does not have such a hard perimeter or such a binary gate-keeping approach, because you find that you need to let in a large number of other parties if you are to do digital business. These include customers, prospective customers, suppliers, service providers and so on. However, you want to let them in only so far, and you want to limit their access privileges to those that are needed for the specific business functions that you want to grant, and no more than that.

An important part of this new model is conceptually like a honeycomb, with many cells, each with its own perimeter protecting it from intrusion. Granting access to one cell of the honeycomb does not imply granting access to any of the other cells. Figure 10-20 shows this conceptual model of security.

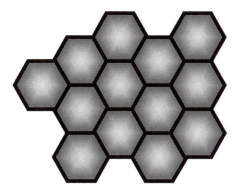

Figure 10-20: The Honeycomb Model of Security

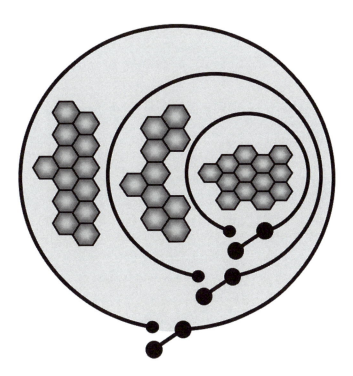

Figure 10-21: An Egg and Honey Combination Model of Security

The egg and honey combination model

This honeycomb model alone will not suffice. A more practical model of enterprise security that opens up the enterprise is a combination of concentric eggshell-type perimeters, each with a gateway and with the honeycomb type of cells within each concentric zone. We show this egg and honey conceptual model in Figure 10-21.

Multi-tiered security domains

In this egg and honey combination model there are a series of zones or security domains, each with a more stringent security policy than the one before. So, to get through the outer gateway a party needs to be:

- Registered (do you know who he is and have you got him on your books?);

- Authenticated (can he prove his identity?);

- Authorised (have you granted him privileges to enter this domain under the terms of the domain policy?)

Hierarchical filtering

To get through subsequent inner gateways the party needs to be authorised to a higher level of privilege and in particular needs to have a valid business reason to get to the honeycomb at that level. Access to individual honeycomb cells is also granted or denied according to specific business need.

Eggshells are usually physical domain boundaries

These security domains represented by the concentric eggshells are usually physical (sub-domains of the network or perhaps whole computer systems attached to the network), and the access control at these gateways is implemented through a physical access control mechanism such as a firewall.

Honeycombs are usually logical domain boundaries

The cells of the honeycomb are also security sub-domains, each with its own policy on access. These are more likely to be logical (applications within a physical computer, logical functions within an application program, or logical data sets within an application database). In this case the access control mechanism is a logical access control software sub-system, either within the application software itself, or within the database management system, or within the operating system.

The overall access control strategy is a combination of the eggshell and honeycomb approaches

Both the physical access control mechanism (firewall) and the logical access control mechanism (a software sub-system) are responsible for delivering an access control service. They work together, implementing a layered series of filters, and mapping the trust model and authorisation model that represents the real business. In this way you can achieve the granularity of control that you need to manage and control the business.

Eggshell maps to network security and honeycomb maps to application security

Bearing in mind what was said in an earlier section of this chapter about the differences between network security and application security, you can basically classify the eggshell mechanism as being a network security device, and the honeycomb mechanism as being an application security device.

Use these concepts to model your business

We strongly recommend that you adopt these modelling techniques and apply them to your business:

- What are the domains and how do they relate to one another?

- How many concentric eggshells do you need?

- What are the honeycombs and how many cells does each need?

- What privileges are associated with each domain (each eggshell and each honeycomb cell?

Using these techniques helps you to create simple models representing highly complex environments

It will take a little while to develop these conceptual models, but once you have them and you have validated them, then the design process becomes very straightforward. You can clearly see how many firewalls you need and where they should be positioned. You can also see how many levels of logical access control you need and how many roles you will need at each level – the role being equivalent to a single honeycomb cell. You will have represented what seemed at first to be a very complex environment by a model whose simplicity is beautiful.

VPN Concept

Virtual private networks (VPNs) are seen by some organisations as the way to provide a secure business environment, but there are some limitations to be considered.

A VPN uses point-to-point encryption within the network layer to provide a series of secure pipes along which private business data can be transmitted without being capable of being read by an eavesdropper (see Figure 10-22). In addition, by virtue of the fact that the application data stream is completely encrypted, it is also infeasible for an outsider to make changes to the transmitted data without this being detected.

There are some issues to consider here. If you construct a secure pipe between two domains without regulating the flow at each end of the pipe, then all that the pipe does is to connect the two domains to form a single domain. In Figure 10-22 you see three physically remote domains interconnected with encrypted pipes to form a single logical domain.

This is perfectly acceptable if the security policy and the ownership of the remote domains are identical, but if they are not, then the secure pipe becomes a means by which one domain can attack

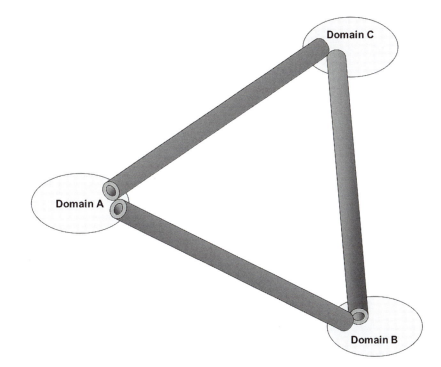

Figure 10-22: The VPN Concept Using Encrypted Pipes

the other. In this case you still need the firewall to regulate the flow of data between the two domains connected by the secure pipe, as shown in Figure 10-23. You need a regulator (firewall) at each end of the pipe (in each domain) because each domain must be responsible for setting and enforcing its own security policy.

Typically a VPN is built by using embedded encryption and decryption in the firewalls that provide the secure interface to a hostile network such as the Internet. The standardised approach to achieving this is to use the IPSec protocol – a secure version of the IP protocol that provides encryption and/or authentication within the IP packet level protocol.

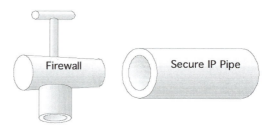

Figure 10-23: Using a Firewall to Regulate Flow in Secure Pipe

A VPN tunnel through a firewall can be built but has disadvantages

However, the IPSec functionality can be embedded in any end-system and so may tunnel through the firewall (if the firewall rules allow) right up to an application server. The downside of this approach is that the firewall can no longer monitor the contents of the packets because they are encrypted, and so VPNs are usually terminated at the firewall.

For extranet VPNs, the VPN client resides on the PC

At the client end, if the client is outside the firewall, such as in the implementation of an extranet, then the VPN client resides on the user's PC and the VPN runs all the way up to this platform (see Figure 10-24)

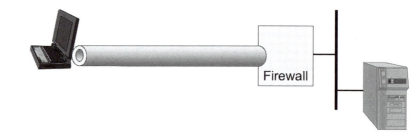

Figure 10-24: VPN Implementation of an Extranet

Firewall Concept

A firewall is a network security gateway

A firewall is a security gateway that sits on the boundary between two network domains, enforcing the security policy of one of those domains (usually the internal corporate domain), and regulating the flow of network traffic into and out of that domain. Firewalls have the job a preventing unauthorised traffic flows, and of detecting unauthorised attempts to penetrate the security boundary created around the protected domain

Firewalls have limitations that are not always well-understood

When it comes to securing data networking environments, especially those in which an internal corporate network is to be connected to an external hostile network such as the Internet, most organisations will choose to use a firewall. However, the limitations of firewalls seem to be poorly understood, consider some of the key issues.

The corporate domain is an island in the Internet sea

Firstly, the Internet is so pervasive that it effectively surrounds your enterprise domain. Think of the private corporate domain as being a small island in a large ocean called the Internet (see Figure 10-25).

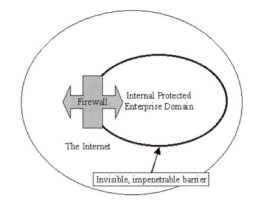

Figure 10-25: The Corporate Domain as an Island in the Internet Sea

The firewall alone is ineffective – you need a good security perimeter, too

As soon as this concept is clearly understood, it becomes obvious that the firewall alone will do little, because the firewall can only regulate traffic that is directed through it. If the boundary around the rest of the domain is leaky, and if traffic flows into and out of the domain other than through the firewall, then the firewall is ineffective and may as well not be there. For example, if a member of staff purchases a modem and installs this in her PC without authorisation, and then uses it to make dial-up connections to an ISP, then the firewall cannot intervene. So, to make a firewall work properly, you need to implement the invisible, impenetrable barrier also shown in Figure 10-25.

The remainder of the perimeter is mostly cultural

This barrier is mostly not a technical thing – it is a combination of policy, procedure, behaviour, awareness, and so on, without which the firewall cannot be effective. To implement good firewall-based network security, you need good security culture throughout your enterprise.

You also need a clear firewall policy

The firewall itself must also be properly configured and managed. Firewalls allow certain traffic (because it is required for legitimate business purposes) and disallow other traffic (because it is not required for legitimate business purposes). So you must be clear about what you will allow and what you will block at the firewall. This is the firewall security policy, and without a properly stated policy, the firewall will probably not offer the correct protection.

The firewall configuration needs proactive management

Even when you have the policy correct, you must continue to monitor and check that the policy is properly implemented and that the firewall is correctly configured according to this policy. Many people think that firewalls are essentially technical gadgets that work in isolation. As you can see from this discussion, nothing could be further from the truth.

Security Lifetimes and Deadlines

SABSA® Matrix cross-reference

Please refer to Chapter 3, Figure 3-3 and Chapter 7, Figure 7-6, the SABSA® Matrix, Conceptual layer, Time column, where you will see a cell entitled Security Related Lifetimes and Deadlines. In Chapter 7, Figure 7-5 this also appears as key deliverable of the conceptual security architecture. This section explains in detail the main lifetime and deadline concepts that you need to consider.

Registration Lifetimes

Fixed lifetimes prevent accumulation of dormant registrations

Each registered entity is registered for a fixed period of time, after which the registration expires and must be renewed. This prevents the build-up of dormant registrations, which are not in use because the entity is no longer operational.

One to three years is a typical lifetime

A typical registration lifetime would be in the range of one to three years. However, some registrations are much longer. An example of this is the registration of each individual citizen at birth and the assignment of a social security number that remains operative for the entire life of that individual.

Certification Lifetimes

Digital certificates must also be expired

A registered entity can be issued with a set of digital certificates with which to authenticate messages and exchange encryption keys. These digital certificates also have fixed lifetime, after which the certificate expires and cannot be used.

Certificate life is less than registration life

The digital certificate lifetime should never exceed the registration lifetime, because if it did, the certificate holder would be in possession of apparently valid credentials when his or her registration had actually expired.

Expiry is checked as part of acceptance of a certificate

All entities making use of certificates of other entities must check the expiry date as part of the certificate verification process.

Cryptographic Key Lifetimes

Cryptographic keys must be limited in their exposure to cryptanalysis

All cryptographic keys must have a fixed operational lifetime determined by an expiry date, to limit the time that they are exposed to possible cryptanalysis by opponents. Some keys may also be limited in exposure by the amount of usage that they are allowed. In this case the keys should expire either on the reaching of the expiry date or on reaching the usage threshold, whichever is the sooner.

Signature keys are retired from use, but previous signatures may still need to verified

Digital signature keys should have two lifetimes: one for the period over which signatures can be made and the other for the period of time over which those signatures remain valid and can be verified in operational use. The former should expire before the latter. Archiving requirements will determine the signature verification lifetime.

Lifetime depends on security policy

The actual lifetimes to be used are to be specified in the security policy of the security domain that owns the keys. Factors to consider are the type of usage, the strength of the algorithm, the key length, the system architecture and other relevant factors that influence the assessment of vulnerability to cryptanalysis.

Cryptographic keys may be archived for data recovery, implying an extended lifetime

Cryptographic keys may also need to be archived for the purposes of data recovery. In these circumstances a second lifetime should be specified, to ensure that the keys are kept in archived form for as long as is required to grant access to the data over its expected archive lifetime. For most business data this period will be several years and may potentially be indefinite.

Policy Lifetimes

Policy decays over time and needs renewal

Security policies also have lifetimes. Over a period of time security policy often decays in terms of its effectiveness and its appropriateness, and there comes a point when it needs to be reworked.

Policy should stable between renewal times

It is a bad idea to make frequent policy changes because this leads to confusion and undermines confidence in the policy, but there should be a policy review cycle, perhaps every three or four years, when policies are subjected to scrutiny to make sure that they are still appropriate. This review often provides an opportunity to make changes that have become necessary to keep the policy up-to-date.

Rule Lifetimes

Rules to implement policies may need to change frequently.

It is important to distinguish between policies (at the logical level) and rules (at the physical level). Whilst the policy should stay relatively unchanged, the rules needed to implement that policy may need to be changed quite frequently to keep up with rapid changes in technology, new attack modes and exploits.

Password Lifetimes

Passwords should be expired according to the security policy of the domain

All passwords should be subject to enforced expiry at the end of a specified lifetime. The actual lifetime to be employed is a matter of security policy of the domain in which the password is to be used.

Minimum lifetimes should also be applied to passwords

Passwords may be expired voluntarily before the end of their lifetime, but it is also essential to have a minimum lifetime before which the password cannot be expired. This value is usually selected to be one day (24 hours), but its actual selection is a matter for security policy in the domain. This minimum password lifetime prevents an uncooperative user resetting new passwords immediately and thus returning to the previous value that should have been retired from use.

History files of previous passwords may be implemented

It is even more effective to maintain a history file of previously used passwords to ensure that they are not reused until several new generations of passwords have expired and been retired, but the precise application of this technique is also a matter for security policy in the domain.

Token Lifetimes

Issuing physical tokens is logistically demanding

Issuing tokens such as smart cards to large user communities requires considerable logistical support. The tokens have to be processed individually to program them with user-specific data, and then distributed securely to the users. An initial password also has to be distributed to the user through another channel to prevent the token and password being stolen together during distribution.

Frequent redistribution needs to be avoided

This means that you must avoid having to redistribute tokens too frequently, otherwise the costs would be prohibitive. Tokens (such as smart cards) should therefore be renewed every two to three years. They are mechanically capable of sustaining this lifetime, but it is also important to ensure that any cryptographic keys stored on the smart card or other token over its entire lifetime without being changed are of sufficient strength to withstand this level of exposure to cryptanalysis.

Token issue should be staggered

Token issue should be staggered over the business year to provide a smooth operational workload for the business unit that handles this function.

Message Time to Live

Undeliverable messages have to be managed

Messages can sometimes become difficult or impossible to deliver. In order to prevent denial of service resulting from the build-up of undeliverable messages, all levels of messaging should incorporate the concept of 'time to live'.

Time to live determines when delivery attempts are abandoned

This means that the message has a finite lifetime within which it should be delivered. If it has failed to be delivered in this time then the attempt to deliver it is abandoned.

Actions on expiry of time to live

The action to be taken on failure is a matter of policy within the domain. However the actions that are possible include:

- Discard message, without notifying the sender;

- Discard message, with a return message to notify the sender (not guaranteed to be delivered);

- Discard message and send a priority notification back to the sender to give high assurance that the sender discovers the non-delivery;

- Implement a positive acknowledgement service, whereby all messages delivered are acknowledged (either explicitly, or implicitly using sliding windows[31]), with a NAK (negative acknowledgement) in case of failure, or a time-out window at the sender in case the NAK fails to be returned.

Stored Data Lifetimes

Data storage should have a defined lifetime

Every application or service that stores data should be analysed to define the storage lifetime business requirements for the data.

Storage lifetime may apply to each phase of storage

There may be several phases in the overall storage lifetime, beginning with memory-cached data, moving to on-line disk-stored data, and finally off-line archived data.

Archiving lifetime for backup data

The archiving lifetimes should also be defined for backup copies of data.

Continued support for reading long-term archived data

One of the most important aspects of managing long storage lifetimes of electronic data (with lifetimes in the order of several decades) is maintaining the technologies and technical products that will be needed to retrieve the data. For example, magnetic tapes become useless if the tape machines needed to read them are no longer supported. Physical degradation of storage media is also a problem that must be understood and managed, because over time the quality of magnetic media will often decay to a point where the medium is no longer readable.

Data Secrecy Lifetimes

Secrecy lifetimes depends on business need and policy

The secrecy of some data has to be maintained for many years. The actual periods of time required are a matter of policy determined by the policy authority that governs the business area concerned. For example, in many jurisdictions, privacy law applies to personal information stored and processed during the lifetime of the human subjects, but not once they are dead.

Solutions must be selected with long-term secrecy requirements in mind

It is essential to plan technology solutions that are capable of maintaining these secrecy lifetimes without failing through the passage of time. This impacts upon the selection of cryptographic algorithms and key lengths, taking into account likely advances in technology over the intended lifetime where these advances might make the cryptography easier to attack[32]. This is a difficult area that needs careful strategic planning and expert advice.

---

[31]A 'sliding window' is a contiguous range of message sequence numbers (say eight or 16) within which a new message is allowed to be received, even though some of the messages earlier in the sequence window have not yet been received. The window extends forwards from the last positively acknowledged message. Messages with sequence gaps still outstanding behind them are not acknowledged. When the trailing end of the window has all been filled with received messages (including any backfilling of gaps in the sequence) a positive acknowledgement is sent for the last message in the completed sequence, and this implies that all previous messages up to and including that sequence number are now received and acknowledged. The window automatically slides forward so that its trailing edge is at the newly acknowledged position, and its leading edge now includes fresh sequence numbers that may be received.

[32]As an example, differential power analysis was an entirely new approach to attacking cryptosystems.

User Session Lifetimes

When a user session is opened following a login, there should be a maximum lifetime for which that session can stay open. This limits the risk of sessions being kept alive long after they are no longer needed, which leads to waste of resources and can also result in abuse of the session be an unauthorised party. Session lifetimes should be specified in the order of a few hours, to match patterns of working hours for authorised personnel.

System Session Lifetimes

In some cases it is wise to introduce a session concept even for continuous processes that never stop (such as middleware messaging). This enhances performance in secure data communications. A session context is established, in the form of security associations between the communicating entities, so that fast, efficient, symmetric cryptographic techniques can be used. Amongst the important state variables in the security context are the session keys, used for either authentication or confidentiality or both.

The session keys must be renewed from time to time to limit their exposure to cryptanalytic attack, which leads to the concept of a session lifetime. In general session lifetimes in these circumstances are expected to be in the order of 24 hours.

However, in dial up connections, the session lifetime may be considerably shorter because the duration of the dial-up call itself is short, and this determines the session boundary.

Response Time-Out

Sometimes a message or a service request fails to reach the target, or after having reached the target and being serviced, the response fails to be returned all the way to the original requestor. In these circumstances a response time-out can be implemented to ensure that the requesting process or entity is not left hanging indefinitely.

Actual time-out values are a matter for local domain policy and depend upon the circumstances of the request, especially the business environment. Who is waiting? What is the actual business activity? And how long will they be patient?

Care must also be exercised if transactions are timed-out at a client (requestor) but which have actually reached the server and been serviced but simply failed to be notified to the requestor. The server must monitor requests to ensure that an incoming request from a client is not a repeat of a previous request, assumed by the client to have been lost, timed out at the client, but actually serviced by the server. There are several mechanisms that can be used to implement this control.

Inactivity Time-Outs

When end-users log in to a system, they frequently forget to log out again. It is not an uncommon experience to find that an end user leaves his or her desk (to go to a meeting, to go to lunch, to go home, to go on vacation), leaving an open session logged in on the desktop computer.

This provides an opportunity for someone else in the area to walk up to the machine and abuse the open session for unauthorised purposes. When one considers that statistically it is more likely that a security incident will be launched from inside the organisation rather than outside, this can be a serious vulnerability. To minimise the problem, an inactivity time-out is used. This means that the system monitors end-user activity, and if the end user is inactive for a given period of time, then the system assumes that the user has left the desktop machine unattended, and a time-out is implemented to suspend the open session.

Actions on a time-out

There are two alternatives for action taken:

- Completely close the session, disconnecting from the application and requiring a complete login procedure to restart application.

- Suspend the session, holding the context as it was, including all open files, active applications and so on. A simple re-authentication of the end-user restores the session to its stored context.

The action chosen depends on circumstances

For dial-up connections the first of these options is usually implemented. For LAN connections or permanent WAN connections, the second option is usually used.

Time-out values are a policy matter

Actual time-out thresholds are a matter for local security policy. However, periods of time in the order of 10 to 15 minutes are frequently used.

Context-Based Access Control

Time of day, day of week can be used to set access control contexts

Context-based access control uses a set of context parameters to make access control decisions in real time. These context parameters include time of day, day of week, location of terminal and type of network connection (LAN, WAN, dial-up). Thus it is possible to construct access privilege rules that limit access to certain times of day and days of the week. Typically, access rights are granted during normal working hours but not outside of those hours.

Context rules can be local or central, depending on policy

Context-based privilege rules can be associated with roles, either on a central basis or on a local basis. The actual selection of those rules is a security policy issue within each security domain.

Replay Protection

Replay of previous messages can be a serious attack scenario

In distributed information systems one possible style of attack is for an opponent to capture whole messages or data exchanges and replay them later to gain some advantage. This replay attack is especially a problem with authentication exchanges, because the opponent can eavesdrop without being detected, collect the login authentication data (such as a password) and then replay the data at a later time to masquerade as the authorised user.

To prevent message replays, trusted time stamps can be used

Even if the data is encrypted, this attack can still be made to work, if the encrypted data structure is reused. To avoid this problem a special field is often introduced into the message which has a one-time value, never to be used again. This field is often called a 'nonce value', used only once and never repeated.

One-time values allow detection of replays

Nonce values are constructed by means of:

- Time stamps, with a short lifetime over which the message bearing that time stamp is acceptable;

- Random numbers used in challenge-response protocols;

- Sequence numbers that are checked off by both parties;

- Some combination of these techniques.

Time is a useful concept for a nonce value, provided the time source can trusted

Using time stamps for nonce values is an attractive technique because it does not require a state variable to be stored for the nonce. However, there are other security-related considerations. If a time stamp is used as a nonce value then it is also important that the clock on the receiving system that will be used to verify the currency of the time stamp is set to the correct time. This also means that you need to ensure that it cannot be maliciously manipulated to accept a replay of an expired time stamp. This introduces the need for a trusted time service.

Nonce values detect replays – they do not prevent them

Remember also, nonce values do not prevent replays – they merely allow them to be detected – which implies some recovery action to follow.

Trusted Time

Trusted time service is an important common security service

A trusted time service is needed as part of the security infrastructure. This means that any computing device can synchronise its clock to a trusted time source, using a trusted communications protocol to obtain the time value.

Trusted time service provides reliable time stamps for any applications that need them

One of the important applications of this service is to provide confidence that time stamps used as nonce values to defeat replay attacks can be relied upon to be accurate and that clocks used to compare against those received nonce time values can also be relied upon to be accurate.

Time Stamps

Some applications require trusted time stamps

Applications also use trusted time for business control purposes, where reliability of the time source can be a significant business risk. This is especially true in the banking industry where banking deadlines and cut-offs can cause significant loss of overnight interest payments.

Trusted time can be delivered from the security infrastructure

Trusted time service can be made available to all applications as a common security service through the common security services API, as described earlier in this chapter.

Time Performance Issues

Security processing impacts performance

Security processing can have a substantial impact upon time performance. The type of processing that particularly has this effect is computation of cryptographic values, especially when public key cryptography is in use.

Cryptographic processing poses the greatest problem

The computation of a digital signature and the decrypting of a public key-encrypted message are the most demanding processes. Next most demanding are the verification of digital signatures and the encryption process using a public key, but these are orders of magnitude faster. Much faster still are the symmetric cryptographic techniques.

Hardware accelerator modules increase performance

The use of dedicated, special-purpose cryptographic hardware accelerator modules increases performance for cryptographic processing but may still not solve the problem from a business perspective.

Avoid heavy dependence on cryptographic processing that impacts time-critical processes

You need to avoid heavy cryptographic processing in situations where system performance would be adversely impacted. The most important architectural effect of this is the use of symmetric cryptographic techniques for data encryption in the middleware layer or for encrypting application messages. Public key cryptography is then restricted in use to the exchange of symmetric session keys, one for data authentication and one for data encryption. It is also important to examine the process design carefully to minimise heavy cryptographic work, as can be seen in the following case study.

Case Study: Cryptographic Processing in an IBFS Application[33]

The IBFS retail banking division has 10 million customers. The customer details are held on a customer file as a series of 10 million records. For security reasons each record is encrypted.

The bank has an application that processes standing orders for customers. This runs once every day. The steps of the processing are:

1.	FOR record #1 TO record #10,000,000	
2.	Retrieve customer record	100 µs
3.	Decrypt customer record	785 µs
4.	Are there any standing orders due today?	5 µs
5.	IF YES process standing orders ELSE GOTO step 6	50 µs
6.	NEXT record	5 µs

Next to each step is the time taken to execute the step in microseconds. On average 10% of the customer accounts are due for a standing order on any specific day. Total execution time per record is 945 microseconds if standing orders are processed, or 895 if not. The total run time for the application is $((0.9 \times 895) + (0.1 \times 945)) \times 10 = 9,000$ seconds or 2.5 hours.

By re-designing the application so that (a) the standing order date information is duplicated in the customer record in plaintext (unencrypted) and (b) reversing the sequence of process steps 3 and 4, the process becomes:

1.	FOR record #1 TO record #10,000,000	
2.	Retrieve customer record	100 µs
3.	Are there any standing orders due today?	5 µs
4.	IF YES decrypt customer record ELSE GOTO step 6	785 µs
5.	Process standing orders	50 µs
6.	NEXT record	5 µs

The total execution time per record is now 945 microseconds if standing orders are processed (unchanged) but only 110 microseconds where there are no standing orders. The total application run time is now $((0.9 \times 110) + (0.1 \times 945)) \times 10 = 1,935$ seconds or 32.25 minutes.

Redesigning the process has eliminated nine million record decryptions, saving 7,065 seconds out of a total of 9,000 seconds, which is a 78.5% saving.

---

[33]With thanks to Stan Dormer for the idea

Disaster Recovery Time Targets

Disaster recovery must be achieved within business critical deadlines

Disaster recovery refers to the recovery of business information systems following a major incident that causes an interruption in service. It is important that a careful analysis is made of the business needs for recovery of services and the time-criticality of various information services, so that appropriate designs can be developed that will maintain these time targets.

Speed of recovery must be traded off against cost

There is a considerable trade-off between the cost of providing recovery, and the time target to be achieved. If really needed, virtually non-stop 365 day by 24-hour service can be maintained, but its pushes the costs up to a very high level. The business needs and justifications must be worked out in detail in preparation for disaster recovery planning, remembering that the only goal is to create effective business continuity, whatever that turns out to be.

Assessing the Current State of your Security Architecture

SABSA® methodology process-flow cross-reference

In Chapter 7, Figure 7-5, you will see an additional deliverable called 'Assessment of current security status of the enterprise'. This is a tactical deliverable, designed to provide the backdrop for designing a programme of work that will deliver some quick wins (see Chapter 8 under the heading Long-Term Confidence of Senior Management).

Planning for a programme of quick wins

You will need to look at the Business Risk Model from the contextual security architecture and the control objectives that you have added to it as part of the work done in defining the conceptual security architecture. The question to ask at this stage is: What is the current state of the enterprise security architecture? You need to attempt to document this in a form that will enable you to conduct a gap analysis against the logical security services definition at the next stage of the architectural development process – the logical security architecture.

To Summarise: Conceptual Security Architecture

The conceptual security architecture provides the big picture, the helicopter view and the strategic plan for your enterprise security architecture.

The business and everything about the business that can be considered to be an asset in need of protection against a range of risks is conceptualised into a standardised, normalised form – the SABSA® Business Attributes Profile.

The assets identified in the Business Attributes Profile are used to drive a risk assessment method that presents a prioritised view of the enterprise risks. This risk assessment is used to develop a set of control objectives that conceptualises the needs of the enterprise for mitigating the risks.

Layering techniques are an important conceptual approach to developing enterprise security architectures. The strength and effectiveness of the enterprise security architecture is improved by adopting a strategy of multi-layered security services. The infrastructure architecture is also modelled as a series of layers, and security services are placed within these layers to provide the most appropriate combination of services.

Other major strategies for the enterprise security architecture are also described in some detail. These include a strategy for authentication, authorisation and audit, built around role-based access control; a strategy for secure service management; a strategy for systems assurance; a directory services strategy and a public key infrastructure strategy.

At the conceptual security architecture level, people or organisational units and any technical elements that represent them (such as applications) are regarded as security entities, and their interactions are conceptualised as entity relationships. The degree of trust that exists in such entity relationships drives the needs for securing the communications between the entities.

There are various levels of trust, largely depending upon the degree to which the parties know one another. In a business environment this knowledge is derived from a registration process, which for high levels of trust must be rigorous and searching.

Trust between two entities can be either one-way or two-way, and in some cases a third party entity intervenes, in which case the trust is transitive. Sometimes these third parties act as trust brokers. The concept of a trust broker is essential to some business models.

However complex the trust relationships become, they can always be analysed into a series of component parts, all of which are simple one-way trust relationships. This method of analysis renders all trust relationships capable of being understood in detail.

The security domain is an important concept that is used to build up domain models of real businesses, providing a means to understand how different security policies can co-exist, governed by different policy authorities, and how these different security policies interact.

This domain modelling approach helps you to understand how networks and applications are intertwined with one another and how their security policies differ so as to achieve the appropriate continuous level of security across the enterprise.

These domain models also allow the development of sensible conceptual approaches to providing security in business environments that make use of the Internet, including providing protection by the deployment of virtual private networks and firewalls.

The time dependency of security is conceptualised through a series of security-related lifetimes and deadlines, and many of these concepts are briefly described.

During the development of the conceptual security architecture there is an opportunity to document the existing state of the enterprise security architecture. This current status provides the baseline against which a series of 'quick win' projects can be planned and executed.

Part 3: Design

This part of the book is entitled 'Design'. It is about how you develop the logical security architecture, the physical security architecture and the component security architecture. This preamble looks at what exactly is meant by these words, starting with some dictionary definitions to help you understand the language being used.

de+sign vb. 1. to work out the structure or form of (something), as by making a sketch, outline, pattern, or plans. 2. to plan and make (something) artistically or skilfully. 3. (tr.) to form or conceive in the mind; invent. 4. (tr.) to intend, as for a specific purpose; plan. 5. (tr.) Obsolete. to mark out or designate. ~n. 6. a plan, sketch, or preliminary drawing. 7. the arrangement or pattern of elements or features of an artistic or decorative work: the design of the desk is Chippendale. 8. a finished artistic or decorative creation. 9. the art of designing. 10. a plan, scheme, or project. 11. an end aimed at or planned for; intention; purpose. 12. (often pl.; often foll. by on or against) a plot or hostile scheme, often to gain possession of (something) by illegitimate means. 13. a coherent or purposeful pattern, as opposed to chaos: God's design appears in nature. [C16: from Latin d_sign_ re to mark out, describe, from DE- + sign_re to mark, from signum a mark, SIGN] — **de+'sign+ a·ble** adj.

de+sign+er n. 1. a person who devises and executes designs, as works of art, clothes, machines, etc. 2. a person who devises plots or schemes; intriguer.

lo+gic n. 1. the branch of philosophy concerned with analysing the patterns of reasoning by which a conclusion is drawn from a set of premises, without reference to meaning or context. See also **formal logic**, **deduction** (sense 3), **induction** (sense 3). 2. the system and principles of reasoning used in a specific field of study. 3. a particular method of argument or reasoning. 4. force or effectiveness in argument or dispute. 5. reasoned thought or argument, as distinguished from irrationality. 6. the relationship and interdependence of a series of events, facts, etc. 7. chop logic. to use excessively subtle or involved logic or argument. 8. Electronics, computer technol. the principles underlying the units in a computer system that perform arithmetical and logical operations. [C14: from Old French logique from Medieval Latin logica, from Greek logikos concerning speech or reasoning]

log·i+cal adj. 1. relating to, used in, or characteristic of logic. 2. using, according to, or reduced from the principles of logic: a logical conclusion. 3. capable of or characterised by clear or valid reasoning. 4. reasonable or necessary because of facts, events, etc.: a logical candidate. 5. Computer technol. of, performed by, used in, or relating to the logic circuits in a computer. — **'log·i+'cal+i·ty** or **'log·i+cal+ness** n.

physical adj.   1. of or relating to the body, as distinguished from the mind or spirit. 2. of, relating to, or resembling material things or nature: the physical universe. 3. of or concerned with matter or energy. 4. of or relating to physics. 5. perceptible to the senses; apparent: a physical manifestation.

com+po+nent n.   1. a constituent part or aspect of something more complex: a component of a car. 2. Also called: **element** any electrical device, such as a resistor, that has distinct electrical characteristics and that may be connected to other electrical devices to form a circuit. ˜adj. 3. forming or functioning as a part or aspect; constituent. 4. of or relating to components: the component catalogue. [C17: from Latin comp_nere to put together, from p_nere to place, put]

Design

The design phase of the security architecture lifecycle is where you work out the structure and form of both the technical and managerial aspects of your secure business systems.

What you create through this design activity is a coherent and purposeful pattern by which all the elements of your secure business systems fit together.

The activity requires skill and inventiveness on the part of the designer – the one who devises and executes the designs.

Logical Security Architecture

The logical security architecture describes the relationships and interdependence between the various elements of your secure business systems.

It deals with the reasoned, logical flow from one step to the next in the secure processing of business information.

It also describes the security architecture at the level of logical entities that have identity, meaning, function and structure but no physical embodiment.

To present an analogy with the human being, these logical descriptions are the mind and spirit of the security architecture as opposed to its body.

Physical Security Architecture

The physical security architecture describes the hard material presentation of your secure business systems. As an example, at the logical level we talk of services, but at the physical level we identify the servers, being interested now in the size, capacity, performance, throughput, number and location of the physical devices that deliver the logical services.

Physical architecture is perceptible to the senses – you can see, feel and touch it.

Using again the analogy with the human being, physical architecture describes the body of the security architecture as opposed to its mind or spirit.

Component Security Architecture

At the level of the component security architecture you see the constituent parts of something more complex.

Each component is an element of the whole, and these elements are assembled together according to the designs embedded in the physical security architecture, which in turn supports the functional service model at the logical layer.

Chapter 11: Logical Security Architecture

The logical security architecture develops more detail to flesh out the bones of the conceptual framework that you have developed at the second layer of the security architecture model. The logical layer is largely concerned with the functional view of security, defining a comprehensive set of functional requirements. It does not at this stage pay attention to the security mechanisms that will be used to deliver those functions – these are part of the physical security architecture at the next layer down.

In this chapter you will learn about:

- An information architecture model that distinguishes between knowledge, information and data;

- The differing needs for securing static information and dynamic information;

- How a security policy is used as a logical encapsulation of business requirements;

- The need to have security policies at different levels of granularity related to one another in a hierarchical security policy architecture framework;

- The wide range of logical security services that are needed to implement security policies;

- How security services are grouped into the layers of the multi-tiered approach to security already described in Chapter 10;

- How security services are integrated into a series of logical security architectures, including:

    - Certificate management architecture;

    - Directory service architecture;

    - Access control architecture;

    - Entity authentication architecture;

    - Service management architecture;

    - Incident response architecture.

- Detailed descriptions of the most commonly deployed individual security services.

- How entities are arranged into a framework called a schema, along with the various attributes that describe the entities and how this logical schema is used to structure a directory service;

- The definition of security domains within the network, the middleware and the applications so as to manage successfully a set of security policies set by different security policy authorities that govern these various domains;

- How security domains can also be used to achieve segregation of groups of entities within the extended enterprise;

- The security management activities involved in the security processing cycle;

- The use of a short-term security improvements programme to maintain momentum whilst the longer term architectural work progresses.

Business Information Model

SABSA® Matrix cross-reference

Please refer to Chapter 3, Figure 3-3 and Chapter 7, Figure 7-8, the SABSA® Matrix, Logical layer, Assets column, where you will see a cell entitled Business Information Model. It is not the task of a security architecture team to develop the Business Information Architecture, and so in Chapter 7, Figure 7-9 you will see that this is assumed to be a pre-existing model.

Information Architecture

Information is the logical representation of the real business

Information is the logical representation of the real business. In Chapter 2 (see Figure 2-1) the idea of an information architecture was introduced. You will find there a brief introduction to this concept.

Knowledge, information and data – how they are related

In this chapter this idea is expanded further, to help you to understand more fully the logical assets that you are working to protect. One distinction that you need to clarify is that between data, information and knowledge.

These three ideas are associated with different layers of the architecture model. Table 11-1 explains each one and their inter-relationships.

Table 11-1: Abstraction Levels of the Real Business

SABSA® Layer	Abstraction Level	Explanation
Contextual	Business	The real business context
Conceptual	Business Knowledge	Information that has been given business value and related to business context through interpretive or reflective intellectual activity of a human
Logical	Business Information	Data that has been transformed and structured to have business meaning and relevance through intelligent analysis and synthesis
Physical	Business Data	Raw facts and quantities that form the inputs and outputs of business processes and that are processed and stored during process execution

The properties of information

At the logical architecture layer you have business information. Information has the following properties:

- Information is a logical representation of something real. For example a 'real customer' is represented in your information system by 'customer information'. This information includes everything you need to know about the customer to do business with him or her. It starts with name, address, telephone number and goes right through every detail of your business relationship with that customer.

- Information is structured data – organised into fields, records, files, tables, databases.

- Information structures are related to one another both in hierarchical and peer-to-peer relationships.

- Information is time-related – the currency of information or its historical context is important.

- Information is independent of location – the information exists independently of the physical location of the underlying data. However, access to information may be location-dependent.

- The quality of information depends not only on the content of the underlying data but also on the structure used to present the information and the analytical tools applied. All the relevant data may be there, but the information needed may not be apparent. Anyone who has tried to navigate and find out useful things on a poorly designed web site will immediately understand this point!

- The success of information is best measured in terms of the user experience of using it.

- When one talks of information assets, these are secondary assets – representing the real primary business assets that you want to protect.

Static and Dynamic Information

Static information has long-term stability

Static information is that which does not move or change in the short term. Examples of static information include:

- Master records and files (such as customer information);

- Executable object code;

- Configuration information for systems and applications;

- Historical information, including all stored audit trails, all historical transaction records, and all historical message records.

Dynamic information is unstable and changes

Dynamic information changes and moves in the short term and might only have a short lifetime between being created and destroyed. Examples of dynamic information include:

- Real-time free-format messages such as used in e-mail;

- Real-time structured application messages such as database queries using SQL;

- Real-time transaction information[1];

- System and service management real-time information exchanges.

---

[1] Note that stored transaction information and stored message information are included above under static information along with other historical records.

The protection of both static and dynamic information requires security services such as:

- Confidentiality protection;

- Integrity protection;

- Availability protection.

Additionally, the protection of dynamic information requires security services such as:

- Authenticity of source;

- Non-repudiation.

However, many more of the Business Attributes can be applied directly to the protection of information. You might find it an interesting exercise to refer back to the taxonomy of Business Attributes in Figure 6-3, Chapter 6 and run through the list. How many of the Attributes can be applied directly to information?

Business Transactions

Business transactions are a special case of dynamic information. Protecting them implies some specific security services:

- **Business user identification:** to identify uniquely every business user;

- **Business user authentication:** to verify the identity of every business user, as a prerequisite to granting access to business resources and services;

- **Business user authorisation:** to ensure that every business user has been authorised for access to the functions and information that he needs to carry out legitimate business activities and that access to other, unauthorised functions and information is specifically prevented;

- **Business entity authentication:** to ensure that all business entities taking part in business transactions are who they claim to be;

- **Business transaction integrity protection:** to ensure that business transactions are completed as expected and that they are protected from unauthorised modification, duplication, replay, delay or deletion;

- **Business transaction authentication:** to ensure that all business transactions are initiated by authenticated entities;

- **Business transaction non-repudiation:** to give assurance that all entities involved in a business transaction cannot later deny having participated in the transaction.

Security Policies

Please refer to Chapter 3, Figure 3-3 and Chapter 7, Figure 7-8, the SABSA® Matrix, Logical layer, Motivation column, where you will see a cell entitled Security Policies. Security policies and security policy architecture also appear as key deliverables of the logical security architecture in Chapter 7, Figure 7-9. Both of these deliverables are addressed in this section, although you will also need to read Chapter 14 (Security Policy Management) to complete your understanding of how to develop them. They are built on the concepts of security policy, security domain and security policy authority that were introduced as part of the conceptual security architecture in Chapter 10.

The Meaning of Security Policy: A Theoretical View[2]

Security policies are statements of what type of security and how much should be applied to protect the business in various ways. Security policy is positioned at the logical layer of the security architecture model and is derived directly from a number of drivers in the conceptual layer. The Business Attributes profile and the control objectives are strong drivers of security policy. So are aspects of the Security Entity Model and Trust Framework and the Security Domain Model.

A security policy defines what is meant by security within a security domain, the high-level rules for achieving this security and the activities that are to be authorised to achieve security objectives. The policy also defines how entities outside the domain are allowed to interact with entities inside the domain. For a definition and explanation of security domains please refer back to Chapter 10.

The domain owner sets the security policy for the domain. The owner may delegate implementation of the security policy to a lower security authority that acts on behalf of the domain owner. Such a delegated security authority is effectively the custodian of the domain. For a discussion on ownership and custody, please refer to Chapter 14, under the section Outsourcing Strategy and Policy Management'.

Thus, a security authority is an entity responsible for the implementation of a security policy on behalf of the owner (and may also be the owner). The security authority may delegate the enforcement of a security policy (or parts of it) to other entities within the security domain.

The security policy is determined by the business requirements for information management and information systems, following an assessment of the possible operational risks. Operational risk assessment is discussed in Chapter 9 and operational risk management is the subject of Chapter 15.

The security policy states what should be done but as far as possible avoids any reference to particular technical solutions. For this reason security requirements are expressed in terms of generic security services. Security services are discussed in detail in a later part of this chapter.

Security Policy Architecture

Security policy exists at a number of different levels, and hence it is useful to conceive of a hierarchically layered security policy architecture. Figure 11-1 provides and example for such a layered architecture.

You have probably seen similar layered diagrams of security policies before, but this is different because it does not have as its top layer the corporate information security policy – this appears on the second layer. The reason is that information security management is only one of several disciplines involved in corporate operational risk management, and information security management needs to be closely integrated with several other related operational risk management disciplines, especially physical security management and business continuity management.

This means that there are policy statements that are applicable to all these related disciplines. It is

---

[2]The theoretical ideas here are drawn mostly from ISO/IEC 10181: 'Security Frameworks for Open Systems', 1996.

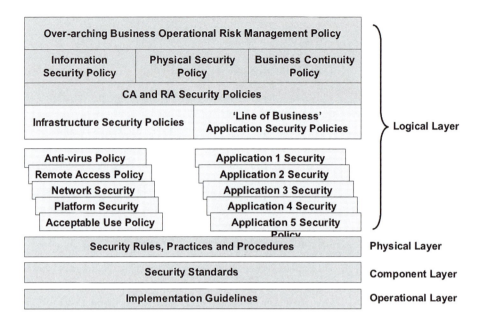

Figure 11-1: A Suggested Hierarchical Policy Architecture

better not to repeat these same statements under different policy headings but to assemble them together into an integrated, overarching top-level policy. Such a top-level policy is addressed to all employees throughout the enterprise.

Cross-reference to Chapter 14 and Chapter 15

There is a much more detailed discussion of this integration of operational risk management in Chapter 15, but for the present time you need to understand how this integration affects the structuring of the information security policy architecture. As a part of the logical security architecture you will need to determine what is the appropriate policy architecture for your enterprise and which policies you will need at each level. Within this policy architecture you will also need to populate it with the policies themselves, but the process for you to develop your detailed policies is described in Chapter 14 (see also Chapter 3, Table 3-2, operational architecture at the logical layer). Figure 11-1 also shows a number of lower layers of documentation that support the policies – these too are discussed in detail in Chapter 14.

Security Services

SABSA® Matrix cross-reference

Please refer to Chapter 3, Figure 3-3 and Chapter 7, Figure 7-8, the SABSA® Matrix, Logical layer, Process column, where you will see a cell entitled Security Services. Logical security services also appears as a key deliverable of the logical security architecture in Chapter 7, Figure 7-9. In this section the most common security services are introduced and described.

Security services are logical descriptions, not physical

The security services are logical services – specified independently of what physical mechanism might be used to deliver them. They are driven from the layer above, most specifically from the Business Attributes Profile, the control objectives and the security strategies.

Common Security Services and Their Descriptions

In Chapter 10 the concept of multi-tiered security was introduced and presented in Figure 10-2 as a layered model of security services including:

- Prevention services;

- Containment services;

- Detection and notification services;

- Event collection and event tracking services;

- Recovery and restoration services;

- Assurance services.

This is now explored in greater depth by presenting a detailed list of security services under each of these six defensive strategy headings – see Table 11-2. In subsequent sections each security service is described. You will need to decide which of these services you require in your enterprise security architecture to meet the requirements and policies that you have derived. However, no list of security services will ever be complete, and you should not take this one to be so. It is a useful guide and is reasonably comprehensive.

Table 11-2: Security Services by Defensive Strategy

Defensive Strategy	Security Services
Prevention	Entity Security Services:
	• Entity unique naming
	• Entity registration
	• Entity public key certification
	• Entity credentials certification
	• Directory service
	• Entity authorisation
	• Entity authentication
	• User authentication
	• Device authentication
	Communications Security Services:
	• Session authentication
	• Message origin authentication
	• Message integrity protection
	• Message content confidentiality
	• Security measurement and metrics
	• Security administration (privilege management)
	• User support
	• Physical security services
	• Environmental security services

Defensive Strategy	Security Services
	• Non-repudiation
	• Message replay protection
	• Traffic flow confidentiality
	Application and System Security Services:
	• Entity authorisation
	• Logical access control
	• Audit trails
	• Stored data integrity protection
	• Stored data confidentiality
	• Software integrity protection
	• Software licensing management
	• System configuration protection
	• Data replication and backup
	• Software replication and backup
	• Trusted time
	• User interface for security
	Security Management Services:
	• Security policy management
	• Security training and awareness
	• Security operations management
	• Security provisioning
	• Security monitoring
	• Security measurement and metrics
	• Security administration (priviledge management)
	• User Support
	• Physical Security Devices
	• Environmental security services
Containment	Entity authorisation
	Stored data confidentiality
	Software integrity protection
	Physical security
	Environmental security
	Security training and awareness

Defensive Strategy	Security Services
Detection and Notification	Message integrity protection
	Stored data integrity protection
	Security monitoring
	Intrusion detection
	Security alarm management
	Security training and awareness
	Security measurement and metrics
Event Collection and Event Tracking	Audit trails
	Security operations management
	Security monitoring
	Security measurement and metrics
Recovery and Restoration	Incident response
	Data replication and backup
	Software replication and backup
	Disaster recovery
	Crisis management
Assurance	Audit trails
	Security audit
	Security monitoring
	Security measurement and metrics

Security Service Integration

Security services need to work together

A critical aspect of the logical security architecture is fitting these various security services together into a single integrated whole. Figures 11-2 and 11-3 show two high-level views of this integration. Figure 11-2 shows some of the major security services and how they logically interact with one another.

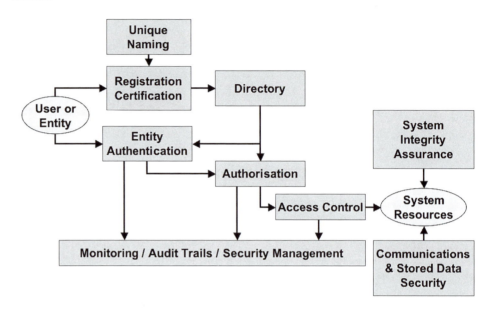

Figure 11-2: Integration of the Major Security Services

Integrating key security services

Figure 11-3 shows a high-level logical architecture of the directory service and how it integrates with a number of other key elements that provide security services. This diagram is a logical architecture representation that expands some of the concepts shown in Chapter 10, Figure 10-3 which depicted a conceptual architecture of security infrastructure, including these common security services.

Entity Security Services

This group of security services act on or for security entities. Security entities are defined in Chapter 10.

Unique Naming

Uniqueness is critical

For each entity there must be a unique name to prevent confusion over which entity is being referenced. The structure and syntax of this name will depend upon the type of entity (application entity, middleware entity, human user, etc.). There must be a set of syntax rules and a service that creates and registers these names for new entities.

Registration

Registration prevents unauthorised participants

Each entity is registered as being part of the community of entities in the overall universal domain governed by your security architecture. Registration is an important security control in its own right, because if an entity can become registered, it can fairly easily obtain privileges. The importance of the strength of the registration process has been discussed in Chapter 10.

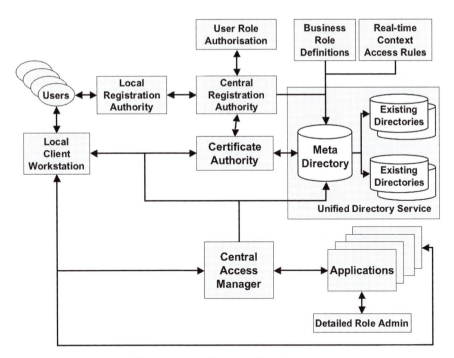

Figure 11-3: Logical Architecture of the Directory and Associated Services

Public Key Certification

Public key certification prevents unauthorised public keys being used

An entity that has been registered needs to participate in interactions with other entities. If public key cryptography is in use and public key infrastructure is included in the overall security architecture, then each registered entity requires a set of private keys and a set of matching certified public keys. There must therefore be a service (run by a certification authority) by which the entity can generate the public and private key pairs and submit the public keys for certification. Public key certification prevents an unauthorised, unregistered entity from becoming a fraudulent participant in the business community being secured.

Credentials Certification

Credentials certification prevents unauthorised credentials being used

In a distributed systems environment where a role-based access control strategy is adopted, the entity roles and other possible credentials information are sent across the network from the central access manager (CAM) to the target application server. The target server needs to trust the credentials contained in that package of information. It trusts the CAM, but it must also be assured that what it receives is the same as sent out by the CAM. This can be achieved by wrapping all the necessary credentials in a form of certificate that has been digitally signed (and thereby certified) by the CAM security authority. These certificates are sometimes known as authorisation certificates or privilege attribute certificates (PACs).

Directory Service[3]

Directory service is a complex critical piece of infrastructure

The directory service is built on four basic models:

- The directory information model;
- The directory-naming model;
- The directory functional model;
- The directory security model.

Directory Service Information Model

The directory holds an entry on every object

The information model defines the types of data and basic units of information that you can store in your directory. This model defines the building blocks for your directory. The basic unit of information is a directory entry, which is a collection of information about an object.

Objects of a similar type belong to an object class

Objects are of different types, and each of these types is known as an object class. Some object classes refer to real-world physical objects such as people and devices. Others can refer to abstract objects such as roles. The following are possible examples of object classes:

> objectClass: person
>
> objectClass: role
>
> objectClass: device
>
> objectClass: site
>
> objectClass: building
>
> objectClass: top

Object classes can be sub-classes of other super-classes

Some object classes are sub-classes of a higher-level object class (called a super-class). Thus the object class 'building' is a sub-class of the object class 'site'. There is a single top-level object super-class to which all other object classes belong as sub-classes. This root object class is called 'top'.

An entry is a set of attributes describing the object

A directory entry comprises a set of attributes[4]. Each attribute describes one of the traits of the object being described. Consider an object from the object class 'person'. Its directory entry (description) contains its 'distinguished name', the object classes to which it belongs, and the set of attributes.

In the following example, the abbreviations used have the following meanings:

> dn – distinguishedName
>
> ou – organisationalUnit
>
> uid – userIdentifier
>
> cn – commonName
>
> sn – surName

---

[3]A major source for the information in this section is *Understanding and Deploying LDAP Directory Services*, Timothy A. Howes, Mark C. Smith and Gordon S. Good, Macmillan Network Architecture and Development Series, 1999, ISBN 1-57870-070-1, Chapter 3: 'An Introduction to LDAP'.

[4]Some caution is required here understanding the use of the term attribute. Its usage here in the context of directories is quite different from its usage in the SABSA® Business Attributes Profile.

Each attribute has a type and one or more values, for example:

> dn: uid=wsmith, ou=asset_management, ou=people, ou=ibfs
>
> objectClass: top
>
> objectClass: person
>
> cn: William Smith
>
> cn: Bill Smith
>
> sn: Smith
>
> eMail: wsmith@am.ibfs.com
>
> telephoneNumber: +1 123 456 7890

Syntax rules support search and matching operations

Each attribute type also has a syntax that controls what types of data can be used for the values of that attribute. The syntax rules also contain information on how the directory matches values when searching:

- For the syntax rule caseIgnoreString applied to the attribute sn, the values 'smith' and 'Smith' are the same and would be matched.

- For the syntax rule caseExactString applied to the attribute sn, the values 'smith' and 'Smith' are different and would not be matched.

Directory Service Naming Model

A distinguished name reflects the structure in the directory tree

The distinguished name is the result of a naming model that arranges the objects in a hierarchical logical structure, as shown in Figure 11-4.

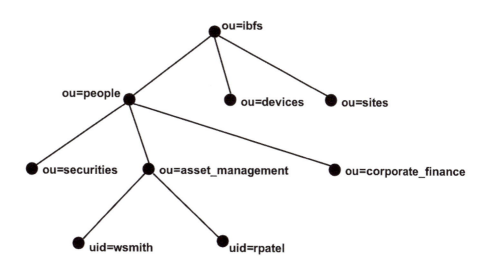

Figure 11-4: A Hierarchical Naming Model for a Directory

Directory Service Functional Model

Directory functions provide access and management

The functional model of the directory describes the operations that you can perform on the directory to interrogate it, to populate it and to manage it. These functions are implemented through a set of protocols. The X.500 standard defines four different protocols, each with its own function[5]. One of these, Directory Access Protocol (DAP) provides directory access. It has been found to be complex in implementation and in operation.

Access is provide through an access protocol

DAP has now been overtaken in popularity by Lightweight Directory Access Protocol (LDAP), which provides all directory access and management functions in a single protocol. LDAP is a client-server protocol. The server agent is in the directory server, and every user of the service has the LDAP client software (user agent) installed on the remote computer – often a PC.

LDAP functional groups

The functions provided by LDAP are arranged in groups:

- Interrogation operations;

- Update operations;

- Authentication and control operations;

- Extended operations (LDAP version 3 only – allowing new operations to be added).

A search engine is used to match entries

To make these functions work there is a sophisticated search engine in the server that can apply a variety of matching algorithms and filters.

Directory Service Security Model

Directory services are critical infrastructure needed by all other applications and services

The directory service is one of the most important security services. It provides a trusted repository for all entity information and is used by all other security services that need that information. Thus as well being a security service in its own right, it requires several integrated security services to maintain its own security and integrity.

Authentication and access control are needed to protect the directory

The directory must be subject to sophisticated access control, so that users are able to get access only to subsets of entity credentials for which they are authorised. The directory access methods should require user authentication and cryptographic protection of the data exchanges.

LDAP supports standard authentication methods

LDAP version 2 supports only simple authentication using passwords. However, LDAP version 3 uses the SASL[6] framework to offer support for multiple authentication methods, including strong authentication methods using cryptographic authentication exchanges.

Access control is an issue for the implementer

Apart from requiring authentication to gain access, there is no standardised access control model defined in LDAP. This means that each implementer has to define and implement his or her own access model within the structure of the directory itself, defining rules and ACLs[7] that control what a specific user can do once inside the directory.

Other security services are needed to protect the integrity and availability of the directory services

The integrity and availability of the directory service must also be protected, almost at all costs, since without directory services almost no other service can remain operable. Suitable directory security management services must be applied:

- Physical access control to the directory servers and their location;

---

[5]X.519: The Directory – Protocol Specifications

[6]See RFC 2222: 'Simple Authentication and Security Layer (SASL)', RFC 2444: 'The One-Time-Password SASL Mechanism', and RFC 2245: 'Anonymous SASL Mechanism'.

[7]ACL: access control list

- Environmental protection to prevent fire, flood, structural instability and other environmental problems from interfering with directory service availability;

- Sophisticated service management and monitoring of the directory and its service availability;

- Logical access control with a severely limited set of privileged users and limited transitivity and inheritance to avoid the problem of uncontrolled inheritance, in which everything gains access to everything else;

- Strong user authentication for privileged directory administrators and operators;

- A highly resilient directory service infrastructure:

  - No single points of failure;

  - Replication of records from the master directory server to a series of slave directory servers, providing both resilience in case of a single component failure, and performance handling through load sharing and local request handling;

  - Resilience against denial of service attacks.

Inter-operability suggests international standards The directory must also be inter-operable with other directory infrastructures, which implies conformance to industry standards such as LDAP or X.500, probably the first of these.

Authorisation Services

Authorisation is multi-faceted Authorisation services prevent unauthorised entities gaining unauthorised access. There are three distinct parts to an authorisation service. They can be followed on Figure 11-3.

- The first part is an off-line service, in which a registered entity is granted privileges by a registration authority (either centrally or locally) and those privileges are stored against the entity name as attributes of the entity in the directory. If role-based access control is being used, the privileges are in the form of authorised roles, the roles having been created in advance.

- The second part of the service is the local off-line administration of authorisations at target servers, associating specific local privileges with roles.

- The third part is the real-time on-line authorisation of a request made by an entity. The CAM first authorises the request on the basis of the role in the entity credentials (is the entity allowed to use this application service?), and these credentials are then forwarded to the target application server. The target server uses the trusted role in the credentials to grant specific privileges to the entity based upon the role associations set up earlier in off-line mode.

Entity Authentication

Authentication of a claimant to a verifier Entity authentication means that one entity that claims a certain identity (the claimant) proves to the satisfaction of another entity (the verifier) that he or she really is the entity claimed.

External reference of authentication Entity authentication is a huge subject in its own right, and a book of this wide scope cannot go into it in great detail. For those with an interest in pursuing the subject further there is a good reference in ISO/IEC 10181[8].

---

[8]ISO/IEC 10181-2: 'Security Frameworks in Open Systems: Part 2: Authentication'.

Defining terms

Figures 11-5 to 11-9 summarise the logical flows of the common authentication scenarios that are discussed in detail in ISO/IEC 10181. To understand the diagrams there are some important definitions:

- Authentication information (AI) – information used for authentication purposes (such as passwords, cryptographic keys, random numbers);

- Exchange AI – information exchanged between a claimant and a verifier during the process of authentication (such as a one-time password);

- Claim AI – information used by a claimant to generate exchange AI needed to authenticate to a verifier (such as a password or cryptographic key);

- Verification AI – information used by a verifier to verify an identity claimed through exchange AI (such as a previously registered password or cryptographic key);

- Authority verification AI – verification AI used specifically and exclusively by the authority;

- Authority claim AI – claim AI used specifically and exclusively by the authority.

Possible parties to a scenario

Figure 11-5 defines all the possible parties and the possible AI instances that can exist in the various scenarios.

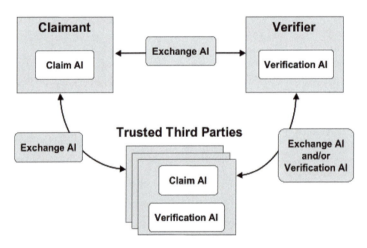

Figure 11-5: Logical Relationships and Types of Authentication Information

No trusted third party

Figure 11-6 is the scenario where no trusted third party is involved and the claimant and verifier interact directly, as in direct password verification.

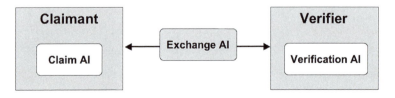

Figure 11-6: Direct Authentication Without a Trusted Third Party

Third party intermediary

Figure 11-7 is the scenario where a trusted third party acts as an intermediary, intercepting the authentication exchange and the verifier trusts the intermediary to have verified the claimant. This is also called in-line authentication. The initial authentication exchange when using an authentication-server architecture is of this type (see Chapter 10, Figure 10-8). The subjects (claimants) interact initially only with the authentication server and, depending upon the decision taken by that server, may later interact directly with the target application servers.

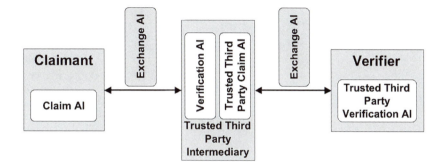

Figure 11-7: Indirect In-Line Authentication

Key distribution for on-line authentication

Figure 11-8 shows on-line authentication, where the trusted third party sets up an initial authentication exchange with each party, which then allows the claimant and verifier to exchange authentication information directly with one another. Cryptographic key distribution servers work this way.

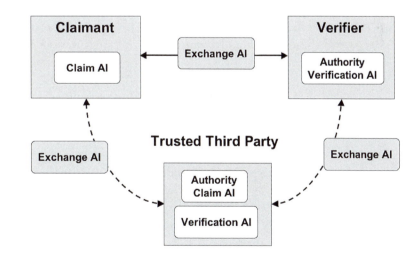

Figure 11-8: On-Line Authentication

Public key certificates for off-line authentication

Figure 11-9 shows off-line authentication, where the verifier obtains authentication information in advance from the trusted third party that allows verification of the claimant in real time later on. Public key certificate authorities operate in this mode.

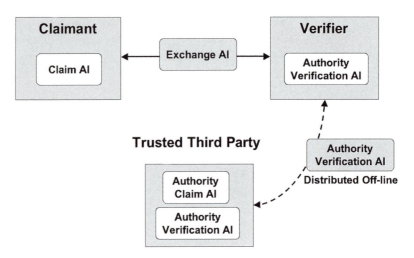

Figure 11-9: Off-Line Authentication

User Authentication

Users are special entities

User authentication is a special case of the generalised entity authentication discussed above. In this case the claimant is a human user. You must consider the human-to-machine interaction as a special part of the overall exchange.

Users should be decoupled from the extended authentication exchanges

In Chapter 10 (see Figure 10-9) there is a discussion about the decoupling of a user from the network authentication exchanges, reducing the user interaction to a local exchange between the human user and the local terminal or PC. This is a case of indirect in-line authentication (see Figure 11-7 above). The user is the claimant and the PC or terminal is the trusted intermediary. The user has a password (or other piece of claimant authentication information such as a PIN or a biometric) that is entered into the PC. This may be verified locally, or may be used to construct the authentication information to be sent on in the second stage (such as happens in the Kerberos protocol).

User AI may be supplied in many ways

There are several ways that the human user may be locally authenticated to the intermediary PC:

- The AI is a password only;

- The AI is a password together with some information read directly from a physical token device such as a smart card or magnetic stripe card;

- The AI is generated using a smart token device (which is actually just another trusted intermediary, activated by a password or PIN);

- The AI is generated by scanning some biometric property of the human user.

Device Authentication

Device authentication is simply a case of entity authentication

Device authentication is a special case of the generalised entity authentication discussed above. In this case the claimant is a device that has embedded into it a suitable piece of claim AI. The AI can be an IP address or fixed password for low levels of trust or a physically protected cryptographic key for higher levels of trusted interaction.

Communications Security Services

There are threats to remote communications between entities

Communications security services protect the communications between remote entities from a number of threats. The main threats are those perpetrated by an eavesdropper who listens in and possibly alters the message flow or a saboteur who mounts a denial of service attack.

Session Authentication

Session authentication protects a communications session from being hijacked

When two parties establish a communications session between them there is a threat from an unauthorised eavesdropping third party that the session will be hijacked, either during the session setup or at some time during the session itself. Such a style of attack is often called a man-in-the-middle attack. The opponent may completely take over from one of the participants and masquerade as that participant, or may instead stay as a middleman altering the exchanges of information that pass between the original parties.

A mutual authentication exchange is required

To minimise the vulnerability to this type of threat the session can be authenticated. The session setup is handled through a mutual authentication exchange that may or may not involve a trusted third party (see Figures 11-5 to 11-9 above). Both parties can adopt the roles of both claimant and verifier, mutually verifying each other's identity.

The best session authentication uses cryptographic methods and keys exchanged during the authentication handshake

To secure the session over its entire lifetime the exchanged authentication information should include some secret cryptographic keys not disclosed to the eavesdropper. Various secure key exchange mechanisms can be used for this (see Chapter 12, Security Mechanisms section). These keys are then used to authenticate every data exchange between the two parties throughout the session. This does not prevent the opponent from making changes to the exchanged data, but it does mean that any such changes will be immediately detected. Action can then be taken to deal with the attack.

SSL[9] is a good example of session authentication with strong mechanisms, although in this case the authentication is usually limited to authenticating the only the server and rarely the client.

Not all vendor claims to provide authentication in their products are necessarily sound

You need to be careful when assessing vendor products and certain protocols. Just because a product specification claims to provide session authentication as a service does not mean the vendor or the protocol designer has specified a strong mechanism to deliver that service. A good example is the so-called authenticator in SNMP[10] version 1. This is the 'community name' of the community of devices to which the managed device belongs. Beyond all this jargon the authentication is actually achieved by a fixed, plaintext password that is shared between all devices in the community. Not a strong mechanism![11]

Message Origin Authentication

Proving that a message came from the claimed origin

When a message is delivered to a recipient it usually contains information about its origin –who sent it. However, there is a threat that an unauthorised party can send a message pretending to be someone else. To minimise this vulnerability the message can be authenticated using a cryptographic mechanism (see Chapter 12, Security Mechanisms section). Each message is individually

---

[9] SSL: Secure Sockets Layer
[10] SNMP: Simple Network Management Protocol
[11] SNMP version 3 incorporates strong cryptographic authentication mechanisms.

authenticated to allow the recipient to verify the claimed identifier in the message. This is a special case of entity authentication as discussed above and shown in Figures 11-5 to 11-9.

Message Integrity Protection

Proving that a message remains unchanged

Even if a message originates from an authentic source, there is a threat that an eavesdropping third-party opponent can alter it in some way during its transport through the network. To minimise the vulnerability to this attack the contents of the message can be authenticated by use of a cryptographic mechanism such as a message authentication code (MAC) or a message integrity checksum (MIC, see Chapter 12, Security Mechanisms section). Each message is individually authenticated for its contents. Any unauthorised changes will be detected, and appropriate action can be taken.

Origin and contents authentication can be combined

If the contents include the identifier of the originator, then the same mechanism can be used to provide both services – origin authentication and contents authentication.

Message sequencing can also be protected

If the message contents include a sequence number that is held as a state variable[12] at both sender and receiver, then an attack that attempts either to change the sequence of messages or to delete one of the messages in the sequence altogether can also be detected.

Message Replay Protection

Protecting against the replay of previous messages

There is a threat that an opponent may capture a transmitted message and replay the same message at a later time, perhaps several times over. By doing so the opponent could masquerade as an authorised user and conduct a faked login, or he could alter the contents of payment messages to gain some financial advantage.

A one-time value protects against replays

As a further extension of message integrity protection, if a nonce value is incorporated into the message contents it is possible to detect this attack and take appropriate action. A nonce value is a value that occurs only once and can never be repeated. Such one-time values are constructed from time stamps, random numbers, sequence numbers, or more often, combinations of these types of number. If time stamps are used, the time service must be a trusted service – see below.

Message Content Confidentiality

Preventing the disclosure of message contents

To protect the contents of a message from unauthorised disclosure to eavesdroppers the payload of the message can be encrypted using a suitable mechanism (see Chapter 12, Security Mechanisms section).

Non-Repudiation

Protecting against repudiation of a sent message

When a message is sent by a sending party to a recipient it is sometimes important for business reasons to prevent the sender from later attempting to deny that the message was sent or the recipient from later denying that the message was received. A non-repudiation service provides this assurance, either by use of an asymmetric cryptographic mechanism or by use of a trusted third-party logging mechanism (see Chapter 12, Security Mechanisms section). In the case of providing proof of receipt, a non-repudiable acknowledgement message needs to be created and sent.

---

[12]See Chapter 5 – Finite state machine models.

Traffic Flow Confidentiality

Sometimes seeing activity is enough to draw conclusions about events

In some circumstances it may be sufficient for an opponent to know simply that there is a peak volume of message traffic, even if all the messages are encrypted. By looking at the surrounding environment, the timing and the sources and destinations of the messages, the opponent may be able to draw some intelligent conclusions about what the messages are saying. For example, in a military environment it could become apparent that an attack is about to be launched.

Hiding peaks and troughs in traffic volumes

To minimise the vulnerability to this type of traffic analysis, a traffic flow confidentiality service hides the volumetric flow of messages. The mechanism used (see Chapter 12, Security Mechanisms section) is usually some type of dummy messaging to show a continuous smooth volume of traffic.

Application and System Security Services

Application security focuses on authorised access control

This group of security services protects applications and systems from attack or abuse. Mostly they are in some way concerned with preventing or revealing unauthorised access or unauthorised actions by those who have been granted authorised access.

Authorisation

Previously discussed under entity security services

Authorisation has already been discussed under the heading of Entity Security Services above. You should read that section and this one in conjunction with one another, since they discuss different aspects of authorisation services.

Roles provide a means to simplify access management

Setting up the roles for an application service or a community of resources is a policy matter for the security authority responsible for policy in that domain. The process requires a careful analysis of business needs to identify the roles that should be used. The aim should be to create only a few roles to minimise role access administration at target servers. In some applications it may be acceptable to have only one role (you belong to the application community or you do not).

Roles can be used to segregate duties

The business analysis of role requirements may include the creation of roles that are mutually exclusive so as to segregate duties. Thus a user entity may not possess both of these roles. It will be the responsibility of the application domain security authority to ensure that this policy is upheld in the granting of roles to requesting entities.

First level central access control is also based on role

When a real-time access request for an application service is received, the CAM makes intelligent first-level access control decisions based upon:

- The role of the requesting user entity;
- The static role associations registered under the resource object to which access is being requested.

Real-time role association depends upon a number of factors

The real-time dynamic association of a role to an entity during an access request is dependent on several things:

- The static role(s) stored in the directory as an attribute of that entity;
- Inheritance of role attributes under the directory schema;
- Pre-condition rules stored with a roles object in the directory:

- Preventing illegal role combination assignment;

- Preventing illegal security association assignment;

- Controlling transitivity within allowed limits;

- Configuring delegation controls;

- Checking and enforcing specific user conditions and constraints;

- Post-condition rules stored with a roles object in the directory:

  - Controlling of real-time interactions between roles;

  - Controlling of real-time interactions between roles and other directory objects;

  - Defining logical security domains by role group membership;

  - Setting real-time limits on transitivity and delegation.

- Context-*based* access control rules such as:

  - Time of day;

  - Day or week;

  - Location of client workstation;

  - Remote access method (for example, leased line vs. dial-up).

Access Control

Theoretical models have been discussed previously

Theoretical models for access control have been described at a conceptual level in Chapter 10. You may find it useful to refer back to that section now.

Three types of access control service

Access control services may govern both physical and logical domains, and access control mechanisms may also be physical or logical in their nature. There are three types of access control service:

- Controlling access to physical domains such as sites and buildings using physical mechanisms such as gates, doors, locks, guards;

- Controlling access to logical domains such as systems, applications, files, records and databases using logical access control mechanisms such as permissions and software decision-making functions;

- Controlling access to physical domains such as hardware platforms and networks using logical access control mechanisms (permissions and software decision-making functions).

Audit Trails

Providing evidence for later examination

Audit trails provide historical evidence of activity for monitoring purposes or forensic examination purposes. Protecting the integrity of the audit trail itself becomes an issue in some circumstances, since tampering with an audit trail may cover up unauthorised activity. Thus a robust audit trail service needs not only mechanisms for capture and storage of the event information but also mechanisms to protect the integrity of that stored information.

Case Study: Premature Release of Prisoners

'The Los Angeles County Board of Supervisors ordered the Sheriff's Department and the district attorney's office Tuesday to investigate two recent incidents in which suspected killers were mistakenly released from county jails.' [Timothy Williams. The Los Angeles Times. Los Angeles, Calif.: 30 August, 1995, p.3]

In the investigation that followed it appeared that there had probably been interference with the computer systems and that the data records for these two prisoners had been altered, resulting in the automatic generation of the release papers.

However, it was impossible to be certain, since the computer system used for managing this information had a very poor access control regime in place, and large numbers of court officials and other administrators had read-and-write access to these records.

There was also no audit trail of the transactions made, and hence no accountability for any information changes. It was obvious that someone had tampered with the records and that by simply changing the information they had arranged for the unauthorised early release of the prisoners, but there was no evidence that could prove this had happened, and no evidence that could begin to identify the perpetrator.

Stored Data Integrity Protection

Protecting against changes in stored data

Just as message data in transit can be subject to unauthorised alteration, deletion or resequencing by an eavesdropper, stored data can suffer the same fate between the time it is stored and the time it is retrieved for use. The security mechanisms for detecting such modification are the same as for transmitted data – using a MAC or a MIC (see above under Message Integrity Protection and Chapter 12, Security Mechanisms section).

Access control is one of the methods

The use of physical and logical access control mechanisms also helps to prevent the unauthorised access that would lead to such unauthorised modification of the stored data.

Stored Data Confidentiality

Preventing disclosure of stored data

This service prevents unauthorised disclosure of stored data. Several mechanisms are available (see Chapter 12, Security Mechanisms section) including encryption, physical enclosure of the data store and logical access control.

Software Integrity Protection

Greatest threat is from viruses and the like

Software integrity is a huge problem. The most significant threat comes from malicious software in the form of viruses, worms, macro viruses, and Trojan horses.

Hackers can also insert malicious code

Rogue software may also be inserted into a system manually by a hacker who has already penetrated to a level of high privilege and installs malicious code objects for future use.

Multiple mechanisms are needed

The mechanisms used to implement the services to defend against malicious attack include anti-virus scanning tools, change-detection mechanisms such as checksums and quarantine environments for testing newly imported software before it is released.

You cannot completely eliminate the problem

It should be noted that it is impossible to prevent software being attacked in real business systems. Your only real defence is to try to catch as many infectious agents as possible before they do too much damage and to be ready to clean up when inevitably some of those agents penetrate your defences. There is no such thing as the silver bullet that kills all malicious code. As Dorothy Denning says[13]: 'The problem of protecting against malicious code would always be a "learn as we go" business.'

Malicious characteristics are 'undecidable'

Fred Cohen has proved[14] that it is impossible to examine a piece of code and decide whether it is malicious unless it is a piece of malicious code you have seen before. He says, 'precise determination of a virus by its appearance is undecidable.' It is one of those many undecidable questions in computing, such as the 'halting problem'[15].

New software must be acquired from trusted sources

Software integrity-protection services also include the acquisition and distribution of third-party software packages to ensure that software is obtained from reputable sources and that it is clean of malicious infections when it is acquired. For organisations that develop their own software, either for internal use or for distribution to others, the process of releasing and publishing the software also needs to be controlled.

Mechanisms are discussed later

The delivery of a software integrity protection service utilises a number of security mechanisms (see Chapter 12, Security Mechanisms section).

Software Licensing Protection

Software licence control needs similar approaches to integrity protection

The same mechanisms that support the publishing and distribution of software to protect its integrity can also be used to ensure that you comply with software licensing and copyright protection by controlling the release and use of licensed software.

System Configuration Protection

Protecting the integrity of configuration data

The configuration of a system includes both the executable software, including scripts, and the configuration data that many of the executable files need to perform their function. All of these files and the directory structure in which they are stored need to be protected from unauthorised changes. This service is usually delivered by applying a number of security mechanisms including:

- Anti-virus scanning;

- Use of checksums to check the integrity of files and directories;

- Use of scanning tools comparing the actual configuration with a stored configuration policy file.

---

[13]'The Limits of Formal Security Models', National Computer Systems Security Award Acceptance Speech, Dorothy E. Denning, October 18, 1999

[14]Fred Cohen, 'Computer Viruses – Theory and Experiments', 7th Security Conference, DOD/NBS, September 1984.

[15]A.M.Turing. 'On Computable Numbers, with Application to the Entscheidungs Problem' Proc. London Math Soc, 42(2):230-265 (1936) cited in F.Cohen, 'Computational Aspects of Computer Viruses', *Computers & Security*, Volume 8 (1989), Number 4, pp.325–344.

Data Replication and Backup

Data backup for system recovery

To enable recovery of a system following a disaster incident the data must be backed up. This replication, backup and restoration service must cover:

- Regular backup copying process;

- Backup media management: labelling, indexing, off-site secure storage, retrieval, etc.;

- Data restoration process;

- Backup and recovery sub-system testing.

Software Replication and Backup

Software backup for system recovery

Whilst data must be backed up on a regular basis to have available the latest version, software should be backed up on the basis of a master copy of the latest release. Software should not be backed up from the system, since this may incorporate alterations into the backups. This service provides a library of backup masters from which software can be reinstalled in the event of recovery operations.

Trusted Time

Time is used as a universally agreed value

In distributed systems time is often used as a means of agreeing certain aspects of a protocol. One specific application of time is to include a time stamp into a protocol data unit to prevent message delay, message replay or message re-sequencing by an unauthorised eavesdropper. These time stamps are protected from alteration by using a cryptographic protection mechanism.

The source of time values must be protected from tampering

However, even if the opponent cannot tamper with the message itself, if he can tamper with your clock he may still be able to persuade you to accept a message that is out of time because you no longer know what the time really is. So, the provision of a trusted time service is a critical piece of security infrastructure.

User Interface for Security

Ease of use is critical for successful security

The user interface should be easy to use and present no significant obstacles to legitimate business activities – otherwise it brings the security services into disrepute. The principal elements of a well-designed security user interface are:

- Easy-to-use strong authentication;

- Single sign-on to all applications;

- GUI-based login screens and operational messages;

- Easy navigation through hierarchical menus and hypertext.

Security Management Services

Security management is both procedural and technical

Security management services fall into two groups: procedural security management services and technical security management services. The possible list of such services is almost endless, but some key examples are included here.

A logical architecture for technical security management

In the case of the technical security management services there is a basic logical architecture that describes how they work. Figure 11-10 shows this.

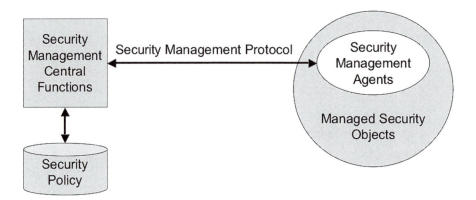

Figure 11-10: Logical Architecture of Security Management Services

Security management means applying policy throughout the environment

The use of the term 'security policy' in this schematic is a loose one. It means all of the policies and standards that drive the configuration and management of the managed security objects. A security management agent is a software sub-system embedded in the managed end-system that handles the security management protocol and implements the instructions from the security management centre. The security management protocol has primitives such as GET, SET and TRAP as found in most protocols for systems management and network management.

Security Policy Management

Policies also need to be managed

This service (or rather group of services) falls under both types – procedural and technical. The creation and agreement of polices and standards is clearly a procedural process – it is the subject of the discussion in Chapter 14. The application of those policies to the management of objects, as shown in Figure 11-10, is a technical set of services.

Security Training and Awareness

Discussed in more detail in the operational layer

This again is a group of services rather than a single service, and is entirely procedural in its nature. This entire programme is discussed again in more detail in Chapter 14.

Security Operations Management

Uses the same logical architecture

This is a set of services involving both procedural services and technical services. The logical architecture model shown in Figure 11-10 shows how the technical services are delivered. The procedural management aspects are discussed in Chapter 17.

Security Provisioning

Uses the same logical architecture

These services deal with configuring the managed security objects shown in Figure 11-10. There are also procedural aspects to these services, which are discussed in Chapter 17.

Security Administration (Privilege Management)

Uses the same logical architecture

The administration of access privileges is a special case of security provisioning. Once again the underlying logical architecture is as shown in Figure 11-10. The procedural aspects are discussed in Chapter 17.

Security Monitoring

Reporting status from the distributed agents

Security monitoring is another sub-set of the security management services built on the logical architecture in Figure 11-10. The security management agents report back status information to the security management centre. The procedural aspects of this are discussed in Chapter 17.

Security Measurement and Metrics

Measuring performance against targets

At the security management centre the data collected by the security monitoring service must be collated and analysed to report management information, including measurement of performance in the form of agreed metrics. (Note: there is a key difference here between raw data that is collected and information that is created by collation and analysis – an example of what was discussed at the beginning of this chapter – see Table 11-1).

Things that can be measured

Some of the performance elements of the environment that might be measured include:

- Security services response times;

- Preservation of security policy across domains;

- Confirmation that the authorisation and authentication process is functioning properly;

- Confirmation that non-repudiation and notarisation services are operating correctly;

- Relationship between the actual observed system behaviour and standard security baselines for diagnostic and planning purpose.

Approaches to developing suitable security metrics

Developing appropriate security metrics is important to the evolution enterprise security architecture. The end result of this activity will be to know with confidence whether the security management systems are working and how well. Several approaches to this endeavour are available:

- The first is to create a reference system by which components of the production system are compared. This is accomplished by paralleling portions of the production system with the reference system and comparing functionality in terms of throughput and integrity.

- Another testing method would include sampling line activity and subjecting the sample to FFA (Fast Fourier Analysis)[16] to ensure encryption is functioning properly and to test for unexpected or unauthorised traffic.

- Inspection tools, automated when possible, can be acquired or developed to test actual resource configurations against standards or expected configurations.

---

[16]Fast Fourier Analysis is an advanced mathematical technique. Refer to mathematical texts for an explanation.

- The interactions of numerous quasi-intelligent entities on a modern distributed computing network tend to cause the environment to move towards the nature of a complex adaptive system and increasingly become subject to chaos. It may be necessary to assess at what point this is likely to occur and take steps to bound or limit the eventuality. Failure to anticipate this situation may lead to significant unwelcome results. Research is probably needed to clarify this possibility. Modelling and simulation tools are needed to address these issues. This is one of many areas where enterprises cannot afford to ignore on-going research programmes and must endeavour to acquire external support services to keep them informed of new developments.

Security Alarm Management

Handling unexpected events reported by agents

Security alarms are reported from managed objects in the form of an unsolicited TRAP primitive in the security management protocol (see Figure 11-10). These alarms are handled and managed by services at the security management centre. They feed into the incident response services.

Intrusion Detection

Detecting an attempted intrusion

If a break-in or attempted break-in takes place, it must be detected as soon as possible and reported so that incident-response services can take appropriate action. The service is implemented through the deployment of detection agents as in Figure 11-10, and the correlation, collation and analysis of this information at the security management centre.

Things that might signal an intrusion

Indicators of intrusion incidents can include:

- Multiple instances of the same user;
- Failed logon attempts;
- Attempted access to unauthorised resources;
- Unusual network loading conditions;
- Components failing integrity tests;
- Unknown source addresses;
- Detection of certain attack signatures by specialised intrusion-monitoring software. The agents are deployed to monitor both host platforms and network components.

The overall logical architecture for an intrusion detection system is shown in Figure 11-11.

Incident Response

Responding to security incidents

Incident response services deliver actions in response to detected security incidents. In many cases an incident or group of incidents will require a decision process – what should be done next? The decision about what action to take can in some cases be automated and in other cases will require human intervention.

Steps in an incident response process

The logical steps required for an appropriate incident response include:

- Data collection;
- Data normalisation and collation;

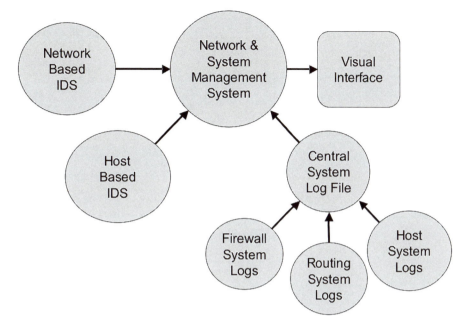

Figure 11-11: Logical Architecture for Intrusion Detection

- Data analysis;

- Incident assessment and conclusions;

- Presentation;

- Response alternatives;

- Response decision;

- Response action management.

Automated response or manual response? The first action as the result of a reported condition once analysed is to determine whether an automated response is adequate or not. This decision can be made based on error type or number of errors and can be controlled by scripts or logic engines. For example, an instance of a particular error type may be determined to be addressable by an automated response, whereas multiple instances may require human action. This could be an instance of a single resource failure as opposed to multiple resource failures.

Progressive problems? The second decision involves any correlated error conditions. In most cases of system failure, it becomes progressive and may require rapid action to contain damage.

Minimal sustainable configurations for fall-back A good approach is to develop worst-case scenarios and analyse your network and application resources so that a minimum sustainable configuration is known and can be quickly implemented. This would include physical domain segmentation, human intervention, firewalls at critical domain boundaries, alternate communications links and other required resources.

The overall logical architecture for incident response and management is shown in Figure 11-12.

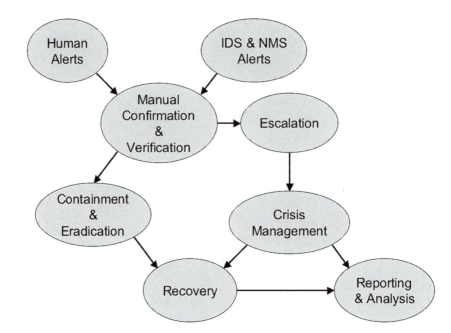

Figure 11-12: Logical Architecture for Incident Response

User Support

Handling user-related security problems

Many operational problems experienced by users of systems and applications are security-related. The potential impacts of unresolved problems are lost production time and bringing the security services into disrepute amongst the user community. There must be adequate user support services through the help desk function to manage these problems and ensure their timely resolution.

Disaster Recovery

Recovering after a major incident

Disaster recovery relies essentially either on organisational measures, or on technical measures that have a broader scope than security. It is often regarded as part of business continuity management (see the section on BCM in Chapter 17).

Many mechanisms are involved

The mechanisms that support disaster recovery services include:

- Taking appropriate backups of data and software;
- Providing backup management: labelling, indexing, storage;
- Off-site storage;
- Data recovery and restoration procedures;
- Redundancy of hardware and communication lines for resilient operations;
- Recovery plans and procedures;
- Contingency sites;
- Incident management responsibilities;
- Activation plans.

Crisis Management

Handling the organisational aspects

Crisis management is an organisational and process-based service that is needed to handle serious incidents. It is an extension and escalation of the incident management services described above. It is discussed again in detail in the section in Chapter 17, Business Continuity Management section.

System Audit

Reporting on the status of security

Security audit services provide for the independent collection and analysis of system records. These are usually organised by a specialised security audit team. The techniques and mechanisms used include both manual record collection and analysis and the use of automated system auditing tools that compare actual system configurations against expected configurations. The entire subject of security auditing is discussed in greater detail in Chapter 16, Assurance Management.

Physical Security

Security of the physical sites and buildings

Physical security services include the following:

- Site design and construction, including buildings and site perimeters;
- Guarding perimeters of controlled areas;
- Authorisation of personnel for physical access to controlled areas;
- Authentication of personnel at physical access points;
- Visitor handling;
- Contractor handling;
- Maintenance activity handling.

Personnel Security

Ensuring the honesty and integrity of personnel

Personnel security services include the following:

- Hiring policies on employment history, criminal records, qualifications;
- Background checks, vetting and reference checking;
- Training and awareness for all personnel;
- Disciplinary processes.

Environmental Security

Securing against environmental threats

Environmental security services include the following:

- Site selection;
- Fire prevention;
- Fire detection;
- Fire quenching;
- Flood prevention;
- Climate control;

- Electrical power protection;

- Other critical services protection.

Entity Schema and Privilege Profiles

SABSA® Matrix cross-reference

Please refer to Chapter 3, Figure 3-3 and Chapter 7, Figure 7-8, the SABSA® Matrix, Logical layer, People column, where you will see a cell entitled Entity Schema and Privilege Profiles. This also appears as a key deliverable of the logical security architecture in Chapter 7, Figure 7-9. In this section the notion of a schema is explained, and its application in structuring the security attributes of all enterprise entities is described.

Entity Schemas[17]

A schema is a rule-set for what information can be stored

A schema is a set of rules that determines what data can be stored in a database or directory. (For a discussion on the directory, objects and attributes, please refer to section on directory services earlier in this chapter.)

A schema has many benefits

The purpose of the directory schema is to:

- Help maintain the integrity and quality of the data stored in the directory;

- Reduce duplication of data (polyinstantiation);

- Impose constraints on the size, range and format of data objects stored in the directory;

- Provide a well-documented and predictable method for directory-enabled applications and services to access and modify the collection of directory objects;

- Help to slow down the effects of directory entropy, in which over a period of time with constant use by many entities, the contents of the directory tend to move towards chaos.

Changes to data are checked against schema rules

Before a directory server stores a new or modified entry, it checks the entry's contents against the schema rules. Whenever directory clients or servers compare two attribute values, they consult the schema to determine what comparison algorithm to use.

Schema components

The components of a schema are:

- Attributes (attribute types and attribute values);

- Attribute syntax rules;

- Object classes.

Attributes type definition

An attribute type definition includes:

- A unique name identifying the attribute type;

- An object identifier (OID[18]) that also uniquely identifies the attribute;

---

[17]A major source for the information in this section is *Understanding and Deploying LDAP Directory Services*, Timothy A. Howes, Mark C. Smith and Gordon S. Good, Macmillan Network Architecture and Development Series, 1999, ISBN 1-57870-070-1, Chapter 7, 'Schema Design'.

[18]OID is a concept within ASN.1 (abstract syntax notation 1), which is discussed in a little more detail in Chapter 12 under the heading Security Related Data Structures.

- An indication of whether the attribute is single-valued or multi-valued;

- An associated attribute syntax and set of syntax rules;

- A usage indicator (which applications use this attribute);

- Restrictions on the range and size of the values that may be stored in the attribute.

Objects belong to one or more object classes

An object class is used to group objects that have something in common, usually real-world objects of the same type, such as people, printers or network devices. A single directory entry describes an object that can belong to one or more object classes. Thus a network printer belongs to the objects class 'printers' and to the object class 'network devices'.

Object class definition

An object class definition includes:

- A name that uniquely identifies that class;

- An object identifier (OID) that also uniquely identifies that class;

- A set of mandatory attributes that *must* be included in the entry describing the object;

- A set of optional attributes that *may* be included in the entry describing the object[19];

- An object kind (structural, auxiliary or abstract)[20].

Role Association[21]

Roles are associated with objects through special attributes

The association of a role with an entity is achieved by defining for the entity object an attribute that carries the assigned role. Such an attribute might be called 'roleAssignment'. Since an entity may have more than one role, this attribute can be multi-valued, with more than one occurrence in the object entry:

dn: uid=wsmith, ou=asset_management, ou=people, ou=ibfs

objectClass: top

objectClass: person

cn: William Smith

roleAssignment: internetUser

roleAssignment: accountingClerk

You need to design the schema to fit your needs for role management

In designing the schema you need to define suitable attributes for role management. Depending upon your requirements and your design decisions, the attribute may be mandatory or optional in the object class definition. (Do you foresee an object in this class that has no role whatsoever?)

The roles themselves are identified through business analysis

You will need to define the logical roles that are to be mapped to groups of users through attributes. This can only be achieved by a thorough business analysis of the job functions and how privileges need to be allocated to run the business. You should aim to minimise the number of roles whilst still maintaining sufficient granularity to achieve segregation of job types and their access privilege profiles.

---

[19]Attributes that are not included in either the mandatory or optional list *may not* be used.

[20]To explain this aspect would go far beyond the scope of this book.

[21]Abbreviations (dn, ou, uid, cn) used in this section are explained earlier in the chapter in the section headed Directory Service.

Some common role types	Some of the main role types may include:

- User roles;
- Business manager roles;
- System manager roles;
- Operations management roles;
- Administrator roles;
- Auditor roles.

Examples of specific roles	Within each of these role groups you will need finer levels of granularity depending upon your analysis of the business models. For example in a financial accounting department, roles might be:

- Financial director;
- Financial controller;
- Accounting supervisor;
- Accounting clerk;
- Financial auditor.

Authorisation, Privilege Profiles and Credentials

Authorisations stored as data structures	Many aspects of authorisation are discussed in other parts of this chapter. The discussion in this section focuses on the storage of authorisations in the form of privilege profiles, privilege attribute certificates or credentials. All these terms mean roughly the same thing.
Storing roles in the directory	If you are using role-based access control, then all that needs to be stored in the directory entry for the entity being granted authorisation is the associated role (or roles). This is achieved through defining attributes for the entity object – see above in the section Role Association.
Storing other types of credentials in the directory	For other types of access control management, where roles are not used, a similar approach can still be taken. Whatever forms the package of information that you call the entity's credentials, this information can be put into an attribute or set of attributes in the directory entry for the object.
Roles and credentials are also stored as objects that describe what they can do	Roles or credentials or whatever you call them are also probably objects in their own right. So you might define an object class called 'role', which has a set of attributes that define a role. When an entity object has a roleAssignment value, you can cross reference in the directory to match the value of the name of a role object to the value of roleAssignment so as to find out what that role means.

Certificates and Tickets

Certificates and tickets are cryptographically protected sets of credentials	Often a set of credentials is protected cryptographically, either to protect its integrity or its confidentiality or both. Such a structure is often called a certificate (if an asymmetric cryptographic technique is applied) or a ticket (if a symmetric cryptographic technique is applied).
Certificates are sometime stored as attributes of an object with which they are associated	Certificates can sometimes be enduring data structures that could be stored in the directory as objects or as attributes of objects. For example, a digital certificate is usually stored as an attribute of the directory object representing the entity to which that certificate has been issued.

Tickets tend to be transitory in their lifecycle

Some certificates and all tickets are transitory objects that have limited lifetimes (up to a few hours generally speaking) – that is, they are temporary credentials. The most useful thing to do for these would be to define an object class in the directory and to store an enduring template of the transitory structure to be used.

Security Domain Definitions and Associations

SABSA® Matrix cross-reference

Please refer to Chapter 3, Figure 3-3 and Chapter 7, Figure 7-8, the SABSA® Matrix, Logical layer, Location column, where you will see a cell entitled Security Domain Definitions and Associations. Security Domains and Associations also appears as a key deliverable of the logical security architecture in Chapter 7, Figure 7-9. This section describes the most important types of security domain that you will need to define.

Network Domains

Logical domain specification is a powerful tool

The logical specification of a network into domains is a very useful step in developing your enterprise security architecture. The important thing to remember in doing this is the definition of a domain – a set of security elements that are all subject to the same security policy. This definition is what mainly drives your thinking in segregating one domain from another.

Be clear about the difference between 'logical' and 'physical'

It is also important to remember what is meant by 'logical'. When you look at the diagram in Figure 11-13, you will find no servers – only services. You will find no computers, no firewalls, no routers, no VPNs, no equipment boxes of any sort, since these are all physical elements and form part of the physical architecture. To help you to distinguish the difference, this same example is replicated in Chapter 12 showing a version of the physical architecture that can be used to build this logical architecture. That diagram is very different and contains physical boxes. Note also that the lines that join the boxes in Figure 11-13 are not cables – they are logical channel connections that may have any type of physicality, both in media type and topology.

An example

Consider a large corporate organisation and refer to Figure 11-13 to see how the logical network architecture is developed in response to the business needs.

The example organisation has many business units and changes structure over time

The enterprise has a number of different business units. Each line of business is potentially subject to different security policy restrictions regarding the sharing and disclosure of information. Additionally, over time the shape and size of the business changes, because new businesses are acquired or existing businesses are sold. Some business units are not wholly owned but are joint ventures with other companies. For all these reasons it is a good idea to conceive each business unit as a separate logical domain, so that domains can be added or removed painlessly according to changes in business structure, and so that potential differences in security policy between one business unit and another are easily implemented.

There are numerous business partners who are granted limited access through a partner services domain

The organisation has a number of business partners – suppliers, major customers and service providers – that are given access to certain corporate information and services. To facilitate this, a logical domain is created called 'partner services' in which are grouped all of the service elements to manage these external partner interactions. This partner services domain is a buffer zone to prevent any direct external access to corporate applications and to ensure that only the desired application functionality and information is externalised.

An extranet is used for external connections

Each of these partners has its own logical domain with its own security policies, but to connect them into the partner services domain an extranet domain is introduced. This is a networking

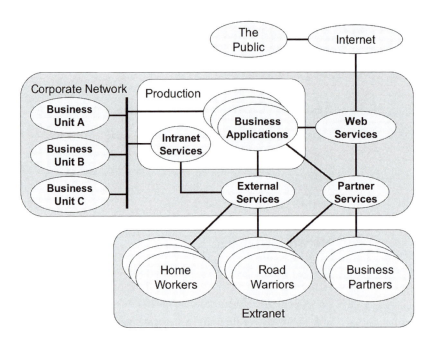

Figure 11-13: Logical Network Architecture Diagram

domain that allows parties outside the corporate network domain to connect into services that are inside the corporate network domain – in this case partner services. External partners can be added or removed as required.

No assumptions are made about the physical implementation of the extranet

Note again the difference between logical and physical architectures. An extranet is a logical definition. At this stage no assumptions are made about how that extranet will be physically implemented, and there are several alternatives available, including the use of VPN technology, the Internet, direct dial-up or all of these.

There are home workers and road warriors

The organisation also has a number of people who regularly work from home, and a number of people who are on the road needing to communicate from lap-tops with mobile telephone connections, from hotel rooms, from business centres or from airport business lounges (the road warriors). Both these groups of people need to have access to certain business applications, but security policy does not allow direct external access.

The external services domain provides a buffer zone

To facilitate this external access, another logical domain is created as a buffer zone called 'external services' through which the application functionality and information that needs to be externalised can be delivered securely and safely to those externally located employees. Access to the external services is made through the extranet as for external business partners.

The intranet domain must be externalised through external services

Additionally, both these groups of people are company employees and need to have access to a variety of information services and office automation support services that are bundled into a service package called intranet services. This package of services is available both internally and externally to all employees. For the externally located employees access is via the external services domain with connection made through the extranet.

Road warriors also need the partner services domain

The road warriors are responsible for the relationships with external business partners, and so their external access through the extranet also gives access to the partner services domain so that they can monitor activity with the external business partners whose relationships they manage.

The production domain is an inner sanctum to protect the business applications

No one except the data centre operations staff has direct hands on access to production business applications and the intranet services. These applications and services are contained in an inner sanctum domain called 'production'. Business users gain access through an inter-domain multi-layered architecture that is conceptually like that described in Chapter 10 (see Figure 10-24).

Public web access through the Internet

Finally, the public at large are also given access to the web services through the Internet.

The logical domain map is a critical design step

If you examine Figure 11-13 carefully you will see that the arrangement of the logical networking domains delivers both the required access and the required segregation of policies. Once you have this logical domain definition it is easy to move forward to a physical design (see Chapter 12). If you miss out this logical step, believing that you can move straight to the physical design and thus cut a corner to save time, beware! It is actually very difficult to design the physical architecture without this intermediate step, and you will almost certainly design a physical network that does not fully meet the requirements. If you doubt this, try it!

Middleware Domains

Middleware provides services integration

The middleware is the services integration layer of the infrastructure. It provides transparency of location for application servers, application clients and common services used by applications.

Middleware has within it a number of common service domains

In Chapter 10 there is a discussion of the types of common security service and the delivery of such services through a conceptual layer called middleware. At the logical architecture layer this leads you towards a definition of a number of service domains in the overall middleware domain. Figure 11-14 shows a typical configuration.

This domain model is a different view of the same infrastructure seen in the network domain model

When comparing this diagram with that in Figure 11-13, it might be useful to make an analogy between these views and the different architectural views of a building. Figure 11-13 is the equivalent of a plan view of the building, looking down from above. Figure 11-14 is the equivalent of the side elevation view of the building, looking horizontally from the side.

Your logical domain model should be specific to your business

The domains shown in Figure 11-14 are generic. Your logical domain architecture should be specific,

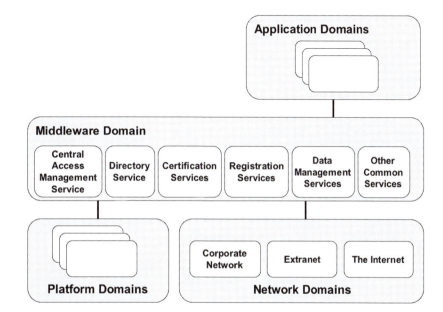

Figure 11-14: Logical Domain Model of the Middleware Layer

showing exactly which services you plan to have and in the case of different logical entities offering services (such as different registration authorities), how many of each there are.

Each service domain can be exploded up to a more detailed logical architecture view

You can then take each one of these service domains and explode it into the next level of detail by representing all the logical elements within that domain. An example of this is shown in Figure 11-15 with the development of a logical architecture for the directory services.

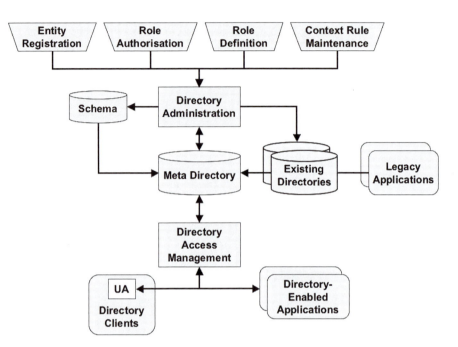

Figure 11-15: Logical Architecture of the Directory Service

Application Domains

Application sub-domains are roles

Each application is a logical domain, subject to a security policy for that application. This application domain has sub-domains, which are best mapped onto the roles, each role being a logical sub-domain[22].

Users are in a people domain, information in an information domain

The real users are actually part of another domain, which you can call the 'people domain', and the information resources used by the application are part of an 'information domain'. There are mappings from these external domains into the application domain to associate people and information resources with the roles.

The extended application domain includes people and information

The 'extended application domain' includes these external logical components. Thus an extended application domain comprises:

- Roles –the roles and functions and information associated with each role and the user-to-role mappings;

- Functions associated with each role;

- Users;

- High-privilege users – administrators, managers, auditors, operators, maintenance staff;

[22]Note that application domains and sub-domains tend to be always logical, rarely physical.

- User groups;

- Information resources accessed by each role.

Figure 11-16 shows this in diagrammatic form.

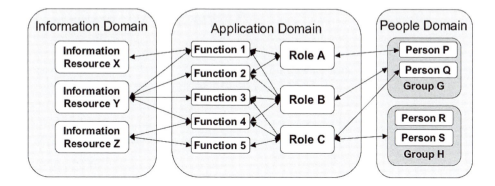

Figure 11-16: The Extended Application Domain

Security Service Management Domains

The security service management domain

The security service management domain comprises:

- The managed security objects and their management agents;

- The security management information database;

- The security service management functions (within security service management applications);

- The security management personnel.

A special case of an extended application domain

This is a special case of the extended application domain logical architecture shown in the previous section. Figure 11-17 shows this special case.

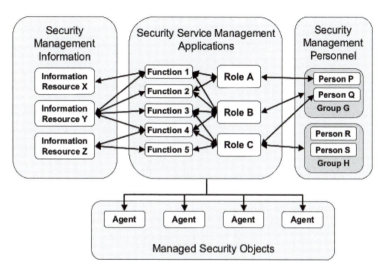

Figure 11-17: Security Service Management Logical Domain Architecture

Policy Interactions Between Domains

Domain interactions depend upon domain policies

The interactions between entities in different domains are governed by the way in which their domain policies govern the interactions.

An example of sub-domains and their policies

Take for example the situation shown in Figure 11-18. Domain 1 and Domain 2 are independent domains, but they are both sub-domains of Domain 3. Alice and Bob (A and B) are registered members of Domain 1, having been registered by the security authority SA1. They are subject to a security policy set by SA1. Similarly Xavier and Yvonne (X and Y) are members of Domain 2, having been registered by SA2 and subject to the security policy set by SA2. The authorities SA1 and SA2 are both registered by SA3, the security authority that governs Domain 3. SA3 sets the security policy for Domain 3, which in turn applies throughout both Domains 1 and 2. The sub-domains have their own additional policies that supplement that handed down from the super-domain. The policies of the two sub-domains cannot (by definition) conflict with the policy of the super-domain.

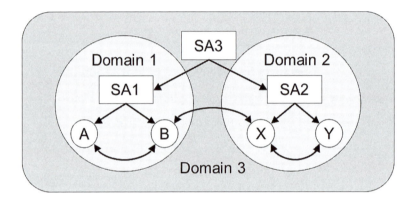

Figure 11-18: Interactions between Logical Domains

Policy interactions in the example

When Alice and Bob interact, they do so governed by the security policy of SA1. Similarly Xavier and Yvonne interact governed by the security policy of SA2. However, when Bob and Xavier interact they are governed essentially by the security policy of Domain 3, constrained by any additional policy requirements placed on them by both SA1 and SA2. They cannot behave as they might if only operating with their home domain.

Security Processing Cycle

SABSA® Matrix cross-reference

Please refer to Chapter 3, Figure 3-3 and Chapter 7, Figure 7-8, the SABSA® Matrix, Logical layer, Time column, where you will see a cell entitled Security Processing Cycle. This also appears as a key deliverable of the logical security architecture in Chapter 7, Figure 7-9. This section expands on the meaning of this idea.

The security processing cycle activities

The security processing cycle involves a number of security management activities such as:

- Introducing and registering new organisational entities;
- Introducing and registering new users;
- Setting up authorised privileges;

- Registration renewal;

- Certificate issue and renewal;

- Provisioning and configuring equipment throughout the environment.

Automated security processes

There are also a number of automated processes, such as for setting up and closing down sessions, and for handling messages that have a defined time to live so that they are discarded if they prove to be undeliverable.

Defining the logical flow of each process

To define the logical flow of each of these processes you will need to adopt a systematic method. Here are some of the key considerations:

- What is your complete list of security processes?

- What event initiates each of these processes?

- What event closes the process?

- What intermediate stages are there in the process where it moves from one state to another?

- What events trigger the transition of the process from one intermediate state to another?

A more formal approach could use finite state machine modelling

This is a relatively informal approach, but what is being described here is a loose version of finite state machine modelling. If you want to adopt a more rigorous approach, refer back to Chapter 5 where finite state machine modelling is described in more detail. It can be applied here to each of your security processes to define their precise operational cycle.

Security Improvements Programme

SABSA® Methodology process flow cross-reference

Please refer Chapter 7, Figure 7-9, where the Security Improvements Programme is a key deliverable of the logical security architecture.

Achieving quick wins

The Security Improvements Programme comprises a series of short-term projects aimed at achieving quick wins. The projects are planned as a result of a gap analysis performed after the logical security architecture has been designed, comparing that design to the current status assessment generated during the development of the conceptual security architecture.

Keeping senior management satisfied

The purpose of this programme is to maintain the momentum of the security programme whilst the longer-term architectural work is in progress. In particular its purpose is to ensure that senior management see a frequent flow of deliverables resulting from the investment in the security architecture development programme.

To Summarise: Logical Security Architecture

Business information is the logical representation of the real business. Hence the information assets needing protection are secondary assets that logically represent the true primary assets – the business itself.

The overall logical representation of the business is through the information architecture, which must pre-exist the development of the logical security architecture. This information architecture should distinguish between knowledge (conceptual layer), information (logical layer) and data (physical layer).

Information itself is either static or dynamic, and depending upon which of these classes it falls under, it has different needs for security services to protect it.

The logical representation of the business requirements for information security is expressed through security policy. Security policies are high-level statements of what sort of security and how much security is needed, but they do not state how that security is to be delivered.

Security policy exists at a number of levels of granularity and applies to a number of different domains. These different security policies are inter-related through a logical security policy architecture framework.

Security policy is implemented through a series of security services. These security services are logical services – specified independently of what physical mechanism might be used to deliver them. They are driven from the conceptual security architecture layer above, most specifically from the Business Attributes Profile, the control objectives and the security strategies.

Security services are grouped together under headings that describe their function in the multi-tiered approach to security described in Chapter 10. Hence there are security services for prevention, containment, detection and notification, event collection and event tracking, recovery and restoration, and assurance.

Logical security architectures are created by the integration of these security services into a meaningful whole. Authentication services, directory services, certificate management services, access control services, intrusion management services, and many more, all interlock to form the overall logical security architecture.

The directory service is pivotal to the success of your logical security architecture. It provides the repository for all logical representations of entities and their security-related attributes. The directory schema describe the logical relationships between these various entities and their related attributes. Privilege management is achieved by suitable structuring of the schema and rules for inheritance and transitivity.

The definition of security domains to map the real business domains (both logical – such as a business unit, and physical – such as a building) is a key tool for setting out the overall structure of your logical security architecture. Each domain has an associated security policy. From this logical domain model it is relatively simple to progress to the physical architecture layout at the next layer down, but without the logical domain model it can be difficult to construct a physical architecture that really represents the true business requirements.

The security processing cycle describes the set of security management activities needed to manage the time-related aspects of the logical security architecture.

Finally, whilst the main security architecture work progresses, a security improvements programme can be launched to achieve some quick wins based on a gap analysis between the designed logical security architecture and the known current status of the enterprise security programme.

Chapter 12: Physical Security Architecture

The physical security architecture is the builder's view of life – the bricks and mortar of your enterprise security architecture. The previous chapter looked at logical functionality and flow. Now you need to look at physical boxes, how many of them, where they are located, their size and performance and how much bandwidth you need to connect them together. You also need to look at the physical data structures that are used to realise logical information structures and at the physical security mechanisms that implement the logical security services.

In this chapter you will learn about:

- How business information at the logical layer is mapped onto data structures such as files and databases at the physical layer;

- How the physical security mechanisms embedded within file management and database management systems can be applied to deliver the security services called upon from the logical layer;

- The use of rules, practices and procedures to provide the detailed implementation of security policies;

- The mapping of physical security mechanisms to deliver logical security services;

- How cryptographic mechanisms are used to deliver security services;

- Why vulnerabilities in security mechanisms are often difficult to foresee and how these hidden weaknesses can be exploited;

- The types of physical security mechanisms that can be used to deliver user security and application security services;

- The physical security mechanisms available for providing security on host platforms and within the network infrastructure;

- Recent advances in hardware security mechanisms;

- How to use security mechanisms to implement security-related time-constraints and sequence constraints.

Business Data Model

SABSA® Matrix cross-reference

Please refer to Chapter 3, Figure 3-3 and Chapter 7, Figure 7-8, the SABSA® Matrix, Physical layer, Assets column, where you will see a cell entitled Business Data Model. It is not the task of a security architecture team to develop the Business Data Model itself, and so in Chapter 7, Figure 7-10 you will see that this is assumed to be a pre-existing model to be updated with relevant security data. However, there are many mechanisms embedded within the data storage and management systems that can be applied for security purposes, and these are discussed in this section. The application of these mechanisms forms part of the overall deliverable in Figure 7-10 marked as Security Mechanisms.

Physical layer focuses on data

The logical architecture layer is concerned with information, and at the beginning of Chapter 11 the differences between knowledge, information and data were discussed. Now, in the physical layer, the focus is on data.

This means files and databases

This means that you are concerned with the physical organisation and management of data so that it supports information and knowledge at the higher architecture layers. This physical data management involves:

- File structures, including record structures and field structures;
- File management tools, including directory management;
- Databases structures;
- Database management systems (DBMSs).

File and Directory Access Control

File systems offer discretionary access control

File management systems are a featured sub-system of almost every operating system. Typical examples are the file management capabilities within the UNIX operating system family or within the MS Windows NT/2000 operating system family. These types of operating systems offer discretionary access control, meaning that each file has an owner and that at the discretion of the owner the file can be shared with other users or groups of users.

Files have permissions set by their owners

Each file and each directory (which is just a file of files) has permissions set to control what actions can be taken by the owner and by others who have been granted access at the discretion of the owner.

Files are locked during access to prevent concurrency conflicts

Another aspect of file security is protecting the integrity of the file by use of a file locking mechanism. This means that if one user is accessing a file, another cannot do so until the first user has closed the file. If this were not so, then different users would be making changes to the file concurrently, and it would soon become corrupted as the different changes conflicted with one another.

More details under platform security

For a wider discussion of operating system security and how these file security mechanisms fit into the bigger picture, see the Platform Security section later in this chapter.

File Encryption

File encryption as a means to protect confidentiality

Encryption of data is discussed later on in this chapter under the heading of Security Mechanisms. One of the ways that encryption can be applied is to encrypt entire files, selected records within a file or selected fields within a record. Choice of encryption algorithm depends upon the lifetime over which the stored data needs to be protected from disclosure.

Tamper-resistant devices can protect keys from disclosure

The main challenge with using file encryption is how to manage the encryption keys. If the solution is to put the keys in another file, then no advantage has been gained. Encryption keys (or rather decryption keys) must be placed in a physically secure location, which implies some sort of tamper-resistant hardware device. (There is a discussion on tamper resistance in the Hardware Security section later in this chapter.)

Hierarchical key management can be used

Alternatively the data keys can be controlled by a master key that is derived from a passphrase[1] and not stored anywhere on the system. A master key is a key-encrypting key used to encrypt a population of working keys or data keys so that they can be stored securely in an ordinary file. When a data key is required for use, it is retrieved from the file and decrypted using the master key. There is then only a single key – the master key – that has to be given a physically secure method of storage.

You need to be careful regarding the real entropy level of a password used to derive a master key

If the master key is derived from a user passphrase that is not stored, there is an issue regarding the potential strength of the passphrase and the key that is derived from it. Key strength and password or passphrase strength are measured the same way – in terms of their entropy. Entropy is a measure of the randomness contained within the data. Redundancy of data reduces the entropy. Entropy is measured as the number of truly random bits in a unit of data, as opposed to redundant bits. Text that is readable by humans (such as natural-language passwords and passphrases) has high levels of redundancy in it, and hence the entropy density is low. For example, normal English-language text can be bit-encoded using ASCII to produce a string of characters, each of which has eight bits. However, this encoded English text has a real average entropy level of approximately 1.3 bits per character, because it is highly redundant in its structure (which makes it easy to read). This means that on average, 6.7 bits per character are redundant (8 minus 1.3).

The entropy of the passphrase must be at least equal to the required entropy of the derived master key

A common and naive mistake is to assume that a 16-character ASCII-encoded string can provide 128 bits of cryptographic key. If you want to have an English-language passphrase that contains 128 bits of entropy so that you can derive a 128-bit master key from it (and really achieve 128-bit strength), then you need a phrase that is 128/1.3 = 99 characters in length. That presents the user with a double problem – first he has to remember a 99-character string (although this can be simplified by making it into a normal English-language phrase or sentence – hence the term 'passphrase'), and second, the user has to type in this string with perfect accuracy. Nevertheless this approach provides a workable solution with high levels of key security.

The passphrase needs a physical secure backup for data recovery purposes

There is also a secondary (but no less important) issue associated with using a passphrase that is not stored on the system. If the user forgets the passphrase, there is no other way to get the master key that is needed to decrypt the data keys that in turn are needed to decrypt the data. So, if you lose the passphrase, you lose the data – period! This means that for data recovery purposes the passphrase MUST be stored in written form in a physically secure location such as a safe.

Practical key-management systems use these various methods

Various combinations of tamper-resistant hardware devices, encrypted key files and passphrase-derived master keys are to be found in practical key-management schemes.

Cryptographic integrity checksums can be used on files

Cryptographic techniques can also be used to enhance file-integrity protection by computing cryptographic checksums on each file or each record and storing those with the file. If an unauthorised change is made, this can be detected, although this may not help to recover the original data. Once again, as with all cryptographic mechanisms, managing and safely storing the authentication keys is the main challenge.

---

[1] A passphrase is like a password, only longer and comprising several words.

Database Security

The DBMS offers a much richer set of functions

Database management systems are much more sophisticated than file systems, offering much more extensive data management facilities.

Concurrency of access is automatically managed

One principal difference is that a database management system offers concurrent access to a large number of users to the same data resources and must manage this without allowing the data to become corrupted by conflicting changes made by concurrent users. In a file system the entire file is locked when a user is accessing it, but it would be unthinkable to lock the database so that only one user at a time could make use of it. The locking mechanism has to be at a much finer granularity within the database structure.

Database hierarchy

Database locking is at the record level. The hierarchy of data structures in a database is shown in Figure 12-1.

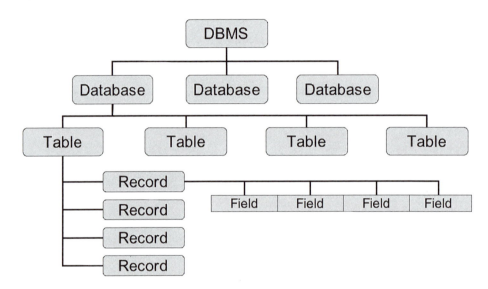

Figure 12-1: Data Structure Hierarchy in a Database Management System

A database comprises tables

Thus, a sales database might contain a number of tables, including a customer table, orders table and a products table.

Tables comprise records

The customer table contains a number of customer records, one for each customer.

Records have fields

The customer record comprises several fields, such as customer number, customer name, address, credit limit, etc.

The DBMS automatically protects integrity

The functional (logical) description of database integrity control that is achieved through the record locking mechanism is:

- Atomicity of transactions:

    - If the transaction terminates normally, the alterations to data are made permanent (committed).

    - If not, then no alteration is made.

    - That is, the transaction is atomic (indivisible) and cannot be split.

- Recoverability of transactions – the recovery sub-system of the database management system behaves such that the database contains:

    - All the effects of committed transactions;

    - None of the effects of uncommitted transactions.

- Serialisability of transactions:

    - Each transaction accesses shared data without interfering with other transactions.

    - When two or more transactions execute simultaneously, the database operations are interleaved.

    - The interleaving is such that one transaction must be completed before the next can begin.

DBMS sub-systems To achieve this a database management systems has certain sub-systems:

- Transaction manager – to pre-process the data and transactions;

- Scheduler – to control ordering and serialisation;

- Recovery manager – to manage transaction commitment and abortion;

- Cache manager – to act directly on stored data.

DBMS mechanisms Database recovery is managed through a series of mechanisms:

- Database backup to create checkpoints, usually:

    - Full backups on a weekly basis;

    - Incremental backups daily.

- 'Before' image journaling – taking an image (copy) of the record before a transaction and storing it in a 'before image' journal table;

- 'After' image journaling – taking an image (copy) of the record after a transaction and storing in an 'after image' journal table;

- After restoring the database to a checkpoint, providing roll-back from the saved checkpoint to a previous business position by running the transactions in the before-image journal in reverse chronological order against the checkpointed database until the desired point is reached;

- After restoring the database to a checkpoint, providing roll-forward from the saved checkpoint to a future business position by running the transactions in the after-image journal in chronological order against the checkpointed database until the desired point is reached.

Security Mechanisms in SQL Databases

SQL is used for database access SQL (structured query language) is the ANSI standard language that allows you to access a database. It supports:

- Execution of queries against a database;

- Retrieval of data from a database;

- Insertion of new records in a database;

- Deletion of records from a database;

- Updating records in a database.

SQL can be used to implement security mechanisms

You can use many of the functions within SQL databases specifically to implement security mechanisms. These are summarised here:

- Each user has a user account just as in an operating system such as UNIX. To login as a given user, a password must be entered. Password management is similar to that in UNIX.

- There are three classes of user:

  - System administrator – has access to and controls all databases in the entire DBMS;

  - Database administrator – has access to and controls a given database;

  - User – has access privileges as defined by the system administrator or the database administrator.

- Groups are used with group identifiers and group passwords, just as in UNIX.

- A user is often mapped to an application that makes automated database access but can also be mapped to a human user who makes direct database access without an intervening application, such as through the use of OLTP.[2]

- User and group privileges granted by an administrator can be assigned to:

  - Specific tables;

  - Specific views;

  - Specific procedures.

- In an SQL program the commands for managing user privileges are GRANT and REVOKE. The SQL syntax is:

  GRANT action_list ON object_name TO user_list

  Where:

  action_list can include: SELECT, INSERT, UPDATE, DELETE, EXECUTE;

  object_name can be one of: table_name, view_name, procedure_name;

  user_list can include: user_name, group_name, public;

- SQL supports mechanisms to protect the integrity of data in the database records, such as:

  - UNIQUE columns in tables to prevent data from being duplicated incorrectly;

---

[2]OLTP: on-line transaction processing

- Creating views with the WITH CHECK option to force underlying table updates to conform to constraints on value ranges;

- COMMIT and ROLLBACK functions to allow mistakes to be corrected;

- BEFORE IMAGE and AFTER IMAGE journaling with CHECKPOINTS to allow database recovery to a specific business position.

- You can use views to provide restricted access to a table. This provides a mechanism for fine control over access by specified users. The user gets access only to the view, which is a sub-table of the main table. It might contain only certain records (rows) or only certain fields (columns). Figure 12-2 shows a diagrammatic representation of a view within a table. In fact a view is much more flexible than is suggested by this diagram because it can be defined across multiple tables.

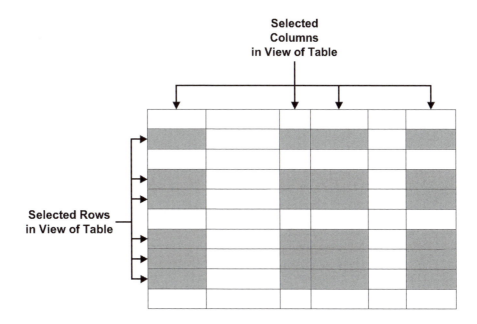

Figure 12-2: A Database View Within a Table

- You can define as many views as you like, and these may overlap one another in any way, so there is great flexibility to provide differential access rights to individual users or groups of users. As an example, if one of the fields (columns) in a personnel table is 'salary', then individuals are not given access to other peoples' salary details. However, department heads are given a view of the table that includes the salaries of those staff members who report to them, but no others.

- Stored procedures are effectively macros of SQL commands bound together and executed as a whole. This allows you to define whole tasks and make them available to users without giving them the use of the individual raw commands. Thus you can grant quite sensitive operations to a user but only in the context of the macro and thus under close control.

- Triggers are procedures whose execution is triggered when certain logical conditions occur. There are four types of triggers:

- BEFORE statement – executes immediately before a particular statement in the SQL program;

- AFTER statement – executes immediately after a particular statement in the SQL program;

- BEFORE row – executes immediately before a row in a given table is to be processed;

- AFTER row – executes immediately after a row in a given table has been processed.

Statement triggers fire once for the statement, regardless of the number of rows processed by that statement.

Row triggers fire on every row processed.

You can use a trigger as you use a procedure, but they are more powerful because of the trigger mechanism. They are very useful to apply security rules, such as:

- Time limits for updates 08:30 to 18:00 Monday to Friday, using a BEFORE statement trigger to check the time;

- Preventing employees from accessing their personal customer account details when they are both a customer and an employee, using a BEFORE row trigger to check the identity of the user.

Privilege conflicts are resolved in real time

Privilege levels in an SQL database system are not checked in advance and may be in conflict at execution time, and so there is a hierarchy of privileges to decide which will prevail:

- Procedures and triggers use tables and views;

- Views use tables;

- The hierarchy of privilege levels is:

    - Procedure – which overrides the privileges of a:

    - Trigger – which overrides the privileges of a:

    - View – which overrides the privileges of a:

    - Table.

Extensive audit logging

Most SQL database management systems also provide extensive audit logging to monitor database activity, with audit records being written to special system tables. If these are insufficient for your needs, you can extend and customise the audit logging by using triggers so as to create your own customised audit log tables.

Implementing roles in a DBMS

Roles can be implemented in an SQL database by assigning a user ID to a role (such as PAYROLL_CLERK) and controlling this within the application. This role can be mapped to several different individual human users of the application. The application should be designed to pass across an identifier for the specific user being assigned to the role so that this can be entered into a customised audit trail table in the database to provide individual accountability. The DBMS must also be configured to allow multiple concurrent sessions under the single role user ID.

Resource limitations

A DBMS also allows the administrator to limit access by users to resources. Resource limits are grouped together in sets called profiles, and a profile is assigned to one or more users for ease of administration. Limits can be placed on any or all of the following:

- CPU time;

- Number of concurrent sessions;

- Idle time per session;

- Input and output in logical data blocks.

Mandatory access control as an extension

Some vendors of DBMS products have implemented 'mandatory access control' to comply with various trusted-systems[3] criteria. This is achieved by labelling each object (row in a table) with a compulsory security classification in the form of an extra field (column). Users (subjects) are also assigned clearance levels. The DBMS automatically manages the matching of subject clearance level to object classification to control access.

Multi-level secure implementations can be clumsy

However, the implementation of multi-level secure systems can become complex and performance can be poor. Here is what Dorothy Denning[4] tells us of her personal experiences in this field:

> 'I learned my second lesson on the limits of models in the mid-80s while working at SRI. I was part of a project to develop a model for a multilevel-secure database system based on views. Our model, which we called SeaView, grew progressively more complex as we attempted to address the real issues. Any hope of usability had been killed by a concept called polyinstantiation, which involved instantiating multiple data values within a single field of a record, all with different security classifications.

> 'Polyinstantiation was needed to satisfy the mathematical models of multilevel security, but it got uglier and uglier the deeper we went. I learned then that security models could lead to dreadful systems that nobody would ever use.'

Distributed Databases

Logical unity – physical distribution

A distributed database is one that is logically a single database but is physically distributed over several servers – perhaps at several geographically separated sites. This brings some additional challenges for managing database integrity and consistency.

Managing independent failures

The main problem is that one part of the distributed system can fail quite independently of any other part. Thus to maintain the concept of atomicity of transactions you need some additional functionality, since if one part of the database has committed a transaction and another part is unable to complete the commitment, then they may become desynchronised.

Two-phase commitment

The solution is to implement two-phase commitment of transactions. It works like this:

- Each physical location has its own independent resource manager.

---

[3]Such as TCSEC (Trusted Computer Systems Evaluation Criteria – also known as 'Orange Book') level B1 or ITSEC (IT Security Evaluation Criteria) level F-B1/E3

[4]'The Limits of Formal Security Models', National Computer Systems Security Award Acceptance Speech, Dorothy E. Denning, 18 October 1999

- Each resource manager controls its own local resources and maintains its own recovery log.

- One resource manager acts as co-ordinator for a distributed transaction (usually the one that initiates the transaction).

- All participating resource managers in a particular transaction prepare for the transaction by writing the effects of the transaction into non-volatile storage in their logs.

- At this stage they can each either COMMIT (make the transaction permanent) or ROLLBACK (erase the effects of the transaction).

- The co-ordinator awaits a message from participating resource managers to hear that they have all reached this stage.

- The co-ordinator writes an entry in its own log to record this status.

- The participants are all instructed to COMMIT the transaction.

- When all have signalled to the co-ordinator that the commitment is completed, the transaction is completed.

- If at any stage there is a signal that a resource manager has failed to complete normally, or there is a timeout because a resource manager is unable to respond, then the co-ordinator issues the command to ROLLBACK.

- There is still the possibility that one of the resource managers that has already committed has now gone off-line and cannot roll back. This is detected by the co-ordinator, and a manual recovery operation is instigated. A similar approach is needed if the co-ordinator fails before overall completion.

Data Storage

Physical storage on disks uses RAID for resilience

Files and databases need to be stored on physical disks, and one of the potential threats is the catastrophic failure of the disk system, such as a through a head crash. To reduce the impact of such an event, disks can be configured in redundant arrays of inexpensive disks[5] (known as RAID). There are various levels of protection in the RAID scheme, as follows:

- RAID 0: data striping across all the physical disks in the array to reduce the amount of loss from individual records if one of the disks in the array fails but without any parity information to reconstruct damaged data. There is no true redundancy in this solution, and hence its inclusion in the RAID definition is marginal.

- RAID 1: simple disk mirroring, with data written simultaneously to two or more disk drives.

- RAID 2: data striping across physical disks in the array with additional parity bits (Hamming codes) for error detection and error correction.

---

[5]In 1987 Patterson, Gibson and Katz at the University of California Berkeley published a paper entitled 'A Case for Redundant Arrays of Inexpensive Disks (RAID)'.

- RAID 3: striping on a byte-by-byte basis to maximise distribution across the surfaces of the disk array, with the parity bytes on a separate physical disk. If any single drive fails it can be completely reconstructed from the remaining drives.

- RAID 4: similar to RAID 3 but with the striping on a block basis. RAID 4 has a different performance and cost profile from RAID 3, and the best choice depends upon the profile of read/write activity.

- RAID 5: Similar to RAID 4 but with the parity distributed amongst the drives. Again the performance profile differs, although the cost profile is the same. Best choice depends upon the read/write activity profile of the system and is especially suited to multi-user environments with many short, random write operations.

Security Rules, Practices and Procedures

SABSA® Matrix cross-reference

Please refer to Chapter 3, Figure 3-3 and Chapter 7, Figure 7-8, the SABSA® Matrix, Physical layer, Motivation column, where you will see a cell entitled Security Rules, Practices and Procedures. You will find this same title associated with a deliverable of the physical security architecture shown in Chapter 7, Figure 7-10. This section looks at aspects of this deliverable.

Rules are the interpretation of policies

At the logical security architecture layer you have security policies, as discussed in Chapter 11. These now get turned into sets of rules and into practices and procedures at the physical architecture layer.

Security Rules

Rules support automated decision making

A rule is a specific filter against which automated decisions are made by security sub-systems. For example, rules are used in the following types of security sub-system:

- Firewall rules – to determine what types of traffic are allowed or disallowed;

- Database rules – to determine what types of access and what types of actions are allowed or disallowed (see the previous section for details);

- File system rules – to make decisions about access to data.

ACLs contain rules

Rules are often built into access control lists (ACLs). An access control list is made up of access control entries (ACEs), each of which contains one or more rules.

Rules are absolute – no interpretation is needed

The key difference between security rules (in this context) and security policies is that whilst policies may require interpretation, rules do not – they are absolute and unequivocal.

Security Practices and Procedures

Security practices describe behaviours

Security practices are generic descriptions of how to accomplish certain objectives in security management. Usually the term 'practice' is used as part of a phrase such as 'good practice' or 'best practice'. This implies adopting an approach that has been found to work well in other places. Security practices are more specific than security policies and imply a definite behavioural content to them, but they are not so specific as security procedures.

Security procedures give step-by-step instructions

Security procedures are documented step-by-step instructions on how specific tasks are to be performed. A procedure is specific to a particular platform or product and deals with the detail of how that specific technical environment works. A new release of a given product may require the procedure to be re-written because the product is now slightly different to the previous release and needs a different set of steps.

Procedures are product-specific

Thus a procedure for backing up data on one type of computer platform will probably not be applicable to another different computer platform and would need to be modified to be useful. However, the practices of data backup will be the same for both computers, because they involve the same generic steps.

Guidelines provide good advice

Another term that is used in this general context is 'guidelines'. These are generally non-specific, like practices, but they tend to be more in the style of giving good advice to people about how to behave in order to comply with policy and in order to exhibit good practice. Guidelines require intelligent interpretation.

Implementation guidelines provide additional advice in specific circumstances

In the policy architecture hierarchy shown in Chapter 11, Figure 11-1 (also Chapter 14, Figure 14-1) there is a lower layer of documentation called Implementation Guidelines. These are intended to cover situations where, given a specific policy and a standard that supports it, it may still not be clear how to build a specific piece of infrastructure. The implementation guideline gives advice on how to achieve this. However, it is less specific than a procedure.

Cross-reference to Chapter 14

The discussion in Chapter 14 provides concrete examples to help you to understand the subtle relationships between these various layers of documentation.

Security Mechanisms

SABSA® Matrix cross-reference

Please refer to Chapter 3, Figure 3-3 and Chapter 7, Figure 7-8, the SABSA® Matrix, Physical layer, Process column, where you will see a cell entitled Security Mechanisms. Security Mechanisms also appears as a key deliverable of the physical security architecture in Chapter 7, Figure 7-10. In this section the most common security mechanisms are mapped to the logical security services already introduced in Chapter 11. Some of these security mechanisms – mainly those with a cryptographic basis – are discussed in some greater detail in this section. Others, such as data management mechanisms, are discussed in other parts of the chapter.

A mechanism implements a service

A security mechanism is a physical means by which a logical security service is implemented. Some security mechanisms have already been discussed in the earlier sections of this chapter, describing how database and file system mechanisms could be used for security purposes.

Some (but not all) security mechanisms are described in ISO standards

Some security mechanisms have been classified in ISO standards, such as in ISO 7498-2.[6] Others that are described here have been added because the authors think they are important (such as the various database management mechanisms already mentioned). However, there are many more mechanisms that you will encounter that will also serve you well in this context, and you should not consider any of the lists that are provided here to be exhaustive – they are not.

Mapping Security Mechanisms to Security Services

Mapping mechanisms to services

Table 12-1 shows the mapping of the security mechanisms described here to the security services that are described in Chapter 11.

---

[6]ISO/IEC 7498-2: 1989, 'Information Processing Systems, Open Systems Interconnection – Basic Reference Model – Part 2: Security Architecture'.

Table 12-1: Mapping Security Mechanisms to Security Services

Logical Security Services	Physical Security Mechanisms
Entity Unique Naming	Naming standards
	Naming procedure
	Directory system
Entity Registration	Registration policy
	Registration authority system
	Registration procedure
Entity Public Key Certification	Certification policy
	Certification authority system
	Certification procedure
	Certificate syntax standards
	Certificate publishing mechanism (directory)
	Certificate revocation list (CRL)
	CRL publishing and management (directory)
Entity Credentials Certification	Certification policy
	Certification authority system
	Certification procedure
	Certificate syntax standards
	Certificate publishing mechanism (directory)
	Certificate revocation list (CRL)
	CRL publishing and management (directory)
Directory Service	Directory system
	Directory access protocols
	Directory object and attribute syntax rules
	Directory replication
Entity Authentication	Login procedure
	User passwords and tokens
	Client user agents for authentication
	Authentication exchange protocols
	Authentication server system
	Directory system
Session Authentication	Mutual two-way and three-way authentication exchanges
	Session context (finite state machine)
Message Origin Authentication	Message source identifiers, protected by:
	Message integrity checksums
	Digital signatures
	Hashing

Logical Security Services	Physical Security Mechanisms
Message Integrity Protection	Message integrity checksums
	Digital signatures
	Hashing
Message Replay Protection	Message nonce values protected by message integrity checksums
Message Contents Confidentiality	Message contents encryption
	Encryption key management
	Routing control to physically secure networks
Non-Repudiation	Digital signatures
	Notarisation servers
	Transaction logs
	Trusted third party certification and arbitration
Traffic Flow Confidentiality	Traffic padding
Authorisation	Roles
	Fixed role associations with entities
	Real-time role association with entities
	Authorisation certificates
Logical Access Control	Local access control agents
	Local role access control lists (ACLs)
	Central access manager (CAM)
	CAM role ACLs
	Central application access control agents
	Central application role ACLs
	Database management system mechanisms
	File system mechanisms
Audit Trails	Event logs
	Event log integrity protection mechanisms
	Event log browsing tools
	Event log analysis tools
	Reporting tools
Stored Data Confidentiality	Logical access control mechanisms
	Physical access control mechanisms
	Stored data encryption
	Media storage security
	Media disposal procedures
Stored Data Integrity Protection	Message integrity checksums
	Digital signatures
	Hashing

Logical Security Services	Physical Security Mechanisms
Software Integrity Protection	Development lifecycle controls
	Delivery and installation controls
	Production system configuration control
	Production system change control
	Production system management authorisation
	Crypto-checksums on object code images
	Regular inspection of object code images and checksums
	Anti-virus tools
Software Licensing Protection	Software metering
System Configuration Protection	Production system configuration control
	Production system change control
	Production system management authorisation
	Cryptographic checksums on configuration data files
	Regular inspection of configuration data files and checksums
Data Replication and Backup	Regular backup copying
	Backup media management: labelling, indexing, transport, storage, retrieval, media recycling, media disposal
Software Replication and Backup	Master software media management: labelling, indexing, transport, storage, retrieval
Trusted Time	Secure time server with clock
	Secure time server protocols
User Interface for Security	GUI login screens
	GUI security message screens
	Single sign-on mechanism
	Ergonomic design of authentication devices
	Help desk for security problem resolution
Security Policy Management	Data content monitoring and filtering
	Real-time system monitoring
Security Service Management	Security service management sub-system
	Secure management protocols
	Management agents in managed components
	Access control at all agents and sub-systems security alarms
Security Training and Awareness	Training courses
	Training manuals and documentation
	Publicity campaigns
Security Operations Management	Operator authentication mechanisms
	Operator activity logs
	Operations event logs

Logical Security Services	Physical Security Mechanisms
Security Provisioning	Security service management sub-system
	Secure management protocols
	Management agents in managed components
	Access control at all agents and sub-systems security alarms
Security Administration	Security service management sub-system
	Secure management protocols
	Management agents in managed components
	Access control at all agents and sub-systems security alarms
Security Monitoring	User activity logs
	Application event logs
	Operator activity logs
	Management event logs
	Event log browsing and analysis
	Reporting
	Real-time system monitoring and alarms
Security Measurements and Metrics	Cryptographic test mechanisms
	Inspection tools
	Penetration testing
	Statistical tests
Security Alarm Management	Security alarms
	Security alarm monitoring
Intrusion Detection	Intrusion signature analysis on network traffic
	Real-time system monitoring
	Alarms
Incident Response	Data collection and analysis
	Incident assessment procedures
	Response action management procedures
User Support	Help desk
	Trouble ticketing system

Logical Security Services	Physical Security Mechanisms
Disaster Recovery	Data backups
	Software backups
	Data restoration procedures
	Off-site backup storage
	Backup media management: indexing, labelling, transport, storage, retrieval, recycling, disposal
	Redundancy of hardware
	Redundancy of communications lines
	Recovery plans
	Recovery procedures
Crisis Management	Vested authority in a crisis manager and crisis management team
	Assessment procedures
	Escalation procedures
	Activation procedures
System Audit	Independent inspection
	Regular scanning with system audit tools
Physical Security	Secure premises with locks and guards
	Locked rooms for servers, operations and communications
	Physical protection for cabling
	Authorisation procedures
	Identification badges and visitor procedures
	Supervision of contract engineers
Personnel Security	Hiring, background checking and vetting procedures
	Training courses, booklets, publicity campaigns
	Disciplinary procedures
Environmental Security	Site-selection procedures
	Fire prevention, detection and quenching
	Flood avoidance, detection and removal
	Air temperature and humidity controls
	Electrical power protection mechanisms

Many mechanisms require little additional explanation

Many of the security mechanisms listed in Table 12-1 are simple and obvious in their nature, and there is no attempt here to explain each one in detail – there is no need. Other mechanisms (such as the DBMS mechanisms, the directory system mechanisms and access control mechanisms) are discussed in detail elsewhere.

Some mechanisms are described in more detail

However, some of the security mechanisms are technically detailed in nature, especially those of a cryptographic type. The following sections describe a few selected mechanisms in slightly greater detail, and the selection is made on arbitrary grounds as to whether or not the authors judge that more detail will be both helpful to you and within the scope of this book.

Full details can be found in specific references beyond the scope of this book

For more detailed information on other security mechanisms, and indeed for full details of those mechanisms described below, you are recommended to research in other books more focused at this level of detail and with vendor organisations who provide tools and products that contain these mechanisms. The following sections do not purport to be an in-depth tutorial on cryptography, but if you are a newcomer to this subject they should be helpful to you in explaining how cryptography works – what it can do, and also by inference what it cannot do.

Cryptographic Mechanisms and Their Uses

Cryptography supports four fundamental services

Cryptography has some very specific roles to play in securing information. There are four fundamental security services that can be implemented using cryptography:

- Confidentiality – preventing the unauthorised disclosure of information;

- Integrity – protecting information content from being altered in any way without this being detected (you cannot prevent the alterations by using cryptography but you can ensure they will be detected);

- Authenticity – proving that information originated from an authentic trusted source;

- Non-repudiation – preventing a dishonest party from later denying (repudiating) the authenticity of information provided by that party.

If the service is not a variation of these four, cryptography is not the answer

There are various ways to present these services, as can be seen in the service-to-mechanism mapping in Table 12-1 above. However, if the security service you want to provide cannot be in some way presented as a variation of one of these four, then cryptography is not the right mechanism for your solution.

Cryptographic strength is most dependent upon key-length

The strength of cryptographic mechanisms is mostly related to the number of bits in the cryptographic key and hence the number of possible key values (see the discussion on entropy earlier in this chapter in the section on File Encryption). This assertion assumes that there are no specific analytical weaknesses in the algorithm and that the cryptanalyst must rely on searching the entire key space to find the key value being used.

Whatever the mechanism, key management is an issue

The main constraint on using cryptographic mechanisms in information systems is the need to manage the keys. This must be done securely and efficiently. This is discussed in a little more detail in a later section below.

Encryption[7] Mechanisms

The encryption process transforms plaintext into ciphertext

An encryption mechanism transforms original raw data (called plaintext) into an enciphered form of the data (called ciphertext). If a good quality encryption algorithm is used the transformation is complex and opaque, such that it is infeasible for an opponent to analyse the ciphertext (a process called cryptanalysis) so as to discover the original plaintext. In most cases the transformation is controlled by an encryption key. This is an additional piece of data that influences the transformation. For a given plaintext, if you change the key you will obtain a different ciphertext. The mapping of the ciphertext result to the key is similarly opaque such that the opponent cannot determine the value of the key by cryptanalysis. Figure 12-3 shows this process in simple diagrammatic form.

---

[7]The terms 'encryption' and 'decryption' are used here, but in many ISO standards the terms used are 'encipher' and 'decipher' because these words are culturally neutral in all countries and all languages.

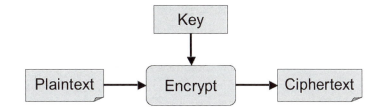

Figure 12-3: The Encryption Process

Ciphertext is safely transmitted or stored, then later recovered through decryption

If the purpose of using the encryption mechanism is to hide the plaintext from an opponent, during transmission over a network or perhaps during storage on a computer system, but later to recover the plaintext in its original form, then the transformation must be reversible. The reverse process is called decryption. In some cryptosystems the key used for decryption is the same as the one used for encryption. These systems are known as symmetric.

Asymmetric cryptosystems use different keys for encryption and decryption

However, there is a class of cryptosystem where the reverse transformation requires a different (but mathematically related) key, and these are called asymmetric for obvious reasons. The asymmetric algorithms are also commonly known as public key cryptosystems because the encryption key can be published and only the decryption key needs to be kept private. Figure 12-4 shows a fully reversible cryptosystem. For symmetric algorithms, 'key 1' and 'key 2' are equal. For asymmetric algorithms they are related but different, and knowledge of 'key 1' does not reveal 'key 2'.

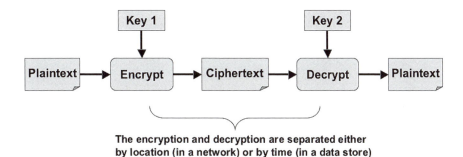

The encryption and decryption are separated either by location (in a network) or by time (in a data store)

Figure 12-4: A Reversible Cryptosystem

One-way (irreversible) functions have many applications

Not all cryptosystems are reversible, and there are good applications for one-way functions as cryptographic algorithms. The storage of passwords in a password file is one such example. You want to make sure that if someone steals the file they cannot reverse the encryption and recover the plaintext passwords. The way to check a submitted password is to encrypt it and compare the ciphertext result with the stored ciphertext in the password file. Such a system is still vulnerable to so-called dictionary attacks, but direct decryption of the stored password is not feasible.

Successful key management is the main challenge in any cryptographically secured system

To make any cryptosystem work in practice it is essential that all secret keys (in the case of symmetric cryptography) and all private keys (in the case of asymmetric cryptography) are protected and not revealed to an opponent (who might be an insider). This is the greatest challenge in building secure cryptographic systems, because you must be able to communicate the keys between collaborating trusted parties without disclosing them to others. The subject of key management is extensive and complex, and a detailed treatment is well beyond the scope of this book. Some more high-level insights are provided in the approaches in a later section of this chapter.

Data Integrity Mechanisms

Cryptographic checksums called seals, MACs and MICs

Cryptography can be applied to generate secure checksums or seals that provide a mechanism for detecting any changes to the target information. These seals are also known as message authentication codes (MACs) or message integrity checksums (MICs) in some contexts. The method used is to process the entire data contents to be protected through a cryptographic transformation that produces a short checksum value.

Hashing does not require a key, although it can be applied as keyed hashing

If the checksum algorithm does not require a cryptographic key, then the method is called hashing. Hash values are usually used within digital signature functions to improve overall efficiency and speed (see below), but there is also a variation of the MAC technique called hash-MAC or HMAC – also known as keyed hashing.

The checksums are regenerated by the recipient and compared with the original received checksums

Figure 12-5 shows the generic scheme for attaching seals to data structures – either transmitted messages or stored data records. Note that the data structure itself is not encrypted and is still visible as plaintext. A seal is created by the sender and attached as an additional field in the data structure. At the receiver, the received seal is stripped off and put to one side, a new seal is generated using the same key as was used by the sender, and the two seals are compared. If they are the same, then there is a high level of assurance that the data has not been altered between the two seal-generating events.

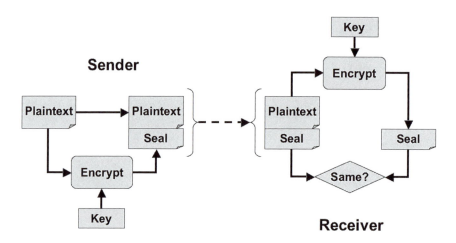

Figure 12-5: Using a Seal to Check the Integrity of Data

Key management is also required

As with any application of cryptography, the method works only if a key management service is provided to make the keys available wherever they are needed whilst not revealing them to an opponent.

Public Key Certificates

Public key cryptography

Where asymmetric cryptographic techniques are used each participating entity has a key pair. One of these keys of a key pair is published and available to all other participants. This key is known as the public key. The other key of the pair must be kept completely private and not disclosed to any other participant – called the private key.

Although public keys are known to all and therefore not confidential, they must be authentic. An opponent could steal your identity and publish his own public key pretending to be you, unless there is some mechanism to prevent this happening. The mechanism used is called certification. Every public key in the community has to be certified by a trusted authority. The trusted certification authority (CA) digitally signs each public key to create a public key certificate. It is the certificate that is published for all to use. To be sure that you are using an authentic public key, you must first check the signature of the certification authority in the certificate.

Digital Signature Mechanisms

Digital signatures prove integrity and authenticity and support non-repudiation

Digital signatures are based on the application of asymmetric (public key) cryptographic techniques. The private key is used to create the signature, and the public key is used to verify the signature. Public keys must be certified as described above. Digital signatures prove both the integrity of the data content and authenticity of the data source. The signatures are also non-repudiable.

Efficiency requires a two-stage process with an intermediate hash value

To apply an asymmetric cryptographic algorithm directly onto the target data would in most cases be very inefficient, take a long time to execute and create a signature the same size as the original data. There are also some disadvantages in terms of making the cryptanalyst's job easier. To create an efficient practical digital signature system you use a two-stage process. First the data is hashed to create a short hash value. This hash value is digitally signed and attached to the message by the signatory. The verifier must rehash the message and also recover the original hash from the received signature, then compare these two hash values. If they are the same, there is a high level of assurance that the signature was made by the authentic signatory. Figure 12-6 shows this schematically.

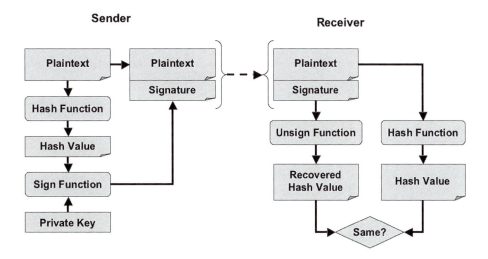

Figure 12-6: Digital Signature Mechanism

Authentication Exchange Mechanisms

The mechanisms for authentication exchanges

In Chapter 11 the logical flow of various authentication exchanges is discussed. Here these are developed to the physical mechanism stage.

One-way, two-way and three-way exchanges

Traditionally in describing authentication exchanges the two parties – prover and verifier – are known as Alice and Bob, abbreviated to A and B in the diagrams. There are three basic authentication exchange mechanisms that Alice and Bob can use – one-way authentication, two-way authentication and three-way authentication[8]. There are many different specific standard protocols for realising these mechanisms, but these protocols are fundamentally all the same in the generic way they work using time stamps or random numbers.

One-way authentication based on a security association

In one-way authentication Alice is the prover and Bob the verifier. Alice authenticates herself to Bob. Bob does not authenticate himself to Alice. The authentication relies on Alice and Bob having previously created a security association in which they share at least one secret cryptographic key. The creation of this security association may or may not involve the participation of a trusted key-distribution server. In some of the protocols the exchange itself is not between Alice and Bob but through a trusted server. In some authentication exchange protocols the cryptographic algorithms are symmetric and in others they are asymmetric. However most boil down to something very like the exchange shown in Figure 12-7.

$$E_{AB}\{ SK, T, B\}$$

A ⟶ B

Where: $E_{AB}\{...\}$ means 'encrypted under a key previously agreed
between Alice and Bob to be used by Alice
SK is a random session key for use in this session
T is a time-stamp
B is Bob's name

Figure 12-7: One-Way Authentication

Extending to session authentication

The session key can be used throughout the rest of the session either to encrypt data or to provide integrity checksums. If you want both of these functions then two session keys can be exchanged, one for each.

Preventing the replay attack

The time stamp gives a limited life to this authentication exchange and prevents it from being replayed by an opponent pretending to be Alice at another time. However, Alice and Bob must agree on what time it is and must have a trusted time service to set their clocks. If Bob's clock can be manipulated, then an opponent can replay out-of-time messages and masquerade as Alice to Bob. The inclusion of Bob's name prevents an opponent from using the message to masquerade as Alice to any other of Alice's friends apart from Bob.

Two-way authentication is an extension of one-way authentication

In two-way authentication, the simple one-way protocol is reflected back allowing Bob also to authenticate himself to Alice. Now you can have different session keys for each direction of the session. Figure 12-8 shows the exchange schematically.

Three-way authentication uses random numbers in place of timestamps

The three-way authentication exchange replaces time stamps with random numbers. These exchanges are sometimes known as challenge-response protocols because the first message from Alice to Bob contains a random number challenge from Alice. In this case Alice is the verifier and Bob is the prover. Bob must prove his authenticity by successfully decrypting Alice's message, extracting the random number and sending it back to Alice re-encrypted under his own

---

[8]The terms 'one-way', 'two-way' and 'three-way' refer to the number of exchanges, not the number of parties involved. In all three cases there are two parties to the exchange, Alice and Bob. Refer to X.509 for the definitive description of these three cases. [ITU-T Recommendation X.509 (1997 E): Information Technology – Open Systems Interconnection – The Directory: Authentication Framework, June 1997].

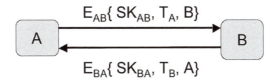

$$E_{AB}\{ SK_{AB}, T_A, B\}$$

$$E_{BA}\{ SK_{BA}, T_B, A\}$$

Where: $E_{XY}\{...\}$ means 'encrypted under a key previously agreed between entity X and entity Y to be used by entity X'
SK_{XY} is a random session key for use in the X-Y direction
T_X is a time-stamp made by X
X is entity X's name (and X is either A or B)

Figure 12-8: Two-Way Authentication

authentication key. At the same time he sends his own random number challenge to Alice, who must then in turn prove her own authenticity by extracting Bob's random number, re-encrypting it under her own authentication key and sending it back to Bob. Figure 12-9 shows the generic exchanges schematically.

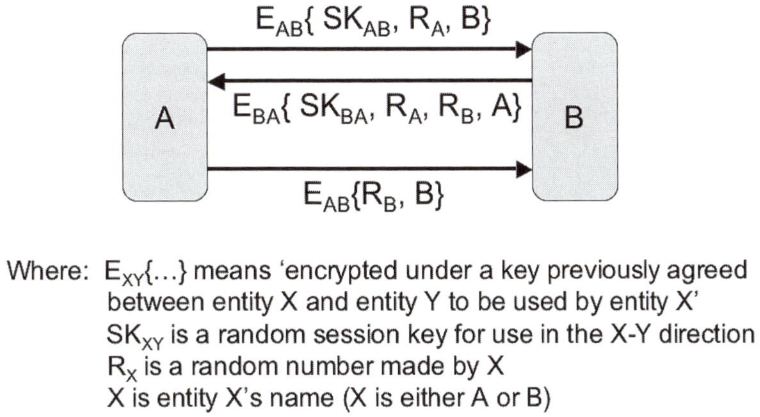

$$E_{AB}\{ SK_{AB}, R_A, B\}$$

$$E_{BA}\{ SK_{BA}, R_A, R_B, A\}$$

$$E_{AB}\{R_B, B\}$$

Where: $E_{XY}\{...\}$ means 'encrypted under a key previously agreed between entity X and entity Y to be used by entity X'
SK_{XY} is a random session key for use in the X-Y direction
R_X is a random number made by X
X is entity X's name (X is either A or B)

Figure 12-9: Three-Way Authentication

Cryptographic Key Management Mechanisms

Key management could occupy its own book

Throughout the foregoing sections attention has been drawn to the need for efficient, secure key management. One could write an entire book of similar size to this one just on this topic alone, and so you will understand that scope is an issue here. There are however a few things that should be said in a book of this type.

Principles of key management

There are some general principles of key management that are worth considering:

- However strong the cryptographic algorithms might be, if the keys are poorly managed and can be learned by an opponent, the overall system is weak.

- In general it is a bad idea to allow human beings to have knowledge of cryptographic keys. Humans are often the weakest link in any security system. Even the most honest and high-integrity individuals have their price that will induce them to give up the keys. A cynical view? Well that price may not be money or other wealth. If you point a gun at someone's head the price becomes their own life. It probably gets worse if you point a gun at the heads of their children. It is actually very unfair to place employees in a position where they can be subjected to this type of duress.

- It is often impossible to avoid some human knowledge of some keys somewhere in the system, usually to ensure that when all the technology has broken you can still recover the system manually. However, these are emergency conditions that should occur infrequently. The way to make this work is to split the key knowledge amongst two or more individuals and require them each to enter their own key component. Thus no single individual can be subjected to duress.

- Key management should in all other ways be completely automated, using key-encrypting keys to move working data keys around from one place to another.

- A truly random number generator should be used to generate new keys so as to ensure that they are not predictable. Software random number generators cannot fulfil this requirement, because they always use some seed value that might be predictable, and they always use some mathematical function that is eventually cyclical.

- Tamper-resistant devices can protect keys from unauthorised disclosure.

- Keys should be limited in their exposure to cryptanalysis. This exposure is defined in terms of both the number of ciphertext samples that an opponent can collect and the time that the opponent has to work on those samples. These can be traded off against one another. Thus, a data key used for bulk data encryption or authentication generates large quantities of cipher text and should be changed frequently. A key-encrypting key used only for exchanging other keys generates small samples of ciphertext and can have its lifetime extended. These principles are fundamental to the construction of key management hierarchies.

- Different keys should be used for different functions, different parties and different channels to ensure cryptographic separation of logical communications that may share the same physical bandwidth.

The key management life-cycle

Key management covers the entire lifecycle of keys and everything that happens from them from birth to death:

- Generation of keys;

- Communication and distribution of keys;

- Storage of keys;

- Entry and installation of keys;

- Checking the validity of keys;

- Usage of keys;

- Changing the active key;

- Archiving of keys;

- Destruction of keys;

- Audit of key operations and usage;

- Key backup and recovery;

- Emergency reserve keys.

Cryptographic Services Physical Architecture

Two basic cryptographic architectures

There are two fundamentally different physical architectures for providing cryptographic services in a distributed system:

- The in-line architecture, providing cryptographic services in the networking layers of the system architecture, as shown in Figure 12-10;

- The on-line architecture, providing cryptographic services at the applications layer of the system architecture, as shown in Figure 12-11.

Figure 12-10: In-Line Cryptographic Services Architecture

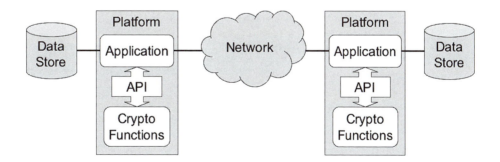

Figure 12-11: On-Line Cryptographic Services Architecture

In-line architecture for network-level encryption

The in-line cryptographic architecture can provide the following types of network security service:

- Physical layer (OSI layer 1) confidentiality implemented by encrypting the entire bit stream using in-line pairs of link encryption units.

- Link layer (OSI layer 2) confidentiality implemented by encrypting the payloads in HDLC frames or in Ethernet packets, using functionality embedded in the network interface card (NIC).

- Network layer (OSI layer 3) confidentiality and integrity checking implemented by encryption and integrity checksums over the payloads in packets of the network protocol (either X.25 or IP). IPSec transport mode services are of this type, using additional software functionality in the IP stack. IPSec in tunnel mode also provides a certain amount of traffic flow confidentiality. There are external in-line intelligent X.25 encryption products on the market for use in legacy X.25 networks.

- Transport layer (OSI layer 4) session authentication implemented with cryptographic authentication exchanges. Additionally, transport packet payload confidentiality can be implemented by encryption. SSL[9] services are of this type, using additional software functionality in the TCP stack.

Peer-to-peer key management

Key management for the in-line cryptographic architecture is most likely to be on an in-line peer-to-peer basis, although for OSI layer 3 encryption systems there may be a key distribution server.

On-line architecture for application level cryptographic services

The on-line architecture can support these application-level services:

- Confidentiality of transmitted data in the payload of application data structures. The confidentiality can apply to the entire payload or to selected fields within it.

- Integrity checking of transmitted data in the payload of application data structures. The integrity check can apply to the entire payload or to selected fields within it. The selected field option is especially useful in cases where the values of some fields vary over the lifetime of the data structure and therefore cannot be included in an integrity checksum.

- Authentication of the source of transmitted application data structures.

- Peer-to-peer application level authentication using cryptographic authentication exchanges.

- Non-repudiation of transmitted application data structures.

- Encryption of application data stored in files or databases.

- Integrity checking of application data stored in files or databases.

- User and other entity authentication services based on cryptographic authentication exchanges, such as those provided in the CAM architecture described in various parts of this book.

Sophisticated key management using master key hierarchies

The key management for the on-line cryptographic architecture can be highly sophisticated, including the storage of large numbers of keys in the data store. To keep the stored keys secure they are encrypted under a higher-level key-encrypting key, sometimes called a master key. The master keys can be stored in a physically secure, tamper-resistant hardware unit, which may also offer accelerated processing for cryptographic computations and a hardware random number generator (RNG) for key generation. This type of special hardware unit is sometimes known as a hardware security module (HSM). There are many refinements that can be incorporated into this

---

[9]SSL: Secure Sockets Layer

generic on-line architecture. It offers by far the most flexible approach to providing cryptographic services to applications.

Application types
Typical applications where this type of on-line cryptographic architecture can be used are:

- E-mail and all similar store-and-forward messaging applications;

- Interactive messaging services;

- File transfer applications;

- Financial payment systems and money transfer systems in banking applications;

- Point-of-sale and cash machine authorisation systems based on bank cards with PINs (personal identification numbers);

- Secure eCommerce, eProcurement and similar applications.

Strength of Cryptographic Mechanisms

Some broad indications of cryptographic strength
It is not the intention to provide an extensive tutorial on cryptographic algorithms, but when you come to select your architectural components (see Chapter 13) you will be confronted by vendor literature that mentions specific cryptographic algorithms and key lengths. You will need to know what it is you are being told, and you will need to have some yardstick by which to judge the claims of strength. To help you with that a summary is included in Table 12-2 that gives broad indications of relative strengths of commonly encountered algorithms.

Table 12-2: Comparison of Cryptographic Strengths of Algorithms

	Symmetric	Asymmetric	Hashing/MACs
	Bit numbers indicate key length	Bit numbers indicate modulus length	Bit numbers indicate hash value length
Weak	DES 40-bit RC4 40-bit	RSA 256-bit	
Medium	DES 56-bit CAST 64-bit	RSA 512-bit Diffie-Helman 512-bit DSA 512-bit	ANSI X9.9 MAC 32-bit
Strong	Triple DES 112-bit IDEA 128-bit RC4 128-bit	RSA 1024-bit Diffie-Helman 1024-bit DSA 1024-bit	MD5 128-bit SHA-1 160-bit
Very Strong	AES 192-bit AES 256-bit	RSA 2048-bit ECC 300-bit	SHA-256 256-bit SHA-384 384-bit SHA-512 512-bit

Algorithm strength is not the only important factor
However, you must be careful because algorithm strength is not the only indicator of the level of security. The other two major constraints that must be considered are:

- The key management scheme – does it prevent the keys from being revealed? How are the keys managed?

- Cryptographic protocols – are they robust against replay attacks, man-in-the-middle attacks, spoofing attacks, dictionary attacks, etc.?

Cryptographic design and assessment is a job for an expert

To make a proper cryptographic assessment of a secure system is a job for an expert, and the authors recommend that as soon as you move beyond the trivial purchase of packaged encryption products you should get such expert advice.

Other Cryptographic Mechanisms

Some other cryptographic techniques

The discussion here has mentioned a few of the most commonly encountered cryptographic mechanisms, but there are many more that you may encounter. Some of these are listed here:

- Zero knowledge proofs;
- Secret sharing schemes;
- Multi-party signatures;
- Dual signatures;
- Blind signatures;
- Elliptic curve cryptography;
- Quantum cryptography (see also below in the section on The Future of Cryptographic Mechanisms.

The Future of Cryptographic Mechanisms

Strength depends on the attack capabilities of the opponents

Security mechanisms of all types will evolve, but the cryptographic mechanisms deserve a special mention. The strength of cryptographic algorithms is entirely dependent upon the power available to attack them. To some extent this is governed by Moore's Law,[10] but there are two new quantum technologies appearing[11] just over the horizon that are both predicted to have a major impact on cryptography of the future.

Quantum computing may threaten public key cryptography as a useful technique

The first of these is the quantum computer. Assuming that investment in research and development and the passage of sufficient time allows a practical working quantum computer to be built, then such a device is predicted to have a dramatic effect on reducing the time taken to solve the complex mathematical problems that underpin public key cryptography. Such problems are typified by the integer factorisation problem, in which the complexity of factorising the product of two very large prime numbers grows exponentially as the size of the numbers is increased. However, the quantum computer holds the prospect of being able to search the solution space in a mere fraction of the time needed by a conventional computer. The effect of this new approach is many orders of magnitude greater than the effect of Moore's Law, which applies to traditional computing hardware. This could sweep away much of the powerful technology based upon these types of asymmetric algorithm, leaving the industry with a major problem.

Quantum cryptography may provide the new key management solution

Ironically the second of these quantum technologies offers hope of a replacement for the public key-based key management schemes that may at some date become unusable as a result of quantum computers. This second technology is quantum cryptography, and is in no way related

---

[10]An observation first made by Gordon Moore, co-founder of Intel, that the power of computer hardware doubles approximately every 18 months and is expected to continue to do so until at least 2020.
[11]At the time of writing in 2005.

to the development of quantum computers. Quantum cryptography is based upon the quantum polarisation properties of single photons of light. You can generate a photon with a given polarisation and transmit it, and a receiver can measure the polarization. This can be used to encode and transmit data bits – one bit per photon. However, in making the measurement the receiver disturbs the polarisation, and this can be detected. Thus, any eavesdropping on the photon channel is guaranteed by the laws of physics to be detectable, and there is no way for the eavesdropper to avoid this consequence.

Workable systems for quantum cryptography are close at hand

The application of quantum cryptography is seen as providing key management channels that are 100% secure – a novel concept. The raw bandwidth of a photon channel is many megabits per second, but much of this is used up in synchronisation and error correction protocols between the sender and receiver. At the time of writing this there are working laboratory quantum cryptography systems providing actual key management bandwidths of around one kilobit per second over distances exceeding 50 kilometres using both fibre optic cable and laser-through-air implementations.[12] The commercial exploitation of this technology is likely to follow in the next few years.[13]

Vulnerabilities in Security Mechanisms

All security mechanisms have potential vulnerabilities

It is important to recognise that every security mechanism potentially has vulnerabilities in its design that may not be apparent to the designers. You will constantly hear about new vulnerabilities in all sorts of tools and products on the market. You must wonder sometimes why the designers cannot just be careful and get it right. Well, the truth is, it is not that easy to achieve, and you must be prepared constantly to test for vulnerabilities in your security mechanisms through the use of professional penetration testing teams who are skilled at winkling out these weaknesses.

Two cases studies provide some insight

To provide some small insight into how vulnerabilities arise and why designers do not see them, here are two very different mechanism case studies. One is cryptographic, and other is a secure door-entry system of a type used in many data centres.

Vulnerability Case Study 1

One of the divisions of IBFS was using passwords to authenticate users in a client-server application. The user of the application entered a username and a password into a login screen on the client PC, and this was sent across the internal LAN to the server where it was verified. If the verification was successful then the session was opened.

Then the use of the application was extended to some branch offices whose connection into the head office was through a public dial-up service. There was some concern that this would expose the passwords to external opponents who could simply intercept the dial-up communications, either at the local loop to one of the buildings or at an intermediate exchange.

It was decided that to protect the passwords from being revealed, an additional routine would be called in the client software to encrypt the password before

---

[12]Mark Hillery, 'Quantum cryptography: Code-breakers confounded', *Nature* **421**, 224-225, (16 Jan 2003, News and Views

[13]Erica Klarreich, 'Quantum cryptography: Can you keep a secret', *Nature* **418**, 270-272, (18 Jul 2002), News Feature

sending it. The server could then decrypt the received password before checking it. Simple! The designers even designed a reasonable but easy-to-implement key management scheme, the detail of which is irrelevant.

So what is wrong with this design? The problem is that in order to attack the system from the outside you do not need to decrypt the password. What the server expects to receive is an encrypted password. So the opponent can listen on the line, capture the encrypted password, and replay the same encrypted password at another time so as to masquerade as the authentic user.

To make the system secure against interception and replay, the password block must have a nonce value inserted – a value that is used only once and never repeated, and which is tracked by both client and server. Such values are typically time stamps, random numbers or sequence numbers, or a combination of these value types. The password block then becomes a one-time value that cannot be re-used.

The failure is of the protocol, not the algorithm

This is not a failure of the cryptographic algorithm – it is a failure of the cryptographic protocol, and as such is the simplest example of a major problem in cryptographic system design. The error here was chosen because it is the most obvious, but there have been examples of protocol failures that were thought for a long time to have been well designed and robust. Many of those failures involve some sort of replay attack; others are often based upon a dictionary attack. Cryptographic protocol design is a subtle business and should not be undertaken by amateurs. Using homegrown protocols as in this case study is a recipe for a disaster. You are strongly advised not to do it.

Vulnerability Case Study 2

The data centre at IBFS runs on 365 by 24 basis. However, the night shift is a low-profile affair, with one single operator on duty for much of the time.

The data centre building is a high-tech design with all the latest technology to secure the perimeter. There is a portion of the building that is for general office use, and then there is the computer suite itself. The only way into the computer suite is through one of a pair of glass tubular doors that allow only one person at a time to pass through.

The authorised person uses a smart card in a reader device next to the door to open the outside of the tube, then removes the card and steps into the tube. A weight sensor on the floor determines when there is someone standing in the tube and the outer door closes. There is a 15-second delay and then the inner door opens allowing the user to walk into the computer suite. To get out of the computer suite again you need to do the same thing in reverse, using a card reader on the inside. So, it is essential to carry your card with you.

There was a rumour going around that one of the male night-shift operators was bringing his girlfriend into the suite to keep him company during the night. The data centre manager heard these rumours and thought this unlikely because of the highly secure door entry system. Even if the girl were a small person, it was simply infeasible for two people to get into the tube together.

The rumours persisted, and the manager became uneasy. She arranged for a

CCTV camera to be installed in a hidden place to monitor activity at the door. The next day she viewed the tape and was astonished.

The operator had arranged a time for his girlfriend to arrive when everyone else had left the building. He came out of the suite and went to the outer door of the building to let her in. They went together to the door to the computer suite. The operator entered normally. He then fetched a heavy box of listing paper used on the high-speed printer and put it into the tubular door. He had inserted his card before putting in the paper, and now he withdrew it again, placing it on top of the box of paper. The door operated as if a person were in there. When the outer side doors opened the girlfriend took out the box and put it on one side. She then used the card to enter.

To exit again the procedure was reversed. One of them went out, put the box of paper back into tube with the card on top. The other then removed the box and took it back to whence it came, and then exited normally.

Once again this is a protocol failure

The door mechanism operated normally and remained strong. What failed was the protocol for using the door. Vulnerabilities are often subtle, and that is why designers do not see them. However strong and well-designed you think your security mechanisms are, you should never be overconfident, and you should always get other people to try to crack them as a test. The vulnerabilities usually lie in the unplanned functionality or in the abuse of the protocol for using the mechanism.

User and Application Security

SABSA® Matrix cross-reference

Please refer to Chapter 3, Figure 3-3 and Chapter 7, Figure 7-8, the SABSA® Matrix, Physical layer, People column, where you will see a cell entitled Users, Applications and the User Interface. This also appears as a key deliverable of the physical security architecture in Chapter 7, Figure 7-10. This section describes the security mechanisms that are commonly applied to implement user security and application security. Among these mechanisms is the user password, which is an important element of the security user interface, and there is some discussion of the issues that surround the use of this mechanism.

Security mechanisms to implement application-level security services

In Chapter 11 the security services applicable to users and applications are discussed at some length. The security mechanisms by which these services are implemented are fairly straightforward. They include:

Directory Mechanisms

- Object class definitions;
- Attribute syntax definitions;
- Directory access protocols;
- Directory access control mechanisms;
- Directory user authentication mechanisms;
- Inheritance checking mechanisms.

Central Access Manager (CAM) Mechanisms

The CAM makes real-time decisions

The CAM examines every access request and processes it against pre-condition and post-condition rules stored with role objects in the directory to determine real-time access decisions to applications and systems.

Database Mechanisms

DBMS mechanisms can be used for application security

These are discussed in some detail earlier in this chapter. They provide an important toolkit for building application and user security into systems.

File System Mechanisms

File security mechanisms can provide application security

These are also discussed in some detail earlier in this chapter, with further detail in the section below, Platform Security.

Operating System Mechanisms

Discussed elsewhere under platform security

These are discussed in more detail in the following section, Platform Security.

Application Mechanisms

Mechanisms built by application developers

These can be anything that the application designers choose to incorporate into the application code. They are most likely to focus on access control mechanisms:

- Access control lists (ACLs) made up of access control entries (ACEs);
- Subject privileges built into ACEs;
- Object labels and ACEs;
- Context-based rules for access (time, location, etc.);
- Event logs and transaction logs for audit trail purposes.

User Authentication Mechanisms

Proving a user's identity

These can include:

- Usernames and passwords;
- One-time passwords produced by intelligent tokens;
- Smart cards;
- Magnetic stripe cards;
- Biometrics;
- Multi-factor authentication.

Password Management

Password management raises a number of important issues to be considered

Passwords are totally ubiquitous in information systems, and everyone is familiar with their use. However, they can be misused and abused unless there is some careful thought given to their selection and their usage. This section discusses some of the key issues regarding passwords.

- Users need to have individual passwords to ensure accountability for their actions. If they share a password as a group then this is not possible. Not only is it impossible to identify who might have misused their privileges, but innocent users in the group then fall under suspicion.

- Users need to understand the importance of not disclosing their password to anyone, since once they have done so, they are open to abuse by that other party, but they will be accountable. The usual 'good practice' advice is not to write down a password so that others can find it, and not to give a password to someone else to log on under your account.

- Users should not select a password that is easily guessed because it is the name of a family member, their car registration number or something similar.

- The password should never be identical to the username.

- Minimum password length: The longer is a password the more entropy it has and the more difficult it becomes for an opponent to mount a brute-force dictionary attack to search for the password with a password-cracking program.

- Use of characters other than pure alphabetic characters increases the entropy even further, making the password-cracking task even more difficult.

- However, be aware that with a highly parallel cracking engine, most passwords can be cracked in a finite time. They provide only a finite level of security, but the level can be maximised with increased length and use of a broad character set. (Refer to the section on time-based security in Chapter 9 for more about the time taken to mount a successful attack.)

- Enforcing password changes on a regular basis (usually around every 30 days) is part of the regular information security management culture and thought to be good practice. It is even embodied in ISO17799. However, as far as the authors are aware there is no scientific research that underpins this practice.[14] It seems to be based purely on anecdotal wisdom. Why 30 days? This is probably not good practice at all, because if you confront users with many passwords, each with different syntax rules, each associated with different usernames, and each requiring to be changed on different cycles, the potential for confusion and forgotten passwords is huge. How will the normal user deal with this? He will certainly write down the passwords in a place of easy reference because otherwise it is all too difficult to manage.[15] Once that happens, the basic rule of non-disclosure is broken[16].

---

[14]The authors would be very pleased to hear from anyone who can supply references to scientific research on password changing cycles and the relative security merits of frequency of change.

[15]For a good case study see 'Users are not the enemy: security design for human and organisational factors', M. Angela Sasse, University College, London.

[16]There is a much wider issue to consider here. Tony Sale, during his presentation at COSAC 99, claimed that not only password change but security procedures in general are a mathematical misconception. For example length and syntax rules on a password actually reduce the number of possible permutations. In particular in discussing the breaking of the Enigma code in the Second World War he claimed that capture of the German security procedure book, which mandated the frequency of change and the order of cogs, dramatically reduced the power of Enigma and contributed greatly to the Allies' ability to break it.

- A more common-sense view (but still lacking proper scientific research) is that if you have a good password with strong syntax and you are sure that it has not been disclosed, you should keep it alive for several months – perhaps a year.[17]

- You should definitely change a password immediately if you believe it has been disclosed.

- You should always change the default passwords set by vendors for delivery of systems and applications, since these are known to anyone. The abuse of default passwords is a common vulnerability.

Platform and Network Infrastructure Security

SABSA® Matrix cross-reference

Please refer to Chapter 3, Figure 3-3 and Chapter 7, Figure 7-8, the SABSA® Matrix, Physical layer, Location column, where you will see a cell entitled Platform and Network Infrastructure. This also appears as two key deliverables of the physical security architecture in Chapter 7, Figure 7-10 – one is sub-titled Physical Layout and the other Capacity Plan and Resilience Model. This section describes the most important security mechanisms that are used to provide security within the platform and network infrastructure. It also discusses aspects of the physical layout and topology of this infrastructure.

Resilience

Infrastructure should resilient and fault-tolerant

Physical network and platform infrastructure should be built in resilient configurations to incorporate a degree of fault tolerance. The amount of fault tolerance (and hence the cost of providing it) will depend upon the business requirements for resilience and continuity of operations.

The main principles of resilient design are:

- Avoidance of single points of failure by ensuring that there is always an alternative mechanism for delivering a given function or service;

- Redundancy of hard physical components such that if one fails another is available to take its place;

- Backup and restoration procedures for all soft physical components such as software and data;

- Recovery procedures worked out in advance for all foreseeable failure scenarios;

- Automated recovery and reconfiguration where possible;

- Extensive event logging, monitoring and reporting to help foresee possible failures before they occur and to help recovery by providing evidence of the nature of the failure.

---

[17]There is a mathematical calculation in Appendix C of the 'Green Book' – 'US DoD Password Management Guidelines CSC-STD-002-85' published in 1985 which suggests that, provided that the password file is not exposed to dictionary attacks and that the password attack is only by guessing and submission through the login interface, there is no significant difference in vulnerability by extending the life of a password from six months to 12 months, and furthermore, that the optimum length of a password is eight or nine random characters (depending upon number of characters in the available alphabet) and the optimum length for a passphrase is three words chosen randomly from a dictionary of 23,300 words.

In applying these principles to the design of network topologies, a number of specific approaches are commonly used:

- Multiple communications cables and channels, often with diverse physical routing;

- Separation of cable routes from buildings to avoid all the multiple cables suffering the same physical failure such as when the road is dug up;

- Alternative telephone exchanges for routing of third-party telco lines from a given site;

- Alternative telco carriers where local market conditions allow this;

- Dynamic automated re-routing and re-configuration to create a self-healing network based on a multi-path network of switches and connections;

- ISDN or dial-up fallback for leased line connections;

- Regular testing and monitoring of these various resiliency features to ensure they are operating correctly;

- Duplicate frames and frame-rooms in buildings where external telecommunications lines are terminated and connected into the infrastructure of the building;

- Physical and environmental security of communications rooms and computer rooms.

Resilient host platforms

The same principles are also applied to providing highly resilient host platform facilities for applications:

- Dual processing facilities in separate data centres, often geographically separated by several hundred kilometres;

- Fault-tolerant computer systems with special operating systems or middleware that automatically organises data mirroring or distributed processing;

- RAID[18] configurations for data storage (discussed in detail in an earlier section of this chapter).

Performance and Capacity Planning

Capacity planning and performance management are closely related to resilience

The whole issue of system performance has to do with being able to deliver both the processing power and the communications bandwidth required to handle the volumes of information to be processed and transported. Thus the entire disciplines of capacity planning and performance tuning are highly relevant to the overall provision of secure, resilient information-processing services to meet the business requirements. However, a detailed discussion on these topics is a little beyond the scope of this book.

Platform Security

Host computers run applications

Platforms are host computers. The host can be anything from a small personal computer up to a super-computer. The word host does not imply any specific size or type of computer; merely that it is capable of hosting some application software.

A platform is hardware plus operating system

A platform is generally thought of as a combination of the underlying hardware together with the operating system. Hence people talk about a UNIX platform or a Windows 2K platform. Platform

---

[18]RAID: redundant arrays of inexpensive disks

security is therefore focused upon how the operating system should be configured and operated to meet the various business requirements for security. Here some of the main functions and mechanisms available for managing platform security are summarised.

DAC file security is a standard approach

The generic file-security mechanisms and process-security mechanisms that one finds in most commercial operating systems are based on a discretionary access control (DAC) policy and include:

- Each real user associated with a user account to control access by that user;

- Unique username and identifier[19] for each user account;

- Groups of users with a group name and group identifiers;

- Password for each user account or group account, with password aging, minimum password length, account lock-out after successive failed logins, and a variety of related mechanisms depending on the precise operating system;

- A super-user[20] account that has access to everything and controls the system;

- Mapping of physical devices (such as disks and printers) onto logical file structures to control access to these devices;

- Files and directories created by a user being owned by that user who can at his or her discretion grant access privileges to other users;

- Differentiated access privileges including such rights as: read data, write data, create file, delete file, execute program and modify privileges;

- A home directory for each user under which to create and store other directories and files;

- A login program or script to control the view of the system that is granted to the user;

- A security kernel to enforce process security based on the privilege granted to a process. A separate process control block in main memory represents each individual process. Within that process control block is a field containing the user identifier (UID[21]) of the owner of the process – the user who runs the program. The privileges associated with that UID are used to control the actions of the process as it executes.

- An ability for some programs to set the user identifier to a higher privilege value than that of the person who runs the program so as to grant higher privileged access under the careful control of an approved program[22];

- Event logs at various levels capture event data for investigations and forensic analysis;

- One-way encrypted password files to prevent easy decryption of stored passwords;

- Password files stored in a super-user-privileged directory to minimise the risk of these files being stolen.

---

[19]Such as the 'UID' in UNIX and the 'SID' in Windows

[20]In UNIX the root' account, in Windows the administrator account

[21]The term UID is from UNIX. Other operating systems have a similar identifier that is conceptually the same as the UID.

[22]In UNIX this is the SUID facility. It can be seen both as a security-strength and as a security-weakness, depending upon how it is used.

Some of the major security issues in these types of operating system are as follows:

- The super-user is all-powerful and can do anything to any file in any directory. If an opponent can gain super-user privilege there is no limit to the damage that he can inflict.

- Carelessly coded programs that allow the user identifier to be set to a higher privilege level than that of the process owner are one of the ways in which an opponent can gain higher privileges. Thus if it is possible to elevate the privilege level and then break out of the constraints of the program, the opponent has gained great advantage.

- Trojan horse attacks are a major source of threat. If an opponent can arrange for a Trojan version of a highly privileged system utility to be run (possibly with super-user privilege), then the opponent can take control of the system.[23]

- Writeable directories are a major vulnerability, since they allow files to be added, renamed or removed from the directory, whatever the permissions on the file itself.

In order to run a secure production environment for business applications, these are some of the good practice guidelines for managing the platform:

- There should be a written security policy supported by detailed standards aimed at those with operational responsibility for maintaining the operational security of the platform.

- Production platforms must be segregated from development platforms and test platforms.

- File and directory permissions should be carefully designed as part of the application to meet the business requirements.

- There should be stringent change control on all executable files.

- There should be regular scanning to detect changes in any authorised executables and to detect the unauthorised installation of any other executables.

- There should be strict control over maintenance procedures, for both hardware and software, with close independent supervision.

- All non-production executable software should be removed from the production platform. Especially there should be no editors, code compilers, linkers or other software development tools stored on the platform. If these are needed for emergency maintenance they must be loaded temporarily under strict supervision and completely removed afterwards.

- There should be a strict process for accepting and releasing new versions of production software.

- All default system accounts should either be removed completely or at the very least have their passwords changed to strong values that are kept secret.

- The super-user account ***must not*** be used for routine operations.

This last statement is highly controversial and will upset many system managers who regard the platform as their own private territory. The approach to handling system operations should be as follows:

---

[23]A classical example is described in *The Cuckoo's Egg*, Clifford Stoll, Pan Books, ISBN 0-330-31742-3.

- All routine operations tasks should be fully analysed to define what accesses are required to fulfil the job.

- Captive scripts or programs should then be constructed that run with super-user privilege where needed, without granting full super-user status to the person running the utility.

- Every single routine operations task should be subjected to this treatment.

- The platform can then be managed for day-to-day operations without the super-user account ever being required.

- The super-user account should be protected by a secret password that is written down and locked in a safe under the control of a senior manager who does not personally have any hands-on computer operations duties.

- If an emergency arises that can only be handled by releasing the super-user password, then the senior manager will make that decision.

- If so-called emergencies are happening on a regular routine basis, then the analysis of routine operations tasks needs to be reworked and new captive utilities added to cover these recurring events.

- Once the super-user account has been used, the password must be changed and the new one stored in the safe.

- Password setting should be the responsibility of a security administration team that has no responsibility for computer operations.

Super-user access is not the way to run professional operations

In the opinion of the authors, any production shop that runs routinely with computer operators sharing the super-user password to operate the platforms by issuing raw command-line syntax is a disaster waiting to happen. However, this can be seen in practice in a number of computer centres!

Hardware Security

Lack of security at the physical hardware level has been a major issue since the invention of electronic computers

A major problem that has dogged computer security since the first computers were developed has been how to provide security at the physical hardware level. Whatever logical control systems have been built in software, if you cannot control the hardware, you cannot control the software execution environment, and hence it is always possible for unauthorised software to be loaded and executed, taking overall control of the machine and subverting much of the security provided through other authorised software. The successful exploitation by computer viruses, Trojan horses and hacking is a direct result of this problem.

Traditional physical security has been through secure physical enclosure of the site, or by using tamper-resistant modules

There are two ways in which a certain amount of hardware security has been achieved in the past:

- By physically surrounding the entire computing platform and its peripherals in a secure building – known as a computer centre or a data centre. Physical access to the building and to rooms within the building is controlled, with only trusted, authorised personnel being allowed access so as to operate the computer equipment. Rigorous procedures are enforced to control the release of software into this environment. This is the traditional model for providing secure computing on mainframe systems. On a smaller scale this approach is sometimes implemented as a computer room within an ordinary office building.

- By building tamper-resistant[24] computing equipment, in which the physical boxes of the computers are protected from unauthorised use. This approach has especially been used to provide secure storage and processing for cryptographic keys used for authentication, authorisation, integrity protection and non-repudiation – both secret (symmetric) keys and private (asymmetric) keys. Tamper-resistant techniques are many and various, with different levels of resistance being available[25]. Some levels of tamper-resistance are specified in FIPS[26] publications[27], and others that exceed these standards are available from highly specialised vendors of cryptographic equipment.

These approaches suffer from limitations

Whilst these methods work, they have severe limitations:

- The use of a tamper-resistant module (TRM) for providing the traditional host security module (HSM) architecture still requires the application software and the main host platform to be surrounded by a physically secure computer suite, otherwise the application software can be compromised, and whatever authorisation decision is taken inside the secure TRM, once that decision is exported back to the application, it can be subverted. The TRM is only a slave to the application and has no control over the security of the application itself. Figure 12-12 shows the HSM architecture.

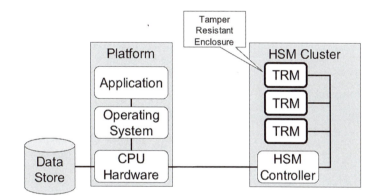

Figure 12-12: Traditional HSM Architecture Using TRMs

- The secure computing suite is inappropriate when the platform to be secured is a personal computing device – a desktop or laptop PC or a PDA. Thus the TRM approach has little to offer in a personal computing environment. The use of smart cards on personal computers is architecturally the same as the use of HSMs on mainframes, as smart cards (like the HSM) provide secure storage and some secure processing, but they suffer the same limitation – if you cannot trust the application, then there are numerous malicious attacks that can succeed.

---

[24]Some people talk about 'tamper-proof' equipment, but this is a strong claim indeed – almost any type of defence has some vulnerability to a more sophisticated attack than was envisaged by the defenders. 'Tamper-resistant' is a much more realistic term.

[25]Andrew J Clark, 1996, 'Tamper Resistance and Cryptovariable Protection', available at www.primarykey. co.uk/Andy/Papers/tamper01.pdf

[26]FIPS: Federal Information Processing Standard

[27]FIPS PUB 140-1 and FIPS PUB 140-2, 'Security Requirements for Cryptographic Modules'.

New secure hardware architectures are needed

The way to solve these problems in the personal computing environment is to develop new hardware architectures that incorporate inexpensive physical security at the chip level.

Intel has announced its LaGrande Architecture for secure hardware

The Trusted Computing Group[28] (TCG) is an industry standards body that promotes open industry standards for trusted computing hardware building blocks and software interfaces across multiple platforms. One of the leading players in the TCG is Intel. At the time of writing, Intel has announced[29] its LaGrande Architecture. This is likely to make a huge step forward in the development of secure commercial client computing platforms. The LaGrande Architecture is aimed at developing secure client hardware platforms, where a client is defined as any computing platform to which users have direct access and which can initiate communications with other platforms.

Intel's LaGrande is aimed at beating malicious software attacks

LaGrande is designed to counter the group of threats characterised by malicious software attacks of all kinds. Malicious software can:

- Read memory and expose secret information held there;

- Change memory and alter the values of data or the functionality of software code;

- Manipulate input or output;

- Change requests for information from other devices.

Design principles for LaGrande

The design principles of LaGrande are:

- Protected execution of trusted code;

- Attestation – proving the trustworthiness of the hardware platform and its current configuration;

- Sealed storage of data and code;

- Trusted communication channels and paths for input and output through keyboards, graphics displays and other peripherals.

A new generation of hardware architectures

It is beyond the scope of this book to provide a detailed description of a specific vendor's products, but it is clear that this initiative from Intel is the first of a new generation of hardware architectures that will soon be adopted by hardware developers, platform vendors, OEMs, software vendors and ICT infrastructure architects.

Informing the user about a trusted path remains an intractable problem

There still remains one issue that is difficult to resolve. The concept of a trusted path requires the cooperation of the user. The user must be informed when the trusted path is in place and must modify his behaviour accordingly – 'only perform these sensitive input/output tasks when you know that there is a trusted path'. How is the user to be informed of this trusted path status? Perhaps through some symbol on the screen, as in the case of the padlock that indicates the presence of a secure HTTP session over SSL; or perhaps by an illuminated LED on the peripheral device. Can this indicator be spoofed by unauthorised software? Of course it can! Hmmm.

---

[28]Refer to Chapter 12 under the section Security Standards for more information about the TCG. See also www.trustedcomputinggroup.org

[29]Intel Developer Forum, September 2003, David Grawrock, Chief Security Architect, Intel. See ftp:// download.intel.com/technology/security/downloads.scms18-ltarch.pdf

Network Topology

Carrying forward the example from the previous chapter

In Chapter 11 under the heading of Network Domains the logical architecture of networks is discussed. A specific example set of business requirements for a large corporate organisation is described and the logical network domain model for this set of requirements is shown in Figure 11-13. You may now wish to refer back to that section the refresh your recollections of it, since that same example is now used again to convert the logical domain model into a physical network topology model.

Physical network topology

Figure 12-13 shows the physical topology for the example. It comprises real boxes – routers, firewalls, server platforms, client platforms, etc., and real network connections, both LAN and WAN. This is quite a different diagram from that in Figure 11-13, and yet it is the physical representation of the logical model that was in the earlier diagram. What is clear is the mapping between the two. Once you have accurately captured the logical domains it is relatively straightforward to design the physical implementation of them. However, it is difficult to miss out the logical domain step and still get the physical topology correct.

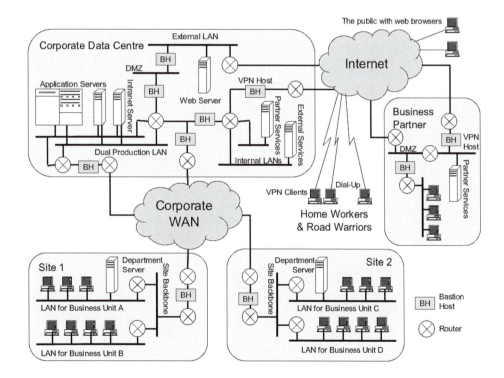

Figure 12-13: Physical Network Topology Diagram

Main features

The main features to look for are as follows:

- The production domain is contained behind internal firewalls in the data centre. The firewall architecture comprises a combination of dual-homed bastion hosts and screening routers.

- The public Internet access to the web services is via a screening router that leads only to the external LAN on which the web server is positioned. This screened sub-net is then double-buffered from the production domain by two bastion hosts, separated by a DMZ.[30]

- Internal firewalls on all corporate WAN connections isolate this domain from all other domains.

- The VPN host (another dual-homed bastion host) gives a second double-buffered route to the Internet and supports traffic from home workers and road warriors and from the business partners – this traffic forms the logical extranet services.

- VPN clients are used for home workers and road warriors, to construct the physical implementation of the logical extranet.

- A VPN host is used at each business partner, again to construct the extranet connection to those domains. Note that this VPN host is part of the deployment of the main organisation and implements the main organisation VPN security policy, whereas the secondary bastion host shown in the business partner site is owned entirely by the business partner, enforcing their security policy and protecting them from attack by any party, including the main organisation. The other router connecting the business partner DMZ directly to the Internet also belongs to the business partner and is not involved in handling traffic to or from the main organisation.

- The partner services and external services servers are on separate screened sub-nets well away from the main production domain.

- No one has direct access to the main application servers in the data centre except for the data centre operations staff. All user access is via internal firewalls across the corporate WAN, and all extranet access is via intermediate servers – never directly to the applications themselves.

- The partner services communications run at application level between the partner services server in the data centre and a remote partner services server installed at each business partner site.

Directory Topology

Physical directory topology

In Chapter 11 the logical architecture of a directory service is discussed. Here the physical implementation of that service is considered. The key issues to be addressed in the physical topology are:

- Resilience;

- Service availability;

- Performance, including response time;

---

[30]DMZ – demilitarised zone – on which no services are deployed. This double-buffering technique is adopted here because of the high level of threat from the public Internet. For a more detailed description of this double buffering approach, refer to Siyan, K. and Hare, C., 1995, *Internet Firewalls and Network Security*, published New Riders Publishing, ISBN 1-56205-437-6 (pp 292-3).

- Balance between enquiries and updates;
- Replication strategy.

Figure 12-14 shows a diagrammatic representation of a typical directory physical topology.

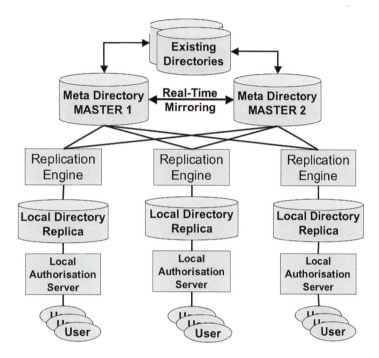

Figure 12-14: Directory – Physical Topology

Resilient real-time mirrored masters

For resilience purposes the architects have chosen in this case to maintain two separate copies of the master directory, with real-time mirroring of updates between the two masters. This means that if one of the master directory servers goes off-line and cannot be reached, or even worse, gets destroyed, the other one will have a complete copy of the directory for continued operations. An even greater degree of resilience could be achieved by having three separate master copies.

Geographical separation

To avoid the duplicated masters suffering the same destructive event, these are maintained on separate sites, probably in different geographical locations separated by hundreds of kilometres. For an international organisation it would be normal practice to site these servers on different continents. So, Master 1 might be in London and Master 2 in New York. For the triple-resilient model Master 3 might be in Singapore, Hong Kong or Sydney.

Traffic management is an issue

If every user making an enquiry were to make direct access to these masters, even given multiple masters, then there is a potential hazard of traffic congestion. The bandwidth needed to service all directory enquiries directly from the masters would be prohibitively expensive, with a great risk of overload if any of the bandwidth were lost even temporarily. There is also the likelihood that the response time experienced by each user would be unacceptably long, especially at times of peak loading.

Replica slaves provide the solution here

A much better solution is to provide local slave servers carrying replicas of the masters and for user enquiries to be handled locally. This cuts down on total long-distance traffic, thus saving costs, and creates a much more resilient model where it is easier to carry out realistic capacity planning and to provide a much more resilient service. It also provides a much shorter return route for each client enquiry, thus minimising the response time. The replication itself is handled by a series of replication engines as shown in Figure 12-14.

Frequency of replication

This approach does however raise the question of the replication strategy – how frequently should updates to the masters be replicated to the local copies? There is a middle path to be found which balances traffic volumes and costs against service levels related to the up-to-date condition of the local directory server.

Managing consistency and convergence

Immediately following an update from a master, a replica server can be said to be consistent and convergent with the masters. As time passes and updates are made to the masters – but not yet replicated out to the slave servers, then the replicas become inconsistent and divergent.

Replication and currency of information

One of the factors to consider might be the potential liability incurred by replica slave directories holding out-of-date credentials, such as revoked public key certificates. You must make some trade-off decisions here based upon business requirements and the type of data held in the directory.

Dual local connections

To improve resilience even further, users may be offered local directory service from more than one slave replica, such that if one is unavailable the other can handle the enquiries. However, your capacity planning must take into account potential peak loads when certain replicas are unavailable.

Traffic patterns and convergence requirements influence your choice of physical architecture

One thing that is implicit in this master-slave topology is that directory updates can be made only to one of the mirrored masters. The distributed community of slave replicas is to handle directory queries only – not updates. If you have a directory where frequent updates are required from widely distributed directory clients then you will need a different topology. Similarly if divergence is a major business issue for you, another topology might work better. However, this book is not primarily about directory architecture, and so the example of physical topology is confined to this one case.[31]

Close integration of the directory and the CAM is a feature of physical implementation

One last feature of Figure 12-14 is the inclusion of local authorisation servers. In the overall architectural infrastructure model that has been developed incrementally throughout this book the use of role-based access control built around a central access manager (CAM) has featured prominently. This single centralised logical service is similar to and closely associated with the directory service. It is therefore essential that you reflect the physical topology of the CAM in your overall directory design, adopting a distributed architecture for this specialised infrastructure management application. Wherever there is a slave replica for the directory, there should also be a distributed slave authorisation server, which uses as its database the directory itself.

Control Structure Execution

SABSA® Matrix cross-reference

Please refer to Chapter 3, Figure 3-3 and Chapter 7, Figure 7-8, the SABSA® Matrix, Physical layer, Time column, where you will see a cell entitled Control Structure Execution. This also appears as

---

[31]For more detailed reading on the physical architecture of directories you are recommended to *Understanding and Deploying LDAP Directory Services*, Timothy A. Howes, Mark C. Smith and Gordon S. Good, Macmillan Network Architecture and Development Series, 1999, ISBN 1-57870-070-1, Chapter 9, 'Topology Design' and Chapter 10, 'Replication Design'.

a key deliverable of the physical security architecture in Chapter 7, Figure 7-10. This section expands on the meaning of this idea.

Mechanisms for implementing control points in the flow of activities and events

In Chapter 11 the security processing cycle is discussed. This is the logical flow of processes that manage the various lifetimes and deadlines that were identified at the conceptual architecture level in Chapter 10. Now in this chapter you need to look briefly at the security mechanisms by which you can implement the series of control points in those processes so as to enforce the security-related time-constraints and sequence constraints.

These mechanisms are relatively simple. They include such things as:

- Date and time fields embedded in renewable data structures such as certificates. The certificate cannot be used once its expiry date has been passed, because every potential recipient checks this date as a routine control point in the acceptance process.

- Date and time fields in configuration files that tell you when a control event needs to be executed, with a regular lookup function to compare the current date and time with the event threshold. As an example, you may have a threshold set to update your virus-scanning package every few days[32], and the configuration file holds the next date and time when this event is due.

- Automated timers that are set running at the opening of a period that has a maximum lifetime. This could be a login session lifetime of several hours, or an inactivity timeout of several minutes, or a protocol timeout of several seconds. Once the timer expires an interrupt is generated that triggers the execution of a control point and terminates the wait state.

To Summarise: Physical Security Architecture

Business data is managed by means of a number of file management, database management and directory management systems, all of which have many mechanisms built into them that can be applied for implementing security.

Physical data storage systems can be designed to ensure that data is not lost during a physical failure of an individual data storage device.

Security rules, practices and procedures, integrated with the application of various security mechanisms, are used as the physical implementation of logical security policies.

Security mechanisms in general can be mapped onto the set of logical security services developed at the logical security architecture layer. The available types of security mechanism vary widely.

It is almost impossible to create a security mechanism that does not have some form of vulnerability, and often these vulnerabilities are difficult to predict until an opponent finds a means to exploit them.

Cryptographic mechanisms are applied to provide high levels of assurance of confidentiality, authenticity, integrity and non-repudiation. These mechanisms cover encryption and authentication, using both symmetric and asymmetric crypto-systems. They also require cryptographic key management mechanisms and physical hardware security mechanisms to protect cryptographic keys in storage and in use.

---

[32]Expert opinion varies on exactly how many days, but in a private e-mail communication on 14 May 2003, Niels Bjergstrom, Editor of Information Security Bulletin and an expert in the field of malicious software, suggested that every one or two days is currently the appropriate update threshold.

Security mechanisms for protecting user privileges and the applications that they use are mainly focused around user authentication and access control. The user password is an important and ubiquitous security mechanism in this context but has many issues that need to be considered carefully. Tokens and biometrics can be used to strengthen user authentication procedures.

The security mechanisms applied in the ICT infrastructure (platforms and networks) include those deployed to manage resilience, capacity and performance. They also include the entire range of possibilities for physical layout design and topology.

The embedded security mechanisms within operating systems are be used to control access to platforms of all types, but they tend to be impotent against the threat posed by malicious software.

Physical protection from interference with software running on a computing platform (such as the unauthorised installation of malicious software) is achieved through physical security of sites, building and rooms, physical access control for authorised personnel, robust procedures for software installation and release, and tamper-resistant equipment for specialised applications.

In the future it is likely that there will be a significant shift towards the use of tamper resistance at the chip level, allowing physically secure hardware platforms to be deployed for personal use, including PCs, PDAs and digital telephones. This will bring about a major change in the ability to defend against malicious software threats.

Finally, the physical control of time dependency and sequencing is achieved through specialised time-sensitive security mechanisms.

Chapter 13: Component Security Architecture

The component security architecture is the tradesman's view of life – the specialised tools and product components of your enterprise security architecture. This chapter looks at a selection of these components but stops short of discussing any specific brand or vendor. This is because (1) it is not appropriate to comment on one versus another here and (2) the marketplace changes so rapidly that the authors have focused on writing as timelessly as possible by sticking to generic principles. To find specific tools and products you must do your own research. As before, the chapter structure follows the cells in the Security Architecture Matrix at this layer, although at this level there is little to say on most of the cells.

In this chapter you will learn about:

- How standards are needed to achieve consistency and inter-operability between security architecture components;

- The role of ASN.1 and XML as fundamental syntax standards on which many other standards are built;

- The major international, national and industry sector standards-making bodies and their main contributions in providing security-related standards;

- The most commonly used components in terms of security products and tools, together with a brief overview of their main functional features;

- Functional security standards based upon XML, including web services comprising various modular building blocks and protocols;

- The positioning of security protocols within the hierarchical protocol stack.

Detailed Data Structures

SABSA® Matrix cross-reference   Please refer to Chapter 3, Figure 3-3 and Chapter 7, Figure 7-8, the SABSA® Matrix, Component layer, Assets column, where you will see a cell entitled Detailed Data Structures. In Chapter 7, Figure 7-11 you will also see a deliverable entitled Detailed Security Data Structures. This section discusses the basic syntax standards that are used to create standardised data structures for the security-related protocols that are used to exchange this data.

Inter-Operability

Smooth integration requires compatible interfaces

At the component layer of any architecture it is essential that the various components selected from different vendors should be capable of being plugged together to build integrated structures. This means that they must have compatible interfaces – otherwise systems integration becomes very difficult.

International and de facto standards help to provide the compatible interfaces

The best way to achieve integration of individual components is to select components that have compatible interfaces – usually internationally standardised interfaces or de facto industry standardised interfaces to support ease of integration and inter-operability. This quality should be one (amongst others) that guides your search for suitable tools and products.

Syntax rules for exchanged data structures is an important area for standardisation

One specific area of standardisation is in the data structures that your components exchange. If they do not agree precisely on syntax rules and protocols then they will not communicate successfully. This is where you need to look for compliance with recognised standards, whether or not they are formal.

Abstract Syntax Notation (ASN.1)

ASN.1 is used to build protocols

One important international standard is abstract syntax notation number one (ASN.1). ASN.1 is described in ISO/IEC 8824. It is a strongly typed language especially designed for specifying application-layer protocol data units for communications protocols of all sorts. In the context of security it is used for defining data structures in security-related protocols, such as authentication exchange data structures, digital signatures, seals and digital certificates.

There are built-in types

The language has a number of built-in types that act as initial building blocks. These include the simple types: BIT STRING, BOOLEAN, CHARACTER STRING, ENUMMERATED, INTEGER, OCTET STRING, NULL and REAL.

Standard types for time values

Other built-in types include UTCTime – Co-ordinated Universal Time (GMT[1]) and GeneralizedTime, which is a local date and time including a difference from GMT.

Different types of character string

The CHARACTER STRING type also has various in-built classes defined, including GraphicString, IA5String[2], NumericString, PrintableString, TeletexString, VideotexString and VisibleString.

Structured types

There are structured types: SEQUENCE, SET and CHOICE which can be used to construct new types by combining the simple types. The following example shows how these are used to construct protocols:

ClientServerProtocol ::= CHOICE

      {

           clientRequest   [0]   ClientRequest

           serverResponse   [1]   ServerResponse

      }

Example protocol

This protocol is a structured type that has two possible data units. The first is a request from client to server. It is referenced by the identifier clientRequest and is of the type ClientRequest. The second is a response from server to client, referenced by the identifier serverResponse and of the type ServerResponse. Each of these two types now gets defined in the next level of detail.

---

[1]GMT: Greenwich meantime at longitude 0 degrees

[2]IA5: international alphabet number 5 – a specific set of characters

ClientRequest ::= SEQUENCE

{

    reqRefNumber   [0]   INTEGER

    clientName   [1]   IA5String

    reqTime   [2]   UTCTime

    clientPayload   [3]   ClientPayload

}

ServerResponse ::= SEQUENCE

{

    respRefNumber   [0]   INTEGER

    reqRefNumber   [1]   INTEGER

    serverName   [2]   IA5String[3]

    respTime   [3]   UTCTime

    serverPayload   [4]   ServerPayload

}

Hierarchical type definitions   This leaves two more types, ClientPayload and ServerPayload to be defined at the next level of detail, and so on until everything has been resolved down to simple built-in types or OBJECT IDENTIFIERS (see below).

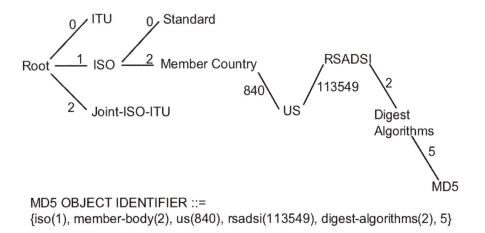

MD5 OBJECT IDENTIFIER ::=
{iso(1), member-body(2), us(840), rsadsi(113549), digest-algorithms(2), 5}

Figure 13-1: The ASN.1 OBJECT IDENTIFIER for the MD5 Algorithm

---

[3]See Footnote 2.

Object identifiers for registered universal objects

The OBJECT IDENTIFIER provides an external reference to an ASN.1 object that has been described and registered by one of a number of international authorities. The reference itself appears as a series of integer numbers, which are the node numbers on a hierarchical tree structure beginning at the root. Thus the OBJECT IDENTIFIER for the MD5[4] algorithm is {1,2,840,113549,2,5}. Figure 13-1 shows how this string is constructed from the tree.

Binary encoding rules for ASN.1

Also included in the ASN.1 standards are the encoding rules, which can be the basic Encoding Rules (BER) or the Distinguished Encoding Rules (DER). The DER definition represents a later improvement (in 1993) that guarantees a unique encoding of every object. Actual encoding is achieved through the use of special compilers.

Extensible Markup Language (XML)

XML is extremely flexible and can be used to create any type of 'document'

XML is a meta-language that allows you to create specialised application-level languages for specialised client-server interactions. 'Documents' are created using these specialised languages. In this context 'document' refers to any structured information and so can describe any information that needs to be exchanged for eBusiness purposes. Thus, in addition to text, a document may contain graphics, mathematical equations, structured numerical information such as tables and charts, executable code, interface descriptions, object meta-data (such as MPEG metadata) and much more.

XML is the new generation of what used to be EDI

In effect XML has become the new generation mechanism for what was originally called electronic data interchange (EDI). However, XML is many times more powerful than the old EDI syntax because of its ultimate flexibility. Also, whereas originally EDI was focused around simple point-to-point file transfers, XML is supported by the more powerful web technologies.

XML supports any type of electronic business and thus requires in-built security mechanisms

The significance of XML from a security perspective is that over the coming years you will see an explosion of the application of XML and its derivatives to all types of electronic business activity. Thus where those activities require protection of confidentiality, integrity, authenticity, non-repudiation, authorisation, accountability and many other similar attributes, mechanisms are needed within XML to deliver that protection.

XML security standards are already available

There are already many such specific mechanisms being developed within the XML standards, beginning with simple building blocks such as XML Encryption and XML Signature. These and others are described in more detail in later sections of this chapter.

Relationship between ASN.1 and XML

XML has a much greater range of application than ASN.1

ASN.1 and XML are neither in conflict nor in competition. They do different jobs in different ways. ASN.1 was developed as a tool for specifying data communications protocols in a traditional sense, whereas XML is intended for use in encoding document exchanges. The difference is subtle, because an XML document exchange is in fact an elaborate data communications protocol.

XML is less efficient than ASN.1, but with bandwidth abundance this is unimportant

However, there is another very clear difference, in that ASN.1 produces binary encoded data, whereas XML produces text-encoded data. There is an ongoing debate as to whether XML should be used because it is much less efficient than binary encoding, taking up greater bandwidth. However, the bandwidth revolution in which huge bandwidths have become available at low cost has rather taken away the anxiety about efficiency. It is rather like the situation where the need to fit all computer software into 512KB of memory disappeared once the price of computer memory

---

[4]MD5: message digest algorithm number 5 – a specific hashing algorithm from RSA Security Inc.

and CPU power fell to minimal levels. Once that happened the size and efficiency of the object code became a non-issue.

Where efficiency is important, ASN.1 still has a role

Where efficiency is more of an issue because the communications protocol is implemented in a real-time embedded system such as a router, ASN.1 has an important role. Where the interaction is truly in the business applications layer, XML provides much greater flexibility, the bandwidth is available to support it, and performance is not so critical.

ASN.1 structures are found embedded in XML documents

Additionally, because XML can embed any types of data, including binary data objects, you will also see ASN.1 data structures inside XML documents. A particularly relevant example is the X.509 digital certificate, which is specified in ASN.1 and binary-encoded but which will often be sent as part of an XML document.

Standard Security Data Structures

Examples of security-related data structures

There are many security-related data structures that are already or will be in the future standardised. These types of structure include:

- Digital signatures;

- Digital certificates;

- Other cryptographic syntax standards;

- Certificate management protocols;

- Time protocols;

- Authentication exchanges;

- Authorisation certificates and other credentials documents;

- Security policy documents with standardised structures in XML.

XML offers the possibility of far more sophisticated data structures

The last bullet point is especially interesting, because it shows where XML technology is going. The possibility now exists to describe large complex documents in standardised formats that can be created and interpreted by automated processes. This will support even greater automation of high-level security management processes that would have been impossible with previous technologies.

Security Standards

SABSA® Matrix cross-reference

Please refer to Chapter 3, Figure 3-3 and Chapter 7, Figure 7-8, the SABSA® Matrix, Component layer, Motivation column, where you will see a cell entitled Security Standards. In Chapter 7, Figure 7-11 you will also see a deliverable entitled Security Standards. This section summarises the main standards-making bodies that operate in the area of information security and also provides an overview of the focus of each body. Web site addresses are provided to facilitate your own further research on up-to-date standards.

Standardisation allows components to be integrated into systems

If every component were built to a unique interface specification, nothing would ever work together. So, standards are needed to ensure that that many different components can be integrated to form a larger system. Having agreed that a standard should make every thing the same, you then find that there are so many standards from which you can choose!

There are many different standards from many standards bodies

There are literally hundreds and hundreds (possibly thousands by the time you read this) of internationally recognised standards for various aspects of security. In this chapter the various standards-making bodies and types of standards that they address[5] are summarised. There is no attempt to include a comprehensive list of all the standards because (1) such lists are not very interesting and (2) they go out of date very quickly as new standards are published. To find out the most recent standards you are advised to look up the current activities under each of the standards bodies listed.

International Organisation for Standards (ISO)

ISO is worldwide

The International Organisation for Standardisation (ISO) is a worldwide federation of national standards bodies from more than 140 countries, one from each country.

Supporting world business

ISO is a non-governmental organisation established in 1947. The mission of ISO is to promote the development of standardisation and related activities in the world with a view to facilitating the international exchange of goods and services, and to developing cooperation in the spheres of intellectual, scientific, technological and economic activity.

ISO has important security standards

ISO's work results in international agreements that are published as international standards. There are many ISO standards that address information security and the security of information systems and networks, some of which are referred to at various points throughout this book.

See www.iso.org for more details.

International Electrotechnical Commission (IEC)

Bringing national and international standards into alignment

The International Electrotechnical Commission (IEC) is the leading global organisation that prepares and publishes international standards for all electrical, electronic and related technologies. These serve as a basis for national standardisation and as references when drafting international tenders and contracts.

In the area of electrotechnical standards

Through its members the IEC promotes international co-operation on all questions of electrotechnical standardisation and related matters, such as the assessment of conformity to standards, in the fields of electricity, electronics and related technologies.

Defining 'electrotechnical'

The IEC charter embraces all electrotechnologies including electronics, magnetics and electromagnetics, electroacoustics, multimedia, telecommunication, and energy production and distribution, as well as associated general disciplines such as terminology and symbols, electromagnetic compatibility, measurement and performance, dependability, design and development, safety and the environment.

Overlap with ISO

Where the activities of the IEC and ISO overlap, standards are published jointly. Thus many of the standards in the area of information and communications technology are joint ISO/IEC standards, and this includes the security-related standards.

See www.iec.ch for more details.

---

[5]Many of the summaries below are borrowed directly from the text published by the bodies themselves. The authors feel that the organisations' descriptions of themselves are probably the most useful to you. A top-level web site address is also included for each so that you can pursue your own research into the detail of the standards from each body.

Internet Engineering Task Force (IETF)

Co-ordinates working groups
for Internet standards

The Internet Engineering Task Force is a large open international community of network designers, operators, vendors, and researchers concerned with the evolution of the Internet architecture and the smooth operation of the Internet. It is open to any interested individual. The actual technical work of the IETF is done in its working groups, which are organised by topic into several areas (e.g., routing, transport, security). Much of the work is handled via mailing lists. The IETF holds meetings three times per year.

Much activity on security
standards

The IETF working groups are grouped into areas, and managed by area directors (ADs). The ADs are members of the Internet Engineering Steering Group (IESG). At the time of writing the IETF has 19 working groups in the security area, including work programs on PKIX, SMIME, IPSec, TLS and others.

Organisational hierarchy

The Internet Architecture Board (IAB) provides architectural oversight. The IAB also adjudicates appeals when someone complains that the IESG has failed. The IAB and the IESG are both chartered by the Internet Society (ISOC) for these purposes. The general area director also serves as the chair of the IESG and of the IETF and is an ex-officio member of the IAB.

An RFC is an Internet
standard

Each distinct version of an Internet standards-related specification is published as part of the Request for Comments (RFC) document series. This archival series is the official publication channel for Internet standards documents and other publications of the IESG, IAB, and Internet community. The current index of RFCs and downloadable copies of individual RFCs are to be found on the IETF web site, together with details of ongoing work programs.

See www.ietf.org for more details.

Common Criteria

International harmonisation
of security product
evaluation

The Common Criteria standard represents the outcome of a series of efforts to develop criteria for evaluation of IT security that are broadly useful within the international community. In the early 1980s the Trusted Computer System Evaluation Criteria (TCSEC – 'Orange Book') was developed in the United States. In the succeeding decade, various countries began initiatives to develop evaluation criteria that built upon the concepts of the TCSEC but were more flexible and adaptable to the evolving nature of IT in general.

Brings the North American
and European evaluation
criteria together

In Europe, the Information Technology Security Evaluation Criteria (ITSEC) version 1.2 was published in 1991 by the European Commission. This was the result of joint development by the nations of France, Germany, the Netherlands and the United Kingdom. In Canada, the Canadian Trusted Computer Product Evaluation Criteria (CTCPEC) version 3.0 was published in early 1993 as a combination of the ITSEC and TCSEC approaches. In the United States, the draft Federal Criteria for Information Technology Security (FC) version 1.0 was also published in early 1993, as a second approach to combining North American and European concepts for evaluation criteria.

Addressing a global market
place

Work had begun in 1990 in the International Organisation for Standardisation (ISO) to develop a set of international standard evaluation criteria for general use. The new criteria were to be responsive to the need for mutual recognition of standardised security evaluation results in a global IT market.

The Common Criteria version 1.0 was published in 1996, followed in 1998 by version 2.0.

See www.commoncriteria.org for more details.

American National Standards Institute (ANSI)

The US National standards body

The American National Standards Institute (ANSI) is a private, non-profit organisation that administers and coordinates the US voluntary standardisation and conformity assessment system. The institute's mission is to enhance both the global competitiveness of US business and the US quality of life by promoting and facilitating voluntary consensus standards and conformity assessment systems, and safeguarding their integrity.

Relevant standards series

ANSI has been active in standardising many areas of information security. The relevant standards series are:

* X3 Information Processing Systems: This includes many security-related standards, especially those that standardise cryptographic algorithms and their modes of use.

* X9 Financial Services: In this area ANSI has long been a world leader in the development of standards for security of financial transactions and messaging.

See www.ansi.org for more details.

British Standards Institute (BSI)

The UK national standards body

The BSI is the national standards body for the United Kingdom. The most important contribution to the information security arena is the development of BS7799: 'A Code of Practice for Information Security Management'. This has been moved into the international space as ISO/IEC 17799. Another very relevant standard is BS15000: 'IT Service Management', which is also moving to international acceptance as ISO/IEC 15000.

Business continuity management standard being developed

At the time of writing another British Standard that is under development addresses business continuity management. This is currently available as a publicly available specification (PAS) – PAS 56: 'Guide to Business Continuity Management'.

See www.bsi-global.com for more details.

International Telecommunication Union (ITU)

Standards for international telecommunications

The International Telecommunications Union (ITU) is an inter-governmental organisation established in 1865 when international telegraphy was new. When, in 1947, the United Nations was formed, the ITU became a specialised agency of the UN responsible for telecommunications. Thus it represents the public telecommunications interests of more than 170 countries. Amongst its activities is the establishment of standards. Until 1993 the ITU had two separate standards-making arms: the Comité Consultatif International Téléphonique et Télégraphique (CCITT) and the Comité Consultatif International des Radiocommunications (CCIR).

Some alignment with ISO and IEC

Thus many of the earlier standards are labelled as CCITT[6] or CCIR, whereas now they are all under the direct control of the ITU and labelled as such. Just to add to the confusion, there is also dual labelling of many standards with both ISO/IEC numbers and ITU numbers – which are different.

See www.itu.int for more details

---

[6]Many of the original CCITT X-series standards, including X.400, X.500, and X.509, are very relevant to information security.

Institute of Electrical and Electronics Engineers (IEEE)

Technical engineering standards

The Institute of Electrical and Electronics Engineers (IEEE) is a non-profit, technical professional association of more than 377,000 individual members in 150 countries. Through its members, the IEEE is a leading authority in technical areas ranging from computer engineering, biomedical technology and telecommunications, to electric power, aerospace and consumer electronics, among others. The IEEE has nearly 900 active standards with 700 under development.

Many adopted by ISO and IEC

In the area of local area networking, many IEEE standards have been adopted by ISO/IEC. With regard to LAN security, the IEEE set up committee 802.10 to develop a Standard for Interoperable LAN Security (SILS).

See www.ieee.org for more details.

Information Systems Audit and Control Association (ISACA)

Standards for information systems audit

With more than 26,000 members in over 100 countries, the Information Systems Audit and Control Association® (ISACA®) is a recognised global leader in IT governance, control and assurance. Founded in 1969, ISACA sponsors international conferences, training events and a global knowledge network (K-NET), administers the globally respected Certified Information Systems Auditor™ (CISA®) designation earned by more than 29,000 professionals worldwide and the new Certified Information Security Manager™ (CISM™) designation, and develops globally applicable information systems (IS) auditing and control standards.

Focus on IT governance

An affiliated foundation undertakes leading-edge research in support of the profession. The IT Governance Institute established by the association and foundation in 1998, assists enterprise leaders in their responsibility to make IT successful in supporting the enterprise's mission and goals.

CobiT is an important standard

In particular, the Control Objectives for Information and Related Technology (CobiT) standards, now in their third edition, are a result of work by ISACA.

See www.isaca.org for more details.

Object Management Group (OMG)

Standards for object-oriented architectures

Founded in April 1989 by eleven companies, the Object Management Group™ (OMG™) began independent operations as a not-for-profit corporation. Through the OMG's commitment to developing technically excellent, commercially viable and vendor independent specifications for the software industry, the consortium now includes approximately 800 members. The OMG is moving forward in establishing the Model Driven Architecture™ as the 'Architecture of Choice for a Connected World'™ through its worldwide standard specifications including CORBA®, CORBA/IIOP™, the UML™, XMI™, MOF™, Object Services, Internet Facilities and Domain Interface specifications.

New security protocol standard

Of particular interest to information systems security architecture is the CORBA[7] CSIv2[8] protocol.

See www.omg.org for more details.

---

[7]CORBA: Common Object Request Broker Architecture

[8]CSIv2: Common Secure Inter-Operability Version 2

Organisation for Advancement of Structured Information Standards (OASIS)

Promoting web services and XML through standards

OASIS is a not-for-profit, global consortium that drives the development, convergence and adoption of eBusiness standards. Members themselves set the OASIS technical agenda, using a lightweight, open process expressly designed to promote industry consensus and unite disparate efforts. OASIS produces worldwide standards for security, web services, XML conformance, business transactions, electronic publishing, topic maps and interoperability within and between marketplaces.

UN sponsorship

OASIS has more than 600 corporate and individual members in 100 countries around the world. OASIS and the United Nations jointly sponsor ebXML, a global framework for eBusiness data exchange. OASIS operates xml.org, a community clearinghouse for XML application schemas, vocabularies and related documents.

Primary body for XML development

OASIS was founded in 1993 under the name SGML Open as a consortium of vendors and users devoted to developing guidelines for interoperability among products that support the Standard Generalized Markup Language (SGML). OASIS changed its name in 1998 to reflect an expanded scope of technical work, including the eXtensible Markup Language (XML) and other related standards.

See www.oasis-open.org for more details.

The World Wide Web Consortium (W3C)

Developing the full potential of the web though standards

The World Wide Web Consortium develops interoperable technologies (specifications, guidelines, software, and tools) to lead the web to its full potential. W3C is a forum for information, commerce, communication, and collective understanding. It was created in October 1994 to lead the World Wide Web to its full potential by developing common protocols that promote its evolution and ensure its interoperability. W3C has around 450 member organisations from all over the world.

See www.w3.org for more details.

Organisation for Economic Co-operation and Development (OECD)

World economic development

The OECD groups 30 member countries sharing a commitment to democratic government and the market economy. With active relationships with some 70 other countries, non-government organisations and civil society, it has a global reach. Best known for its publications and its statistics, its work covers economic and social issues from macroeconomics, to trade, education, development and science and innovation.

Security management guidelines

The specific relevance of the OECD to security is the publication in 2002 of its 'Guidelines for the Security of Information Systems and Networks: Towards a Culture of Security'.

See www.oecd.org for more details.

US Federal Government

US government standards

US Federal Information Processing Standards publications (FIPS PUB) are developed and published by the National Institute of Standards and Technology (NIST). The primary application of these standards is in building government systems. However, because vendors of government systems also sell into the commercial world, these standards often become important outside the immediate government domain.

US DOD standards In addition there are various Department of Defense (DOD) standards, which for the same reasons sometimes become important in commercial environments.

See www.itl.nist.gov/fipspubs/ for more details.

Standards Australia (SAA) and Standards New Zealand (SNZ)

Australian standards Standards Australia was founded in 1922, originally called the Australian Commonwealth Engineering Standards Association. As early as 1929 this name clearly failed to reflect the mission and the name was changed to the Standards Association of Australia. In 1988, it changed again to Standards Australia. In 1990 a wholly owned subsidiary business was established, SAI Global Assurance Services, to manage the rapidly expanding certification activities. In 1999 the original association status was abandoned and the organisation was incorporated as an Australian company, becoming Standards Australia International Limited.

New Zealand standards Standards New Zealand is the trading arm of the Standards Council, a crown entity operating under the Standards Act 1988. The Standards Council, an appointed body with representatives from all sectors of the community, oversees the development and adoption of standards and standards-related products.

Security focus There are some useful Australian standards on managing the security of information, risk management and corporate governance. Some of these standards are harmonised with those of Standards New Zealand.

See www.standards.com.au and www.standards.co.nz for more details.

Japanese Industrial Standards Committee (JISC)

Japanese industrial standards JISC consists of many national committees and plays a central role in standardisation activities in Japan. The task of JISC is the establishment and maintenance of Japanese Industrial Standards (JIS), administration and accreditation of certification, participation and contribution in international standardisation activities and development of measurement standards and technical infrastructure for standardisation.

See www.jisc.go.jp/eng/ for more details in an English-language version.

European Computer Manufacturers Association (ECMA)

Vendor collaboration on standards ECMA International is an industry association founded in 1961 and dedicated to the standardisation of Information and Communication Technology (ICT) Systems.

The aims of ECMA are:

- To develop, in co-operation with the appropriate national, European and international organisations standards and technical reports in order to facilitate and standardise the use of ICT systems.

- To encourage the correct use of standards by influencing the environment in which they are applied.

- To be freely copied by all interested parties without restrictions.

Feeds into international standards

For over 40 years ECMA has actively contributed to worldwide standardisation in information technology and telecommunications. More than 335 ECMA standards and 85 technical reports of high quality have been published, more than 40% of which have also been adopted as international standards.

Security focus

One of the most important ECMA projects was Project Sesame, which developed an architecture for a centralised authentication service. The member manufacturers who participated on the project created products based upon this architecture. ECMA also supports a number of IT Security standards and technical reports.

See www.ecma-international.org for more details.

European Telecommunications Standards Institute (ETSI)

European telecommunications standards

ETSI (the European Telecommunications Standards Institute) is a not-for-profit organisation whose mission is to produce the telecommunications standards that will be used for future decades throughout Europe and beyond.

Serving the market needs of its members

Based in Sophia Antipolis, in the South of France, ETSI unites 768 members from 55 countries inside and outside Europe, and represents administrations, network operators, manufacturers, service providers, research bodies and users. Its members, who are also responsible for approving its deliverables, determine the institute's work programme. As a result, ETSI's activities are maintained in close alignment with the market needs expressed by its members.

See www.etsi.org for more details.

European Forum for Electronic Business (EEMA)

Forum for electronic business

EEMA is the premier European forum for electronic business. Formed in March 1987, it is an international, non-profit organisation which provides an independent forum for all participants in electronic business.

Diverse membership

EEMA has many members from users, hardware and software vendors, and government bodies to public and private systems and service providers. The scope of the membership includes large national and multi-national companies involved in business transactions using:

- IT security, including: trusted service provision, digital certificates and PKI;

- EDI and XML;

- E-mail;

- Directories;

- The Internet and the World Wide Web;

- E-commerce best practices;

- Wireless messaging;

- Unified messaging.

Promoting the use of electronic business

As the leading European professional association in the electronic marketplace, EEMA's role is to help members utilise the wide range of electronic business communications, technologies and services available to improve corporate effectiveness. This involves not only education of the business community regarding the uses and availability of electronic business but also addressing industry issues through the relevant international and governmental bodies.

See www.eema.org for more details.

Wi-Fi Alliance

The Wi-Fi Alliance is a non-profit international association formed in 1999 to certify interoperability of wireless local area network products based on IEEE 802.11 specification. Currently (in late 2003) the Wi-Fi Alliance has 205 member companies from around the world, and 915 products have received Wi-Fi® certification since certification began in March of 2000. The goal of the Wi-Fi Alliance's members is to enhance the user experience through product interoperability.

See www.weca.net for more details.

Trusted Computing Group (TCG)

Industry-wide interest

The Trusted Computing Group (TCG) is an industry standards body comprising computer manufacturers, device manufacturers, chip manufacturers, software vendors, and others with a stake in enhancing the security of the computing environment across multiple platforms and devices.

Platform and device security

TCG develops and promotes open industry standards for trusted computing hardware building blocks and software interfaces across multiple platforms, including PCs, servers, PDAs and digital telephones. The objective is to enable greater security for data storage, online business practices and online commerce transactions whilst protecting privacy and individual rights.

Replaced the TCPA

TCG replaced its predecessor, the Trusted Computing Platform Alliance, and adopted the previously published specifications of the TCPA as its initial specifications. This included the Trusted Platform Module (TPM) specification (version 1.1b).

See www.trustedcomputinggroup.org for more details.

International Security Forum (ISF)

Dedicated to practical research in information security

The International Security Forum (ISF) is an international association of over 250 leading organisations that fund and co-operate in the development of practical research about information security. Over the past 13 years the ISF has invested more than $40 million in providing authoritative, best-practice material for its members. The ISF's output is the most comprehensive and integrated set of reports anywhere in the world about the process of managing information risk.

See www.securityforum.org for more details.

Vendor Standards

Standards are driven by the vendor community

It is good to remember that in the end most international standards are driven by the large vendors, because they are the ones who are most represented on the standards-making bodies. Their motivation is to drive the market forward by ensuring that their potential customers can find uses and applications for their products and services, either to be compliant or by providing the support for interoperability.

Some vendors issue their own standards

In some cases individual vendors forge ahead on their own, simply because the formal standards-making bodies take years to agree and they have a more urgent agenda (although the informality of the IETF RFCs and Internet Drafts avoids this problem completely). Famous examples of security standards driven by vendors are:

- The Public Key Cryptography Standards (PKCS) from RSA Security (www.rsasecurity.com) which have later become the foundation for many Internet RFCs and Drafts.

- Secure Sockets Layer (SSL) from Netscape, later published as an Internet Draft (www.ietf.org).

Internal Security Standards

Consistent good practice across the enterprise

As well as the various international, national and industry standards that promote interoperability, you will need your own internal security standards to promote consistency and good practice across your enterprise. Internal security standards will include the following:

- Platform security standards for each type of platform in use in your enterprise, stating the standards for configuring and operating those platforms;

- Cryptographic standards, defining which algorithms and protocols are to be used for certain applications, usually aligned with external standards;

- Password management standards, dealing with password length, password syntax, frequency of change, etc.;

- Physical security standards for various types of site, buildings and installations;

- Document standards for all types of security-related documents, including intranet publications;

- Secure communications interface standards for connecting applications to the enterprise infrastructure;

- User interface standards for providing consistent user login.

Security Products and Tools

SABSA® Matrix cross-reference

Please refer to Chapter 3, Figure 3-3 and Chapter 7, Figure 7-8, the SABSA® Matrix, Component layer, Process column, where you will see a cell entitled Security Products and Tools. In Chapter 7, Figure 7-11 you will also see a deliverable entitled Security Products and Tools. This section provides a high-level taxonomy of security products and describes the common features and functions of each one.

Common types of security component

Table 13-1 tabulates some of the most common types of security tools and products and gives an overview of the most commonly found features of those components.

Table 13-1: Security Tools and Products

Component Type	Common Features/Mechanisms
Anti-piracy tools	Preventing the illegal copying and distribution of software
Anti-theft devices	Preventing the theft of equipment items such as PCs
Anti-virus scanners	Scanning for known viruses and other malicious software, and repairing any damaged files (although the repair may not be perfect and therefore may not be the correct way to proceed)
Biometric devices	Providing personal authentication based on measurement of a bodily feature – such as fingerprint, retina pattern, and facial geometry
Boot-protection software	Preventing the booting of a PC from a diskette to get unauthorised access to the hard drive
Business continuity planning and disaster recovery planning tools	Supporting the collection and management of planning information
CCTV monitoring	Physical site surveillance
Computer forensics tools	Recovering deleted data and piecing together a history of activity
Content filtering for e-mail	Detecting and filtering out unacceptable content
Content filtering for web browsing	Detecting and filtering out unacceptable content
Cryptographic hardware	Providing high-performance cryptographic processing, high-security key storage, secure time source, random number generation for key management, tamper-resistant enclosures
Cryptographic software tool-kits	Run-time libraries for data encryption, authentication, digital signatures and certificate processing
Data back-up management systems	Copying and storage management, and restoration to a previous business position
Directory products	Providing directory services
Document safes	Protecting documents from theft and fire damage
E-mail encryption and authentication products	Providing privacy and authentication for e-mail messages
Enterprise security management tools	Managing a wide range of security services across multiple platforms
Fault-tolerant computing solutions	Resilient computing platforms that will survive failure of components
File encryption products	Encrypting files either for transmission or for storage
Firewalls	Filtering network traffic according to source, destination and content to allow only authorised traffic
Intrusion detection systems	Looking for unauthorised activity from intruders both in the network and on host platforms
LAN security products	Providing security functionality in local area networks
Operating platforms	Logical access control and integrity protection
Personal authentication tokens and devices	Multi-factor authentication of users
Physical security alarms	Intruder alarms and fire alarms in buildings and computer suites
PKI software	Digital certificate management and the cryptographic services that it supports

Risk assessment tools	Software packages to capture and process risk data
Role-based access control solutions	Centralised role-based access control management and authentication of users
Secure middleware products	Providing secure node-to-node communications and an API for applications to call security services
Security auditing tools	Automated inspection tools to check the configuration of an operating platform or application
Security shells	Add-on software products to provide additional levels of access control to standard operating systems
Single-sign-on authentication service solutions	Centralised authentication servers integrating distributed applications and providing an authentication front end with single sign on
Smart cards	A self-contained computer on a plastic card with its own on-board authentication and access control functions
Software licence management tools	Managing the distribution of licensed software to ensure compliance with the licence
Uninterruptible power supplies	Protecting against electrical power failure
VPN products	Virtual private networks built using IPSec or SSL
Vulnerability scanning tools	Looking for holes in the network or host configurations
Wireless security products	Preventing eavesdropping and authenticating nodes

Identities, Functions, Actions and ACLs

SABSA® Matrix cross-reference

Please refer to Chapter 3, Figure 3-3 and Chapter 7, Figure 7-8, the SABSA® Matrix, Component layer, People column, where you will see a cell entitled Identities, Functions, Actions and ACLs. In Chapter 7, Figure 7-11 you will also see a deliverable of the same name. This section discusses the main functional security protocol standards and their application. It is focused around the web-services standards that are currently being used to build the infrastructure for digital business.

Web Services

Modular components of web applications

The term 'web services'[9] refers to modular component functions that can be integrated to form the building blocks of web applications. The following is a usable definition of web services:

> Web Services Definition
>
> 'Web services' are self-contained, self-describing, modular applications that can be published, located, and invoked across the web. They perform black-box functions, which can be anything from simple requests to complicated business processes.
>
> Once a web service has been deployed other applications (and other web services) can discover and invoke the deployed service. Access to web services is through use of standard Internet protocols. The web service interface is defined strictly in terms of the messages that the web service accepts and generates.

---

[9]At the time of writing in 2005 'web services' is an emerging area of technology, and when you read this there will have been many new developments. The best place to start looking for up-to-date information is on the World Wide Web Consortium (W3C) site, which is at www.w3.org.

Figure 13-2 shows the overall architecture of web services.

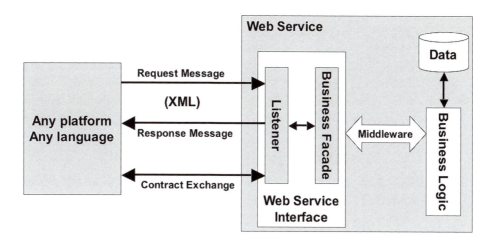

Figure 13-2: Web Services Architecture

Decoupling XML from business logic

The main points to note in Figure 13-2 are:

- The consumer of a web service can be written in any language and supported on any platform. The only constraint is that it must comply with the XML message interface to the web service.

- The 'listener' is a service-agnostic component that simply receives and sends XML messages. It does not interpret the messages and therefore is generic to all web services.

- The 'business façade' interprets the messages and is thus specific to the web service. It translates messages between the external XML message interface and the internal interface to the business logic. The internal interface is based on whatever existing middleware architecture you happen to have to integrate your existing business applications.

Requirements for implementing web services

To implement a web services architecture you need the following components:

- A standard way to represent data (XML representation of data and an XML schema [see next section for an explanation] to define data types);

- A common, extensible, message format (SOAP[10] supported over HTTP);

- A common, extensible, service-description language (WSDL[11]);

- A way to discover services located on a particular web site (Disco[12]);

- A way to discover service providers (UDDI[13]).

[10]SOAP: Simple Object Access Protocol – a lightweight protocol to exchange information. Part of the SOAP specification defines a set of rules for using XML to represent data. Another part of the specification defines extensible message formats.. (See also a later section for more explanation.)
[11]WSDL: Web Services Description Language – an XML-based 'contract' language developed jointly by Microsoft and IBM to allow developers to create and interpret 'contracts' of what a web service is offering.
[12]Disco: Discovery Protocol – defining a format for a 'discovery document' that can be retrieved from a known URL to find out the details of the services offered at that URL
[13]UDDI: Universal Description, Discovery and Integration – a mechanism for web services to be advertised and for consumers to locate them

XML Schema

XML schema define the specific vocabulary to be used in a given application

You were introduced earlier to the idea of XML as a meta-language – used to create new customised languages for specific applications. In creating such a new application language there must be some agreement about shared vocabulary and processing rules that are to be applied in response to the instruction encoded in the application language. This set of common definitions is created through XML schema. The schema define the structure, content, syntax and semantics of the XML documents to be used. It is written using the XML Schema Definition Language, and it allows the rules that have been devised by humans to be interpreted by machines.

Simple Object Access Protocol (SOAP)

SOAP is a simple, lightweight messaging framework

This is a peer-to-peer message exchange protocol for use in a decentralised, distributed environment, providing many-to-many connectivity. Fundamentally it is a stateless, one-way message paradigm,[14] but it can be used as a building block to create application-specific, state-dependent message exchanges such as request/response pairs of messages. It is formally specified as an XML information set.

The messages comprise a body and a header

The message structure is similar to that of most other conventional message protocols, with a message header and message body. The header contains routing and processing information, and the body contains the end-to-end payload content sent by the originator and intended for the final recipient. See Figure 13-3.

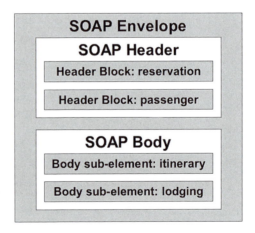

Figure 13-3: SOAP Message Structure

Routing is handled through a series of SOAP Nodes

SOAP messages are handled through a series of SOAP Nodes at which they are received, examined and then sent forward to the next node on their routed journey. There are sending nodes, receiving nodes and intermediary nodes. The nodes process the routing of the messages according to the information in the message headers.

Web Services Security and Trust

Security service definitions are changing quickly

As a part of the overall XML-based web services development there are a number of specific standards addressing security and trust in this environment. At the time of writing[15] this is a fast-

---

[14] Rather like sending a holiday postcard to which no reply is expected.
[15] Time of writing: 2005

moving area of development, and so quite possibly when you read this things will have changed considerably. In view of that the detail is kept to a minimum here. You will need to go and research the most up-to-date position.[16]

XML Encryption

Encryption of XML documents

XML Encryption[17] is an open standard that defines techniques for using XML to represent encrypted XML and other data. It permits encryption of an entire XML document, of specific elements, or just of specific element content. Any encryption algorithm can be used, specified in the <EncryptionMethod> element.

XML Signature

Digital signatures on XML documents

XML Signature (XML-SIG)[18] is an open standard for creating an XML-based digital signature for data of any type, including XML data. The signed data may reside within the same XML document as the signature, or it may be located elsewhere. The signature itself is in the form of a short digest, which may optionally be encrypted as well. Any signature algorithm can be used, specified in the <SignatureMethod> element of the signature data.

SOAP Extensions: Digital Signature

Digital signatures on SOAP messages

This extension to the SOAP standard provides an open-standard method for digitally signing SOAP messages. It is based either on XML Signature or on other non-XML signature standards if required.

XML Key Management

Key management for XML applications

The XML Key Management Specification (XKMS)[19] integrates PKI and digital certificates with XML applications. It comprises two parts:

- XML Key Information Service Specification (X-KISS) – defining a protocol for a trust service that resolves public key information contained in XML-SIG elements.

- XML Key Registration Service Specification (X-KRSS) – allowing a client to delegate all or part of the tasks needed to process the 'key information' elements of an XML structure to a dedicated web service that offers this service. This allows the main application to be protected form the potential complexity of handling a variety of underlying PKI standards, including X.509/PKIX, SPKI and PGP.

Support for basic services

These services provide support for XML digital signatures and XML data encryption services.

Security Service Markup Language (S2ML)

A language focused on security management

Security Service Markup Language (S2ML)[20] enables inter-operable secure eBusiness transactions through XML. It provides a common language for exchanging security information in support of

---

[16]A good place to start is a whitepaper entitled 'XML Trust Services Overview' published by Verisign. Also go to www.xml.com, www.w3.org and www.oasis-open.org and follow the trails from there.

[17]XML Encryption: XML Encryption Syntax and Processing. See www.w3.org

[18]XML-SIG: XML Signature Syntax and Processing. See www.w3.org

[19]Jointly developed by Microsoft and Verisign

[20]S2ML: Security Service Markup Language. See www.w3.org

B2B and B2C transactions. The type of information exchanged is authentication, authorisation and user profile information (ACLs). Because it is XML-based, the information exchange is independent of the platforms used by the participants and independent of the transport protocols used.

Unique identification

S2ML utilises uniform resource identifiers (URIs) as means of unique identification (naming) of entities. A URI can also be used to identify a role (as in role-based access control).

Authentication and authorisation

S2ML also provides specific syntax for distributing and exchanging authorisation information, authentication information and trust assertions.

Trust assertions address wide issues of trust

A trust assertion[21] is an extension of the digital certificate concept – except that whereas a digital certificate makes assertions about the trustworthiness of an identity, a trust assertion has much wider applicability, allowing trusted statements to be made about any type of information or transaction.

Implementing conceptual trust models

Trust assertions can be used to implement the conceptual trust models that are described in Chapter 10 of this book.

Deployment of trust services as a special type of web service

S2ML has been designed specifically to support the deployment of trust services. A 'trust service' is a special type of web service, concentrating the delivery of this specialised service on specialist service providers. Thus eBusiness applications do not need to implement their own trust services since they can obtain them from specialist providers. As with any trust brokerage, the degree of trust depends upon the credibility of the service provider, which has nothing at all to do with technology.

Premium trust services

It is expected that a market will emerge for premium trust services such as:

- Payment gateway services;

- Credit rating services;

- Authentication services;

- Transaction authorisation services;

- Role-based authorisation services for an entire business community;

- Confidential information repositories (such as shared databases of patients' health care records) that support trusted consortia for sharing sensitive business information;

- Enterprise-level authentication and role-based authorisation services.

Future developments

For those services that have a real market, there will undoubtedly be developments of even more specialised protocols based on XML but aimed at the provision of a specific service.

New standards

It is also clear that the emergence of these common, transparent, open standards provides an easy mechanism for the implementation of third-party services, thus promoting even further the possibilities for managed security services and managed trust services.

Security Assertion Markup Language (SAML)

Supporting security assertions

Security Assertion Mark-up Language (SAML)[22] is specifically designed to create security

---

[21]XML Trust Assertion Service Specification (X-TASS). See www.oasis-open.org
[22]SAML: Security Assertion Markup Language. See www.oasis-open.org

assertions. It provides a framework for exchanging security information between business partners over the Internet. It is similar to and modelled on the earlier S2ML, but it is not the same. One suspects that in the future these two may be merged into one standard.

The key benefits of SAML are:

- It is an open standard, designed to work with any industry-standard transport protocol such as HTTP, SMTP and FTP or with multiple XML document-exchange frameworks such as SOAP.

- It provides inter-operability between end users, service providers and brokers, without any of these parties needing to change their local security solutions.

- It provides single-sign-on across multiple web sites under multiple ownership for communities of enterprises that from trusted consortia business level for sharing information

Web Services Security Language (WS-Security)

Another method of supporting security assertions

Web Services Security Language (WS-Security)[23] is based on the use of XML Encryption and XML Signature. It enhances SOAP with methods to protect confidentiality and integrity and to exchange security information. Several types of security token can be attached to a message as a mechanism to implement these services. The tokens hold a number of claims, similar to the assertions in SAML.

Lightweight approach

Compared to SAML it is lighter, requiring far less infrastructure for its implementation. However, as a consequence it is functionally less rich, and in particular does not provide the single-sign-on that is implicit in SAML.

Not fully functional

However, SAML does not support confidentiality services and relies on SSL or TLS at a lower layer to provide this. This approach is deeply flawed insomuch as the application has no control over and no signalling channel with the SSL/TLS level of the stack and cannot tell whether or not the confidentiality service is switched on. WS-Security on the other hand includes confidentiality at the application layer using XML Encryption.

Competing approaches

At the time of writing[24] WS-Secure and SAML are competing for dominance. It is possible that one will prevail over the other, but a much more attractive outcome would be that they will merge into one standard, bringing together the strong points of both and letting go of the weaknesses. Only time will judge this competition. This is a fast-moving area, and no doubt by the time the reader is considering these matters there will have been several new developments and publications.

eXtensible Access Control Markup Language (XACML)

Expressing security policy to implement access control

XACML[25] is an XML-based common security policy language for expressing information system access policy. This can be used to express security policy so as to implement access control systems in a variety of applications. In particular the access control models in Chapter 10 of this book, and especially the conceptual model shown in Figure 10-7, are typical of the kind of system that can be implemented using XACML.

---

[23]WS-Security: Web Services Security Language. See www.oasis-open.org

[24]Time of writing: Autumn 2004

[25]XACML: eXtensible Access Control Markup Language: See www.oasis-open.org

Combining and resolving the interaction of complex rules

It provides a method for combining individual rules and policies from distributed entities into a single policy set that applies to a particular decision request. The ability to handle this level of complexity is a huge advantage, since the intersection of a widely varying set of access rules can be very confusing. Some of the complexities that can be resolved include:

- Dealing with subjects acting in different capacities;

- Making authorisation decisions based on the combined attributes of:

    - Subject;

    - Resource (object);

    - Environment;

- Action or function requested (See Figure 13-4).

- Assessing the contents of an information resource;

- Dealing with distributed policy components.

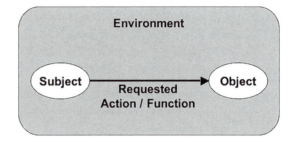

Figure 13-4: Elements of a Complex Access Control Decision

eXtensible Business Reporting Language (XBRL)

Automated reporting of business and financial information

XBRL is an open standard of the XML family that provides a standard interface for the automated reporting of business and financial information. It is becoming of interest in the area of compliance reporting to industry regulators and is an important element in the construction of highly integrated operational risk management systems of the type described later in this book in Chapter 15 (see Figure 15-9).

Statutory and compliance reporting using XBRL

XBRL enables automated data collection and report submission to support the consumption and analysis of business information. It will be used increasingly for statutory reporting of accounting information in compliance with multiple accounting standards and for regulatory reporting of other compliance information.

Advantages of XBRL

The main advantages of using XBRL are that it is:

- Platform-independent;

- Globally inter-operable;

- Less expensive and more efficient than manual methods.

XML Benefits

Benefits of using XML

The business benefits[26] of using XML and its derivatives are that it:

- Enables international media-independent electronic publishing;

- Saves businesses money by enabling use of inexpensive off-the-shelf tools to process data;

- Saves training and development costs by having a single format with a wide range of uses;

- Increases reliability, because user agents can automate more processing of documents they receive;

- Provides a foundation for the Semantic Web, enabling a whole new level of interoperability and information exchange;

- Encourages industries to define platform-independent protocols for the exchange of data, including electronic commerce;

- Allows people to display information the way they want it, under style sheet control;

- Enables long-term re-use of data, with no lock-in to proprietary tools or undocumented formats.

XML Security Architecture Issues

Malicious code insertion is the main style of attack

The main attacks against XML-based systems are by means of executable malicious code inserted into XML documents. To counter this type of attack several architectural approaches are needed:

- All XML documents must be signed to detect unauthorised changes, insertions, deletions or replays.

- XML tunnelling through conventional network-level firewalls needs to be controlled and managed by means of XML application-level firewalls (see below).

Security architecture must address these attacks

The XML family provides a rich combination of security mechanisms embedded within the various protocols, but if application architects and programmers fail to design for an appropriate set of security services to be implemented through these mechanisms, then there will be no security advantage. There is a huge risk that all the common mistakes are being made all over again with these new technologies, despite the availability of the solution components.

XML Firewalls

XML firewall design principles

XML application-level firewalls are much more sophisticated than IP firewalls. The principles of XML firewall design are:

- Access must be controlled on the basis of a combination of:

  - Applications (web services) requested;

  - APIs (functions) requested;

  - User identities (service requestors);

---

[26]Quoted from www.w3.org/XML/Activity.html

- XML or SOAP messages;

- URLs.

- The firewall must decide whether or not a given XML message may access a specific operation or a specific web service;

- Access must be decided according to the authorisations for given service requestor identity and role.

XML firewalls should be operated to provide the following security services:

- Authorisation – against registered roles;

- Authentication – of requestor identity, based on signature verification;

- Access controls – role-based;

- Audit trails – event logging;

- Administration – of users, privileges, roles, etc.;

- Decryption and re-encryption to open up the XML documents for inspection;

- Integration with directories, PKIs, single sign-on systems, etc., to support full application-level security architecture.

Non-Web Applications

Non-web applications are not covered in this chapter because of lack of space

A choice has been made to feature in the foregoing sections some of the most important current component developments in the web services and XML space. However, the provision of the Functions, Identities, Actions and ACLs that characterise this cell of the security architecture matrix is equally applicable across all types of applications, including those you would describe as legacy applications. The description of all of these various components is, however, well beyond a reasonable scope for this book.

Processes, Nodes, Addresses and Protocols

SABSA® Matrix cross-reference

Please refer to Chapter 3, Figure 3-3 and Chapter 7, Figure 7-8, the SABSA® Matrix, Component layer, Location column, where you will see a cell entitled Processes, Nodes, Addresses and Protocols. In Chapter 7, Figure 7-11 you will also see a deliverable of the same name. This section describes some more security-related protocols and describes how these fit into the hierarchical protocol stack.

Protocol Stack

Positioning of security protocols in the stack

Figure 13-5 shows the positioning of various important security-related protocols in the protocol stack. Those that provide application security have been discussed in the previous section. This current section is looking at the component level of the network infrastructure, and so discusses the lower level protocols. The processes in this infrastructure stack are always client and server processes, and these are all client-server protocols.

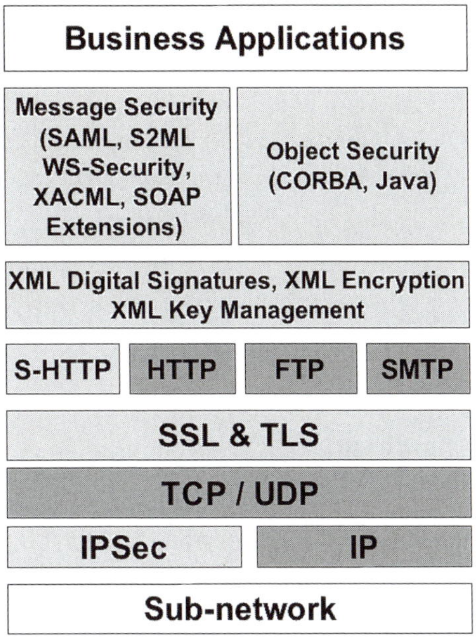

Business Applications

Message Security (SAML, S2ML WS-Security, XACML, SOAP Extensions)	Object Security (CORBA, Java)

XML Digital Signatures, XML Encryption XML Key Management

S-HTTP	HTTP	FTP	SMTP

SSL & TLS

TCP / UDP

IPSec	IP

Sub-network

Figure 13-5: The Infrastructure Stack and Security-Related Protocols

Hypertext Transfer Protocol (HTTP)

Simplicity and ubiquity

HTTP is the underlying protocol for communicating between a web client (browser) and a web server. It has been a huge success for two reasons:

- Simplicity – the web architecture is simple for all participants:

  - A client user types in an URL[27] address and gets connected transparently to a web site. By clicking on objects at the site that represent other URLs, the user navigates from page to page and from site to site. The user sees the logical information structure of the web but not its physical structure.

  - A web site can be created using a simple markup language (HTML). Construction is made even easier by using low-cost power tools that create web pages.

  - There are thousands of Internet service providers (ISPs) who will host your web site as a managed service at competitive prices.

- Ubiquity – by setting up a web server you automatically join a global community. Every personal computer sold has an in-built web-browser, and as a browser user you get immediate access to the entire global community of web sites. Wherever and whoever you are, the web is available to you.

A common transport protocol for everything XML

All of the specialist security services protocols that are discussed in the previous section (XML Encryption, XML Signature, XKMS, SOAP Extensions, S2ML, SAML, WS-Security, XACML) rely on a transport protocol to carry them between client and server, and HTTP is the basic workhorse for this task.

---

[27]URL: universal resource locator

Secure HTTP (S-HTTP)

Modified HTTP

S-HTTP is a modified version of HTTP. It was designed to secure HTTP connections and is described in an Internet Draft from June 1998. It provides a wide variety of mechanisms for confidentiality, authentication, and integrity. The system is not tied to any particular cryptographic system, key infrastructure, key certification scheme or cryptographic format.

Secure encapsulation of HTTP

S-HTTP allows HTTP messages to be encapsulated in various ways. Encapsulations can include encryption, signing, or MAC-based authentication. This encapsulation can be recursive, and a message can have several successive security transformations applied to it. S-HTTP also includes header definitions to provide key transfer, certificate transfer and similar administrative functions.

HTTPS

HTTP over SSL

Do not be confused! HTTPS is NOT the same as S-HTTP (described above). HTTPS is simply unmodified HTTP run over either SSL or TLS (the official IETF SSL replacement – see below).

SSL and TLS

SSL is a vendor standard

Secure Sockets Layer was developed by Netscape and as such is a proprietary protocol. However, it has been published and is widely implemented by many vendors. SSL version 3 was published in November 1996 as an Internet Draft.

TLS is an Internet RFC

Transport Layer Security (TLS) is the official non-vendor protocol from the IETF that replaces SSL and is specified in RFC 2246, 1999. There is an IETF working group focused on developing TLS.

The benefits are often misunderstood

The functions and benefits of SSL and TLS are much misunderstood by many (most?) people. There is a popular myth that once you see the padlock icon on your browser screen telling you that you are communicating with the server over an SSL-secured link, everything is nice and secure and there are no worries. Now consider exactly what that padlock implies.

Strong encrypted pipe with server-side authentication

SSL provides a strongly encrypted pipe (see Chapter 10, Figures 10-25, 10-26 and 10-27 for this concept) between the server and the client browser. Thus any data transmitted along the pipe will be safe from eavesdroppers on the connection. When the SSL session is established, there is an authentication handshake between the client and the server that ensures that the server has a valid SSL certificate, and so server-side authentication is automatic. Although SSL is capable of being configured to provide client-side authentication as well, it is rarely implemented, and in all cases where you use SSL to access a public Internet site it is not implemented. Thus the padlock tells you that you have established a strongly encrypted pipe directly to a server that has a valid SSL certificate.

What are the real benefits?

So much for the mechanisms – but what benefits does this confer? Here are some questions and answers:

Q: Does SSL help you to trust the server to be run by an honest, well-managed organisation?

A: No, because pretty much anyone can apply for a certificate, pay the money and get one. To run an SSL server you will merely have to prove that you exist and have that name, but the certificate authority will register you without checking anything about your honesty. There is no implied business trust in SSL certificates.

Q: Is your data kept confidential during transmission to the server?

A: Yes it is, but once it arrives it may be stored on the server for some time, and the server may be easily hacked from outside to allow theft of the information once it is on the server. SSL only protects the transmission along the pipe. What happens afterwards depends on other things about server security.

Q: Can you be sure that the server belongs to the organisation that you believe it represents?

A: Only if you are very careful about checking the name in the URL. (Go back and read again the IBFS Internet Bank case study in Chapter 9). People with fake names can get SSL certificates.

Q: Will your transactions be protected from unauthorised changes?

A: Only whilst they are in the pipe. Malicious software already on your client PC could make unauthorised changes before the data is transmitted. Also, once the data emerges from the pipe at the server end, the SSL protection stops – so it then depends on how much you trust the server – and SSL cannot help with that.

Q: Will SSL provide non-repudiation of a business transaction?

A: Definitely NOT! All the SSL mechanisms provide transitory protection during transmission. Once the data arrives, any encryption is stripped off and discarded, and any implied authentication is lost with it. There is no audit trail of digital signatures or message authentication codes that can be retrospectively matched to business transactions for proof of sending.

Q: Will the fact that SSL was used help to resolve any disputes about the business transactions?

A: Sorry, no. There is no audit trail of security on the transaction. There is no way of even proving that the SSL was switched on and working at the time of the transaction, because the business application has no visibility of that.

Q: Does SSL protect against fraud?

A: No, because the fraud is usually perpetrated by someone at the client end or by someone at the server end, and SSL cannot control what these parties do.

Q: Why then is SSL promoted as the solution to eBusiness security requirements?

A: Because most people do not understand its limitations. It provides a strong encrypted pipe that protects against eavesdropping on and alteration of the transmissions. That is all it does, and it does it very well. However, securing eBusiness transactions takes much, much more than that.

SSL/TLS is only one component of a holistic security architecture

The conclusions to be drawn from this discussion are that whilst SSL is not the complete solution to securing eBusiness applications, it is an important component. However, it is only one component in what has to be a holistic security architecture, addressing all the potential threats, not just those associated with transmission.

IPSec

IPSec summarised: payload encryption and packet authentication

IPSec is a large group of standards describing how cryptographic security is integrated into the IP packet layer. There are two basic approaches: Encapsulating Security Payload (ESP) and IP Authentication Header (AH). The key management is handled by the Internet Key Exchange protocol (IKE). There are also two modes of applying the encryption – transport mode and tunnel mode.

Limited traffic flow confidentiality

Transport mode reveals the original IP source and destination addresses, whereas tunnel mode hides them and reveals only the addresses of the IPSec gateway. Thus tunnel mode provides a limited degree of traffic flow confidentiality in addition to packet payload content confidentiality.

Flexible use of algorithms

There is no mandatory encryption algorithm specified in the standards. Vendor support for certain algorithms is the only real constraint. The authentication is achieved by use of keyed hashing (HMAC). MD5, SHA-1 and SHA-256 are the currently supported hashing algorithms.

Ongoing work

The IPSec standards are under continuous development by the IPSec working group of the IETF[28].

Often misunderstood in terms of what it can do

As with SSL, there is much misunderstanding about what IPSec delivers. It is certainly an excellent technology for building a virtual private network (VPN). As such it will provide blanket data confidentiality and perhaps limited traffic flow confidentiality down in the network packet layer. It will also guarantee the authenticity of all nodes in the IPSec network, preventing any rogue nodes from being introduced.

Not an application security mechanism

However, like SSL, IPSec has no way of communicating with the application layer, and so it offers no direct assurance or trust to the application. The application has no way of knowing whether or not IPSec is switched on and working, or whether all or only part of the network is encrypted and authenticated. Specifically IPSec does not provide any authentication or non-repudiation for applications.

IPSec provides network security

IPSec is a technology for providing network security, and is not a technology for providing application security. (See Chapter 10 for a full discussion on placing of security services in different layers and the differences between network security and application security.)

DNSSec

Extension of DNS

To complement the security mechanisms within IPSec it is also necessary to secure the DNS[29] lookups, otherwise the overall security of the network can be compromised beyond the control of IPSec. To achieve this there is an extension to DNS defined in RFC 2535 called DNSSec.

Authenticating DNS lookups

DNSSec applies digital signatures (using RSA or DSA) to authenticate DNS requests and responses. It also provides authenticated storage and distribution of public keys used for its own purposes and for other network-level secured protocols. DNSSec does not provide confidentiality for DNS traffic.

---

[28]For up-to-date information see www.ietf.org/html.charters/ipsec-charter.html

[29]DNS: domain name system – allows Internet domain names to be mapped to raw IP addresses

SASL

Simple Authentication and Security Layer (SASL) is described in RFC 2222. It is a generic, flexible security protocol that adds authentication support to connection-based protocols through the uses of registered mechanisms. Servers may support one or more of the registered mechanisms in which case a secure connection can be negotiated. SASL also allows a proxy client with one identity and credentials to authorise on behalf of another entity.

Security Step-Timing and Sequencing

Please refer to Chapter 3, Figure 3-3 and Chapter 7, Figure 7-8, the SABSA® Matrix, Component layer, Time column, where you will see a cell entitled Security Step Timing and Sequencing. In Chapter 7, Figure 7-11 you will also see a deliverable of the same name. This section expands a little on this subject.

The timing and sequencing of security steps is primarily driven by business requirements, such as user expectations, business deadlines, volume throughput requirements, and so on. However, in this cell of the SABSA® Matrix you must deal with the nuts and bolts of how that timing and sequencing is to be achieved in practice. Much of this will depend upon the performance and efficiency of the various components that you have assembled to build the architecture.

There is a detailed design task to be executed that focuses on how each component performs and how the timing of their individual operations can be interlocked to deliver the ultimate business requirements. Look back to the case study in Chapter 10 under the section headed Time Performance Issues, which discusses the design of a process that involves decryption of database records. This will help you to understand the type of issue that can face you. In developing your detailed designs at the component layer, it is the interaction between components that you must consider. The actual sequencing of component operations may be different from the logical business flow, simply to gain better performance efficiency.

To Summarise: Component Security Architecture

One of the critical success factors for a security architecture at the component level is compatibility, consistency and inter-operability between the various components. This is achieved through standards – international, national and industry sector standards.

Components exchange data, and hence one of the most critical areas for standardisation is the data structures and the protocols that are used to make the exchanges. Fundamental syntax standards such as ASN.1 and XML are essential to the construction of higher-level protocol standards.

There are numerous standards-making bodies, each with a specific focus and in many cases overlapping in their areas of standardisation. There is no hard rule that tells you which is the most appropriate standard to pick, and the variety of possible choices can be confusing, but in the end it comes down to which ones are adopted widely across the community that needs interaction.

New standards are being developed and published all the time, making this area somewhat of a moving target. To be aware of the most recent developments and of upcoming new developments you need to carry out up-to-date research on the various standards-making bodies and the individual vendors who are members of those bodies. The web site addresses in this chapter will help you to accomplish this.

The security products and tools that are marketed by the vendor community fall into a number of generic categories, each with a common set of features and functions. The chapter contains a high-level taxonomy of these products to help you to understand which components you might include at this level of your enterprise security architecture. However, the list cannot be exhaustive, and new products and tools are being launched all the time, so once again, up-to-date research is called for when you are selecting your components.

Many of the standards to which security products and tools comply are standard communications protocols at various levels. It is important to understand the functionality of each of these protocols – what they can do and what they cannot do – and also to understand their relative positioning within the hierarchical protocol stack, which in turn governs the functionality and business benefits that they can bring you.

Part 4: Operations

This part of the book is entitled Operations. It maps onto the third and fourth stages of the SABSA® Lifecycle – Implement and Manage and Measure. It is also about how you develop and apply the operational security architecture, which is the view of the facilities manager. It is concerned with keeping the security of processes and systems fully operational over their entire lifetime. Once again the dictionary definitions of key words are used as a starting point for this part of the book, examining exactly what these words mean.

op+er·a+tion n.   1. the act, process, or manner of operating. 2. the state of being in effect, in action, or operative (esp. in the phrases in or into operation). 3. a process, method, or series of acts, esp. of a practical or mechanical nature.

op+er·a+tion+al adj.   1. of or relating to an operation or operations. 2. in working order and ready for use. — **op+er·'+tion+al+ly** adv.

Operations

Operations are the series of actions, the processes, the methods and the manner of operating business systems.

Business operations are concerned with the day-to-day running of the business using repeatable and reliable processes and procedures that provide expected outcomes.

For some of these operations, special technical tools are required, or at least, by providing such tools, operational reliability, repeatability, efficiency and effectiveness can be improved.

Operational Security Architecture

The operational security architecture relates to the operation of secure business systems.

It describes the processes, procedures, methods and actions by which business systems are operated in a secure manner.

It also describes the special tools that are used to enhance the efficiency, effectiveness and security of business operations as a whole and business systems operations in particular.

Style of Part 4

In this Part 4 of the book you will see a change of stylistic approach, since the chapters and their sections do not follow every cell of the SABSA® Matrix as in Parts 2 and 3. This is because much of what this layer is about has been described in great detail in many other books already on the market, and there is no merit in repeating work that other authors have already done well.

If you refer back to Chapter 3 in Table 3-4 you will see that this operational security architecture layer is broken out into five sub-layers, and if this part of the book were to attempt to cover all the 30 cells shown in that table, it would become another full book in its own right. The authors have therefore selected a few pertinent topics that they regard as worthy of discussion here. Cross-references to the SABSA® Matrix are provided to help you understand where they fit into the overall architectural model.

Chapter 14: Security Policy Management

Security policy is the logical embodiment of the enterprise business requirements for security and control. It can therefore be seen as something that, once determined, is a key driver of the operational security management programme as a whole. This chapter looks at various aspects of security policy and how it is managed.

In this chapter you will learn about:

- Security policy as the logical model of your business requirements for security and risk mitigation;

- How to use security policy as a means to develop a strong security culture by affecting human attitudes and behaviour;

- How to use risk assessment as the means to select the appropriate level of security policy;

- The trade-off between complexity and granularity of security policy on the one hand and efficiency of security policy management on the other hand;

- How to construct a hierarchical security policy architecture that is aligned with the layers of the SABSA® Model;

- How to set up an organisational structure that supports the creation, implementation and management of security policy;

- How to manage security policy in an environment of outsourced technical services by applying the concepts of ownership and custody.

The Meaning of Security Policy

SABSA® Matrix cross-reference

Please refer to Chapter 3, Figure 3-3 and Chapter 7, Figure 7-8, the SABSA® Matrix, Logical layer, Motivation column, where you will see a cell entitled Security Policies. Security Policies and Security Policy Architecture also appear as key deliverables of the logical security architecture in Chapter 7, Figure 7-9. In Chapter 11 there is a brief discussion about these two deliverables, since they fit into the SABSA® Matrix row (Logical Security Architecture) that is addressed by that chapter. However, as is explained in Chapter 11, the process of policy making and policy management is more appropriately addressed as part of the operational security architecture (see also Chapter 3, Table 3-2, Operational Security Architecture at the Logical Layer) and hence is the subject of this chapter.

A Theoretical View

Cross-references to Chapter 11 and Chapter 10

There is a section in Chapter 11 with this same title. You will find it useful to go back now to Chapter 11 and re-read that section as an introduction to the discussion here. The theoretical basis for security policy comes from the concepts of security domain and security authority as described in Chapter 10 (Conceptual Security Architecture), and you may also find it useful to remind yourself of that discussion.

A Cultural View

Policy is more than just words

On one level a security policy appears to be words on a piece of paper – a purely physical document that lives in the filing cabinet in your office or in electronic format on your Intranet. However, if your security policy is simply pieces of paper or screens with words on them, it has no value to the organisation, and you may as well discard it.

Security policy means something that is alive and well in the behaviour of the organisation

Security policy should be a living, breathing thing. It represents a culture that exists in the organisation. It describes the way in which people behave when doing their work. It is a mindset that has been accepted and bought into at all levels of the organisation. It is a message to the workforce from the management to tell them what is expected of them, and the results of it can be seen everywhere in the way that business processes are carried out.

Security policy is unique to each enterprise

Security policy is not something that you can lift from a textbook, and so this book does not include sample security policies for you to copy. Security policy is a statement of business requirements for security, translated into a logical structure that can be consistently applied, monitored and measured. Your security policy should be unique to your business. It communicates the intentions of your management team for managing risk and enforcing security in your organisation.

Structuring the Content of a Security Policy

How should a policy be structured?

Through long experience of working in a wide range of client organisations the authors have seen many different ways of structuring security policies. Some approaches work better than others. So what is the right way to approach the structure and content of a security policy?

The purpose of a policy is to influence behaviour

In Chapter 8 you were introduced to the Rules for Influencing Opinion or Behaviour. Refer back to those rules now. One of the applications of those rules that is listed there is in the writing of security policies.

The critical driver for making your decisions about structure and content of a security policy should be:

- What is the purpose of this security policy?

Its purpose is not to sit on a shelf

If your only purpose is to get a tick in the box when the auditor comes around, then it doesn't really matter what approach you take – you just want some shelf-ware. However, it unlikely that collectors of shelf-ware will be readers of this book, so that is probably not what you want.

Ask yourself whom you are trying to influence

What you probably want from a policy is a means to influence the mindset and hence the behaviour of certain people in your organisation. So that is the place to begin. Define the community of people to whom this security policy is to be addressed. The key question is:

- Whose behaviour are you trying to influence?

If the question is too difficult, the scope of the policy is probably wrong

If when you try to define this community it turns out to be too difficult, then you have chosen the wrong scope for your policy. Go right back to the beginning and ask again – what identifiable groups of people do you want to influence in mindset and behaviour? Make a list of these groups. Then for each group consider, what sort of security policy do you need to influence this group? Some people are in more than one group and will need to be aware of more than one policy.

Do not include material that has no relevance influencing the target audience

Remember the key message of the Rules for Influencing Opinion and Behaviour – that you should confine your content to only that which you think is relevant to influencing the target audience. Do not include irrelevant material 'just because it's there'. Keep your message concise and to the point. Focus on the objective – to make them think and behave differently.

Policy Hierarchy and Architecture

The highest-level policy states senior management intentions

Given the principles set out in the previous section, you will need policies aimed at different groups of people. One policy – the top-level corporate security policy – is aimed at everyone. This policy is short and high-level. It is issued with the authority of the chief executive officer and should carry his or her signature. This corporate policy is a message from the CEO to everyone. The message is:

'Listen up everyone and pay attention! If you want to work here, this is the sort of outfit that we are. This is the way we behave. This is how we do business. If you really want to be one of us, do it this way. If not, you'd probably better move on.'

Detailed policies focus on specific groups of people and activities

Below this corporate level security policy there will be other more-detailed policies that are aimed at specific sub-groups of people, although some of these more detailed polices may also be applicable to everyone (such as an Acceptable Use Policy). These secondary policies add more flesh on the bare bones of the corporate security policy. They also do it in carefully targeted ways to ensure that you do not bury the nuggets in a whole lot of dross.

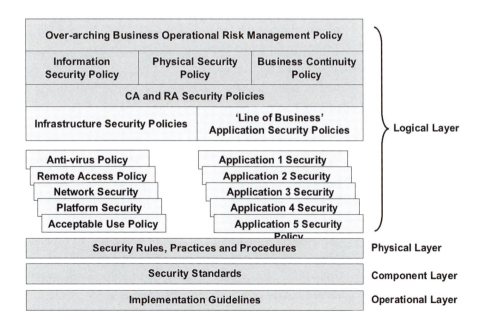

Figure 14-1: A Suggested Hierarchical Policy Architecture

The set of policies needed depends upon your business

It is not possible to prescribe here the set of policies that you will need, for the simple reason that the authors do not know the target groups of people in your business and because your target groups will differ from those of another reader. Instead, here is some guidance on how to arrange those policies into a policy architecture and how to structure supporting documentation to help the implementation of the policies.

Hierarchical model for policy architecture

The concept of hierarchical policy architecture has already been introduced in Chapter 11, and there is a suggested hierarchical model shown in Figure 11-1. That model is discussed again here in some detail, and so it is reproduced for convenience in Figure 14-1.

Top-level operational risk management policy

The top-level policy (Overarching Business Operational Risk Management Policy) is suggested so as to bring together all the common themes of operational risk management across all of the operational risk management disciplines. There are policy statements that are applicable to all these related disciplines, and it is better not to repeat these same statements under different policy headings but to assemble them together into an integrated, overarching top-level policy. Such a top-level policy is addressed to all employees throughout the enterprise.

Information security is part of operational risk management

At the next layer there are policies to diversify operational risk into its constituent disciplines. For the purposes of this book only the three domains of information security, business continuity and physical security are considered. You probably also need other operational risk management policies such as Health and Safety Policy, but to include these other areas would be straying beyond the scope of this discussion.

CA and RA policies

The third level for policies in Figure 14-1 shows CA and RA Security Policies. These refer to the certification authorities and registration authorities that one would expect in an enterprise security architecture built around the concept of public key infrastructure and digital certificates. In such an environment, potentially there will be a number of domains in which entities are registered and issued with digital certificates. The authorities that control these domains – the certification authorities and registration authorities – have policies stating their requirements for security within the domains.

Specific policies provide more detail

At the fourth level in Figure 14-1 is the place for specific infrastructure policies, including examples such as Anti-Virus Policy, Remote Access Policy, Network Security Policy, Platform Security Policies and Acceptable Use Policy. Also at this level are the individual business applications policies. These might be divided by line of business, or by individual business application, or both. The decision as to how to split up these policies will be driven by the granularity and variability of business risk across these sub-domains. There is further detailed discussion of this topic later in the chapter under the headings System Classification and Application System Security Policies.

The lower layers of the hierarchy contain supporting documents

Below all these various policies are a number of layers of supporting documents. These are various levels of detailed documents that help you to know how to implement policy at the nuts-and-bolts level – such as password syntax standards and how often a password should be changed.

Rules, practices and procedures align with the physical layer

At the fifth level of the policy hierarchy come the security rules, practices and procedures. All of the policies are aligned with the logical security architecture, as indicated in the introductory paragraphs of this chapter. However, the security rules, practices and procedures are aligned with the physical security architecture (see Chapter 12 for a detailed discussion).

Standards align with the component layer

At the sixth level of the policy hierarchy the security standards are aligned with the component security architecture (see Chapter 13 for a detailed discussion). These standards include both external standards – international, national and industry sector standards – and internal standards.

Implementation guidelines are sometimes needed

Finally, at the base of the hierarchy is a layer where you can place documents that provide implementation guidelines, where these are appropriate. This layer is likely to be sparsely populated because these guidelines are needed only in certain circumstances. Implementation guidelines are part of the operational security architecture at the Component layer (see Chapter 3, Table 3-2), because they give you advice about how to use or implement certain tools or products.

Example

The following example should help you to differentiate between these various types of document.

Example: Data Backup Policy

Policy Statement (Logical layer): All application systems must have a regular weekly full data backup, with a daily incremental backup on other days.

Procedure (Physical layer): This is how you backup Application ABC hosted on Platform PQR:

> Step 1…
>
> Step 2…
>
> Etc.
>
> (NB: The procedure itself is a security mechanism at the physical security architecture layer, but executing the procedure is an operational activity – see Chapter 3, Table 3-2, Operational Security Architecture at the Physical layer).

Internal Standard (Component Layer): Backup tapes must be of minimum quality 'X' in accordance with ISO YYYY and must be retired after 'Z' uses. Labelling and indexing standards are… etc.

Implementation Guideline (Operational Security Architecture at the Component layer): There are two software packages you can use to perform backups on Platform PQR, but Tool A is recommended over Tool B because you will find it easier to use. When you install it, the following configuration parameters are recommended… etc.

Corporate Security Policy

The highest level of security policy

Now take another look now at the highest level of policy – the corporate-level policies. These remarks may apply to any of the policies referred to in the top two layers of the policy architecture depicted in Figure 14-1.

Corporate security policy is a topic in ISO 17799

ISO/IEC 17799[1] sets out the objectives for a corporate information security policy as being:

'To provide management direction and support for information security. Top management should set a clear direction and demonstrate their support for and commitment to information security through the issue of an information security policy across the organisation.'

Points to consider in writing a corporate security policy

Your corporate level policies should address the following points:

- A policy at this level should come from the most senior level of management. Preferably it should be personally signed and issued by the CEO.

---

[1]ISO/IEC 17799:2000 'A Code of Practice for Information Security Management'.

- To get such senior sponsorship, you will need to invest many months in developing the policy, mostly in a process of wide consultation across the organisation to ensure that it represents a consensus view and is not just the personal opinions of an individual.

- The policy should refer to business risk management as the primary driver. It should state senior management's expectations for limiting the organisation's risk exposure. Key business risks might be specifically mentioned.

- The need for security and risk management should be related to the overall business goals of the organisation.

- The policy should provide a strong mandate, instructing the management at all levels and the employees at large to behave in certain ways and holding them accountable for doing so.

- The policy should formally delegate responsibility with phrases like 'divisional directors are responsible for...' 'line managers are responsible for...' and 'all staff are responsible for...'

- It might mention the issues of ownership and custody.

- It might specifically mention compliance with laws, regulations and contracts.

- It should refer to a reporting process for suspected security incidents.

- It should mention the need for education and training and the provision of a centre of expertise to provide internal advice and support on security matters.

- It should refer to other documents where more detail can be found.

Policy Principles

Principles that may help you to frame policy statements

There are a number of principles that may help you in formulating security policies. These are not presented as something to which you must slavishly adhere. Indeed some of these principles may be counter to your intentions in some circumstances. Look on them merely as a resource from which you can draw inspiration.

- **Least privilege principle** – Users and system processes should be given the least authority and minimum access to resources required to accomplish a given task (but see the discussion below for some qualification of this principle).

- **Accountability principle** – All significant system and process events should be traceable to the initiator.

- **Minimum dependence on secrecy principle** – Controls should still be effective even if an opponent knows of their existence and knows their mode of operation.

- **Control automation principle** – Wherever possible, automatic controls should be used rather than controls that depend on human vigilance and human behaviour.

- **Resiliency principle** – Systems should be designed and managed so that in the event of breakdown or compromise the least possible damage and inconvenience is caused.

- **Defence in depth principle** – Controls should be layered such that if one layer of control should fail, there is another different type of control at the next layer that will prevent a security breach.

- **Approved exception principle** – Policy exceptions should always have management approval.

- **Secure emergency override principle** – Controls must only be bypassed in predetermined and secure ways. Systems are at their most vulnerable when normal controls are removed for emergency maintenance or other similar reasons. There should always be procedures and controls to minimise the level of risk in these circumstances.

- **Auditability principle** – It must be possible for an independent expert to verify that the system conforms to the security policy. A necessary, but not totally sufficient condition for this is that the system must be able to record security related events in a tamper-resistant audit log.

More About the Least-Privilege Principle

Least privilege is proven to work well in some circumstances

The least-privilege principle is a longstanding security policy principle that you will find stated in any serious text on information security, and without doubt it is an important principle in many circumstances. For example, at the level of platform security, it works very well.

Where knowledge is more important than information, least privilege is of questionable value

However, the authors have a serious concern that at the application level – dealing with application information – that is, true business information – it will actually be counter-productive to the goals of an organisation leveraging the power of the knowledge economy. The principles here require that an organisation can use existing business information to create new business knowledge (refer to Table 11-1 in Chapter 11 for the clear distinction between these two terms). The whole basis of data mining is developed from this idea. Thus, for a user to be able to create new business knowledge, access to all business information may be required.

The role of knowledge engineer may require a special privilege profile

One way to view this issue, which does not then violate this least-privilege policy principle, is that those whose job function is to be a knowledge engineer (or something of the kind) require access to all business information all of the time, and this is just a special case of the least-privilege principle. Whichever way you view this, you should be aware of this issue and ensure that your approach to information security policy does not inhibit genuine business activity related to knowledge.

Case Study: The 9/11 Commission Report[2]

One of the key findings of the 9/11 Commission was that the need-to-know principle – the principle of least privilege – was central to the failure of the various intelligence agencies to piece together knowledge from the vast amounts of information potentially at their disposal.

The recommendations in the Executive Summary of the report, under the heading Unity of Effort: Sharing Information, includes the following statement:

'The US Government has access to a vast amount of information. But it has a weak system for processing and using what it has. The system of "need to know" should be replaced by a system of "need to share".'

Could there be a more powerful example?

---

[2]See www.9-11commission.gov/report/911ReportExec.pdf

Information Classification

Information classification is one way to manage security policy

One way to approach security policy and its implementation is to classify information into one of several classifications, each of which has an associated security policy. Thus, once classified, that information must be handled under the terms of the associated security policy.

Information classification is originally a military concept to protect differing levels of secrecy

The concept of information classification is one that has been developed over many centuries in military and government organisations. The focus has traditionally been on differing requirements for secrecy, depending upon the information to be protected. Thus it is usual to define several levels of classification, such as top secret, secret, confidential and restricted, leaving everything else unclassified by default. Each document (or object) is classified at one of these levels. Each object is also protectively marked to ensure that its classification is obvious and can be used to make decisions as to how it should be handled, according to the relevant security policy.

Objects are classified, and subjects are security-cleared for access to a level of classification

The people (subjects) who might gain access to documents (objects) are given security clearance at one of these levels. Thus someone who is cleared to secret level can read any document classified up to and including secret, but is not allowed to read documents classified as top secret. This matching of subject clearance levels to object classifications is at heart of multi-level secure systems (MLS).

Multi-level secure systems handle multiple levels of classification simultaneously

Multi-level secure systems are computer systems, usually in military or government establishments, which simultaneously handle objects at multiple levels of classification and subjects at multiple clearance levels. The Bell-LaPadula model[3] is a formal description of access control in multi-level secure systems. The basic rules are summarised as 'no read from a higher level' and 'no write to a lower level'.

Classification has also been applied to data integrity

The idea was then transported to data integrity. Differing levels of integrity protection can be defined, such as 'sensitive for personal health and safety', 'sensitive for business mission'; 'sensitive for business function' and by default everything else is 'non-sensitive'. The issue here is not unauthorised disclosure of information but unauthorised error-contamination of high-integrity information. The Biba model[4] formally describes a multi-level secure system managing multiple levels of integrity. The basic rules are summarised as 'no write to a higher level' and 'no read from a lower level' – the opposite of the Bell-LaPadula model.

Complex classification schemes can make business operations difficult

Whilst these models are all well and good in theory, in practice they prove to be difficult to make operational and useful. Even in the military environment for which these models were developed they pose many practical difficulties, and they need to be applied with great care to ensure that the systems delivers useful functionality to their user community.

If classification is also applied to availability the complexity increases

The situation can get worse. Once you move beyond the military and government arena into commercial business, the emphasis is rarely on secrecy. Continuous availability and integrity are usually much more important business drivers. Thus many people have tried to take the basic concept of classification (as conceived for secrecy) and move it not only into integrity but also to availability. To do this you classify your data (or systems, or applications) according to their criticality for business continuity: highly critical, critical and by default non-critical.

Many classification schemes outside of the military environment are not clearly focused on meeting a business need

Now you potentially have a three-dimensional matrix containing 60 different cells (if you take the classifications described here – 5 for secrecy **x** 4 for integrity **x** 3 for criticality). That implies 60

---

[3]D. Bell and L. LaPadula, 1975, 'Secure Computer Systems: Unified Exposition and Multics Interpretation', ESD-TR-75-306, Mitre Corporation.

[4]K. Biba, 1975, 'Integrity Considerations for Secure Computing Systems', MTR-3153, Mitre Corporation.

different ways of handling information, according to combined classification and its associated security policy. It is at this point that you start to ask the question: 'Why are we doing this?' If the answer is: 'Because we can', then it is time to throw the whole lot in the trash can. If the answer is: 'Because it fulfils a useful business purpose', then you might keep it. However, in the experience of the authors, application of these classification schemes outside of their original military and government area of application usually falls into the 'Because we can category' and rarely (never?) do they fulfil a useful business purpose.

Classification leads to complex handling procedures for those who create and have access to documents and files

Just supposing you can justify a classification scheme on business grounds, you still have many operational problems. Each classification category needs rules that determine how it gets classified at that level, in accordance with the security policy. Everyone who creates documents or objects that might be at that level needs to know those rules and needs to apply them rigorously. All documents need to be given a protective marking. Then the people who may receive the documents need to know how to handle them. Someone cleared to a high level may have to manage several levels of classification, must know the different handling procedures for each and must apply them rigorously. This is all a lot of hard work. It has an adverse effect on efficiency and upon the flow of information in the business, and it has a high cost.

Classified information tends to drift upwards in the classification stack

There is another problem. Because it is unusual for items to be downgraded in their classification, information tends to drift upwards in the hierarchy, usually attaining a higher classification that it really needs. This over-restrictive regime tends to inhibit real business activity.

Be clear about the added value and business purpose of a classification scheme

In conclusion, if you already have or are considering implementing an information classification scheme, think carefully about the issues:

- Do you really need this for business purposes?

- What added value will it bring, and at what cost?

- How will it work in practice?

- How much user training and support will it require?

- Can it be made simpler and easier to operate?

- Will it really be used, or will it soon fall into disrepute and disuse?

- Does it really deliver any benefit?

- Should you really reject this approach altogether?

ISO 17799 mentions classification without a clear business focus

It is interesting to note that ISO/IEC 17799 mentions information classification as an approach but does not enter into any of the discussion you have seen above about the value or difficulty of classifying objects and handling classifications. Reading the text of that Code of Practice one suspects that the advice falls into the category of 'because you can', since no real business value proposition is offered.

System Classification

System classification offers a more practical way to manage security policy

A much more useful way to approach classification as a means to manage security policy might be to classify systems or applications according to the level of business risk (high/medium/low) revealed through a risk assessment. (See Chapter 9 for a method of assessing business risk. There is also a detailed discussion of risk in Chapter 15.) The reason to do this is to set a security policy for each level of risk and to associate each system with a specific control regime – a standard set of controls that must be applied to protect the application system according to the level of business risk as specified in the associated security policy[5].

Granularity is manageable with this approach

You can diversify this to another level by having the risk level stated for each of a small number of Business Attributes (such as confidential, integrity protected and available) because the standard control regime for each will be slightly different. Thus a system may be classified as high-risk for available, medium-risk for integrity-protected and low-risk for confidential. By reference to the security policies and control standards for each of these risk and attribute categories you can see what should be the complete set of controls to protect the system to an appropriate level of security as specified in the security policies.

There are many benefits

The benefits of this approach are:

- It provides a method of ensuring a consistent, standardised approach to enforcing security policy across multiple systems and applications in a large, complex organisation where there are potentially hundreds (even thousands) of application systems.

- Although there are many, many application systems, only a limited number of security policies (one for each risk and attribute category) are maintained to apply to those systems.

- It ensures that the level of security and control on each application system is matched to the perceived business risk for that system and is in line with security policy appropriate to that level of risk.

- It is completely transparent to the user community, which does not have to get involved with any decisions about how to handle a specific document, because the system managers apply the security policy control regime at the system level, not the user level.

- It makes the job of security auditing of systems much simpler, because it removes subjective judgement and introduces an objective set of criteria for the audit. The audit team now can check:

  - Has the business risk assessment for the application system been carried out properly?

  - Have the business risk categories for the application system been correctly stated?

  - Does the control regime for the application system comply with the security policy and the standard controls that are associated with the risk categories allocated to the system?

  - If gaps are found between the control standards and the actual application system, is there a good reason? Are there other mitigating circumstances? What remedial actions are required?

---

[5]The security policy document should point to procedures, practices and standards documents specified in detail at lower levels of the policy architecture. The policy itself does not contain details of individual controls.

CA and RA Security Policies

CA and RA policies are specific to PKI-based architectures

The security policies for certification authorities and registration authorities are specifically focused upon managing the authorisation of registrants and embodying that authorisation in a logical format in a digital certificate in PKI-based enterprise security architecture.

CA and RA Policy issues

CA and RA security policies must cover the following issues:

* Processes used to register entities and issue them with certificates;

* Security management for the CA and RA ICT systems;

* Validity periods for an entity encryption public key certificate;

* Validity periods for an entity-signing key;

* Validity periods for an entity verification public key certificate (which must be greater than or equal to lifetime for the entity-signing key;

* Validity periods for lower-level CA signing (certification) keys;

* Lifetimes for certificate revocation lists (CRLs) after which they must be discarded and new versions obtained.

Certificate Policy (CP)

PKIX standards describe a CP and CPS

The PKIX[6] standards include RFC 2527: 'Internet X.509 Public Key Infrastructure Certificate Policy and Certification Practices Framework'. This describes a standard approach to publishing a certificate policy (CP) and a certificate practices statement (CPS).

CP definition

The PKIX definition of a certificate policy is:

> 'A named set of rules that indicates the applicability of a
> certificate to a particular community and/or class of application
> with common security requirements. For example, a particular
> certificate policy might indicate applicability of a type of certificate
> to the authentication of electronic data interchange transactions
> for the trading of goods within a given price range.'

Level of assurance associated with a certificate

The critical message from a CA when it issues a digital certificate is that the certificate user (the relying party) can be assured that the public key embedded in the certificate is bound to the entity named as the certificate subject (the subscriber). However, the level of that assurance will depend upon many factors, including the entire set of processes and controls applied by the CA and RA in registering the certificate subject and issuing the certificate. Thus the CP alone is insufficient to provide this assurance. The CPS is a much more informative document in this respect.

Certificate Practices Statement (CPS)

CPS definition

RFC2527 provides a template for developing a certificate practices statement and defines a CPS as:

> 'A statement of the practices which a certification authority
> employs in issuing certificates.'

The CPS explained

The CPS is a declaration by the CA of its detailed operational practices used for registering a

---

[6]X.509 based public key infrastructure. See www.ietf.org

certificate subject (subscriber) and issuing the certificate to that subject. The purpose of the CPS is to provide collateral for a certificate user (relying party) to assess the trustworthiness and level of assurance that can be associated with a business transaction digitally signed by the subscriber and verified by the relying party using the certificate.

Part of a legally binding contract

The CPS will usually either be itself a legally binding document that commits the CA to certain levels of liability or be referred to in support of another similarly legally binding contract, regulation or statute. For the CPS to be legally binding on the relying party in accepting the business transaction, there needs to be a clear legally binding contract between the relying party and the CA, which in many circumstances may be difficult to establish. If there is to be any chance of the relying party being bound in this way, it is essential for the certificate itself to embed a direct reference to both the CP and the CPS.

Online publishing of a CP or CPS

One possibility for publishing the CP and CPS and providing a direct reference in the certificate is to provide them with ISO standard object identifiers (OIDs). This gives each one a globally unique identifier. It is also possible to use extension fields in X.509 version 3 certificates to contain reference pointers to these policies and practices, by reference to their OIDs or to the URLs where the policies and practices statements may be found. In future it is also likely that XML-based policy documents will used as a means to make a policy available online in a way that can be used to drive automated implementation of the policy and practices.

Relationship between a CP and a CPS

The CP and CPS are orthogonal

A CP and a CPS have an orthogonal relationship, since they come from different perspectives and have different functions. A CP is aligned with a certificate type and may apply across multiple CAs, whereas a CPS is aligned with an individual CA and may apply across multiple certificate types, each with its own CP.

CPS supports trust, whereas a CP supports inter-operability

A CPS is published by a CA with the specific intention of informing certificate subscribers and certificate users (relying parties) about the operational practices used in the issuance of certificates. It is aimed at promoting the trustworthiness of the certificate authority and its service offering. A CPS tends to be a detailed, comprehensive document that describes not only what is done but also how it is executed. It describes a service offering that is almost certainly unique and proprietary in its nature. A CPS is therefore much more detailed than a CP but does not focus aspects of inter-operability between certificates issued by this CA and those issued by other CAs. On the other hand, a CP forms the basis of providing inter-operable services between multiple CAs, for a specific certificate type used in a specific application.

Application System Security Policies

System classification as a means to simplify security policy management

If you adopt the approach described earlier in this chapter whereby each application system is risk-assessed against a few Business Attributes (such as confidential, integrity-protected and available) then you will need an application system security policy for each risk and attribute category – nine in this case, as shown in Figure 14-2.

Efficiency and consistency

This small number of application system security policies can be applied to a large number of application systems, making the process of policy setting and policy management efficient and also ensuring consistent risk management practices across all applications.

Granularity is traded off against efficiency

If this approach seems not to provide the granularity of security policy that you require for

	Low Risk	Medium Risk	High Risk
Confidential	Policy 1	Policy 2	Policy 3
Integrity-protected	Policy 4	Policy 5	Policy 6
Available	Policy 7	Policy 8	Policy 9

Figure 14-2: The Application Systems Security Policy Matrix

business purposes, then you can of course have an individual risk assessment for each application, based upon the entire Business Attribute Profile for the line of business supported by that application. This will be less efficient in terms of effort but will provide a much more finely tuned security policy.

An alternative policy matrix Another possibility is to have a set of security policies for each risk level paired with each line of business. This provides another efficiency gain by limiting the total number of policies in use. Figure 14-3 shows this approach. You may then be able to make further efficiency gains by combining certain lines of business together because the differences in their security policy requirements are minor.

	Low Risk	Medium Risk	High Risk
Line of Business A	Policy 1	Policy 2	Policy 3
Line of Business B	Policy 4	Policy 5	Policy 6
Line of Business C	Policy 7	Policy 8	Policy 9
Line of Business D	Policy 10	Policy 11	Policy 12
Line of Business E	Policy 13	Policy 14	Policy 15

Figure 14-3: The Line-of-Business Security Policy Matrix

Issues to be addressed in application security policy The issues to be addressed in an application system security policy are concerned with the Six As of application security, as described in Chapter 10 in the section entitled Security Services in the Application Layer:

- Authorisation (the process of granting a privilege);

- Authentication (the process of verifying identity);

- Access control (the process of making access decisions based on checking authorisations and authenticating identity);

- Audit (the process of writing, storing and reviewing records of all access attempts, decisions and outcomes);

- Administration (administering privileges and all associated activities);

- Application-to-application communications security.

Platform Security Policies

Policies are needed for platforms of all types

A platform is a combined hardware box and its operating system. It may be used to host a single application, or more often, multiple applications. Platforms include supercomputers; mainframes; mid-range servers; PCs; laptops, PDAs and every other type of computer along that continuum.

Security policy depends on both the technology and the environment

One important distinguishing factor with regard to security policy is the operating system, but there may also be key aspects of the hardware (such as its portability and the environment in which it might be used) that will also drive the security policy.

Potentially there are an almost infinite number of combinations of hardware and operating system that you might need to support, but hopefully you have an ICT strategy that limits the number of platform types so as to improve efficiency of administration and support – security policy being just one of the areas to be managed.

Granularity of policy needs to be limited for efficiency

One security policy per platform type

You will need to categorise your platforms into a number of types that are reasonably homogenous across each type (such as servers running Solaris 3.x or laptops running Windows 2000 Pro). Then you will need to develop a security policy (and also associated security standards) for each of these platform types. However there are more issues to consider:

- Should the security policy for the platform be independent of the risk level and security policy for the application being hosted?

- If application risk level is to be taken into account, in the case of multiple applications being hosted on the same platform, will the platform security policy be 'system high' (that is, appropriate to the highest-risk application)?

Cost/benefit trade-offs

The more granularity you introduce, the more complex and the less efficient becomes the process of managing the security policies. Hence there are real cost/benefit trade-offs to be made in deciding the level of granularity at which security policy will be formulated.

Strategic principles of platform security policy

The issues to be addressed in a platform security policy are those identified in Chapter 10 in the section entitled Security Services in the Information Processing Layer. The main strategic principles driving your platform security policies will be:

- To reduce vulnerabilities in the information processing platforms and infrastructure;

- To segregate and isolate production platforms and environments from those used for development and testing;

- To provide and maintain highly trusted execution environments for highly sensitive data processing;

- To provide secure storage environments for highly sensitive non-volatile stored data.

Network Security Policies

A security policy for each network domain and sub-domain

You will almost certainly need to develop a security policy that governs the entire enterprise network domain and applies to all parts of it. You may also need to develop a number of network sub-domain security policies, depending upon the nature of your business and the degree of separation that you require between these sub-domains. Once again, efficiency can be traded against complexity and granularity, but in the networking domain this is unlikely to be as great an issue as it is with applications or platforms.

Security policies for VPNs and firewalls

Where you have implemented VPNs, these will need to be governed by a security policy – perhaps one for all VPNs. Firewalls also need a security policy that gets converted into rules at the physical layer (see Figure 14-1) for configuring the firewall.

Strategic principles of network security policy

The issues that your network security policies will need to address and the strategic principles of network security are described in Chapter 10 in the section entitled Security Services in the Information Transfer (Network) Layer.

Other Infrastructure Security Policies

Security policies for a variety of infrastructure elements

There are other aspects of ICT infrastructure that will need specific security policies. These may include:

- General infrastructure security policies:
    - Anti-virus and other malware policy;
    - Remote access policy;
    - Acceptable use policy;
    - User authentication policy.
- Specific infrastructure security policies (see Chapter 10 for guidance on the issues to be addressed):
    - Middleware security policy;
    - Data management security policy;
    - Security management services security policy;
    - Directory service security policy.

Security Organisation and Responsibilities

Managing information security requires an organisational framework

Who within the enterprise is responsible for information security? The correct simple answer is 'everyone', but the full answer is more complicated than that. Clearly, as with any management issue, there is a hierarchy of responsibilities, which implies that there is an organisational structure dedicated to information security management, including security policy making. What should that structure look like?

This framework must begin at board level

It must start at the very top, with the company board and the chairman. At this level there is a responsibility to the shareholders to ensure that their investments are being properly managed. This falls under the general umbrella of corporate governance and includes the setting of high-level risk management policies.

The CEO leads executive responsibility

At the next level are the chief executive officer (CEO) and the other members of the executive management team who report to the CEO. They must execute the directions from the board and take executive responsibility for all aspects of corporate risk management. This includes the management of information security. To make this possible this executive team must set up a specific organisational framework to manage all aspects of corporate security in general and information security in particular.

You need someone at director level to take the senior management lead

To quote ISO/IEC 17799: 'It is recommended that one member of the management team should take lead responsibility for co-ordinating information security policy'. This is essential. If the organisational framework is to be useful and to have the necessary teeth to get anything done, it must be seen by everyone in the enterprise to be led and directed from the most senior levels. If it is not, then the message sent is that information security is not really a serious issue and people need not pay attention.

The director in charge is a part-time role

This director in charge[7] of information security could be any member of the senior management team. It is unlikely that such an appointment would be a full-time commitment to this responsibility. It is more likely that one of the existing senior management team will take this on as part of a portfolio of duties.

The director chosen should be a natural champion of information security

So which director should it be? If this is really going to work, then the director should be someone who is genuinely the flag-bearer for the information security cause. This person needs to be fully committed and a strong believer in the benefits of an enterprise security programme – someone who will fight for the cause at meetings and who will proactively promote information security cultural values at every opportunity, driving the programme forward.

It is best to segregate this director role from any IT responsibility to provide the business focus

However, there is one director who should be avoided in making the choice of the director in charge of information security – the IT director. If this responsibility is placed with IT then it sends the wrong message. It is essential that information security be understood by everyone to be a business issue and not an ICT issue. The more involvement there is from the IT department, the less people will understand the true business emphasis.

A management steering group provides the forum for discussion of information security issues

Another clear recommendation from ISO/IEC 17799 is the formation of a management steering group at which major security policy and strategy issues get discussed. This will provide 'clear direction and visible management support for security initiatives'. Such a steering group should meet perhaps three or four times a year and should be chaired by the director in charge identified above. It should bring together wide business representation, and the agenda should be prepared in advance to ensure that the time is used to good effect.

The steering group must have powers and responsibilities that attract senior members to attend meetings

The terms of reference and power of this steering committee are critical to its success. If it is not vested with any real power, then the senior people who are supposed to attend will always be busy doing something else and will always delegate someone else to go to the meeting instead. You will then finish up with a junior committee that is a talking shop and which adds little value to the process of managing enterprise information security. You have to create an environment in which the senior members of the steering group regard it as important to attend because important decisions will be taken that they want to influence. Perhaps the best way to achieve this is to give the steering group the power to award financial budget. Nothing gets attention more quickly than serious money.

The chief information security officer leads the operational development of information security

There are other positions of authority and leadership that need to be defined. In an organisation

[7]There can be confusion between different cultures in different countries as to the terminology for senior managers. We (the authors) are UK folk, and to us the term 'director' is definitely senior management, whereas in the USA it has less weight. There you would expect a vice-president or senior vice-president to be taking this lead role. Wherever you come from, you know what is the appropriate terminology – use your own terms, but make sure that the role is positioned at a senior level.

of any real size it will be usual to have someone in a position called 'information security manager' or 'information assurance manager' or something like it. The term 'chief information security officer' (CISO) is emerging in some organisations. This is a full-time job with a mission to lead and develop information security activities on a number of fronts. There are two important points to make regarding this job:

- If the job title is IT Security Manager, this immediately sends the message that this an IT issue (a technical issue) and that business people need not concern themselves with it. This is a poor cultural message.

- It must be clear that this post-holder is not responsible for the security of information in the business. This post-holder is a centre of expertise to help and advise others, to develop methods and processes that will support others in managing information security, and to provide leadership in shaping the information security agenda and development programme. The responsibility for securing business information falls to everyone in the enterprise, starting at the chairman and chief executive officer and cascading downwards through the line management. Every line manager must accept this responsibility and be held accountable.

Other roles in the management of information security

There are a number of other roles that need to be fulfilled. How these roles are integrated into the organisational framework will depend very much on the enterprise and how it is organised. Here are some of the roles that can be identified:

- Security administration: setting up and managing user access privileges;

- User support: a help desk to solve security-related user problems;

- User awareness and management awareness development in security matters;

- Specific education, training and skills development for those with specific security responsibilities;

- Security audit – possibly as part of an internal audit function;

- System security administration: configuring IT systems (both platforms and applications) to comply with security policies and standards;

- Departmental security champions – people within business units who act informally as a focal point and a communications channel for information security matters;

- Contracts with third-party organisations – making sure that information security issues are addressed in commercial contracts and service level agreements, especially in the case of contracting for out-sourced IT services or similar.

There needs to be a liaison group for communication with those with varied and distributed roles for information security management

There needs to be some kind of co-ordination framework for these various people who may be widely distributed across the organisation. You may need another level of committee below the steering group, called the Information Security Liaison Group. This is an informal group, probably led and chaired by the CISO, the purpose of which is to communicate with this distributed community of people who have an interest in information security. The meetings are an opportunity to listen to their problems, their moans and their successes, so as to get feedback on what is happening out in the field. The meetings are also an opportunity to disseminate new information on policies and processes, to stimulate morale amongst these front-line troops and to co-ordinate the activities of this community. The liaison group is a two-way communications channel of a very practical type. It is not a policy-making or decision-making group, although it may feed suggestions for policy upwards to the Information Security Management Steering Group.

The hierarchical committee model for information security management

Figure 14-4 summarises the various committees that play a part in the governance of information security management, indicating the leadership for each. This is followed by a summary for each of its main roles.

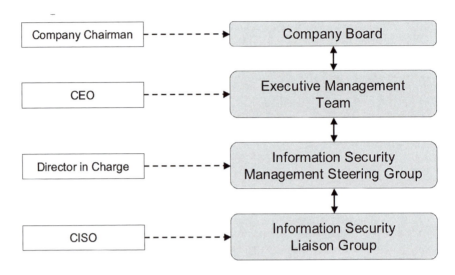

Figure 14-4: Governance Structure for Information Security Management

Board responsibilities

The company board is responsible for:

- Overall corporate governance;

- Setting goals and expectations for risk management.

Executive team responsibilities

The Executive Management Team is responsible for:

- Ratifying policies approved by the Information Security Management Steering Group;

- Approving major budgets for information security initiatives and programmes.

Steering group responsibilities

The Information Security Management Steering Group is responsible for:

- Reviewing and approving corporate security policy and subordinate policies, as developed and proposed by the CISO after wide consultation throughout the enterprise;

- Approving and supporting major initiatives to develop the enterprise information security programme, culture and architecture;

- Developing and submitting to the Executive Team for approval all major budgets for information security related activities;

- Monitoring major information security-related threats to the enterprise business;

- Approving specific methodologies and processes for information security management across the enterprise;

- Promoting the visibility of business support for information security activities;

- Monitoring and reviewing significant security incidents.

Liaison group responsibilities

The Information Security Liaison Group is responsible for:

- Providing a communications channel to listen to views, ideas and inputs from all those with operational responsibilities for some aspect of information security;

- Providing a dissemination channel to communicate new policies, processes and methodologies to all those with operational responsibilities for some aspect of information security;

- To find resolution for operational problems or to escalate these if immediate resolution is not possible.

Line management responsibilities

Line management is responsible for:

- Owning the corporate information assets on behalf of the enterprise;

- Depending upon the function of the department, playing the role of owner, custodian or user with respect to corporate information assets (see below under the section on Outsourcing[8] for descriptions of these roles);

- As owners, authorising access by users, and as custodians, enforcing the authorisations created by owners;

- Ensuring compliance with corporate information security policies, practices, procedures and standards throughout the span of control;

- Developing awareness of information security issues and a strong culture of information security management throughout the span of control.

Security Culture Development

Everyone needs to understand their responsibilities

Information security is everyone's responsibility. However, this can only work if everyone understands that proposition and knows how to discharge that responsibility. Thus it is important to develop a strong information security culture right across the organisation.

Corporate policy signed off by the CEO sends a strong message

The first key component of this culture is a corporate information security policy statement signed off at the most senior level of executive management – the CEO. Everyone must see this policy as the lynchpin of the information security stance of the organisation. It is a deeply cultural message from the CEO that says:

> 'Listen carefully and pay attention. This how we do things around here. This is the type of enterprise that we are. This is the type of people that we are. This is how we do our business. This how we behave and conduct ourselves. If you want to be one of us and you want your face to fit, this is how you will behave too. Otherwise you had better consider your position here.'

Everyone must understand and live by the policy

Having the policy written down is not enough. A real policy is one that lives and breathes in every action that anyone in the organisation takes. Everyone must know the policy intimately, be consciously aware of it and use it to guide their everyday actions and behaviour.

---

[8]Although these notions of ownership and custody are described as useful for managing an outsourced service, they are equally useful for internal relationships.

There needs to be constant attention to raising awareness

That takes strong awareness, and strong awareness can be developed only by constantly bringing the issue to the attention of people. Even if you raise awareness to a high level at a given point in time, if you neglect it after that, the awareness decays and dies. People forget. People leave and new people arrive. So you need a campaign that will constantly renew the awareness level by a continual series of reminders that never stops.

Developing an information security brand is one way to maximise awareness

One approach to running a continuous information security awareness campaign that is known to have been successful is the use of a security brand. When a retailer wants to make the public aware of a product, the marketing campaign is used to build a brand – something that is easy to identify and easily remembered. Whenever you see the logo or hear the jingle, you instantly and unconsciously are reminded of that product and no other. Think about the 'Intel Inside' brand on computers. You know what it looks like, and you can hear the little jingle in your head.

The brand is used in every context of information security management

Now, if you can adopt that approach to branding information security in your enterprise you really can build up some lasting, durable awareness. To maintain the awareness level you just need to keep repeating the brand message – on login screens, on notice boards, on internal newsletters, on documents, on intranet pages, on training materials, on presentations, on e-mail signatures, on letterheads, on mouse mats, on coffee mugs, on desk tidies, on calendars, – everywhere! Because the message is totally consistent it builds up a powerful and memorable impact. If on the other hand you have a different message each time, with different colours and images, nothing hangs together, and it all gets lost in the noise.

Line managers must set a good behavioural example

One key driver of awareness and commitment throughout the organisation is the example set by management. Managers at all levels must set a good example by abiding by the policy at all times and by pointing out compliant behaviour as well as non-compliant behaviour. Managers must be on the case at all times, never letting the issue of security slip, especially when things have gone wrong.

A 'no-blame' culture encourages openness and team-based improvement

On the other hand, a culture of blame will only encourage people to cover up mistakes. Much better to have a 'no-blame' culture in which everyone is encouraged to admit their mistakes, to own them on a team basis even though an individual may have made a mistake, to use the experience as a means to learn lessons, and to embark on a process of continuous improvement and development. Such an approach develops strong team values and keeps morale high.

Sometimes malice and negligence need to be disciplined

However, there are circumstances where blame and retribution are appropriate. These are cases where an individual, either with deliberate malice or with reckless negligence, has caused a major loss event which should have been prevented had that individual behaved properly. It is a matter of scale. Sometimes people are so reckless, malicious or incompetent that they need to be punished and possibly removed. It is therefore essential to have in place an appropriate disciplinary process as part of the overall human resources management process.

Reporting of incidents can help to track progress

Regular consistent reporting of security incidents is an important part of cultural development. It works best in the open, no-blame culture described above, because there are no inhibitions to reporting an incident in those circumstances. In these circumstances the number and type of incidents can sometimes be used as a metric of success. However, be careful here, since there are two possible pitfalls of using incidents as a measurement of success:

- When you have a major security awareness campaign, awareness rises, people are more likely to notice security incidents that they previously ignored, and they are more likely to report them in their newly aware state – so the number of reported security incidents shows a sharp rise! You must anticipate this and manage expectations accordingly.

- If you have a target for numbers of reported incidents that is linked into any kind of bonus or reward scheme, or is even used as a general measure of success for a manager or department, then you encourage non-reporting. There are numerous examples of 'league tables', especially imposed by governments, which measure one organisational unit against another, in which it seems that those at the top of the table are more skilful at manipulating the reported events than those at the bottom.

A co-ordinated training programme

Another aspect of security culture development is the education and training programme. There are a number of different types of education and training that should be undertaken, according to the specific business needs of the enterprise. These include:

- Brief induction training for all new employees to ensure that they are fully aware of the security policy and that they understand how to apply it to their everyday activities;

- Specific technical training for anyone whose job includes a technical activity relevant to maintaining the enterprise security stance. This will include people in IT systems development and IT systems operations;

- Professional career development for those with specific information security responsibilities, such as following a course leading to a Master of Science in Information Security, or preparing for CISSP examinations;

- Short courses on various aspects of information security, including new issues as they arise, such as new threats, new solutions, new products and new technologies.

Outsourcing Strategy and Policy Management

There are three main issues to be addressed with regard to outsourcing strategy:

- The security of outsourced IT services;

- The security of business information handled by service provider to which non-IT business process operations are outsourced;

- The outsourcing of operational security management services.

IT services are often outsourced

Many organisations outsource activities that are regarded as non-core business. For an enterprise that is not an IT services company, the operational management of ICT is often a prime candidate for such outsourcing. This includes both standard data centre operations and also call centre operations based on computer-telephony integration. The management of security of the ICT systems and the business information they process must be addressed as a part of the outsourcing contract.

Non-IT activities are also outsourced

Non-IT business activities are also frequently outsourced, and in this area there is currently a huge growth, motivated mainly by a desire to reduce headcount and to take advantage of low-cost labour resources in offshore locations. Those activities that are components of business processes but which do not add real value to the process are the main candidates for outsourcing. For example, an insurance company might outsource a purely administrative function such as claims handling[9], but in doing so it hands over to a third party huge amounts of confidential, business-critical information. There are obvious information security management issues to be addressed here.

---

[9]Although this is a real example of what is actually happening, some would argue that for an insurance company claims handling is a core process, since it impacts heavily on the customer relationship.

*Principles for managing
the security of outsourced
services*

There are some principles that should guide your thinking on managing the security of outsourced services:

- You should NEVER outsource any type of security policy making activity. Setting policy is a business issue that you MUST keep in house.

- For policies already made in house, their implementation is well suited to being outsourced, provided that you maintain and manage the relationship between you and the outsourcing service provider.

- The outsourcing contract must explicitly address security management and how it is to be executed. Far too many outsourcing deals are put together without due regard for this aspect of the relationship, and hence in the post-contract phase when there are problems, there is no adequate remedy.

- The outsourcing contract should refer to a specific security management process, in which the points of contact are specified on each side, and a protocol is described for raising issues on either side, for handling security incidents, for escalating persistent problems and for generally managing the entire relationship with regard to security management.

- Accompanying the security management process there should be a security management organisational structure on both sides with clear responsibilities defined for each post holder.

- There should be a security target document that has been agreed between the parties and which forms an integral part of the service level agreement (SLA). This security target document should specify what the parties agree to be the meaning of 'secure' and 'secure operations'. It should set some metrics by which the performance of the outsourcing service provider can be judged as being inside or outside an acceptable level of service provision in the management of security. The Business Attributes Profile tool that was described in Chapter 6 should help with this.

- The responsibilities and liabilities of each party to the agreement must be spelled out in detail so that there are no hidden surprises in the post-contract phase.

- Assessing business risk, specifying business security requirements, granting authorisations and setting policy are matters to be retained by the business folks in the customer organisation. Do not attempt to outsource any of these activities, although you may seek help from third-party consultants.

- Implementing decisions and policies handed over by the business people is what an outsourcing service provider does for a living. All of the operational and administrative work can be outsourced.

- The best way to ensure that these principles are all observed is to make security management a key topic for discussion during the pre-contract phase. Get all the issues out on the table, explore them fully and resolve the differences BEFORE you sign the contract.

*Concepts of ownership and
custody are useful in the
outsourcing model*

Some important concepts that will also help to clarify the nature of the relationship between a service customer and a service provider are those of owner and custodian. The owner can own either the service or the data used by the service, or both. Figure 14-5 shows the relationships between the various players in this scenario, including the users.

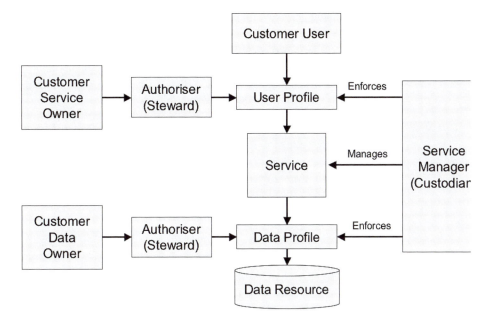

Figure 14-5: The Relationships Between Owners, Users and Custodians

For maximum clarity the model assumes separate ownership of the service and the data. If you find this confusing, the following case study should help to clarify the concepts.

Example of Separate Ownership of Service and Data

The IBFS Retail Banking Company has 10 million retail customers. These customers are all registered in a single central customer database, with full details of their names, addresses, account details, credit history, etc. The vSenior Vice-President, Global Customer Services, owns the customer database (and the data in it).

Many retail customers are issued with plastic cards (debit cards and credit cards). There is a division in the bank that deals with everything to do with plastic cards, called the Card Services Division. The vice-president heading this division owns the service that handles requests from customers for cards, authorises the requests and issues the cards. This division also deals with lost cards, card fraud incidents, blacklisting, hot-listing etc.

The VP, Card Services owns the card services applications and the services that they deliver to customers. The SVP, Global Customer Services owns the customer data that these applications use.

Both the running of the main customer database and its immediate applications, and the physical creation and distribution of plastic cards have been outsourced by the bank to a service provider called Intergalactic Data Services. This service provider manages all the operational services and data management on behalf of both bank owners.

Service owners authorise use of the service The owner of the service is responsible for authorising users of that service and for granting a privilege profile that allows them access to certain service functionality. Service owners are usually senior managers who do not themselves sit at a terminal entering authorisations into the computer system. So, someone on their team actually does the work – in the model these people are called authorisers or stewards (see Figure 14-5). Once a user has been authorised, a privilege profile is handed over to the service manager who is the custodian of the service. The job of the custodian is to manage the service on behalf of the service owner, and to enforce all rules, policies and authorisations set by the owner.

Data owners authorise use of the data

As in the IBFS case study above, the service in Figure 14-5 uses data that is under separate ownership. The data owner also has a team of authorisers or stewards. The privilege profiles created here are not for users but for services. They grant access to the database on the basis of what a particular service needs to carry out its functions. Once again, the service manager is the custodian who looks after the database on behalf of the data owner, and enforces the rules, policies and authorisations set by the owner.

The model works for both internal and external service providers

This model works for an internally provided service management function, but it works equally well for an outsourced service provider relationship. In fact once you adopt this conceptual model for how the relationships work, understanding the respective roles, responsibilities, and liabilities in an outsourcing contract is made very easy, which in turn improves your ability to manage an outsourcing contract.

Managing the interface with the outsourced service provider

There is another aspect to managing the security of outsourced service – how to assess risk and set policy, and how to audit the policy compliance of the service provider. Figure 14-6 shows how this can be achieved.

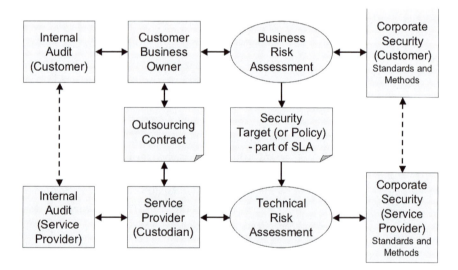

Figure 14-6: Policy Setting and Compliance Monitoring for Outsourced Services

Responsibilities for each party to the arrangement

The model in Figure 14-6 assumes that both the parties have an internal audit department and that both have an internal corporate security team. If these teams do not formally exist on one or both sides of the relationship, then these functions will still need to be fulfilled by some other functional unit. The job of the internal corporate security team in both cases is to create and support security standards and methods (such as a risk assessment method). The customer organisation carries out a business risk assessment and uses this to set policy and to write the security target document in which its requirements for security are expressed. The service provider organisation carries out a technical risk assessment to ensure that it can continue to meet the requirements set out in the security target document.

The internal audit group checks the correct operation of these internal processes in both cases. These internal audit groups need to liaise and to share information to ensure that the relationship is harmonious. Similarly the corporate security groups on both sides will find that some degree of communication and cooperation will help to promote smooth and harmonious working of the relationship. However, the main interactions between the two parties are through the formal points of contact that manage the outsourcing contract.

To Summarise:

The theoretical basis for applying security policy (as discussed in Chapter 10) is embedded within the definition of a security domain, which is a set of security elements subject to the same security policy, defined and enforced by a single security policy authority.

Security policy is the logical representation of the business requirements of the organisation for mitigating risk and enforcing security and control (at the logical layer of the SABSA® Model) and is defined according to the needs of the various business domains. These domains can be arranged into a hierarchical layered policy architecture model, and below this, other layers of supporting documentation are defined (procedures and standards), aligned with the lower layers of the SABSA® Model.

Security policy is much more than a mere set of statements – it represents the culture of the enterprise and describes how people approach their work and how they behave with regard to security matters. For this reason you should begin writing a security policy from the point of view that you want to influence the attitudes and behaviour of a specific community of people. The policy should speak clearly to that group of people, in appropriate language and sticking strictly to the messages that the group needs to hear. You should omit any material not relevant to this mission.

There are a number of commonly used policy principles that will help you to decide on the content of your policies, but these should not be taken as absolute truths, since they may or may not be appropriate to the business needs of your enterprise. There are also many useful guidelines on policy content embedded in Chapter 10 of this book, where the conceptual bundles of security services are discussed under various headings.

Information classification is one possible way to simplify security policy management, with certain security policies being associated with certain classes of information. It is commonly used in military and government environments. However, there are many difficulties and additional complexities that accompany this approach, and so it is probably unworkable in a commercial environment.

Much more useful as an approach is the classification of application systems, based upon a business risk assessment for each one. This produces a limited number of classifications and hence a limited number of security policies that need to be maintained and enforced. This approach can help to balance the competing needs for granularity of policy and efficiency of policy management.

In addition to security policies for business applications and their associated domains, there are also a number of infrastructure domains, each of which needs an appropriate security policy.

In order to develop, approve, publish, maintain, implement and enforce this range of security policies there needs to be an organisational structure and a governance framework, starting with the roles and responsibilities of the board and working down through the organisation to ensure that policy management is appropriately handled at every level. Investment in development of a strong security culture is an essential element of a successful security policy programme.

Where certain services are out-sourced to a third-party service provider, it is essential to keep in-house the function of policy making but to transfer to the service provider many of the functions of policy implementation and enforcement. The key conceptual roles in the governance framework that make this possible are those of owner (the enterprise) and custodian (the service provider).

Chapter 15: Operational Risk Management

The key driver for your enterprise security architecture is business risk. This chapter examines in detail the management of risk within your business operations. It discusses operational risk management in general terms but constantly focuses back onto the specific needs for managing operational risk in the context of business information security.

In this chapter you will learn about:

- What operational risk management really means;

- The breadth of risk types that you need to consider;

- The regulatory regimes that are bringing operational risk to the top of senior management agendas;

- The complex interactions between different types of operational risk;

- The qualitative and quantitative methods that can be applied for assessing and analysing operational risk;

- How to create a strategic enterprise-wide operational risk management framework;

- The most well-known external standards for operational risk management;

- How to mitigate risk by the selection and implementation of controls;

- How to conduct a risk-based security review;

- Approaches to risk financing, risk transfer and risk retention using insurance and related techniques;

- How to design a risk management dashboard for information security related risk monitoring and reporting.

Introduction to Operational Risk Management

SABSA® Matrix cross-reference

This chapter is relevant to the cell of the SABSA® Matrix entitled Operational Risk Management on the Operational row and in the Motivation column (see Chapter 3, Figure 3-3 and Chapter 7, Figure 7-8).

'Operational risk kills organisations. It is difficult to define, and harder still to measure, but until you can measure it, you cannot control it'.

Risk Magazine, November 1998.

Operational risk seen from different perspectives

Operational risk means different things to different people. If you ask several of them what they mean by operational risk management, here are some of the answers that you might get back:

- The prevention of loss (auditor's view)

- Cost-effective risk financing (insurance manager's view)

- Managing volatility (finance director's view)

Risk management involves trading off one risk against another

Operational risk management is a trade-off – if there is a risk associated with taking a particular course of action, there is also a risk of not doing so. Furthermore, individual risks interact in complex ways, and if you mitigate one risk you almost certainly increase at least one other risk in response. You therefore need to take a broad view of operational risk so as to manage it successfully. The aims of operational risk management are to:

- Understand the enterprise risk profile in detail;

- Make well-informed risk-mitigation and risk-taking decisions;

- Minimise the overall cost to the organisation, taking into account the widest possible view.

Cross-reference to Chapter 9

In Chapter 9 of this book you have already been introduced to operational risk as an important part of the contextual security architecture. You should go back and re-read that part of Chapter 9 now as an introduction to the new material presented here. The topics covered in that discussion include:

- Risk modelling in terms of assets, threats, impacts and vulnerabilities;

- A threat-modelling framework based on threat domains, threat agents, threat categories and threat scenarios;

- The capabilities, motivations, amplifiers, catalysts and inhibitors that apply to threat agents;

- The SABSA® Method for qualitative risk assessment;

- Risk mitigation.

Definition of operational risk

The definition of operational risk can be somewhat elusive. There are some specific definitions available, such as that provided by the New Basel Accord for the banking industry (see the case study later in this chapter), but there is no standardised precise definition that has broad applicability across different industry sectors. What is certain is that operational risk has a wide scope. Table 15-1 shows some of the categories of operational risk that you may need to consider, along with some possible mappings to related information security and ICT concerns.

Table 15-1: Operational Risk Categories

Operational Risk Areas	Description	Information or ICT Mapping
Facilities and Operating Environment Risk	Loss or damage to operational capabilities caused by problems with premises, facilities, services or equipment	Business continuity management for ICT facilities
Health & Safety Risk	Threats to the personal health and safety of staff, customers and members of the public	Confidentiality of home addresses and travel schedules
Information Security Risk	Unauthorised disclosure or modification to information, or loss of availability of information, or inappropriate use of information	All aspects of information and ICT security
Control Frameworks Risk	Inadequate design or performance of the existing risk management infrastructure	Business process analysis to identify critical information flows and control points
Legal & Regulatory Compliance Risk	Failure to comply with the laws of the countries in which business operations are carried out, or failure to comply with any regulatory, reporting and taxation standards, or failure to comply with contracts, or failure of contracts to protect business interests	Compliance with data protection legislation and cryptographic control regulations Accuracy, timeliness and quality of information reported to regulators Content management of all information sent to other parties
Corporate Governance Risk	Failure of directors to fulfil their personal statutory obligations in managing and controlling the company	Information security policy making, performance measurement and reporting
Reputation Risk	The negative effects of public opinion, customer opinion, market reputation and the damage caused to the brand by failure to manage public relations	Controlling the disclosure of confidential information Also presenting a public image of a well-managed enterprise
Strategic Risk	Failure to meet the long-term strategic goals of the business, including dependence on any estimated or planned outcomes that may be in the control of third parties	Managing the quality and granularity of information on which strategic business decisions are based (such as mergers, acquisitions and disposals)
Processing and Behavioural Risk	Problems with service or product delivery caused by failure of internal controls, information systems, employee integrity, or by errors and mistakes, or through weaknesses in operating procedures	All aspects of information systems security and the security-related behaviour of employees in carrying out their tasks
Technology Risk	Failure to plan, manage and monitor the performance of technology-related projects, products, services, processes, staff and delivery channels	Failure of information and communications technology systems and the need for business continuity management

Operational Risk Areas	Description	Information or ICT Mapping
Project Management Risk	Failure to plan and manage the resources required for achieving tactical project goals, leading to budget overruns or time overruns or both, or leading to failure to complete the project The technical failure of a project or the failure to manage the integration aspects with existing parts of the business and the impact that changes can have on business operations	Management of all information security-related projects
Criminal and Illicit Acts Risk	Loss or damage caused by fraud, theft, wilful neglect, gross negligence, vandalism, sabotage and extortion	Provision of security services and mechanisms to prevent all types of cyber crime
Human Resources Risk	Failure to recruit, develop or retain employees with the appropriate skills and knowledge, or to manage employee relations	Need for policies protecting employees from sexual harassment and racial abuse through corporate e-mail systems
Supplier Risk	Failure to evaluate adequately the capabilities of suppliers leading to breakdowns in the supply process or sub-standard delivery of supplied goods and services Failure to understand and manage supply-chain issues	Outsourced service delivery of ICT or other business information-processing activities
Management Information Risk	Inadequate, inaccurate, incomplete or untimely provision of information to support the management decision-making process	Managing the accuracy, integrity, currency, timeliness and quality of information used for management decision support
Ethics Risk	Damage caused by unethical business practices, including those of associated business partners; issues include racial and religious discrimination, exploitation of child labour, pollution, environmental and so-called green issues and behaviour to disadvantaged groups	Ethical collection, storage and use of information Management of information content on web sites, Intranets and in corporate e-mails and instant messaging systems
Geopolitical Risk	Loss or damage in some countries caused by political instability or by poor quality of infrastructure in developing regions or by cultural differences and misunderstandings	Managing all aspects of information security and ICT systems security in regions where the enterprise has business operations but where there are special geopolitical risks
Cultural Risk	Failure to deal with cultural issues affecting employees, customers or other stakeholders; these include language, religion, morality, dress codes and other community customs and practices	Management of information content on web sites, Intranets and in corporate e-mails and instant messaging systems
Climate and Weather Risk	Loss or damage caused by unusual climate conditions, including drought, heat, flood, cold, storm and winds	Business continuity management for ICT facilities

Regulatory Drivers for Operational Risk Management

Corporate Governance

Cleaning up the corporate act

There is a continuing pressure from both governments and industry regulators to clean up the corporate act so as to improve the quality of corporate governance and the accountability of senior executives in the face of governance failures. This has largely been in response to an alarming number of major corporate governance failures in many countries, but especially in the USA, the UK and other parts of the EU.

Drivers for increased regulation

There have been the major corporate frauds, including Enron, WorldCom, Shell and Parmalat. There have also been the spectacular failures of corporate strategy, such as at The Equitable Life, and the breathtaking failures of operational control, such as at Barings Bank. The entire financial services industry in the UK continues to be dogged by the scandal of mis-selling of life assurance and pensions products, and there is growing shareholder militancy, especially amongst institutional shareholders such as pension funds managers, resisting the phenomenon of fat-cat pay-offs for failed executives. Additionally, the harmonisation of regulations across an increasingly globalised economy is leading to a general raising of the standard for compliance, as regulators pursue the highest common factor approach to align regulations across a number of nation states, as is happening in the EU.

Recent governance regulations

In the following sections there are brief descriptions of some of the most important recent developments in the corporate governance regulation and compliance arena.

Sarbanes-Oxley (USA)

Financial reporting transparency

The Sarbanes-Oxley Act of 2002 was signed into law on 30 July 2002 in the wake of a series of financial scandals involving Enron and WorldCom. The act stipulates important changes to the financial regulatory requirements of publicly traded companies. Key requirements are:

- Board oversight of financial accounting for publicly traded companies;

- Maintenance of an audit trail and financial records for a minimum period of seven years;

- Independent external audit – not linked to other business consulting services – to eliminate conflict of interest;

- Provision for confidential, anonymous whistle-blowing regarding corporate wrongdoing;

- Executive certification of quarterly or annual financial reports;

- Management assessment of internal controls;

- Accelerated real-time financial reporting;

- Code of ethics;

- Corporate and criminal fraud accountability;

- White-collar crime penalty enhancements.

Patriot Act (USA)

Government surveillance

The USA Patriot Act of 2001 was signed into law on 26 October 2001, following the 9/11 terrorist atrocities, and its purpose is to facilitate the investigation of potential terrorist activity. It is highly controversial because it was rushed into law in a few weeks, and yet it is highly complex, being 342 pages long and making changes to 15 other statutes. Some of the major concerns expressed by some commentators include:

- Expanded government surveillance with reduced checks and balances regarding the justification for that surveillance;

- A very wide scope, not all of which is obviously focused on the investigation or prevention of terrorism.

Archiving of all corporate communications

Whatever you might think of this legislation, one of the key impacts for information management in corporate US organisations is the requirement to gather and archive ALL documents and communications for a period of seven years. This requirement seems to be totally pervasive, and potentially includes all call logs, all corporate e-mails and all corporate instant messaging.

Basel II (Banking Industry)

Representing banking supervision in the G10 countries

The Basel Committee on Banking Supervision is a committee of banking supervisory authorities that was established by the central bank governors of the Group of Ten (G10) countries in 1975. It consists of senior representatives of bank supervisory authorities and central banks from Belgium, Canada, France, Germany, Italy, Japan, Luxembourg, the Netherlands, Sweden, Switzerland, the United Kingdom and the United States.

Central banks and national regulators

The committee is one of several committees set up under the auspices of the Bank for International Settlements[1] (BIS). The Basel Committee meets regularly four times a year. It has about 30 technical working groups and task forces, which also meet regularly. The 10 countries are each represented by their central bank and also by the authority with formal responsibility for the prudential supervision of banking business where this is not the central bank.

Harmonisation of national regulations

The committee does not possess any formal supranational supervisory authority, and its conclusions do not have legal force. Rather, it formulates broad supervisory standards and guidelines and recommends statements of best practice in the expectation that individual authorities will take steps to implement them through detailed arrangements that are best suited to their own national systems.

The first Basel Accord addressed credit risk

The Basel Capital Accord was published by the Basel Committee on Banking Supervision in 1988 and sets down the agreement among the G10 central banks to apply common minimum capital standards to their banking industries, to be achieved by 1992. The objective was to introduce international convergence of capital measurement and capital standards. The standards are almost entirely addressed to credit risk, the main risk incurred by banks.

Market risk was included under various amendments

In recent years, five amendments to the accord have been agreed, for four of which specific changes to the text of the original accord have been published. The fifth of these amendments, which introduces parallel capital requirements for market risk, does not include amendments to the original 1988 text. This amendment was issued as a separate document in January 1996 and is published as *'Amendment to the capital accord to incorporate market risks'*. Operational risk is not addressed either in the original 1988 accord or in any of the subsequent amendments.

---

[1]BIS is at http://www.bis.org/

The New Basel Accord includes operational risk

The New Basel Accord (known also as Basel II) currently being developed by the Basel Committee on Banking Supervision extends the existing requirements for banks to make capital allocations against risk exposure. The New Basel Accord now includes operational risk as well as credit risk and market risk. This major change recognises two things. First, that operational risk represents a black hole in risk management across the banking industry as a whole, because it is impossible to calculate any meaningful value at risk (VAR) without reliable statistical data on operational losses, and these data do not currently exist. Second, that many banking institutions have begun to tackle this problem in recent years by developing quantitative approaches to measuring VAR with regard to operational risk. The Basel Committee wants to encourage these developments by offering the incentive of reduced capital allocation traded against improved sophistication of risk measurement.

Supervision and public disclosure of risk management practices

In addition, the New Basel Accord introduces a new three-pillar approach, in which Pillar 1 is the existing allocation of capital against VAR, Pillar 2 is the enhanced supervision of risk management in banks by national banking regulators, and Pillar 3 is improved public disclosure to market participants with regard to each bank's risk exposure and risk management practices.

Gramm-Leach-Bliley Act (USA)

Privacy for banking customers

The Gramm-Leach-Bliley was enacted on 12 November 1999 in an effort by Congress to regulate privacy of consumer financial information. Under the act, financial institutions are required to ensure the privacy of financial information provided by their customers. In particular, consumers have specific privacy protection when they obtain financial products or services from a financial institution for personal, family or household use. The privacy regulations came in to effect on 13 November 2000.

HIPAA (USA)

Standards for electronic transmission of health care information

The purpose of the Health Insurance Portability and Accountability Act of 1996 is to improve the Medicare and Medicaid programmes set up under the Social Security Act, and to enhance the efficiency and effectiveness of the health care system by encouraging the development of a health information system through the establishment of standards and requirements for the electronic transmission of certain health information.

Information security is explicitly included

HIPAA has major implications for the management of health information, including the security of such information. There are specific sections of the act that specify the need for standards covering:

- Technical capabilities of health record systems;

- Cost/benefit evaluation of security measures;

- Training requirements related to information security;

- Audit trails for computerised systems;

- Security policies and security procedures;

- Risk assessment to protect against 'reasonably anticipated threats' and:

  - To protect the integrity and confidentiality of health information;

  - To prevent the unauthorised use or disclosure of health information.

- The use of electronic signatures on digitally transmitted documents or transactions.

CAD3 (EU)

EU harmonisation of Basel II implementations

The European Union new Capital Adequacy Directive (known as CAD3) is designed to facilitate the transposition of the New Basel Accord into EU legislation. It will overwrite the existing rules and extend the scope of the New Basel regime to all credit institutions and investment firms across the EU, which at the same time is expanding to become a community of 25 countries.

Combined Code, Turnbull, Smith and Higgs (UK)

Standards of governance for listed companies

The Combined Code on Corporate Governance is a UK code of best practice, prepared by the Hampel Committee in 1998. It applies to companies listed on the London Stock Exchange. The key points of the Combined Code that apply to operational risk management are:

- Principle D.2 of the code states that 'The board should maintain a sound system of internal control to safeguard shareholders' investment and the company's assets'.

- Provision D.2.1 states that 'The directors should, at least annually, conduct a review of the effectiveness of the group's system of internal control and should report to shareholders that they have done so. The review should cover all controls, including financial, operational and compliance controls and risk management'.

- Provision D.2.2 states that 'Companies which do not have an internal audit function should from time to time review the need for one'.

Statement in the annual report of a listed company

The London Stock Exchange listing rules require that a listed company incorporated in the UK must include in its annual report statements regarding its compliance with the Combined Code.

Turnbull Report: guidance on the Combined Code

The document entitled 'Guidance for Directors on the Combined Code' (also known as the Turnbull Report[2]) issued by the Institute of Chartered Accountants in England and Wales sets out some specific guidance on risk management and how to be compliant with the Combined Code. It states that the board must consider:

- The nature and extent of the risks facing the company;

- The extent and categories of risk that it regards as acceptable for the company to bear;

- The likelihood of the risks concerned materialising;

- The company's ability to reduce the incidence and impact on the business of risks that do materialise;

- The costs of operating particular controls relative to the benefit thereby obtained in managing the related risks.

Problems of transparency for shareholders

A key feature of the Combined Code approach to corporate governance is self-regulation by companies on the basis that they either comply with best practice or explain to their shareholders why they do not comply. The problem with this has been that the explanations to shareholders have tended to be inadequate, being rather unspecific, boilerplate in their nature and somewhat obscure. For a time it seemed that shareholders had neither the resources nor the will to challenge this unsatisfactory operation of the Combined Code.

Improving transparency for shareholders

A string of high-profile corporate governance failures that provoked increasing shareholder

---

[2]'Internal Control: Guidance for Directors on the Combined Code', ICA, September 1999. See www.icaew.co.uk

militancy created the head of pressure that led to the Higgs Review[3] and the Smith Report[4], both of which have been used to strengthen the Combined Code in a reissued version in June 2003. The strengthening of the code includes some specific recommendations including:

- Clear segregation of the position of chairman of the board from that of chief executive officer;

- Increased roles, responsibilities and accountability for non-executive directors;

- More non-executive directors providing increased independence and better informed, more experienced boards;

- Greater transparency and accountability in the boardroom and in the audit process;

- Closer relationships between non-executive directors and shareholders;

- Protection of the independence of the external auditors by restricting the delivery of other services (such a management consultancy) that might lead to a conflict of interest.

Integrated Prudential Sourcebook (UK)

The FSA Integrated Prudential Sourcebook

In the UK the Financial Services Authority (FSA)[5] regulates all banking, insurance and other financial services activities. Its overall set of regulations are embodied in the FSA Handbook, but a part of that handbook is the Integrated Prudential Sourcebook that deals expressly with risk-based prudential requirements for the management of financial services firms. These include standards for managing:

- Credit risk (the risk of lending);

- Market risk (the risk of investing on financial markets);

- Operational risk;

- Insurance risk;

- Liquidity risk (the risk of running out of liquid assets – cash!);

- Group risk (the risk of belonging to a group of companies).

The main thrust of the Integrated Prudential Sourcebook is in two areas:

- Ensuring that the firm has adequate financial resources:

  - Solvency requirements;

  - Capital adequacy requirements.

- Ensuring that the firm has in place appropriate systems and controls.

It is this last bullet point that has a huge regulatory impact on the management of operational risk in general and information security in particular.

FSA requirements for operational risk management

The FSA has issued very specific advice on how it expects regulated firms to manage operational risk, and this advice is contained in a consultation paper (CP142) entitled 'Operational Risk Systems and

---

[3]'Review of the Role and Effectiveness of Non-Executive Directors', Derek Higgs, 20 January 2003. See www.dti.gov.uk

[4]'Audit Committees Combined Code Guidance', Sir Robert Smith, 20 January 2003. See www.dti.gov.uk

[5]See www.fsa.gov.uk

Controls'. This is closely aligned with the New Basel Accord requirements for operational risk management, but as well as the four domains (People, Processes, Systems and External Events) of Basel II, a fifth domain is introduced specifically addressing Outsourcing.

21 CFR Part 11 (Pharmaceuticals Industry, USA)

The use of electronic documents in the food and drug industries

Title 21 of the Code of Federal Regulations Part 11 (21 CFR Part 11) is the section of the United States government rules and regulations document that applies to all the Food and Drug Administration (FDA) program areas and applies to the security and use of electronic records and electronic signatures.

Compliance mandated for all pharmaceutical firms

All organisations and persons within the United States who market, or intend to market, pharmaceutical products, pharmaceutical systems, or participate in pharmaceutical research, must comply with the controls, procedures and requirements for using computer applications, systems and devices detailed in 21 CFR Part 11.

Creating trust and privacy in electronic documents

The goal of the regulation is to ensure the trustworthiness, privacy and reliability of electronic data, documents and signatures transmitted to the FDA. These transmissions occur when:

- The FDA requires a timely review and approval of safe and effective new medical products so as to protect and promote public health;

- The FDA needs to conduct efficient audits of required records;

- The FDA needs to pursue regulatory actions.

Computer security and sound business practice

The regulation requires the applicable organisations and persons to demonstrate their ability to develop and maintain reliable and secure computer systems, in addition to having sound business practices and processes around these systems.

Electronic recordkeeping is not mandated, but where it used, compliance with the regulations is mandated

The regulations set forth in 21 CFR Part 11 became effective on 20 August 1997. 21 CFR Part 11 applies to all FDA program areas but does not mandate electronic recordkeeping. 21 CFR Part 11 describes the technical and procedural requirements that must be met if a person or company chooses to maintain records electronically and use electronic signatures. 21 CFR Part 11 applies to those records required by the FDA predicate rule and to signatures required by the FDA predicate rule, as well as signatures that are not required but appear in required records.

FAA, CAA and Others (Civil Aviation Industry)

Regulation of the civil aviation industry

In the USA the Federal Aviation Administration (FAA) regulates the civil aviation industry, with a particular focus on protecting the aviation-related safety of people both in the air and on the ground. In the UK the Civil Aviation Authority (CAA) manages these responsibilities. Other countries have similar organisations fulfilling similar roles.

Licensing of people, organisations and aircraft

The regulations cover amongst other things the licensing of aircrew, air mechanics, engineers, air traffic controllers, aircraft, airports and airlines. In all cases there is a significant paper trail of documents that contain evaluations, maintenance histories, medical examinations, qualifications, authorisations, designs, test results and configuration details – everything that is needed to provide assurance of the air-worthiness of an aircraft, the competence of an aircrew member, an air mechanic, engineer or an air traffic controller, or the suitability of an airport or airline to operate in the industry.

Licensing implies documentation, much of it in electronic format

However, in the 21st century the so-called paper trail is much more likely to be in electronic format, and hence there are huge implications for managing the integrity and availability of this information. Without the proper documentation, and aircraft cannot take off and an aircrew member, air mechanic, engineer or air traffic controller cannot work, so the operational impact of losing control of this information is potentially substantial.

Data Protection Legislation (EU)

European protection of information held on private individuals

The concept of data protection (meaning legally protecting the privacy, integrity and use of information gathered and held relating to private individual citizens) is a European one. There is a European Union directive requiring all EU member countries to legislate for data protection and for these laws in each nation state to follow a harmonised set of guidelines that apply on a EU-wide basis.

Defined concepts

The EU laws have very specific definitions of the important concepts:

* Personal data;

* Processing;

* Data subjects (individuals who are subjects of personal data);

* Data controller;

* Data processor;

* Recipient;

* Third party.

The eight principles

There are also eight principles that characterise the legislation:

* Personal data shall be processed fairly and lawfully.

* Personal data shall be obtained only for one or more specified and lawful purposes and shall not be further processed in any manner incompatible with that purpose or those purposes.

* Personal data shall be adequate, relevant and not excessive in relation to the purpose or purposes for which they are processed.

* Personal data shall be accurate and, where necessary, kept up to date.

* Personal data processed for any purpose or purposes shall not be kept for longer than is necessary for that purpose or those purposes.

* Personal data shall be processed in accordance with the rights of data subjects under the legislation.

* Appropriate technical and organisational measures shall be taken against unauthorised or unlawful processing of personal data and against accidental loss or destruction of, or damage to, personal data.

* Personal data shall not be transferred to a country or territory outside the European Economic Area unless that country or territory ensures an adequate level of protection for the rights and freedoms of data subjects in relation to the processing of personal data.

A major driver for information security

This legislation is a major contributor to the regulatory drivers for operational risk management and information security management across all EU member states.

The Complexity of Operational Risk Management

A Case Study: The Banking Industry

The banking industry as a case study through which to explore the complexity of operational risk

Operational risk management is an issue in every industry, and especially so with the rising tide of regulation that affects all organisations and which is primarily aimed at improving the quality of corporate governance. These various drivers for operational risk management have been discussed above. However, the industry where most progress on operational risk management appears to have been made in recent years is the banking industry, and this provides an industry case study on which to base a discussion on operational risk management so as to explore some of its complexities.

Case Study: Operational Risk Management in the Banking Industry

The inclusion of operational risk in the New Basel Accord ('Basel II') is a major innovation. Banks will in future be required to allocate capital against a measured value at risk (VAR) for operational risks. Previously capital has only been allocated against potential losses under the headings of credit risk (the risk of lending) and market risk (the risk of investing on financial markets).

During recent years there has been a growing emphasis on the use of highly automated technical systems in the banking industry, much of it associated with the growth of electronic banking. There have also been many large-scale mergers and acquisitions amongst banks that test to the limit the viability of newly integrated systems and position the merged banks as high-volume service providers. At the same time there has been a major shift towards outsourcing the operation of these technical systems to third-party service providers. All of this suggests that operational risk exposures in banks are substantial and growing, and yet the industry as a whole has no real grasp on how large or small this risk may be, and whether it has the potential to trigger systemic failures across a number of banks. These then are the key drivers for introducing operational risk into the New Basel Accord.

Within the Basel II framework, operational risk is defined as 'the risk of losses resulting from inadequate or failed internal processes, people and systems, or external events.' Some commentators often say that operational risk refers to all risks not included under credit risk or market risk, but this is not true under this definition in the New Basel Accord. It includes internal and external fraud risks, risks associated with employment practices and workplace health and safety, risks associated with clients, products and business practices, risks of damage to physical assets, risks of business disruption and system failures, legal risks, risks of failure in execution, delivery and process management and other sundry unspecified operational risks. However, this definition specifically excludes reputation risk, strategic business risk and systemic risk. The use of the word 'losses' also needs clarification, since it is not the intention of the

New Basel Accord to require capital allocation against all indirect losses such as opportunity cost.

Variations in Mathematical Complexity

Exclusions may seem to be ducking the issue, but by sticking to the simpler areas the accord stands more chance of implementation

The exclusion of reputation risk, strategic risk and systemic risk from the New Basel Accord is reasonable on the grounds that the Basel Committee wishes to build on the rapidly developing internal assessment techniques in the operational risk arena and wishes to provide banks with incentives to improve those techniques even further. These incentives are in the form of reduced capital allocations where the more sophisticated risk measurement approaches are used. The operational risk measurement techniques being developed are quantitative and based upon applying statistical models to estimate value at operational risk. To include those risks that are excluded would present the banks with huge difficulties in implementing the accord, since it is clear that the mathematical models for those risks are far more complex than for operational risk within the definition.

As new advanced risk-modelling techniques emerge these may lead to more inclusions

Taking reputation risk as an example, anecdotal evidence suggests that reputations can survive a long series of serious events without too much damage, and that the small amounts of damage suffered can be quickly recovered. Then, one day an event comes along that does not seem different from its predecessors, but it turns out to be the straw that breaks the camel's back, and at this point the reputation of the firm collapses catastrophically. This catastrophic failure is far more complex than the losses incurred under the more straightforward operational risks, and its quantitative modelling would be a major challenge if it were included at the present time. It is possible that, had these more complex risks been included in the New Basel Accord, the entire initiative would have failed through being too difficult to implement. No doubt the Basel Committee has an eye on the future for inclusion of these more complex risks when the techniques for modelling them have evolved to a sufficiently usable level.

Statistical Modelling

Incomplete data on the 'tail' risks may present a problem – because these are the catastrophic risks that one most seeks to mitigate

However, this does raise a number of concerns about whether the New Basel Accord is really solving the operational risk problem in the banking industry in terms of preventing banks from failing catastrophically. A cynic might comment that the New Basel Accord requires a bank to measure certain operational risks 'because it can' and that those areas that are too difficult to measure are excluded, yet it these very exclusions where the largest potential business impacts are to be found. Reputation risk, systemic risk and strategic risk are all more likely to be 'tail risks', meaning that they are very low probability events with very high impact, found in the 'tail' of the statistical probability distribution (see Figure 15-1).

Computing value at risk

The computation of a value at risk (VAR) for a particular loss event is usually around some formula that has the fundamental structure:

$$\underset{\text{Impact}}{\underset{\text{loss}}{\text{VAR} = \text{Value of}}} \times \underset{\text{Threat}}{\overbrace{\text{Probability}}} \times \underset{\text{Vulnerability}}{\text{Probability of}}$$

		Probability of Loss	
VAR =	Value of Potential loss	x Probability of the event	x Probability of failure of controls
	Impact	x Threat	x Vulnerability

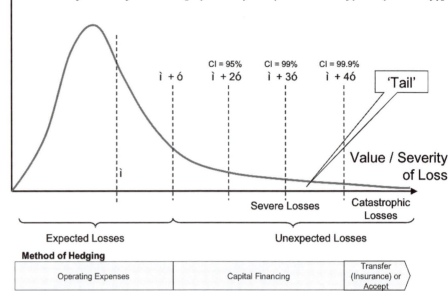

Figure 15-1: The Statistical Distribution of Operational Loss Events

Fitting a probability distribution for the frequency of loss events

The probability of a loss occurring within a given one-year period is theoretically based upon, and the product of, two separate probabilities: the probability that the threat event will occur within that period; and, given that the event occurs, the probability that the controls will fail and an impact will be experienced. In practice it is difficult to separate out these two factors, and if one is to model the combined loss distribution from historical data, such a separation is unnecessary. The technique is as follows:

- Collect historical data on the frequency of loss events;

- Statistically analyse the data (the sample) to determine the parameters of the sample: mean and standard deviation for frequency of losses over a one-year period;

- Use the sample parameters to estimate the population statistics: population mean (μ) and population standard deviation (σ) for the frequency of losses within a given one-year period;

- Fit the empirical data to a theoretical distribution – in this case the Poisson distribution is the most suitable;

- Carry out a 'goodness of fit test' using the χ^2 test of significance;

- Use the fitted distribution as the assumed distribution for the frequency of loss events within a one-year period.

Fitting a probability distribution for the size of losses

However, as well as the frequency of losses, the size of the loss is also statistically distributed, and so this too must be incorporated into the overall loss distribution. Once again the historical data can be used to model this second distribution:

- Collect historical data on the size of losses;

- Statistically analyse the data (the sample) to determine the parameters of the sample: mean and standard deviation for size of losses;

- Use the sample parameters to estimate the population statistics: population mean (μ) and population standard deviation (σ) for the size of losses;

- Fit the empirical data to a theoretical distribution – in this case the Lognormal distribution is the most suitable;

- Carry out a 'goodness of fit test' using the χ^2 test of significance;

- Use the fitted distribution as the assumed distribution for the size of loss events.

Using Monte Carlo methods to generate the combined loss distribution

Now you use a Monte Carlo simulation to combine these two distributions into a single loss distribution. The two theoretical distributions are used as the inputs into the Monte Carlo simulation, randomly selecting sizes and frequencies of loss events based on the theoretical distributions already modelled and generating output data for the final combined loss distribution. A typical example of the combined loss distribution obtained is shown in Figure 15-1.

Designating expected losses

In the diagram the probability distribution is Poisson-like, with an asymptotic probability density curve to the right-hand side, forming the tail of the distribution. The mean (μ) and standard deviation (σ) are the key parameters of the distribution. The greatest proportion of loss events fall within the range:

$$0 < \text{loss value} < \mu + \sigma$$

Designating severe and catastrophic losses

That is below the mean plus one standard deviation, and you might choose to call this range the expected losses – the cost of doing business. That leaves the tail losses as being unexpected losses, and you might choose to divide this range again at ($\mu + 2\sigma$) into severe losses and at ($\mu + 4\sigma$) into catastrophic losses. The aim of applying controls is to push the mean (μ) as far to the left as possible (to minimise the mean value of losses) and to minimise the standard deviation (σ) so that the ranges up to ($\mu + 2\sigma$) and ($\mu + 3\sigma$) are reduced. That would allow you to designate severe and catastrophic losses at four, five or even six standard deviations to the right of the mean, thus greatly reducing the probability of these types of loss. In most practical cases roughly 95% of events will fall below ($\mu + 2\sigma$). This is called the 95% confidence interval. The 99% confidence interval is at approximately ($\mu + 3\sigma$), and the 99.9% confidence interval is at approximately ($\mu + 4\sigma$).

Basel II capital adequacy requirements

The capital adequacy requirements of Basel II are that sufficient risk capital must be held to cover losses over a one-year period up to a 99.9% confidence interval. The capital must cover both expected and unexpected losses in this range and must also cover all risk types (as defined within the accord) and all lines of business.

Limits of Statistical Models

The need to collect and collate loss data systematically

However, there are complex problems associated with applying statistical methods. Measuring the actual statistical parameters (mean and standard deviation) can be done only if you have suitable loss-event data available, and one of the major problems facing those who wish to pursue quantitative statistical methods for operational risk is that such statistical data is usually not available. At best there is patchy, inconsistent, largely anecdotal information about previous losses. Even if you do accumulate a well-populated loss database, then there is still the problem that measuring the past history may not be a good indicator of the future – an issue that is discussed in more detail later in this chapter.

Pushing the limits of computational errors – problems in the tail risk areas

In the case of catastrophic tail risks the value of a potential loss is close to infinity in terms of the firm's ability to absorb it, and the probability of a loss event occurring is close to zero. The multiplication of infinity by zero yields a mathematically indeterminate result, and so the application of simple VAR computations in these cases is dubious. There is also the problem that one cannot accurately estimate a very low probability by looking at a loss database that contains zero occurrences of that event. The sample of previous events is simply not available to provide the input data, and you have to rely entirely on values of mean and standard deviation for predicting tail probabilities. At that point the potential errors in your measured values of μ and σ can become very significant. For all sorts of reasons, the mathematical models needed here are far more complex.

Complex Interactions between Risk Silos

The problem of silo thinking in enterprise-wide risk management

There is yet another aspect of complexity to be considered. Operational risk is in itself a complex and integrated thing. Just because you classify risks into silos for the convenience of identifying and managing them does not mean that they actually possess that discrete granularity. In practice, risks are interlinked in a complex web of interactions. Mitigating one operational risk almost always increases at least one other risk area, and hence the actions to manage and mitigate operational risks are often in conflict with one another[6]. This is frequently misunderstood and overlooked, because attempts to separate operational risks for classification purposes can suggest that they are discrete. This is certainly a problem with the public perceptions of risks that relate to everyday living, and many risk professionals do not always maintain sufficient awareness of this complexity when dealing with operational risk in the workplace. One fact that greatly exacerbates this problem is that operational risk management in most organisations is fragmented across many different functional departments[7], each with detailed knowledge of its own risk area, but without the visibility of how their mitigating actions affect and conflict with risk management goals in other departmental areas.

Ambiguity in classifying risks – when is an exclusion not excluded?

The excluded risk areas under the New Basel Accord are also clearly linked with many of the risks that are included. For example, almost any operational risk that has a serious impact has the potential to damage the reputation of the firm. In another example, if a firm makes a poor strategic acquisition of another firm so as to move into a new business area, and this attempt to diversify fails causing heavy financial losses, then it is clearly an outcome of a strategic risk event, yet it may well have been caused in part by failure of a due diligence process which is well within the New Basel Accord definition of operational risk. Nothing is ever simple!

Different perspectives for different requirements

To understand more fully the complexity of this high level of integration between risk areas one needs to look behind the definition of the term 'risk' itself. The definition of operational risk provided in the New Basel Accord focuses upon the underlying causes of loss (the threats), rather than on the nature of the losses themselves. This perspective is especially useful for managing operational risk in financial institutions and for introducing control regimes to mitigate risks.

---

[6]Consider the conflict between protecting the safety of occupants of a building by providing easily opened escape doors in case of fire, and the requirements to keep all the doors locked so as to prevent unauthorised access. There have been many tragic events, especially in nightclubs and similar venues, where this conflict has led to multiple deaths and injuries.

[7]Typically there is a corporate security team, a legal team, an insurance team, an ICT security team, a public relations team, a health and safety team, and so on, each working relatively independently of one another and unaware of the conflicts between each others' risk areas.

Measuring actual loss events is often of more practical use than attempting to analyse their causes

However, for the purposes of measuring operational risk and especially for providing standardised definitions of loss quantification that can be shared and pooled across different banks, it is more useful to focus upon actual measurable events. These events may have several contributory causes interacting with one another, many of which are not easily understood. To make capital allocation against these potential events the bank must translate the outcome of the event (business impact) into an effect on the P&L of the bank. Thus operational risk needs to be viewed and analysed from a number of different perspectives.

Approaches to Risk Assessment

Quantitative Methods

Lack of consistent complete loss data makes quantitative assessment difficult

Operational risk is a hot topic, mostly because it represents a huge area of corporate risk, but at the present time is extremely difficult to it tie down to numerical, quantitative analysis. The main issue is the lack of available, reliable, consistent data on which to perform statistical analysis. The holy grail of operational risk management is to be able to analyse historical loss data and make predictions about the future. Based upon this analysis one would then plan, implement, manage and operate a range of controls designed to meet these predictions.

Quantitative operational risk data would allow proper risk-adjusted cost calculations

One would also have the potential to make risk-adjusted computations of both operating costs and operating revenues by factoring in the risks that are taken to achieve those revenues and costs. A risk-adjusted cost, risk-adjusted revenue and hence a risk-adjusted profitability would be much more accurate measures of financial performance since they are potentially more sustainable into the future. The following case study should help to explain this idea.

Case Study: The Cost of Computer Virus Control

A small company had a number of PCs. The ICT manager of this company decided that the computer virus problem is overrated and that this company would not implement any special anti-virus software, processes or procedures. The amount of data interchange with the outside world was known to be small, and in the opinion of this Manager, the risk was negligible.

All went well for two years, and the CEO of the company was very pleased that the ICT department was able to keep down its costs to such a low level. Then, about six months into the third year, the company suffered a major virus infection that was initially introduced through an e-mail (the use of e-mail had been rapidly expanding over this period). The effect was severe. The entire business operations of the company were affected for several weeks. Productivity was hit and revenues were decimated. Customers were unable to be serviced, and many took their business elsewhere. What a piece of bad luck!

Only risk-adjusted cost is a measure of true long-term cost

The problem here was that the approach to calculating cost did not include any notion of risk. It is easy to keep your short-term costs down if you take enormous risks, but the longer-term view is different – because sooner or later the risks will bite and the costs of those events will be borne. In any risk management decision there is a view of the total cost being the cost of control plus the cost of losses (see Figure 15-2), and if this is not a risk-adjusted cost then it is illusory and unsustainable over the longer term. In this case study over the first two years both the cost of control and the cost

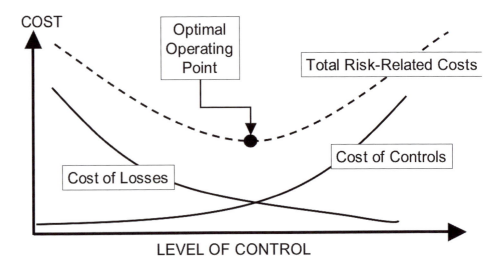

Figure 15-2: Optimising the Risk-Related Total Cost

of losses were zero, but that cannot be sustained forever, because the risk factor was missing from the calculation. To be able to make these risk-adjusted calculations you would need numerical risk factors, and for this you need the historical data.

The past is not necessarily a good predictor of the future

There is another problem though. Even if you had complete, accurate data on the history of loss events, the past is not necessarily a good predictor of the future, since new threats are emerging all the time, and the relative importance of existing threats is in a continual state of flux. Examples of new threats include the computer virus, unknown before the early 1980s, and the rising threat of international terrorism in the early 21st century. New threats can emerge at any time and are difficult to predict. If you rely upon historical data only, you will never predict them.

Operational risk is a black hole in corporate risk accounting

The fact that operational risk is such an elusive thing to measure creates a major business problem. It is known to be a widespread and diverse problem, yet with no reliable method of measurement of how large it is it remains a problem of unknown seriousness – a kind of black hole in the risk accounting practices of the world's businesses.

The banking industry is concerned about systemic failure caused by operational risk

As you have seen from the discussion on the proposed New Basel Accord, the banking industry is especially concerned, because whilst they have nailed down credit risk and market risk with sophisticated statistical methods, the failure to similarly address operational risk leaves the industry possibly facing the systemic risk of banks failing and by doing so bringing down a chain of other banks, rather like a line of upright dominoes toppling into one another. That is precisely why the Basel Committee has developed a new accord.

Qualitative Methods

Qualitative methods as a pragmatic approach

What is more commonly found, and indeed often much more useful from a management decision support perspective, is to treat operational risk assessment on a purely qualitative basis. In Chapter 9 of this book the SABSA® Risk Assessment Method is explained in detail, and this provides a good example of this type of qualitative risk assessment approach. The use of this qualitative method allows the risk profile to be presented to senior management in a traffic light chart, showing red, amber and green lights for qualitative levels of risk.

Assessing Criticality – Business Impact

Business impact assessment

One aspect of measuring risk is to assess how critical a risk event outcome might be to the business. The questions to be answered are: Does it matter? Do you care? If so, how much? The process of answering these questions is often called business impact assessment.

Thresholds and bands for impact

Business impacts can be measured either qualitatively or quantitatively. The qualitative approach is to define a number of bands. The simplest, and the one used in the SABSA® Method (see Chapter 9) deals with only three bands:

- High impact: could potentially do great damage to the business;

- Medium impact: could do significant damage to the business;

- Low impact: only minimal damage to the business;

Various levels of granularity

Some other methods use similar bands but at greater levels of granularity, such as four, five or 10 bands.

Quantitative methods for business impact assessment

Quantitative methods of measuring business impact tend to focus on financial value equivalence – what is the cost of a particular event in dollars or euros? On the more strategic types of impact, where reputation is at stake, this can be difficult to achieve with any accuracy, but some people use the potential fall in share price for a publicly traded company as being an equivalent measure of reputation. Other specific approaches to making quantitative calculations of business impacts include:

- Annual loss expectancy (ALE);

- Value at risk (VAR) – see earlier discussion;

- Risk-adjusted return on capital (RAROC)

Categories of business impact

Whether you decide to use qualitative or quantitative methods for assessment of business impact, it is useful to categorise business impact types as a tool for helping to assess the overall impact value, since the impact for a given event may be of several different types concurrently. The following checklist is one that provides a useful breakdown of business impact categories:

- Loss of revenue income;

- Loss of capital value;

- Increased operating costs;

- Opportunity costs;

- Damage to reputation;

- Bad publicity;

- Loss of key customers;

- Loss of key suppliers;

- Loss of market share;

- Loss of management control over the business;

- Damage to the entire market;

- Damage to customer confidence;

- Damage to employee confidence and morale;

- Damage to investor and shareholder confidence;

- Breach of the law or regulations leading to:

  - Fines;

  - Withdrawal of operating licence;

  - Custodial jail sentences for senior executives.

The business impact assessment process   In Figure 15-3 there is a flowchart representing a typical business impact assessment process, in this case based upon having constructed a SABSA® Business Attributes Profile as described in earlier chapters.

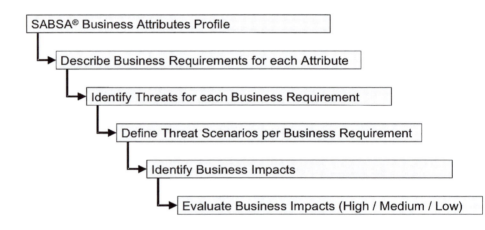

Figure 15-3: Business Impact Assessment Process

Assessing Likelihood – Probability

Compound probability of an event   The likelihood of an event causing a business impact is a product of two separate probabilities:

- The probability that the event will occur (the level of the threat);

- The probability that when the event occurs the controls will fail (the level of vulnerability).

Issues with statistical methods   Threat assessment and vulnerability assessment have already been discussed in Chapter 9, and you are referred back to that discussion now. However, it is worth noting once again that threat assessment can be difficult to conduct on a statistical basis, since historical data is often not available, history is not necessarily a good predictor of the future, and the threats and their respective levels change constantly. That is why an alternative method of assessing threats has been described in Chapter 9.

Unreliable data is a major issue for quantitative methods   The actual quantitative probability values for vulnerability are also rather difficult to compute, since upon what data would you base your calculations? That is why many risk professionals prefer to avoid playing guessing games with numbers that are unreliable and stay instead within the bounds of qualitative assessment methods.

Operational knowledge and experience is the key to vulnerability assessment

Vulnerability assessment techniques vary according to the circumstances, but in general require a range of intellectual input from various knowledgeable people. These will include those with operational experience on the ground, such as business operations staff and technical operations staff, and also external expert advisors who have experience in a broader field of activity than this one organisation. The joint experience of these people is best extracted through brainstorming workshops. The goal is to achieve broad agreement and buy-in across the team.

Technical vulnerability assessment tools

There are also specific technical methods for assessing vulnerability in business information systems. These include:

- System testing;

- System auditing;

- Vulnerability scanning using automated tools;

- Penetration testing (discussed in more detail in Chapter 17);

- Dependency tree modelling (discussed in more detail in Chapter 5)[8].

Managing Operational Risk

Risk Management Strategies

Doing business requires risk taking

You cannot do business without taking risks. To control costs, you need to take risks. To gain revenues, you need to take risks. The question is, how much risk? That will depend upon the size of the risks, the potential costs, the potential gains and your particular appetite for risk.

Risk management balances losses and opportunities

The aim of risk management is to balance the various risks taken by the organisation providing an optimal overall balance between cost, risk and revenue. Taking a risk is as much an opportunity for profit as it is a potential for loss. For every possible action you can take, there is a risk of taking that action and a risk of not taking that action. The risks of one course of action play against the risks of an alternative course of action, and the components of risk in a complex series of business actions also interact with one another in complex ways. To manage these risks you need to model the risks in a suitable way and then optimise the model. Risk modelling and risk assessment have been discussed in previous sections.

Risk management means deciding what to do about risks you have identified

Once you have assessed, analysed and modelled your risks so as to understand them, possible risk management strategies include:

- Reduce or mitigate the risk by increasing the level of control and thereby increasing costs;

- Transfer the risk to another party (such as by insurance), again increasing costs;

- Avoid the risk by avoiding that business activity, thus reducing revenue opportunities;

- Delay the risk until another time (if possible), thus delaying the costs, but also delaying the revenue opportunities;

---

[8]See also www.conceptlabs.co.uk and www.dependency.com

- Compensate for the risk by offsetting against other benefits associated with it – making a cost/benefit analysis to justify risks;

- Spread the risk (if possible) to gain advantage by using the statistical spread of risk events;

- Accept the risk (there is always a residual level of risk that must be accepted) because you cannot do business without taking risk and you need to grasp this opportunity;

- Reject the risk – not a real risk at all!

Risk Management and Corporate Governance

Corporate governance implies sound risk management

Enterprise risk management (ERM) refers to the management of the entire set of risks facing the enterprise – reputation risks, strategic risks, financial risks and operational risks. The only place where this high-level enterprise-wide view can be taken is at the board of directors, and hence the responsibility for enterprise risk management is inextricably linked to the corporate governance function of the board. The board must put in place risk management processes that apply across the entire enterprise.

Enterprise Risk Management Framework

The board must have an enterprise risk management framework

The board of directors must define how the management of risk will be handled in general across the enterprise. Within this enterprise framework will be a description of how you will actively manage your operational risks.

The ERM framework is all-encompassing

The risk management framework sets the context in which corporate risks are managed, in terms of how they will be identified, analysed, controlled, monitored and reviewed. It must be consistent and comprehensive, with processes that are embedded in everyday management. With regard to operational risk, such a framework will need to cover:

- Board oversight of operational risk management, with policies being set by the senior management to communicate downwards their requirements for managing operational risk, and regular real-time reporting upwards to inform senior management of the success and progress of the implementation of those policies. This oversight is part of what is often called governance.

- Definition of roles and responsibilities with regard to the management of risk at all levels of the organisation.

- The processes, procedures, standards, tools, facilities and documentation that are needed for risk management.

- A roll-up strategy for aggregating and consolidating operational risk data and reporting it through a series of dashboards to senior management, whilst at the same time preserving sufficient transparency and granularity in the consolidated figures to reveal major hot spots of risk down in the detail.

- Automated enterprise risk systems for risk-event sensing and capture, risk data collection and analysis, and application of the risk data to calculate risk-adjusted key performance indicators (KPIs).

- A no-blame enterprise risk management culture that encourages more honesty in risk event reporting and reduces the temptation to cover up mistakes.

- Enterprise-wide integration of risk management to avoid the problems of silo risk management in which the interaction between different types of operational risk is not understood.

- A good model and mapping of your business processes so that you can analyse each process and sub-process to identify where the operational risks are located within this process framework.

- A business process-based risk assessment and analysis methodology that is used to describe, quantify and prioritise operational risks in your business. As part of this there should be a defined framework for measuring risk in terms of both its likelihood and its potential business impact, as well of a method of determining the organisation's risk appetite or risk tolerance.

- The incorporation into your business processes of control points where risks have been identified and controls are to be applied to mitigate those risks.

- A risk register in which all of the significant business risks are recorded, including your operational risks, with an analysis of each risk and the actions being taken to mitigate the risk (see below for a more detailed discussion of risk registers).

- A method of defining risk objectives and associating these with key risk indicators (KRIs), and a means to monitor and report on those KRIs in real time, especially with the goal of providing advanced warning of potential risk events before they occur.

- Effective, efficient management of compliance with policies, regulations and legislation to limit operational risk.

- An enterprise-wide, pro-active programme of risk measurement, risk management and risk mitigation, including risk awareness for all employees.

Enterprise risk management conceptual model

Figure 15-4 shows a three-dimensional model that conceptualises the Board view of the enterprise risk management framework. The three dimensions are the:

- Risk dimension: having a hierarchical taxonomy of risks classified and grouped so as to provide a framework for risk identification;

- Enterprise organisation dimension: ensuring that risk is understood and managed at every level of granularity within the enterprise organisational model;

- Process dimension: ensuring that all major process-related aspects of risk management are addressed.

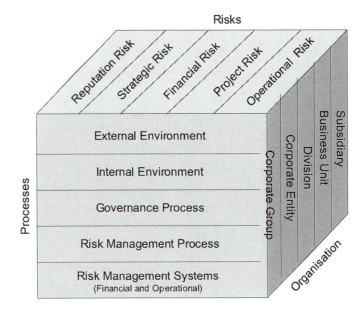

Figure 15-4: Enterprise Risk Management Framework

The external threat environment

The front face of the cubic framework (the process dimension) has five process components that must be taken into account by the board. Each of these is broken out into a more detailed model in the following five figures. Figure 15-5 shows the external environment as a series of external forces putting pressure on the enterprise. All of these external forces are sources of risk (threats).

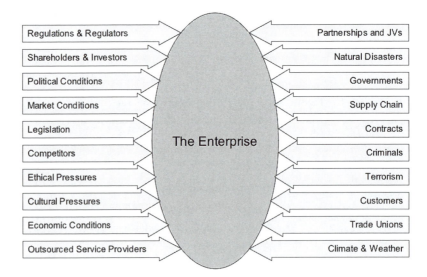

Figure 15-5: The External Environment

The internal enterprise environment

Figure 15-6 shows the various components that comprise the internal environment, conceptualised as a wheel with the corporate policies that communicate the board's intentions as the hub around which all other internal components revolve. Once again, all of these internal components are potential sources of risk (threats).

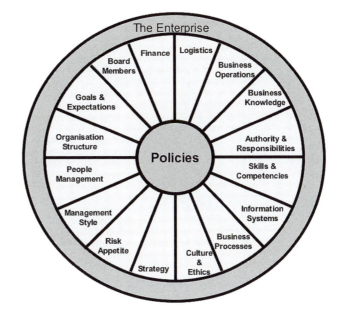

Figure 15-6: The Internal Environment

The corporate governance process

Figure 15-7 shows the corporate governance process itself, which is just another example of the type of feedback control look introduced in Chapter 5, Figure 5-4.

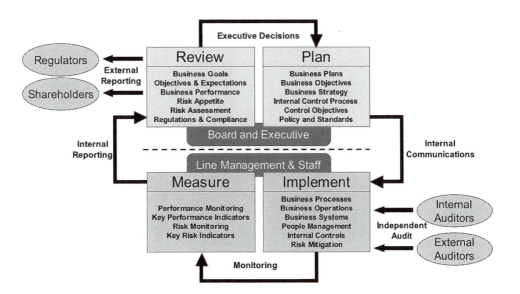

Figure 15-7: The Governance Process

The risk management process

Figure 15-8 shows a generic risk management process, which is yet another example of the type of feedback control loop introduced in Chapter 5, Figure 5-4. This risk management process is a subset of the governance process shown in Figure 15-7 and can be overlaid onto that earlier diagram.

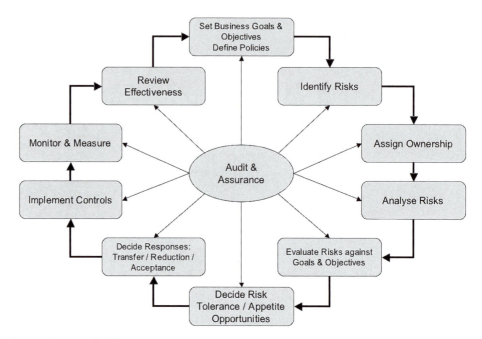

Figure 15-8: A Generic Risk Management Process

Conceptual architecture of an operational risk management system

Figure 15-9 provides a conceptual architecture view of an operational risk management system – an ICT system used to manage and co-ordinate all operational risk management activities and information.

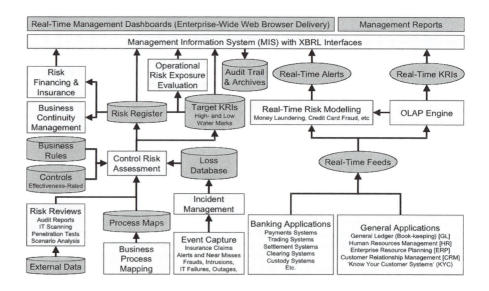

Figure 15-9: An Operational Risk Management System

Risk Management Standards

There are many commercial risk assessment and risk tracking products on the market, and some of those may have enough market penetration to claim to be *de facto* standards. However, there is one true national standard available – the Australian and New Zealand Standard for Risk Management AS/NZS 4360:1999[9]. The overall risk management process described in AS/NZS 4360 is shown in

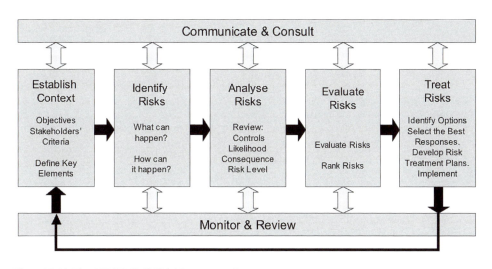

Figure 15-10: The AS/NZS 4360 Risk Management Process

Figure 15-10. By referring back to Figure 15-8 and by analysing the flow you will see that this AS/NZS 4360 process is essentially a specific example of the type of generic risk management process shown in the earlier diagram.

Although there is no international equivalent of AS/NZS 4360, the International Organisation for Standardisation (ISO) has recently issued a background document, ISO/IEC Guide 73: 'Risk Management – Vocabulary – Guidelines for use in standards'. This document standardises the concepts and language to be used in other standards.

Risk management standards are also available from several professional membership bodies, such as the joint standard issued in the UK by AIRMIC[10], IRM[11] and ALARM[12]. The risk management process from this standard is shown in Figure 15-11.

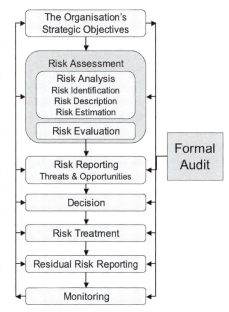

Figure 15-11: The AIRMIC/IRM/ALARM Risk Management Process

---

[9]There is a new draft version of this standard available at the time of writing, yet to be finalised.

[10]AIRMIC: Association of Insurance and Risk Managers (UK)

[11]IRM: Institute of Risk Managers (UK)

[12]ALARM: the national forum for risk managers in the UK public sector

The risk management process described in the AS/NZS 4360 framework bears many striking similarities to the SABSA® approach, although both were developed independently of one another. The AS/NZS 4360 process (which begins with risk description and risk assessment) is as follows:

AS/NZS 4360 Step 1: Establish Context

This means understanding what, from a business perspective, is at risk. It has two main phases, each of which covers several aspects:

- Descriptive phase:

    - Determine the business objectives.

    - Define the measurable success criteria for these objectives (covering all aspects of success).

    - Create measurements of risk (qualitative or quantitative).

    - Make a clear distinction between measuring the likelihood of a risk event and the impact of its occurrence.

    - Take into account stakeholders' concerns and objectives.

- Creative phase:

    - Split the entire enterprise into components: key elements.

    - Focus thinking on these key elements.

    - Stimulate creative thought through workshops and brainstorming sessions.

    - Speak specific risk-oriented language.

AS/NZS 4360 Step 2: Identify Risks

- Determine what can happen and how it can happen.

    - Cover both threats and vulnerabilities.

    - Checklists may be used, but you should avoid preconditioning expectations.

    - Checklists can help to verify the completeness of the identification process.

    - The recommended approach is a structured brainstorming workshop.

    - A secondary approach is to use questionnaires, surveys or interviews by skilled consultants.

    - You should include a creative assessment of the future – what might happen?

AS/NZS 4360 Step3: Analyse Risks

- Assign to each risk a significance rating using simple impact versus likelihood scales.

- Where risks are complex, custom-modelling techniques should be used.

- The outcome is an initial view of the significance of each risk, but it is recognised that at first pass ratings can be either too high or too low.

AS/NZS 4360 Step 4: Evaluate Risks

- Apply a screening process to ensure the system does not become bogged down with too many risk items.

- Prioritise the risks relative to the complete set taking into account known priorities and the supporting business requirements.

AS/NZS 4360 Step 5: Treat Risks

- Determine what you will do about each risk, both in terms of preventive measures and contingency arrangements.

- Calculate and sign off on the residual risk after the risk treatment plan has been applied – the business accepts this level of residual risk.

The steps are bound together by ongoing communication, consultation, monitoring and review

Each of these steps is linked into an ongoing communications and consultation process and also into a continuous monitoring and review process (see Figure 15-10). The latter ensures that there is an iterative process rather than a one-shot approach. The intention is to review only changes, but this assumes that there is a pre-requisite process in place for managing and tracking these changes.

The output is fed back as part of the iterative process

There is also a feedback loop from Step 5 to Step 1 whereby results of the Risk Treatment phase are fed back into the Establish Context phase as part of the continuous iterative process (see Figure 15-10). As with the generic process model in Figure 15-8, that feedback loop can be mapped onto the feedback control loop concept introduced in Chapter 5 and shown in Figure 5-4. The annotated version of this diagram in Figure 15-12 shows how the AS/NZS 4360 standard process maps onto the loop.

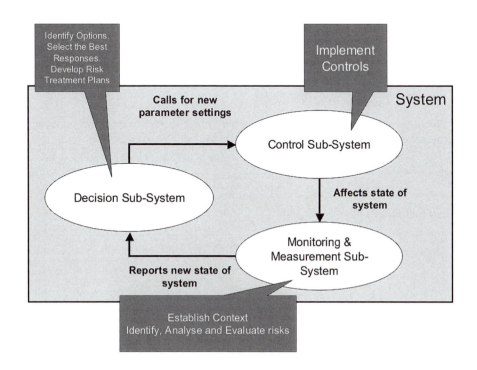

Figure 15-12: The AS/NZS 4360 Process as a Feedback Control Loop

Fundamental similarity between standards

Refer also to the AIRMIC/IRM/ALARM process in Figure 15-11. You will see that this too has a similar feedback control loop built into it. These processes are fundamentally the same, differing only in minor details of description and language.

The Risk Register

Risk register as the repository of all enterprise risks

The purpose of a risk register is to record details of all risks that have been identified, together with their analysis and plans for how those risks are to be treated. The risk register is an important component of the overall risk management framework. It will include ALL risks – not just operational risks. It can be focused either on the enterprise as a whole or on specific projects where it is used to maintain the register of project risks over the lifetime of the project.

Example structure for a risk register

An example of a risk register, in the form of a table, is shown in Table 15-2. This table could be maintained as a simple document in either a word processing format or a spreadsheet format, but it is more likely to be stored in a database. Many of the fields in the table have a defined set of options, which can be stored in sub-tables and entered from drop-down menus. Each risk entry in the table has a unique identifier to avoid any confusion in cross-referencing risks to other documents.

Assigning ownership of risk is critical to successful risk management

An important parameter recorded in the risk register is the owner of each risk – the person who owns responsibility for actions relating to that risk. The action plans and status reports may be detailed and thus unsuitable to be included in a table of this sort. One way to handle this issue is to use the table cells as entries of URLs or hyperlinks where the full documents can be found. This makes navigation of the risk register quick and efficient.

Classify risks according to type

The risk type field records a type such as operational, strategic, reputation, credit, market, liquidity, etc., so as to accommodate many different types of risk in the risk register.

Keep track of how recently the register has been updated to ensure currency and timeliness

It is important to record when the risk item was identified and added to the register, when the entry was last updated, and for some items, when they were closed. However, closed items should be maintained for historical analysis purposes, perhaps being transferred to a separate 'closed risks' register table.

The risk register is an information repository that requires its own authorisation and access control

Access to the risk register must be controlled to maintain its integrity and confidentiality. Some items recorded in the register may be sensitive and thus not for wide publication. These confidential items can be flagged by adding an extra field to the table record structure. The integrity of all item entries is also important, so you need a security policy for the register that defines who should be

Table 15-2: An Example of a Risk Register

Risk ID	Risk Name	Risk Type	Threat Description	Business Impact Description & Rating (H/M/L)	Vulnerabilities & Overall Likelihood (H/M/L)	Risk Category Rating (A/B/C/D)	Owner	Date Identified	Last Updated	Actions Planned (URL)	Current Status Report (URL)	Date Closed

able to update the table and who can read it. Table 15-3 shows an example of possible roles and how you might organise access control and authorisation. You might also want to create an audit trail by setting up a risk register transactions table which records all additions, changes and deletions in the risk register table itself.

Table 15-3: Role Management Example for Risk Register Access Control

Role	Privileges
Risk Manager	Full access to the entire table and the only role with Delete access
Risk Owner	Read access to all entries Create/Write/Update access to owned entries
Risk User	Read access to all entries
Restricted Risk User	Read access only to entries flagged as unrestricted

Benefits of Good Risk Management

Good risk management delivers many benefits

There are many benefits to be gained from a good operational risk management programme. These include:

- Keeping the senior executive managers and board members out of jail;

- Being able to continue to hold an operating licence in a regulated industry (such as civil aviation, pharmaceuticals, banking or insurance);

- Avoiding fines for corporate non-compliance with regulations and legislation;

- Cost reduction through reduced operational losses and improved efficiency of operational business processes;

- Reduced requirements for both regulatory and economic capital allocation;

- Improved shareholder value and confidence, which is especially valuable in times of crisis when shareholder trust is stressed to its maximum limits;

- Better measures of true business performance through the use of risk-adjusted key performance indicators (KPIs);

- Competitive advantage through improved decision support and market intelligence based upon more accurate risk-adjusted management information;

- More-reliable forecasting for new business plans, again based upon more accurate risk-adjusted management information;

- Improved relationships with industry regulators.

Risk Mitigation

Types of Control

Controls are applied to mitigate risks

Risk mitigation is the process of introducing controls to reduce the frequency or severity of a business impact. This can be done in a number of different ways, depending upon the type of control:

- Deterrent control – reduces a threat;

- Preventive control – reduces a vulnerability;

- Corrective control – reduces an impact;

- Detective control – detects a problem and triggers other controls.

There different types of control

The way in which these different types of control interact with the components of risk is shown in Figure 15-13.

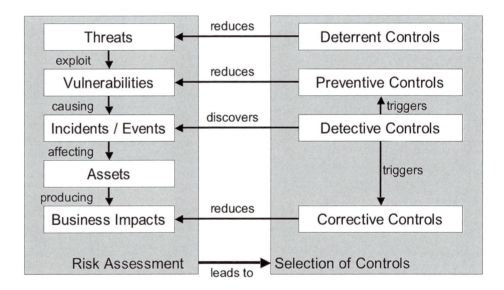

Figure 15-13: The Types of Control and How They Work

Levels of Control

Control decisions should be supported by a cost/benefit analysis

The conceptual strategies for layering controls have already been discussed in Chapter 10 (see Figures 10-1 and 10-2). In order to fulfil the optimisation goals of risk management, one must carry out a cost/benefit analysis of each control – is the total cost of this control greater or less than the total cost equivalent of the risk reduction being achieved through this control? Only if the cost of control is less than the cost of the risk will it be cost-effective to implement the control. The overall goal is to minimise the total cost of losses, as is suggested by the diagram in Figure 15-2.

Good risk management through the application of controls requires you to seek the middle path

Another diagram that presents this idea in a different way is in Figure 15-14. If the investment in control is low but the risk is high, then this suggests over-exposure to risk, but if the investment in control is high in response to a low level of risk, this suggests that the cost of control is excessive. In risk management one is always searching for that middle ground where the optimum position is to be found – the appropriate level of control.

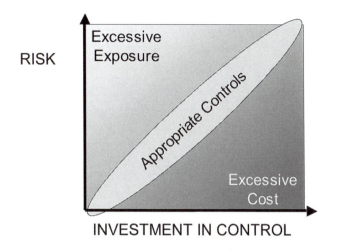

Figure 15-14: Appropriate Levels of Control

Risk-Based Security Reviews

A risk-based security review of an existing system is similar to carrying out a 'before the fact' risk assessment

Conducting a risk assessment of an existing system is similar to but subtly different from carrying out the risk assessment described in Chapter 9 as part of the development of an enterprise security architecture project. The difference is that in the enterprise architecture development one is providing for a generic set of systems, whereas in a risk-based system security review, the specifics of the system are already known.

The risk-based assessment process for existing systems

In order to illustrate the risk assessment to be applied to a specific business information system, a case study example is used here. However, before embarking on the details of the example, Figure 15-15 shows the overall risk assessment process that is applied.

Case Study: The Brief

The Interstellar Travel Engineering Company (ITEC) asked a team of specialist information risk consultants to conduct a review of the risks it faced in its main business information system and a review of the security of that system with regard to mitigating and managing those risks.

The company wanted to receive a report highlighting any key risk areas, with clear justified recommendations for additional controls in areas where the risk was judged to be unacceptable, and an assurance that once the new controls were applied the risks would be reduced to an acceptable level.

The consulting team used the following method to fulfil the client's requirements:

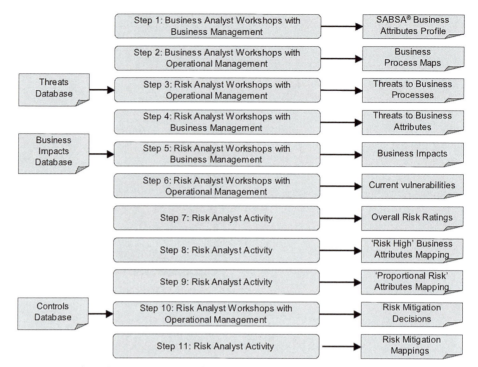

Figure 15-15: The Risk Assessment Process for Reviewing the Security of Existing Systems

Case Study Step 1: Develop the Business Attributes Profile

Using the SABSA® Business Attributes Profile method and by engaging the management team of ITEC in a series of workshops, the consultants developed the Business Attributes Profile, including the relevant Business Attributes, their detailed definitions within the ITEC context, the metric types, the measurement approach to be taken for each and the performance targets for each attribute.

Establishing the business requirements for security and control

This first step is necessary to understand the business requirements for information security in the broadest possible terms. It utilises the methodology already introduced in Chapters 6 and 7 of this book. The management team involved in this part of the process are those who can speak for the business as a whole – senior managers.

Case Study Step 2: Map the Business Processes

By engaging with business operational managers in all departments where operations were supported by the business information system, and using a specialised business process mapping software tool to aid productivity, the consultants built detailed process maps, showing high-level processes, broken down at lower levels into sub-processes, and so on until a level of granularity was achieved that facilitated full understanding and knowledge of the processes.

Mapping the business processes

In order to identify, describe and analyse business operational risks within a business information system, you need to have a good understanding of the business processes that are supported by the system, including knowing which parts of the process are automated and which parts are manual. The best way to achieve this understanding is to examine detailed process maps. If these are not available, then you need to build them as part of this exercise. Those who can help build these maps are managers with hands-on operational responsibility at the detailed level.

Case Study Step 3: Analyse the Business Processes

Using the threats database and business process maps the consultants worked step by step through each business process, in workshop sessions with the relevant operational managers, to determine at every stage of the processes what the requirements were for security and control, and what threats put those requirements at risk.

Identify risks in business processes

These results are tabulated into a Risk Assessment Working Table columns 1 to 4 as shown in Table 15-4.

The column details are as follows:

Column 1	The Risk ID	This is a unique identifier introduced at this stage for future cross-referencing.
Column 2	Business Process Reference	Each component of each business process map must be systematically indexed for reference, and this index is cross-referenced here.
Column 3	Business Requirement	This is a description of the business requirement for security and control within this business process component.
Column 4	Threat Description	This describes the threats perceived as putting at risk the business requirement in Column 3.

Table 15-4: Sample Layout for Risk Assessment Working Table

1	2	3	4	5	6
Risk ID	Bus. Proc. Ref.	Business Requirement	Threat Description	Business Attributes	Performance Targets

Table 15-5: Sample Layout for 'Risk Mitigation Working Table'

1	2	3	4	5	6
Risk ID	Bus. Proc. Ref.	Business Requirement	Threat Description	Current Risk Rating	Proposed Improvements to Mitigate Risk
				A (red)	
				B (amber)	
				A (red)	
				B (amber)	

7		8	9		10
Business Impact		Current Controls	Current Vulnerabilities		Risk Rating
	H			H	**A** (red)
	H			M	**B** (amber)
	H			L	**C** (green)
	M			H	**B** (amber)
	M			M	**B** (amber)
	M			L	**C** (green)
	L			H	**C** (green)
	L			M	**C** (green)
	L			L	**C** (green)

7	8	9	10
Cost Factor (H/M/L)	Difficulty Factor (H/M/L)	Projected Vulnerability Level	Projected Risk Rating
		L	**C** (green)
		L	**C** (green)
		L	**C** (green)
		L	**C** (green)

Case Study Step 4: Associate the Business Attributes

The consultants then cross-referenced the business requirements and the threat descriptions in Columns 3 and 4 of the Risk Assessment Working Table to the Business Attributes Profile, registering those Business Attributes that were affected by each identified threat, and also the Performance Targets associated with each Business Attribute.

Associate the process-embedded risks with the Business Attributes

These results are tabulated into Columns 5 and 6 of the Risk Assessment Working Table as shown in Table 15-4. Note that for any given identified threat, there may be more than one Business Attribute affected, and hence the table rows are split at this point to accommodate as many Business Attributes as are required.

The column details are as follows:

Column 5	Business Attributes	The Business Attributes are cross-referenced from the Business Attributes Profile.
Column 6	Performance Targets	For each Business Attribute the Performance Targets are picked up, again from the Business Attributes Profile.

Case Study Step 5: Describe the Business Impacts

Once again using brainstorming techniques with appropriate management workshops, the consultants then assessed the business impact resulting from each threat materialising, based upon the potential failure to meet the Performance Targets specified in the Business Attributes Profile.

Capture types and severity of business impact

These results of Step 5 are tabulated in Column 7 of the Risk Assessment Working Table as shown in Table 15-4. This column has a main column for a description of the business impact and a sub-column for the impact to be rated as high, medium or low.

The column details are as follows:

Column 7	Business Impact	A description of the business impact arising from this threat, possibly based on the impact categories listed in the section entitled Assessing Criticality earlier in this chapter
Sub-column	Impact Rating	A rating of high, medium or low, as defined in the section entitled Assessing Criticality earlier in this chapter

Using the Business Attributes Profile to normalise the measurement of impact

You may be wondering at this point, 'Why not just go straight to the business impact assessment from the threat stage, without bringing in the Business Attributes?' The reason for using the Business Attributes Profile is to normalise all impact assessments against the performance targets agreed by senior management. There is a potential problem if this is not done that individual operational managers will either underestimate or overestimate the true level of business impact, and this problem is experienced in many risk assessment methodologies. By referencing everything back to a Business Attributes Profile that has an enterprise-wide applicability, the variability of opinion is eliminated from the process, and the results are far more meaningful and reliable.

Case Study Step 6: Assess Current Vulnerabilities

For this stage of the assessment the consultants assembled a different team that included some of the operational managers who understood the manual details of the business processes but also those technical experts who could speak with authority on the workings of the information systems that were used to automate parts of the business processes. The workshops focused upon describing the current controls relating to the identified threats, and hence the residual vulnerabilities that might exist.

Additionally a number of purely technical assessments were made using vulnerability scanning tools and a specialist penetration testing team. The results of these technical assessments were fed into the workshop sessions for discussion and evaluation.

Assess vulnerabilities

These results of Step 6 are tabulated into Columns 8 and 9 of the Risk Assessment Working Table as shown in Table 15-4. Column 9 has a main column for a description of the current vulnerabilities and a sub-column for the overall current vulnerability to be rated as high, medium or low.

The column details are as follows:

Column 8	Current Controls	
Column 9	Current Vulnerabilities	A description of the business impact arising from this threat, possibly based on the impact categories listed in the section entitled Assessing Criticality earlier in this chapter
Sub-column	Current Vulnerability Rating	A rating of high, medium or low, where:
		High = current controls are poor and it is very likely that the controls will fail
		Medium = controls are fair, but may fail
		Low = current controls are good and unlikely to fail

Case Study Step 7: Assess Overall Risk Rating

The consultants now assessed the overall risk rating based upon the rating values of business impact and current vulnerability.

Calculate overall risk rating

This is a simple exercise using the mapping matrix shown in Table 15-6. The results are entered into Column 10 of the Risk Assessment Working Table as shown in Table 15-4. The cells of this matrix can be colour-coded red, amber or green, depending upon the risk rating.

Table 15-6: Risk Category Mapping Matrix

		Business Impact		
		Low	Med	High
Vulnerability	High	C green	B amber	A red
	Med	C green	B amber	B amber
	Low	C green	C green	C green

	Meaning of Risk Rating
A red	Unacceptable – system fails the review
B amber	Business risk decision needed
C green	Acceptable without further consideration

Ratings indicate pass, fail or management decision needed

Rating A is a clear fail, and rating C is a clear pass, but rating B is more complex. This indicates that there is a significant risk that could be reduced with additional control but that there is a management decision involved as to whether to accept this risk or to increase the level of control.

Senior management reporting is through the Business Attributes Profile

However, for senior management, who have bought into the Business Attribute Profile and who do not get involved in system details, the results need to be reformatted into the Business Attributes Profile itself, so that these decisions on acceptability can be taken at the right level of management.

Case Study Step 8: Map Risk-High Ratings to Business Attributes Profile

Using the information from the Risk Assessment Working Table (Table 15-4) the consultants extracted all the instances of each Business Attribute and presented a diagram showing each of the Business Attributes as a single instance, with each one colour-coded according to the highest risk rating recorded for this Attribute. This is called the Risk-High Business Attributes Current Status diagram.

Colour coding re', amber or green displays the worst case risk category in the Business Attributes Profile

The purpose of this risk-high diagram is to show to senior management the Business Attributes Profile (with which it is already familiar) colour-coded such that each Business Attribute shows up a red, amber or green light according to the highest risk recorded as affecting that attribute. This is a worst-case scenario. Figure 15-16 shows a fragment of the Business Attributes Profile as an example.

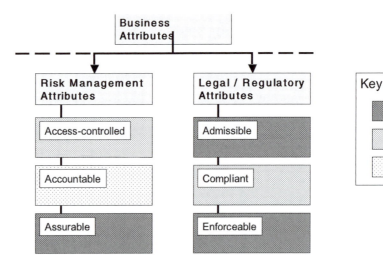

Figure 15-16: The Risk-High Business Attributes Current Status

Case Study Step 9: Map Proportional-Risk Ratings to Business Attributes Profile

The consultants also constructed a second diagram using the same extracted information from Step 8. This second diagram also showed each of the Business Attributes as a single instance, but this time with each one colour-coded proportionally according to the spread of risk ratings extracted from the Risk Assessment Working Table (Table 15-4). This second diagram is called the Proportional-Risk Business Attributes Current Status diagram.

Colour coding red, amber or green displays the proportional spread of risk categories in the Business Attributes Profile

The purpose of this second diagram is to juxtapose against the worst-case scenario a more balanced view of the risk ratings. The overall objective in presenting both diagrams together to a senior management team is to help that team to make decisions regarding amber-rated risks. Figure 15-17 shows a fragment of the Business Attributes Profile as an example.

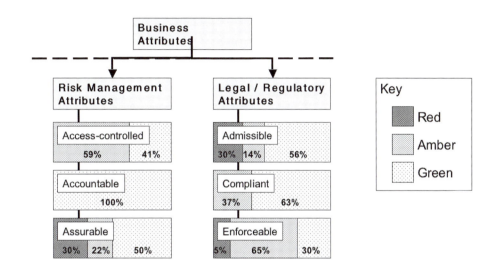

Figure 15-17: The Proportional-Risk Business Attributes Current Status

Case Study Step 10: Risk Mitigation

Working with the same team of operational managers and technical experts used for Step 6, the consultants now considered each threat in turn, together with its associated vulnerabilities, so as to propose improvements to mitigate the risk by implementing additional controls.

Deciding upon risk mitigation

The results of this workshop are entered into a second table called the Risk Mitigation Working Table (see Table 15-5), in which each row represents a threat that showed up with either a red or amber risk rating in the Risk Assessment Working Table.

The table entries show:

Column 1	The Risk ID	This is the same unique identifier used in Table 15-4.
Column 2	Business Process Reference	Same cross-reference as in Table 15-4
Column 3	Business Requirement	Replicated from Table 15-4
Column 4	Threat Description	Replicated from Table 15-4
Column 5	Current Risk Rating	Only red and amber risk ratings are selected for this table.

Column 6	Proposed Improvements to Mitigate Risk	A description of the actions proposed to increase controls so as to mitigate the risk. At this stage there may be a management decision to accept the risk (if it has an amber light), in which case this can be recorded in this part of the table.
Column 7	Cost Factor	What is the potential cost of these actions and new controls, rated as High, Medium or Low?
Column 8	Difficulty Factor	What is the potential level of difficulty of these actions, rated as High, Medium or Low?
Column 9	Projected Vulnerability	After mitigation, what level of residual vulnerability will there be? The usual target will be L.
Column 10	Projected Risk Rating	Mapped from Table 15-6 using the projected vulnerability rating. The usual target will be C.

Case Study Step 11: Map Mitigated Risks to Business Attributes Profile

To complete the presentation to senior management the consultants now constructed two more colour-coded diagrams similar to those produced in Steps 8 and 9. These were respectively the Risk-High Business Attributes Projected Status diagram and the Proportional-Risk Business Attributes Projected Status diagram.

Map Risk High and Proportional Risk to Business Attributes profile

These diagrams are similar to those shown in Figures 15-16 and 15-17, but in this case they refer to the status of the Business Attributes Profile after the risk mitigation has been applied. The intention is that by viewing these simple diagrammatic presentations, senior management will see first a current status showing a number of red and amber lights across the diagrams, but that once the planned mitigations have been implemented, the majority of these will turn into green lights. This is a powerful way to present the business case for the investment needed for the risk mitigation projects that are planned.

Presenting the risk mitigation programme to Senior Management

The mapping of risk ratings back to the Business Attributes Profile also ensures that senior management is presented with the risk profile mapped across a set of performance targets to which it has already signed off, and that an individual operational manager's opinions do not contaminate the senior management view of priorities.

Risk Financing

Risks that remain unmitigated must be financed

Having analysed your risks, you have defined mitigation strategies and selected a series of controls to implement your mitigation. However, not all risks can be mitigated – at least not completely, and so you are now left with a level of risk that may have a business impact on your enterprise and must be treated in some other way.

Risk financing is achieved through insurance

This is where risk financing comes into play, using the concept of insurance. Risk financing is designed to manage the financial impact of a risk event if it occurs. There are two main themes:

- Risk acceptance – self-insurance;
- Risk transfer – taking out insurance through a third-party insurer.

Risk Acceptance

Risk acceptance is necessary to provide a business opportunity

Every enterprise has to have a level of risk that it will accept; otherwise it is impossible to do business. Risk represents both an opportunity to make profit and the potential to make losses. What is important to the enterprise is to manage its risks so as to balance the opportunities against the potential losses for the overall good of the business.

Different organisations have differing levels of risk appetite or tolerance

The amount of risk that an organisation is prepared to take is often known as its risk appetite or risk tolerance. It varies from one enterprise to another depending upon the culture, the industry, the line of business and the potential gains. It is also affected by the spread of risk over several lines of business, several geographic locations or over other structural factors that mean the proverbial eggs are not placed in one basket.

Risk Transfer: The Concept of Insurance

Insurers make a profit because of the statistical spread of loss events

Insurance in its simplest form is familiar to everyone in their personal lives in the form of car insurance, buildings and contents household insurance and life insurance. Each person or household pays a premium to transfer catastrophic risks to an insurance company. The insurer calculates the premiums according to actuarial techniques using statistical data, such that on average the insurer makes a profit, even though it will have to pay out on some claims. The principle is based upon the insurer spreading its risk over many different clients, some of who will sustain losses and make claims, but most of who will not.

The insured takes some limited risk through the excess of the insurance policy

The insurer does not take on the entire risk, since there is usually an excess on the insurance policy – a base sum below which the claimant takes the financial pain. This is in effect the risk tolerance or risk appetite of the individual taking out the insurance. Some policies allow you to choose your own excess depending on how much risk you want to take on yourself. By taking a larger excess you can get a lower insurance premium – in other words you balance the risks of a lower upfront cost against a lower payout if you have a claim, or vice versa.

Risk appetite is influenced by the spread of risks experienced by a given organisation

The level of risk appetite depends on what you can afford to lose. Losses above what you can afford are severe or catastrophic losses, and it is these that you seek to insure against. If you own one house, it makes sense to insure it against fire and other catastrophic events, because if it is destroyed you have lost everything. However, if you owned a thousand houses, as many companies do, it is nonsense to take out fire insurance on all these properties because your risk is already spread, and statistically you are unlikely to have more than one or two of these properties damaged by fire (unless they are crowded closely together). If they are all in same locality you may be unlucky enough to have them all damaged by the same storm, but not so if they are widely spread throughout distant locations.

Insurance is used when the spread of risks is poor and there is high concentration of risk that needs to be financed

The need to insure is therefore calculated on the basis of analysing the risks and looking at the spread that exists. Where you have a high concentration of risk for one type of asset then insurance is likely to be a useful solution. Where the risk is widely spread, self-insurance (that is carrying the financial risk yourself) is likely to be more economic.

Types of Insurance

Types of insurance vary according to business need

It is beyond the scope of this book to provide a detailed account of the insurance industry, but listed here are some of the most important types of insurance that are relevant to information security-related risks.

- Banker's Blanket Bond, also known as a fidelity bond, covering the direct theft of cash or funds either in transit or on premises, employee infidelity and forgery;

- Professional Indemnity (PI) insurance, also known as Errors and Omissions (E&O) insurance, covering failures in human professional judgement;

- Directors and Officers (D&O) insurance covering the liabilities of those with formal responsibilities and liabilities under company legislation;

- Traditional property insurance covering damage and destruction of buildings, equipment, plant, finished goods, raw materials, etc.;

- Traditional crime policies covering theft;

- Specialised computer crime insurance policies covering direct loss of tangible property such as cash, negotiable instruments, securities, etc.;

- Business interruption insurance, protecting a business owner against losses resulting from a temporary shutdown because of fire or other insured peril and providing reimbursement for lost net profits and necessary continuing expenses, including the expense of carrying on business at another temporary location.

Self-Insurance

Self-insurance is applicable where there is a good spread of risks

This concept, in which you retain the financial risk of certain events rather than seek third-party insurance, has been introduced above. It is used where it is more economic to self-insure than to pay insurance premiums to a third-party insurer. It can take several forms.

The cost of doing business is the first level if self-insurance

At the simplest level, self-insurance involves recognising that certain types of operational loss are an inevitable cost of doing business. These regular, predictable levels of loss are simply built into the annual budget and show up as cost items on the profit and loss account of the company.

A premium excess is a type of self-insurance

Self-insurance can also take the form of the excess on an insurance policy, in which a sustainable level of loss is not transferred to the insurer, thus reducing the premiums paid. The value of the excess is set at a level of loss that the insured party feels able to sustain without undue discomfort.

Capital allocations are made against the potential for major catastrophic risk events

For certain types of catastrophic loss, which are not easily or economically insured, and which are far beyond the comfort zone of the policy excess, it is sometimes appropriate to allocate capital reserves on the balance sheet of the company. This means setting aside capital that is not used for any other purpose (other than being invested in an easy access deposit account) but which is then available to cover the cost of any large unplanned and unpredicted loss events.

Self-owned insurance companies offer captives

Yet another form of self-insurance is to set up insurance policies with an insurance company that you own. Such schemes are known as captives. A single parent captive is an insurance company owned and controlled by one company and is used to insure only that company and its subsidiaries. A group captive is an insurance company owned and controlled by two or more non-affiliated organisations that the captive insures. In theory all mutual insurance companies are group captives owned by their policyholders. Also intergovernmental insurance pools are captives owned by the public agencies that they insure.

Captives can also be rented

A variation of the captive concept for those companies not large enough to form their own captive is a rental captive. In this case someone sets up a captive using a front company and rents it out to other companies needing insurance. This rent-a-captive approach is perfectly legal and provides a viable alternative.

Another alternative risk financing arrangement is known as finite insurance. Here the limit of coverage, the time period involved and the premium paid acknowledge the time value of money. Premiums are paid for a finite period of insurance. Risk transfer to a third party takes place but most of the premiums are put into a fund wholly owned by the insured party. This fund accrues interest and pays out losses. At the end of the transaction period all money in the fund is paid back to the insured. The third-party component acts as a type of reinsurance for the self-insured fund in case that fund is unable to meet its claims.

Finally there are now many alternatives to conventional insurance based upon products offered by the capital markets. These include a variety of hedge funds, bonds, options and derivatives specially linked into certain types of risk. This enables a company to construct a special portfolio of risk financing structures especially tailored to its own risk profile and its needs for insurance.

Problems with Insurance

Although many types of direct loss are insurable, most insurance policies have many exclusions and the small print of such policies can be extensive.

One of the most important of these with regard to information security risk is the exclusion of coverage for loss of confidential or proprietary information. It usually comes down to the definition of property, which is defined as something tangible under the terms of the insurance policy. This leaves a huge gap with regard to insurance coverage for information-related risks.

Another important exclusion is indirect or consequential loss. As mentioned above it is possible to get coverage for business interruption caused by certain perils such as fire, but it is generally not possible to get such coverage for business interruptions caused by employee dishonesty or extortion, since indirect losses are excluded from the coverage in fidelity bonds. Similarly, the fidelity bond does not cover any loss incurred by the unauthorised actions of an employee, a customer or any party who had been granted authorised access to a computer system and then abuses those privileges.

As explained above, insurance works because the insurer can spread its losses over many insured clients and make a profit whilst paying out on individual loss claims. However, this starts to break down if the losses of all the clients start to aggregate or accumulate into a massive loss scenario for the insurer. Not only is such business unattractive, but also potentially it could lead to the financial demise of the insurance company, which is in no one's interests. There are therefore concerns about the potential dangers of insuring against single cyber attacks (such as caused by the I Love You and Melissa viruses), which could potentially cause billions of dollars worth of damage across the entire insured population of clients of an insurer.

This type of concern has had a considerable negative effect on the development of new insurance products in the cyber world. Insurance is traditionally based upon actuarial analysis of long histories of statistical loss data, and all traditional insurance works well because of this sound mathematical basis. The types of loss now being faced in the highly automated, information-rich world of cyberspace do not have long histories, and there are no such statistical data on which to perform the analysis.

The insurance industry is cautiously attempting to venture into this new world with innovative insurance products, but it has difficulty in assessing its own overall risks without the proper data.

For this reason insurance products tend to lag behind the development of digital business by a considerable margin.

When you consider that as much as 50 percent of the value of new businesses in the knowledge economy can consist of intangible assets in the form of information (designs, research data, product and pricing information, customer details, digital products such as music, films and games), all of which can easily be stolen, copied, reproduced and distributed on a huge scale, this represents a major problem area of uninsurable risk.

The Risk Management Dashboard

Monitoring and Reporting Key Risk Indicators

Dashboards are used by managers to monitor current status of the business

In Chapter 6 the concept of a Security Management Dashboard has been introduced (see Figure 6-1). Such a dashboard provides the monitoring function in the feedback control loop also introduced earlier in Chapter 5. This approach can be applied to monitoring operational risks of all types and has been mentioned above under the description of an enterprise-wide risk management framework.

Risk management dashboards are needed at all levels of management

Different dashboards are required for different levels of management. The board and executive management need to be shown a series of high-level key risk indicators (KRIs) that tell them about the overall risk exposure of the business as a whole. They also need as many early-warning indicators as possible to allow them to foresee problems that can be minimised if properly managed. Further down the management hierarchy each tier has its own similar needs for a dashboard, showing KRIs that are relevant to the degree of granularity and detail being managed at that level of responsibility.

The SABSA® Business Attributes Profile can be used directly as a risk reporting dashboard

For the information security manager, chief information security officer (CISO) or chief information risk officer (CIRO) the dashboard needs to display KRIs that are focused on their sphere on interest. Using the SABSA® Business Attributes Profile as the main driving force for information security-related risk assessment provides a set of parameters that can be monitored against preset performance targets and can be presented in the form of a risk management dashboard. These can be arranged into any visual form you like, but one obvious way is simply to present the taxonomy diagram in Figure 6-4 (see Chapter 4).

Use traffic light colours and click on for drill-down

Assuming that the Business Attributes taxonomy diagram is used for visual presentation purposes, you can present traffic light colour-coding for each of the Business Attribute boxes. The simplest method is to present a single colour (red, amber or green) for each box, taking the Risk-High status as characterising the entire attribute at that level, as described for presenting the results of risk reviews and shown in Figure 15-16 above.

The drill-down through hyperlinks provides high usability

Each Business Attribute box on the screen can be set up as a hyperlink to another screen showing the detailed analysis for that Business Attribute, including the proportional risk status (see Figure 15-17), details of the measurement approach, the metric types defined, the performance targets that have been set and the metrics that have been collected. Such a dashboard is highly usable and provides detailed analysis behind a red or amber light on the main dashboard at a single click of the mouse.

Ongoing monitoring and collection of data allows you to calibrate the effectiveness of controls

The ongoing monitoring process also allows actual operational data to be collected against each of the performance targets for each of the Business Attributes. This allows you to collect data that measure and calibrate the effectiveness of the controls you have chosen to mitigate the identified risks. The first time you make the selection of controls it has to be done on a fairly subjective basis, but as the data in the risk management dashboard mature you accumulate real metrics on the effect of each individual control or group of controls. Later selections as part of new projects eventually becomes much more objective based upon this performance measurement data.

Many organisations apply a baseline control standard

This capability to calibrate the effectiveness of each control then enables you to take the graphical presentation of the dashboard a stage further. It is often the case that an organisation has a baseline control standard, especially for ICT-related risk mitigation. All controls in the baseline standard are mandatory and must be applied regardless of the risk assessment. However, applying the baseline controls may not mitigate all risks to an acceptable level, leaving some that require special treatment above and beyond the baseline.

Multiple dashboard views of the risk profile

This gives the possibility to show three parallel views of the Business Attributes Profile, either in Risk-High status or Proportional-Risk status. The first view is the green field view[13], before any controls of any kind are applied. Some people call this the pure risk view. You would expect this view to have many red lights showing, since there is no mitigation in place. The second view is after the baseline controls have been applied, and this view should have turned off most of the red lights, leaving only a few that require special treatment, and also leaving a number of amber lights which are somewhat borderline in terms of mitigation. Finally, after special treatments have been applied to address the remaining red (and possibly amber) lights, the view should now be mostly one of green lights. Figure 15-18 shows an example with a single Business Attribute displayed as green field, post-baseline and post-special treatments for both Risk-High and Proportional-Risk status.

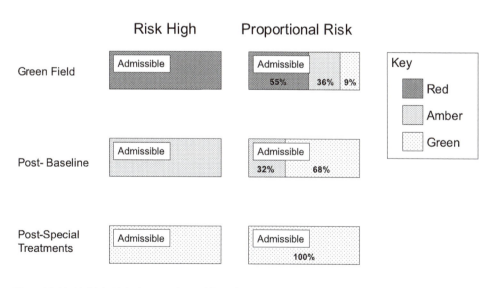

Figure 15-18: Multiple Risk Views on the Dashboard

Risk Reporting using XBRL

XBRL is an XML-based business reporting language

In Chapter 13 there is a discussion of XML (eXtensible Markup Language) and an entire family of interface specifications that can be developed based upon XML. One of the more recent developments

---

[13]This concept of a green field view of risk was introduced in Chapter 9.

in this family is XBRL (XML-based Business Reporting Language). This is used as a standard interface specification for exporting business reports from one business application system to be imported into another business application system.

Specialised sub-sets of XBRL are emerging as an interface standard for risk reporting

One of the interesting developments of this, that at the time of writing is embryonic, is the use of a specialised sub-set of XBRL to generate reports on business risk information. This has important implications for the interfacing of component sub-systems in an integrated enterprise risk management system, and it seems reasonable to predict that there will be much development of risk tools around this concept. Thus you can expect to see the emergence of an XBRL risk reporting standard that will be applied for collecting risk information from a variety of satellite business applications to be aggregated, consolidated and rolled up for reporting through centralised risk reporting dashboards. It is too early to describe exactly how this will work, but it is a development that you should keep in view as it matures.

To Summarise:

Operational risk is complex because it involves the management of a wide range of risks to business operations, and in many cases there are trade-offs to be made between these various risks. There is no universal definition of what is included or excluded from operational risk, although individual industries are focusing on definitions that most suit the business needs of organisations in that specific community.

Operational risk management requires you first to model your risks in a suitable way, to use these models to facilitate risk assessment and risk analysis, and based upon prioritised risk catalogues to make business decisions as to level of risk mitigation that you require in the form of additional controls. An important input in this decision process is the tolerance for risk that you have and the business opportunities that are created by your capacity and appetite for risk-taking.

One of the most powerful drivers for the development of improved operational risk management is the growth of regulations and regulating bodies designed to force large commercial organisations to take corporate governance more seriously and to protect consumers and investors from the downside of reckless risk-taking by senior executives in charge of these large enterprises.

The holy grail of operational risk management is the development of meaningful quantitative measures of risk that can be used to calculate enterprise risk indicators such as value at risk. This implies the use of statistical analysis methods, but the work is currently hindered in many areas by the lack of suitable data to be analysed. Much effort is therefore focused on the collection of historical loss event information into databases that can be used as a reliable source of raw data for analysis and forecasting. One limitation that always affects this approach is that observation of the past is not always a good predictor of the future. Nevertheless a variety of techniques and tools are in use to provide both qualitative and quantitative measures of operational risk.

Risk management strategies involve a blend of risk acceptance, risk avoidance, risk mitigation and risk transfer, and each enterprise must develop its own specific strategy depending upon a range of cultural, financial and operational factors.

One of the greatest challenges faced by all large organisations attempting to develop an enterprise-wide operational risk management strategy is the need to integrate risk information from a wide variety of risk silos so as to gain an enterprise view of its overall risk position. This can be done only by using ICT-based solutions to handle the large amounts of information involved, but at the time of writing it is clear that no full-scale integration out-of-the-box solutions are available on the market. Enterprise risk management systems are more likely to be built by integrating a number of out-of-the-box generic components (such as business performance tools and business process management tools) to create a custom solution for managing operational risk at enterprise level in the context of the specific organisation.

Enterprise risk management systems aim to provide a series of risk management dashboards appropriate to various levels of management to facilitate real-time risk reporting and early warning of developing risk problems so that avoidance action can be taken. The system itself is not enough – what is also needed is an enterprise-wide risk management framework of responsibilities, policies, governance and processes.

Residual risks that cannot be removed or mitigated economically are often financed through some type of insurance programme, which embraces the purchase of several different types of risk financing products and services.

Chapter 16: Assurance Management

Not only does an organisation need to plan and execute an appropriate information security programme, but the senior management team also needs to have a means by which it can check that this is so – to provide assurance that all is well in this respect. This chapter examines the various aspects of providing such assurance.

In this chapter you will learn about:

- The broad meaning of the term 'assurance';

- Setting up and managing an enterprise-wide audit framework for assuring the information security management processes;

- How to use international standards as the basis for an enterprise-wide audit framework and for certifying auditors;

- Technical auditing of information systems to provide assurance of their correctness and completeness with regard to security management;

- Managing the assurance process for systems and software development;

- Managing the assurance process for live production in an ICT systems operations environment;

- Assuring the integrity and acceptable use of software and systems in a live business environment;

- The principles of functional testing and how to create a multi-phased testing strategy to support systems assurance;

- Assurance of systems for final acceptance through user acceptance testing and operational acceptance testing;

- How penetration testing can contribute to the assurance of post-delivery and live operational systems.

Assurance of Operational Continuity

SABSA® Matrix cross-reference Please refer to Chapter 3, Figure 3-3 and Chapter 7, Figure 7-8, the SABSA® Matrix, Operational layer, Assets column, where you will see a cell entitled Assurance of Operational Continuity.

Additionally, Framework for Assurance of Operational Continuity appears as a key deliverable of the operational security architecture in Chapter 7, Figure 7-12.

Operational continuity is related to the SABSA® Business Attributes Profile

'Operational continuity' should be taken in its very broadest sense here. Within the SABSA® methodology that means that you need assurance that all of the Business Attributes in your SABSA® Business Attributes Profile are being provided at a level compatible with the performance targets that you have set for each one (see Chapter 6).

Assurance is provided by inspection of some sort

Assurance has been touched upon previously in this book in Chapter 3, under the section entitled The Inspector's View. The inspector's view is concerned with providing assurance that the architecture is complete, consistent, robust and fit-for-purpose in every way. There are several types of inspection activity that are used to provide assurance:

- Security audits and security reviews of an organisational unit against a suitable code of practice (such as ISO/IEC 17799[1]);

- Security audits and security reviews of a system against a set of pre-determined security standards that have been deemed to be appropriate under the security policy (see Chapter 14);

- System assurance through the application of controls for:

  - Systems development;

  - Systems operations (especially with regard to production facilities in a data centre);

  - Systems integrity protection with regard to malicious software attacks from any quarter;

  - Systems use by the wider community of system business users.

- Functional testing as part of the systems development lifecycle:

  - Unit testing;

  - Integration testing;

  - System validation testing;

  - User acceptance testing;

  - Operational acceptance testing.

- Quality assurance of application systems:

  - Code reviews;

  - Coverage validation for each phase of testing.

- Penetration testing of:

  - Systems under test before release into production;

  - Operational production systems.

Detailed discussions follow

The following sections of this chapter examine in greater detail each of these approaches to providing assurance.

---

[1]ISO/IEC 17799:2000: 'Code of Practice for Information Security Management'.

Organisational Security Audits

The Audit Programme

A summary of the audit and review programme

The process of auditing and reviewing the security of business processes, business systems and ICT infrastructure is a major strategic programme of activity. Such a programme will need to address all of the following points:

- Establishing the business drivers for security and for security audit;

- Defining the general approaches and strategy for security audit;

- Levels of assurance required as a result of a security audit;

- Setting out pre-audit work;

- Defining security targets (how much security is needed);

- Establishing the audit baseline;

- Designing the audit work program;

- System assessment and analysis using both automated tools and interviews with key staff;

- Penetration testing (probing for weaknesses, including by the use of social engineering);

- Assessing the systems and software development environment;

- Assessing the operational environment;

- Security audit reporting;

- Responding to audit reports and tracking progress.

There are external standards that are used as audit frameworks

There are several external standard frameworks available for you to consider for adoption in your organisation. Perhaps the most important of these are (1) the CobiT® Framework and (2) ISO/IEC 17799/BS 7799. Both will ensure that you address a wide range of important audit issues within an internationally accepted common framework.

CobiT®[2] as an Audit Framework

CobiT® is from the IT Governance Institute

CobiT® (Control Objectives for Information and Related Technology) has been developed by and is published by the IT Governance Institute[3], which in turn is associated with ISACA[4] and ISACF[5].

CobiT® addresses the broad issues of ICT governance

CobiT® is not just about the security of information systems. It has a much broader scope, dealing with all aspects of governance of information systems. For some organisations this will be a more appropriate approach to ICT audit than, for example, ISO/IEC 17799, which is specifically security-focused.

CobiT® is mature and represents international opinion

CobiT® is mature, having been through several published versions over many years, and is comprehensive, having benefited from broad international input through the CobiT® Steering Committee.

---

[2]CobiT® is a registered trademark of the Information Systems Audit and Control Foundation.
[3]See www.ITgoverance.org or www.isaca.org
[4]SACA: Information Systems Audit and Control Association
[5]ISACF: Information Systems Audit and Control Foundation

The complete CobiT® package consists of six publications:

- CobiT® Management Guidelines: focused upon the effective integration of the management of both business processes and business information systems. The main elements are:

    - Maturity models;

    - Critical success factors;

    - Key goal indicators;

    - Key performance indicators.

- CobiT® Executive Summary: designed for consumption by the time-pressed decision maker, comprising an explanation of:

    - CobiT®'s key concepts;

    - CobiT®'s principles.

- CobiT® Framework: explains how ICT processes deliver the information that the business needs to achieve its objectives. Key elements are:

    - Business processes and objectives supported by ICT processes;

    - Thirty-four high-level control objectives, one for each ICT process, grouped in four domains;

    - Seven information criteria (effectiveness, efficiency, confidentiality, integrity, availability, compliance and reliability) that are necessary for the ICT processes to support the business objectives;

    - ICT resources (people, applications, technology, facilities and data) that are also necessary for the ICT processes to support fully the business objectives.

- CobiT® Audit Guidelines: providing an outline of activities to be performed corresponding to each of the 34 high-level control objectives.

- CobiT® Control Objectives: A comprehensive set of policy statements required to maintain control in a constantly changing environment. The control objectives are structured hierarchically into:

    - Four domains;

    - 34 high-level control objectives;

    - 318 specific, detailed control objectives (control activities).

- CobiT® Implementation Tool Set: designed to facilitate the implementation of CobiT®, relate lessons learned from organisations that quickly and successfully applied CobiT® in their work environments and assist management in choosing implementation options. It comprises:

    - Management Awareness and ICT Control Diagnostics;

    - Implementation Guide;

    - Frequently asked questions;

- Case studies from organisations currently using CobiT®;

- Slide presentations that can be used to introduce CobiT® into an organisation.

ISO/IEC 17799:2000 and BS7799-2:2002 as an Audit Framework

Using the ISO/IEC 17799 ISMS as an audit standard

ISO/IEC 17799:2000 (Code of Practice for Information Security Management) started life as a British standard and has since been adopted as an international standard. Some people pedantically argue that as a code of practice, it is not really a standard, but what is important is that it is a common internationally recognised framework for planning and implementing the corporate Information Security Management System (ISMS). It can also fulfil the role of an audit framework for evaluating the suitability of the existing corporate Information Security Management System.

ISO/IEC 17799:2000 is a management standard, not a technical standard

It is important to understand that ISO/IEC 17799:2000 addresses topics in terms of policies and general good practices. The document specifically identifies itself as 'a starting point for developing organisation-specific guidance.' It states that not all of the guidance and controls it contains may be applicable and that additional controls not contained may be required. It is not intended to give definitive details on how to do things – rather it is a general guide to what you should do. Hence there are almost no technical details, and the document focuses upon good business practices. ISO/IEC 17799:2000 is a management standard, not a technical standard. It addresses the following major topics:

- Establishing organisational security policy;

- Organisational security infrastructure;

- Asset classification and control;

- Personnel security;

- Physical and environmental security;

- Communications and operations management;

- Access control;

- Systems development and maintenance;

- Business continuity management;

- Compliance.

BS 7799 in two parts

The British Standard from which ISO/IEC 17799:2000 is derived is in two parts:

- BS 7799-1:1999: Code of Practice for Information Security Management (the same content as ISO/IEC 17799:2000);

- BS 7799-2:2002: Information Security Management Systems – Specification with Guidance for Use (a description of a model process for setting up and managing an ISMS).

ISO/IEC 17799 will not move to integrate Part 2

It seems that at the time of writing there is no intention on the part of ISO/IEC JTC1 to generate the ISO/IEC equivalent of BS 7799-2.

The process for managing the ISMS

BS 7799-2:2002 promotes the adoption of a process approach for establishing, implementing, operating, monitoring, maintaining and improving the effectiveness of an organisation's ISMS. It states that such a process approach encourages users to emphasise the importance of:

- Understanding business information security requirements and the need to establish policy and objectives for information security;

- Implementing and operating controls in the context of managing an organisation's overall business risk;

- Monitoring and reviewing the performance and effectiveness of the ISMS;

- Continual improvement based on objective measurement.

The PDCA model   The standard specifically describes a model process that can be applied to achieve these objectives, called the Plan-Do-Check-Act (PDCA) model. Figure 16-1 shows a summary of this model.

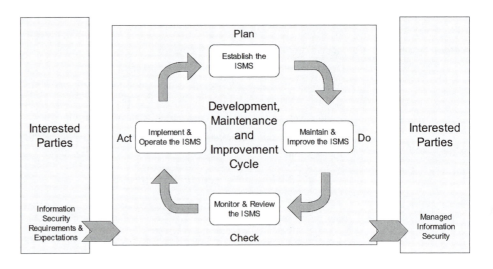

Figure 16-1: The BS 7799-2:2002 PDCA Process Model

BS 7799-2 control objectives and controls   Annex A of BS 7799-2:2002 contains a comprehensive list of control objectives (all cross-referenced to the various sections of ISO/IEC 17799:2000), each with identified controls that can be used to meet that control objective. No such list can ever be complete, but this one does provide a great amount of material from which to draw ideas.

BS 7799-2 implementation guidance   Annex B of BS 7799-2:2002 provides practical guidance notes on how to implement the PDCA model process. There are also cross-references between the BS 7799 standard and the principles in the OECD Guidelines for the Security of Information Systems and Networks[6].

Cross references to other management systems   Annex C gives cross-references between this management system standard (the ISMS) and two other management system standards – BS EN ISO 9001:2000 (the quality management system – QMS) and BS EN ISO 14001:1996 (the environmental management system – EMS). Another useful standard that is cross-referenced in BS 7799-2:2002 is the ISO/IEC 13335 'Guidelines for the Management of IT Security'[7].

Internal ISMS auditing   The use of the standard for conducting internal audits is specifically addressed in BS 7799-2:2002

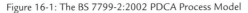

[6]'OECD Guidelines for the Security of Information Systems and Networks – Towards a Culture of Security'. Paris: OECD, July 2002. www.oecd.org

[7]BS ISO/IEC TR 13335-3:1998, *'Guidelines for the Management of IT Security — Part 3: Techniques for the management of IT security'* and BS ISO/IEC TR 13335-4:2000, *'Guidelines for the Management of IT Security — Part 4: Selection of Safeguards'*.

Annex B section B.4.5 – Internal ISMS Audit:

'The overall objective is to check over a specified regular audit period (which should last no more than one year) that all aspects of the ISMS are functioning as intended. A sufficient number of audits should be planned so that the audit task is spread uniformly over the chosen period. Management should ensure that there is evidence that confirms that:

> a) The information security policy is still an accurate reflection of the business requirements;

> b) An appropriate risk assessment methodology is being used;

> c) The documented procedures are being followed (i.e. within the scope of the ISMS) and are meeting their desired objectives;

> d) Technical controls (e.g. firewalls, physical access controls) are in place, are correctly configured and working as intended;

> e) The residual risks have been assessed correctly and are still acceptable to the management of the organisation;

> f) The agreed actions from previous audits and reviews have been implemented;

> g) The ISMS is compliant with this standard.

> The audits will need samples of current documents and records and involve interviews with management and staff.'

Qualified Auditor Status

Qualified auditors for CobiT® and BS 7799

Both CobiT® and BS 7799 have provision for accreditation of qualified auditors who are recognised as having the necessary knowledge and expertise to carry out audits against the relevant standard.

The CISA qualification

In the CobiT® universe the relevant qualification is the CISA (Certified Information Systems Auditor). The requirements for CISA certification are:

- Successful completion of the CISA exam. The exam is offered annually at nearly 200 sites around the world in 10 languages during the month of June.

- Satisfy the work experience requirement pertaining to professional information systems (IS) auditing, control or security activity. Education waivers are available. The CISA Bulletin of Information gives details (www.isaca.org/exam1.htm).

- Adhere to the Information Systems Audit and Control Association's *Code of Professional Ethics* (www.isaca.org/standard/code2.htm).

- Comply with annual continuing education requirements (www.isaca.org/cisacep1.htm).

Alignment of CobiT® and CISA

Although CobiT® is not specifically tested on the CISA examination, the CobiT® control objectives or processes do reflect the tasks identified in the CISA Practice Analysis. As such, a thorough review of CobiT® is recommended by ISACA for candidate preparation for the CISA examination.

Qualified BS 7799 ISMS auditors

Under the BS 7799 regime, an organisation can be formally certified for BS 7799 compliance by a UK Accreditation Service (UKAS) accredited body. These accredited bodies employ qualified ISMS auditors who have been trained and qualified especially for the task. A professional ISMS auditor completes an independent formal review of the Information Security Management System (ISMS). The aim of the review is to confirm that the ISMS is both effective and appropriate.

The ISMS audit

The ISMS auditor will check for:

- Completeness – Have all parts of BS 7799 been covered?

- Relevance – Is the interpretation of BS 7799 relevant for the organisation?

- Implementation – Is the Information Security Management System (ISMS) being followed?

ISMS statement of applicability

The ISMS auditor will require a Statement of Applicability (SOA). This is a document that lists all requirements in BS 7799 Part 2, with:

- An explanation of how the organisation complies with them;

- An explanation and justification of any deviations from them.

Grades of ISMS auditor

The International Register of Certified Auditors (IRCA) operates a certification scheme for ISMS auditors covering four grades:

- ISMS Provisional Auditor;

- ISMS Auditor;

- ISMS Lead Auditor;

- ISMS Principal Auditor.

Criteria for becoming qualified as an ISMS auditor

Candidates are evaluated against requirements that reflect the key skills, knowledge and experience that define competence and which the ISMS auditor needs to have and demonstrate during an audit. The evaluation criteria specify the education, work experience, auditor training and auditing experience needed by an applicant to qualify for registration at each of these grades.

System Security Audits

Security Auditing

Security auditing defined

For the purposes of this book security auditing is the process of verifying that a system complies with all of the security policies, operational procedures and security standards that apply to its operation. However, the term tends to mean different things to different people. Much of what some people label as security auditing is what others would describe as penetration testing. It does not really matter what your definition is, provided that you are clear about it when communicating with others on the subject. In this book penetration testing is dealt with in a separate section later in this chapter.

Three types of auditing activity

Within the definition given above there are three distinct types of security audit activity:

- Daily event monitoring and follow-up to look for violations of policy, procedure and standards. This is best achieved through the use of automated log scanning tools that create exception reports to be followed up manually.

- Routine periodic inspections of system parameters to ensure continued compliance with security standards. This is best achieved by the use of automated tools that scan all system files and directories, comparing the parameter settings with the preferred settings (that are usually stored in a policy file) and creating exception reports for manual follow-up.

- Periodic reviews of system construction and operations to ensure compliance with security policies, procedures and standards. Audit experts, possibly assisted by checklists of issues to be investigated, achieve this through manual information gathering and reporting.

Security audit strategy Your security audit strategy should preferably include all three of the above approaches since they all contribute differently to the overall process of assurance. Your strategy should address the following points:

- Definition – What do you mean by the term 'security audit'?

- Expertise – Who will carry out the security audits, and what training and ongoing professional development do they need?

- Tools and techniques – What is the standard tool-kit that is to be used for executing your security audits?

- Audit work planning – What is the scope of a security audit and the resources required?

- Execution – What is the methodology to be used for security auditing?

- Reporting – What is the style and content of security audit reports, the expected consumers of these reports and the objectives for a report, and what value will reporting add?

Standards for Security Auditing

Auditing against accepted standards The most important prerequisite for conducting a security audit is a written definition of what the auditors expect to find in an ideal world – usually embodied in security policies and security standards documents. The audit process, whether it be manual or automated, is one of comparing the actual configuration parameters found in the operational system against the theoretical configurations described in the policy and standards documents. In theory they should match perfectly. In practice they rarely do so. The mismatch has a variety of causes, including:

- The laws of thermodynamics that tell us that entropy (chaos) tends to increase over time as orderly patterns and symmetry decay through a wide range of natural processes (have you ever tried keeping a garden?);

- Mistakes are made in setting up systems;

- Some people think they know a better way to do it;

- New releases of software bring changes in configuration, often to make the new software 'work properly';

- Inexperienced or ignorant personnel make changes to make things easier without understanding fully the ramifications of their actions.

Case Study: The Network Engineers

It has happened in real life many times.

The network team is monitoring network performance. Something is wrong – the throughput simply is not what it should be.

Someone on the team asks: 'Is it those damned encryptors that are playing up again?'

'Try turning them off and see what happens.'

'There! That's much better!'

Different people have different priorities.

Creating the policies and standards – Chapter 14

In order to provide the necessary security policies and standards against which a system security audit can be conducted, there is a whole strategic field of activity needed to create and maintain those policies and standards. This activity is the subject of Chapter 14 of this book, and you may wish to refer back to that chapter now to remind yourself of the range of policies and standards that are required in order to support an effective programme of system security audits.

System Assurance Strategy

Development Controls

Balancing the risks: speed versus assurance

The systems development activity is critical to the assurance of the systems being developed. However, there is a potential conflict of business requirements here, since there is always acute pressure to bring new systems into production quickly (driven by fast time to market), yet by hurrying too much you run a severe risk of putting into production a system that is not fit for purpose.

Risks conflict here, as in many other areas

This is yet another one of those instances where one operational risk conflicts with another risk. To mitigate the risk of missing a business opportunity you must take additional risks with lack of assurance. Conversely, to achieve a high level of assurance you increase the risk of delaying the release into production and thus missing a valuable business opportunity.

Finding the balance: risk management

Clearly there is some middle ground that you must seek out, and the exact position of this middle ground is for you and your enterprise to define. That is the nature of business risk management.

Problems in small ICT departments

Some of the segregation controls suggested below are also difficult to achieve in a small ICT department where the development and production activities are necessarily blurred by lack of staff and lack of physical resources.

Development control strategy

Bearing all that in mind, the development controls that you should implement include:

- An end-to-end development process with a complete audit trail and sign-off at each significant stage, from business requirements capture through to putting new application software into production, providing assurance that there are no holes in the process whereby sub-standard code could be accidentally or maliciously incorporated into the application.

- A key characteristic of a successful development process is traceability – being able to trace the entire development path of a specific application from concept through to production, with documented authorisations at each key stage.

- Periodic independent audits of the development environment and activity to ensure that the end-to-end process is being properly implemented and that the control points are being observed.

- Creation of an audit trail (through the end-to-end process) for each and every system that is developed, so that any individual system can be audited for its history right from the beginning of the development process.

- There should be complete segregation of the development and production environments. No system development work should be allowed on a production machine, and no system developer should have any access to a production machine.

- Emergency system maintenance work may require development staff to have limited access to production facilities for a limited time under strict supervision, but this should be minimised, and the definition of an 'emergency fix' needs to be defined carefully in business terms.

- There should be comprehensive version controls and version archiving under the control of an appointed software librarian who is one of the systems development team. There are specialised tools on the market that make this easy to implement.

- Only approved, authorised software tools are to be used for development purposes – no private tools or utilities, including the sorts of scripts, macros and programs that some developers write for their own use and sometimes share with colleagues. If these tools are needed, they should be officially developed, tested and released. If not, they should be banned.

- A series of development standards and approved methodologies to be used by all development staff to ensure consistency and to make it possible for development staff to take over or verify each other's work.

- Peer review of critical work packages to check their correctness.

- A full programme of module testing, integration testing, system testing and regression testing carried out by people other than those who cut the code.

- User acceptance testing in a separate testing environment that is segregated from both the development environment and the production environment.

- Test data and live data to be completely segregated.

- Technical risk assessment to identify particular threats and potential vulnerabilities, such as:

    - New software development language;

    - New development tools;

    - New methodologies;

    - New delivery technology;

    - New code;

    - Inexperienced development staff;

    - Hostile delivery environment.

High-level software development lifecycle Systems are developed, tested, accepted and put into live production. Figure 16-2 shows a typical high-level view of the lifecycle of this process for the development of the software components of a system.

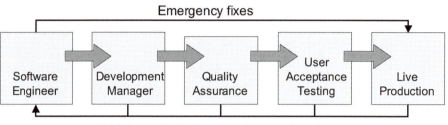

Figure 16-2: High-Level Software Development Lifecycle

Code flows from one stage to the next The software engineer designs and constructs code modules and tests them to make sure they are ready for handover to the development manager. The development manager organises independent testing of the modules, the integration of the modules, and the testing of the integrated sub-systems and system, by delegating to other software engineers ('*It is impossible to test your own programs.*'[8]). The completed system is handed over to the quality assurance team for testing before delivery to the user sponsors. Once delivered, the users perform acceptance testing, after which the system is handed over to the operations team to be put into live production.

Failed code goes back to the beginning If at any stage any part of the system fails, then the relevant modules are demoted all the way back to the beginning for rework, retest and reintegration. The process of functional testing of software is described in more detail later in this chapter.

Emergency fixes need to be supported with a special process There is, however, a possibility that for business-critical applications some emergency fixing will be required to keep the business running. This should be followed up immediately by a formal change request to go through the full rework process to replace the faulty application with one that has been properly repaired. It is dangerous in the long term to rely on live systems that are running with emergency patches in place, since there may be other faults (bugs) related to these emergency patches that the lack of full testing has not revealed.

Regression testing Once an accepted software module has been patched or repaired, the best practice is to go back to the beginning of the lifecycle and retest and reintegrate. This is known as regression testing.

Vendor security patches – emergency fix or not? An interesting conflict that can arise here is regarding security patches. You must make a decision as to whether you regard all vendor security patches as emergency fixes to be applied immediately or whether they should be tested and evaluated before they are applied, with the potential outcome that you may decide not to apply a specific fix.

Risks and costs are always being balanced However, cost and risk always need to be balanced, and so you will almost certainly have to live in an imperfect world. This is especially true in environments where the business driver for fast time to market is paramount and systems are developed using the fashionable high-speed approaches such as application prototyping, rapid application development (RAD) and extreme programming. It all depends on which risks you want to take and is constrained by the cold reality that you cannot simultaneously mitigate them all.

---

[8]Stephen Rakitin, *Software Verification and Validation: A Practitioner's Guide*, Artech House, 1997, ISBN 0-89006-889-5

Production Controls

The key control strategies for live production environments include:

- The production environment should be completely segregated from the development environment and from any testing environments.

- Segregation of duties should prevent development staff from having access to production systems, and other sensitive functions should be segregated where appropriate.

- There should be a complete ban on the storage of software development tools and utilities (editors, compilers, linkers, etc.) on live production systems. The only executable code available should be the applications and the system software required to run these applications. All other tools and utilities should be removed.

- A formal, rigorous change-control process should allow no change to the production environment without approval. This applies to both hardware changes and software changes. Formal responsibilities for approval should be assigned to people with suitable knowledge and with appropriate authority.

- A formal configuration-management process should embrace:

  - Requirements management;

  - Inventory management;

  - Change management;

  - Release management;

  - Data management;

  - Records management;

  - Document control;

  - Library management.

- New releases of systems should come through the formal systems-development lifecycle, including the entire cycle of testing and acceptance.

- There should be a reversal procedure for every planned release in case it fails and the systems need to be restored to the previous release version.

- There should be periodic logical scans of software and configuration data files in live systems to ensure that no unauthorised changes have occurred.

- There should be prevention of operator access to maximum privilege level access (such as root access in UNIX systems) by ensuring that all routine operations tasks are fully encapsulated in scripts or utility programs. The use of root privilege should be reserved for emergency fixes only, should be independently supervised and should require authorisation from a senior operations manager.

- Physical security over the machine rooms in which live production hardware is housed should ensure that only authorised operations personnel are granted access.

- Documented and tested incident management procedures should be created to handle system failures.

- Master backups of all current releases of production software and configuration data should exist to facilitate the rebuilding of systems in case of failure.

- Regular backup of all production data should be available to facilitate restoration of production systems to an acceptable previous business position in case of failure.

Software Integrity and Anti-Virus Strategy

Multi-tiered strategy   The objective of this strategy is first to prevent contamination by malicious executables[9], and if this fails, to detect the contamination as soon as possible, to contain it and to remove it. This is simply a microcosm of the overall strategic model described earlier in Chapter 10 and shown in Figure 10-2.

Malicious code defined   Malicious software can come from various sources:

- Self-replicating malicious software that comes from outside the enterprise. Viruses, certain types of Trojan horses, and worms are all examples of this type of attack vehicle. The destructiveness of the payload varies greatly.

- Malicious mobile code in the form of Java applets, ActiveX, various types of mobile script, remote database queries using SQL[10], OQL[11] and other query mechanisms.

- Code maliciously inserted into a program or system by a member of the systems development team or the systems operation team, or by an external hacker who has gained unauthorised access to a system. These types of malicious object are often Trojan horses, logic bombs or time bombs.

Control techniques   Possible techniques for tackling these problems include:

- Scanning stored files and directories for known malicious code (such as in conventional virus scanning);

- Scanning stored files and directories for unexpected changes;

- Real-time monitoring of the execution environment for unauthorised execution paths;

- Filtering and scanning imported digital materials at the perimeter of the enterprise, including scanning of diskettes, CDs and other media items, and the real-time filtering carried out in a firewall or other security gateway;

- Setting control rules on web browsers to prevent or monitor the execution of certain types of mobile code objects, possibly through the use of digitally signed objects from trusted sources;

- Software object authentication on installation;

- Software object authentication on boot-up;

---

[9]'Executables' includes object code directly executed at machine level, interpreted source code executed under a run-time system and scripts written in a wide variety of scripting languages and tools.
[10]SQL: structured query language
[11]OQL: object query language

- Implementation of secure coding practices as part of the development standards for in-house software development;

- Code audit of in-house developed software to check for Trojan code before release into live production (this is both difficult and expensive and should be considered only for extremely high-assurance systems).

Control strategy Strategic controls should include:

- An enterprise policy requiring the use of authorised, licensed software only, distributed through a corporate procurement function. This includes the use of open source and public domain software, which the enterprise may choose to use, but such software should be acquired, tested and officially distributed by the enterprise. Individual employees should not take it upon themselves to introduce public domain software, and doing so should constitute a disciplinary offence.

- An enterprise policy aimed at all employees to make them aware of the malicious software issues and mandate acceptable behaviour patterns.

- A corporate standard for the configuration of e-mail clients and web browsers to reduce the vulnerabilities of infection to acceptable levels.

- An ongoing awareness programme to ensure that employees behave sensibly and in particular know to be suspicious of certain types of e-mail attachments and web downloads.

- The deployment and regular use of anti-virus[12] detection software from a reputable supplier of these products, with regular frequent updates. This should be used to scan all corporate systems and to scan all incoming files on magnetic media, in e-mail attachments, through FTP transfers and any other means of file import.

- The reinstallation of any damaged software using the original installation files (or possibly a known good backup of these).

- As a last resort, if original software installation files have been lost, the deployment and use of anti-virus repair software[13], which is normally part of an anti-virus package.

- The use of appropriate housekeeping measures for backup and restoration of both software (from masters) and data (from recent operational copies).

- An incident management process to deal with malicious software contamination incidents.

Acceptable Use

Acceptable use defined 'Acceptable use' refers to the use of corporate information systems for acceptable purposes. Unacceptable purposes are those that are illegal, unauthorised or so grossly anti-social as to cause offence to people both inside and outside the enterprise.

---

[12]The phrase 'anti-virus' has a wide meaning as used here. It includes the detection and repair of viruses, Trojan horses, worms, macro-viruses and any other form of malicious software that has a replication mechanism to spread it from one system to another.

[13]Malware alters files in many different ways, and anti-virus software cannot possibly take all of these into account to restore a perfect image of the original file when repairing.

Unacceptable use examples Unacceptable use might include such activities as:

- Browsing pornographic web sites from corporate computers, and possibly downloading and storing pornographic materials;

- Browsing gambling sites and using corporate time to gamble;

- Sexual harassment of colleagues through the corporate e-mail system, by sending unwelcome suggestive or sexually explicit materials, including pornographic images;

- Harassing colleagues though the corporate e-mail system by sending racially or religiously abusive materials that will cause offence to the recipients;

- Wasting corporate time by browsing web sites that have no relevance to one's job;

- Incurring unacceptable communications costs by accessing unauthorised web sites or premium-rate telephone numbers;

- Using corporate information systems for administering private business interests;

- Using corporate computing facilities to hack into other computer systems, both inside and outside the enterprise;

- Loading and playing unauthorised games on corporate computer systems.

Content management strategy The strategic controls should include:

- An Acceptable Use Policy to ensure that all employees are aware of the corporate position and know what constitutes acceptable use and unacceptable use (which varies from one organisation to another).

- The deployment of content-filtering software to ensure that the most offensive items and the illegal items can be detected.

- A disciplinary process by which employees who violate the Acceptable Use Policy are 'brought to book' both as a punishment to them and a deterrent to others.

Functional Testing

Principles of Functional Testing

Functional testing defined Functional testing is carried out against a functional test specification, which in turn is developed from a functional requirements specification (FRS). The FRS is a specification of a system at the logical architecture level. It specifies the entire set of functions that the system will perform. It is at the logical level because it does not tell you how those functions will be implemented in physical terms or what precise mechanisms will be used to deliver the functions[14].

Black box testing Functional testing is often called black box testing. A black box is something into which you cannot see, thus you have no notion of how it works. It has inputs, which you can see, and outputs,

---

[14]What is described here is the ideal scenario. In reality, those who write function requirements specifications often misunderstand this distinction between logical and physical architecture, and there are many FRS documents in existence that go into details of physical mechanisms. The pitfall of this sloppy approach is that a physical architecture is designed before the wider range of functional requirements are captured and understood, and the resulting design fails to deliver fully the business requirements – often by being constrained by ill-informed design decisions taken too early in the process.

which you can also see, but you cannot see its internal mechanisms through which it makes the functional transformations of inputs to outputs. It is a logical description, not a physical one.

White box testing

In contrast, white box or glass box testing is carried out in the full knowledge of how the mechanisms inside the box work. If you refer back to the earlier section on development controls and the software development lifecycle (see Figure 16-2), the software engineers who carry out module testing usually apply white box testing.

Using black box testing

Once a software module has passed its individual test regime (sometimes called unit testing), the next phases (integration testing and system testing) are often carried out using black box tests. Black box testing is also used by the quality assurance team in testing the system as a whole, by the user acceptance testing team and by the operational acceptance testing team. Black box testing is also usually applied in carrying out regression tests.

Regression testing

Regression testing is carried out to retest a system after modifications have been made, usually to fix a fault that has been discovered. The purpose of regression testing is to ensure that no new bugs have been introduced during the modifications.

Verifying the absence of unwanted functionality is difficult

The specification of a black box functional test is designed to test the system against a range of possible input scenarios and to verify that the system function being tested produces the expected outputs. Key tests are at the boundaries of the expected inputs (just inside the boundary, on the boundary, just outside the boundary). The objective is to test that the system performs all the functions that have been specified, and that for each function it works precisely as specified.

This provides you with assurance that the system performs all the functions that it should. However, it is much more difficult to verify that the system does not have any unwanted functionality. This is especially important for safety-critical systems, as previously discussed in Chapter 9.

Testing Strategy

Key elements of a testing strategy

Managing the testing process requires suitable testing strategy to have been developed. Key elements of this testing strategy include:

- A test plan – what is to be tested, why, how, where, when and by whom?

- Testing methods – chosen for their suitability for the specific type of test, including possibly:

    - White box tests;

    - Black box tests;

    - 'Act like a customer' (ALAC) tests (for systems testing);

    - Top-down, bottom up and outside-in tests (for incremental integration testing);

- Testing personnel – who will carry out each type of test?

- Acceptance criteria – what level (if any) of failures can be tolerated and at what level of assurance will you deem that a test has been successfully passed?

- Test schedule – which specific list of tests will be carried out, at what stage, in what order and by whom?

• Test environments – what infrastructure in the form of software stubs, simulators, emulators and scaffolding is required for each test?

Multi-phased functional testing

Carrying out the range of functional tests is a multi-phased process. Figure 16-3 shows the main phases that you should expect to see in testing a new software system. It is essential as part of the testing strategy to specify the exit criteria for each phase and the entry criteria for each phase (at what point can you move on to the next phase).

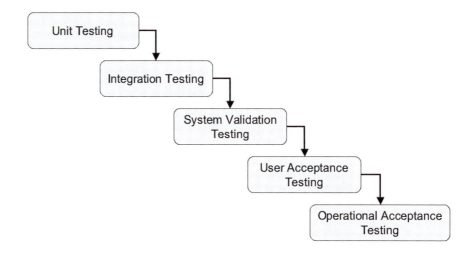

Figure 16-3: Phases of Testing for a Software System

Unit Testing (or Module Testing)

Testing of each individual software module

The objective of a unit test is to find bugs in the logic, data (both local and global) and algorithms within a single software module. All independent paths through the software module should be identified and exercised. The specifications of data being imported to or exported from the module should be checked for consistency – do they match the interface specification of the modules on the other side of the interface?. The boundary conditions should be specified and tested to ensure that the module works correctly around its boundaries. Error handling should also be tested to ensure that any possible errors are trapped and handled.

Part of the code development process – debugging as you go

Unit testing is often not really regarded as a separate testing activity but is carried out as an integral part of the coding process – a debugging activity by the software engineers generating the code. The integral nature of this activity within the coding task means that it is relatively informal with little or no test documentation generated before, during or after the tests.

Exhaustive white box testing approach at the unit level

Such testing is obviously white box in its nature, since those carrying out the tests are intimately familiar with the inner structure of the module being tested. They are looking to gain their own assurance that this inner structure is of sound quality, and in doing so they are exercising all the known aspects of the internal structure to ensure that every possibility is explored. This exhaustive approach is possible only at the level of small units. Once the integration process begins and complexity grows it would be an infinitely difficult task to continue with exhaustive white box testing across the integrated system.

A testing infrastructure is needed

Each module is tested in isolation and thus requires suitable investment in developing the testing infrastructure of software stubs and scaffolding. This infrastructure should be prepared in advance so that it is available as soon as the coding activity begins.

Integration Testing

Testing the integration of already tested modules

Once each of a series of modules has been tested in isolation through unit testing, they can be integrated together to build larger and more complex components of the overall system. Even though the modules have been individually tested, integration testing is needed because:

- Modules may interact in a way that produces an adverse effect, not obvious when the modules are viewed independently;

- Errors and imprecise calculations can become magnified as they are passed from one module to another;

- Modules may be contending for shared resources which may affect performance and at its worst can cause deadlock (two modules each holding a resource that the other needs and both not releasing the held resource until they get the resource for which they are waiting – which will never happen);

- In real-time systems the timing is critical, and this can only be seen in total by viewing the interaction of the various modules;

- There may still be interface problems not revealed by the unit testing phase;

Integration testing needs to be planned along with the integration itself

It is important to design the integration process and the integration testing methods together. Depending upon how you approach integration, it may be best to choose a top-down, bottom-up or outside-in approach to integration testing. Each approach has its own strengths and weaknesses and its own suitability, but that discussion is beyond the scope of this book.

System Validation Testing

Validating the functionality of the system as a whole

System validation testing is carried out by a separate quality assurance team that has not been involved in the development of the system in any way. The objective of system validation testing is to verify that the system meets all the requirements specified in the system requirements specification. The term 'system' may well imply the integration of both software and special hardware, although in many business systems the hardware will be a standard platform, and what is really being tested is the software and its ability to use the standard hardware.

Ensuring that system validation test development is future-proofed

Documentation of the system validation testing process is critical to the overall lifecycle management for the system, since much of the development of tests and test environments will carry forward to future releases. Three key documents are:

- The system validation test plan, defining the goals, objectives, resource estimates and schedules;

- The system validation test procedure with detailed test scripts;

- The system validation test report presenting the results of the formal validation testing.

Complexity limits the feasibility of exhaustive testing

The system complexity may be such that it is infeasible to test every possible combination of inputs to the system and record all possible combinations of outputs. If this is the case then the combinations of functionality to be tested must first be prioritised – which is where the act-like-a-customer' approach is useful since the tests are based upon what an end user is most likely to do with the system.

System validation testing must look not just at pure functionality, since the system requirements specification will specify such aspects as performance. Hence performance testing is an important element in the validation process.

User Acceptance Testing (UAT)

User acceptance testing is the phase that follows system validation. The developers and their quality assurance team have now prepared the system to a point where they are satisfied that it can be handed over to the end users. It is now time for the end users to carry out their own tests to ensure that the system being delivered meets the requirements stated in the user requirements specification.

The testing phase begins with the development of an acceptance test plan, which details what tests will be carried out, what the expected outcomes of those tests will be, and what are the criteria for acceptance. The test plan should also set out the expected responses from the various interested parties (users, project development team, vendors, consultants, contractors) in case issues and problems are identified. The process for resolution should also be clearly defined, including the responsibilities of the various parties.

It is often useful to apply a qualitative classification scheme to categorise problems so as to decide how they should be processed. Each category needs to have the responsibilities and required actions defined. A six-point scale as follows is the type of classification scheme that can be helpful (although three- or four-point scales are often used):

1. Complete Failure – it is impossible to continue with the testing because of the severity of this problem;

2. Critical Problem – testing can continue but the system cannot go into live production with this problem;

3. Major Problem – testing can continue but this feature will cause severe disruption to business processes in live operation;

4. Medium Problem – testing can continue and the system is likely to go live with only minimal changes to the agreed business processes;

5. Minor Problem – both testing and live operations may progress; this problem should be corrected, but little or no changes to business processes are envisaged;

6. Cosmetic Problem – for example concerning colours, fonts, pitch size; however if such features are key to the business requirements (such as the readability of the screen) they will warrant a higher severity level.

The final expected outcome of the user acceptance testing phase is that the system is accepted by the users for transfer into live production and the person with authority on the user side signs off formal acceptance, possibly with a number of conditions specified as part of the acceptance.

Operational Acceptance Testing (OAT)

Operational acceptance testing is concerned with whether or not the ICT operations group is prepared to accept the new application system as being suitable for integration into the operational production environment. Often the operation of the system will be carried out by a third party under an ICT services outsourcing agreement, so this phase of testing is quite different from the user acceptance testing.

The users are concerned to test whether or not they are getting the right business functionality. The operators are concerned only with the ease with which the system can be operated under the service level agreement and how it can be supported throughout its operational lifetime. The main scope of operational acceptance testing is to validate the following points:

- Stability and robustness:

  - Verification of continuous operation over an extended period;

  - Verification that services restart correctly on reboot of any server OR that documented procedures exist for service restarts.

- Event capture:

  - Verification that a user error message is generated following an incomplete or failed user transaction;

  - Verification that all failures, errors and other significant events (such as exceeding high- and low-water marks for pre-emptive capacity management) are logged.

- Resilience:

  - Verification that the system will operate continuously through the failure or controlled shutdown of individual system components;

  - Verification that the system will have sufficient levels of redundancy to ensure that committed availability targets under the service level agreement (SLA) can be maintained;

  - Verification that any application-specific data mirroring and failover functions are working correctly as expected.

- Systems monitoring:

  - Verification that comprehensive error reporting and alerting supports effective troubleshooting and problem diagnosis;

- Verification that pre-emptive alerting (such as approaching a capacity threshold or a preventive maintenance cycle) allows for pro-active management of system issues;

  - Verification that operator procedures are documented for all required control interventions.

- Performance management and service level reporting:

  - Verification that performance monitoring data supports detection of performance issues and measurement against agreed service levels;

- Verification that automated reports meet the requirements for service level reporting;

- Verification that observed system performance is consistent with the performance requirements under the SLA;

- Verification that all application failures are logged with time stamps to enable downtime reporting.

- Software deployment:

    - Verification that all software can be deployed within the available deployment window;

    - Verification that all software to be deployed meets the quality standards of the operations group;

    - Verification that all software changes and releases can be reversed out within the deployment window in case of deployment failure.

- Systems operations:

    - Verification that all support and maintenance processes and procedures are operable;

    - Verification that automated housekeeping tasks are in place to archive log files and prevent disk space from becoming full;

    - Verification that all routine housekeeping tasks are automated;

    - Verification that procedures for starting and stopping services and for any other routine operations tasks are fully documented;

    - Verification that the specified capacity management tools are installed and configured so as to produce the expected output.

- Impact on other systems and regression testing of other systems:

    - Verification that applications do not cause disruption to other applications running in the same client environment;

    - Verification that applications do not cause disruption to other applications running in the same mid-tier server environment;

    - Verification that applications do not cause disruption to other applications running in the same mainframe environment.

- Security manageability:

- Verification that all hardware platforms are 'hardened' according to the operations group's internal security standards;

    - Verification that any user support provided by the business user community meets the internal standards of the operations group;

    - Verification that the system adheres to all relevant internal operational security standards of the operations group;

- Verification that system account information and system passwords can be changed and managed according to documented procedures.

- Backup and recovery

  - Verification that a reliable automated backup solution is in place, including notifications of backup failures;

  - Verification that restoration from backup can be completed successfully within the available business window.

Operational sign-off and acceptance The final expected outcome of the operational acceptance testing phase is that the system is accepted by the operations group for transfer into live production and the person with authority on the operational side signs off formal acceptance, possibly with a number of conditions specified as part of the acceptance.

Software Quality Assurance

Software QA defined Software quality assurance is concerned with monitoring and continuously improving the software development process, making sure that any agreed standards and procedures are followed and ensuring the problems are identified and resolved.

Good quality software Good quality software will exhibit the following characteristics:

- Reasonably bug-free (within the context of the application);

- Delivered on time and within budget;

- Meets the user requirements and expectations;

- Is operable, supportable and maintainable.

Other aspects of software QA Although much of what has been described in the foregoing sections is concerned with software quality assurance in a wide variety of ways, there remain a few software QA issues not yet addressed here. These include:

- Source code reviews and inspections:

  - Peer review as a regular procedure;

  - Verification of adherence to internal coding standards.

- Reviews of testing strategies and plans:

  - Coverage validation for each phase of the testing cycle – do the planned tests cover everything that they should cover?

CMMI to benchmark development process maturity As a benchmark of maturity of the software development process in a given organisation the best available model is the CMMI[15] from the Carnegie Mellon University Software Engineering Institute. (See Chapter 6 for a general discussion on capability maturity models.)

Penetration Testing

Penetration testing for dynamic systems Functional testing is relatively static in its nature, testing one function at a time with selected inputs and looking to see what outputs are produced. In reality systems are dynamic in their behaviour and

---

[15]CMMI: Capability maturity model integration. See www.sei.cmu.edu/cmmi/

so need to be tested in dynamic scenarios. This leads to the concept of penetration testing or intrusion testing.

Up-to-date expertise is required

Penetration testing is designed to test an operational system to see if there are vulnerabilities that can be exploited to gain unauthorised access privileges and thus attack the system. It is a fast-moving area of expertise that requires constant research into new exploits and vulnerabilities and development of new testing tools. It is a job for experts and specialist companies who keep up to date.

Levels of penetration testing

Penetration testing can cover a number of different levels of system access, including:

- Internal network penetration – attempting to attack the network from inside the enterprise;

- Static analysis of computer-generated logs and firewall rule sets;

- On-host auditing – ensuring the security policies and standards have been rigorously applied on host platforms;

- Vulnerability assessment – automated scanning of networks and systems for known vulnerabilities (new ones emerge continually);

- External network penetration – attempting to attack the network from external locations, including from the Internet;

- Application testing – attempting to subvert applications by manipulating data inputs, looking for unwanted functionality;

- Source code analysis – looking for poor coding practices or suspicious routines;

- Wireless and mobile telephony penetration testing – for systems that employ these technologies;

- PABX auditing and testing – looking for poor configuration that could lead to penetration of corporate voice and data systems;

- War dialling – automatically dialling specified ranges of telephone numbers to look for useful service that could be exploited by an opponent to attack your network;

- Remote access server (RAS) testing – to look for vulnerabilities that could be exploited by an opponent to penetrate your network;

- Social engineering – to test whether your people can be socially engineered into revealing passwords or into allowing unauthorised personnel into control areas of your buildings.

Case Study: Penetration Testing of a Web Casino

A casino operator decided to set up a web-based casino, offering a number of games of chance through the web interface. Players could choose from a wide variety of the usual games – blackjack, poker, roulette and so on. Using modern graphics the site was made to look very attractive, dynamic and interesting – with all the action of a real casino.

Players had to register with the site, providing a username and password for login, and a credit card authorisation to cover their stakes. They could purchase chips using the credit card and then play with these chips, just as in a real casino. If they won they could then cash in the chips and have them credited back to the card.

A great deal of thought had been put into making the site look good and to providing games that would capture the attention of the gambling community. Obviously fraud is an issue in casinos, so the credit card interface was robust. Another key threat in the world of casinos is cheating at the game itself, but in a web interface the casino has ultimate control. The player cannot touch anything because there is no physical presence, and the possibility of socially engineering or colluding with casino staff is also eliminated, so the web casino seemed much easier to secure than the real thing.

Despite all the careful design the casino operator decided that before going live with the site it would be wise to call in some specialist penetration testing experts to see if they could find any exploits by which the casino could be cheated or defrauded. It was a wise decision.

The mindset of the casino operator had been conditioned by years of experience of running real casinos. Thus some of the things that can be done on a web interface had not been considered. The exploit that they found was so simple that it defies belief, and yet you can see how conventional thinking led to the problem. The penetration testers started to manipulate the data inputs into the gambling application, and the key input here is how much stake you want to gamble. By entering negative numbers into the stake field it was possible to force a win every time. Of course nobody ever bet a negative stake in real casino.

The problem was fixed before it went live.

Developing a penetration testing strategy

In putting together your penetration-testing strategy you should consider the following points:

- Use external experts – this is not a game for amateurs.

- Choose an expert service supplier with depth of expertise and multiple testing tools.

- In choosing your experts, be wary of ex-hackers and convicted criminals. You are potentially opening your systems to people with dangerous skills, so trust in the integrity of penetration testers is a major issue.

- Use more than one firm to supply these services and rotate them. They have different tools and different experts, so that what one team misses might be found by another.

- Organise a regular programme of tests for existing systems and applications – new vulnerabilities and new exploits emerge all the time.

- Test new systems and applications and new releases of existing systems before they go live.

- Make sure that the contract with the testing services supplier is clear about responsibilities and liabilities on each side. You will have to give them authorisation to work on live system interfaces, but you must restrict what they can do next if they discover an exploit. The risk is that live production systems will be brought down by a test that succeeds in penetrating the system.

- If you decide to carry out tests on a separate test environment rather than a live environment, then try to replicate the live environment as closely as possible, and accept that there may be a risk that you cannot achieve this. If the environment changes then an exploit that failed may now be successful. Thus a test system that was impenetrable may not guarantee the same properties for the live system.

To Summarise:

Within the SABSA® methodology 'assurance' means being assured that all of the Business Attributes in your SABSA® Business Attributes Profile are being provided to a level compatible with the performance targets that you have set for each one.

Assurance is provided through a number of inspection processes and thus corresponds to the Inspector's View described in Chapter 3. Inspection includes various types of audit process as well as a wide range of testing processes. An assurance strategy requires that a wide range of these techniques be used at different times to achieve different specific objectives.

Organisational security audits are focused on reviewing the management processes against accepted standards. Both CobiT® and BS 7799[16] can be used as internationally accepted standards for this purpose. Both provide a suitable audit framework within which an audit programme can be developed. Both also support the certification of qualified auditors who can carry out the audit work in an assured way.

Technical system security audits are based upon a blend of daily event monitoring, periodic checks on the compliance of system parameter settings with policies and standards, and reviews of the overall construction and operation of the system.

Systems assurance also requires an end-to-end, traceable and auditable systems development process, a documented and auditable systems operations process, and processes to assure the integrity and acceptable use of the systems in the hands of business end users.

A further pillar in the systems assurance strategy is the use of testing to assure the functionality, performance and operability of a system, especially during system development and preceding system acceptance for transfer into a live production mode.

Once the system is live, penetration testing is often used to ensure the continued robustness of the security of the system against all known threats and exploits.

---

[16]ISO/IEC 17799:2000 covers only BS 7799-1:1999 and thus technically is not suited to the assurance of the Information Security Management System (ISMS) as described in BS 7799-2:2002.

Chapter 17: Security Administration and Operations

The foregoing chapters of this book have focused heavily on the strategic and tactical aspects of managing an enterprise information security programme. In this final chapter the emphasis is wholly upon the day-to-day operations that keep that programme moving forward.

In this chapter you will learn about:

- Running an integrated programme of operational security management, based upon the framework set out in ISO/IEC 17799:2000;

- Developing a culture in which all personnel have direct responsibility for enterprise security;

- Raising and maintaining awareness of security issues and practices throughout the enterprise business user community;

- Using conventional personnel management processes as a means to support security management;

- Segregating duties in activities where there is high risk of fraud or similar abuse of privilege;

- Managing the physical and environmental security of corporate sites, buildings and equipment;

- Protecting daily operations through the use of well-defined key operating procedures and strict change control;

- Ensuring that major changes are properly managed through a change management programme;

- Managing security incidents that occur so as to minimise the impact, recover quickly and learn lessons by analysing their causes;

- Protecting the live ICT production systems environment by segregating it from all development and testing of systems;

- Capacity planning as a means to prevent operational problems and failures;

- How to minimise the risk associated with putting a new business system into live production by applying acceptance processes and release-management controls;

- Applying good housekeeping practices to protect the live production systems from failure. Measures include malicious software protection, data backup and recovery, operational event logging, media handling, network operations, software licence management;

- Managing the operational aspects of interacting with and exchanging information with third parties;

- Managing outsourced contracts for both mainstream ICT operations and ancillary services;

- Asset control and configuration management;

- Service level agreements and the part they play in the wider management of business relationships;

- Training and security awareness development of operational and administrative staff;

- Service monitoring and reporting;

- Event log management and the provision of audit trails;

- Forensic investigations;

- Problem tracking and problem management;

- Providing three-level user support through a help desk;

- Provisioning of systems with up-to-date configuration data;

- Financial management in relation to enterprise security operations;

- Enforcing access control policies through operational processes for user access management, system-level privilege management, password management and the management of access by authorised third parties;

- Managing legal and regulatory compliance with regard to information security, including compliance with regulations governing the deployment and use of cryptographic technology;

- Security-specific operations, including the management of security services, security mechanisms, security components and system users;

- Outsourcing certain security operations to specialist providers of managed security services;

- Evaluating, selecting and procuring commercially available security products and services;

- A business-process-centric approach to business continuity management.

Introduction to Security Management and Administration

SABSA® Matrix cross-reference   This chapter is relevant to the four cells of the SABSA® Matrix on the operational architecture row. Respectively these are: Security Service Management and Support (Process column), Application and User Management and Support (People column), Security of Sites, Networks and Platforms (Location column), and Security Operations Schedule (Time column) – see Chapter 3, Figure 3-3 and Chapter 7, Figure 7-8.

This chapter also needs to be read in conjunction with the section in Chapter 11 entitled Security Management Services – a description of the logical architecture needed to support security management and administration. The emphasis here in this chapter is different from that in Chapter 11, focusing on the operational procedures that run parallel with the logical security architecture and which are a part of the overall operational security architecture.

The Operational Prevention Process

Prevention brings together many threads A critical aspect of ongoing security operations is the co-ordination of a prevention process that brings together many different threads of operational activity. Figure 17-1 shows some of the major components of this process.

Figure 17-1: Main Components of the Operational Prevention Process

Routine operational management is also required When you examine Figure 17-1 you will notice that many of the threads that it draws together have already been discussed, especially in Chapters 14, 15 and 16. What is added here in this chapter is a discussion of the routine, ongoing operations and administrative functions that keep your information security management fully operational on a day-to-day basis.

The International Standard: ISO/IEC 17799:2000

The basic operational and administrative framework is described in ISO/IEC 17799:2000 ISO/IEC 17799:2000, 'Code of Practice for Information Security Management' is a high-level model for everything that might be considered to be in the realm of information security management. Chapter 14 of this book discusses the application of ISO/IEC 17799:2000 to security policy management, security organisation, and asset classification and control. Chapter 16 discusses risk management, which is an important concept within ISO/IEC 17799:2000. In Chapter 15 there is a description of how to use ISO/IEC 17799:2000 as an audit framework. Here in this chapter it is used again as the basic framework covering all aspects of information security administration and operations. The most relevant sections of the standard for this purpose are:

- Section 6: Personnel security;

- Section 7: Physical and environmental security;

- Section 8: Communications and operations management;

- Section 9: Access control;

- Section 10: Systems development and maintenance;

- Section 11: Business continuity management;

- Section 12: Compliance.

Managing the People

Security Responsibilities

Information security is part of everybody's responsibility

There is an unfortunate perception in many organisations that security is the responsibility of a few people who have job titles that include the word 'security'. One of the principal goals of any information security programme must be to address this misconception and to ensure that everyone understands that information security is part of *everyone's* responsibility. There are a number of operational measures that will help you to reach this objective:

- Make sure that information security responsibility is mentioned appropriately in every job description and every contract of employment and include confidentiality agreements in contracts of employment;

- Relate this personal responsibility to the real corporate risks and ensure that each person understands the part they play as part of the wider community of staff;

- Reinforce this message of personal responsibility by direct reference to it in the corporate information security policy;

- Introduce these concepts at the earliest possible opportunity – at recruitment interviews and staff induction meetings;

- Provide adequate training and education to ensure that all employees are fully aware of their personal responsibilities and also trained in the techniques that they need to apply in their work so as to fulfil these responsibilities;

- Monitor the compliance stance and attitude of each individual throughout their employment, and use appraisal reviews to draw attention to both shortcomings and successes in the fulfilment of these responsibilities;

- Provide mandatory operational procedures for reporting security incidents of all types and ensure that all employees are aware of their duty to make such reports and that they know the mechanisms by which the reports are submitted;

- If necessary, for special types of event you may wish to provide an anonymous whistle-blowing facility to protect an employee from intimidation by a more senior and powerful person who may be abusing that power.

Personnel Management

Making sure that the people employed by the enterprise are trustworthy and of good character is a primary line of defence. There are a number of standard operational measures that can help to weed out those with a tendency to dishonesty, fraud or other criminal activity:

- Carry out proper employment screening and vetting to ensure that people with a record of irresponsibility or criminality are excluded from the beginning. This screening process should include:

  - Character references – one professional and one personal;

  - Verifying the contents of an applicant's CV or application form and ensuring that all periods of time are accounted for and checked;

  - Confirmation of all claimed academic or vocational qualifications;

  - Independent verification of identity;

  - Possibly personal credit checks where an employee will be handling large sums of money (although being in debt is not a crime and not an indicator of criminal intent).

- Supervise staff through suitable management frameworks, and use this supervision not only for monitoring quality of work but also to keep track of other issues that might affect an employee's performance, loyalty and honesty, including personal family life, financial difficulties, psychological difficulties or changes in lifestyle. When there are alarming signals, ensure that authorised follow-up action is taken within the framework of the organisation's human resources polices and the relevant employment law, but tread carefully and beware of being cavalier in making accusations that will lead to industrial relations difficulties. Operational risk is a many-faceted thing, as discussed in Chapter 16.

- Ensure that there are well-documented procedures, within the local employment law and approved by qualified legal advisors, for dealing with any incidents involving personnel. Such incidents will include any type of suspicion of wrongdoing.

- Provide clear documented policies and procedures as to how a 'leaver' is to be handled. Staff members who leave do so under one of several circumstances, each of which needs its own tailored approach:

  - Staff who leave of their own volition to go to another job (Why are they leaving – unhappy? Career move? More money? Following their spouse or partner?);

  - Staff who retire voluntarily under normal or early retirement rules;

  - Staff who face compulsory retirement because they reach the age of retirement but who otherwise wish to continue to work;

  - Staff who are dismissed for misconduct or under-performance;

  - Staff who are made redundant, possibly as part of a wider programme of downsizing.

- Establish a formal disciplinary process for dealing with employees who are careless or negligent in fulfilling their duties, or who maliciously and knowingly disobey instructions, policies, procedures and practices affecting information security management. It may be necessary to collect and preserve evidence in cases where formal prosecution is considered or where the employee may dispute the disciplinary action or seek legal counteraction (see later in this chapter under Forensic Investigations).

Segregating Duties

Segregating duties and implementing dual control increases security

Long before computers were introduced, the banking industry in particular has long understood the benefits of segregating duties. For example, if you had a vault storing large quantities of money there would be two locks. Each lock had its own key, and each key would be assigned to a different person. No individual person could open the vault alone. The principle is often known as dual control.

Dual control has many ways of being implemented

The same principle has been adopted into modern banking in electronic systems. A high-value transaction has its details entered by one person (a clerk), but is authorised for release by another person (a manager). A system change is authorised by one person (a manager) but implemented by another (an engineering technician). There are many similar examples.

Fraud prevention measures often apply dual control

Each organisation should consider where this principle might be applicable and how it can be implemented. The most common application of this technique is in the prevention of fraud – ensuring that no one person can commit a fraud without another person detecting it. A typical dual control procedure would be the task of raising a purchase order being segregated from the task of signing off the receipt of goods to authorise an invoice for payment. This prevents an individual inside the organisation from colluding with an outsider to submit fraudulent invoices for goods not delivered or to submit multiple invoices for the same batch of delivered goods.

Delegation to deputies protects business continuity

It is important to ensure that normal business productivity is not hindered by a dual control procedure. In particular you need to make provisions for deputies who can act on behalf of an authoriser who might not be available at the required time, whilst still maintaining the original segregation – so, a deputy cannot be a person authorised to perform the other part of the segregated task.

Independent monitoring or auditing is one solution

One way to implement the dual control principle that leaves most opportunity for proper segregation is to make one person the monitor or auditor who simply checks on the activity of the other person and reports unexpected behaviour.

Beware of collusion amongst close friends or relatives

You also need to consider the possibility of collusion between two people who hold the two duties in a dual control procedure. You need to take the wider view sometimes, since conspiracy between several people in a chain of control can be a problem. There are certain regular exclusions that you should apply, such as members of the same family or close friends. It works best if the two people are as segregated as much as possible both in their work interaction and in their social and domestic interaction, but this may be impractical – especially in small organisations. If you need to take risks of this type for purely practical operational purposes, you may need additional risk mitigation in the form of enhanced audit trails and supervisor monitoring.

Enforced Annual Leave

Keeping a fraud hidden often needs constant attention

If a member of staff is running an ongoing fraud against the employer, keeping that fraud hidden often depends upon that person maintaining continuous control over some activity or over a set of records. These are the people who never take leave, never take sick leave (even when they are ill) and always work overtime – often alone in the premises.

Enforced annual leave is a good way to reveal ongoing frauds

A useful personnel management control that has often been successful in revealing frauds is to insist that in any one annual leave year, everyone at every level of seniority MUST take at least one continuous week of annual leave (but preferably two continuous weeks) and that their job MUST be done by someone else during that period of leave.

Managing Physical and Environmental Security

Physical security is based upon enclosed areas with impenetrable perimeters

Physical security depends upon the effective definition of security perimeters and the control of access both in and out of those secure areas enclosed within the perimeters. These perimeters include:

- Site perimeters;
- Building perimeters;
- Internal perimeters of secure areas where sensitive processing activity or secure storage takes place;
- Locked cabinets, storage cupboards, 'dark'[1] equipment rooms and storerooms.

Authorised access through the perimeter requires suitable controlled access points

As well as maintaining the integrity of the perimeter boundary with impenetrable walls and fences and locked doors and windows, there is also a need to provide authorised access points such as controlled gates and doors. These may be controlled either by automated access control mechanisms or by security personnel such as security guards or reception staff.

Segregation of duties must be applied to guarding activities

The duties of the guards must be segregated from those who are guarded (as described in the section above on dual control and segregation of duties).

Access is allowed only by authorised personnel

Only authorised personnel are allowed through these controlled points, and identification badges should be shown at the access point and worn visibly inside all controlled areas. Authorised visitor procedures should ensure adequate escort and supervision at all times. This includes the procedures for supervising on-site contractors and temporary staff. Delivery and loading areas also require special control arrangements.

Equipment and services require protection from malicious tampering

Live operational equipment rooms, electrical power supplies and other essential services, communications connections and cabling runs require protection against both malicious and accidental tampering, and also against environmental threats such as fire, water damage, smoke and physical damage. The safety of personnel who handle or come into contact with equipment is also of paramount importance.

Procedures are needed for equipment maintenance and removal

Electrical, electronic and mechanical equipment should be maintained and inspected in accordance with documented maintenance and support procedures. There should also be special procedures for the authorised removal of equipment and for its possible authorised use or repair off site. All changes to equipment configurations should be subject to rigorous change control policies and procedures. Equipment authorised for disposal or re-use should be cleansed of any residual data before removal from site.

Theft is controlled by ensuring that all valuable items are locked away

The malicious theft or accidental loss of information both on paper and on electronic or electromagnetic media should be controlled through clear desk and clear screen policies and

[1]The term 'dark' is often used to describe an unmanned equipment operations area.

procedures, and suitable locked storage facilities should be provided for such items when not in immediate use. Inventory control should be applied to all items of equipment and sensitive storage media, with comprehensive logging of all items stored or removed for whatever purpose.

Managing ICT Operations and Support

Operating Procedures

All key operating procedures should be documented in detail

The key to successful day-to-day operations of all business processes, including the operation of both information processing and data communications systems, is that all expected procedures (whether routine or emergency) have been worked out and documented in fine detail. This means that even if the staff members who are familiar with these tasks are unavailable, a new member of staff has access to a full description of each and every task that needs to be performed.

Considerations in documenting these procedures include:

* Detailed step-by-step processing task descriptions;

* Scheduling requirements and constraints, including interdependencies between systems and earliest or latest start times to harmonise with business deadlines and cut-offs;

* Instructions and guidance for handling errors and exceptions during processing;

* Support contacts in case of unexpected technical or operational difficulties;

* Handling instruction for special output media;

* Recovery and restart procedures in case of system failure.

Change Control

Change control maintains the stability of the operating environment

Another key contributor to the stability of ongoing operations is rigorous change control over the operational environment. All changes to equipment configurations, software configurations, operational data and the operating procedures themselves must be subject to this change control regime.

The change control process should address the following points:

* Identification of significant proposed changes and capture of the details;

* Impact assessment for each potential change;

* Formal evaluation and approval for each proposed change;

* Documentation of each change with adequate communication of the details to all affected parties and updates to all appropriate records including the configuration database and the business continuity plans;

* Clear responsibilities for change implementations, including responsibility and procedures for reversing out and recovering from failed changes;

* Quality assurance of the change implementation;

* Post-implementation testing of each change.

Change Management

It is easy to confuse the two terms 'change control' and 'change management' because they sound similar, but they have very different meanings. Change control has been described above. Change management refers to the management of a major change across the entire enterprise. The impacts of such a major change will be far reaching and need to be managed carefully.

An example of such a change would be for an organisation that has so far had no formal framework for managing information security making a decision to implement a BS7799-compliant ISMS (see Chapter 16 for a detailed discussion of this topic). Such an implementation requires a major change project.

Issues to be considered and managed in such a change project are:

- Building executive-level sponsorship and championship;
- Defining goals and objectives;
- Planning the investment required;
- Business process development;
- Cultural development;
- Infrastructure development;
- Managing the interfaces with customers, suppliers and regulators;
- Identifying success factors;
- Identifying obstacles and barriers;
- Adopting a change management methodology;
- Overcoming resistance;
  - Estimating organisational change capacity and speed;
  - Employee resistance;
  - Manager resistance.
- Project team structure and membership;
- Communications to the management and staff – messages to be delivered and methods of delivery;
- Training for new skills;
- Dealing with redundant skills and the whole HR, personnel management, industrial relations scenario;
- Retaining valued employees;
- Rewarding positive behaviour and discouraging negative behaviour;
- Use of external consultants and change management models.

Even with small-scale change projects, many of these issues need to be addressed. Change management must therefore be an integral part of any information security administration and operations programme, in which changes will necessarily be introduced from time to time.

Incident Handling

Many diverse types of incident need to be handled

In any operational environment there will be incidents that need to be handled in the course of events. Types of incidents can include:

- System failures and loss of service;

- Denial of service;

- Errors from incomplete or inaccurate business data;

- Breaches of confidentiality;

- Unauthorised changes.

Incident impact assessment is the first step

Some of these incidents will be minor, whilst others will have the potential to cause severe damage to the business. When an incident first occurs it is often difficult to tell which what the potential outcome will be, and so one of the first responses is to assess the severity of the incident.

Incident management is largely an operational process

In Chapter 11 of this book there is a description of the logical architecture for incident management as a service, including incident detection and incident response. Much of the incident response service is implemented through operational handling procedures, the focus of the discussion here.

The procedures for incident handling

The incident handling procedures should cover:

- Receiving the alarm that draws attention to an incident;

- Identification and analysis of the cause of the incident;

- Potential business impact assessment and prioritisation of the incident (triage);

- Reviewing options for remedial actions;

- Planning and implementation of remedies, both to remove the cause and to recover the effects of the incident (and also to prevent its recurrence);

- Collection and preservation of audit trails and similar forensic evidence for analysis and for use in possible legal proceedings and contractual negotiations;

- Communication with those parties affected by the incident;

- Reporting the incident and the responses to an appropriate authority.

Potential conflict between incident management and problem management

If your organisation has adopted an IT management framework for incident control such as ITIL, BS15000 or AS8018, you should take extra care in developing additional procedures and protocols in this area to define and handle security incidents. Such frameworks implement a segregation of duties between incident management (where the primary focus is on rapidly recovering service levels to the customer) and problem management (where the primary focus is on understanding the cause of incidents, the relationships between incidents and preventing recurrence). These roles often operate in conflict: the incident manager wants the system brought back up while the problem manager needs it to stay down for investigation. This is of particular sensitivity in the area of security where many incidents are not known problems but the result of new threats, which may be very difficult for help desk staff to identify. Special procedures are therefore required for:

- Identification and classification of a security incident;

- Reporting and escalating the security incident;

- Investigation of the security incident;

- Criteria for management decisions to balance the conflict between restoring service, containing a potential new problem and investigating the incident;

- Handling information relevant to a security incident; for example, if the incident is inappropriate or illegal use of computer resources it would be inappropriate for the help desk or incident-management systems to openly display and record the sensitive details of who was involved.

Segregating System Development from Operational Production

Good practice requires separation of system development and systems operations

The issue of segregation of system development and system operation has already been discussed in Chapter 16 under the section entitled System Assurance Strategy. The summary of the operational requirements is as follows:

- System development facilities, test facilities and live production facilities should be completely segregated from one another.

- The rules for transfer of new software from development or test into production should be clearly defined and documented and should include an authorisation process involving a responsible and accountable manager.

- No development activity should be allowed on a live production system, with the possible exception of emergency fixes that are carried out under strictly supervised special procedures.

- On a live production system the only software that should be allowed is application software and the underlying system software needed to run that application. All software development tools, editors, compilers, linkers, loaders, system utilities and any similar tools that can be used to generate new software code should be completely banned from all live production machines.

- Even for emergency fixes, the diagnostics should be carried out on the live system, the software fix should be made on the development system, tested on the test system and the new code patch should then be promoted and installed on the live system. There should be no need for software tools to be executed, or indeed reside, on the live system.

Capacity Planning

Capacity planning has several areas of application

Capacity in business information systems includes a number of different types:

- Processing power;

- Memory size;

- Disk (and other media) storage capacity;

- Communications bandwidth;

- Input and output volumes;

- Staffing levels;

- Accommodation requirements (according to the footprints of equipment items and staff working space);

- Ancillary services requirements (such as electrical power and air conditioning).

Capacity planning deals with future requirements

As time progresses there is a tendency for each of these capacity requirements to grow. The operational activity of capacity planning is concerned with:

- Monitoring the utilisation of current capacity, including the statistical variability in terms of peaks and troughs using mean and standard deviation parameters;

- Monitoring the rate at which spare capacity is being consumed and plotting trends;

- Based upon these observations, making predictions and forecasts about future capacity needs against timelines;

- Planning ahead to ensure that the required capacity is available when the time arrives.

Lack of capacity leads to business interruptions

Having insufficient capacity can cause serious business interruptions through system failures caused by overloads.

Case Study: Not Counting on the Capacity of Census Interest

In 2002 the UK Government Public Records Office (PRO) put the 1901 UK census data online. The web site was launched on 2 January 2002 with the aim of catering for a maximum of 1.2 million users in a 24-hour period. However by noon on the first day, just three hours after being launched, 1.2 million users per hour were trying to access the site, with the same level of demand continuing during the next few days. The site had to be withdrawn five days after its launch following a consistent volume of visits from users of about 1.2 million users an hour. There was severe embarrassment for the PRO.

The site was reopened seven months later and now caters for between 8,000 and 10,000 web users every day. A report by the UK National Audit Office (NAO) said the level of interest in the web site had not been expected by the PRO, which had 'developed a pre-launch strategy based on a low key launch'. The NAO report said the PRO was taken by surprise by the level of press interest in the site, while launching it during a holiday period meant more web users were able to access it from home.

The NAO report says this demand overwhelmed the site and led the PRO and its contracted service provider to close it and launch a technical investigation. The site was closed until reopening on a limited basis in August 2002, before being made fully available in November the same year.

According to the NAO report, the principal lessons are:

- Transfer commercial risk to the service provider, to be funded, where possible, from revenues earned from the service and secure an interest in further revenues thereafter;

- Recognise the distinction between commercial risk, which can be

> transferred to third parties, and reputation risk, which usually remains with the contracting party;

- – Make a realistic assessment, as far as possible, of usage and put in place a capacity management strategy that will successfully divert unexpected overloads experienced in practice;

- – Where appropriate, carefully select both the rate and timing of the launch of the new services to maximise the opportunity to resolve unforeseen problems before peak demand has built up;

- – Before the service goes live, develop an agreed post-launch disaster recovery strategy.

The key recommendations for the National Archives are as follows:

- – Monitor closely the web site's ongoing financial performance;

- – Work with the contractor to maximise the marketing opportunities and revenues from the web site;

- – Include in its corporate plan an early appreciation of how the completion of the 10-year contract with the contractor will be managed.

System Acceptance and Release Management

Acceptance testing requires both UAT and OAT

Acceptance testing is discussed in Chapter 16 as part of the entire cycle of testing that underpins system assurance. There are two very different areas of acceptance testing that need to be planned and executed before a system is put into live production:

- • User acceptance testing (UAT): testing the business functionality to ensure that it matches the requirements of the operational business process and hence meets the needs of the end users;

- • Operational acceptance testing (OAT): testing to ensure that the system is capable of being operated by the operations team within the terms of the service level agreement.

Refer to Chapter 16

For a detailed discussion of each of these types of acceptance testing, the reader is referred to Chapter 16.

Ongoing release management

Once accepted, a system should be subject to an ongoing release management programme, including the release of upgrades and patches.

Protecting Against Malicious Software

Strategy for malicious software protection

Malicious software includes a wide variety of viruses, Trojans, worms and the like. The core of a strategy to protect live operational systems against malicious software is:

- • Good awareness and good behaviour among the user community;

- • Appropriate control of access to systems based upon business need;

- • A strict change control regime;

- • Automated scanning of all data and software imports through e-mail, web access, file transfer, etc.

Refer to Chapters 11 and 16 For a detailed discussion of this topic, the reader should refer to Chapter 16: section entitled Software Integrity and Anti-Virus. Refer also to Chapter 11: Software Integrity Protection.

Data Backup and Recovery

Data backup enables disaster recovery Operational data is changing all the time and thus it is essential to take regular, frequent backup copies of the most recent version. The objective is to be able to recover the business data (following some type of failure or disaster) to a previous business position that is acceptable to the business users under the terms of the service level agreement.

Backup strategy Depending upon the business needs, the backup strategy may be based upon conventional weekly full data backups with daily incremental backups. For a more demanding set of business requirements, real-time online data mirroring may be needed.

Backups require testing Whatever the type of backup mechanism in use, it should be tested regularly to ensure that it is working properly and that backup copies are actually being created. The mechanism for restoration using the backup copies should also be tested. These restoration tests should include verification that the restoration can be accomplished within the window of time available in the business day.

Case Study: The Phantom Backups

A small software house was keenly aware that its assets were largely in the code that it produced. A fully automated high-speed tape backup system was acquired and installed to protect against major failure of the development system and in particular to protect against failure of the disks on which the development files were stored.

Secure off-site storage was rented, and a regular daily routine was established whereby an incremental backup was run every evening and a full weekly backup every Friday evening. A member of staff was paid overtime rates to execute these procedures after everyone else had finished work. The tape was taken to the off-site storage, and the tapes were recycled on a monthly basis, so that a complete month's backups were always available, giving plenty of depth to the backup strategy. No tape was used more that 10 times, after which it was retired and destroyed.

This backup regime had been in place for around 18 months, running as smoothly as clockwork. Then there was a major disk crash on the main development system. The disk was beyond repair or recovery and so a new disk unit was purchased, and the task began of restoring the data from the backup tapes.

It soon became clear that the tapes that had been so carefully stored away were completely blank. Not a single tape in the entire month of tapes had any backup data on it. There were a few tapes that had been recycled and brought back – these too were blank. It was impossible to tell when the backup writing system had failed (had it ever worked?), but certainly it was more than a month ago, and there were no backup copies of any sort available.

There was a simple but completely critical step missing from the backup procedures that this firm had put in place – verifying that the backup tapes actually had data written to them and that they could be used to achieve a restoration of the business information.

Case Study: Time Travelling

A major computer operations production facility for a credit card processing firm was based upon a large mainframe computer with huge disk storage facilities and extensive input/output equipment. This was by anyone's standards a very large-scale operation, processing card transactions and billing for many millions of cardholders and running on a 24-hours by 7-days-a-week basis. Production never stopped.

The backup regime was solid, based upon tape backups of both data and current versions of application and system software.

The management then commissioned a study to find out how long it would take to complete a full business restoration following a complete system failure. The answer was 27 hours – more than a whole business day, so you could never catch up.

The solution lay in a change of system architecture, both logically in terms of real-time mirroring, and physically in terms of upgrades to the processing power and channel bandwidths.

Managing backup media   There should be defined operational procedures both for making backup copies and for restoring system data using the backups. There must also be standards and procedures for managing backup media (tapes, disks, CDs). Please refer to the later section in this chapter on media handling.

Operational Logging

Operator logs record operator activity   There are many system logs maintained automatically by both applications and system software. However, there is also a need for certain manually maintained logs with regard to operational activity itself.

Operator log specifications   Operator logs should include the name of the operator making the entry, the date and time, and the nature of the entry, such as:

- System starting and finishing times;
- System errors and other events and corrective actions taken;
- Confirmation of completion and correctness of input and output runs.

Media Handling

Media types   The media to which this section refers includes all removable computer generated output media, including:

- Magnetic media: disks, diskettes, tapes and tape cassettes (including voice recordings);
- Optical media: CDs and other optical device media;

- Printed paper output and other specialised printed media;

- Carbon paper, one-time printer ribbons and other quasi-media of a similar type.

Media handling procedures The secure handling of such media requires controlled operational procedures, including:

- Secure and permanent erasure of all data from magnetic or optical media that is no longer required by the organisation;

- Authorisation for the removal of any media items from the premises of the organisation, whether or not for disposal purposes;

- A complete audit record of all media items: their creation; their use; their storage; their erasure, their removal and their disposal;

- Secure storage facilities for all media items, including off-site storage for backup media;

- Secure media handling procedures and standards, including those for:

  - Media quality standards and acquisition;

  - Naming, labelling and indexing;

  - Secure storage and retrieval procedures;

  - Environmental considerations such as temperature, humidity, electromagnetic fields and physical stability;

  - Secure transport to and from authorised locations;

  - Procedures for caring for and maintaining stored media;

  - Recycling, lifetime management and retirement;

  - Secure disposal and destruction.

Ensure that equipment for media support is still available In addition to the management of the media items you also need to ensure that old, archived, stored media can still be read back using the correct media read/write sub-systems. It has happened many times that data stored on old media types cannot be accesses because the equipment needed has been superseded, is no longer supported and no longer available in the organisation. (When did you last see an 8-inch or even a 5.25-inch floppy drive?)

Case Study: Banking on the Backups

A major European bank was required by law to retain account information for a period of seven years. It was also required to disclose the information on request by law enforcement agencies or the court system.

It had an extensive backup procedure, the tapes were tested for content at the time of backup, the restore process was tested at the same time, and then the tapes were stored in duplicate both on site in a fireproof safe and off site.

In 1999 the bank received an order from the court system to disclose information relating to transactions made in 1993. They duly retrieved the relevant backup tapes but to their horror discovered that they were unable to read them.

In the intervening years their physical architecture had changed beyond all recognition and equipment thought to be now redundant had been disposed of, including the tape drives used to write and read the old backup tapes. The bank had to engage the expensive services of a specialist forensic recovery company to retrieve the information from the old media.

Network Operations

Network operations procedures

There are a number of additional operational controls (over and above those such as change control and capacity planning already described elsewhere in this chapter for generic operational security) that are required to ensure that data networking remains secure. These include:

- Segregation of responsibilities and activities for network operations from those associated with computer systems operations;

- Clear responsibilities and operating procedures for the operation of remote networking equipment;

- Clear responsibilities and operating procedures for cryptographic key management where cryptographic networking equipment has been deployed.

Software Licence Management

Controlling the use of software licences

In order to comply with the terms of commercial software licenses, an organisation needs to put in place a number of specific controls that might include:

- A published corporate software licence compliance policy which defines the legal use of software and organisation's stance on copyright protection and compliance with licence agreements;

- Standard procedures for software acquisition and deployment;

- Ensuring that all staff are aware of the policy and procedures around software acquisition and that there is a robust disciplinary process for dealing with those who violate the policy;

- Maintaining a comprehensive asset register of all commercial software products acquired and in use, the number of run-time copies in use, the location of the machines on which they run, the location of the master copies (CD or diskettes) and documentary proof of possession of the requisite licences;

- Ensuring that for site licenses the maximum permitted number of run-time users is not exceeded;

- Ensuring that unauthorised, unlicensed software is not in use or installed on corporate computing platforms, especially end user PCs.

Information Exchange

Processes for controlling information exchange

Many organisations need to exchange information for business purposes. These exchanges need to be controlled through a number of operational measures, including:

- Risk assessment to reveal the threats, impacts and vulnerabilities associated with information exchanges;

- Procedures and standards to protect the information in transit, according to the requirements derived from the risk assessment, including specific procedures for sending and receiving the information;

- Formal agreements and contracts between the parties exchanging information to define clearly the roles, responsibilities and liabilities of each party.

Information exchange mechanisms

The mechanisms for exchanging information can vary widely. Each mechanism requires its own threat and vulnerability assessment. The most frequently encountered mechanisms for which you will require standards and procedures include:

- Physical transport of media items such as disks, tapes and paper documents;

- Web-based electronic commerce;

- File-transfer based EDI[2];

- Electronic mail and file attachments;

- Voice telephony and voice mail;

- Video conferencing;

- Web conferencing and web-casting;

- Fax transmissions;

- SMS text messaging;

- IRC-based instant messaging (IM) and the constantly emerging multimedia versions of this type of service.

Outsourcing Contractor Management: Ancillary Services

Examples of outsourced ancillary services

It is common to outsource many ancillary and support services to a third-party contractor. Typical examples include:

- Hardware and software maintenance and support;

- Cleaning services;

- Catering services;

- Security guarding services;

- Specialist consulting services.

Controlling on-site contractor personnel

The employees of these third-party contractors often work on site, and in many cases they need either physical access to the operations areas of your buildings and to certain equipment, or logical

---

[2]EDI: electronic data interchange

access to corporate information systems. It is therefore essential to address specifically these access requirements.

Access management processes

Issues to address include:

- Access privileges to be granted;

- Entry passes and passwords to be issued, and on who's authority and based upon what criteria;

- Degree of supervision and escorting to be applied;

- Times and modes of access;

- Procedures for withdrawal and termination of access rights;

- Codes of behaviour for contractor employees with reporting and disciplinary processes;

- Liabilities of the contractor for their employees' behaviour;

- Contents of third-party contracts to cover compliance with the organisation's security polices and procedures;

- Specific contractor employee confidentiality agreements.

Outsourcing Contractor Management: ICT Operations

Processes for managing outsourced ICT operations

Outsourcing of the entire ICT operations activity implies a highly demanding set of requirements for operational security management, since much of this is transferred into the hands of the outsourced service provider. In this section are some additional issues (above and beyond those already covered in the foregoing section) to be addressed with regard to general outsourcing of ICT operations. Later in the chapter there is also a detailed discussion of Managed Security Services – where the security management itself is outsourced.

Issues to be addressed

The main issues with outsourcing ICT operations include:

- Clear and unambiguous definition of the services being outsourced, and a risk assessment showing the information security risks that are associated with these services;

- Compliance with legal requirements for information security;

- Contractual agreement of security responsibilities, liabilities and obligations between the parties and ensuring that all the contractor's employees are aware of these;

- Maintaining and testing the confidentiality and integrity of the service customer organisation's business assets;

- Protecting the intellectual property rights (IPR) of the parties;

- The selection, deployment and operation of physical and logical information security controls;

- The processes for transferring staff where appropriate;

- The minimum service levels to be maintained even under disaster recovery conditions;

- The methods, processes and criteria for monitoring and reporting performance against the targets set in the service level agreement (SLA);

- The levels of physical security to be applied to protecting the operations centre and the equipment within it;

- The rights of the service customer to audit the way in which the service provider meets the information security requirements;

- Responsibilities, processes and procedures for sharing security management between the two parties;

- The processes to be used for identifying, reporting, escalating and handling security incidents.

Asset and Configuration Management

The asset register

The most basic form of asset management is the creation and maintenance of an asset register (or inventory) in which all the assets are catalogued together with any relevant information about the assets (such as location, identification data such as a serial number, date of acquisition, original value, present value, ownership and security classification). The types of assets that need to be included for information security management purposes include:

- Information assets: databases and data files (including backup copies), system documentation, user manuals, training materials, operational and support procedures, continuity plans, fallback arrangements, archived information;

- Software assets: application software, system software, development tools and utilities;

- Physical assets: computer equipment and peripherals, communications equipment, magnetic media, ancillary equipment, accommodation, furniture and office equipment;

- Services: communications services and general utilities (such as heating, lighting, electrical power, water and air conditioning).

Configuration management defined

Whereas asset inventories record lists of hardware and software items, they do not record the relationships between them. These relationships between the various ICT components are the objective of configuration management. Thus configuration management involves the unique identification, recording and reporting of components, their version, constituent components and relationships. Items that need to be under configuration control include: hardware, software, data structures, licences, documentation and people.

Benefits of asset management and configuration control

The benefits of good configuration management include:

- Support for change control and change management by ensuring that the impact of all configuration changes can be traced and tracked;

- Effective deployment of software and hardware;

- Improved resource planning;

- Improved financial planning;

- Improved risk management;

- Maintaining the stability and security of the operational environment;

- Improved business continuity and disaster recovery;

- Improved control over legal and contractual responsibilities such as licence management and copyright protection;

- Reduced complexity of configurations;

- Improved problem resolution and hence higher levels of service delivery.

Service Level Agreement (SLA) Management

The service level agreement explained

A service level agreement (SLA) is a formal document describing the service to be provided by a service provider to a service customer. It should be formalised whether or not the service provider and customer are separate commercial entities. It is just as applicable in the case where the service provider is another department or business unit within the same commercial organisation as the service customer.

Change control over the SLA

The SLA is subject to change control, as is the service that it describes. The key word is 'agreement' – between the two parties – and hence any changes must be renegotiated and subject to agreement.

Addressing operational security in the SLA

Operational security management is one of the major topics that must be addressed within the SLA. The document should describe:

- Security obligations, responsibilities and liabilities between the parties;

- The points of contact, communication channels and methods, and the management process for handling security issues;

- Escalation procedures;

- Complaints process;

- Rights of the service customer to audit the service provider activities;

- Security service performance targets;

- Reporting against security service performance targets;

- Security incident identification, handling escalation and resolution;

- Remedies and penalties for failure to reach the agreed service levels;

- Disaster recovery and priorities following a service failure.

Business Relationship Management

Formal agreements are the safety net

The relationship between a service provider and a business user of those services is defined, controlled and managed through a number of operational control mechanisms discussed in this chapter, including contracts, SLAs, policies and processes. However, in many ways these formal frameworks represent only a safety net – a fallback position for when the relationship sours.

Success depends upon a good relationship

A key success factor in any operational service provision, whether to an internal or an external customer, is to develop and maintain a good working relationship between the two parties. Such relationships are what gets business done, and they need attention and nurture for them to grow and flourish. This may seem to be a wishy-washy and ill-defined topic area, but in fact the investment of effort on business relationship management will bring much greater returns than much of the effort that is necessarily put into keeping in place that safety net of contracts and SLAs.

Goals of relationship management

The goals of business relationship management should be:

- To know your customer, understand the business and be aware of the business drivers and constraints;

- To use that understanding to interpret technical requirements more accurately by understanding the true business requirements that lie behind them;

- To understand the subtle cultural differences between different organisations in your portfolio of customers. On the surface they may seem to be very similar, but in cultural terms can be very different.

Techniques for relationship management

To achieve these goals there are a number of techniques that can be used:

- Regular customer liaison meetings at the business management level (not the technical management level) with the objective of managing customer expectations, perceptions and satisfaction;

- Periodic service reviews with the customer, focused around the SLA, past performance and future requirements, but again with the business management level in the customer organisation;

- Objective reporting to the customer organisation of the service provider performance in terms of costs, service levels and workloads handled to try to head off subjective judgements supported by anecdotal evidence;

- Customer satisfaction surveys, with visible, proactive follow-up of any problems or issues that these surveys reveal.

Operations Staff Training and Awareness Development

Training in skills and procedures

All members of staff with systems operations responsibilities need to be properly trained in the skills and procedures for carrying out their duties. This will include:

- Training on all regular operational tasks;

- Training on all emergency and disaster management tasks;

- Training on security-related procedures, polices and rules;

- Training on the recognition, identification, reporting, escalation and handling of all security-related incidents;

- Awareness training on general security issues and policies;

- Training in the use of specialised security management tools.

Service Monitoring and Reporting

Keeping the business informed

Service monitoring and reporting encompasses all measurable aspects of the service. The purpose of such monitoring and reporting is to provide the business with timely, reliable, clear, concise and meaningful reports to support decision making. The reports enable the business management to review the effectiveness and efficiency of the services being provided, the service levels being achieved and the workloads being handled.

Types of reporting　The types of reports to be made available include:

- Workload management reports;

- Problem management reports;

- Financial reports;

- Asset and configuration management reports;

- Change control reports.

Supporting service development and improvement　The reports can be used as a source of reliable data to support service development and improvement. There are two main categories of report:

- Reactive reports: showing information on past events and allowing an analysis and trend comparison of error rates, outages and cost overruns, so that attention can be paid to improving these aspects of service provision and management;

- Proactive reports: providing early warning of significant events and enabling preventive actions to be taken beforehand.

Tailoring the reports to the needs of the recipient　Raw metrics are rarely helpful to a manager. The presentation of metrics needs to be tailored to the individual needs of the manager, and presented in a clear concise form that tells that manager what he wants to know – no more and no less. The concept of a management information dashboard as discussed in Chapter 6 is relevant here.

Event Log and Audit Trail Management

Logging significant events for audit purposes　Event logging is used to record any system event that may have significance to the management of the services. The log of events creates an audit trail of what has happened. This audit trail must be stored for an agreed period of time to facilitate historical analysis and investigation.

Event types　Included amongst these significant events are those that have some significance for security management. These will include:

- Exceptions – events which are unusual and beyond the pattern normally expected;

- Failed login attempts;

- Successful logins and subsequent logoffs;

- Access to any especially sensitive information resources that have been flagged for access event logging;

- Use of privileged resources such as administrator or root identities;

- Errors or failures in any logical or physical system components;

- Security alerts from anti-virus software, firewalls and intrusion detection systems;

- Expiry of security credentials and authorisations.

Event log formats　The event log records must contain sufficient data to make them useful. Typical fields in an event log record will include:

- Data and time of the event;

- User identifiers associated with the event;

- Logical or physical location, or both;

- Event type (may be encoded to economise of log storage space);

- Any other context information needed to explain the full nature of the event.

Event log storage

Some audit trails are kept for short periods of time and are often stored in a finite area of storage operated on a rolling first-in-first-out (FIFO) basis. Thus as new event data is captured, the oldest event data is overwritten, and the store contains only the most recent set of events.

Event log archiving

In other circumstances it may be more appropriate to keep audit trails for several years, in which case the most recent event logs are kept online and the older material is archived every month or so.

Tools for event log management

Whatever type of audit trail is appropriate, it will normally be stored in chronological order and you will need to have suitable tools to manage and search the event information. These tools include a number of capabilities:

- Searching for certain event types or certain identifiers;

- Searching for certain combinations and patterns of events, using normal database or search engine query functions (AND, OR, NOT, XOR) to combine conditional searches for combinations of fields in the records;

- Statistical analysis of event patterns, frequencies and severity;

- Archiving, indexing and retrieving event logs.

Forensic Investigations

A detailed discussion is beyond the scope of this book

Information system forensics is a large and growing field of specialised activity, and it is well beyond the scope of this book to attempt to describe it in any detail. However, as a brief overview the main issues are discussed here.

Forensic investigation is focused upon the collection and preservation of evidence, usually so that such evidence can be presented in a court of law, but it could also be in support of an internal disciplinary process. This immediately identifies a number of important goals for forensic investigations:

- Maintaining the continuity of the chain of evidence;

- Preserving the integrity of the evidence – preventing the evidence from becoming contaminated either during or after the process of it being collected;

- Ensuring that the evidence will be admissible under the rules of the court and the relevant laws;

- Building up the appropriate weight of evidence – its quality and completeness.

The forensics process has certain key goals

The main elements of the forensic investigation process needed to achieve these goals are:

- Planning the investigation:

  - Setting the goals, objectives and scope;

- Establishing the principles;
- Defining the protocols.

- Seizing the evidence;
  - Tools required;
  - Conduct of the seizure process.

- Analysis of the evidence;
  - Tools required;
  - Logical analysis processes;

- Establishing the history of captured digital evidence;
  - Detecting and overcoming data hiding tools and techniques used by data owners to disguise incriminating evidence;
  - Handling encrypted forensic material.

- Reporting;
  - Written reports;
  - Expert witness statements and court appearances.

Forensic investigation is best carried out by trained and experienced experts

If you have a problem that requires forensic investigation then the best thing to do is to call in some experts; this is not a job for amateur first-timers. Inappropriate actions can jeopardise potential criminal prosecutions or internal disciplinary hearing. The priority is to preserve the 'crime scene' as completely as possible. This is best achieved by leaving it undisturbed and calling in expert assistance at the earliest opportunity. Such expertise can be found in the specialist teams of various law enforcement agencies, or in some specialist consultancies[3] that can carry out investigation on a private commercial basis.

Problem Tracking and Management

Problem management seeks to eradicate causes

Problem management differs from incident management in that its main goal is to detect the underlying causes of an incident and to eradicate or circumvent those causes both in the immediate and long-term future.

There can be conflicts with incident management

Problem management and incident management can be in conflict with one another. The objective of managing an incident is to restore the service as soon as possible, whereas problem management requires the investigation of the causes, which can delay the service recovery.

Two main types of problem management

Problem management can be divided into two main classes:

- Reactive problem management: managing problems already identified and resolving them within agreed service times so as to minimise the business impact of the problem;

- Proactive problem management: analysis of incidents so as to prevent recurrence and leading to improvements in the service. Service reports and incident reports (see earlier sections in this chapter) are fundamental to the proactive problem management process.

---

[3]For example, see www.inforenz.com

The problem management process

The problem management process includes:

- Investigation and diagnosis;

- Impact and urgency assessment so as to prioritise problem management tasks;

- Provision of workarounds to maintain short-term service levels whilst the problem is investigated and resolved;

- Resolution of problems;

- Communicating information to those who need to know the outcome of the problem resolution;

- Monitoring and tracking the status of outstanding problems and checking progress against service level targets;

- Escalation of major problems to appropriate levels of authority;

- Problem record closure on completion to ensure all details are captured;

- Major incident handling;

- Problem reviews;

- Incident and problem prevention.

Help Desk and User Support

Co-ordination of user-related problems

The help desk is a central point through which user problems or issues are reported and subsequently managed and co-ordinated. It is an integral part of the service management function and is responsible for bringing resources together to address a problem or other issue. It is an important part of the problem management infrastructure.

Help desk support characterises the user perception of service levels

For the user community, whether they are internal users or external users (customer users), the help desk is probably their main human interface with the service provider. They contact the help desk when they have problems, and their judgement and assessment of the service provider is largely influenced by their experiences of interacting with the help desk personnel and functions. This support service therefore has a great impact upon the reputation of the service provider.

Specialised technology support is an important part of the help desk infrastructure

Help desk functions are supported by advanced call-centre technology solutions, including computer-telephony integration (CTI), e-mail and web forms for fault reporting. Behind these various communications channels is a trouble-ticketing system into which all user calls are logged and through which they are subsequently tracked. The trouble-ticketing system also measures help desk service level performance and provides statistical analysis of fault types, mean time to repair (MTTR), mean time between failures (MTBF) and other useful statistical measures of performance.

Three-level support

Help desk support is usually organised on three levels:

- Level 1 support:

  - Provided by help desk agents with broad expertise and knowledge, in direct contact with users making calls;

- Supported by basic diagnostic tools, information lookup tools and access to asset databases and configuration data;

- Providing the immediate resolution of common problems and answering frequently asked questions;

- Capturing information about more complex problems and questions that need to be referred to the second level of support.

- Level 2 support:

  - Provided by a team of expert analysts with specific product and system knowledge;

  - Providing the resolution of more advanced problems and questions that require greater technical knowledge than is generally available in the Level 1 support team;

  - Supported by deep technical expertise and the resources to carry out detailed research, problem simulation and fault replication on test systems;

  - Capturing information about more complex problems and questions that need to be referred to the third level of support;

  - Relieving frontline agents of the burden of dealing with complex, protracted investigations, thus leaving the Level 1 team available to deal with the larger volume of shorter duration calls. This means that the variation in average call handling time can be allowed for in the planning and forecasting process to assist in the accurate prediction of the number of agents needed to handle the workload overall (see the earlier section in this chapter on capacity planning).

- Level 3 support:

  - Provided by the development team that designed and built the product, system or component; this will often be at a third-party vendor;

  - Providing the resolution of problems that involve major intervention, often in the form of a patch to fix a fault in the product or system;

  - Often requiring new hardware or software to be shipped and installed at the user location.

Help desk support is often focused upon security-related user problems

Help desk support, especially at Level 1, is extremely important in the management and administration of information systems security, since in most organisations the majority of user calls are security-related. Forgotten passwords, locked user accounts and incorrect privileges make up a huge number of the problems that users encounter in day-to-day business operations.

Provisioning

Dynamic setting up and configuration of components in complex distributed processing environments

In ICT operations and service management the term 'provisioning' refers to the dynamic process of setting up, loading, configuring, co-ordinating and launching new components in a complex distributed-processing environment. The term is most likely to be applied in organisations that provide services to a large number of paying customers, such as network service providers. However it can equally well be applied internally in the context of managing a large distributed population of desktop PCs and workstations, or any similar large-scale distributed-management system.

The provisioning process

Provisioning includes the following activities:

- Selecting remotely the hardware item or customer account to be provisioned;
- Loading appropriate software (operating system, device drivers, middleware and applications);
- Customising and configuring the remote system, software, networking devices and storage resources;
- Starting newly loaded software;
- Making the system ready for operation.

Security provisioning as a sub-set

Security provisioning refers to the setting up and configuration of security-related software and parameters, including:

- Creating, amending and deleting user IDs and their associated accounts;
- Setting and resetting user passwords;
- Administering user access privileges and authorisations;
- Loading and updating anti-virus software;
- Loading and configuring firewall rules;
- Configuring VPNs;
- All operational activities involved in cryptographic key management.

Financial Management

Budget management for operational services

The provision of operational services has many financial implications, which must be dealt with by the management functions running these services. The issues that need to be addressed include:

- Cost management: providing the operational services within a predetermined budget and cost accounting to track where the expenditure has been made;
- Pricing and charging: for services provided to paying service customers;
- Budgeting and forecasting: setting out the financial plans for future periods;
- Contingency management: dealing with unforeseen and unbudgeted items.

Access Control Management

Refer to Chapters 10 and 14

Access control concepts are described in detail in Chapter 10 and access policy management based upon information and system classification is discussed in Chapter 14. It may be useful for you to read those sections again in conjunction with this one.

Access Control Policy

Business requirements drive access policies

Access privileges granted to individual users or to groups of users should be based upon business requirements. Thus the starting point for developing an access control policy must be the clear definition of these business requirements, taking into account a wide range of issues discussed in Chapter 14. Other aspects of access control are discussed in detail in Chapter 10. The main relevant considerations to be drawn from those two chapters include:

- Information classification;

- System classification;

- Identity management and federated[4] identity management;

- Mandatory access control rules imposed by central management versus discretionary access control rules imposed at the discretion of user-owners;

- Consistency of access control rules across multiple systems and networks which form different policy domains;

- Compliance with legislation and contractual arrangements;

- Policy principles;

- The possible limitations of applying the least-privilege principle[5];

- Role-based access control to simplify administration and improve centralised control;

- Context-based access control rules that are dependent on the context of the end user login (different rules for different times of day or days of the week, different rules for different end user locations, different rules for an end user as an employee and as a customer of the same organisation);

- Strength of the user authentication mechanisms to be used;

- The authorisation process and the model for ownership, custody and use;

- The access-related parts of the SABSA® Business Attributes Profile.

User Access Management

Operational management and administration of user access privileges

Once the access control polices have been determined, these must be applied to individual users and groups of users, based upon business authorisations granted to those users by an appropriate authority. This requires a considerable amount of operational management and administration.

The user access management process

The major operational issues to be addressed include:

- User registration and deregistration;

- Issuing users with unique identification in the form of user IDs or distinguished names to ensure that actions of a user can be linked unambiguously to that user for accountability purposes;

- Creating system authorisations (privileges or permissions) based upon business level authorisations (job functions and responsibilities);

---

[4]Federated identity management: a system that allows individuals to use the same user name, password or other personal identification to sign on to the networks of more than one enterprise in order to conduct transactions.

[5]For a detailed discussion on this refer to Chapter 14.

- Administering (create, amend, delete) the changing pattern of user registrations, user identities and user authorisations for 'joiners', 'movers' and 'leavers';

- Checking user identity (authenticating a user) and system authorisations during system login;

- Recording all login and access control events, whether successful or failed access attempts, and reviewing the audit logs thus created;

- Reviewing system access privileges from time to time to check that they reflect real business access requirements and that the configuration of privileges has not decayed over time;

- Periodically reviewing and removing any redundant user accounts on a system;

- Ensuring that default user accounts that are configured by the vendor when the system is delivered and commissioned are either completely removed or else have had their passwords changed to a strong value. This includes accounts to be owned and used by the vendor for maintenance purposes (whether remote or local) during the operational lifetime of the system.

Case Study: Default Accounts Give Default Access

A small business had purchased a computer system from a well-known vendor. The company itself had little computer expertise but needed to automate certain accounting functions and similar business activities with standard off-the-shelf software packages. When the system was delivered it had been installed, configured and commissioned by the computer vendor's field service engineers.

Only authorised members of staff in the finance department were allowed to use the computer system. However, it became clear over time that other people were able to access the computer records of the company, and the finance director, who had overall responsibility for the computer system, was at a loss as to how this was happening. All the authorised staff had individual accounts and had been told to choose strong passwords and not to share them with anyone else.

What the finance director had not appreciated was that there were two default accounts that had come preconfigured when the system was delivered. One account was named 'System' with a preset password of 'Manager', and the other was named 'Field' with a preset password of 'Service'. Both accounts were of the highest privilege level, providing access to all parts of the system. Anyone who knew about these default accounts could access anything they wanted.

Managing System-Level Privileges

Use of raw system-level accounts is best avoided

Some accounts (such as those mentioned in the case study above) provide high levels of access privilege for the purposes of systems management or maintenance. The use of these accounts is therefore potentially very dangerous since they are all-powerful. Their use in a raw form, even by those authorised and trained to use them, is best avoided.

System-level privileges should be encapsulated to restrict activities under routine circumstances

Much safer is the practice of creating utility tools that run with the privileges of these accounts but which strictly control the functionality available (often known as encapsulation). Every known routine management task is enabled through a series of functions of the tool. Thus the highly privileged user is decoupled from the raw system, and any errors or mistakes will not have a direct impact on the system itself – the tool prevents incorrect actions from being made.

Raw system privilege is reserved for emergencies only

The passwords to the direct privileged accounts should then be kept secret and locked in a safe for release only in genuine emergencies when the normal, routine tools cannot fix the problem, and raw, high-privileged access is required for a short time.

Cultural barriers often obstruct professional considerations

There are some operational environments where the culture is that 'real men (and women) are not afraid of raw command-line access'. It is a culture of the geeky, eccentric techno-nerd, who takes great pride in knowing intimately every single system command and every possible parameter and switch that can be used with it. Such system managers tend to regard the computers they manage as their personal playground, and their special knowledge maintains their powerful control over the system. It might be great fun, and in an academic environment it may be acceptable, but it is no way to run a professional operational production shop.

Password Management

Refer to Chapter 12

In Chapter 12 there is a sub-section headed Password Management in which the discussion covers both the design issues and the operational issues. Please refer back to that sub-section now for coverage of this topic.

Third-Party Access Management

Types of third-party access

There are many valid business reasons why operational access must be granted to third parties. There are two main types of access to be considered:

- Physical access to offices, store rooms, equipment rooms, computer rooms and filing cabinets;

- Logical access to information systems and databases.

Legitimate third-party access

The types of third parties for whom there are good reasons for granting operational access to might include:

- Service providers such as:

  - Telecommunications engineers;

  - Hardware and software maintenance engineers and support personnel;

  - Utilities engineers (electrical power, water, gas);

  - Cleaning staff, catering staff, security guards and other similar ancillary service providers;

- Consultants.

- Trading partners such as:

- Customers;

- Suppliers;

- Joint venture partners.

- Short-term, temporary contract staff and students on work-placements;

- Regulators;

- External auditors.

Principles of managing third-party access

The general aspects of managing outsourcing partners are discussed in two earlier sections of this chapter. Here in this section the focus is on a more detailed discussion of the specific access management considerations. These include:

- The attention paid in the general information security policy to managing third-party access;

- Risk assessment of specific third-party activities and functions to identify where special access controls might be needed;

- Specific authorisation responsibilities and procedures for granting, reviewing and revoking third-party access rights;

- Determining the extent to which access is required to enable the *bona fide* business activities of the third parties;

- Permitted access methods and time periods for access;

- The extent to which third-party access needs to be supervised and monitored.

Third-party access policy in relation to the policy architecture

The discussion in Chapter 14 on security policies includes the suggestion of a hierarchical policy architecture in which a number of specific security policies might be formulated to deal with specific areas of security management. Figure 14-1 shows such a hierarchy. Although not specifically shown in Figure 14-1, a third-party access policy would be an appropriate item to include alongside the Remote Access policy, Anti-Virus policy and others in that group.

Compliance Management

Compliance in the Realm of Information Security Management

Specific information security compliance requirements

Compliance with international and national laws and with industry regulations is discussed previously in a broad context in Chapter 15. Here the focus is upon compliance with laws and regulations that are specific to information security and its management.

Elements of compliance strategy

The main elements of a successful compliance strategy are:

- Making sure you identify comprehensively all relevant laws and regulations and understand their applicability to the business operations of your organisation. The identification should also be extended to your contracts with third parties to ensure that you are complying with all contractual obligations that you have made.

- Implementing appropriate procedures to protect intellectual property rights, both those owned by your organisation and those owned by other parties. This will especially include protection of copyright of both documents and software and preventing unauthorised copying and distribution.

- Retaining and safeguarding organisational records that must be archived for certain periods to meet legal and regulatory requirements. These will always include corporate financial accounting records, but in some industry sectors other records may be subject to similar mandatory requirements.

- Protecting the privacy of personal information as required in the EU by data protection legislation and in the USA by such laws as the Gramm-Leach-Bliley Act (see Chapter 15).

- Preventing the misuse of corporate information-processing facilities in compliance with internal corporate policies.

- Ensuring compliance with the regulations governing the use of cryptographic controls (a detailed discussion appears in the next section of this chapter).

- Ensuring that the collection of evidence complies with the rigorous rules of evidence and that evidence will be admissible when presented in a court of law (see the earlier section in this chapter on forensic investigations).

- Providing assurance that there is compliance with all internal information security policies and standards. This is the subject of extensive discussion in Chapter 16.

Cryptographic Regulations

Governments exert control over cryptographic technology

Cryptographic technology, especially high-performance cryptographic hardware, has powerful implications for national security. Most governments regard it as a dangerous tool in hands of enemies of the state. These enemies can include hostile nations, terrorist organisations (both domestic and international) and organised crime gangs.

Cryptographic technology is treated in the same way as weapons technology

Because of this most countries treat cryptographic technology in exactly the same way as munitions or armaments. This means that there may well be restrictions on:

- Export of cryptographic products;

- Import of cryptographic products;

- Manufacture of cryptographic products;

- Domestic use of cryptography in information systems;

- Export and import of encrypted data across national borders.

Complying with regulations requires detailed attention

This poses a management issue for corporate enterprises that need to comply with the laws of each and every country in which they have business operations. It is particularly complicated by the fact that every country is unique and has its own version of cryptographic control, so you must understand the detailed picture in every country of interest. It is even more complicated by the fact that the details are not necessarily made crystal clear by every government, some choosing to reserve judgement and generally make it up as they go along. Even in countries where there is a clear policy, this policy can change from time to time and needs to be tracked.

544 Enterprise Security Architecture

Important international
agreements

There are some attempts to co-ordinate policy between nations, but these inter-country agreements may still hide differences, especially in the way the agreements are implemented through national legislation. The important agreements (at the time of writing[6]) are:

- The Wassenaar Arrangement on Export Controls for Conventional Arms and Dual-Use Goods and Technologies, signed in 1996 by 31 countries and last revised in December 1998. Each member state has to implement the provisions of the Wassenaar Arrangement in national legislation for them to have effect.

- The Council of Europe, a multi-country organisation with 43 member states, adopted the Convention on Cybercrime in November 2001, signed by 26 of the 43 member states, and also by Canada, Japan, South Africa and the United States. The focus is upon access by law enforcement agencies to information, including the provision of decryption keys for data that has been encrypted. As with the Wassenaar Arrangement, national legislation is needed to implement the convention.

- The European Union regulates the export of dual-use goods, including cryptography, by the Council Regulation (EC) No 1334/2000, setting up a European Community regime for the control of exports of dual-use items and technology (*Official Journal* L159, 30 January 2000), in force since 29 September 2000. This regulation follows the Wassenaar Arrangement but provides some liberalisation of export between EU member countries.

This issue must be
proactively managed

So, if you are a multi-national or international organisation, or even if you operate only in one country, how should you manage this issue? Good advice is to be proactive – never put your head in the sand and hope it will go away – it won't. A good code of practice is:

- Make a register (or inventory) of all counties where you have business operations, noting the types of operational use of information in terms that are relevant to these regulations.

- Set up a robust process by which every time you consider opening a new operation in a new country, or significantly changing your business operations in an existing country, you update the register.

- For each country, identify as best you can the current legal and regulatory situation[7] and enter this information in the register.

- For each country in your register identify the government department or agency through which the regulations are managed and controlled and try to establish a relationship and a dialogue with that agency. The objective of such a relationship is to discuss your intentions and to understand as fully as possible the local regulations so as to ease the path of any authorisations that you might require.

- Keep liaison going with these government agencies so as to keep up to date on developments. Hopefully you can see any significant changes coming in advance of them being in force and make plans accordingly.

- Keep your register up to date in every respect and use it as a tool for supporting your management decisions in this sensitive area.

---

[6]Time of writing: January 2005

[7]A good starting point is http://rechten.uvt.nl/koops/cryptolaw/index.htm. However, this is research site that attempts to give the best up-to-date picture. It is not necessarily correct in every detail, and you may not want to rely on the information there to cover your legal liabilities.

Security-Specific Operations

Security Service Management

Refer to Chapters 10 and 11

The needs for security service management are discussed in Chapter 10 (Conceptual Security Architecture) and in Chapter 11 (Logical Security Architecture). Those discussions are also relevant in considering the operational security architecture. Please refer back to Chapter 10 under section entitled Security Service Management Strategy and Chapter 11 under the section entitled Security Management Services.

Security Mechanism Management

Processes for managing security mechanisms

The management of security mechanisms requires a number of operational processes, procedures and tools. The mechanisms to be managed include the following:

- Cryptographic key management;

- Security parameter communication and synchronisation to support security associations;

- Maintenance of access control lists (ACLs) and user privilege profiles;

- Managing the process of data backup and restoration;

- Media management, including labelling, indexing, transport, storage (off-site), retrieval, media recycling and lifetime control;

- Virus signature maintenance and distribution;

- Intrusion signature maintenance and distribution;

- Firewall rule maintenance;

- Event log file management and archiving.

Security Component Management

Processes for managing security components

At the component level there are a number of operational management processes:

- Product evaluation, selection and procurement (see below in the later section for a detailed discussion on this topic);

- Supplier relationship management;

- Supplier contract management;

- Project management for developments, implementations and roll-outs;

- Trusted build process management for new implementations – ensuring the authenticity, provenance and traceability of all hardware and software components incorporated into a system as it is constructed;

- Component lifecycle management, including scheduled maintenance programmes, replacement of worn parts and consumables, repair of faults, and retirement and disposal at the end of useful life.

User Management

Processes for user management

A very large proportion of security administration and security operations are focused around the management of user identity and user privileges:

- Registration of new users;

- Authorisation of user privileges by the business;

- Implementation of the authorised privileges;

- Adding, amending and deleting user registrations and credentials on system security databases;

- User support (help desk) to resolve user access problems (see the section on help desk earlier in this chapter);

- Problem tracking and management;

- Password management, updating and changing;

- System account management of high-privilege accounts for applications, systems operators and managers, and auditors.

Managed Security Services

Outsourcing the management of certain operational security services

There is a current trend towards the outsourcing of certain operational security services, and a new market is developing in managed security services. The types of service that are potential candidates for this approach include:

- Managed VPNs;

- Managed firewalls;

- Managed authentication service;

- Managed S-NOC[8] operations;

- Managed intrusion detection and prevention;

- Managed anti-virus screening;

- Managed content screening;

- Penetration testing;

Outsourcing strategy is discussed in Chapter 10

Vulnerability scanning. Various service providers offer some or all of these services on an outsourced basis. Outsourcing in general is discussed in Chapter 10 under Outsourcing Strategy. Here some of the issues are briefly revisited with a particular focus on managed security services.

Benefits of outsourcing managed security services

There are various benefits that will make the adoption of management security services attractive. These include:

- Cost reduction, because the service provider can reach the economies of scale;

- Focus your attention on core business activities rather than dissipating your efforts on peripheral activities;

---

[8]S-NOC: secure network operating centre

- Expert attention to security operations from a specialist service provider to whom it is a core business;

- Herd immunity – by joining a large community of customers being serviced by the same provider, ensuring that any new attack will affect only one or a few of those customers, the remainder being protected by the knowledge and skill gained from the early attacks.

Issues to be addressed

However, there are also various issues to be addressed, including:

- Will you lose control?

- Who will own the risk?

Strategic principles for outsourcing managed security services

What is the split of responsibilities?To ensure that these issues are adequately addressed you should adopt the following strategic approach and principles:

- Adequate definitions of the responsibilities and liabilities of the two parties:

  - In the outsourcing agreement;

  - Legally binding.

- An organisational structure that formalises ownership on both sides;

- Full exploration of all security issues during the pre-contract negotiations;Policy making is a business responsibility;

- Policy implementation is a service provider responsibility;

- Management process ownership:

  - Authorisation by customer business managers;

  - Administration by the service provider;

  - Monitoring compliance with the SLA by both parties;

  - Independent third-party audit to ensure compliance with best practice.

- A Security Target document describing the customer's primary requirements for security;

- Supporting documents to assist both sides with implementation.

Who is responsible and who is liable?

In defining the responsibilities and liabilities, the following questions arise:

- Who is responsible for what?

- Who is liable for what?

- What are the penalties?

Responsibilities and liabilities

Broadly the split should be:

- The customer is responsible for:

  - Business security risk assessment and policy making;

  - Management of business processes and systems using the outsourced services;

  - Authorisation of business users.

The service provider is responsible for:

- Security infrastructure management;Meeting the terms of the SLA.

Product Evaluation and Selection

Procurement of security products needs careful evaluation

Procuring security products and tools is no different than doing so for other items. However, it is surprising how many times one encounters sloppy practices in making such choices. The contract and pricing is usually dealt with by a specialised purchasing department, which means this gets careful professional attention. Where the deficiencies usually arise is in the technical evaluation and selection process.

ITTs are often badly written

One major problem can be the invitation to tender (ITT) document that is sent out to potential vendors. Government departments and agencies favour the formal tendering process so as to eliminate nepotism, fraud and back door deals, all of which is laudable. However, the formal tendering process with its rigid rules and explicit exclusion of negotiation of the technical specification can be problematic in cases where those who create the tender documents do not really understand what it is they are procuring.

A poor ITT makes it difficult for a vendor to make a good bid

There are numerous examples of ITTs that ask for the wrong thing or ask for it with significant lack of insight. This poses a difficult problem for a vendor who, under the rules of the tendering process, must respond to the ITT as issued but who can see instantly what the customer should have been asking for. At this stage of the tendering process it is too late to put forward that advice.

More effort should be invested in getting the ITT right

The solution to this problem is that those who write ITTs should first thoroughly research the area, and in particular should hold informal discussions with all the leading vendors to gain a good understanding of the issues and solutions. Sometimes the issue is to do with structuring and phasing of the project, and at other times is it to do with the technical approach to be taken. The problems generally arise when the buyers try to specify in detail the technical solution, when they should stick rigidly to specifying their requirements, and let the vendors suggest solutions, which may differ greatly from one to another.

First understand what the marketplace has to offer

It is best to get the vendor community to feed you the information that you will use in specifying your requirements, so that the ITT is geared up to what the industry can supply. Then your tendering process is focused on looking only for the best vendor with the best solution and the best value, rather that looking for someone to build a solution you have specified that may not be the right one.

If necessary get some help from consultants to write the ITT

If you really do lack the skills and knowledge to write an informed ITT, get an independent consulting firm to help you write it. It will be money well spent. There is an added value proposition here too, in that the consultants can go on to help you evaluate the tenders that have been submitted. Experienced consultants can add huge value through their ability to ask the awkward questions and expose all the issues for the selection team to make the best-informed decision. As one client put it: 'I want you to bowl some googlies[9]'.

RFIs and RFPs are more flexible than tenders

The use of independent consultants is also applicable if you go down the more flexible route of asking vendors for proposals through a request for proposal (RFP) process. This process is used by commercial firms rather than government agencies and has less rigidity than the tendering process.

---

[9]In cricket the googly is an off-break ball bowled with a leg-break action. The batsman is taken by surprise by the unexpected direction of the spin.

However, the RFP can still be a problem if those who write it are ill-informed. The best way to approach this is first to send out a request for information (RFI) so as to learn what the vendor community can offer. Following that you can arrange meetings and presentations with the most promising vendors to learn in detail what they can offer. All this is in advance of any formal proposals. Only when you understand fully exactly what it is you want to procure do you commit to a formal RFP, in response to which you will receive formal proposals to evaluate. This still leaves headroom for subsequent negotiation of both the specification and the contractual terms.

Selection criteria must be clear from the outset

Then you come to the evaluation process itself. How should you judge one proposal or tender against another? The key to success is to set out clearly in advance what your selection criteria are going to be, and this should be made clear through your ITT or RFP document. In the end the overriding criterion for a decision is that you have the greatest confidence in the selected vendor to fulfil your requirements. Along the way to building this confidence is an evaluation of the vendor's compliance with your functional requirements.

Business Attributes can be used to construct an evaluation plan

As an example of how this can done, a Business Attributes Profile as described in Chapter 10 can be used as the framework for developing the RFP. This is particularly attractive to the business team since they need not become involved in any technical specifications – the Business Attribute profile is a specification of business requirements, not technical solutions. Once the Business Attributes Profile has been agreed, this can be used as the main basis for an RFP to a short-list the major systems vendors.

Case Study: Vendor Selection for a Secure Banking System

Consultants were asked to assist with the specification of new secure banking system. In the course of the consulting activities the consultants helped the client to build a Business Attributes Profile. The client embraced this methodology enthusiastically, especially those people in the business who for the first time began to see a real linkage between specifying business requirements and specifying a technical system to meet those requirements.

Once the Business Attributes Profile had been agreed, they used this as the main basis for an RFP to a short-list of two major systems vendors, both with globally recognised names. The vendors were asked to make their responses to a set of requirements based on each and every Attribute in the Business Attributes Profile. The responses were assessed as to their level of compliance with each requirement, at levels of 0%, 25%, 50%, 75% and 100%.

The client then produced a pair of charts similar to the one shown in Figure 6-3 in Chapter 6, but covering only the attributes in the profile. These charts were colour coded according to the level of compliance for each attribute and were used as a couple of slides to help the Architecture Board reach a decision as to which vendor should be selected. This was the shortest meeting the Architecture Board has ever had, because the visual result of this approach was instantaneous and stunning. The charts are reproduced in Figures 17-2 and 17-3 (pages 556 and 557) exactly as the client used them. Vendor A has a 'cool' chart with lots a greens and blues, whereas the chart for Vendor B is 'hot', covered in red and orange. Vendor A was awarded the contract.

Weighted scoring can be applied

You may not choose to use this exact approach, although it has many merits to recommend it. However, the techniques of scoring and colour-coding applied in any format are extremely useful to help you get the appropriate vendor ranking for your selection process. If you have criteria at different levels of importance, then weighted scores can be used so that the weights are appropriate to the level of importance for each selection criterion.

Also applicable to evaluating outsourced service delivery

This case study above shows the charts for vendor evaluation, but a similar approach is also commonly used for reporting service levels in an outsourced service delivery environment.

Business Continuity Management

BCM is an important aspect of operational management

Business continuity management (BCM) is a huge topic in its own right that could occupy a separate book. However, it deserves some mention in this chapter, and this section first describes a business-process based approach to BCM, followed by a checklist of the main activities that should in your BCM programme. For additional guidance you are recommended to the Publicly Available Specification (PAS 56) from the British Standards Institute[10].

Business Process Based Approach to BCM

A process-centric approach is most logical way to tackle business continuity management

There are various approaches that are used in business continuity management and planning, but the most logical must be to start with the business processes, since BCM is essentially all about maintaining the continued operation of these processes. However, this approach does imply that as a prerequisite you already have good documented models of your business processes, broken down into a series of hierarchical layers of sub-processes, sub-sub processes and so on.

Meta-processes in large enterprises

In a large organisation there might be around 10 high-level business processes (often called meta-processes), with names such as:

- Develop product offerings;

- Bring product offerings to market;

- Acquire customer orders;

- Fulfil customer orders;

- Manage and administer the business.

Top-down business process analysis

Each of these processes can be analysed into another level of detail of sub-processes, some of which are in parallel and some in series. Figure 17-4 shows a simple example of this top-down process analysis.

---

[10]BSI PAS 56: 'Guide to Business Continuity Management'. See www.bsi-global.com

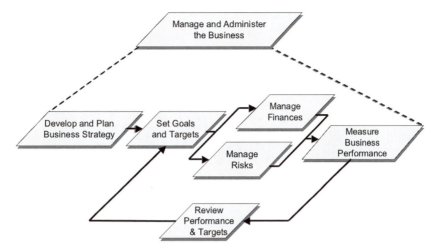

Figure 17-4: Example of Top-Down Business Process Analysis

Achieving up-to-date process models with delegated ownership requires a sophisticated software tool

Overall, if there are 10 'Level 1' processes, and on average each of these can be analysed into around 10 sub-processes, which in turn can each be analysed into 10 sub-sub-processes at the next level of detail, then potentially the total number of detailed processes grows exponentially at each level, as shown in Figure 17-5. This means that you will need a professional automated tool to carry out this analysis, to store all the detail, keep the model up to date, and delegate process ownership at each level of detail to those with operational responsibility. However, if you can achieve this type of business process analysis there are major business benefits, one of which is that you have an excellent model for business continuity management.

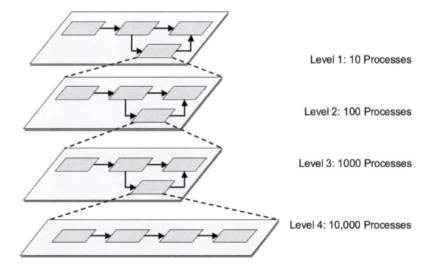

Figure 17-5: Multi-Level Business Process Analysis

The BCM process

Starting with your business process model, the overall BCM process (which is itself part of the process model) is as follows (see also Figure 7-6 for a diagrammatic representation):

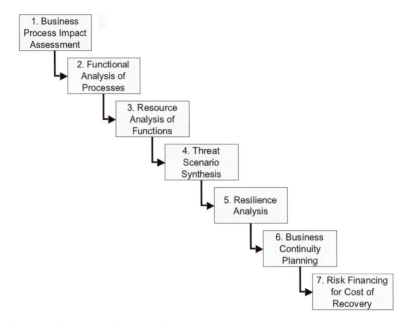

Figure 7-6: The Business Continuity Management Process

Step 1: Business Process Impact Assessment

- Identify and map business processes;

- Assess the business impact of loss of each business process;

- Classify the business processes into three or four bands:

- Band A: Critical – loss of this process will destroy the business;

- Band B: Severe – loss of this process will cause persistent, severe damage to the business;

- Band 3: Significant (Optional band) – loss of this process will cause significant damage;

- Band 4: Other: damage caused by loss of this process can be absorbed.

Step 2: Functional Analysis of Business Processes

- Select the processes classified as Band A or Band B;

- Analyse all the sub-processes down to single functional steps to discover all the process and functional components needed to keep this high-level process in continuous operation.

Step 3: Resource Analysis of Functions

- For each sub-process or function identified in Step 2, what resources are needed and how much of each resource (people, ICT services, accommodation, equipment, communications, raw materials)?

Step 4: Threat Scenario Synthesis

- For each resource identified in Step 3, what high-level threat scenarios put that resource at risk?

- Focus here on effects, not causes.

Step 5: Resilience Analysis

- For each resource/scenario combination, are the current resources provided with sufficient resilience for the overall business to withstand the scenario? In particular, are there any single points of failure?

Step 6: Business Continuity Planning

- What additional resource protection is needed to provide the required level of resource resilience so that the overall business can withstand the threat scenarios? Such as:

  - Preventive measures to avoid the threats materialising;

  - Containment measures to limit the damage;

  - Redundancy of resources to avoid single points of failure and to provide fall-back capacity;

  - Incident management plans;

  - Recovery plans to resume business following an incident;

  - Crisis management plans;

  - Training and awareness.

Step 7: Risk Financing for Cost of Recovery

- Insurance and related services.

Checklist of BCM Activities

Checklist of BCM activities

This checklist is a brief summary of the activities in a BCM programme. It should help you to ensure that you are covering all the bases:

- Understanding the business need:

  - Business goals and objectives for BCM;

  - Business impact analysis – critical processes;

  - Business process analysis – vulnerable functions;

  - Risk assessment – prioritisation.BCM strategy development:

  - Prevention strategy: resilience;

    - Risk reduction;

    - Robust technical systems;

- Contingency;

- Stand-by.Containment strategy: business resumption;

- Contingency sites and facilities;

- Alternative ways of working;

- Prioritisation of business operations.Incident handling strategy: crisis management;

- Leadership;

- Escalation;

- Activation;

- Communication;

- Public relations.Recovery strategy: resources and actions needed for recovery;

- Scenario planning;

  - Temporary and permanent;

  - Physical and logical;

  - Total and partial.

- Priorities;

  - Resource levels;

  - Timescales.Resource analysis – what's needed?

  - People;

  - ICT;

  - Telecommunications;

  - Infrastructure;

  - Facilities;

  - Documents;

  - Services;

  - Logistics.Insurance strategy: cost recovery;

- Risk financing;

- Insurable risks;

- Self-insurance.Developing plans and solutions:

- Centralised planning;

- Distributed and localised planning;

- Guidelines for planners;

- Integration of plans;

- Maintenance of plans.

- Implementation support:

  - Project management;

  - Budget management;

  - Guidelines for implementers.

- BCM leadership and organisation development:

  - Responsibilities;

  - Leadership and sponsorship;

  - Governance;

  - Management structure;

    - Planning management;

    - Crisis management;

    - Incident management.

  - Skills and resources;

  - Policy;

  - Relationship to change management.

- Crisis management integration:

  - Across all aspects of crisis management;

  - Reputation and brand protection;

  - Public relations management;

  - Senior management training and briefing.

- BCM culture development:

  - Education;

  - Awareness;

  - Training.

- Assurance through audit:Testing plans and solutions;

  - Rehearsal of procedures;

  - Maintenance of plans and solutions;

  - Audit.Operational management:

  - Emergency response;

  - Crisis leadership and organisation;

Figure 17-2: Colour-coded Evaluation of Vendor A

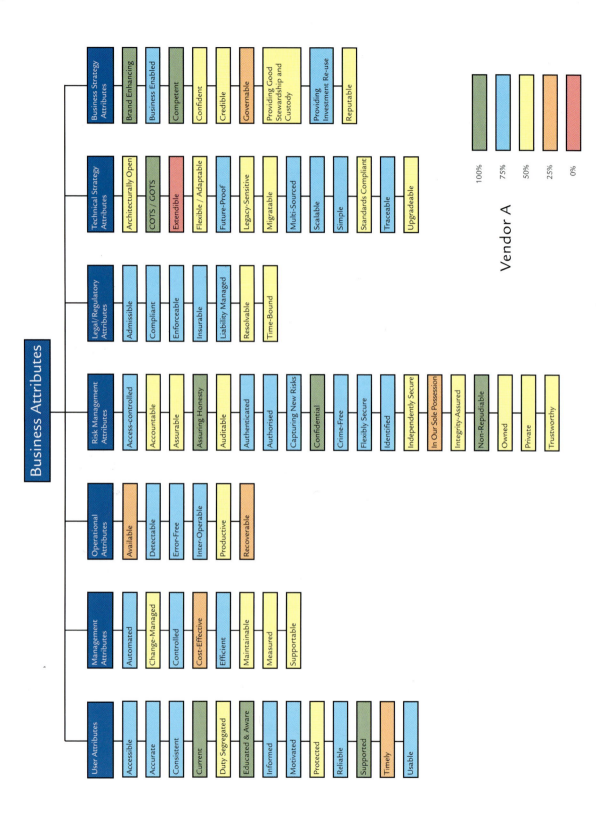

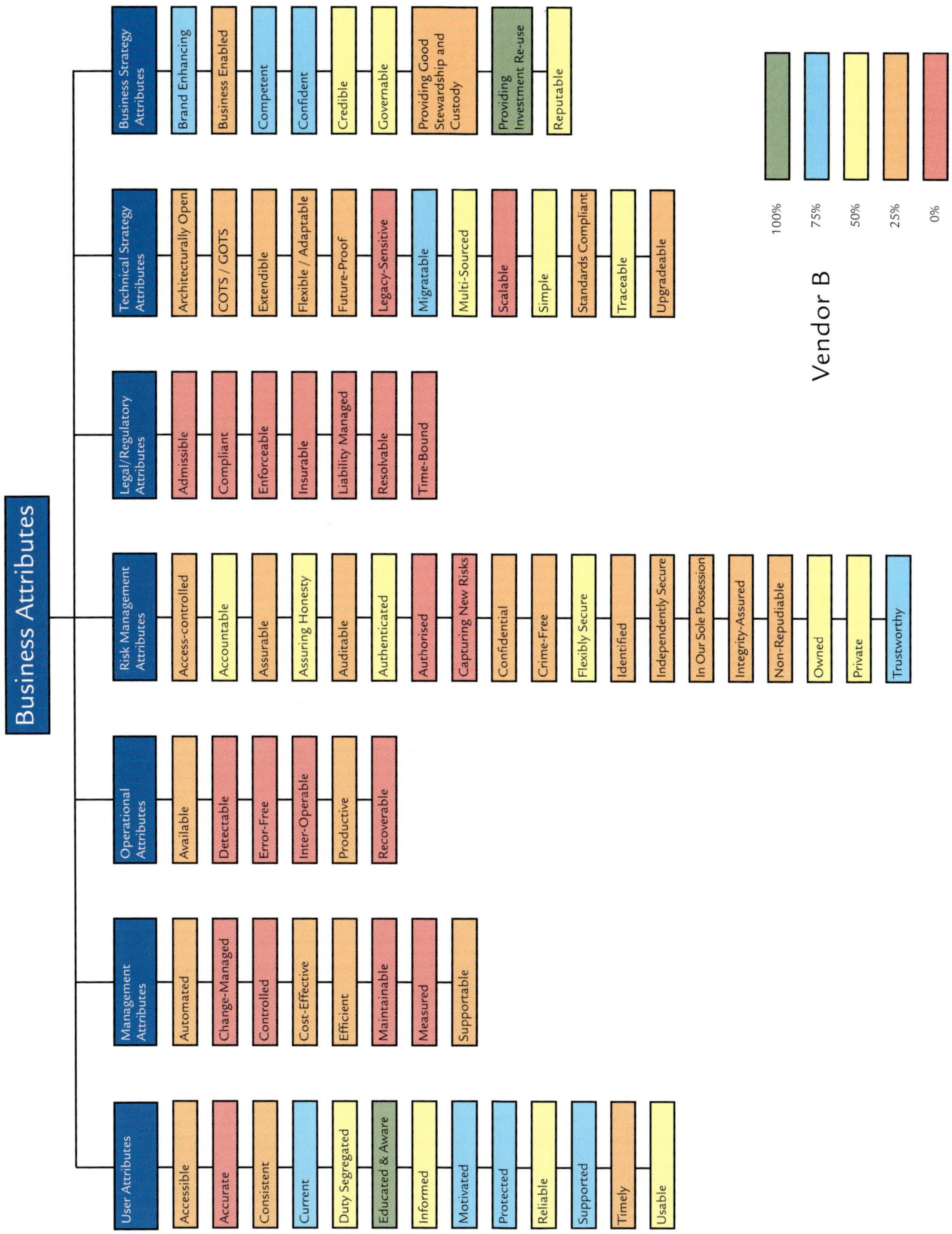

Figure 17-3: Colour-coded Evaluation of Vendor B

- Teams;

- Command and control;

- Communications;

- Resources;

- Scheduling. Third-party products and services:

- Consultancy;

- Methodologies;

- Software tools for planning;

- Event management and notification tools;

- Incident management tools;

- Training courses;

- Professional bodies;

- Recovery facilities and equipment;

- Off-site on-line backup;

- Publications.

To Summarise:

Much of the operational security architecture layer in the SABSA® model consists of a variety of operational and administrative processes that are performed on a day-to-day basis to maintain enterprise security. These activities embrace the operational management and support of the entire range of security services for applications, users, sites, buildings, networks and platforms. They cover the bulk of the material contained in ISO/IEC 17799:2000: Code of Practice for Information Security Management.

Managing the people-related security operations is an especially important part of what has to be done to keep operational security up-to-date and at an acceptable level of quality. This includes such items as ensuring that everybody has a clear understanding of their personal responsibilities for security, that they are aware of the issues, that they are properly trained to carry out specific security-related tasks, and that there is a general culture taking security seriously across the enterprise.

To reduce the risk of fraud, certain security-sensitive operational tasks are often split between two or more individuals who do not interact on a personal level either during normal working or in their social and domestic lives. This is known as dual control.

Physical and environmental security of sites, buildings and certain rooms and of specialised equipment and document storage cabinets is implemented through secure perimeters and controlled access points. Those who control who have access (the guards) and the people who make the access should be segregated under the dual control principle.

Day-to-day ICT operations and support are a critical part of maintaining operational security. To ensure consistency and to avoid dependency on the knowledge of individuals, all procedures should be well-documented and kept up-to-date. Both the procedures and the operating environment should be subject to strict change control, and any major changes in working practices need to be planned and executed carefully under a change management programme.

Amongst the standard procedures used will be those for handling security incidents, with the objective of eliminating operational problems, restoring normal operations, and learning lessons from the experience.

To protect the live operational production environment in a data processing facility, it should be highly segregated from all development and test systems. There should be strict rules enforced regarding the acceptance of new software, the release of new code and system maintenance activities in the production domain. Capacity planning and management is also critical to the long-term stability of production systems. Housekeeping operations, including malicious software prevention, data backup and recovery, operational logging, media handling, network operations, software licence management, asset control and configuration management are also critical to running a successful production operation.

There needs to be a special set of arrangements for dealing with third parties. These include business partners (customers, suppliers, regulators) with whom information is exchanged electronically, and also outsourcing contractors who supply ICT operations services and a variety of ancillary services. The principal tool used to manage the business relationships with these third parties is a service level agreement.

Managing operational security also embraces a number of other activities of diverse nature. These include training and awareness development for operational staff, service monitoring and reporting, event log and audit trail management, forensic investigations, problem tracking and management, help desk and three-level user support, provisioning, financial management.

Managing access control is perhaps one of the most important of the operational security activities. It must be based upon access policies that have been explicitly stated and authorised at an appropriate level of management. Implementation of these policies is then the task of operational security staff. The activities include the administration of user accounts, the control of highly privileged system accounts, password management and management of authorised third-party access.

Compliance with relevant laws and regulations is another area where operational security teams become involved, particularly where those laws or regulations relate specifically to information security issues. This includes the management of corporate activity with respect to the rules governing the use and deployment of cryptographic technology.

There are some security-specific operations for managing security services, security mechanism, security components and the user community. Some of these activities can be outsourced to third-party providers of managed security services. The specification and procurement of security products and services is also part of operational security management.

Finally, there is a huge overlap between security management and business continuity management, although the latter is far too large a subject to cover in detail in this book. However, by taking a business-process-centric view of business continuity management, many of the principles of risk assessment and risk mitigation described in this book can be applied.

Appendix A: List of Acronyms

The following acronyms are used in various parts of the book.

ACE	Access control entry (in an access control list)
ACK	Acknowledgement
ACL	Access control list
ADSL	Asynchronous digital subscriber line
AES	Advanced encryption standard
AH	Authentication header
AI	Authentication information
AIRMIC	Association of Insurance and Risk Managers (UK)
ALARM	The national forum for risk managers in the UK public sector
ALE	Annual loss expectancy
ANSI	American National Standards Institute
API	Application program interface
ASCII	American standard code for information interchange
AS/NZS	Australian standard and New Zealand standard
ASN.1	Abstract syntax notation number 1
B2B	Business-to-business
B2C	Business-to-consumer
B2G	Business-to-government
BCM	Business continuity management
BER	Basic encoding rules
BIS	Bank of International Settlements
BSC	Balanced scorecard
BSI	British Standard Institute
CA	Certificate (or certification) authority
CAA	Civil Aviation Authority (UK)
CAM	Central access manager
CAST	Carlisle Adams and Stafford Tavares (an encryption algorithm)
CCIR	Comité Consultatif International des Radiocommunications
CCITT	Comité Consultatif International Téléphonique et Télégraphique

CCTV	Closed-circuit television
CD	Compact disk
CEO	Chief executive officer
CERT®	No longer really an acronym – it refers to the Carnegie Mellon University co-ordination centre (CERT/CC®), which is a major reporting centre for Internet security problems. 'CERT Notifications' are published daily to alert the world to new issues regarding Internet security. CERT/CC® was the very first computer security incident response team, and the original acronym comes from that.
CIO	Chief information officer
CISA	Certified Information Systems Auditor
CISM	Certified Information Security Manager
CISO	Chief information security officer
CFO	Chief financial officer
CFR	Code of Federal Regulations
CISA	Certified Information Systems Auditor
CMM	Capability maturity model
CMMI	Capability maturity model integration
CobiT	Control Objectives for Information and related Technology
COE	Common operating environment
CORBA	Common object request broker architecture
CP	Certificate policy
CPS	Certification practices statement
CPU	Central processing unit
CRL	Certificate revocation list
CRM	Customer relationship management
CSF	Critical success factor
CSI	Computer Security Institute
CSIv2	Common Secure Inter-operability Version 2
CTI	Computer-telephony integration
CTO	Chief technical officer (or chief technology officer)
CTCPEC	Canadian Trusted Computer Product Evaluation Criteria
DAC	Discretionary access control
DAP	Directory access protocol
DBMS	Database management system
DEA	Data encryption algorithm
DER	Distinguished encoding rules
DES	Data encryption standard
Disco	Discovery protocol
DIT	Directory information tree
DMZ	Demilitarised zone
DNS	Domain name system
DNSSec	Secure DNS

DOD	Department of Defense (USA)
DSA	Digital signature algorithm
ECC	Elliptic curve cryptography
ECMA	European Computer Manufacturers Association
EDI	Electronic data interchange
EEMA	European Electronics Manufacturers' Association
ERM	Enterprise risk management
ESP	Encapsulating security payload
ETSI	European Telecommunications Standards Institute
EU	European Union
FAA	Federal Aviation Administration (USA)
FDA	Food and Drug Administration (USA)
FFA	Fast Fourier analysis
FIFO	First-in-first-out (a queuing algorithm)
FIPS PUB	U.S. Federal Information Processing Standards publications
FRS	Functional requirements specification
FSA	Financial Services Authority (UK)
FSM	Finite state machine
FTP	File transfer protocol
G10	The 'Group of Ten' countries
GMT	Greenwich mean time
GUI	Graphical user interface
HDLC	High-level data link control (protocol)
H-MAC	Hashed message authentication code
HR	Human resources
HSM	Hardware security module
HTML	Hypertext markup language
HTTP	Hypertext transfer protocol
HTTPS	HTTP run over either SSL or TLS
I-4	International Information Integrity Institute
IA5	International alphabet number 5
IAB	Internet Architecture Board
IBFS	Intergalactic Banking and Financial Services – a fictional organisation used in this book for a running case study
ICMP	Internet control message protocol
ICT	Information and communications technology
IDEA	International data encryption algorithm
IEC	International Electrotechnical Commission
IEEE	Institute of Electrical and Electronics Engineers
IESG	Internet Engineering Steering Group
IETF	Internet Engineering Task Force
IKE	Internet key exchange protocol

IM	Instant messaging
I/O	Input/output
IP	Internet protocol
IPAK	Information Protection Assessment Kit
IPR	Intellectual property rights
IPSec	IP security protocol
IRC	Internet relay chat
IRM	Institute of Risk Managers (UK)
IS	Information systems
ISACA	Information Systems Audit and Control Association
ISACF	Information Systems Audit and Control Foundation
ISF	Information Security Forum
ISMS	Information security management system
ISO	International Standards Organisation
ISOC	Internet Society
ISP	Internet service provider
IT	Information technology
ITIL	IT Infrastructure Library
ITSEC	IT Security Evaluation Criteria
ITT	Invitation to tender
ITU	International Telecommunications Union
JISC	Japanese Industrial Standards Committee
JTC	Joint Technical Committee
JV	Joint venture
Kb	Kilobit
KB	Kilobyte
KGI	Key goal indicator
KPI	Key performance indicator
KRI	Key risk indicator
LAN	Local area network
LDAP	Lightweight directory access protocol
LRA	Local registration authority
MAC (1)	Message authentication code
MAC (2)	Media access control (as in 'MAC address')
MAC (3)	Mandatory access control (as in multilevel secure systems)
MD5	Message digest algorithm number 5
MIC	Message integrity checksum
MIS	Management information system
MLS	Multi-level secure system
MOF	Meta object facility
MPEG	Moving picture experts group

MTBF	Mean time between failures
MTTR	Mean time to repair
NAK	Negative acknowledgement
NAO	National Audit Office (in the UK)
NBS	National Bureau of Standards
NIC	Network interface card
NIST	National Institute of Standards and Technology
OASIS	Organisation for Advancement of Structured Information Standards
OAT	Operational acceptance test(ing)
OECD	Organisation for Economic Co-operation and Development
OID	Object identifier
OLAP	On-line analytical processing
OLTP	On-line transaction processing
OMG	Object Management Group
OQL	Object query language
ORB	Object request broker
OSI	Open systems inter-connection
P&L	Profit and loss
PA	Process area (in the context of Capability Maturity Models)
PABX	Private automatic branch exchange
PAC	Privilege attribute certificate
PBX	Private branch exchange
PC	Personal computer
PDA	Personal digital assistant
PDCA	Plan-Do-Check-Act
PDF	Portable data format
PGP	Pretty Good Privacy
PIN	Personal identification number
PKCS	Public key cryptography standards
PKI	Public key infrastructure
PKIX	X.509-based PKI
PPP	Point-to-point protocol
PRO	Public Records Office (in the UK)
QA	Quality assurance
RA	Registration authority
RAD	Rapid application development
RAID	Redundant array of inexpensive disks
RAROC	Risk-adjusted return on capital
RAS	Remote access server
RBAC	Role-based access control
RC4	Ron (Rivest)'s code number 4

RDA	Remote database access
RFC	Request for comment (an Internet standards document)
RFI	Request for information
RFP	Request for proposal
RNG	Random number generator
RPC	Remote procedure call
RSA	Rivest, Shamir and Adleman
RTSS	Real-time settlement system
RoI	Return on investment
S2ML	Security service markup language
SAA	Standards Australia
SABSA®	Sherwood Applied Business Security Architecture
SAML	Security assertion markup language
SASL	Simple authentication and security layer
SGML	Standard generalized markup language
SHA	Secure hash algorithm
S-HTTP	Secure hypertext transfer protocol
SILS	Standard for Interoperable LAN Security
SLA	Service level agreement
SLIP	Serial line interface protocol
SMIME	Secure multi-purpose mail extensions
SMS	Short message service
SMTP	Simple mail transfer protocol
SNMP	Simple network management protocol
S-NOC	Secure network operating centre
SNZ	Standards New Zealand
SOA	Statement of applicability
SOAP	Simple Object Access Protocol
SPKI	Simple public key infrastructure
SQL	Structured query language
SSE-CMM	System security engineering capability maturity model
SSL	Secure sockets layer (protocol)
SVP	Senior vice-president
TCG	Trusted Computing Group
TCP	Transmission control protocol
TCPA	Trusted Computing Platform Alliance
TCSEC	Trusted Computer Systems Evaluation Criteria
TLS	Transport layer security (protocol)
TMN	Telecommunications management network
TPM	Trusted platform module
TRM	Tamper resistant module

UAT	User acceptance test(ing)
UDDI	Universal description, discovery and integration
UML	Unified modelling language
URI	Uniform resource identifier
URL	Universal resource locator
VAR	Value at risk
VDU	Visual display unit
VP	Vice-president
VPN	Virtual private network
WAN	Wide area network
W3C	World Wide Web Consortium
WSDL	Web services description language
WWW	World Wide Web
X.25	The serial number of an international standard packet switching protocol
X.500	The serial number of an international standard for The Directory
X.509	The serial number for the international standard Directory Authentication Framework
XACML	Extensible access control markup language
XBRL	XML business reporting language
X-KISS	XML key information service specification
XKMS	XML key management specification
X-KRSS	XML key registration service specification
XMI	XML metadata interchange
XML	Extensible markup language
XML-SIG	XML signature syntax and processing
XOR	Exclusive OR (a digital binary operation)
X-TASS	XML trust assertion service specification

Index

Note to Reader: The following letter indicators are used with the page references: "*t*" for tables, "*f*" for figures, and "*n*" for notes.

Numbers

A

C

M